Morningside Heights and Harlem
12
11
9
10
Central Park
Upper East Side
4
5
Upper Midtown
8
Lower Midtown
RIVER
N
0 kilometres 2
0 miles 1

★ **Cathedral of St John the Divine** 12
See pages 224–5

★ **Solomon R Guggenheim Museum** 11
See pages 186–7

★ **Metropolitan Museum** 10
See pages 188–95

★ **St Patrick's Cathedral** 5
See pages 176–7

★ **United Nations** 8
See pages 158–61

★ **Grand Central Terminal** 6
See pages 154–5

STAR SIGHTS FURTHER AFIELD

★ **The Cloisters** *See pages 234–7*

★ **Botanical Garden** *See pages 240–41*

★ **International Wildlife Conservation Park** *See pages 242–3*

★ **Brooklyn Museum** *See pages 248–51*

NEW YORK

EYEWITNESS *TRAVEL GUIDES*

NEW YORK

Main contributor:
ELEANOR BERMAN

DORLING KINDERSLEY
LONDON • NEW YORK • SYDNEY • MOSCOW

A DORLING KINDERSLEY BOOK

PROJECT EDITOR Fay Franklin
ART EDITOR Tony Foo
EDITORS Donna Dailey, Ellen Dupont
DESIGNERS Steve Bere, Louise Parsons, Mark Stevens
EDITORIAL ASSISTANT Fiona Morgan

MANAGING EDITOR Douglas Amrine
MANAGING ART EDITORS Stephen Knowlden, Geoff Manders
SENIOR EDITOR Georgina Matthews
SERIES DESIGN CONSULTANT Peter Luff
EDITORIAL DIRECTOR David Lamb
ART DIRECTOR Anne-Marie Bulat
PRODUCTION CONTROLLER Hilary Stephens
PICTURE RESEARCH Susan Mennell, Sarah Moule
DTP DESIGNER Andy Wilkinson

CONTRIBUTORS
Lester Brooks, Patricia Brooks, Susan Farewell

MAPS
Andrew Heritage, James Mills-Hicks, Chez Picthall,
John Plumer (Dorling Kindersley Cartography)

PHOTOGRAPHERS
Max Alexander, Dave King, Michael Moran
ILLUSTRATORS
Richard Draper, Robbie Polley, Hamish Simpson

SUPERVISING EDITOR IN NEW YORK
Mary Ann Lynch
•
This book was produced with the assistance of
Websters International Publishers.

Film outputting bureau PLS (London)
Reproduced by Colourscan (Singapore)
Printed and bound by Graphicom (Italy)

First published in Great Britain in 1993
by Dorling Kindersley Limited
9 Henrietta Street, London WC2E 8PS
Reprinted with revisions 1994, 1995 (twice), 1997

A CIP CATALOGUE RECORD IS AVAILABLE FROM THE BRITISH LIBRARY.

ISBN 0-75130-011-X
•

Every effort has been made to ensure that the information in this
book is as up-to-date as possible at the time of going to press.
However, details such as telephone numbers, opening hours,
prices, gallery hanging arrangements and travel information are
liable to change. The publishers cannot accept responsibility for
any consequences arising from the use of this book.

We would be delighted to receive any corrections and
suggestions for incorporation in the next edition.
Please write to the Managing Editor, Eyewitness Travel Guides,
Dorling Kindersley, 9 Henrietta Street, London WC2E 8PS.

THROUGHOUT THIS BOOK, FLOORS ARE REFERRED TO IN ACCORDANCE
WITH AMERICAN USAGE, IE THE "FIRST FLOOR" IS AT GROUND LEVEL.

CONTENTS

**Baseball star,
Babe Ruth
(1895–1948)**

INTRODUCING
NEW YORK

South Manhattan skyline

Vesuvio Bakery, SoHo

Trump Tower, Upper Midtown

The New York City Ballet

Tug boat at the North Wind Undersea Institute Museum

TRAVELLERS' NEEDS

Bagel from a New York deli

SURVIVAL GUIDE

Solomon R Guggenheim Museum, Upper East Side

HOW TO USE THIS GUIDE

THIS EYEWITNESS TRAVEL GUIDE helps you get the most from your stay in New York with the minimum of practical difficulty. The opening section, *Introducing New York*, locates the city geographically, sets modern New York in its historical context and describes the regular highlights of the New York year. *New York at a Glance* is an overview of the city's specialities. The main sightseeing section of the book is *New York Area by Area*. It describes all the main sights with maps, photographs and detailed illustrations. In addition, five planned walk routes take you to parts of New York you might otherwise miss.

Well-researched tips on where to stay, eat, shop, and go for entertainment are found in *Travellers' Needs*. *Children's New York* lists highlights for young visitors, and the *Survival Guide* shows you how to do anything from posting a letter to using the subway.

NEW YORK AREA BY AREA

Manhattan has been divided into 15 sightseeing areas, each described separately. Each area opens with a portrait, summing up the area's character and history and listing all the sights to be covered. Sights are numbered and clearly located on an *Area Map*. After this comes a large-scale *Street-by-Street Map* focusing on the most interesting part of the area. Finding your way about each area is made simple by the numbering system. This refers to the order in which sights are described on the pages that follow.

Sights at a Glance lists the sights in the area by category, including: Historic Streets and Buildings, Modern Architecture, Museums and Galleries, Churches, Monuments, Parks and Squares.

The area covered in greater detail on the *Street-by-Street Map* is shaded red.

Numbered circles pinpoint all the listed sights on the area map. Trump Tower, for example, is ❷

1 The Area Map

For easy reference, the sights in each area are numbered and located on an Area Map. *To help the visitor, the map also shows subway stations, heliports and ferry embarkation points.*

Photographs of facades and distinctive details of buildings help you to locate the sights.

Colour-coding on each page makes the area easy to find in the book.

Travel tips help you reach the area quickly by public transport.

2 The Street-by-Street Map

This gives a bird's eye view of the heart of each sightseeing area. The most important buildings are illustrated, to help you spot them as you walk around.

A locator map shows you where you are in relation to surrounding areas. The area of the *Street-by-Street Map* is shown in red.

Trump Tower ❷ is also shown on this map.

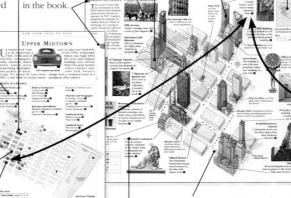

A suggested route for a walk takes you past some of the area's most interesting sights.

Red stars indicate the sights that no visitor should miss.

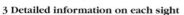

NEW YORK AT A GLANCE

Each map in this section concentrates on a specific theme: *Museums, Architecture, Multicultural New York, Celebrated New Yorkers*. The top sights are shown on the map; other sights are described on the following two pages and cross-referenced to their full entries in the *Area by Area* section.

Each sightseeing area is colour-coded.

The theme is explored in greater detail on the pages following the map.

---

3 Detailed information on each sight

All important sights in each area are described in depth here. They are listed in order, following the numbering on the opening Area Map. *Practical information is also provided.*

PRACTICAL INFORMATION

Each entry provides all the information needed to plan a visit to the sight. The key to the symbols is inside the back cover.

Map reference to Street Finder at back of book

Address

Sight Number

Trump Tower ❷

725 5th Ave. **Map** 12 F3.
[832-2000. **M** 5th Ave-53rd St.
Garden level, shops open 10am–6pm
Mon–Sat. **Building open** 8am–10pm
daily. **Adm free.** *See* **Shopping** p311.
📷 ♿ *Concerts.* 🍴 🔲 🔲

Opening hours

Telephone number

Services and facilities available

Nearest subway station

---

4 New York's major sights

These are given two or more full pages in the sightseeing area in which they are found. Important buildings are dissected to reveal their interiors; museums have colour-coded floor plans to help you find particular exhibits.

The Visitors' Checklist provides the practical information you will need to plan your visit.

The facade of each major sight is shown to help you spot it quickly.

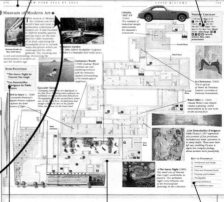

Red stars indicate the most important works of art or exhibits on view inside, or the most interesting architectural details of the building.

A colour key helps you find your way easily around the collection.

Floors are referred to in accordance with American usage, ie the "first floor" is at ground level.

INTRODUCING
NEW YORK

Putting New York on the Map

NEW YORK is a city of over seven million people, covering 301 sq miles (780 sq km). The city gives its name to the state of New York, the capital of which is Albany, 156 miles (251 km) to the north. New York is also a good base from which to visit the historic towns of Boston and Philadelphia, as well as the spectacular Niagara Falls.

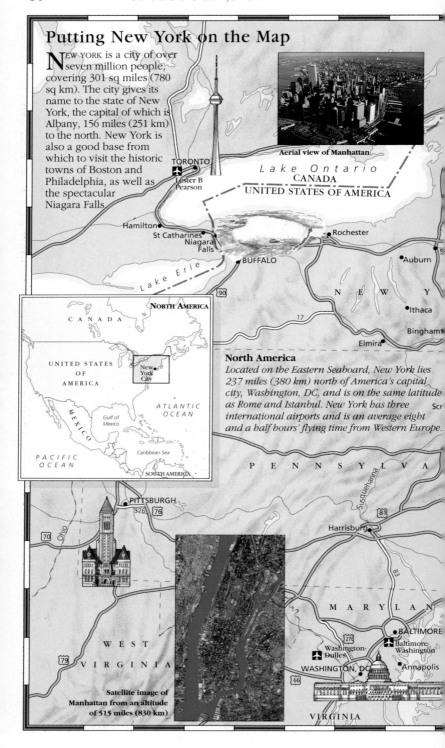

Aerial view of Manhattan

TORONTO
Lester B Pearson

Hamilton
St Catharines
Niagara Falls

BUFFALO

Lake Ontario

CANADA
UNITED STATES OF AMERICA

Lake Erie

90

Rochester

Auburn

N E W Y

Ithaca

Bingham

Elmira

North America

Located on the Eastern Seaboard, New York lies 237 miles (380 km) north of America's capital city, Washington, DC, and is on the same latitude as Rome and Istanbul. New York has three international airports and is an average eight and a half hours' flying time from Western Europe.

NORTH AMERICA

CANADA

UNITED STATES OF AMERICA

New York City

ATLANTIC OCEAN

MEXICO
Gulf of Mexico

Caribbean Sea

PACIFIC OCEAN

SOUTH AMERICA

17

Scr

P E N N S Y L V A

PITTSBURGH

376 76

Ohio

70

79

Susquehanna

Harrisburg

81

83

M A R Y L A N

BALTIMORE

Washington-Dulles

Baltimore-Washington

WASHINGTON, DC

Annapolis

66

W E S T

V I R G I N I A

VIRGINIA

270

Satellite image of Manhattan from an altitude of 515 miles (830 km)

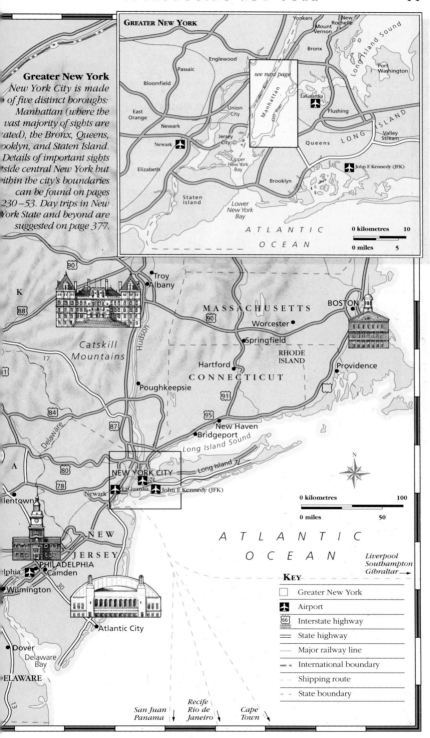

GREATER NEW YORK

Greater New York
*New York City is made
of five distinct boroughs:
Manhattan (where the
vast majority of sights are
ated), the Bronx, Queens,
ooklyn, and Staten Island.
Details of important sights
side central New York but
ithin the city's boundaries
can be found on pages
230–53. Day trips in New
ork State and beyond are
suggested on page 377.*

Yonkers
New Rochelle
Mount Vernon
Bronx
Englewood
Passaic
Bloomfield
East Orange
Newark
Union City
Jersey City
Newark
Elizabeth
Upper New York Bay
Staten Island
Lower New York Bay

Long Island Sound
Port Washington
La Guardia
Flushing
Queens
Valley Stream
Brooklyn
John F Kennedy (JFK)

see next page

Manhattan

LONG ISLAND

ATLANTIC OCEAN

0 kilometres   10

0 miles   5

Troy
Albany

MASSACHUSETTS
Worcester
Springfield
BOSTON

Catskill Mountains
Hudson

RHODE ISLAND
Hartford
CONNECTICUT
Providence

Poughkeepsie

New Haven
Bridgeport
Long Island Sound

Delaware

NEW YORK CITY
Long Island
Newark La Guardia John F Kennedy (JFK)

N

0 kilometres   100

0 miles   50

ATLANTIC OCEAN

Liverpool
Southampton
Gibraltar →

llentown

NEW JERSEY
PHILADELPHIA
elphia Camden
Wilmington

Atlantic City

Dover
Delaware Bay

ELAWARE

KEY

☐	Greater New York
✈	Airport
66	Interstate highway
=	State highway
—	Major railway line
▬ ▬	International boundary
- -	Shipping route
- -	State boundary

San Juan
Panama

Recife
Rio de
Janeiro

Cape
Town

Manhattan

MOST OF THE SIGHTS described in this book lie within 15 areas of Manhattan. Each of these has its own section in the book. If you are short of time, you could restrict your sightseeing to one or two areas. Many of New York's oldest and newest buildings rub shoulders in Lower Manhattan. It is from here, too, that you can take the Staten Island ferry for breathtaking views of the famous skyline and the Statue of Liberty. The Theater and Midtown districts offer Fifth Avenue's glittering shops as well as museums, entertainment and landmark skyscrapers such as the glorious Chrysler Building. Museum Mile on the Upper East Side is a cultural paradise and, since it runs alongside Central Park, you can stop to rest on the way and watch New York at play.

PAGES 138–47
*Street Finder maps
8, 11–12*

PAGES 128–37
*Street Finder maps
7–8*

PAGES 106–13
*Street Finder maps
3–4*

PAGES 100–5
*Street Finder map
4*

Chelsea and
the Garment
District

Grams
and r
Flatir
Distr

Greenwich
Village

SoHo
and
TriBeCa

Eas
Villa

Lower
East Side

Lower
Manhattan

Seaport
and the
Civic
Center

PAGES 80–91
*Street Finder maps
1–2*

PAGES 92–9
*Street Finder maps
4, 5*

PAGES 64–79
*Street Finder maps
1–2*

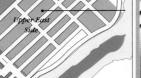

Morningside Heights and Harlem

PAGES 208–17
*Street Finder maps
11–12, 15–16*

PAGES 218–29
*Street Finder maps
19–20*

Upper West Side

Central Park

Upper East Side

Theater District

Upper Midtown

Lower Midtown

H U D S O N   R I V E R

PAGES 202–7
*Street Finder maps
12, 16*

PAGES 180–201
*Street Finder maps
12–13, 16–17*

PAGES 164–79
*Street Finder maps
12, 13–14*

PAGES 148–63
*Street Finder maps
9, 12, 13*

PAGES 114–19
*Street Finder maps
4, 5*

PAGES 120–27
*Street Finder maps
8, 9*

0 kilometres   2

0 miles   1

THE HISTORY OF NEW YORK

FROM ITS FIRST sighting almost 500 years ago by Giovanni da Verrazano, New York's harbour was the prize that all of Europe wanted to capture. The Dutch first sent fur traders to the area in 1621, but they lost the colony they called New Amsterdam to the English in 1664. The settlement was re-christened New York and the name stayed even after the English lost the colony in 1783 at the end of the War of American Independence.

A shell-work cloak worn by an Indian chief

THE GROWING CITY
In the 19th century, New York grew rapidly and became a major port. Ease of shipping spawned manufacturing, commerce was king and great fortunes were made. In 1898, Manhattan was joined with the four outer boroughs to form the world's second largest city. From 1800 to 1900, the population grew from 79,216 to 3 million people. The city became America's cultural and entertainment mecca as well as its business centre.

THE MELTING POT
The city continued to grow as thousands of immigrants moved there to seek a better life. Overpopulation meant that many lived in slums. The mix of cultures has enriched the city and become its defining quality. Today its nine million inhabitants speak 80 languages.

Manhattan's skyline took shape as the city grew skyward to make space for its ever-increasing population. Throughout its history, the city has experienced alternating periods of economic decline and growth, but in both good times and bad, it remains one of the world's most vital cities.

The following pages illustrate significant periods in New York's history.

A deed signed by New Amsterdam's last Dutch governor, Peter Stuyvesant, in 1664

The southern half of Manhattan and part of Brooklyn in 1767

Early New York

Indian husk mask

MANHATTAN WAS a forested land populated by Algonquian-speaking Indians when the Dutch West India Company established a fur trading post called New Amsterdam in 1625. The first settlers built houses helter-skelter, so even today the streets of Lower Manhattan still twist. Broadway, then called by the Dutch name Breede Wegh, began as an Indian trail known as the Weekquaesgeek Trail. Harlem has also kept its Dutch name. The town was unruly until Peter Stuyvesant arrived to bring order. But the colony did not produce the expected revenues and in 1664 the Dutch let it fall to the English, who renamed it New York.

GROWTH OF THE METROPOLIS

☐ *1664*   ☐ *Today*

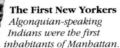

Seal of New Netherland
The beaver pelt and wampum (Indian shell beads) on the seal were the currency of the colony of New Netherland.

FIRST VIEW OF MANHATTAN (1626)
The southern tip of Manhattan resembled a Dutch town, down to the windmill. Although shown here, the fort had not yet been built.

Dutch ships

The First New Yorkers
Algonquian-speaking Indians were the first inhabitants of Manhattan.

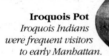

Iroquois Pot
Iroquois Indians were frequent visitors to early Manhattan.

Indian Village
Algonquian Indians lived in longhouses on Manhattan before the Dutch arrived.

Indian canoe

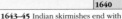

TIMELINE

1524 Giovanni da Verrazano sails into New York harbour

1624 Dutch establish first permanent trading post

1626 Peter Minuit buys Manhattan from the Indians

1653 Wall is built for protection from Indians; adjacent street is called Wall Street

1600   **1620**   **1640**

1609 Henry Hudson sails up the Hudson River in search of the Northwest Passage

1625 First black slaves brought from Africa

1643–45 Indian skirmishes end with temporary peace treaty

1647 Peter Stuyvesant becomes colonial governor

1654 First Jewish settlers arrive

Dutch Delftware
Colonists brought this popular tin-glazed earthen-ware pottery from Holland.

Manhattan Skyline
The Strand, now Whitehall Street, was the site of the city's first brick house.

Tiger timbers

WHERE TO SEE DUTCH NEW YORK

Dug up by workmen in 1916, these remnants of a Dutch ship, the *Tiger*, which burned in 1613, are the earliest artefacts of the period and are now in the Museum of the City of New York (see p197). Rooms in the museum, as well as in the Morris-Jumel Mansion (see p233) and the Van Cortlandt House Museum (see p238), display Dutch pottery, tiles and furniture.

Purchase of Manhattan
Peter Minuit bought the island from the Indians in 1626 for $24 worth of trinkets.

Dutch windmill

Fort Amsterdam

Peter Stuyvesant
The last Dutch governor was a tyrant who imposed strict laws – such as an edict closing all the city's taverns at 9pm.

1660 First city hospital established

1664 British forces oust Dutch without a fight and change name to New York

1676 Great Dock built on East River

1698 Trinity Church dedicated

1660 **1680** **1700**

The surrender of New Amsterdam to the British

1680s Bolting Laws give New York exclusive right to process and ship grain

1683 First New York city charter established

1689 Merchant Jacob Leisler leads revolt against taxes and takes over the city for two years

1693 Ninety-two cannons installed for protection; area becomes known as the Battery

1691 Leisler sentenced to death for treason

Colonial New York

U NDER BRITISH RULE, New York prospered and the population grew rapidly. The bolting of flour (grinding grain) was the main commercial enterprise. Ship-building also flourished. As the city prospered, an elite emerged, and fine furniture and household silver were made for use in their homes during the colonial period. During more than a century of governing New York, Britain proved more interested in profit than in the welfare of the colony. The Crown imposed many hated taxes and the spirit of rebellion grew, although loyalties were divided, especially in New York. On the eve of the Revolution, New York was the second largest city in the 13 colonies, with 20,000 citizens.

Colonial gentleman

Colonial currency

GROWTH OF THE METROPOLIS
☐ *1760* ☐ *Today*

Bedroom

Dining room

Colonial Street
Pigs and dogs roamed free on the streets of colonial New York.

Kas
This Dutch-style pine wardrobe was made in New York's Hudson River Valley around 1720.

Shipping
Trade with the West Indies and Britain helped New York prosper. In some years, 200 or more vessels visited the port.

TIMELINE

1702 Lord Cornbury appointed colonial governor; he often wore women's clothes

1711 Slave market set up at the foot of Wall Street

1720 First shipyard opens

| 1700 | 1710 | 1720 | 1730 |

1710 Iroquois chief Hendrick visits England

1725 *New York Gazette*, city's first newspaper, is established

1732 First city theatre opens

Captain Kidd
The English pirate, William Kidd, was a respected citizen, loaning a block and tackle to help build Trinity Church (see p68).

VAN CORTLANDT HOUSE
Frederick Van Cortlandt built this Georgian-style house in 1748 on a wheat plantation in what is now the Bronx. Today a museum (see p238), it shows how a well-to-do Dutch-English family once lived.

West parlour

WHERE TO SEE COLONIAL NEW YORK
Colonial buildings are open to the public at Historic Richmond Town on Staten Island (see p252). Fine examples of colonial silver and furniture are on display at the Museum of the City of New York (see p197).

Richmond Town General Store

Colonial Kitchen
Plain white cheese, called "white meat", was often served in place of meat. Waffles, introduced by the Dutch, were popular. Fresh fruit was rare, but preserved fruits were eaten.

Pewter baby bottle   **Cheese mould**   **Waffle iron**

Decorative carvings
A face carved in stone peers over each of the front windows.

Sucket fork, for eating preserved fruits

1734 John Peter Zenger's libel trial upholds freedom of the press

1741 Slave uprising creates hysteria; 31 slaves are executed, 150 imprisoned

1754 French and Indian War begins; King's College (now Columbia University) founded

British soldier

1759 First jail built

1740   **1750**   **1760**

1733 Bowling Green becomes first city park; first ferries to Brooklyn

King's College

1762 First paid police force

1763 War ends; British gain control of North America

Revolutionary New York

George Washington, Revolutionary general

DUG UP INTO TRENCHES for defence, heavily shelled by British troops and scarred by recurring fires, New York suffered during the War of American Independence. But despite the hardships, the citizens continued to enjoy cricket games, horse races, balls and boxing matches. The city had long been a loyalist stronghold, but after the British took it in 1776, loyalists from other states flocked there. American troops did not return to Manhattan until after the peace treaty had been signed in 1783.

GROWTH OF THE METROPOLIS

☐ *1776*   ☐ *Today*

Battle Dress
The American army wore blue uniforms, while the British wore red.

British soldier

Soldier's Haversack
American soldiers in the War of American Independence carried their supplies in haversacks.

TOPPLING THE KING
New Yorkers tore down the statue of King George III in Bowling Green and melted it down to make ammunition.

American soldier

Battle of Harlem Heights
Washington won this battle on 16 September 1776. But since he did not have enough troops to hold the New York, he had to retreat, leaving it to the British.

Rioter

Death of a Patriot
While working behind British lines in 1776, Nathan Hale was captured and hung without trial by the British for spying.

TIMELINE

1765 British pass Stamp Act; New Yorkers protest; Sons of Liberty formed	**1767** New duties imposed with Townshend Act; after protests, the Act is repealed	**1770** Sons of Liberty fight British in the "Battle of Golden Hill"

1774 Rebels dump tea in New York harbour to protest taxes

1760   1770   178

St Paul's Chapel

1766 St Paul's Chapel completed; Stamp Act repealed; Statue of George III erected on Bowling Green

General William Howe, commander in chief of the British troops

1776 War begins; 500 ships under General Howe assemble in New York harbour

Fire Fighters

Fires had long threatened the city, but during the war a series of fires nearly destroyed it. In the wake of the patriot retreat, on 21 September 1776, a terrible fire razed Trinity Church and 1,000 houses.

Leather fire bucket

Flags of the Revolution

Washington's army flew the continental colours, with a stripe for each of the 13 colonies and a Union Jack in the corner. The Stars and Stripes became the official flag in 1777.

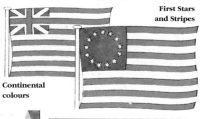

First Stars and Stripes

Continental colours

Statue of George III

General Washington Returns

Washington received a hero's welcome when he re-entered New York on 25 November 1783 after the British withdrawal.

Cheering patriots

WHERE TO SEE THE REVOLUTIONARY CITY

In 1776, George Washington used the Morris-Jumel mansion in upper Manhattan as a headquarters *(see p233)*. He also slept at the Van Cortlandt House *(see p19 and p238)*. After the war he bid farewell to his officers at Fraunces Tavern *(see p76)*.

Morris-Jumel mansion

1783 Treaty of Paris signed, US wins independence; British evacuate New York

1785 New York named US capital

1784 Bank of New York chartered

1789 George Washington inaugurated as first president at Federal Hall

Washington's inauguration

1790 US capital is moved to Philadelphia

1794 Bellevue Hospital opens on the East River

1790

1792 Tontine Coffee House built – first home of the Stock Exchange

1791 New York Hospital, city's oldest, opens

1801 *New York Post* founded by Alexander Hamilton

1800

1804 Vice President Aaron Burr kills political rival Alexander Hamilton in a duel

New York in the 19th Century

FIRMLY ESTABLISHED as the nation's largest city and pre-eminent seaport, New York grew increasingly wealthy. Manufacturing increased due to the ease of shipping; tycoons like John Jacob Astor made millions. The rich moved uptown; public transportation followed. But big city problems came with New York's rapid growth: fires, epidemics and a financial panic took their toll. With the arrival of great numbers of immigrants, overcrowding occurred and slums grew. In 1846, one out of seven New Yorkers was a pauper.

Governor De Witt Clinton

GROWTH OF THE METROPOLIS
☐ *1840*　　☐ *Today*

Sheet Music
New Yorker Stephen Foster wrote many popular ballads, such as Jeanie With the Light Brown Hair.

Croton Distributing Reservoir was built in 1842. Until then New Yorkers had no fresh drinking water – they relied on deliveries of bottled water.

Keeping Fit
Gymnasiums such as Dr Rich's Institute for Physical Education were established in New York in the 1830s and 1840s.

Omnibus
The horse-drawn omnibus was introduced for public transportation in 1832 and remained on New York streets until World War I.

TIMELINE

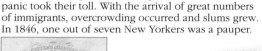

1805 First free state schools established in New York

1811 Randel Plan divides Manhattan into grid pattern above 14th Street

1812–14 War of 1812; British blockade New York harbour

The Constitution, *most famous ship in War of 1812*

1835 Much of old New York razed in city's worst fire

1810	1820	1830

1807 Robert Fulton launches first steamboat, on the Hudson River

1822 Yellow fever epidemic; people evacuate to Greenwich Village

1823 New York surpasses Boston and Philadelphia to become nation's largest city

1827 New York abolishes slavery

1837 New Yorker Samuel Morse sends first telegraph message

The Brownstone

Many terraced houses of brown stone were built in the first half of the century. The raised stoop allowed separate entry to the parlour and ground floor servants' quarters.

Crystal Palace was an iron and glass exhibition hall erected for the 1853 World's Fair.

NEW YORK IN 1855

Looking south from 42nd Street, Crystal Palace and the Croton Distributing Reservoir stood where the Public Library and Bryant Park are today.

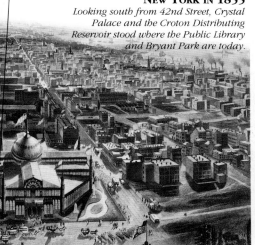

THE PORT OF NEW YORK

New York's importance as a port city grew by leaps and bounds in the early 19th century. Robert Fulton launched his first steamboat, the *Clermont*, in 1807. Steamboats made travel much quicker – it now took 72 hours to reach Albany, which was both the state capital and the gateway to the West. Trade with the West by steamboat and canal boat, and with the rest of the world by clipper ship, made the fortunes of many New Yorkers.

The steamboat *Clermont*

Crystal Palace in Flames

On 5 October 1858, New York's Crystal Palace exhibition hall burned to the ground, just as its predecessor in London did.

Grand Canal Celebration

Ships in New York harbour lined up to celebrate the 1825 Erie Canal opening. In connecting the Great Lakes with Albany, the state capital, on the Hudson River, the canal opened a water link between the Midwest and the Port of New York. New York realized huge profits.

1849 Astor Place riots; ships set sail for California Gold Rush

1851 *New York Times* first published

1861 Civil War begins

1863 Draft riots last four days, many die

1853 New York hosts first World's Fair

1857 Financial panic and depression

1865 Abraham Lincoln lies in state in City Hall

840

1850

1860

Early baseball player

1845 New York Knickerbockers, first organized baseball team, chartered

Clipper ship card

FOR SAN FRANCISCO

FREE TRADE

1858 Vaux and Olmsted design Central Park; Macy's founded

Crowds in Central Park

1842 Croton Reservoir built

The Age of Extravagance

Industrialist Andrew Carnegie

GROWTH OF THE METROPOLIS
☐ *1890*   ☐ *Today*

AS NEW YORK's merchant princes grew ever wealthier, the city entered into a gilded era during which many of its most opulent buildings went up. Millions were lavished on the arts, with the founding of the Metropolitan Museum, Public Library and Carnegie Hall. Luxury hotels like the Plaza and the original Waldorf–Astoria were built, and elegant department stores arose to serve the wealthy. Such flamboyant figures as William "Boss" Tweed, political strongman and king of corruption, and circus man Phineas T Barnum were also larger than life.

Overlooking the Park
The Dakota (1880) was the first grand luxury apartment house on the Upper West Side (see p216).

Palatial Living
Mansions lined Fifth Avenue. When it was built in 1882, W K Vanderbilt's Italianate palace at 660 Fifth Avenue, was one of the furthest north.

Fashion City
Lord & Taylor built a new store on Broadway's Ladies' Mile; 6th Avenue between 14th and 23rd Streets was known as Fashion Row.

BATHING SUITS.

A GREAT SPECIALTY AT
LORD & TAYLOR'S, Broadway and 20th Street, N. Y.
CHEAPEST AND BEST QUALITY OF BATHING SUITS IN THE CITY.

THE ELEVATED RAILROAD
By the mid 1870s, elevated railroads or "Els" ran along 2nd, 3rd, 6th and 9th Avenues. They made travel faster, but left noise, grime and pollution in their wake.

TIMELINE

1867 Brooklyn's Prospect Park completed

1868 First elevated railroad built on Greenwich Street

1870 J D Rockefeller founds Standard Oil

1871 The first Grand Central Depot opens on 42nd St; "Boss" Tweed is arrested and imprisoned

1877 A G Bell demonstrates the telephone in New York

1865   **1870**   **1875**

1869 First apartment house built on 18th Street; Black Friday financial crisis hits Wall Street

The interior of the Stock Exchange

1872 Bloomingdale's opens

1873 Banks fail: Stock Exchange panics

1879 St Patrick's Cathedral completed; first city telephone exchange opened on Nassau Street

Mark Twain's Birthday
Mark Twain, whose 1873 novel The Gilded Age *portrayed the decadent lifestyle of New Yorkers, celebrated his birthday at Delmonico's.*

WHERE TO SEE THE AGE OF EXTRAVAGANCE
The Gold Room in the Henry Villard Houses *(see p174)* is a good place to experience the city's past. Formerly the Music Room, it is now a venue for afternoon tea. The Museum of the City of New York also has two period rooms *(p197)*.

Elevated train

Streetcar

Bowery

The Tweed Ring
William "Boss" Tweed led Tammany Hall, which dominated city government. He stole millions in city funds.

Nast's cartoon of "Boss" Tweed

Tammany Tiger
The Museum of the City of New York has Boss Tweed's cane, which sports a gold Tammany Tiger mascot on its handle.

Rural Fifth Avenue
This painting by Ralph Blakelock shows a shanty-town at 86th Street. Today it is one of New York's most expensive addresses.

1880 Canned fruits and meats first appear in stores; Metropolitan Museum of Art opens; streets lit by electricity

1883 Metropolitan Opera opens on Broadway; Brooklyn Bridge completed

1886 Statue of Liberty unveiled

1891 Carnegie Hall opens

1880

1885

1890

1888 Great Blizzard dumps 22 in (56 cm) of snow

1890 First moving picture shows appear in New York

Grand display of fireworks over Brooklyn Bridge, 1883

1892 Cathedral of St John the Divine begun; Ellis Island opens

New York at the Turn of the Century

Horse-drawn carriage

By 1900, NEW YORK was the hub of American industry: 70% of the country's corporations were based there and the port handled two-thirds of all imported goods. The rich got richer, but for the poor, conditions worsened. In the crowded slums, disease spread, but the immigrants who lived there kept their rich traditions alive. In 1900, the International Ladies' Garment Workers' Union was founded to battle for the rights of the women and children who toiled in the dangerous factories for low wages. But only after the Triangle Shirtwaist Factory fire in 1911 were reforms made.

GROWTH OF THE METROPOLIS

☐ *1914*   ☐ *Today*

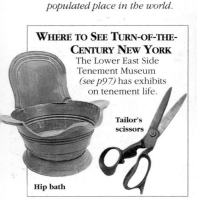

Portrait of Poverty
Almost five times as crowded as the rest of New York, the Lower East Side was the most densely populated place in the world.

No Place to Live
Tenements were unhealthy and overcrowded. They often lacked windows, air shafts or proper sanitary facilities.

WHERE TO SEE TURN-OF-THE-CENTURY NEW YORK
The Lower East Side Tenement Museum *(see p97)* has exhibits on tenement life.

Tailor's scissors

Hip bath

Inside a Sweatshop
Workers toiled long hours for low wages in the overcrowded sweatshops of the garment district. This view of Moe Levy's shop was taken in 1912.

Streetcars on Broadway

TIMELINE

1895 Olympia Theater is first to open in the Broadway area

1898 Five boroughs merge to form world's second largest city

1901 Macy's opens Broadway department store

1895

1900

1896 First bagel served in a Clinton Street bakery

1897 Waldorf–Astoria Hotel opens: the largest hotel in the world

1900 Mayor Robert Van Wyck breaks ground on city's first subway with silver shovel

1903 Lyceum Theater opens – oldest Broadway house still in use

FLATIRON BUILDING

Overlooking Madison Square where Broadway, Fifth Avenue and 23rd Street meet, the 21-storey tower was one of the city's first skyscrapers (1902). Triangle-shaped, it was dubbed the Flatiron Building (see p125).

Underlying steel structure

Elaborate limestone facade

Only 6 ft (185 cm) wide at apex of triangle

Supper in the Saddle

Decadent parties were all the rage, but C K G Billings's horseback dinner at Sherry's restaurant, in 1903, was the talk of all New York.

Plaza Promenade

The section of Fifth Avenue in front of the Plaza Hotel was considered the most elegant in the city.

Ventilated hair piece

High Fashion

In 1900 styles were stiff with wire hoops and bustles worn beneath ornate dresses. Later clothes became softer and more practical.

Long bustle

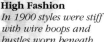

Wire hoops

New York Between the Wars

Entrance card to a speakeasy

T HE 1920s WERE a time of high living for New Yorkers. Mayor Jimmy Walker set the pace, whether squiring chorus girls, drinking in speakeasies or watching the Yankees. But the good times came to an end with the 1929 stock market crash. By 1932, Walker had resigned, charged with corruption, and one-quarter of New Yorkers were unemployed. After Fiorello LaGuardia was elected mayor in 1933, New York began to thrive.

GROWTH OF THE METROPOLIS
☐ *1933*   ☐ *Today*

Exotic Costumes
Chorus girls were a major Cotton Club attraction.

THE COTTON CLUB
This Harlem nightclub was host to the best jazz in town as first Duke Ellington and then Cab Calloway led the band. People flocked from all over the city to hear them.

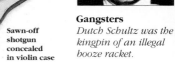

Defying Prohibition
Although alcohol was outlawed, speakeasies, semi-secret illegal drinking dens, still sold it.

Home-Run Hitter
In 1927, baseball star Babe Ruth, hit a record 60 home runs for the Yankees. Yankee Stadium (see p239) became known as "the house that Ruth built."

Sawn-off shotgun concealed in violin case

Gangsters
Dutch Schultz was the kingpin of an illegal booze racket.

TIMELINE

1918 End of World War I

1919 18th Amendment bans alcohol, launches Prohibition Era

1920 American women get the vote

1924 Novelist James Baldwin is born in Harlem

1925 *The New Yorker* magazine is launched

1926 Jimmy Walker becomes mayor

Opening of the Holland Tunnel

1927 Lindbergh flies across the Atlantic; first talking movie, *The Jazz Singer*, opens; Holland Tunnel opened

1929 Stock market crash; Great Depression begins

1930 Chrysler Building completed

1931 Empire State Building becomes world's tallest

1920	1925	1930

Harlem High Life
Banned from many downtown clubs, black artists like Cab Calloway starred at the Cotton Club.

THE GREAT DEPRESSION
The Roaring Twenties ended with the stock market crash of 29 October 1929 which set off the Depression. New York was hard hit: squatters' shacks sprang up in Central Park and thousands were out of work. But art flourished as artists came to work at the Works Projects Administration (WPA) programme, creating murals and artworks throughout the city.

Waiting to receive benefits in 1931

Broadway Melodies
The 1920s were the heyday of the Broadway musical, with a record number of plays opening.

Breakfast menu

Lindbergh's plane,
Spirit of St Louis

Lindbergh's Flight
New Yorkers celebrated Lindbergh's non-stop solo flight across the Atlantic in 1927 in a variety of ways, including a breakfast in his honour.

Rockefeller Center
Millionaire John D Rockefeller drives the final rivet to celebrate the opening of Rockefeller Center on 1 May 1939.

Mass Event
Forty-five million people visited the 1939 World's Fair in New York.

NEW YORK WORLD'S FAIR
1939

1933 Prohibition ends; Fiorello LaGuardia begins three terms as mayor

1940 Queens-Midtown Tunnel opens

1942 Times Square blacked out during World War II; Idlewild International Airport (now JFK) opens

| 1935 | 1940 | 1945 |

1936 Parks Department headed by Robert Moses, new parks created

1939 Rockefeller Center completed

1941 US enters World War II

1944 Black leader Adam Clayton Powell elected to Congress

Postwar New York

SINCE WORLD WAR II, New York has seen both the best of times and the worst. Although established as the financial capital of the world, the city itself almost went bankrupt in the 1970s. Wall Street hit its peak in the 1980s, then experienced its worst crash since 1929. Recently the city has had to cope with racial tensions, and an increase in homelessness and crime. Yet New York always bounces back. The city is the cultural and financial hub of the United States, and while new buildings continue to spring up, many of the city's older buildings, such as Grand Central Station, are being restored.

BILTMORE THEATER
201 WEST 47TH STREET. 582-5340

1967 Hippie musical *Hair* opens on Off-Broadway, then transfers to the Biltmore Theater

1971 Pop artist Andy Warhol has a retrospective show of his work at the Whitney Museum

1953 Merce Cunningham founds dance company

1963 Pennsylvania Station razed

1966 Newspaper and transit strikes

1970 John Lindsay starts second term as mayor

1945 End of World War II

1959 Guggenheim Museum opens

1946 UN headquarters established in New York

1954 Ellis Island closes

1945	1950	1955	1960	1965	1970
MAYORS:	IMPELLITERI	WAGNER	WAGNER	LINDSAY	LINDS
1945	1950	1955	1960	1965	1970

The Beatles

1964 New York World's Fair; race riots in Harlem and Bedford-Stuyvesant; Verrazano Narrows Bridge links Brooklyn and Staten Island; Beatles play at Shea Stadium

1947 Jackie Robinson, first black baseball player in the major leagues, signs with Brooklyn Dodgers

NEW YORK
1964 WORLD'S 1965 FAIR

Souvenir scarf

1968 20,000 anti-establishment hippies gather in Central Park; student sit-ins at Columbia University

Donald Trump

*Andy Warhol with actresses
Candy Darling and Ultra Violet*

1983 Economic boom: property prices
skyrocket; Trump Tower completed by real
estate tycoon Donald Trump, who symbolizes
the "yuppie" wealth of the 1980s

1975 Federal
loan saves New
York from
bankruptcy

1981 New York
regains solvency

1988 Twenty-
five percent of
New Yorkers live
below the
poverty line

1990 David Dinkins, New
York's first black mayor, takes
office; Ellis Island reopens as
an immigration museum

1977 New York
power blackout
lasts 25 hours

1987 Stock
market crash

1993 Rudolph Giuliani
takes office as mayor

1975	1980	1985	1990	1995
BEAME	KOCH	KOCH	DINKINS	GIULIANI
1975	1980	1985	1990	1995

3 World
e Center
pleted

1986 Shock of corruption scandals
rock Mayor Koch's administration;
Centennial
of Statue
of Liberty

1995 The
neglected
Chelsea Piers
are renovated
and open as a
mammoth
sports and
entertainment
complex
(see p136)

NEW YORK AT A GLANCE

THERE ARE ALMOST 300 places of interest described in the *Area by Area* section of this book. They range from the bustling New York Stock Exchange *(see pp70–71)* to Central Park's peaceful Strawberry Fields *(see p206)*, and from synagogues to skyscrapers. The following 16 pages are a time-saving guide to New York's most interesting sights. Museums and architecture each have a section, and there are guides to the people and cultures that have given the city its unique character. Each sight is cross-referenced to its own full entry. Below are the top tourist attractions to start you off.

NEW YORK'S TOP TEN   TOURIST ATTRACTIONS

Ellis Island
See pp78–9.

Empire State Building
See pp134–5.

South Street Seaport
See p84.

Rockefeller Center
See p142.

Museum of Modern Art
See pp170–73.

Central Park
See pp202–7.

Metropolitan Museum of Art
See pp188–95.

Statue of Liberty
See pp74–5.

Brooklyn Bridge
See pp86–9.

Chinatown
See p96.

Park Avenue's relentless flow of traffic

New York's Best: Museums

N EW YORK'S MUSEUMS range from the vast scope of the Metropolitan Museum to the personal treasures of financier J Pierpont Morgan's own collection. Several museums celebrate New York's heritage, giving visitors an insight into the people and events that made the city what it is today. This map features some highlights, with a detailed overview on pages 36–7.

Museum of Modern Art
The world's most comprehensive collection of modern art includes gems such as Picasso's Goat (1950).

Intrepid Sea-Air-Space Museum
Situated on a large aircraft carrier on the Hudson River, this naval museum also traces the progress of flight and undersea exploration.

Pierpont Morgan Library
One of the world's finest collections of manuscripts, prints and books includes this rare French Bible from 1230.

Old Merchant's House
This perfectly preserved 1820s house belonged to a wealthy trader.

Ellis Island
This museum vividly recreates the experiences of many millions of immigrant families.

Ellis Island

HUDSON RIVER

Upper West Side

Theater District

Chelsea and the Garment District

Lower Midtown

Gramercy and the Flatiron District

Greenwich Village

SoHo and TriBeCa

East Village

Lower East Side

Lower Manhattan

Seaport and the Civic Center

EAST RIVER

| 0 kilometres | 2 |
| 0 miles | 1 |

American Museum of Natural History

Dinosaurs, meteorites and much more have fascinated generations of visitors here.

Morningside Heights and Harlem

Central Park

Upper East Side

Lower Midtown

Museum of the City of New York

Costumes, works of art and household objects (such as this 1725 silver dish) create an intricate and detailed picture of New York's past.

Cooper-Hewitt Museum

A wealth of decorative arts are displayed in the handsome setting of Andrew Carnegie's Upper East Side mansion.

Solomon R Guggenheim Museum

Ellsworth Kelly's Blue, Green, Yellow, Orange, Red *(1966) is part of the collection housed in Frank Lloyd Wright's only New York building.*

Metropolitan Museum of Art

Of the millions of works in its collection, this 12th-dynasty Egyptian faïence hippo is the museum's own mascot.

Frick Collection

The collection of 19th-century rail magnate Henry Clay Frick is on show in his former home. Masterpieces include St Francis in the Desert *(about 1480) by Giovanni Bellini.*

Whitney Museum of American Art

This exceptional collection includes many views of New York. One of the best is Brooklyn Bridge: Variation on an Old Theme *(1939), by Joseph Stella.*

Exploring New York's Museums

Richmond Town tobacco tin

YOU COULD DEVOTE an entire month to museums in New York and still not do them justice. There are more than 60 museums in Manhattan alone, half again that number in the other boroughs. The wealth of art and the huge variety of offerings is equal to that of any city in the world, from old masters to old fire engines, dinosaurs to dolls, Tibetan tapestries to African masks. Note that some museums may be closed on Monday as well as on another day. Many stay open late one or two evenings a week, and some have one evening when admission is free. Not every museum charges for admission, but donations are always welcome.

PAINTINGS AND SCULPTURE

NEW YORK is best known for its art museums. The **Metropolitan Museum of Art** houses an extensive collection of American art as well as world-famous masterpieces. The **Cloisters**, a branch of the "Met" in Upper Manhattan, is a treasury of medieval art and architecture. The **Frick Collection** has a superb display of Old Masters. In contrast, the **Museum of Modern Art (MoMA)** has some of the world's most famous Impressionist and modern paintings. **The Whitney Museum of American Art** and the **Solomon R Guggenheim Museum** also specialize in modern art, the Whitney's biennial show being the foremost display of contemporary work by living artists. The cutting edge of today's art is to be seen at the **New Museum of Contemporary Art**, and the work of untrained artists can be seen

at the **Museum of American Folk Art**. The **National Academy of Design** displays a collection of 19th and 20th century art, donated by its members. In Harlem, the **Studio Museum** shows the work of black artists.

CRAFTS AND DESIGN

IF YOU ARE interested in textiles, porcelain and glass, embroideries and laces, wallpaper and prints, visit the **Cooper-Hewitt Museum**, the decorative arts outpost of Washington's Smithsonian Institution. The design collections at **MoMA** are as well known as the paintings, tracing the history of design from clocks to couches. The **American Craft Museum** offers the finest work of today's skilled artisans in mediums from furniture to art glass, while the **Museum of American Folk Art** presents folk forms, from quilts to canes. Silver collections are notable at the **Museum of the City of New York**. The fine displays of native art at the **Museum of the American Indian** include jewellery, rugs and pottery.

PRINTS AND PHOTOGRAPHY

THE SMALL but excellent **International Center of Photography**, is the only museum in New York totally devoted to this craft. Collections can also be seen at the **Metropolitan Museum of Art** and **MoMA**, with many examples of early photography at the **Museum of the City of New York** and **Ellis Island**.

Prints and drawings by great book illustrators, such as Kate Greenaway and John Tenniel, are on show at the **Pierpont Morgan Library**. The **Cooper-Hewitt Museum** has examples of the use of prints in the decorative arts.

FURNITURE AND COSTUMES

THE ANNUAL exhibition of the Costume Institute at the **Metropolitan Museum of Art** is always worth a visit. Also impressive is the American Wing, with its 24 rooms of original furnishings tracing life from 1640 to the 20th century. Period rooms depicting New York in various settings, beginning with 17th-century Dutch, are on view at the **Museum of the City of New York**. There are also some house museums that give a realistic picture of furnishings and life in old New York. The **Old Merchant's House**, a preserved residence from the 1820s, was occupied by the same family for 98 years. **Gracie Mansion**, the residence of the mayor, was the 1799 country house of a wealthy shipping merchant and is open periodically for public tours. The **Theodore Roosevelt Birthplace** is the brownstone where the 26th president of the United States grew up, and the **Abigail Adams Smith Museum** was part of an 18th-century estate.

The Peaceable Kingdom (c1840–1845) **by Edward Hicks, at the Brooklyn Museum**

Corn husk doll, American Museum of Natural History

HISTORY

**Palm pistol at the Police
Academy Museum**

AMERICAN HISTORY unfolds at **Federal Hall**, the first US capital – George Washington took his oath as America's first president on the balcony in April 1789 – and now a museum of constitutional history. For the history of colonial New York, visit the **Fraunces Tavern Museum**. The restored **Ellis Island** and **Lower East Side Tenement Museum** recreate the hardships faced by immigrants. The **New York City Fire Museum** and **Police Academy Museum** chronicle heroism and tragedy, while the **South Street Seaport Museum** recreates early maritime history, complete with the original tall ships.

TECHNOLOGY AND NATURAL HISTORY

**Forest-dwelling bonga, American
Museum of Natural History**

SCIENCE MUSEUMS hold exhibitions from nature to space-age technology. The **American Museum of Natural History** has vast collections covering flora, fauna and cultures from around the world. Here, the Hayden Planetarium offers spectacular laser light shows. The ***Intrepid* Sea-Air-Space Museum** is a repository of technology that chronicles military progress. It is based on the decks of an aircraft carrier.

If you missed a classic Lucille Ball sitcom or footage of the first man on the moon, the place to visit is the **Museum of Television and Radio** which holds these and many other classics of TV and radio.

ART FROM OTHER CULTURES

ARTWORK of other nations is the focus of several special collections. Oriental art is the speciality of the **Asia Society** and the **Japan Society**. The **Jewish Museum** features major collections of Judaica and has changing exhibitions of Jewish life. **El Museo del Barrio** is dedicated to the arts of Puerto Rico, including many pre-Columbian artefacts. For an impressive review of African-American art and history, visit the **Schomburg Center for Research in Black Culture**. Finally, the **Metropolitan Museum of Art** excels in its multicultural displays of art, ranging from ancient Egypt to contemporary Africa.

**Egyptian
mummy,
Brooklyn
Museum**

LIBRARIES

NEW YORK'S notable libraries, such as the **Pierpont Morgan Library**, offer some superb art collections as well as a chance to view pages from rare books. The **New York Public Library** shows a collection which includes manuscripts of many famous works.

BEYOND MANHATTAN

OTHER MUSEUMS worth a visit include **The Brooklyn Museum**, with its one and a half million paintings. The

American Museum of the Moving Image in Queens has a unique collection of motion picture history. The **Jacques Marchais Center of Tibetan Art** is a rare find on Staten Island. Also on Staten Island is **Historic Richmond Town**, a well-restored village dating from the 1600s.

New York's Best: Architecture

Even when following world trends, New York has given its own twist to the turns of architectural fashion, the style of its buildings influenced by both geography and economy. An island city, with space at a premium, must look upwards to grow. This trend was reflected early on with tall, narrow town houses, and later with the city's apartment buildings and skyscrapers. Building materials such as cast-iron and brownstone were chosen for their local availability and practical appeal. The result is a city that has developed by finding flamboyant answers to practical needs. A more detailed overview of New York's architecture is on pages 40–41.

Apartment Buildings
The twin-towered Majestic apartment building is one of four Art Deco blocks on Central Park West.

Cast-Iron Architecture
Mass produced cast-iron was often used for building facades. SoHo has many of the best examples, such as this building at Nos. 28–30 Greene Street.

Post-Modernism
The quirky, yet elegant, shapes of buildings like the World Financial Center, built in 1985 (see p69), mark a bold departure from the sleek steel and glass boxes of the 1950s and 60s.

Brownstones
Built from local sand-stone, brownstones were favoured by the 19th-century middle classes. India House, built in a Florentine palazzo style on Wall Street, is typical of many brownstone commercial buildings.

Map labels:
HUDSON RIVER
Theat Distri
Chelsea and the Garment District
Gramerc and the Flatiro District
Greenwich Village
SoHo and TriBeCa
East Village
Lower East Side
Lower Manhattan

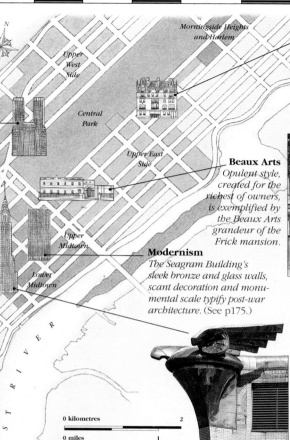

Morningside Heights
and Harlem

Upper
West
Side

Central
Park

Upper East
Side

Upper
Midtown

Lower
Midtown

EAST RIVER

N

0 kilometres   2

0 miles   1

19th-Century Mansions

The Jewish Museum (see p184), formerly the home of Felix M Warburg, is a fine example of the French Renaissance style that typified these mansions.

Beaux Arts

Opulent style, created for the richest of owners, is exemplified by the Beaux Arts grandeur of the Frick mansion.

Modernism

The Seagram Building's sleek bronze and glass walls, scant decoration and monumental scale typify post-war architecture. (See p175.)

The Skyscraper

The glory of New York architecture, these buildings expressed perfectly a blend of practical engineering skill together with fabulous decoration, such as this gargoyle on the Chrysler Building.

Tenements

Constructed as an economic form of housing, for many these buildings were a stark introduction to new lives. Mainly built on the Lower East Side, the apartments were hopelessly overcrowded. In addition, the building's design, with inadequate air shafts, resulted in apartments with little or no ventilation.

Federal Architecture

Federal style was popular in civic architecture of the 19th-century; City Hall combines it with French Renaissance influences.

Exploring New York's Architecture

A Federal-style front door

IN ITS FIRST 200 YEARS, New York, like all of America, looked to Europe for architectural inspiration. None of the buildings from the Dutch colonial period survive in Manhattan today; most were lost in the great fire of 1776 or torn down to make way for new developments in the early 1800s. Throughout the 18th and 19th centuries, the city's major architectural trends followed those of Europe. With the advent of cast-iron architecture in the 1850s, the Art Deco period and the ever-higher rise of the skyscraper, New York's architecture came into its own.

FEDERAL ARCHITECTURE

THIS AMERICAN adaptation of the Neo-Classical Adam style flowered in the early decades of the new nation, featuring square buildings two or three storeys tall, with low hipped roofs, balustrades and decorative elements all carefully balanced. **City Hall** (1811, John McComb, Jr and Joseph François Mangin) is a blend of Federal and French Renaissance influences. The restored warehouses of **Schermerhorn Row** (c1812) in the Seaport district are also in Federal style.

BROWNSTONES

PLENTIFUL AND CHEAP, the brown sandstone found in the nearby Connecticut River Valley and along the banks of the Hackensack River in New

A typical brownstone with stoop leading up to the main entrance

Jersey was the most common building material in the 1800s. It is found all over the city's residential neighbourhoods, used for small homes or small apartments – some of the best examples of brownstone can be found in **Chelsea**. Because street space was limited, these buildings were very narrow in width, but also very deep. A typical brownstone has a flight of steps, called a stoop, leading up to the living floors. Separate stairs lead down to the basement which was originally the servants' quarters.

TENEMENTS

TENEMENTS WERE built to house the huge influx of immigrants who arrived from the 1840s up to World War I. The six-storey blocks, 100 ft (30 m) long and 25 ft (8 m) wide, offered very little light and air except from tiny sidewall air shafts and windows at each end, leaving the middle rooms in darkness. The tiny apartments were called railroad flats after their similarity to railway cars. Later designs had air shafts between buildings but these helped the spread of fire. The **Lower East Side Tenement Museum** has scale models of the old tenements.

CAST-IRON ARCHITECTURE

AN AMERICAN architectural innovation of the 19th century, cast-iron was cheaper than stone or brick and allowed ornate features to be prefabricated in foundries from moulds and used as building facades. Today, New York has the world's largest concentration of full and partial cast-iron facades. The best, built in the 1870s, are in the **SoHo Cast-Iron Historic District**.

The original cast-iron facade of Nos. 72–76 Greene Street, SoHo

BEAUX ARTS

THIS FRENCH school of architecture dominated public buildings and wealthy residential properties during New York's gilded age. This era (from 1880 to about 1920) produced many of the city's most prominent architects, including Richard Morris Hunt (**Carnegie Hall**, 1891; **Metropolitan Museum**, 1895), who in 1845 was the first American architect to study in Paris; Cass Gilbert (**Custom House**, 1907; **New York Life Insurance**

ARCHITECTURAL DISGUISES

Some of the most fanciful forms on the New York skyline were devised by clever architects to disguise the city's essential but utilitarian – and rather unattractive – roof-top water tanks. Look skyward to discover the ornate cuppolas, spires and domes that transform the most mundane of features into veritable castles in the air. Examples that are easy to spot are atop two neighbouring Fifth Avenue hotels: the Sherry Netherland at 60th Street and the Pierre at 61st Street.

Standard water tower

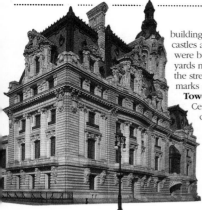

Beaux Arts mansion built for Cornelius Vanderbilt II (1843–99); it has since been demolished

buildings resembled castles and châteaux, and were built around court-yards not visible from the street. Favourite land-marks are the four **Twin Towers** that arose on Central Park West during the peak of Art Deco (1929 to 1931), the Eldorado, Century, San Remo and Majestic. Together they provide the distinctive sky-line seen from the park.

Building, 1928; the **US Courthouse**, 1936); the teams of Warren & Wetmore (**Grand Central Terminal**, 1913; **Helmsley Building**, 1929); Carrère & Hastings (**New York Public Library**, 1911; **Frick Mansion**, 1914); and McKim, Mead & White, the city's most famous firm of architects (**Villard Houses**, 1884; **United States General Post Office**, 1913; **Municipal Building**, 1914).

APARTMENT BUILDINGS

As the city's population grew and space became ever more precious, family homes in Manhattan became much too expensive for most New Yorkers and even the wealthy joined the trend towards communal living. In 1884 Henry Hardenbergh's Dakota (*see p216*), one of the first luxury apartment buildings, started a spate of turn-of-the-century construction on the Upper West Side. Many of the

SKYSCRAPERS

Although chicago gave birth to the skyscraper, New York has seen some of the greatest innovations in this style. In 1902 Daniel Burnham, a Chicago architect, built the **Flatiron Building**, so tall at 300 ft (91 m) that sceptics said it would collapse. By 1913, the **Woolworth Building** had risen to 792 ft (241 m). Soon, zoning laws were passed requiring "set-backs" – upper storeys were stepped back to allow light to reach street level. This suited the Art Deco style. The **Chrysler Building** (1930)

Art Deco arched pattern on the spire of the Chrysler Building

was the world's tallest until the **Empire State Building** (1931) was completed. Both are Art Deco classics, but it was Raymond Hood's **Group Health Insurance Building**, formerly the McGraw-Hill Building, that represented New York in 1932 in the *International Style* architectural survey.

The **World Trade Center** is currently the tallest building, at 1,350 ft (411 m). It represents the "glass box" Modernism style, now superseded by the Post-Modern style, such as the **Citicorp Center** (1977).

No. 245 Fifth Avenue (Apartment Bulding)

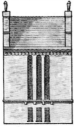

No. 60 Gramercy Park North (Brownstone)

Hotel Pierre (Beaux Arts)

Sherry Netherland Hotel (Beaux Arts)

Multicultural New York

WHEREVER YOU GO in New York, even in pockets of the hectic highrise city centre, you will find evidence of the richly ethnic flavour of the city. A bus ride can take you from Madras to Moscow, Hong Kong to Haiti. Immigrants are still coming to New York, though numbers are fewer than in the peak years from 1880 to 1910, when 17 million people arrived. In the 1980s, a million newcomers, largely from Caribbean countries and Asia, arrived and found their own special corner of the city. Throughout the year you will encounter crowds celebrating one of many festivals. To find out more about national celebrations and parades, see pages 50–53.

Hell's Kitchen
The Irish community first settled here; now they colour Fifth Avenue green for St Patrick's day on 17 March every year.

Little Ukraine
Services are held at Taras Sevchenko Place as part of the 17 May festivities to mark the Ukrainians' conversion to Christianity.

Little Korea
Not far from Herald Square, a small enclave of Koreans have made their niche.

Little Italy
For ten days in September the Italian community gathers round the Mulberry Street area and the streets are taken over by the celebrations of the Festa di San Gennaro.

Chinatown
Every year, around the end of January, Mott Street is packed with revellers as Chinatown celebrates its New Year.

The Lower East Side
The synagogues around Rivington Street reflect the religious traditions of this old Jewish area.

Chelsea and the Garment District

Theatre District

Gramercy and the Flatiron District

Greenwich Village

Soho and TriBeCa

East Village

Seaport and the Civic Center

Lower East Side

Lower Manhattan

0 kilometres   2
0 miles   1

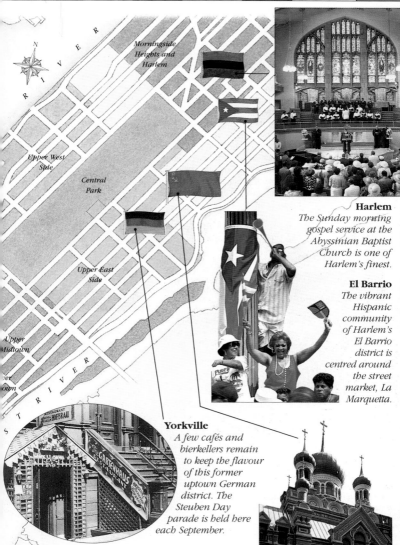

Harlem
The Sunday morning gospel service at the Abyssinian Baptist Church is one of Harlem's finest.

El Barrio
The vibrant Hispanic community of Harlem's El Barrio district is centred around the street market, La Marquetta.

Yorkville
A few cafés and bierkellers remain to keep the flavour of this former uptown German district. The Steuben Day parade is held here each September.

Little India
The restaurants of East 6th Street offer Eastern atmosphere at affordable prices.

Upper East Side
The magnificent St Nicholas Russian Orthodox Cathedral on East 97th Street is a reminder of the dispersed white Russian community. Mass is held in Russian each Sunday.

Exploring New York's Many Cultures

Stained glass at the Cotton Club

EVEN "NATIVE" NEW YORKERS have ancestral roots in another country. Throughout the 17th century, the Dutch and English settled here, establishing trade colonies in the New World. Soon America became a symbol of hope for the downtrodden elsewhere in Europe. Many flocked across the ocean, penniless and with little knowledge of the language. The potato famine of the 1840s led to the first wave of Irish immigrants, soon to be followed by German and other European workers displaced by the Industrial Revolution. Many immigrants have moved from their original neighbourhoods in New York, spreading an estimated 80 languages throughout the city.

Turkish immigrants arriving at Idlewild Airport in 1963

THE JEWS

THERE HAS BEEN a Jewish community in New York since 1654. The first synagogue, Shearith Israel, was established by refugees from a Dutch colony in Brazil, and is still active today. These first settlers, Sephardic Jews of Spanish descent, included prominent families such as the Baruchs. They were followed by the German Jews, who set up successful retailing enterprises, like the Straus brothers. Russian persecution led to the mass immigration that began in the late 1800s. By the start of World War I, there were 600,000 Jews living on the Lower East Side. Today, this area is more Hispanic than Jewish but it holds reminders of its former role as a place of refuge and new beginnings.

THE GERMANS

THE GERMANS began to settle in New York in the 18th century. From Peter Zenger onwards (see p19) the city's German community has championed the freedom to express ideas and opinions. It has also produced giants of industry, such as John Jacob Astor, the city's first millionaire.

THE ITALIANS

ITALIANS FIRST came to New York in the 1830s and 1840s. Many came from northern Italy to escape the failing revolution at home. In the 1870s, poverty in southern Italy drove many more Italians across the ocean. In time, they became a potent political force in the city, exemplified by Fiorello LaGuardia, one of New York's finest mayors.

THE CHINESE

THE CHINESE were late arrivals to New York. In 1880, the population of the Mott Street district was a mere

Eastern States Buddhist Temple, in Chinatown (see pp96–7)

700. By the 1940s they were the city's fastest growing and most upwardly-mobile ethnic group, extending the old boundaries of Chinatown and establishing new neighbourhoods in parts of Brooklyn and Queens. Once a closed community, Chinatown now bustles with tourists exploring the streets and markets, and sampling the restaurant food.

THE HISPANIC AMERICANS

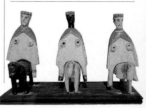

Hispanic religious carving at El Museo del Barrio (see p229)

PUERTO RICANS were in New York as early as 1838, but it was not until after World War II that they arrived in large numbers in search of work. Most live in El Barrio, formerly known as Spanish Harlem. Professionals who fled Fidel Castro's Cuba have moved out of the city itself, but are still very influential in Hispanic commerce and culture. Washington Heights is home to the Dominican and Colombian communities.

THE IRISH

THE IRISH, who first arrived in New York in the 1840s, had to overcome harsh odds. Wretched with starvation, and with barely a penny to their names, they laboured hard to escape the slums of Five Points and Hell's Kitchen, helping to build the modern city in the process. Many joined the police and firefighting forces, rising to high rank through dedication to duty. Others set up successful businesses, such as the Irish bars which act as a focus for the now-scattered New York Irish community.

THE AFRICAN AMERICANS

ARGUABLY the best known black inner city community in the western world, Harlem is notable to visitors today for its gospel singing and unsurpassed soul food. Ancestors of many African-Americans were brought to the US as slaves to work on southern plantations. The move from the south to larger cities in the north began with emancipation in the 1860s. However, it picked up full steam in the 1920s, when the black population rose from 83,000 to 204,000 and Harlem became the centre of a black renaissance *(see pp28–9)*.

THE MELTING POT

OTHER NEW YORK cultures are not so distinctly defined, but are easily found. Ukrainians gather in the East Village, around St George's Ukrainian Catholic Church on East 7th Street. Little India can be spotted by the restaurants along East 6th. The Koreans own many of the greengrocer stalls around Manhattan but more tend to live in the Flushing area. The religious diversity of New York's population can be seen in the Islamic Center on Riverside Drive, the

A woman celebrating at the Greek Independence Day parade

Russian Orthodox Cathedral on East 97th Street *(see p197),* and the new Islamic Cultural Center on 96th Street – Manhattan's first major mosque.

THE OUTER BOROUGHS

BROOKLYN IS by far the most international borough. Caribbean newcomers from Jamaica and Haiti are one of

the fastest growing immigrant groups. West Indians tend to cluster along Eastern Parkway between Grand Army Plaza and Utica Avenue, the route of the lavish, exotically-costumed West Indian Day Parade in September. Recently-arrived Russian Jewish immigrants have turned Brighton Beach into "Little Odessa by the Sea", and the Scandinavians and Lebanese have settled in Bay Ridge and the Finns in Sunset Park. Borough Park and Williamsburg are home to Orthodox Jews and Midwood has an Israeli-Middle East accent. Italians live in the Bensonhurst area. Greenpoint is little Poland, and Atlantic Avenue is home to the largest Arab community in America.

The Irish were among the earliest groups to cross the Harlem River into the Bronx. Japanese executives have favoured the more exclusive Riverdale area. One of the most distinctive ethnic areas is Astoria, Queens, which has the largest Greek population outside the motherland. Jackson Heights is home to a large Latin American quarter, including some 300,000 Colombians. Indians also favour this area and neighbouring Flushing. But it is the Orientals who have transformed Flushing, so much so that the local train has been called "The Orient Express".

The New York police, a haven for Irish-Americans

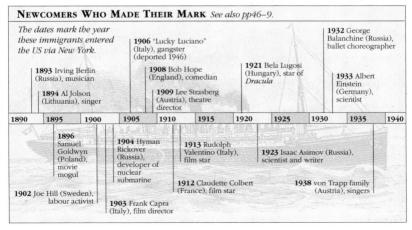

NEWCOMERS WHO MADE THEIR MARK *See also pp46–9.*

The dates mark the year these immigrants entered the US via New York.

1893 Irving Berlin (Russia), musician

1894 Al Jolson (Lithuania), singer

1906 "Lucky Luciano" (Italy), gangster (deported 1946)

1908 Bob Hope (England), comedian

1909 Lee Strasberg (Austria), theatre director

1921 Bela Lugosi (Hungary), star of *Dracula*

1932 George Balanchine (Russia), ballet choreographer

1933 Albert Einstein (Germany), scientist

1890	1895	1900	1905	1910	1915	1920	1925	1930	1935	1940

1896 Samuel Goldwyn (Poland), movie mogul

1902 Joe Hill (Sweden), labour activist

1903 Frank Capra (Italy), film director

1904 Hyman Rickover (Russia), developer of nuclear submarine

1912 Claudette Colbert (France), film star

1913 Rudolph Valentino (Italy), film star

1923 Isaac Asimov (Russia), scientist and writer

1938 von Trapp family (Austria), singers

Celebrated Visitors and Residents

Nearly all New Yorkers have immigrant roots if you go back far enough. Indeed, many of the city's most prominent residents have migrated here, coming to New York to find creative freedom and sometimes fleeing from constraints or repression in their native countries. As a result, some of the most brilliant contributions to New York's colourful history and culture have been made by first-generation immigrants and visitors.

George Balanchine *(1904–83)*
The ballet choreographer migrated from Russia in 1933 and formed the New York City Ballet.

Dylan Thomas
(1914–53)
The Welsh poet drank himself to a tragically early death; he frequented the White Horse Tavern in Greenwich Village.

Marcel Duchamp
(1887–1968)
In 1917 the French Dadaist climbed Washington Square arch to protest against US participation in World War I.

Guiseppe Garibaldi *(1807–82)*
A statue in Greenwich Village honours the Italian freedom fighter who spent four years in exile on Staten Island before returning to unify Italy.

Irving Berlin *(1888–1989)*
Born Israel Baline in Siberia, he grew up on the Lower East Side and composed the all-American White Christmas.

Theater District

Chelsea and the Garment District

Gramercy and the Flatiron District

East Village

Greenwich Village

SoHo & TriBeCa

Seaport and the Civic Center

Lower East Side

Lower Manhattan

HUDSON RIVER

EAST RIVER

Isaac Bashevis Singer
(1904–91)
The Polish Jewish novelist lived on W 86th Street for many years.

Morningside Heights and Harlem

John Audubon
(1785–1851)
America's most famous ornithologist grew up in France. His New York estate was in Washington Heights.

Marcus Garvey
(1887–1940)
Jamaican-born Garvey lived in Harlem during the 1920s, where he was an influential black leader.

Upper West Side

Central Park

John Lennon
(1940–80)
The Liverpool-born musician and his wife, Yoko Ono, made their home on the Upper West Side.

Upper East Side

Harry Houdini
(1874–1926)
The escape artist from Budapest had a vision of his death at the age of 52, and left his house on W 113th Street weeping.

Upper Midtown

Andrew Carnegie *(1835–1918)*
The Scottish-born industrialist and philanthropist's home is now the Cooper-Hewitt Museum (see p184).

Sarah Bernhardt *(1844–1923)*
The French actress attended services at the Little Church Around the Corner (see p127) during her time in New York.

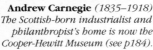

0 kilometres 2

0 miles 1

Jacob Riis *(1849–1914)*
A Danish immigrant, he slept in Bowery doorways before writing How the Other Half Lives, which helped alleviate the squalor in New York.

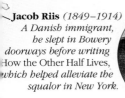

Remarkable New Yorkers

NEW YORK HAS NOURISHED some of the best creative talents of this century. Pop art began in New York, and Manhattan is still the world centre for modern art. The alternative writers of the 1950s and '60s – known as the Beat Generation – took inspiration from the city's jazz clubs. And as the financial capital, many conspicuous capitalists have also made New York their home.

WRITERS

Novelist James Baldwin

AMERICAN LITERATURE was born in New York. *Charlotte Temple, A Tale of Truth,* first published in 1791 by Susanna Rowson (c1762–1824), was a tale of seduction in the city. It was a best-seller for 50 years.

America's first professional author was Charles Brockden Brown (1771–1810), who came to New York in 1791. The novels of Edgar Allan Poe (1809–49), the pioneer of the modern thriller story, expanded the thriller genre. Henry James (1843–1916) published *The Bostonians* (1886) and became the master of the psychological novel, and his friend Edith Wharton (1861–1937) became known for her satirical novels about American society.

American literature finally recieved international recognition with Washington Irving's (1783–1859) satire, *A History of New York* (1809). It earned him $2,000. Irving coined the names "Gotham" for New York, and "Knickerbockers" for New Yorkers. He and James Fenimore Cooper (1789–1851), whose books gave birth to the Western novel, formed the Knickerbocker group of US writers.

Greenwich Village has always attracted writers, including Herman Melville (1819–91) whose masterpiece, *Moby Dick* (1851), was very poorly received at first. Jack Kerouac (1922–69), Allen Ginsberg and William Burroughs all went to Columbia University, and drank with other literati at the San Remo Café in Greenwich Village. Dylan Thomas (1914–53) ended his days at the Chelsea Hotel (*see p137*). Novelist Nathanael West (1902–40) worked in the Gramercy Park Hotel, and his friend Dashiell Hammett (1894–1961) wrote *The Maltese Falcon* while living there. James Baldwin (1924–87), born in Harlem, wrote *Another Country* (1963) on his return to New York from Europe.

ARTISTS

THE NEW YORK School of Abstract Expressionists founded the first influental American art movement. It was launched by Hans Hofmann (1880–1966) with Franz Kline and Willem de Kooning, whose first job in America was as a house-painter. Adolph Gottlieb, Mark Rothko (1903–70) and Jackson Pollock (1912–56) went on to popularize this style. Pollock, Kline and de Kooning all had their studios on the Lower East Side.

Pop Art began in New York in the 1960s with Roy Lichtenstein and

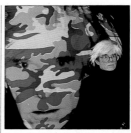

Pop artist Andy Warhol

Andy Warhol (1926–87), who made some of his cult films at 33 Union Square. Keith Haring (1958–90) was a very prolific graffiti artist whose work as a pop artist is now receiving recognition.

Robert Mapplethorpe (1946–89) acquired notoriety for his homoerotic photos of gay men. Jeff Koons has now superceded him as the *bête noire* of the art establishment.

The illusionistic murals by Richard Haas enliven many walls throughout the city.

ACTORS

IN 1849 the British actor Charles Macready started a riot by saying Americans were vulgar. A mob stormed the Astor Place Opera House, where Macready was playing Macbeth, police opened fire, and 22 rioters were killed. In 1927 Mae West (1893–1980) spent 10 days in a workhouse on Roosevelt Island and was fined $500 for giving a lewd performance in her Broadway show *Sex.* Marc Blitzstein's radical pro-labour opera *The Cradle Will Rock,* produced by Orson Welles (1915–85) and John Houseman (1902–88), was immediately banned and the show had to move to

Vaudeville actress Mae West

another theatre. The actors managed to get around the ban by buying tickets and singing their roles from the audience.

The musical has been New York's special contribution to the theatre. Florenz Ziegfeld's (1869–1932) *Follies* ran from 1907 to 1931. The opening of *Oklahoma* on Broadway in 1943 began the age of musicals by Richard Rodgers (1902–79) and Oscar Hammerstein, Jr (1895–1960).

Off Broadway, the Provincetown Players at No. 33 MacDougal Street were the first to produce Eugene O'Neill's (1888–1953) *Beyond The Horizon* (1920). His successor as the major innovative force in US theatre was Edward Albee, author of *Who's Afraid of Virginia Woolf?* (1962).

MUSICIANS AND DANCERS

LEONARD BERNSTEIN (1918–90) followed a long line of great conductors at the New York Philharmonic, including Bruno Walter (1876–1962), Arturo Toscanini (1867–1957) and Leopold Stokowski (1882–1977). Maria Callas (1923–77) was born in New York, but moved to Europe.

Carnegie Hall *(see p146)* has featured Enrico Caruso (1873–1921), Bob Dylan and The Beatles. Record concert attendance was set in 1991 when Paul Simon drew a million people for his free concert in Central Park.

The legendary swinging jazz clubs of the 1930s and 40s are now gone from 52nd Street. Plaques on "Jazz Walk" outside the CBS building honour such famous

Josephine Baker

performers as Charlie Parker (1920–55) and Josephine Baker (1906–75).

Between 1940 and 1965 New York became a world dance capital with the founding of George Balanchine's (1904–83) New York City Ballet and the American Ballet Theater. In 1958, dance choreographer Alvin Ailey (1931–89) started the American Dance Theater, a showcase for modern dance works by a multiracial dance troupe.

INDUSTRIALISTS AND ENTREPRENEURS

Tycoon Cornelius Vanderbilt

THE RAGS-TO-RICHES story is an American dream. Andrew Carnegie (1835–1919), "the steel baron with a heart of gold", started with nothing and died having given away some $350 million. His beneficiaries included public libraries and Universities throughout America. Many other foundations are legacies of wealthy philanthropists. Some, like Cornelius Vanderbilt (1794–1877), tried to shake off their rough beginnings by patronizing the arts.

In business, New York's "robber barons" did what they liked with apparent impunity. Financiers Jay Gould (1836–92) and James Fisk (1834–72) beat Vanderbilt in the war for the Erie railroad by manipulating stock. In September 1869 they caused Wall Street's first "Black Friday" when they tried to corner the gold market, but fled when their fraud was discovered. Gould died a happy billionaire and Fisk was killed in a fight over a woman.

Modern entrepreneurs have included Donald Trump *(see p31),* owner of the Trump Tower, and Harry and Leona Helmsley. Despite Leona's imprisonment for tax evasion, their property empire remains intact and includes such New York sites as the Helmsley Building *(see p156).*

ARCHITECTS

CASS GILBERT (1858–1934), who built such Neo-Gothic skyscrapers as the Woolworth Building of 1913 *(see p91)* was one of the men who literally shaped the city. His caricature can be seen in the lobby, clutching a model of his masterpiece. Stanford White (1853–1906) was as well known for his scandalous private life as for his fine Beaux Arts buildings such as the Players Club *(p126).* For most of his life, Frank Lloyd Wright (1867–1959) spurned city architecture. When he was eventually persuaded to leave his mark on the city, it was in the form of the Guggenheim Museum *(pp186–7).* German-born Ludwig Mies van der Rohe (1886–1969), who built the Seagram Building, did not believe in "inventing a new architecture every Monday morning", although some might argue this is just what New York has always done best.

Musical producer Florenz Ziegfeld

NEW YORK THROUGH THE YEAR

SPRINGTIME IN NEW YORK sees Park Avenue filled with blooms, while Fifth Avenue goes green for St Patrick's Day, the first of the year's many big parades. Summer in the city is hot and humid, but it is worth forsaking an air-conditioned interior to step outside, where parks and squares are the setting for free open-air music and theatre. The first Monday in September marks Labor Day and the advent of comfortable temperatures and the orange-red colours of autumn. Then, as Christmas nears, the shops and streets begin to sparkle with dazzling window displays.

Dates of the events on the following pages may vary. For details consult the listings magazines *(see p353)*. The New York Convention and Visitors Bureau *(see p352)* issues a quarterly calendar of events.

SPRING

EVERY SEASON in New York brings its own tempo and temptations. In spring, the city shakes off the winter with tulips and cherry blossoms in the parks, and spring fashions in the stores. Everyone window shops and gallery hops. The hugely popular St Patrick's Day Parade draws the crowds, and thousands don their finery for the Easter Parade down Fifth Avenue.

Inventive Easter bonnets in New York's Easter Parade

MARCH

St Patrick's Day Parade *(17 Mar)*, Fifth Ave, from 44th to 86th sts. Green clothes, green flowers – even green beer.
Greek Independence Day Parade *(25 Mar)*, Fifth Ave, from 49th to 59th sts. Greek dancing and food.
New York City Opera Spring Season *(Mar–mid-Apr)*, Lincoln Center *(p338)*.
Ringling Bros and Barnum & Bailey Circus *(late Mar–end May)*, Madison Square Garden *(p133)*.

Yellow tulips and cabs shine on Park Avenue

EASTER

Easter Flower Show *(week before Easter)*, Macy's department store *(pp132–3)*.
Easter Parade *(Easter Sun)*, Fifth Ave, from 44th to 59th sts. Paraders in costumes and outrageous millinery around St Patrick's Cathedral.

APRIL

Cherry Blossom Festival *(late Apr–May)*, Brooklyn Botanic Garden. Famous for Japanese cherry trees and beautifully laid out ornamental gardens.
Gramercy Park Flower Show *(last weekend) (p126)*.
Baseball *(Apr–May)*, Major league season starts for Yankees and Mets *(p344)*.
New York City Ballet Spring Season *(Apr–Jun)*, New York State Theater and Metropolitan Opera House in Lincoln Center *(p212)*.

MAY

Brooklyn Bridge Day *(second Sun)*. Celebrations on the bridge *(pp86–9)*.
Martin Luther King, Jr Day Parade *(third Sun)*, Fifth Ave, from 44th to 86th sts. Parade to honour the memory of

Parading in national costume on Greek Independence Day

the assassinated black civil rights leader.
Ninth Avenue Street Festival *(mid-May)*, from W 37th to W 57th sts. A feast of ethnic foods, music and dance.
Washington Square Outdoor Art Exhibit *(last weekend in May and first weekend in Jun)*. Paintings, sculpture and crafts.

AVERAGE DAYS OF SUNSHINE PER MONTH

Jan Feb Mar Apr May Jun Jul Aug Sep Oct Nov Dec

Days of Sunshine
New York enjoys long and light summer days from June to August, with July the month of greatest sunshine. The winter days are much shorter, but many are clear and bright. Autumn has more sunshine than spring, but both are sunny.

SUMMER

NEW YORKERS escape the hot city streets when possible, for picnics, boat rides and the beaches. Macy's fireworks light up the Fourth of July skies, and more sparks fly when the New York Yankees and Mets baseball teams are in town. Summer also brings street fairs, outdoor concerts, and free Shakespeare and opera in Central Park.

Policeman dancing in the Puerto Rican Day Parade

JUNE

Puerto Rican Day Parade *(first Sun)*, Fifth Ave, from 44th to 86th sts. Floats and marching bands.
Museum Mile Festival *(second Tue)*, Fifth Ave, from 82nd to 105th sts. Free entry to museums.
L'eggs Mini-Marathon *(late Jun)*, from Central Park West and W 66th St to Central Park West at W 67th St. Women's road-running race.
Metropolitan Opera Parks Concerts. Free evening concerts in parks throughout the city *(pp338–9)*.
Goldman Memorial Band Concerts *(Jun–Aug)*, Lincoln Center *(p212)*. Traditional band concerts.

Shakespeare in the Park *(Jun–Sep)*. Broadway stars take on the bard at Delacorte Theater, Central Park *(p335.)*
Lesbian and Gay Pride Day Parade *(late Jun)*, from Columbus Circle along Fifth Ave to Washington Sq *(p113)*.
JVC Jazz Festival *(late Jun–early Jul)*. Top jazz musicians perform in various halls in the city *(p341)*.

JULY

Macy's Firework Display *(4 Jul)*, East River. High point of the city's Independence Day celebrations.
American Crafts Festival *(early July)*, Lincoln Center *(p212)*. High-quality crafts.
Chinatown Cultural Festival *(mid-Jul–mid-Sep)*, Chinatown *(pp96–7)*.
Mostly Mozart Festival, *(mid-Jul–end Aug)*, Avery Fisher Hall, Lincoln Center *(pp338-9)*.
NY Philharmonic Parks Concerts *(late Jul–early*

Festivities at a summer street fair in Greenwich Village

Aug). Free concerts in parks throughout the city *(p339)*.
Summer Festival *(Jul–Aug)*, Snug Harbor Cultural Center, Staten Island. Music and art.

AUGUST

Harlem Week *(mid-Aug)*. Films, art, music, dance, fashion, sports and tours.
Out-of-Doors Festival *(mid-Aug–early Sep)*, Lincoln Center. Free dance and theatre performances *(p334)*.
US Open Tennis Championships *(late Aug–early Sep)*, Flushing Meadows *(p345)*.

Independence Day (4 July) fireworks display on the East River

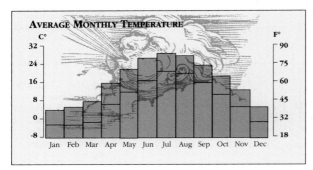

AVERAGE MONTHLY TEMPERATURE

Temperature
The chart shows the average minimum and maximum temperatures for each month in New York. With top temperatures averaging 29° C (84° F) the city can become hot and humid. In contrast, the months of winter, although rarely below freezing, can seem bitterly cold.

AUTUMN

LABOR DAY marks the end of the summer. The Giants and the Jets kick off the football season, the Broadway season begins and the Festa di San Gennaro in Little Italy is the high point in a succession of colourful neighbourhood fairs. Macy's Thanksgiving Day Parade is the nation's symbol that the festive season has arrived.

SEPTEMBER

Richmond County Fair *(Labor Day weekend)*, in the grounds of Historic Richmond Town *(p252)*. New York's only authentic county fair.
West Indian Carnival *(Labor Day weekend)*, Brooklyn. Parade, floats, music, dancing, food.
One World Festival *(second week)*, E 35th St, between First and Second avenues.

Exotic Caribbean carnival costume in the streets of Brooklyn

International antiques, arts and crafts, food.
New York is Book Country *(mid-Sep)*, Fifth Ave, from 48th to 59th sts. Book fair.
Festa di San Gennaro *(third week)*, Little Italy *(p96)*. Ten days of festivities and processions.
New York Film Festival *(mid-Sep – early Oct)*, Lincoln Center *(p212)*. American films and international art films.
Von Steuben Day Parade *(third week)*, Upper Fifth Ave. German-American celebrations.
American Football *(season begins)*, Giants Stadium, home to the Giants and the Jets *(p344)*.

OCTOBER

Columbus Day Parade *(2nd Mon)*, Fifth Ave, from 44th to 86th sts. Parades and music to celebrate Columbus's first sighting of America.
Pulaski Day Parade *(Sun closest to 5 Oct)*, Fifth Ave, from 26th to 52nd sts. Celebrations for Polish-American hero Casimir Pulaski.
Hallowe'en Parade *(31 Oct)*, Greenwich Village. Brilliant event with fantastic costumes.
Big Apple Circus *(Oct–Jan)*, Damrosch Park, Lincoln Center. Special themes are presented each year *(p349)*.
Basketball *(season begins)*, Madison Square Garden. Local team is the Knicks *(p344)*.
New York City Marathon *(last Sun Oct or first Sun Nov)*. From Staten Island through all the city boroughs.

Huge Superman balloon floating above Macy's Thanksgiving Day Parade

NOVEMBER

Macy's Thanksgiving Day Parade *(fourth Thu)*, from Central Park West and W 79th St to Broadway and W 34th St. A joy for children, with floats, huge balloons and Santa.
Christmas Star Show *(Nov–Jan)*, Hayden Planetarium *(p216)*. Re-creation of Bethlehem's sky on the night that Christ was born.
Magnificent Christmas Spectacular *(Nov–Jan)*, Radio City Music Hall. Variety show, with the Rockettes.

Revellers in Greenwich Village's Hallowe'en Parade

AVERAGE MONTHLY RAINFALL

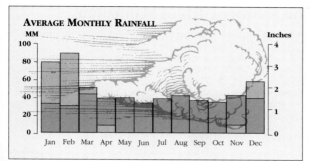

MM | Inches
100 — 4
80 — 3
60 —
40 — 2
20 — 1
0 — 0

Jan Feb Mar Apr May Jun Jul Aug Sep Oct Nov Dec

Rainfall

March and August are the heaviest rainfall months in New York. Rainfall in spring is unpredictable, so be prepared. Sudden heavy snowfalls in winter can cause chaos in the city.

Rainfall

Snowfall

WINTER

NEW YORK is magical at Christmas – even the stone lions at the Public Library don wreaths for the occasion and shops become works of art. From Times Square to Chinatown, New Year celebrations punctuate the season, and Central Park becomes a winter sports arena.

Statue of Alice in Wonderland in Central Park

DECEMBER

Tree-Lighting Ceremony *(early Dec)*, Rockefeller Center *(p142)*. Lighting of the giant Christmas tree in front of the RCA Building.
Messiah Sing-In *(mid-Dec)*, Lincoln Center *(p212)*. The audience rehearses and performs under the guidance of various conductors.
Hanukkah Menorah *(mid–late Dec)*, Grand Army Plaza, Brooklyn. Lighting of the huge menorah (candelabra) every night during the eight-day Festival of Lights.
New Year's Eve. Fireworks display in Central Park *(pp204–5)*; festivities in Times Square *(p145)*; five-mile (eight-km) run in Central Park; poetry reading in St Mark's Church.

JANUARY

National Boat Show *(mid-Jan)*, Jacob K Javits Convention Center *(p136)*.
Chinese New Year *(late Jan)*, Chinatown *(pp96–7)*. Dragons, fireworks and food.
Winter Antiques Show *(late Jan)*, Seventh Regiment Armory *(p185)*. The city's most prestigious antiques fair.

FEBRUARY

Black History Month. African-American events take place throughout the city.
Empire State Building Run-Up *(early Feb)*. Runners race to the 102nd floor *(pp134–5)*.
Lincoln and Washington Birthday Sales *(12–22 Feb)* Big department stores sales throughout the city.
Westminster Kennel Club Dog Show *(mid-Feb)*, Madison Square Garden *(p133)*. Top dog show.

Chinese New Year celebrations in Chinatown

PUBLIC HOLIDAYS

New Year's Day (1 Jan)
Martin Luther King Day (3rd Mon, Jan)
President's Day (mid-Feb)
Memorial Day (end May)
Independence Day (4 Jul)
Labor Day (1st Mon, Sep)
Columbus Day (2nd Mon, Oct)
Election Day (1st Tue, Nov)
Veterans Day (11 Nov)
Thanksgiving Day (4th Thu, Nov)
Christmas Day (25 Dec)

The giant Christmas tree and decorations at Rockefeller Center

The Southern Tip of Manhattan

THIS VIEW OF Lower Manhattan, seen from the Hudson River, encompasses some of the most striking modern additions to the New York skyline, including the instantly-recognizable twin towers of the World Trade Center, and the newer, distinctively-topped quartet of the World Financial Center. You will also catch glimpses of an earlier Manhattan: Castle Clinton set against the green space of Battery Park and, behind it, the noble Custom House building.

LOCATOR MAP

The Southern Tip

World Financial Center
At the heart of this complex is the Winter Garden – a place to shop, dine, be entertained or just enjoy the Hudson River views (see p69).

World Trade Center
Twin 110-storey steel and glass towers (see p72) dominate the skyline. Below is a plaza bigger than St Mark's Square in Venice.

The Upper Room
This walk-round sculpture by Ned Smyth is one of many works of art in Battery Park City (see p72).

An Earlier View
This 1898 photograph shows a skyline now changed beyond recognition.

Detail from the *Upper Room*

Downtown Athletic Club
The Heisman Trophy for football is kept in this fine Art Deco building.

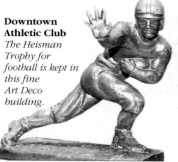

US Custom House
This magnificent 1907 Beaux Arts building now houses the Museum of the American Indian (see p73).

East Coast War Memorial
In Battery Park, a huge bronze eagle by Albino Manca honors the dead of World War II.

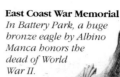

26 Broadway
The tower of the former Standard Oil Building resembles an oil lamp. The interior is still decorated with company symbols.

Bank of New York

17 State Street

26 Broadway

1 Liberty Plaza

Liberty View

Castle Clinton

US Custom House

American Merchant Mariners' Memorial (1991)
This sculpture by Marisol is on Pier A, the last of Manhattan's old piers. The pier also has a clock tower that chimes the hours on ships' bells.

Shrine of Mother Seton
The first US-born saint lived here (see p76).

Lower Manhattan from the East River

AT FIRST SIGHT, this stretch of East River shoreline, running up from the tip of Manhattan Island, is a seamless array of 20th-century office buildings. But from sea level, streets and slips are still visible, offering glimpses of old New York and the Financial District to the west. On the skyline itself, a few of the district's early skyscrapers manage to raise their ornate crowns above their more anonymous modern counterparts.

LOCATOR MAP

☐ East River View

India House
The handsome brownstone at No. 1 Hanover Square is one of the finest of its kind.

Vietnam Veterans Plaza
An engraved green glass memorial dominates the former Coenties Slip, a wharf filled in in the late 19th century, to make a park (see p76).

Hanover Square
A statue of one of the Dutch mayors, Abraham De Peyster, sits near the house where he was born in 1657.

No. 1 New York Plaza

No. 55 Water Street

Barclay Bank Building

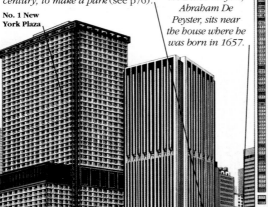

Battery Maritime Building
This historic ferry terminal serves only Governor's Island (see p77).

Downtown Heliport
Air-Sea Rescue and sightseeing flights operate from here.

Delmonico's
High society dined here a century ago.

New York Stock Exchange
Although hidden from view by more modern edifices, this is still the hub of the hectic Financial District (see p70 –71).

No. 40 Wall Street
In the 1940s, the pyramid topped tower of the former Bank of Manhattan was hit by a light aircraft.

No. 70 Pine Street
Replicas of this elegant Gothic-style tower can be seen near the Pine and Cedar Street entrances.

Bank of New York
This serene 1928 interior is part of the bank set up in 1784 by Alexander Hamilton (see p21).

No. 1 Financial Square

New York Stock Exchange

Morgan Bank
Columns from lobby to rooftop are the theme of this striking modern building.

Chase Manhattan Bank Tower

No. 120 Wall Street

Citibank Building

No. 100 Old Slip
Now in the shadow of No. 1 Financial Square, the small, palazzo-style First Precinct Police Department was the city's most modern police station when it was built in 1911.

Carved medallion, No. 100 Old Slip

Queen Elizabeth Monument
The ocean liner that sank in 1972 is remembered here.

South Street Seaport

A S THE FINANCIAL DISTRICT ends, the skyline, as seen from the East River or Brooklyn, changes dramatically. The corporate headquarters are replaced by the piers, low-rise streets and warehouses of the old seaport area, now restored as the South Street Seaport *(see pp82–3)*. The Civic Center lies not far inland, and a few of its monumental buildings can be seen. The Brooklyn Bridge marks the end of this stretch of skyline. Between here and midtown, apartment blocks make up the majority of riverside features.

LOCATOR MAP

☐ *South Street Area*

Pier 17
A focal point of the Seaport, this traditional-style leisure pier is packed with exciting shops, stalls and restaurants.

Stonework on the Woolworth Building

Woolworth Building
The handsomely decorated spire marks the headquarters of F W Woolworth's empire. It is still the finest "cathedral of commerce" ever built (see p91).

National Westminster Bank USA

Seaport Plaza

Transportation Building

Bogardus Building

Maritime Crafts Center
At Pier 15, craftspeople demonstrate traditional seafaring skills such as wood-carving and model-making.

Sweets
This seafood restaurant was in Schermerhorn Row from 1847 to 1993.

Fulton Fish Market
The largest wholesale fish market in the US takes place at the Seaport before dawn.

Police Plaza
Five in One (1971–74), in Police Plaza, is a sculpture by Bernard Rosenthal. It represents the five boroughs of New York.

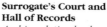

United States Courthouse
The Civic Center is marked on the skyline by the golden pyramid of architect Cass Gilbert's courthouse (see p85).

Municipal Building
Among the offices of this vast building is the Marriage Chapel, where weddings "at City Hall" actually take place. The copper statue on the skyline is Civic Fame *by Adolph Weinman (see p85).*

Surrogate's Court and Hall of Records
Archives dating back to 1664 are stored and displayed here (see p85).

New York Telephone Company

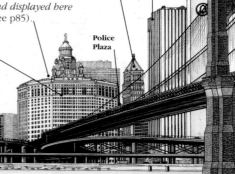

Pace University

Southbridge Towers

Police Plaza

Con Edison Mural
In 1975, artist Richard Haas recreated the Brooklyn Bridge on the side wall of a former electrical substation.

Brooklyn Bridge
Views of, and from, the bridge have made it one of New York's best-loved landmarks (see pp86–9).

Midtown Manhattan

T HE SKYLINE OF Midtown Manhattan is graced with some of
the city's most spectacular towers and spires, from the
familiar beauty of the Empire State Building's Art Deco
pinnacle to the dramatic wedge-shape of Citicorp's modern
headquarters. As the shoreline progresses uptown, so it moves
upmarket. The United Nations complex dominates a long
stretch, and then Beekman Place begins a strand of exclusive
residential enclaves which offer the rich and famous some
seclusion in this busy part of the city.

LOCATOR MAP

▨ *Midtown*

Chrysler Building
*Glinting in the sun by day or lit
up by night, this stainless steel
spire is, for many,
the ultimate
New York
skyscraper*
(see p153).

Empire State Building
*At 1250 ft (381 m), this was
the tallest building in
the world for many
years* (see p134–5).

Grand Central Terminal
*Now dwarfed by its neighbours,
this landmark building is full of
period details, such as this fine
clock* (see pp154–5).

**MetLife
Building**

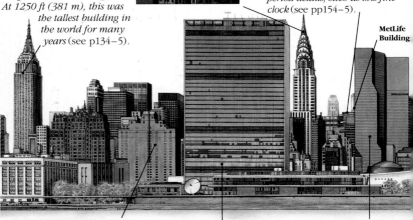

Tudor City
*Built in the 1920s, this
complex is mock Tudor on a
grand scale, with over 3,000
apartments* (see p156).

United Nations
*Works of art from member countries
include this Barbara
Hepworth sculpture,
a gift from Britain*
(see pp158–61).

Nos. 1 and 2 UN Plaza
*Angular glass towers
house offices and the
UN Plaza Hotel* (see
p156 and p280).

General Electric Building
Built of red brick in 1931, this Art Deco building has a tall, spiked crown. The present tenant is RCA Victor (see p174).

Waldorf–Astoria
Twin copper-capped towers rise high above one of the city's finest hotels. The interior is also splendid (see p175).

Citicorp Center
St Peter's Church nestles in one corner of the Citicorp Center with its raked tower (see p175).

Rockefeller Center
The outdoor skating rink and walkways of this complex of office buildings are a great place to people-watch (see p142).

General
Electric
Building

The Nail, by
Arnoldo
Pomodoro,
St Peter's
Church,
Citicorp
Center

No. 866
UN Plaza

No. 100 UN Plaza

Japan Society
Japanese culture, from avant-garde plays to ancient art, can be seen here (see p156–7).

Beekman Tower
Now an all-suite hotel, this Art Deco tower was built in 1928 as a hotel for women who were members of US college sororities.

St Mary's Garden
The garden at Holy Family Church is a peaceful haven.

NEW YORK
AREA BY AREA

LOWER MANHATTAN

THE OLD AND THE NEW con-
verge at the lower tip of
Manhattan, where Colonial
churches and early American
monuments stand in the shadow
of skyscrapers. New York was
born here, and this was the site
of the nation's first capitol.
Commerce has flourished
since 1626, when Dutchman
Peter Minuit made one of

**Minuit memorial on
Bowling Green**

history's most famous property
deals, purchasing the island of
Man-a-hatt-ta from the Algonquin
Indians for beads and goods valued at $24 *(see p17)*. The stakes
have become higher, but finance
remains at the heart of this part of
the city: it is home to Wall
Street, the Federal Reserve
Bank, the World Trade Center
and the Stock Exchange.

Trinity Church at the foot of Wall Street

SIGHTS AT A GLANCE

Historic Streets and Buildings
Federal Reserve Bank ❶
Federal Hall ❷
New York Stock Exchange pp70–71 ❸
Downtown Athletic Club ❽
Cunard Building ❾
Fraunces Tavern Museum ❸
Battery Maritime Building ❶⑥

Museums and Galleries
US Custom House ❶❶
Ellis Island pp78–9 ❶❽

Castle Clinton National Monument ⑳

Monuments and Statues
Statue of Liberty pp74–5 ❶⑦

Churches
Trinity Church ❹
Shrine of Elizabeth Ann Seton ❶⑫

Modern Architecture
World Financial Center ❺
World Trade Center ❻
Battery Park City ❼

Parks and Squares
Bowling Green ❶⓪
Vietnam Veterans' Plaza ❶⑭
Battery Park ❶⑲

Boat Trips
Staten Island Ferry ❶⑮

Bronze statue of a bull,
symbol of Wall Street,
near the Custom House

GETTING THERE

The best subway routes to the tip of Manhattan are the Lexington Ave 4 or 5 trains to Bowling Green; N or R to Whitehall St; or the 7th Ave 1 or 9 trains to South Ferry. For Wall St, take subways 2, 3, 4 or 5 to Wall St, or N or R to Rector Street. The M1, M6 and M15 buses and the M22 crosstown route all serve the area.

SEE ALSO

• *Street Finder*, maps 1, 2

• *Where to Stay* pp274–5

• *Restaurants* pp290–92

0 metres   500
0 yards   500

KEY

Street-by-Street map
Ⓜ Subway station
Ferry boarding point
Heliport

Street-by-Street: Wall Street

No intersection has been of greater importance to the city, past or present, than the corners of Wall and Broad Streets. Three important sites are located here. Federal Hall National Monument marks the place where, in 1789, George Washington was sworn in as president. Trinity Church is one of the nation's oldest Anglican parishes. The New York Stock Exchange, founded in 1817, is to this day a financial nerve centre whose ups and downs cause tremors around the globe. The surrounding buildings are the very heart of New York's financial district.

The Marine Midland Bank rises straight up 55 storeys. This dark, glass tower occupies only 40% of its site. The other 60% is a plaza in which a large red sculpture by Isamu Noguchi, *Cube*, balances on one of its points.

Trinity Building, an early 20th-century Gothic skyscraper, was designed to complement nearby Trinity Church.

The Equitable Building (1915) deprived its neighbours of light, prompting a change in the law: skyscrapers had to be set back from the street.

★ **Trinity Church**
Built in 1846 in a Gothic style, this is the third church on this site. Once the tallest structure in the city, the bell tower is now dwarfed by the skyscrapers that surround it. Many famous early New Yorkers are buried in the churchyard ❹

Wall Street subway (lines 4, 5)

The Irving Trust Company, built in 1932, has an outer wall patterned to look like fabric. In the lobby is an Art Deco mosaic in shades of flame and gold.

No. 26 Broadway was built as the home of the Standard Oil Trust. An oil lamp rests on top of it.

New York Stock Exchange ★
The hub of the world's financial markets is housed in a 17-storey building constructed in 1903. Its visitors' centre explains the history and workings of the Stock Exchange ❸

The Liberty Tower is clad in white terracotta and is in the Gothic style. It was later turned into apartments.

The Chamber of Commerce is a fine Beaux-Arts building of 1901.

STAR SIGHTS

★ **Federal Hall National Monument**

★ **Federal Reserve Bank**

★ **New York Stock Exchange**

★ **Trinity Church**

LOCATOR MAP
See Manhattan Map pp12–13

KEY

– – –   Suggested route

| 0 metres | 100 |
| 0 yards | 100 |

Chase Manhattan Bank and Plaza has the famous Jean Dubuffet sculpture, *Four Trees*, located in the plaza.

★ **Federal Reserve Bank**
In the style of a Renaissance palace, this is a bank for banks. US currency is issued here **❶**

Louise Nevelson Plaza is a park containing Nevelson's sculpture, *Shadows and Flags.*

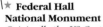

Wall Street is named for the wall that once kept the Algonquian Indians out of Manhattan – this narrow street is now the heart of the city's business centre.

Wall Street in the 1920s

★ **Federal Hall National Monument**
Originally the US Custom House, this Classical building now houses an exhibit about the Constitution **❷**

Federal Reserve Bank ❶

33 Liberty St. **Map** 1 C2. **⟨** 720-6130. **Ⓜ** Wall St. **Open** 8.30 am – 5pm Mon–Fri. **Closed** public hols. **⌀** ♿ ✉

Entrance to Federal Reserve Bank

T HIS IS A GOVERNMENT bank for banks – it is one of the 12 Federal Reserve banks, and therefore issues US currency. You can identify bank notes originating from this branch by the letter B in the Federal Reserve seal on each note.

Below ground is a five-storey vault that serves as the largest storehouse for gold owned by the nations of the world. Each nation's gold is stored in its own compartment within the subterranean vault, guarded by 90-tonne doors. Payments between nations used to be made by physical transfers of gold, but this is no longer so.

Designed by York & Sawyer, the building was completed in 1924. It occupies a full block, and is liberally adorned with fine wrought-iron grillwork. It was inspired by the palaces of the Italian Renaissance.

Federal Hall ❷

26 Wall St. **Map** 1 C3. **⟨** 825-6870. **Ⓜ** Wall St. **Open** 9am–5pm Mon–Fri. **Closed** public holidays. **⌀** ♿ ✉ 🏛

A BRONZE STATUE of George Washington, on the steps of Federal Hall, marks the site where the nation's first president took his oath of office in 1789. Thousands of New Yorkers jammed Wall and Broad Streets for the occasion. They roared their approval when the Chancellor of the State of New York shouted, "Long live George Washington, President of the United States."

The present imposing structure was built between 1834 and 1842 as the United States Custom House, and is one of the finest Classical designs in the city. Display rooms off the Rotunda include the Bill of Rights Room and an interactive computer exhibit about the Constitution.

New York Stock Exchange ❸

See pp70–71.

Trinity Churchyard

Trinity Church ❹

Broadway at Wall St. **Map** 1 C3. **⟨** 602-0872. **Ⓜ** Wall St, Rector St. **Open** 7am–6pm Mon–Fri, 8am–4pm Sat, 7am–4pm Sun. 🏛 11.15am Sun. 📷 except during services. ✉ 2pm daily. **Concerts**. ▯ 🏛

T HIS SQUARE-TOWERED Episcopal church at the head of Wall Street is the third one on this site in one of America's oldest Anglican parishes, founded in 1697. Designed in 1846 by Richard Upjohn, it was one of the grandest churches of its day, marking the beginning of the best period of Gothic Revival architecture in America. Richard Morris Hunt's design for the sculpted brass doors was inspired by Ghiberti's *Doors of Paradise* in Florence.

Restoration has uncovered the original rosy sandstone, long buried beneath layers of city grime. The 280-ft (26-m) steeple, the tallest structure in New York until the 1860s, still commands respect despite its towering neighbours.

Many prominent early New Yorkers were members of Trinity parish. Statesman Alexander Hamilton; steamboat inventor Robert Fulton; and William Bradford, founder of New York's first newspaper in 1725, are among those buried in the venerable graveyard beside the church.

Marble-columned rotunda within Federal Hall

World Financial Center **❺**

West St. **Map** 1 A2. **C** 945-0505.
M 1, 2, 3, 9, A, C, E to Chambers St,
1, 9, N, R to Cortlandt St. **B** M1, M6,
M9, M10, M22.

A MODEL OF URBAN design by
Cesar Pelli & Associates,
this development is a vital
part of the revival of lower
Manhattan. Four office towers
soar skyward, each topped
with a different geometric
shape. Some of the world's
most important financial
companies are headquartered
here, and overpasses link the
Center with its World Trade
counterpart. But this is far
more than an office complex.

At the heart of the Center is
the dazzling Winter Garden, a
vast glass and steel public
space, flanked by 45 restaurants and shops, opening on
to a lively piazza and marina
on the Hudson River. The
sweeping marble staircase
leading down to the Winter
Garden often doubles as
seating for free arts and
events, varying from the
classic to the contemporary in
music, dance and theatre.

Main floor of the Winter Garden

The atrium is a sparkling vault of
glass and steel, 120 ft (36 m) high.

**The "hourglass"
staircase** is used as
extra seating during
concerts in the
Winter Garden.

An esplanade borders the Hudson.　**Cafés and shops** line the atrium.

Sixteen 45-ft (14-m) palm
trees from the Mojave Desert
make this a 1990s version of
the "palm court" of yesteryear.

Inaugurated in 1988 and
still expanding, this is a place
designed for people and for
pleasure, and it has been
hailed as the Rockefeller
Center of the 21st century, by
even the most stringent of
architectural critics.

World Financial Center viewed from the Hudson River

New York Stock Exchange ❸

In 1790, TRADING in stocks and shares took place haphazardly on or around Wall Street but, in 1792, 24 brokers who traded under a buttonwood tree at 68 Wall Street signed an agreement to deal only with each other, and the basis of the New York Stock Exchange was formed. Membership is strictly limited. In 1817 a "seat" cost $25; today it can cost up to a million dollars, and a rigorous test of suitability is required. Visitors can watch the bustle of the trading posts from a gallery overlooking the trading floor. The NYSE has weathered slumps ("bear markets") and booms ("bull markets"), and has seen advances in technology, from tickertape to microchip, turn a local market-place into a global one.

Computerized stock tickers flash a steady stream of prices as fast as the human eye is able read them.

Tickertape Machine
Introduced in the 1870s, these machines printed out up-to-the-minute details of purchase prices on ribbons of paper tape.

Public entrance, Broad Street

WHAT A TRADING POST DOES

The 17 trading posts each consist of 22 groups or "sections" of traders and technology, each trading the stock of up to 10 listed companies.

Post display units show stock prices.

Free-arm CRTs display prices and trades for the specialist.

The pages help on the busy exchange floor, bringing orders from the booths to the brokers and specialists.

The supervisor's job is to monitor the smooth and legal running of the post.

A specialist trades in just one stock at a time, quoting bids to other brokers.

Independent floor brokers handle orders for busy brokerage firms.

Commission brokers work for brokerage firms, and rush between booth and trading post, buying and selling securities (stocks and bonds) for the public.

Clerks process the orders that come in to the trading post via SuperDOT computer, and log the results of trading into the Exchange's Market Data System.

The 48-Hour Day
During the 1929 Crash, Stock Exchange clerks worked non-stop for 48 hours. Their mood stayed cheerful despite the panic outside.

VISITORS' CHECKLIST

20 Broad St. **Map** 1 C3.
📞 656-5168. Ⓜ 2, 3, 4, 5 to Wall St, N, R to Rector St. 🚌 M1, M6, M15. **Visitors' gallery open** 9.15am–4.00pm Mon–Fri (last adm: 2.45pm). **Closed** public hols.
🚫 ♿ 📷 ▯ **Video displays**.

Public viewing gallery

Trading post

Trading Floor
Amid the frenzy of the trading floor, 200 million shares are traded each day for more than 2,000 companies. The advanced electronics that support the Designated Order Turnaround (SuperDOT) computer are carried above the chaos in a web of gold piping.

Great Crash of 1929
On Tuesday, 29 October, over 16 million shares changed hands as the stock market crashed. Investors thronged Wall Street in bewilderment but, contrary to popular myth, traders did not leap from windows in panic.

Members' entrance, Wall Street

TIMELINE

1792 Buttonwood Agreement signed, 17 May		**1867** Tickertape machines introduced		**1903** Present Stock Exchange building opens	**1987** "Black Monday" crash, 19 October. Dow Jones Index drops 508 points
	1844 Invention of the telegraph allows trading nationwide				**1976** DOT system replaces tickertape
1750	**1800**	**1850**		**1900**	**1950**
	1817 New York Stock & Exchange Board created	**1863** Name changed to New York Stock Exchange			**1929** Wall St Crash, 29 October
			1869 "Black Friday" gold crash, 24 September		**1981** Trading posts upgraded with electronic units
	Crowds gather outside during the 1929 Crash		**1865** New Exchange Building opens at Wall and Broad Sreets		

World Trade Center ❻

Map 1 B2. Ⓜ *Chambers St, Rector St.* **Observation Deck** *Two World Trade Center.* ☎ *435-4170.* **Open** *winter: 9.30am–9.30pm; summer: 9.30am–11.30pm daily.* **Adm charge.** 🔲 ♿ *but not to outside viewing platform.* 🍴 🛍 **Commodities Exchange** *9th Floor, Four World Trade Center.* ☎ *748-1006.* **Open** *9.30am–3pm Mon–Fri.* 🚫 ♿ 🎧

Tᴴᴱ 110-ꜱᴛᴏʀᴇʏ twin towers of the World Trade Center dominate the skyline of lower Manhattan. Instead of a steel frame, the enormous weight of each building is supported by an inner wire mesh cage, depriving workers inside of large windows. Spectacular views can only be seen from the top. Critics describe the buildings as giant, upended boxes. Built from 1966 to 1977, the complex consists of five office buildings and a hotel, connected by a vast underground concourse lined with shops and restaurants. The World Trade Center is home to 450 businesses and 50,000 workers. Large numbers of visitors come to see the unparalleled views from the observation deck or the rooftop promenade at Two World Trade Center. The express elevator takes just 58 seconds to reach the 107th floor. At One World Trade Center, make the same speedy ascent to the same level for drinks or dining at the Windows on the World restaurant (*see p295*).

When you look across from one tower to the next, think of Philippe Petit who, on 7 August 1974, stepped out on to a tightrope between towers One and Two, and entertained crowds of amazed office workers for almost an hour with the ultimate high-rise balancing act.

If you've more of a head for high finance than for heights, a visitors' gallery on the ninth floor of Four World Trade Center overlooks the trading floor of the bustling Commodities Exchange.

The tightrope act in progress

Philippe Petit about to step out between the two towers in 1974

Battery Park City ❼

Map 1 A3. Ⓜ *Rector St.* 🔲 ♿ 🍴 🎧

Battery Park City esplanade

Gᴏᴠᴇʀɴᴏʀ ᴍᴀʀɪᴏ ᴄᴜᴏᴍᴏ set the tone for this project in 1983 when he urged the developers: "Give it a social purpose – give it a soul." The city's newest neighbourhood is an ambitious development on 92 reclaimed acres (37 ha) along the Hudson River. The office buildings, restaurants, apartments, sculptures and gardens emphasize quality and are on a human scale.

In due course, Battery Park City will house over 25,000 people. The most visible part is the World Financial Center, four towers centred around the Winter Garden, with its huge atrium lined with palm trees. The total cost has been estimated at $4 billion.

The esplanade which runs along the river is a fine walk, with unobstructed views of the Statue of Liberty.

Downtown Athletic Club ❽

19 West St. **Map** 1 B4. ☎ *425-7000.* Ⓜ *Rector St.* **Lobby open** *to the public, club hours.*

Oɴᴇ ᴏꜰ ᴅᴏᴡɴᴛᴏᴡɴ's most striking buildings, this Art Deco creation from 1926 features a front arcade of arches with a Moorish flavour and a facade of patterned salt-glazed tiles in a range of colours from burnt orange to brown. The tiles have kept their fresh look, thanks to a natural glaze that has resisted the city soot. The rooms of the Club, open to members and their guests, have the calm, sleek atmosphere of an old-fashioned ocean liner.

Downtown Athletic Club facade

Ornate ceiling of the Cunard Building's Great Hall

Cunard Building ⑨

25 Broadway. **Map** 1 C3.
📞 363-9490 Ⓜ *Bowling Green.*
Open *post office hours, see* **Practical Information** *p361.*

STEP PAST the Renaissance facade, through the brass doors and beyond the fine wrought-iron gates of what is now the US Post Office to see the elaborate, domed Great Hall of this fine building of 1921. It was here that tickets were booked on classic liners such as the *Queen Mary* and the original *Queen Elizabeth*, when the Cunard Line was the largest passenger ship company in the world.

The hall has magnificent murals and frescoes, including maps of the world by Barry Faulkner and a remarkable, ornately decorated ceiling. Paintings by Ezra Winter on the supporting vaulting show the ships of Christopher Columbus, John Cabot, Sir Francis Drake and the Viking explorer Leif Eriksson.

Bowling Green ⑩

Map 1 C4. Ⓜ *Bowling Green.*

THIS TRIANGULAR plot north of Battery Park was the city's earliest park, used first as a cattle market and later as a bowling ground. A statue of King George III stood here until the signing of the Declaration of Independence,

when, as a symbol of British rule, it was hacked to pieces and smelted for ammunition *(see pp20–21)*. The wife of the governor of Connecticut is said to have melted down enough pieces to mould 42,000 bullets. The fence, erected in 1771, is still standing, but minus the royal crowns that once adorned it. They met the same fate as the statue. The Green was once surrounded by elegant homes. Beyond it is the start of Broadway, which runs the length of Manhattan and, under its formal name of Highway Nine, all the way north to the New York State capital in Albany.

Top of a column at the US Custom House

Fountain at Bowling Green

US Custom House ⑪

1 Bowling Green St. **Map** 1 C4.
📞 668-6624. Ⓜ *Bowling Green.*
Open *10am–5pm daily.* **Closed** *25 December.* 📷 ♿

ONE OF NEW YORK's finest Beaux Arts designs, this 1907 granite palace by Cass Gilbert is a fitting monument to the city's role as a great seaport, incorporating the talents of the best sculptors and artists of the time. Forty-four stately Ionic columns stand guard, adorned with an ornate frieze. Four heroic sculptures by Daniel Chester French depict four continents as seated women: Asia (contemplative), America (facing optimistically forwards), Europe (surrounded by the the symbols of past glories) and Africa (still sleeping).

Inside, murals by Reginald Marsh decorate the fine marble rotunda, showing the progress of ships into the harbour. Look to your right, opposite the entrance, to see a portrait of movie star Greta Garbo giving a press conference on board ship. In 1973 the US Customs Service moved out, leaving the building empty but for a small bankruptcy court.

The Custom House took on a new function in 1994, when the George Gustav Heye Center of the National Museum of the American Indian was finally unveiled on three floors of the building. The museum's outstanding collection of about a million artifacts along with an archive of many thousands of photographs, spans the breadth of the native cultures of North, Central and South America.

Exhibitions will include new works by contemporary Native American artists as well as changing thematic displays using exhibits drawn from the permanent collection.

Statue of Liberty ⑰

A GIFT FROM THE FRENCH to the American people, the statue was the brainchild of sculptor Frédéric-Auguste Bartholdi and has become a symbol of freedom throughout the world. In Emma Lazarus's poem, which is engraved on the base, Lady Liberty says: "Give me your tired, your poor, Your huddled masses yearning to breathe free." The statue loomed over Paris before its home on Bedloe's Island (now called Liberty Island) was ready. Unveiled by President Grover Cleveland on 28 October 1886, the statue was restored in time for its 100th anniversary.

★ **Golden Torch**
In 1986, a new torch replaced the corroded original. The replica's flame is coated in 24-carat gold leaf.

The crown is the highest level open to visitors.

The frame was designed by Gustave Eiffel who later built the Eiffel Tower. The copper shell hangs by iron bars from a central iron pylon.

A central pylon anchors the 225-tonne statue to its base.

354 steps lead from the entrance to the crown.

Observation deck and museum

THE STATUE
With a height of 305 ft (93 m) from ground to torch, the Statue of Liberty dominates New York harbour.

The pedestal is set within the walls of an army fort. It was the largest concrete mass ever poured.

From her Toes to her Torch
Three hundred moulded copper sheets riveted together make up Lady Liberty.

YOU buy a LIBERTY BOND LEST I PERISH

★ **Statue of Liberty Museum**
Posters featuring the statue are among the items on display.

The original torch now stands in the main lobby.

★ **Views of Lower Manhattan**
Lady Liberty has some of the best views of the city; see them from the observation deck, the crown or the boat.

VISITORS' CHECKLIST

Liberty Island. **Map** 1 A5.
363-3200. M 1, 9, N, R to
South Ferry, 4, 5 to Bowling
Green. M6, M15 to South
Ferry, then Circle Line–Statue of
Liberty Ferry from the Battery
every 30 mins, 9.30am–3.30pm
summer (winter hours vary).
269-5755. **Open** Jul–Aug:
9.30am–5.30pm daily; Sep–Jun:
9.30am–6pm daily. **Closed** 25
Dec. Ferry fare includes entry to
Ellis and Liberty Is. lift to
observation deck only.

Portrait of Liberty
Bartholdi's mother was the model for Liberty. The seven rays of her crown represent the seven seas and seven continents.

Making the Hand
To mould the copper shell, the hand was made first in wood, then plaster.

(left image of statue and model)

A Model Figure
A series of graduated scale models enabled Bartholdi to build the largest metal statue ever constructed.

FRÉDÉRIC-AUGUSTE BARTHOLDI

The French sculptor who designed the Statue of Liberty intended it as a monument to the freedom he found lacking in his own country. He devoted 21 years of his life to making it a reality, even travelling to America in 1871 to talk President Ulysses S Grant and other leaders into funding the statue and installing it in New York's harbour. He said "I will try to glorify the Republic and Liberty over there, in the hope that someday I will find it again here."

Restoration Celebration
On 3 July 1986, after a $69.8 million clean-up, the statue was unveiled. The $2 million firework display was the largest ever seen in America.

STAR FEATURES

★ **Golden Torch**

★ **Statue of Liberty Museum**

★ **Views of Lower Manhattan**

Shrine of Elizabeth Ann Seton ⑫

7–8 State St. **Map** 1 C4. 269-6865 **M** Whitehall, South Ferry. **Open** 6.30am–5.30pm Mon–Fri, 8am–6pm Sat, Sun. frequent.

Elizabeth Ann Seton

Eᴸɪᴢᴀʙᴇᴛʜ ᴀɴɴ Seton (1774–1821), the first native-born American to be canonized by the Catholic Church, lived here from 1801 to 1803. Mother Seton founded the American Sisters of Charity, the first order of nuns in the United States.

After the Civil War, the Mission of Our Lady of the Rosary turned the building into a shelter for homeless Irish immigrant women – 170,000 passed through on their way to a new life in America. The adjoining church was built in 1883. The Mission established and maintains the shrine to Mother Seton.

The house itself was built in 1793, and in 1806 a Federal wing was added, with a curved, columned porch. The Georgian-style and Federal facades have been carefully restored according to an 1859 print. They are all that survives of the early mansions of Lower Manhattan.

Fraunces Tavern Museum ⑬

54 Pearl St. **Map** 1 C4. 425-1778 **M** South Ferry, Bowling Green. **Open** 10am–4.45pm Mon–Fri, noon–4pm Sat. **Closed** public hols, day after Thanksgiving. **Lectures, films.**

Nᴇᴡ ʏᴏʀᴋ's only full remaining square block of 18th-century commercial buildings contains an exact replica of the Fraunces Tavern, originally built in 1719, where George Washington said farewell to his officers in 1783. The tavern had been an early casualty of the Revolution: the British ship *Asia* shot a cannonball through its roof in August 1775. The building was purchased in 1904 by the Sons of the Revolution in the State of New York. Its restoration in 1907 was one of the nation's first efforts to preserve its heritage.

The restaurant on the ground floor has wood-burning fireplaces and a lot of charm. Upstairs is a museum, with changing exhibits of paintings, prints and decorative arts which interpret the history and culture of early America.

Vietnam Veterans Plaza ⑭

Between Water St and South St. **Map** 2 D4. **M** White hall, South Ferry.

Tʜɪs ɪs ᴀ ʀᴀᴛʜᴇʀ sterile multi-level brick plaza with a shopping mall below. However, in its centre is a huge wall of translucent green glass, engraved with excerpts from speeches, news stories and moving letters to families from servicemen and women who died in the war.

Staten Island Ferry – one of the city's best bargains

Staten Island Ferry ⑮

Whitehall St. **Map** 2 D5. 806-6940. **M** South Ferry. **Open** 24hrs daily. **Adm charge.** See **Practical Information** p353.

Tʜᴇ ꜰɪʀsᴛ business venture of a promising Staten Island boy named Cornelius Vanderbilt, the ferry has operated since 1810, carrying island commuters to and from the city and offering visitors

The 18th-century Fraunces Tavern Museum and restaurant

an unforgettable close-up of the harbour, the Statue of Liberty, Ellis Island and Lower Manhattan's incredible skyline. The fare is still the city's best bargain, although it doubled in 1991 – to 50 cents.

Battery Maritime Building ⑯

11 South St. **Map** 2 D4. **M** *South Ferry.* **Not open** to the public.

FROM 1909 TO 1938, the municipal terminal for ferries to Brooklyn operated here on the site of a small wharf known as Schreijers Hoek, from which Dutch colonial ships once set sail for the mother country. At the height of the ferry era, 17 lines made regular runs from these bustling piers, which are used now only by the Coast Guard service for Governors Island.

The building was designed in 1907. Arriving boats face 300-ft (91-m) arched openings guarded by ornately scrolled high columns and adorned with latticework, moulding and rosettes typical of the Beaux Arts period. This is actually a false front of sheet metal and steel, painted green to resemble copper.

Ironwork railing on the Battery Maritime Building

Statue of Liberty ⑰

See pp74–5.

Ellis Island ⑱

See pp78–9.

Castle Clinton National Monument with Liberty Island beyond

Battery Park ⑲

Map 1 B4. **M** *South Ferry, Bowling Green.*

Beaux Arts subway entrance at the corner of Battery Park

NAMED FOR the line of cannon that once protected the harbour, the park is a wedge of green between the water and the crush of buildings, and is one of the best places in the city for gazing out to sea. Over the years, landfill has extended the greenery far beyond its original State Street boundary.

The park is rimmed with statues and monuments, including the Netherlands Memorial Monument and memorials to New York's first Jewish immigrants, early Walloon settlers, the city's first wireless telegraph operators, the Salvation Army and the Coast Guard. Others honoured are Giovanni da Verrazano, the first explorer to see these shores, and also the poet Emma Lazarus.

Castle Clinton National Monument ⑳

Battery Park. **Map** 1 B4. **C** *344-7220.* **M** *Bowling Green, South Ferry.* **Open** 8.30am–5pm daily. **Closed** 25 Dec. 📷 ♿ 🎞 **Concerts.** 🚻

CASTLE CLINTON WAS built in 1807 as a defence post for the artillery. Originally, it stood about 300 ft (91 m) offshore, connected to Battery Park by a causeway; but landfill gradually linked it to the mainland. None of its 28 guns was ever used in battle.

The fort was enclosed in 1824 and became a fashionable theatre known as Castle Garden. Phineas T Barnum introduced "Swedish nightingale" Jenny Lind here in 1850. It later preceded Ellis Island as the city's immigration centre in 1855, processing 7.5 million newcomers. In 1896, the building was remodelled by McKim, Mead & White to become the New York Aquarium, a popular attraction which moved to Coney Island in 1941 *(see p247).*

Now it is a monument, and the main visitors' centre for the National Park Service sites in Manhattan, with exhibits featuring panoramas of New York history. The complex is also the departure point for the Statue of Liberty–Ellis Island ferry *(see p353).*

Ellis Island ⑱

Half of America's population can trace its roots to Ellis Island, which served as the country's immigration depot from 1892 until 1954. Nearly 17 million people passed through its gates and dispersed across the country in the greatest wave of migration the world has ever known. Today the site is a national museum. Exhibits such as *Through America's Gate* retrace the steps through the entry inspections. *Peopling of America* is an electronic map showing the many nationalities that comprise the population. Much of this story is told with photos and the voices of actual immigrants. No other place or museum explains so well the "melting pot" that formed the unique character of New York and the nation.

Main building

The railroad office sold tickets onward to the final destination.

Rail Ticket
A special fare for emigrants led many on to California.

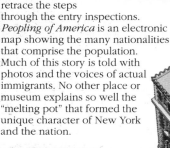

★ **Dormitory**
There were separate sleeping quarters for male and female detainees.

THE RESTORATION

Ellis Island lay in ruins until 1990. A $156 million renewal project replaced the copper roof domes, cleaned the mosaic tiles and restored the interior using any original fixtures that had survived.

The ferry office sold tickets to New Jersey.

★ **Baggage Room**
The immigrants' meagre possessions were checked here on arrival.

Great Hall ★
Immigrant families were made to wait for "processing" in the Registry Room. The old metal railings were replaced with wooden benches in 1911.

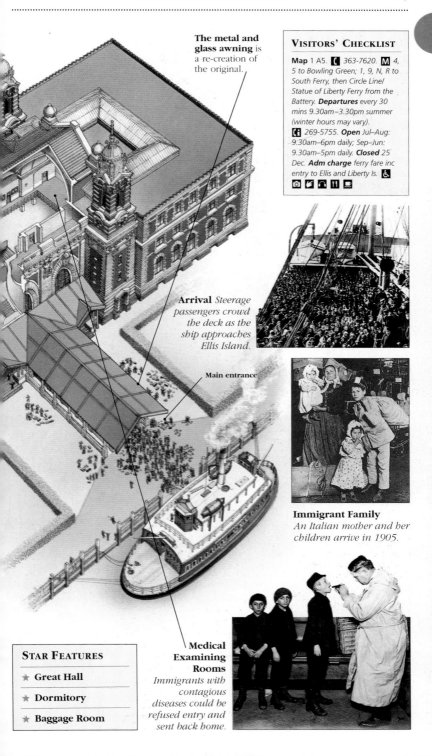

The metal and glass awning is a re-creation of the original.

VISITORS' CHECKLIST

Map 1 A5. **C** 363-7620. **M** 4, 5 to Bowling Green; 1, 9, N, R to South Ferry, then Circle Line/ Statue of Liberty Ferry from the Battery. **Departures** every 30 mins 9.30am–3.30pm summer (winter hours may vary). **f** 269-5755. **Open** Jul–Aug: 9.30am–6pm daily; Sep–Jun: 9.30am–5pm daily. **Closed** 25 Dec. **Adm charge** ferry fare inc entry to Ellis and Liberty Is. **&**

Arrival *Steerage passengers crowd the deck as the ship approaches Ellis Island.*

Main entrance

Immigrant Family
An Italian mother and her children arrive in 1905.

Medical Examining Rooms
Immigrants with contagious diseases could be refused entry and sent back home.

STAR FEATURES

★ Great Hall

★ Dormitory

★ Baggage Room

SEAPORT AND THE CIVIC CENTER

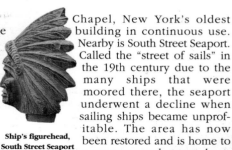

MANHATTAN'S BUSY Civic Center is the hub of the city, state and federal government's court systems and the city's police department. In the 1880s it was the heart of the newspaper publishing business as well. The area is still a handsome enclave of imposing architecture with fine landmarks from every period in the city's history, from the 20th-century Woolworth Building to 19th-century City Hall and 18th-century St Paul's

Ship's figurehead, South Street Seaport

Chapel, New York's oldest building in continuous use. Nearby is South Street Seaport. Called the "street of sails" in the 19th century due to the many ships that were moored there, the seaport underwent a decline when sailing ships became unprofitable. The area has now been restored and is home to a museum and many shops and restaurants. The Brooklyn Bridge, once the largest suspension bridge in the world, lies to the north.

SIGHTS AT A GLANCE

Historic Streets and Buildings
South Street Seaport ❶
Schermerhorn Row ❷
Brooklyn Bridge pp86–9 ❸
Criminal Courts Building ❹
New York County Courthouse ❺
United States Courthouse ❻
Municipal Building ❼
Surrogate's Court, Hall of Records ❽
Old New York County Courthouse ❾
City Hall ❿
Woolworth Building ⓬
AT&T Building ⓮

Churches
St Paul's Chapel ⓭

Parks and Squares
City Hall Park and Park Row ⓫

GETTING THERE
Many subway lines serve the area: the 7th Ave/Broadway 2 and 3 trains to Park Place; the Lexington Ave 4, 5 and 6 to Brooklyn Bridge; the 8th Ave A, C and E to Chambers St and the N and R to City Hall. By bus take the M1, M6, M9, M10, M15, M101/102 or the M22 crosstown.

KEY
⬛ Street-by-Street map
Ⓜ Subway station
River boat boarding point

0 metres   500
0 yards   500

Street-by-Street: South Street Seaport

PART COMMERCIAL, part historical, the development of South Street Seaport has turned the former heart of the 19th-century port of New York, which had long been neglected, into a lively part of the city. Shops and cafés abound; tall ships are once again moored here. The South Street Seaport museum uses the area's historic buildings and many ships to tell the story of New York's maritime past through craft demonstrations, ship tours and river cruises.

★ **South Street Seaport**
Once full of sailors and sailing ships, the seaport is now a lively complex of shops, restaurants and museums ❶

Cannon's Walk is a 19th- and 20th-century block of buildings with an outdoor café, shops and a very lively marketplace.

The Titanic Memorial is a lighthouse built in 1913 in memory of those who died on the *Titanic*. It now stands on Fulton Street.

To Fulton St subway (4 blocks)

Schermerhorn Row
Built as warehouses (1811–13), they now house a number of eateries, including the North Star Pub (see p308) and Sloppy Louie's ❷

The Boat Building Shop lets you watch as skilled craftsmen build and restore small wooden vessels.

At the Maritime Crafts Center wood-carvers and painters can be seen at work on models, ship carvings and figureheads.

Ship in a bottle

The Pilothouse was originally from a steam tugboat built in 1923 by New York Central. The Seaport's admission and information centre is to be found here.

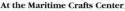

STAR SIGHTS
★ **Brooklyn Bridge**
★ **South Street Seaport**

The Consolidated Edison electrical substation, built in 1975, has an illusionistic mural of the Brooklyn Bridge by Richard Haas on one side to help it blend in with its historic neighbours.

LOCATOR MAP
See Manhattan Map pp12–13

KEY

— — — Suggested route

| 0 metres | 100 |
| 0 yards | 100 |

N

Meyer's Hotel, built in 1873, became a hotel in 1881. Now a bar, it retains a feel of days gone by when markswoman Annie Oakley stayed here.

★ **Brooklyn Bridge**
An engineering wonder when it was built in 1883, the bridge is still remarkable. From the pedestrian walkway there are fine views of the city and the bridge itself ❸

The Fulton Fish Market has been here for over 150 years. Once sold fresh from the boat, the fish now come in by road. The market is only open in the early morning hours *(see p347).*

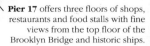

Pier 17 offers three floors of shops, restaurants and food stalls with fine views from the top floor of the Brooklyn Bridge and historic ships.

The paddlewheeler *Andrew Fletcher* is used for river cruises. You can also sail on the schooner *Pioneer,* or the traditional steamboat *DeWitt Clinton (see p355).*

East River harbour at South Street Seaport

South Street Seaport ❶

Fulton St. **Map** 2 E2. █ 732-7678. Ⓜ Fulton St. **Open** 10am–9pm Mon– Sat, 11am–8pm Sun. ⓞ ⓖ ⓥ **Concerts.** ⓗ ⓟ **South Street Seaport Museum** █ 669-9400 ⓘ 748-8600. **Open** 10am–5pm daily (last adm: 4.30pm). **Closed** 1 Jan, Thanksgiving, 25 Dec. **Adm charge.** ⓞ ⓖ ⓥ **Lectures, exhibits, films.** ⓗ ⓟ

THE HEART of New York's 19th-century seaport has been given an imaginative new lease of life. Glitzy stores and restaurants sit harmoniously beside seafaring craft, historic buildings and museum exhibits, with spectacular views of Brooklyn Bridge and the East River from the cobbled streets.

The historic ships docked alongside the piers range from the little tugboat *W O Decker* to the grand four-masted barque *Peking*, the second-largest sailing ship in existence. A 19th-century paddlewheeler offers atmospheric harbour cruises, and there are mini-sailing voyages on the schooner *Pioneer (see p353)*.

The Fulton Fish Market has been here since 1821. Though

Fulton Fish Market at dawn

fish are no longer delivered from boats in the harbour but arrive in refrigerated trucks, many still find the busy morning action an enjoyable sight; however, you'll need to be there before dawn.

Historic seaport restaurant in Schermerhorn Row

Schermerhorn Row ❷

Fulton and South Sts. **Map** 2 D3. Ⓜ Fulton St.

THIS IS THE architectural showpiece of the seaport. Built in 1811 by shipowner and chandler Peter Schermerhorn, on a piece of land reclaimed from the river, the buildings were originally warehouses and counting houses. The opening of the Brooklyn Ferry terminus in 1814, and of Fulton Market in 1822, made the block very desirable property. One of its oldest restaurants – Sloppy Louie's – makes use of the nearby fish market and is justly famous for its bouillabaisse.

The Row has been restored as part of the South Street Seaport development, and it now houses a visitors' centre, shops and restaurants.

Brooklyn Bridge ❸

See pp86–9.

Criminal Courts Building ❹

100 Centre St. **Map** 4 F5. Ⓜ Canal St. **Open** 9am–5pm Mon–Fri. **Closed** public hols.

THIS 1939 BUILDING is Art Moderne in style, with towers reminiscent of a Babylonian temple. The three-storey-high entrance is set back in a court, behind two huge, square free-standing granite columns – an intimidating sight for the accused. The building also houses the Manhattan Detention Center for Men, which was formerly across the street in a building known as "The Tombs" because of its Egyptian-style architecture. The nickname has stuck although the original is long gone. A "bridge of sighs" links the courts with the correctional facility across Centre Street.

The building also houses the night courts, where cases are heard from 5pm to 1am on weekdays.

Entrance to the Criminal Courts Building

New York County Courthouse ❺

60 Centre St. **Map** 2 D1. Ⓜ Brooklyn Br-City Hall. **Open** 9am–5pm Mon–Fri. **Closed** public hols.

BUILT TO REPLACE the Tweed Courthouse (see p90), this new county courthouse was completed in 1926.

The fluted Corinthian portico at the top of a wide staircase is the main feature of the hexagonal building. The austere exterior is offset by a circular-columned interior rotunda featuring Tiffany lighting fixtures, rich marble and ceiling murals by Attilio Pusterla on themes of law and justice. Six wings radiate from the rotunda, each housing a single court and its facilities.

The classic courtroom drama, *Twelve Angry Men,* starring Henry Fonda, was filmed here.

New York County Courthouse

United States Courthouse ❻

40 Centre St. **Map** 2 D1. **M**
Brooklyn Br-City Hall. **Open** *9am–5pm Mon–Fri.* **Closed** *public hols.*

T HIS COURTHOUSE is the last work by noted architect Cass Gilbert, designer of the Woolworth Building. Begun in 1933, the year before his death, it was finished by his son. The 31-storey structure is

United States Courthouse

a pyramid-topped tower set on a classical temple base. The bronzework on the doors is handsome, but the interior lacks the colourful decoration Gilbert had outlined in his sketchbooks. Aerial walkways link the building with its Police Plaza Annex.

Municipal Building ❼

1 Centre St. **Map** 1 C1. **M**
Brooklyn Br-City Hall. 📷 ♿

T HE MUNICIPAL Building, constructed in 1914, dominates the Civic Center and straddles Chambers Street. It was McKim, Mead & White's first skyscraper and houses government offices and a marriage chapel. The exterior, in harmony with the City Hall, has no excess detail to detract from the earlier building. The most notable feature is the top, a fantasy of towers capped by Adolph Wienman's statue *Civic Fame.*

A railway passage (no longer in use) through the base, and the plaza joining the building to the IRT subway station entrance were built as concessions to modern transportation needs. The building has had a far-reaching influence on architectural style; the main building at Moscow University is said to have been modelled on its design.

Surrogate's Court, Hall of Records ❽

31 Chambers St. **Map** 1 C1. **M** *City Hall.* **Open** *10am–3pm Mon–Fri.* **Closed** *public hols.* 📷 ♿ 🚻

A BEAUX ARTS triumph, the original Hall of Records was begun in 1899 and completed in 1911. The elaborate columned facade is of white Maine granite, with a high mansard roof. The figures in the roof area by Henry K Bush-Brown represent man's stages from childhood to old age; the statues by Philip Martiny over the colonnade are of notable New Yorkers

Municipal Building

such as Peter Stuyvesant. Martiny also made the representations of New York in its infancy and New York in Revolutionary times at the Chambers Street entrance.

The Paris Opéra was the inspiration for the twin marble stairways and painted ceiling of the dazzling central hall. The ceiling mosaic by William de Leftwich Dodge features the signs of the zodiac as well as symbols of record keeping.

The Hall of Records holds public records dating back to 1664. A permanent exhibition, *Windows on the Archives,* features historical papers, drawings, letters and photographs illustrating what life was like in New York from 1626 to the present.

Surrogate's Court

Brooklyn Bridge ❸

COMPLETED IN 1883, the Brooklyn Bridge was the largest suspension bridge and the first to be constructed of steel. Engineer John A Roebling conceived of a bridge spanning the East River while ice-bound on a ferry to Brooklyn. The bridge took 16 years to build, required 600 workmen and claimed over 20 lives, including Roebling's. Most died of caisson disease (later found to be the bends) after coming up from the underwater excavation chambers. When finished, the bridge linked Manhattan and Brooklyn, then two separate cities.

Souvenir Medal cast for the opening of the bridge

BROOKLYN BRIDGE
From making the wire to sinking the supports, the bridge was built using new techniques.

Anchorage
The ends of the bridge's four steel cables are fastened to a series of anchor bars which are held in place by anchor plates. These are held down by giant granite vaults up to three storeys high. Their vast interiors were once used for storage.

Granite vault

Cable to tower

Anchor bar

Anchor plate

Vault

Caisson
The towers rose up above caissons, each the size of four tennis courts, which provided a dry area for underwater excavation. As work went on, they sunk deeper beneath the river.

Shaft

Anchor plates
Each of the four cast-iron anchor plates holds one cable. The masonry was built up around them after they were placed in position.

Anchor plates

Central span is 1,595 ft (486 m) long

Vault

Roadway from anchorage to anchorage is 3,579 ft (1091 m)

First Crossing
Master mechanic E F Farrington was the first to cross the river in 1876, riding a traveller rope driven by a steam engine. His journey took 22 minutes.

VISITORS' CHECKLIST

Map 2 D2. Ⓜ 4, 5, 6 to Brooklyn Bridge-City Hall (Manhattan side); A, C to High St, Brooklyn Bridge (Brooklyn side). 🚌 9, 22, 101, 102 (Manhattan side). 📷 ♿

Steel Cable Wire
Each cable contains 3,515 miles (5,657 km) of wire, galvanized with zinc for protection from the wind, rain and snow.

FOUNDATION LINE

Brooklyn Tower (1875)
Two Gothic double arches, each 277 ft (84 m) high, one in Brooklyn, the other in Manhattan, were meant to be the portals of the cities.

Inside the Caisson
Immigrant workers broke up rocks in the riverbed.

JOHN A ROEBLING
The German-born Roebling designed the bridge. In 1869, just before construction started, his foot was crushed between an on-coming ferry and the ferry slip. He died three weeks later. His son, Washington Roebling, finished the bridge, but in 1872 he was taken from a caisson suffering from the bends and became partly paralysed. His wife, under his tutelage, then took over.

MAKING THE CABLES

**Thickness of steel wire
(actual size)**

**End of
wire**

How the Cables Were Made
*Each of the four main cables has
19 strands of 278 steel wires
each. The wires were not twisted,
but laid parallel.*

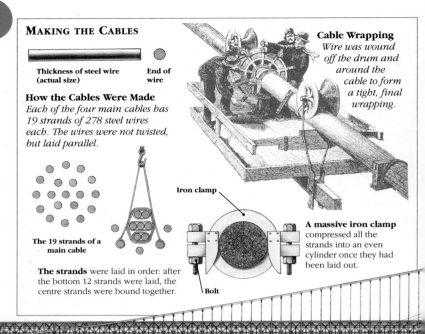

Cable Wrapping
*Wire was wound
off the drum and
around the
cable to form
a tight, final
wrapping.*

Iron clamp

**The 19 strands of a
main cable**

The strands were laid in order: after
the bottom 12 strands were laid, the
centre strands were bound together.

Bolt

A massive iron clamp
compressed all the
strands into an even
cylinder once they had
been laid out.

Bustling Bridge
*This 1883 view from
the Manhattan side
shows the original two
outer lanes for horse-
drawn carriages, two
middle lanes for cable
cars and the elevated
centre walkway.*

Fireworks over the Brooklyn Bridge
Each year, the Fourth of July is celebrated with a firework display.

Panic of 30 May 1883
*After a woman tripped on the
bridge, panic broke out. Of the
estimated 20,000 then on the
bridge, 12 were crushed to death.*

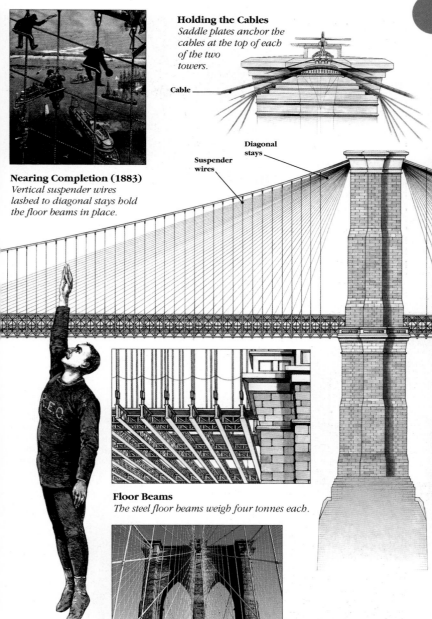

Holding the Cables
Saddle plates anchor the cables at the top of each of the two towers.

Cable

Nearing Completion (1883)
Vertical suspender wires lashed to diagonal stays hold the floor beams in place.

Diagonal stays

Suspender wires

Floor Beams
The steel floor beams weigh four tonnes each.

Odlum's Jump
Robert Odlum was the first to jump off the bridge, on a bet, in May 1885. He later died from internal bleeding.

Elevated Walkway
Poet Walt Whitman said that the view from the walkway – 18 ft (5.5 m) above the road – was "the best, most effective medicine my soul has yet partaken".

Old New York County Courthouse ❾

52 Chambers St. **Map** 1 C1.
Ⓜ *Chambers St-City Hall.* **Open**
9am–5pm Mon–Fri. 🅾️ ♿

P T Barnum's museum blazes as crowds watch from City Hall Park

THIS BUILDING is best known for the scandal it caused. It is nicknamed the "Tweed Courthouse" after the political boss who spent 20 times the budget for the building and pocketed $9 million of the total $14 million cost. "Boss" Tweed even bought a marble quarry, and sold materials to the city at huge profit. Public outrage eventually led to his downfall in 1871 – ironically, he was tried in his own courthouse, and died in a New York jail *(see p25)*.

However, Tweed left behind a handsome Italianate building. Now used to house city offices, it has survived many threats of demolition. Work has begun on a $6.3 million renovation.

City Hall's imposing early 19th-century facade

City Hall ❿

City Hall Pk. **Map** 1 C1. 🄲 *788-3000.* Ⓜ *Brooklyn Br-City Hall.* **Open** *10am–4pm Mon–Fri.* **Closed** *public hols.* 🅾️ ♿ 🎞️ *788-6865.* **Concerts**.

CITY HALL, the seat of New York city government since 1812, is one of the finest examples of early 19th-century American archi-tecture. A stately Georgian building (with a bit of French

Renaissance influence), it was designed by John McComb Jr, the first prominent American-born architect, and French emigré Joseph Mangin.

Marble cladding was not used for the building's rear since it was not expected that the city would ever develop further to the north. In 1954, restoration remedied this and refurbished the interior.

Mangin is usually given credit for the exterior, McComb for the beautiful interior with its fine domed rotunda, the dome encircled by 10 columns. The space beneath it opens on to an elegant double curving marble stairway, leading to the splendid second-floor City Council chambers and the Governor's Room, which houses a portrait gallery of early New York leaders. This magnificent entrance has welcomed rulers and heroes for nearly 200 years. In 1865 Abraham Lincoln's body lay in state in this hall.

Stand on the steps and look to your right to see a statue of Nathan Hale, a US soldier, hanged by the British as a spy in September 1776 during the War of American Independence. His last words – "My only regret is that I have not more lives than one to offer in the service of my country" – won him a permanent place in the history books and hearts of America.

City Hall Park and Park Row ⓫

Map 1 C2. Ⓜ *Brooklyn Br-City Hall.*

THIS WAS New York's village green 250 years ago, complete with stocks and whipping post. It was the scene of pre-Revolution protests against English rule, and there is a memorial to the "Liberty Poles" (symbols of revolt) on City Hall's west lawn. The Declaration of Independence was read to George Washington and his troops here on 9 July 1776.

Later, Phineas T Barnum's American Museum at the Park's southern tip drew the crowds from 1842 until it burned down in 1865. The Park Row building was the site of the Park Theater. From 1798 to 1848, the best actors of the day such as Edmund Kean and Fanny Kemble, per-formed there. Park Row runs along the east side of City Hall Park. Once called "Newspaper Row", it was lined with the lofty offices of the *Sun, World, Tribune* and other papers. Printing

Statue of Benjamin Franklin in Printing House Square

House Square has a statue of Benjamin Franklin with his *Pennsylvania Gazette.*

Time was not kind to the newspaper business. In 1893 New York had 19 daily papers; in 1992 there were four.

Woolworth Building ⓬

233 Broadway. **Map** 1 C2. Ⓜ *City Hall.* **Open** *office hours.*

Bas-relief caricature of architect Gilbert in the Woolworth lobby

IN 1879, SALES clerk Frank W Woolworth opened a new kind of store, where shoppers could see and touch the goods on offer and everything cost five cents. The chain of stores that followed made him a fortune, and changed the face of retailing forever.

The Gothic headquarters of his retail empire, completed in 1913, was New York's tallest building until 1930. It set the standard for the great skyscrapers, and no office building is finer.

Architect Cass Gilbert's soaring two-tiered design, adorned with gargoyles of bats and other wildlife, is topped with a pyramid roof, flying buttresses, pinnacles and four small towers. The marble interior is rich with filigree, sculptured reliefs and painted decoration, and has a high glass-tile mosaic ceiling that almost seems to glow. The lobby is one of the city's treasures. Gilbert showed his sense of humour here, in bas-relief caricatures of the store's founder F W Woolworth counting out his fortune in nickels and dimes; of the estate agent closing a deal; and of Cass Gilbert himself cradling a large model of the building. Paid for with $13.5 million in cool, hard cash, the building has never had a mortgage, and the Woolworth company is still in residence.

St Paul's Chapel ⓭

Broadway. **Map** 1 C2. ☎ *602-0874.* Ⓜ *Fulton St.* **Open** *9am–3pm Sun–Fri.* **Closed** *most public hols.* ✝ *8am Sun.* 📷 ✔ *by appt.* **Concerts**.

IN THE LONG SHADOW of the World Trade Center stands Manhattan's only remaining church built before the War of

The Georgian interior of St Paul's Chapel

American Independence. It is a Georgian gem. The colourful interior, lit by Waterford chandeliers, is the setting for free concerts. The pew where newly-inaugurated George Washington prayed has been preserved. In the churchyard, the Actor's Monument commemorates George Frederick Cooke, who played many great roles at the Park Theater and finally drank himself to death at the Shakespeare Tavern on Fulton Street.

AT&T Building ⓮

195 Broadway. **Map** 1 C2. Ⓜ *Broadway-Nassau.* **Open** *office hours.*

COLUMNS, columns everywhere mark this former headquarters designed by Welles Bosworth from 1915 to 1922. The facade is said to have more columns than any other building in the world, and the interior of the building is a forest of marble pillars. The whole edifice looks like a gigantic square-topped layer cake.

A sea sprite above the door of the AT&T (American Telephone and Telegraph) Building

LOWER EAST SIDE

Nowhere does the ethnic flavour of New York come through more clearly than in lower Manhattan where many immigrants first settled. Here Italians, Chinese and Jews established their own distinct neighbourhoods, preserving their languages, customs, foods and religions in the midst of a strange new land. New immigrants from many different nations now occupy some of these gritty low-rise neighbourhoods, but the old flavour remains. The area brims with enticing restaurants, some of the city's greatest bargains and a spirit found nowhere else. The composer Irving Berlin grew up here. Remembering those days he said: "Everybody ought to have a Lower East Side in their life."

19th-century tin, Lower East Side Tenement Museum

SIGHTS AT A GLANCE

Historic Streets and Buildings
Home Savings of America 1
Police Headquarters Building 2
Little Italy 3
Chinatown 4
Orchard Street 8
Delancey Street 10
Puck Building 12
Engine Company No. 31 14

Parks and Squares
Columbus Park 5

Museums and Galleries
Lower East Side Tenement Museum 7

Churches and Synagogues
Eldridge Street Synagogue 6
Bialystoker Synagogue 9
Old St Patrick's Cathedral 13

Landmark Stores
Schapiro's Winery 11

SEE ALSO

• ***Street Finder***, maps 4, 5
• ***Where to Stay*** pp274–5
• ***Restaurants*** pp290–92
• ***Lower East Side Walk*** pp258–9

GETTING THERE

Chinatown and Little Italy can be reached by subway on the N and R or the Lexington Ave 4, 5 and 6 trains to Canal St, or by taking the M101/102 bus. The Lower East Side is served by the B and D trains to Grand St, the F train to Delancey St or the M15 bus.

KEY

[M] Street-by-Street map
[M] Subway station

Dragon puppet in Chinatown at Chinese New Year

Street-by-Street: Little Italy and Chinatown

NEW YORK'S LARGEST and most colourful ethnic neighbourhood is Chinatown, which is growing so rapidly that it is overrunning nearby Little Italy and the Jewish Lower East Side. Streets here teem with greengrocer stalls, gift shops and hundreds of Chinese restaurants; even the plainest offer good food. What is left of Little Italy can be found at Mulberry and Grand streets, where old world flavour abounds.

★Little Italy
Once home to thousands of immigrants, the scents of Italy still waft from the area's restaurants and bakeries ❸

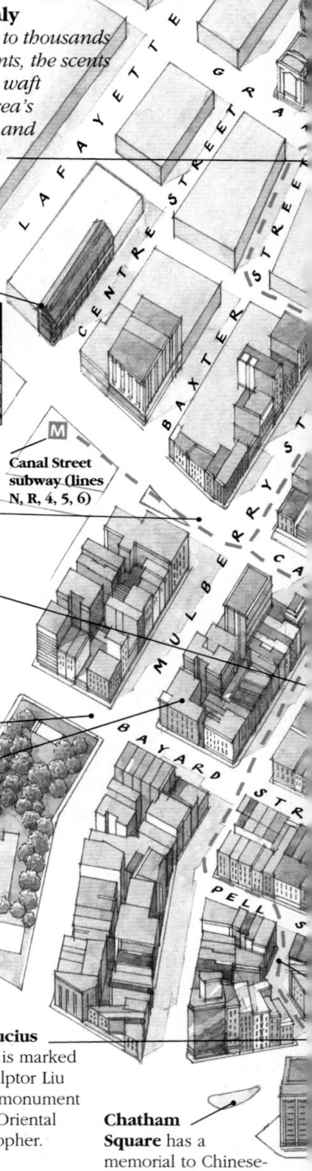

★ Chinatown
Home to a thriving – and still expanding – community of Chinese immigrants, this area is famous for its restaurants and hectic street life. The area truly comes alive around the Chinese New Year in January or February ❹

The Market on Canal Street has a wide range of bargains in new and used clothes and other goods.

Canal Street subway (lines N, R, 4, 5, 6)

The Eastern States Buddhist Temple at No. 64b Mott Street contains over 100 golden Buddhas.

The Wall of Democracy on Bayard Street is covered with newspapers and posters describing the situation in China.

Columbus Park
This park was once the site of 19th century New York's worst slum. ❺

Confucius Plaza is marked by sculptor Liu Shih's monument to the Oriental philosopher.

Chatham Square has a memorial to Chinese-American war dead.

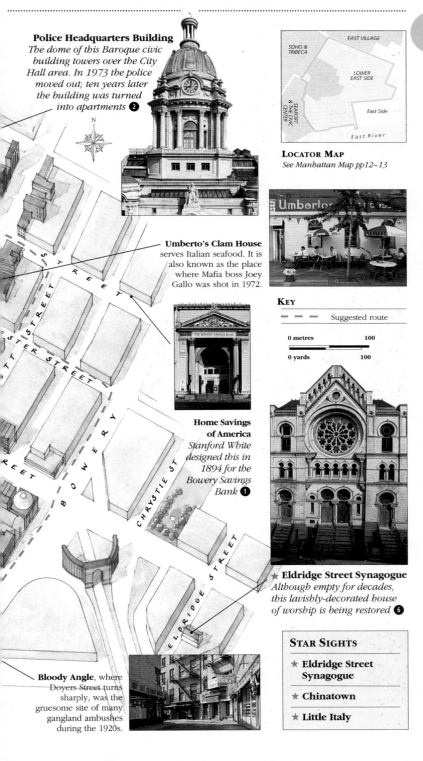

Police Headquarters Building
The dome of this Baroque civic building towers over the City Hall area. In 1973 the police moved out; ten years later the building was turned into apartments ❷

LOCATOR MAP
See Manhattan Map pp12–13

Umberto's Clam House
serves Italian seafood. It is also known as the place where Mafia boss Joey Gallo was shot in 1972.

KEY

= = = Suggested route

0 metres 100
0 yards 100

Home Savings of America
Stanford White designed this in 1894 for the Bowery Savings Bank ❶

★ **Eldridge Street Synagogue**
Although empty for decades, this lavishly-decorated house of worship is being restored ❻

STAR SIGHTS

★ **Eldridge Street Synagogue**

★ **Chinatown**

★ **Little Italy**

Bloody Angle, where Doyers Street turns sharply, was the gruesome site of many gangland ambushes during the 1920s.

Home Savings of America ❶

130 Bowery. **Map** 4 F4. **Ⓜ** *Grand St, Bowery.* **Open** *banking hours.*

IMPOSING INSIDE and out, this Classical Revival building was built for the Bowery Savings Bank in 1894. Architect Stanford White designed the ornamented lime- stone facade to wrap

Detail from Home Savings of America

around the rival Butchers' and Drovers' Bank, which refused to sell the corner plot. The interior is decorated with marbled pillars and a ceiling scattered with gilded rosettes.

By the middle of the 20th century, the bank was a contrast to the Bowery with its vagrants and flophouses.

Police Headquarters Building ❷

240 Centre St. **Map** 4 F4. **Ⓜ** *Canal St.* **Not open** *to the public.*

COMPLETED IN 1909, this was a fitting home for the city's new professional police force. Corinthian columns line the main portico and the end pavilions, and the dome dom- inates the skyline. However, lack of space meant the head- quarters had to conform to an awkward, wedge-shaped site in the midst of Little Italy.

For nearly three-quarters of a century, this was where "New York's finest" came to

work. During Prohibition, Grand Street from here to the Bowery was known as "Bootleggers' Row", and alcohol was easily obtained except when a police raid was due. The liquor merchants paid handsomely for a tip-off from inside police headquarters.

The police moved to new headquarters in 1973, and in 1985 the building was converted into a luxury co- operative apartment project.

Little Italy ❸

Streets around Mulberry St. **Map** 4 F4. **Ⓜ** *Canal St.*

THE SOUTHERN Italians who came to New York in the late 19th century found themselves living in the squalor of "dumbbell" apart- ments. These were built so close together that sunlight never reached the lower windows or back- yards. With over 40,000 people living in 17 small, unsanitary blocks, diseases such as tuberculosis were rife.

Despite the privations of life on the Lower East Side, the community that grew up around Mulberry Street was lively with the colours, flavours and atmosphere of its homeland. These have lingered on, although the Italian population has

dwindled to a mere 5,000 and the boundaries of Chinatown have encroached on the traditional Little Italy.

The most exciting time to visit is during the Festa of San Gennaro, which is held around 19 September (see p52). For nine days each year, Mulberry Street is renamed Via San Gennaro. On the saint's day, his shrine and relics are paraded through the streets. Throughout the feast the milling crowds enjoy music, dancing, fairground sideshows and stalls selling every conceivable kind of Italian food and drink, as well as other ethnic cuisines.

Little Italy's restaurants offer simple, rustic food served in friendly surroundings at reasonable prices.

Italian café in Little Italy

Chinatown ❹

Streets around Mott St. **Map** 4 F5. **Ⓜ** *Canal St.* **Eastern States Buddhist Temple open** *9am–8pm daily.*

THE CHINATOWN of the early 20th century was primarily a male community, made up of immigrants who had first come to California. Wages were sent home to their families in China who were prevented from joining them by US immigration laws. The men relaxed by gambling at mahjong. The community remained isolated from the rest of the city, financed and controlled by its own secret organizations, the Tongs.

Some of the Tongs were simply family associations who provided loans. Others, such as the On Leong and the Hip Sing, who were at war with one another, were criminal fraternities. Tiny, crooked Doyers Street was called "Bloody Angle"; enemies were lured there and set

Stonework figures adorning the Police Headquarters Building

A Chinese grocer tending his shop on Canal Street

upon by gang members waiting around the bend.

A truce between the Tongs in 1933 brought peace to Chinatown. By 1940 it was home to many middle-class families. Immigrants and businesses from Hong Kong also brought postwar prosperity to the community. Today over 80,000 Chinese-Americans live here.

Many people visit the neighbourhood simply to feast on Chinese cuisine, but there is more to do here than eat. There are also galleries, antique and curio shops, and Oriental festivals *(see p53)*. To glimpse another side of Chinatown, step into the incense-scented dimness of the Eastern States Buddhist Temple at No. 64b Mott Street, where offerings are piled up and over 100 golden Buddhas gleam in the candlelight.

Columbus Park ❺

Map 4 F5. **M** *Canal St.*

THE TRANQUILLITY of Columbus Park today could not be further removed from the scene near this site in the early 1800s. The area, known as Mulberry Bend, was a red light district, part of the infamous Five Points slum. Gangs with names like the Dead Rabbits and the Plug Uglies roamed the streets. A murder a day was commonplace; even the police were afraid to pass through. Partly as a result of the writings of reformer Jacob Riis *(see p47)*, the slum was finally pulled down in 1892. Now the park is the only open space in all of Chinatown.

Eldridge Street Synagogue ❻

12 Eldridge St. **Map** 5 A5.
C *219-0888.* **M** *E Broadway.*
Open *Mon–Thu by appt only.*
✪ *Fri at sundown, Sat 9am onwards.* ✷ ✔ *·noon–4pm Sun.* ⟟

WHEN THIS HOUSE of worship was built by the Orthodox Ashkenazi from Eastern Europe in 1887, it was the most flamboyant temple in the neighbourhood. But many immigrant Jews saw the Lower East Side as just the beginning of a new life and later moved up and out. Massive synagogues were no longer needed.

In the 1930s, the huge sanctuary, rich with stained glass, brass chandeliers, marbled wood panelling and fine carving, was closed. Three decades later a group of citizens raised funds for preservation, and restoration is now in progress. A brief audio-visual presentation recounts the history of the synagogue and its renovation.

Even after years of neglect, the facade, with touches of Romanesque, Gothic and Moorish designs, is impressive. Inside, the Italian hand-carved ark and sculpted wooden balcony show why this building was the pride of the area.

Lower East Side Tenement Museum ❼

90 Orchard St. **Map** 5 A4.
C *431-0233.* **M** *Delancey, Grand St.* **Open** *noon–5pm Tue–Fri, 11am–5pm Sat, Sun.* **Closed** *1 Jan, Thanksgiving, 25 Dec.* **Adm charge.**
✷ ✔ ▣ *Lectures, films, videos.*

Street vendor's pushcart (1890s) from the museum

THE INTERIOR of this building is being restored to how it was at the turn of the century. There were no regulations on tenement living conditions until 1879. Many rooms had no windows. Indoor sinks, hallway toilets, even air shafts between buildings were rare. The re-created rooms give a sense of the cramped and deplorable conditions under which so many lived. The museum programme includes changing exhibits about the early immigrants, slide shows and excellent walking tours of the neighbourhood.

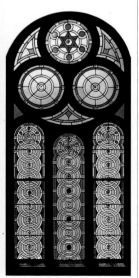

Stained glass from the Synagogue

Orchard Street ❽

Map 5 A3. **M** *Delancey, Grand St.* See **Shopping** *p312.*

JEWISH IMMIGRANTS founded the New York clothing industry on Orchard Street, named after the orchards that once stood here on James De Lancey's colonial estate. For many years the street was filled with pushcarts loaded with goods for sale, much of which were made at home in the teeming tenements of the neighbourhood.

The pushcarts are long gone and not all the shop-keepers are Jewish, but the flavour remains and the stores still close on Saturday, the Jewish Sabbath. On Sunday there is an outdoor market and shoppers fill the street from Houston to Canal look-ing for clothing bargains at any of the 300 shops.

Zodiac mural from the Synagogue

Bialystoker Synagogue ❾

7–11 Willett St. **Map** 5 C4.
C 475-0165. **M** *Essex St.*
⬦ *frequent services.* 📷

THIS 1826 Federal-style building was originally the Willett Street Methodist church. It was bought in 1905 by Jewish immigrants from the Bialystok province in Poland who converted it into a synagogue. For this reason it faces west instead of east, which is traditional. It has a beautiful interior, with lovely stained-glass windows, a

Canal Street Market vegetable stall

three-storey carved wooden ark and murals representing the signs of the zodiac and views of the Holy Land.

Delancey Street ❿

Map 5 C4. **M** *Essex St. See* **Shopping** *p312.*

ONCE A MAJESTIC boulevard, Delancey Street today is little more than an obligatory entrance to the Williamsburg Bridge. The street was named for James De Lancey, whose farm was situated here during colonial days. De Lancey re-mained loyal to George III during the Revolution and fled to England after the war, before his land was seized.

Most of the stores on this once-grand shopping street are now run down, but you can still buy an authentic English bowler hat (not to mention an authentic American Stetson cowboy hat, or almost any other kind of hat) at the Buranelli Hat Company at No. 101 Delancey.

Schapiro's Winery ⓫

126 Rivington St. **Map** 5 B3. **C** 674-4404. **M** *Essex St.* **Open** *10am–5pm Mon–Thu, 10am–2pm Fri, 11am–4pm Sun.* **Closed** *Jewish hols.* **Adm charge.** 📷 ♿ 🎥 *compulsory, every hour, book in advance.*

SCHAPIRO'S was founded in 1899 so that Jewish immigrants to New York could have their traditional kosher wines for the Sabbath

and holidays. It has survived Prohibition, the Depression and the dwindling numbers of local Jewish residents. The owner swears it will still be in business when his grand-children have grandchildren.

Today, Schapiro's produces 32 different types of wine. Though the grapes are now crushed in upstate New York, fermenting and bottling is still done on the premises. The operation can be seen on "quickie" tours; afterwards, you can taste the sweet, thick wine that gave rise to Schapiro's motto: "You can almost cut it with a knife!"

Further east along Rivington Street at No. 150, Streit's Matzoh is another long-established neighbourhood landmark where visitors can

Schapiro's kosher wine

watch the freshly baked unleavened bread rolling off conveyor belts behind the sales counter.

Puck Building

295–309 Lafayette St. **Map** 4 F3. Ⓜ Lafayette. **Not open** to the public.

Puck statue on building's northeast corner

THIS BLOCK-SQUARE architectural curiosity was built in 1885 by Albert and Herman Wagner. It is an adaptation of the German *Rundbogenstil*, a mid-19th-century style characterized by horizontal bands of arched windows and the skilful use of moulded red brick.

The building is part of the city's publishing history. Situated on the edge of Manhattan's old printing district, it housed the satirical *Puck* from 1887 to 1916, a magazine similar to the British *Punch*. At the turn of the century it was the largest building in the world devoted to lithography and publishing.

Today it is used as the site of some of New York's most stylish parties and artiest fashion photography shoots. The only connection remaining to the mythical Puck is the gold-leaf statue on

the third-floor corner of Mulberry and Houston, and the smaller version over the entrance on Lafayette Street.

Walk half a block and you will see a display of *Puck* covers in Bars and Backbars at No. 49 East Houston.

Old St Patrick's Cathedral

263 Mulberry St. **Map** 4 F3. Ⓒ 226-8075. Ⓜ Prince St. **Open** for mass only. ✝ 9.30am, 11am (Spanish), 5.30pm Sat, 12.30pm Sun.

THE FIRST St Patrick's was begun in 1809, making it one of the oldest churches in the city. When fire destroyed the original in the 1860s, it was rebuilt much as at is today, with a somewhat austere exterior. When the archdiocese moved the Cathedral uptown *(see pp176–7)*, this became the local parish church, and it has flourished despite a constantly changing ethnic congregation.

Below the church are vaults containing the remains, among others, of one of New York's most famous families of restaurateurs, the Delmonicos. Pierre Toussaint was also buried here. In 1990 his remains were moved from the old graveyard beside the church to a more honourable burial place in a crypt in the uptown St Patrick's. Born as a slave in Haiti in 1766, Toussaint was brought to New York where he became

Old St Patrick's Cathedral

a prosperous wig-maker as a free man. He later devoted himself to the poor, tending cholera victims and using his money to build an orphanage. The Vatican is now considering him for sainthood.

Engine Company No. 31

87 Lafayette St. **Map** 4 F3. Ⓒ 966-4510. Ⓜ Canal St. **Open** 10am–6pm daily. **Closed** public hols. ▣

IN THE 19TH CENTURY, fire stations were considered important enough to merit memorable architecture and the Le Brun firm was the acknowledged master of the art. This 1895 station is one of their best. The building resembles a Loire château, with its steep roof, dormers and towers, seeming almost fairytale-like in this location.

The present-day tenant is the Downtown Community Television Center, which offers courses, workshops and exhibitions of local filmmakers' and artists' work.

Facade of Engine Company No. 31, in the style of a French château

SoHo and TriBeCa

A RT AND architecture are the twin lures that have transformed these formerly industrial districts. SoHo (South of Houston) was threatened with demolition in the 1960s until preservationists drew attention to the rare cast-iron architecture lining the streets. The plan was scrapped, and artists began to move

Shopfront of a SoHo bakery

into the big loft spaces. Galleries, cafés and shops followed. Brunch and gallery hopping in SoHo is now a favourite weekend outing. As rents rose, artists were priced out of SoHo and began moving down to TriBeCa (triangle below Canal). Now, trendy TriBeCa attracts not only galleries but many of the city's newest restaurants.

Sights at a Glance

Historic Streets and Buildings
Haughwout Building ❶
St Nicholas Hotel ❷
Greene Street ❸
Singer Building ❹

Harrison Street ❾
White Street ❿

Museums and Galleries
Guggenheim Museum SoHo ❺
Museum for African Art ❼

New Museum of Contemporary Art ❻
New York City Fire Museum ❽

Getting There
Take the 6th Ave D or F subway to Broadway-Lafayette; the Lexington Ave 6 to Bleecker St; or the N or R to Prince St. For Canal St, take the 7th Ave/Broadway 1 or 9; the 8th Ave A, C or E; or the Lexington Ave 4, 5, 6, N or R. Bus routes are the M1, M6, and the M21 Houston St crosstown.

See Also

• **Street Finder**, map 4

• **SoHo Walk** pp260

• **Restaurants** pp290–92

0 metres   500

0 yards   500

Key

▨ Street-by-Street map

Ⓜ Subway station

Cast-iron facades on Greene Street

Street-by-Street: SoHo Cast-Iron Historic District

THE LARGEST concentration of cast-iron architecture in the world *(see p40)* survives in the area between West Houston and Canal Streets. The heart of the district is Greene Street, where 50 buildings erected between 1869 and 1895 are found on five cobblestoned blocks. The intricately designed facades were mass-produced in a foundry, but are now rare works of industrial art, well suited to the character of the district.

West Broadway, as it passes through SoHo, combines striking architecture with a string of prestigious art galleries, including Charles Cowles, Hirsch & Adler, Sonnabend, Leo Castelli and Mary Boon. *(See p324.)*

Zona at 97 Greene Street stocks original and imaginative items for the home.

Creature from the Enchanted Forest

No. 72–76 Greene Street, the "King of Greene Street", is a splendid Corinthian-columned building. It was the creation of Isaac F Duckworth, one of the masters of cast-iron design.

Enchanted Forest casts a magic spell, just as its name suggests, selling children's toys and books in a fairytale forest setting. *(See p314.)*

Performing Garage is a tiny experimental theatre that pioneers the work of avant-garde artistes.

★ **Greene Street**
Of all Greene Street's fine cast-iron architecture, one of the best is the "Queen", at No. 28–30, built by Duckworth in 1872, with a tall mansard roof ❸

Canal Street-Broadway subway (2 blocks)

No. 10–14 Greene Street dates from 1869. Note the glass circles in the risers of the iron stoop, which allowed daylight to reach the basement.

No. 15–17 Greene Street is a late addition from 1895, in a simple Corinthian style.

Pace Gallery is one of a clutch of influential galleries housed in a Tuscan-style cast-iron building by Henry Fernbach. *(See p324.)*

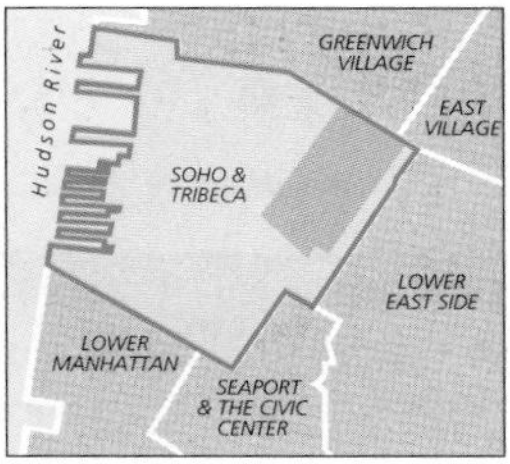

LOCATOR MAP
See Manhattan Map pp12–13

KEY

— — — Suggested route

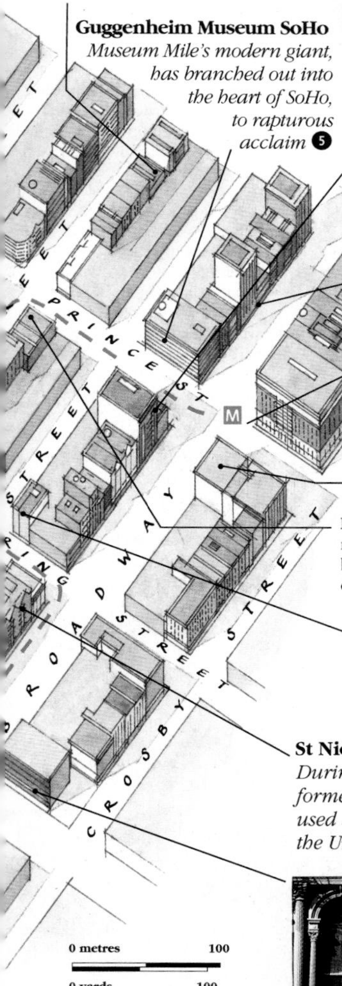

Guggenheim Museum SoHo
Museum Mile's modern giant, has branched out into the heart of SoHo, to rapturous acclaim [5]

★ **Singer Building**
This terracotta beauty was built in 1904 for the famous sewing machine company [4]

New Museum of Contemporary Art
This museum is dedicated to showing innovative work by living artists [6]

Prince Street subway station (lines N, R)

Dean & DeLuca is one of the best gourmet food stores in New York. Its range includes a global choice of coffee beans. *(See p326.)*

Richard Haas, the prolific muralist, has transformed a blank wall into a convincing cast-iron frontage.

No. 101 Spring Street, with its simple, geometric facade and large windows, makes it easy to see how this style led to the rise of the skyscraper.

St Nicholas Hotel
During the Civil War, this former luxury hotel was used as a headquarters for the Union Army [2]

Haughwout Building
In 1857 this was a smart store, featuring the first Otis safety elevator [1]

0 metres 100

0 yards 100

STAR SIGHTS

★ **Singer Building**

★ **Greene Street**

Haughwout Building ❶

88–92 Broadway. **Map** 4 E4.
Ⓜ *Canal St.*

Haughwout Building facade

THIS CAST-IRON building was erected in 1857 for the E V Haughwout china and glassware company, which once supplied the White House. Beneath the grime, the design is superb: rows of windows are framed by arches set on columns flanked by taller columns. Mass-produced sections repeat the pattern over and over. The building was the first to use a steam-driven Otis safety elevator, an innovation which made the skyscraper a possibility.

St Nicholas Hotel ❷

521–23 Broadway. **Map** 4 E4.
Ⓜ *Prince St.*

ENGLISH PARLIAMENTARIAN W E Baxter, visiting New York in 1854, reported of the recently opened St Nicholas Hotel: "Every carpet is of velvet pile; chair covers and curtains are made of silk or satin damask…and the embroidery on the mosquito nettings itself

St Nicholas Hotel in its heyday in the mid-19th century

might be exhibited to royalty." It is small wonder, then, that it cost over $1 million to build – and with profits for that year of over $50,000 it must have seemed money well spent. Its glory was short-lived, however. In the Civil War it served as a Union Army headquarters. Afterwards, the better hotels followed the entertainment district uptown and by the mid-1870s the St Nicholas had closed. There is little left on the ground floor to attest to its former opulence, but look up to see the remains of its once-stunning marble facade.

Greene Street ❸

Map 4 E4. Ⓜ *Canal St.*

Haas mural on Greene Street

THIS IS THE HEART of SoHo's Cast-Iron District. Along five cobblestoned blocks are 50 cast-iron buildings dating from 1869 to 1895. The block between Broome and Spring Streets has 13 full cast-iron facades and Nos. 8 to 34 are the longest row of cast-iron buildings anywhere. Nos. 72–76 are often referred to as the "King of Greene Street" but Nos. 28 –30, the "Queen", are considered to be the finest. The architecture is best appreciated as a streetscape, with row upon row of columned facades. Walk into any of the galleries housed within to see the spacious

interior lofts. At the corner of Greene and Prince Street, the illusionistic muralist Richard Haas has been hard at work, disguising a plain brick side wall as a cast-iron frontage. Look for the detail of the grey cat, which sits primly in an "open" window.

Singer Building ❹

561–3 Broadway. **Map** 4 E3.
Ⓜ *Prince St.*

THE "LITTLE" Singer Building built by Ernest Flagg in 1904 is the second and smaller Flagg structure by this name, and many critics think it superior to the 41-storey tower on lower Broadway that was torn down in 1967. The charmingly ornate building is adorned with wrought iron balconies and graceful arches painted in striking dark green. The 12-storey facade of terracotta, glass and steel was advanced for its day, a forerunner of the metal and glass walls to come in the 1940s and 1950s. The building was an office and warehouse for the Singer sewing machine company, and the original Singer name can be seen cast in iron above the entrance to the store on Prince Street.

Early electric-powered Singer sewing machine

Guggenheim Museum SoHo ❺

575 Broadway. **Map** 4 E3. **C** 423-3600. **M** *Prince St.* **Open** *10am–6pm Sun–Wed, 10am–8pm Fri, Sat.* **Adm charge**.

THIS DRAMATIC gallery opened in 1992 to critical acclaim. Designed by architect Arata Isozake, it features displays which complement those at the main Guggenheim Museum *(see p186)*.

New Museum of Contemporary Art ❻

583 Broadway. **Map** 4 E3. **C** 219-1222. **M** *Prince St.* **Open** *noon–6pm Wed–Fri, Sun, noon–8pm Sat.* **Adm charge**. **Ø** **&** *limited.* **🎤** *Lectures, readings.* **📷**

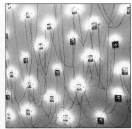

Les Enfants de Dijon by Christian Boltanski, at the New Museum

MARCIA TUCKER left her post as the Whitney Museum's Curator of Painting and Sculpture in 1977 to found this museum. Jeff Koons and the late John Cage are among those whose work has been featured in thematic shows. Tucker exhibits the kind of work she feels is missing from more traditional museums.

Museum for African Art ❼

593 Broadway. **Map** 4 E3. **C** 966-1313. **M** *Prince St.* **Open** *10.30am–5.30pm Tue–Fri, noon–6pm Sat & Sun.* **Adm charge**.

ONE OF ONLY two American museums devoted to African art, these galleries have been ingeniously designed by

architect Maya Lin, creator of the nation's Vietnam Veteran's Memorial. The high-calibre changing shows often tour major museums in America and abroad. The museum also offers lectures, music and dance performances and includes an excellent shop.

1901 La France horse-drawn steam pumper in the City Fire Museum

New York City Fire Museum ❽

278 Spring St. **Map** 4 D4. **C** 691-1303. **M** *Spring St.* **Open** *10am–4pm Tue–Sat.* **Adm charge**. **📷** **&**

THIS SPLENDID museum is housed in a Beaux Arts-style 1904 firehouse. New York City's wonderful collection of fire-fighting equipment and memorabilia from the 18th century to 1917 includes scale models, bells and hydrants. Upstairs, a row of brilliantly gleaming fire engines is neatly lined up for an 1890 parade. Special exhibitions are sometimes held.

Harrison Street ❾

Map 4 D5. **M** *Chambers St.*

SURROUNDED BY modern high-rise blocks, this rare row of eight beautifully restored Federal town houses, with their pitched roofs and distinctive dormer windows, almost seems like a stage set. The houses were constructed in the late 1700s and early 1800s. Two of the buildings were designed by John McComb Jr, New York's first major native-born architect, and were moved from Washington Street, their original site, for preservation purposes. The houses had

previously been used as warehouses and were about to be razed to the ground, when, in 1969, the Landmarks Preservation Commission intervened and helped secure the necessary funding to enable them to be completely restored. They are now privately owned.

On the other side of the high-rise complex is Washington Market Park. This area was formerly the site of New York city's wholesale produce centre. The market moved from this historic district and relocated to the Bronx at the beginning of the 1970s.

White Street ❿

Map 4 E5. **M** *Franklin St.*

WHILE NOT as fine and intricate as some of the SoHo blocks, this sampling of TriBeCa cast-iron architecture shows a considerably wide range of styles. The house at No. 2 has carefully balanced Federal features and a rare gambrel roof, in contrast with the mansard roof of No. 17 (the Alternative Museum). Nos. 8–10, designed by Silesian-born Henry Fernbach, in 1869, have impressive Tuscan columns and arches, with the Neo-Renaissance device of shorter upper storeys to give an illusion of height. In striking contrast, No. 38 is the home of neon artist Rudi Stern's gallery, Let There Be Neon.

Rudi Stern's Let There Be Neon gallery in White Street

GREENWICH VILLAGE

NEW YORKERS call it simply "the Village", and it did, indeed, begin as a country village, an escape for city dwellers during the yellow fever epidemic of 1822. The crazy quilt pattern of streets, reflecting early farm boundaries or streams, could not be made to conform to the city's grid plan, and Greenwich Village

Jazz club flag on West 3rd Street

remained an enclave apart, a bohemian haven that has been home to many celebrated artists and writers. Today it is popular with gays, but on the whole has become mainstream and young; near Washington Square, it is dominated by students from New York University. Non-conformists now often live in the cheaper East Village.

SIGHTS AT A GLANCE

Historic Streets and Buildings
St Luke's Place ❶
No. 75½ Bedford Street ❷
Isaacs-Hendricks House ❸

Grove Court ❹
Jefferson Market Courthouse ❻
Patchin Place ❼
Salmagundi Club ❾
Washington Mews ❿
New York University ⓭

Museums and Galleries
Forbes Magazine Building ❽

Churches
First Presbyterian Church ❿
Church of the Ascension ⓫
Judson Memorial Church ⓮

Parks and Squares
Sheridan Square ❺
Washington Square ⓯

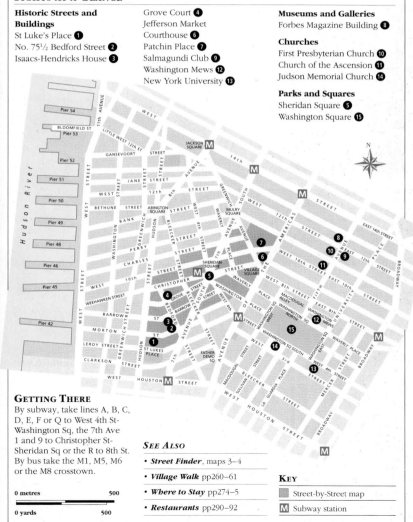

GETTING THERE
By subway, take lines A, B, C, D, E, F or Q to West 4th St–Washington Sq, the 7th Ave 1 and 9 to Christopher St–Sheridan Sq or the R to 8th St. By bus take the M1, M5, M6 or the M8 crosstown.

0 metres   500
0 yards   500

SEE ALSO
• *Street Finder*, maps 3–4
• *Village Walk* pp260–61
• *Where to Stay* pp274–5
• *Restaurants* pp290–92

KEY
▨ Street-by-Street map
Ⓜ Subway station

Billboards on the corner of Christopher Street and Seventh Avenue South

Street-by-Street: Greenwich Village

A STROLL THROUGH HISTORIC Greenwich Village is a feast of unexpected small pleasures – charming row houses, hidden alleys and leafy courtyards. The often quirky architecture suits the bohemian air of the Village. Many famous people, particularly artists and writers such as playwright Eugene O'Neill and actor Dustin Hoffman, have made their homes in the houses and apartments that line these narrow, old-fashioned streets. By night, the Village really comes alive. Late-night coffee houses and cafés, experimental theatres and music clubs, including some of the best jazz venues, beckon you at every turn.

The Lucille Lortel Theater is at No. 121 Christopher Street; it opened in 1955 with *The Threepenny Opera.*

Christopher Street, a part of New York's gay community, is lined with all kinds of shops, book stores and bars.

Twin Peaks at No. 102 Bedford Street began life in 1830 as an ordinary house. It was rebuilt in 1926 by architect Clifford Daily to house artists, writers and actors. Daily believed that the quirky house would help their creativity flourish.

Grove Court
Six houses dating from 1853–54 are set at the back of a quiet leafy courtyard ❹

Chumley's at No. 86 Bedford Street *(see p309),* once a speakeasy, now a restaurant, still seems secret. There is no sign outside, just a small menu.

No. 75½ Bedford Street
Built in 1873 in an alley, this is the city's narrowest house ❷

★ **St Luke's Place**
This beautiful row of Italianate houses was built in the 1850s ❶

To Houston Street subway (2 blocks)

The Cherry Lane Theater, was founded in 1924. Originally a brewery, it was one of the first of the Off-Broadway theatres.

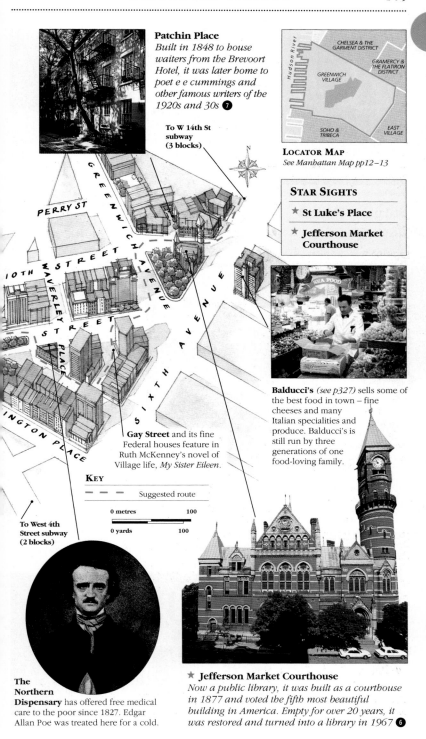

Patchin Place
Built in 1848 to house waiters from the Brevoort Hotel, it was later home to poet e e cummings and other famous writers of the 1920s and 30s **7**

To W 14th St subway (3 blocks)

LOCATOR MAP
See Manhattan Map pp12–13

STAR SIGHTS

★ **St Luke's Place**

★ **Jefferson Market Courthouse**

Balducci's *(see p327)* sells some of the best food in town – fine cheeses and many Italian specialities and produce. Balducci's is still run by three generations of one food-loving family.

Gay Street and its fine Federal houses feature in Ruth McKenney's novel of Village life, *My Sister Eileen*.

KEY

― ― ― Suggested route

0 metres 100

0 yards 100

To West 4th Street subway (2 blocks)

The Northern Dispensary has offered free medical care to the poor since 1827. Edgar Allan Poe was treated here for a cold.

★ **Jefferson Market Courthouse**
Now a public library, it was built as a courthouse in 1877 and voted the fifth most beautiful building in America. Empty for over 20 years, it was restored and turned into a library in 1967 **6**

Row houses on St Luke's Place

St Luke's Place ❶

Map 3 C3. Houston St.

FIFTEEN ATTRACTIVE row houses, dating from the 1850s, line the north side of this street. The park opposite is named after a previous resident of St Luke's Place, Mayor Jimmy Walker, the popular dandy who ran the city from 1926 until he was forced to resign after a financial scandal in 1932. In front of No. 6 are the lamps which always identify a mayor's home in New York. In recent years, the most recognizable house on the block has been No. 10, shown on television as the home of the Huxtable family in *The Cosby Show* (although the series sets it in Brooklyn). This is also the block where the movie *Wait Until Dark* was filmed, starring Audrey Hepburn as a blind girl living at No. 4. Theodore Dreiser, one of several writers, including the poet Marianne Moore, who lived here, wrote his *An American Tragedy* while living at No. 16. One block north, the corner of Hudson and Morton Streets marked the edge of the Hudson River three centuries ago.

Mayor's lamp at No. 6

No. 75½ Bedford Street ❷

Map 3 C2. Houston St. **Not open** to the public.

NEW YORK'S narrowest home, just 9½ ft (2.9 m) wide, was built in 1893 in a former passageway. The poet Edna St Vincent Millay lived here briefly, followed by the actor John Barrymore, and later Cary Grant. Sadly, the three-storey building is now empty and partially boarded up, and there is no plaque.

Just around the corner, at No. 38 Commerce Street, Miss Millay founded the Cherry Lane Theatre in 1924 as a venue for avant-garde drama. It still premieres new works. Its biggest hit was the 1960s musical, *Godspell.*

Cottage on Bedford Street

Isaacs-Hendricks House ❸

77 Bedford Street. **Map** 3 C2. Houston St. **Not open** to the public.

THIS IS THE OLDEST surviving home in the Village, built in 1799. The old clapboard walls are visible to the sides

Isaacs-Hendricks House

and rear; the brickwork and third floor came later. The first owner John Isaacs bought the land for $295 in 1794. Next came Harmon Hendricks, a copper dealer and associate of revolutionary Paul Revere. Robert Fulton, who used the copper for the boilers in his steamboats, was a customer.

Grove Court ❹

Map 3 C2. Christopher St-Sheridan Sq.

AN ENTERPRISING grocer named Samuel Cocks was responsible for this group of six town houses, fitting snugly into an area formed by the bend in the street. (The bends in this part of the Village originally marked divisions between colonial properties.) Cocks reckoned that having residents in the empty passage between Nos. 10 and 12 Grove Street would help his business at No. 18.

But residential courts, now prized as exclusive private addresses, were not considered respectable in 1854 and the low-brow residents attracted to the area soon earned it the nickname "Mixed Ale Alley". O Henry later used this block as the setting for his 1902 work, *The Last Leaf.*

The mid-19th-century town houses at Grove Court

Sheridan Square ❺

Map 3 C2. Ⓜ *Christopher St-Sheridan Sq.*

THIS IS THE HEART of the Village, where seven streets come together in such a maze that early guidebooks called it "the mousetrap". It was named after the Civil War General Philip Sheridan who became commander in chief of the US Army in 1883. His statue stands in nearby Christopher Park.

The Draft Riots of 1863 took place in the square, when mobs revolting against army service tried to lynch freed slaves. More than a century later another famous disturbance rocked the

Sheridan Square scene

square. The Stonewall Inn on Christopher Street was a gay bar that had stayed in business (it was then illegal for gays to gather in bars) by paying off the police. However, on 28 June 1969, the patrons rebelled against this state of affairs and the pitched battle that resulted found police officers barricaded inside the bar for hours while crowds taunted them from outside. It was a landmark moral victory for the budding Gay Rights movement. The inn still stands but is no longer a bar. The Village remains a focus for the city's gay community. The spirited gay Hallowe'en Parade *(see p52)* through the Village, noted for its outrageous costumes, brings thousands out.

Pointed tower of "Old Jeff"

Jefferson Market Courthouse ❻

425 6th Ave. **Map** 4 D1. Ⓒ 243-4334. Ⓜ *W 4th St-Washington Sq.* **Open** 10am–6pm Mon, noon–6pm Tue, Thu, Fri, 1–8pm Wed, 10am–5pm Sat. **Closed** Sun, public hols. ♿

PERHAPS THE MOST treasured Village landmark, "Old Jeff" was saved from the wrecking ball and converted into a branch of the New York Public Library, through a spirited campaign that began at a local Christmas party in the late 1950s.

The site became a market in 1833, named after the former president, Thomas Jefferson. Its fire lookout tower had a giant bell that alerted the neighbourhood's volunteer fire-fighters. In 1865, the founding of the municipal fire department made the bell obsolete, and the Third Judicial District or Jefferson Market Courthouse was built. With its Venetian Gothic-style spires and turrets, it was named one of the 10 most beautiful buildings in the country when it opened in

Statue of General Sheridan in Christopher Park

1877. The old firebell was installed in the pointed tower. It was here in 1906 that Harry Thaw was tried for murdering Stanford White *(see p124)*.

By 1945, the market had moved, court sessions were discontinued, the four-sided clock had stopped and the building was endangered. In the 1950s, preservationists campaigned first to restore the clock, then the whole building. Architect Giorgio Cavaglieri has preserved many of the original details, including the stained glass and a spiral staircase which now leads to a dungeon-like reference room.

Facade and ailanthus tree at Patchin Place

Patchin Place ❼

W 10th St. **Map** 4 D1. Ⓜ *W 4th St-Washington Sq.*

ONE OF MANY delightful unexpected pockets in the Village is this tiny block of small residences lined with ailanthus trees planted in order to "absorb the bad air". The houses were built in the mid-19th century to house Basque waiters from the Brevoort Hotel on Fifth Avenue.

Later the houses became fashionable addresses with many famous writers living here. The poet e e cummings lived at No. 4 from 1923 until his death in 1962. English Poet Laureate John Masefield also lived on the block. So did playwright Eugene O'Neill, and John Reed, who wrote an eyewitness account of the Russian Revolution, *Ten Days That Shook The World* (filmed by Warren Beatty as *Reds*).

**Toy battleship from the
Forbes Magazine Collection**

Forbes Building and Galleries ⑧

62 5th Ave. **Map** 4 E1. 📞 206-5548.
Ⓜ 14th St-Union Sq. **Galleries open**
10am–4pm Tue, Wed, Fri, Sat (times
may vary). 🎟 Thu.

Some architectural critics have called this 1925 limestone cube by Carrère & Hastings pompous. It was originally the headquarters of the Macmillan Publishing Company. When they moved uptown, the late Malcolm Forbes moved in with his financial magazine *Forbes*.

The Forbes Magazine Galleries show Forbes's diverse tastes with Fabergé eggs made for the last Russian Tsar; over 500 antique toy boats; 12,000 toy soldiers; and a signed copy of Abraham Lincoln's *Gettysburg Address*, among other presidential memorabilia. There are also exhibitions of paintings, ranging from French to American Military works.

Salmagundi Club ⑨

47 5th Ave. **Map** 4 E1.
📞 255-7740. Ⓜ 14th St-Union Sq.
Open 1pm–5pm daily. 🚫

America's oldest club for artists is housed in the last remaining mansion on lower Fifth Avenue. Built in 1853 for Irad Hawley, it is now the home of the American Artists' Professional League, the American Watercolor Society and the Greenwich Village Society for Historic Preservation. *The Salmagundi Papers*, the satiric periodical by Washington Irving, gave the club its name. Founded in 1871, the club moved here in 1917. Periodic art exhibits open the late 19th-century interior to the public.

Exterior of the Salmagundi Club

First Presbyterian Church ⑩

5th Ave at 12th St. **Map** 4 D1.
📞 675-6150 Ⓜ 7th Ave-Union Sq.
Open 9am–5pm Mon–Fri. 🕇
12.15pm Mon, Wed, Fri;11am Sun.

This Gothic church was modelled on the Church of Saint Saviour in Bath, England. Designed by Joseph C Wells in 1846, the church's main feature is the brownstone tower. The carved wooden plaques on the altar list every pastor since 1716. The south transept by McKim, Mead & White was added in 1893. The fence of iron and wood was built in 1844 and restored in 1981.

Church of the Ascension ⑪

5th Ave at 10th St. **Map** 4 E1.
📞 254-8620. Ⓜ 14th St-
Union Sq. **Open** noon–2pm,
5pm–7pm daily. 🕇 6pm daily,
9am, 11am, 6pm Sun.
📷 (not during services).

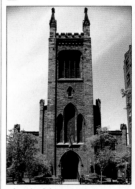

Church of the Ascension

This English Gothic Revival church was designed in 1840–41 by Richard Upjohn, architect of Trinity Church. The interior was redone in 1888 by Stanford White, with an altar relief by Augustus Saint-Gaudens. *The Ascension*, a mural by John La Farge, is above the altar – he designed some of the stained glass too. The belfry tower is lit at night to show off the glowing colours.

In 1844 President John Tyler married Julia Gardiner here; she lived in nearby Colonnade Row *(see p118)*.

Washington Mews ⑫

Washington Sq N at E 8th St.
Map 4 E2. Ⓜ W 4th St.

Built as stables, this hidden block was turned into carriage houses around 1900. The south side was added in 1939. Gertrude Vanderbilt Whitney, founder of the Whitney Museum, lived and worked here.

On the corner of University Place is NYU's French House, remodelled in a French style, where movies, lectures and classes in French are held.

New York University ⓭

Washington Sq. **Map** 4 E2.
998-1212. **M** W 4th St. **Open**
8am–9pm Mon–Sat.

ORIGINALLY CALLED the
University of the City
of New York, NYU was
founded in 1831 as an
alternative to Episcopalian
Columbia University. It is now
the largest private university in
America and extends for blocks
around Washington Square.

Construction of the school's
first building on Waverly
Place sparked the Stone-
cutters' Guild Riot of 1833,
when contractors protested
about the use of inmates from
a state prison to cut stone.
The National Guard had to
restore order. The original
building no longer exists, but
a memorial with a piece of
the original tower can be
seen on a pedestal set into
the pavement on Washington
Square South. Samuel Morse's
telegraph, John W Draper's
first ever photographic

***Bust of Sylvette* by Picasso, between
Bleecker and West Houston Streets**

portrait and Samuel Colt's six-
shooter were invented here.

The Brown Building, on
Washington Place near Greene
Street, was the site of the
Triangle Shirtwaist Company.
In 1911, 146 factory workers
died in a fire here, leading to
new fire safety and labour laws.

A 36-ft (11-m) enlargement
of Picasso's *Bust of Sylvette* is in
University Village.

Judson Memorial Church ⓮

55 Washington Sq S. **Map** 4 D2.
477-0351. **M** W 4th St.
Open 9am–noon, 1pm–5pm
Mon–Fri. **⤴** Sun 11am.

BUILT IN 1892, this McKim,
Mead & White church is
an impressive Romanesque
building with stained glass by
John La Farge. Designed by
Stanford White, it is named
after the first American
missionary sent to foreign
soil, Adoniram Judson, who
served in Burma in 1811. A
copy of his Burmese trans-
lation of the Bible was put in
the cornerstone when the
building was dedicated.

It is the unique spirit of this
church, not the architecture,
that makes it stand out.
Judson Memorial has played
an active role in local and
world concerns and has been
the site of activism on issues
ranging from AIDS to the
arms race. It is also home to
avant-garde art exhibitions
and Off-Off Broadway plays.

Arch on the north side of Washington Square

Washington Square ⓯

Map 4 D2. **M** W 4th St.

NOW ONE of the city's most
vibrant open spaces,
Washington Square was once
marshland through which the
quiet Minetta Brook flowed.
By the late 1700s, the area
had been turned into a public
cemetery – when excavation
began for the park, some
10,000 skeletal remains were
exhumed. The square was
used as a duelling ground for
a time, then as
a site for public
hangings until
1819. The
"hanging elm"
in the northwest
corner remains.
In 1826 the
marsh was filled
in and the brook
diverted under-
ground, where
it still flows; a
small sign on
a fountain at the
entrance to No. 2 Fifth
Avenue marks its course.

The magnificent marble arch
by Stanford White, completed
in 1895, replaced an earlier
wooden version which had
spanned lower Fifth Avenue
to mark the centenary of
George Washington's inauguration. A stairway is hidden in
the right side of the arch. In
1916, a group of artists broke
in, led by Marcel Duchamp
and John Sloan, climbed atop
the arch, and declared the "free
and independent republic of
Washington Square, the state
of New Bohemia".

Across the street is "The
Row". Now part of NYU, this
block was once home to New
York's most prominent
families. The Delano family,
writers Edith Wharton, Henry
James and John dos Passos
and artist Edward Hopper all
lived here. No. 8 was once the
official home of the mayor.

Today students, families and
free spirits mingle and enjoy
the park side by side. A few
drug dealers frequent the
park, but it is safe by day.

**Window on the corner of West 4th
Street and Washington Square**

EAST VILLAGE

Mosaic, facade of St George's Ukrainian Catholic Church

PETER STUYVESANT had a country estate in the East Village, and in the 19th century, the Astors and Vanderbilts lived here. But around 1900, high society moved uptown and immigrants moved in. The Irish, Germans, Jews, Poles, Ukrainians and Puerto Ricans all left their mark in the form of churches, landmarks and the city's most varied and least expensive ethnic restaurants. In the 1960s low rents attracted the "beat generation". Hippies were followed by punks. The area's experimental music clubs and theatres still feature the latest styles. Astor Place buzzes with NYU and Cooper Union students. To the east are Avenues A, B, C and D, a seedy area known as "Alphabet City".

SIGHTS AT A GLANCE

Historic Streets and Buildings
Cooper Union ❶
Colonnade Row ❸
Bayard-Condit Building ❽

Museums and Galleries
Old Merchant's House ❹

Churches
St Mark's-in-the-Bowery Church ❺
Grace Church ❻

Parks and Squares
Tompkins Square ❼

Famous Theatres
Public Theater ❷

SEE ALSO

• *Street Finder*, map 4, 5

• *Where to Stay* pp274–5

• *Restaurants* pp290–92

GETTING THERE
By subway, the Lexington Ave 6 train stop at Astor Place is the most convenient; the area is also served by the M15 and M101/102 buses and the M8 crosstown bus.

| 0 metres | 500 |
| 0 yards | 500 |

KEY

Street-by-Street map

Ⓜ Subway station

Gothic bas-relief on the facade of Grace Church

The interior of McSorley's Old Ale House

Street-by-Street: East Village

A T THE SPOT WHERE Tenth and Stuyvesant streets now intersect, Peter Stuyvesant's country house once stood. His grandson, also named Peter, inherited most of the property and had it divided into streets in 1787. Among the prize sites of the St Mark's Historic District are the St Marks-in-the-Bowery Church, the Stuyvesant-Fish house and the 1795 home of Nicholas Stuyvesant, both in Stuyvesant Street. Many other homes in the District were built between 1871 and 1890 and still have their original stoops, lintels and other architectural details.

Astor Pla[ce] subway (line 6)

Alamo is the title of the 15 ft (4.5 m) steel cube in Astor Place designed by Bernard Rosenthal. It revolves when pushed.

Astor Place saw rioting in 1849. English actor William Macready, playing *Hamlet* at the Astor Place Opera House, criticized American actor Edwin Forrest. Forrest's fans revolted and there were 34 deaths.

Colonnade Row
Now in shabby disrepair, these were once expensive townhouses. The houses, of which only four are left, were unified by a single facade in the European style. The marble was quarried by Sing Sing prisoners ❸

Public Theater
In 1965 the late Joseph Papp convinced the city to buy the Astor Library (1849) as a home for the theater. Once restored, it saw the opening of many famous plays ❷

STAR SIGHTS
★ **Cooper Union**
★ **Old Merchant's House**

★ **Old Merchant's House**
This museum contains the house's original Federal, American Empire and Victorian furniture ❹

★ **Cooper Union**
*Founded by self-
made man Peter
Cooper in 1859,
it still provides a
free education to
its students* ❶

**St Marks-in-the-
Bowery-Church**
*The church was
built in 1799 and
the steeple added
in 1828* ❺

The Stuyvesant-Fish House
(1803–4) was constructed out
of brick. It is a classic example
of a Federal style house.

Renwick Triangle
is a group of 16
houses built in the
Anglo-Italianate
style in 1861.

LOCATOR MAP
See Manhattan Map pp12–13

Stuyvesant Polyclinic
was founded in 1857 as
the German Dispensary
and it is still a health
clinic. The facade is
decorated with the
busts of many famous
physicians and scientists.

St Mark's Place was once
the main street of hippy life.
It is still the hub of the
East Village youth
scene. Funky shops
now occupy
many of the
basements.

Little India, the row
of Indian eateries on
the south side of East
Sixth Street, offers a taste
of India at budget prices.

Little Ukraine is
home to 30,000
Ukrainians. The focus of
the community is St George's
Ukrainian Catholic Church.

KEY

- - - Suggested route

0 metres 100

0 yards 100

McSorley's Old Ale House still
brews its own ale and serves it in
surroundings seemingly unchanged
since it opened in 1854. *(See p309.)*

Great Hall at Cooper Union, where Abraham Lincoln spoke

Cooper Union ❶

30 Cooper Square. **Map** 4 F2.
C 353-4100 **M** Astor Pl.
Open by appointment only, and for
lectures and concerts in Great Hall.
Closed Jun–Aug, public hols. 🚫 ♿

PETER COOPER, the wealthy
industrialist who built the
first US steam locomotive,
made the first steel rails and
was a partner in the first trans-
Atlantic cable venture, had no
formal schooling. To make
education easier for others,
Cooper founded New York's
first free, non-sectarian co-
educational college. Still free,
the school inspires intense
competition for places. The
six-storey building was the
first with a steel frame, made
of Cooper's own rails. The
building was renovated in
1973–74. The Great Hall was
inaugurated in 1859 by Mark
Twain, and Lincoln delivered
his "Right makes Might"
speech there in 1860. Cooper
Union continues to sponsor a
provocative Public Forum.

Public Theater ❷

425 Lafayette St. **Map** 4 F2. **C** 539-
8500 (box office). **M** Astor Pl.
See also **Entertainment** p332.

THE LARGE red brick and
brownstone building that
is the home of the New York
Shakespeare
Festival

began its life in 1849 as the
Astor Library, the city's first
free library, now part of the
New York Public Library. It is
a prime American example of
German Romanesque Revival
style. When the building was
threatened with demolition in
1965, Joseph Papp, founder of
the Shakespeare
Festival,
persuaded
New York City to buy
it as a home for the
company. Renovation
began in 1967,
and much of the
handsome interior
was preserved
during conversion
into six theatres.
Although much of
the work shown is
experimental, the
Public Theater was
the original home
of hit musicals *Hair*
and *A Chorus Line*.
The latter moved
uptown to become the longest-
running Broadway production.

Colonnade Row ❸

428–434 Lafayette St. **Map** 4 F2.
M Astor Pl. **Not open** to the public.

THE CORINTHIAN columns
across these four buildings
are all that remain of a once
magnificent row of nine Greek
Revival town houses. They
were completed in 1833 by
developer Seth Geer, and
were known as "Geer's Folly"
by sceptics who
thought no one
would live so far
east. They were
proved wrong
when the houses
were taken by
such eminent
citizens as John

Jacob Astor and Cornelius
Vanderbilt. Washington Irving,
author of *Rip van Winkle* and
other classic American tales,
lived here for a time, as did
two English novelists, William
Makepeace Thackeray and
Charles Dickens. Five of the
houses were lost when the
John Wanamaker Department
Store razed them early this
century to make room for a
garage. Neglect has been cruel
to the remaining buildings.

Old Merchant's House ❹

29 E 4th St. **Map** 4 F2. **C** 777-1089
M Astor Pl. **Open** 1pm–4pm Sun–
Thu and by appt. **Adm charge**.
🚫 📷 🎧 **Lectures**.

**The original 19th-century iron stove in the
kitchen of the Old Merchant's House**

THIS REMARKABLE Greek
Revival brick town house,
improbably tucked away on
an East Village block, is a
time capsule of a vanished
way of life. It still has its
original fixtures, fittings and
kitchen, and is filled with the
actual furniture, ornaments
and utensils of the family that
lived here for almost 100
years. Built in 1832, it was
bought in 1835 by Seabury
Tredwell, a wealthy merchant,
and stayed in the family until
Gertrude Tredwell, the last
member, died in 1933. She
had maintained her father's
home just as he would have
liked it, and a relative
opened the house as a
museum in 1936. The first-
floor parlours are very grand,
a sign of how well New
York's merchant class lived
in the 1800s.

The Public Theater on Lafayette Street

St Mark's-in-the-Bowery Church ❺

131 E 10th St. **Map** 4 F1. 📞 674-6377. Ⓜ Astor Pl. **Open** 9am–4pm Mon–Fri. **Closed** public hols. 🚫

Oᴺᴇ ᴏꜰ New York's oldest churches, this building, dating from 1799, replaced a 1660 church on the *bouwerie* (farm) of Governor Peter Stuyvesant. He is buried here with seven generations of his descendants and many other prominent early New Yorkers. Poet W H Auden, who was a member of the parish, is also commemorated here.

In 1878, a grisly kidnapping took place in the churchyard, when the remains of department store magnate A T Stewart were removed and held for $20,000 ransom.

The church rectory at 232 East 11th Street is a little-known work, from 1900, by Ernest Flagg. He achieved renown for his Singer Building (*see p104*).

Grace Church ❻

802 Broadway. **Map** 4 F1. 📞 254-2000. Ⓜ Astor Pl. **Open** 10am–5.30pm Mon–Fri, noon–4pm Sat. **Closed** public hols. ⛪ 6pm Wed, 9am, 11am, 6pm Sun. 🚫 ♿ **Concerts**.

Jᴀᴍᴇs ʀᴇɴᴡɪᴄᴋ ᴊʀ, the architect of St Patrick's Cathedral, was only 23 when he designed this church, yet many consider it his finest achievement. Its delicate early Gothic lines have a grace befitting the church's name. The interior is just as beautiful with Pre-Raphaelite stained glass and a handsome mosaic floor.

The church's peace and serenity were briefly shattered in 1863, when Phineas T Barnum

Tom Thumb and his bride at Grace Church

staged the wedding of midget General Tom Thumb here; the crowds turned the event into chaos.

The marble spire replaced a wooden steeple in 1888 amid fears that it might prove too heavy for the church – and it has since developed a distinct lean. The church is visible from afar because it is on a bend on Broadway. Henry Brevoort forced the city to bend Broadway to divert it round his apple orchard.

Grace Church altar and window

Tompkins Square ❼

Map 5 B1. Ⓜ 2nd Ave, 1st Ave.

Tʜɪs ᴇɴɢʟɪsʜ-sᴛʏʟᴇ park has the makings of a peaceful spot, but its past has more often been dominated by strife. It was the site of America's first organized labour demonstration in 1874, the main gathering place during the neighbourhood's hippie era of the 1960s and, in 1991, an arena for bloody riots when the police tried to evict homeless people who had taken over the grounds. The square also contains a poignant monument to the neighbourhood's greatest tragedy. A small statue of a boy

and a girl looking at a steamboat commemorates the deaths of over 1,000 local residents in the *General Slocum* steamer disaster. On 15 June 1904, the boat caught fire during a pleasure cruise on the East River. The boat was crowded with women and children from this then-German neighbourhood. Many local men lost their entire families and moved away, leaving the area and its memories behind.

Bayard-Condict Building ❽

65 Bleecker St. **Map** 4 F3. Ⓜ Bleecker St.

Tʜᴇ ɢʀᴀᴄᴇꜰᴜʟ columns, elegant filigreed terracotta facade and magnificent cornice on this 1898 building mark the only New York work by Louis Sullivan, the great Chicago architect who taught Frank Lloyd Wright. He died in poverty and obscurity in Chicago in 1924.

Sullivan is said to have objected vigorously to the sentimental angels supporting the Bayard-Condict Building's cornice, but he eventually gave in to the wishes of Silas Alden Condict, the owner.

Because this building is squeezed into a commercial block, it is better appreciated from a distance. Cross the street and walk a little way down Crosby Street for the best view.

The Bayard-Condict Building

GRAMERCY AND THE FLATIRON DISTRICT

FOUR SQUARES were laid out by real estate developers in the 19th century to emulate the quiet, private residential areas in many European cities. Gramercy Park, still mainly residential, was one of them. The town houses around the square were

Toy in the Police Academy Museum

designed by some of the city's best architects, and occupied by some of its most prominent citizens. Not far away, pricey boutiques and trendy cafés are moving to the once-dowdy stretch of lower Fifth Avenue just south of the famous Flatiron Building.

SIGHTS AT A GLANCE

Historic Streets and Buildings
New York Life Insurance Company ❷
Appellate Division of the Supreme Court of the State of New York ❸
Metropolitan Life Insurance Company ❹
Flatiron Building ❺
Ladies' Mile ❻
National Arts Club ❽
The Players ❾
Block Beautiful ⓫
Con Edison Headquarters ⓮

Museums and Galleries
Theodore Roosevelt Birthplace ❼
Police Academy Museum ⓬

Churches
The Little Church Around the Corner ⓰

Parks and Squares
Madison Square ❶
Gramercy Park ❿
Stuyvesant Square ⓭
Union Square ⓯

SEE ALSO
- *Street Finder*, maps 8, 9
- *Where to Stay* pp274–5
- *Restaurants* pp290–92

GETTING THERE
The closest subway station is at 23rd St, where the Lexington Ave No. 6 train stops. Buses to the area include the M101/102 on 3rd Ave, and the M1, M2 or M3 on 5th and Madison avenues. The crosstown bus is the M26.

Lizard on a statue in Union Square

KEY
▢ Street-by-Street map
Ⓜ Subway station

0 metres   500
0 yards   500

Con Edison Headquarters by night

Street-by-Street: Gramercy Park

GRAMERCY PARK AND nearby Madison Square tell a tale of two cities. Madison Square is ringed by offices and traffic and is used mainly by those who work nearby, but the fine surrounding commercial architecture and statues make it well worth visiting. It was once the home of Stanford White's famous pleasure palace, the old Madison Square Garden, and a place where revellers always thronged. Gramercy Park, however, retains the air of dignified tranquility it has become known for. Here, the residences and clubs remain, set around New York's last private park, for which only those who live on the square have a key.

★ **Madison Square**
The Knickerbocker Club played baseball here in the 1840s and were the first to codify the game's rules. Today office workers enjoy the park's many statues of 19th-century figures, among them Admiral David Farragut ❶

23rd Street subway (lines N, R)

Statue of Diana atop the old Madison Square Garden

★ **Flatiron Building**
The triangle made by Fifth Avenue, Broadway and 23rd Street is the site of one of New York's most famous early skyscrapers. When it was built in 1903, it was the world's tallest building ❺

A sidewalk clock
found in front of No. 200 Fifth Avenue marks the very end of the once-fashionable shopping area, known as Ladies' Mile.

Ladies' Mile
Broadway from Union to Madison squares was once New York's finest shopping area. A few buildings remain ❻

Theodore Roosevelt Birthplace
The house is a replica of the one in which the 26th American president was born ❼

KEY

 Suggested route

0 metres	100
0 yards	100

National Arts Club
This is a private club for the arts, on the south side of the park ❽

Appellate Court
This small marble palace is said to be the world's busiest courthouse ③

Metropolitan Life Insurance Company
Vast vaulted entrances mark each corner ④

23rd Street subway (line 6)

The Players
Actor Edwin Booth founded this club in 1888 ⑨

Gramercy Park
Only residents can use the park itself, but all can enjoy the peace and charm of the area around it ⑩

The Brotherhood Synagogue was a Friends Meeting House from 1859 to 1975, when it became a synagogue.

The Block Beautiful
This is a tree-lined stretch of East 19th Street. No particular house is outstanding, but the street as a whole is lovely ⑪

Pete's Tavern
has been here since 1903. Short story writer O Henry, a well-known chronicler of the city, wrote *The Gift of the Magi* in the second booth.

LOCATOR MAP
See Manhattan Map pp12–13

New York Life Insurance Company
This spectacular building by Cass Gilbert bears his trademark pyramid-shaped top ②

STAR SIGHTS

★ **Flatiron Building**

★ **Madison Square**

Madison Square ❶

Map 8 F4. **Ⓜ** *23rd St.*

Farragut's statue, Madison Square

Planned as the centre of a fashionable residential district, this square became a popular entertainment centre after the Civil War. It was bordered by the elegant Fifth Avenue Hotel, the Madison Square Theatre and Stanford White's Madison Square Garden. The torch-bearing arm of the Statue of Liberty was exhibited here in 1884.

Quiet once again, it is a lunching spot for neighbourhood office workers, and a place for a stroll to admire the sculptures. The 1880 statue of Admiral David Farragut is by Augustus Saint-Gaudens, with a pedestal by Stanford White. Farragut was the hero of a Civil War sea battle; figures representing Courage and Loyalty arising from the waves are carved on the base. The statue of Roscoe Conkling commemorates a US senator who died of exposure during the great blizzard of 1888. The Eternal Light flagpole, by Carrère & Hastings, honours the soldiers who fell in France during World War I.

New York Life Insurance Company ❷

45 –55 Madison Ave. **Map** 9 A3.
Ⓜ *28th St.* **Open** *office hours.*

This imposing building was designed in 1928 by Cass Gilbert of Woolworth Building fame. The interior is a masterpiece, adorned with enormous hanging lamps, bronze doors and panelling, and a grand staircase leading, of all places, to the subway station.

Other famous buildings have stood on this site. Barnum's Hippodrome was here in 1874, then the first Madison Square Garden opened in 1879. A wide range of entertainments were put on, including the prizefights of heavyweight boxing hero John L Sullivan in the 1880s. The next Madison Square Garden – Stanford White's legendary pleasure palace – opened on the same site in 1890. Lavish musical shows and social events were attended by New York's elite, who paid over $500 for a box at the prestigious annual horse show.

The building had street-level arcades and a tower modelled on the Giralda in Seville. A gold statue of the goddess Diana stood atop the tower. Her nudity was shocking, but far more scandalous was the decadent life and death of White himself. In 1906, while watching a revue in the roof garden, he was shot dead by millionaire Harry K Thaw, the husband of White's former mistress, showgirl Evelyn Nesbit. The headline in the journal *Vanity Fair* summed up popular feeling: "Stanford White, Voluptuary and Pervert, Dies the Death of a Dog". The ensuing trial's revelations about decadent Broadway high society leave modern soap operas far behind.

New York Life Insurance Company's golden pyramid roof

Appellate Division of the Supreme Court of the State of New York ❸

E 25th St at Madison Ave. **Map** 9 A4.
Ⓒ *340 0400.* **Ⓜ** *23rd St.* **Open** *9am–5pm Mon–Fri (court in session from 2pm Tue, Wed, Thu, from 10am Fri).* **Closed** *public hols.* 🚫

Appeals relating to civil and criminal cases for New York and the Bronx are heard here, in what is widely considered to be the busiest court of its kind in the world. James Brown Lord designed the small yet noble Palladian Revival building in 1900.

Statues of *Justice* and *Study* above the Appellate Court

It is decorated with more than a dozen handsome sculptures, including Daniel Chester French's *Justice* flanked by *Power* and *Study.* During the week, the public is invited to step inside to admire the fine interior, designed by the Herter Brothers, including the courtroom when it is not in session. Among the elegant details worth looking out for are the stained-glass windows and dome, the murals and the cabinet work.

Displays in the lobby often feature some of the more famous cases that have been heard in this court. Among the celebrity names that have been involved in appeals settled here are Babe Ruth, Charlie Chaplin, Fred Astaire, Harry Houdini, Theodore Dreiser and Edgar Allan Poe.

Clock tower of the Metropolitan Life Insurance Company

Metropolitan Life Insurance Company ❹

1 Madison Ave. **Map** 9 A4. 📞 578-2211. Ⓜ *23rd St.* **Open** *office hours.* 🚫

IN 1909, THE ADDITION of a 700-ft (210-m) tower to this 1893 building ousted the Flatiron as the tallest in the world. The huge four-sided clock has minute hands said to weigh 1000 lb (454 kg) each. The building is lit up at night, and is a familiar part of the evening skyline. It served as the company symbol "the light that never fails".

A series of historical murals by N C Wyeth, the famed illustrator of such classics as *Robin Hood*, *Treasure Island* and *Robinson Crusoe* (and the father of painter Andrew Wyeth), once graced the walls of the cafeteria. They are now on display in the lobby.

Flatiron Building ❺

175 5th Ave. **Map** 8 F4. Ⓜ *23rd St.* **Open** *office hours.*

ORIGINALLY NAMED the Fuller Building after the construction company that owned it, this building by Chicago architect David Burnham was the tallest in the world when it was completed in 1902. One of the first buildings to use a steel frame, it heralded the era of the skyscrapers.

It soon became known as the Flatiron for its unusual triangular shape, but some called it "Burnham's folly", predicting that the winds created by the building's shape would knock it down. It has withstood the test of time, but the winds along 23rd Street did have one notable effect. In the building's early days, they drew crowds of males hoping to get a peek at girls' ankles as their long skirts got blown about. Police officers had to keep people moving along, and their call, "23-skidoo" became slang for "scram". The stretch of Fifth Avenue to the south of the building was, until recently, rather run down but is fast coming to life with smart shops such as Emporio Armani and Paul Smith, giving the area new cachet and a new name, "The Flatiron District".

Flatiron Building during its construction

Ladies' Mile ❻

Broadway (Union Sq to Madison Sq). **Map** 4 E1 to 8 F4. Ⓜ *14th St, 23rd St.*

Arnold Constable store

IN THE 19TH CENTURY, the "carriage trade" came here in shiny traps from their town houses nearby, to shop at stores such as Arnold Constable (Nos. 881–887) and Lord & Taylor (No. 901). The ground floor exteriors have changed beyond recognition; look up to see the remains of once grand facades.

President Teddy Roosevelt

Theodore Roosevelt Birthplace ❼

28 E 20th St. **Map** 9 A5. 📞 260-1616 Ⓜ *14th St-Union Sq.* **Open** *9am–5pm Wed–Sun (last adm: 4.30pm).* **Closed** *public hols.* **Adm charge.** 📷 🎦 *Lectures, concerts, film, video.* 🚻

THE RECONSTRUCTED boyhood home of the colourful 26th president displays everything from the toys with which the young Teddy played to campaign buttons and emblems of the trademark "Rough Rider" hat that Roosevelt wore in the Spanish-American War. One exhibit features his explorations and interests, the other covers his political career.

Bas relief faces of great writers at the National Arts Club

National Arts Club ⑧

15 Gramercy Pk S. **Map** 9 A5. 🄲 *475-3424.* Ⓜ *14th St-Union Sq.* **Open** *for exhibitions.*

DESIGNED BY Calvert Vaux in 1881–84, this large brownstone was the residence of New York governor Samuel Tilden, who condemned "Boss" Tweed (*see p25*) and established a free public library. The National Arts Club bought the home in 1906, and kept the original high ceilings and stained glass. Members have included most of the top American artists of the late 19th and early 20th century. Early members were asked to donate a painting or sculpture in lieu of a subscription for life membership, and these gifts form the permanent collection. The club is open to the public several times a year for exhibitions.

The Players ⑨

16 Gramercy Pk S. **Map** 9 A5. 🄲 *228-7610.* Ⓜ *14th St-Union Sq.* **Closed** *exc for pre-booked group tours.* 🚫

THIS TWO-STOREY brownstone was the home of actor Edwin Booth, brother of John Wilkes Booth, President Lincoln's assassin. Edwin Booth had architect Stanford White remodel the building as a club in 1888. Although it

was intended primarily for actors, members have included White himself, author Mark Twain, publisher Thomas Nast and Winston Churchill, whose mother, Jennie Jerome, was born nearby. A statue of Booth playing Hamlet can be found across the street in Gramercy Park.

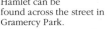

Decorative grille at The Players club

Gramercy Park ⑩

Map 9 A4. Ⓜ *23rd St.*

GRAMERCY PARK is one of four squares (with Union, Stuyvesant and Madison) laid out in the 1830s and 1840s to attract society residences. It is the city's only private park, and residents in the surrounding buildings get keys to the park gate as the original owners once did. A peep through the railings at the southeast corner reveals Greg Wyatt's fountain, with giraffes leaping around a smiling sun.

The buildings around the square were designed by some of the city's most famous architects, including

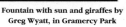

Fountain with sun and giraffes by Greg Wyatt, in Gramercy Park

Stanford White, whose house was located on the site of today's Gramercy Park Hotel. Particularly fine are Nos. 3 and 4, with graceful cast-iron gates and porches. The lanterns in front of No. 4 serve as symbols marking the house of a former mayor of the city, James Harper. No. 34 (1883) has been the home of the sculptor Daniel Chester French, the actor James Cagney and circus impresario John Ringling (who had a massive pipe organ installed in his apartment).

Block Beautiful ⑪

E 19th St. **Map** 9 A5. Ⓜ *3rd Ave, 14th St-Union Sq.*

House facade on the Block Beautiful on East 19th Street

THIS IS A SERENE, tree-lined block of 1920s residences, beautifully restored. None of them is outstanding on its own, but together they create a wonderfully harmonious whole. No. 132 has had two famous theatrical tenants, Theda Bara, silent movie star and Hollywood's first sex symbol, and the fine Shakespearean actress Mrs Patrick Campbell, who originated the role of Eliza Doolittle in George Bernard Shaw's *Pygmalion* in 1914. The hitching posts outside No. 141 and the ceramic relief of giraffes outside Nos. 147–149 are two of the many details to look out for as you walk along the block.

Police Academy Museum ⑫

235 E 20th St. **Map** 9 B4.
🕻 477-9753. Ⓜ *14th St-Union Sq.*
Open *9am–3pm Mon–Fri.* **Closed** *Sat, Sun,* **public** *hols, & for meetings – phone in advance to confirm.* 🎦

A COLOURFUL SALUTE to "New York's finest", the museum possesses one of the largest collections of police force memorabilia anywhere. On display are daily registers describing illicit liquor raids during the Prohibition era, sensational axe murders, bank robberies and kidnappings. There is a whole arsenal of weapons – nightsticks, billy clubs and an enormous gun collection. Also on display are antique uniforms and caps, and every badge issued by the Police Department since 1845. On a more sombre contemporary note, an educational exhibit details the tragic consequences of the twin scourges of drug addiction and youth gangs.

Gangster Al Capone's gun, at the Police Academy Museum

Stuyvesant Square ⑬

Map 9 B5. Ⓜ *14th St-Union Sq.*

T HIS OASIS, in the form of a pair of parks divided by Second Avenue, was part of Peter Stuyvesant's original farm in the 1600s. It was still in the Stuyvesant family when the park was designed in 1836; Peter G Stuyvesant sold the land to the city for the nominal sum of $5 (much to the delight of those living nearby, who saw real estate values jump). A statue of Stuyvesant by Gertrude Vanderbilt Whitney stands in the park. The park separated the Stuyvesant area from the poorer Gas House District.

The towers of Con Edison (right), Metropolitan Life and the Empire State

Con Edison Headquarters ⑭

145 E 14th St. **Map** 9 A5. Ⓜ *3rd Ave, 14th St-Union Sq.* **Museum** 🕻 460-6244. **Open** *9am–5pm Tue–Sat.* **Closed** *public hols.*

T HE CLOCK TOWER of this building from 1911 is a local landmark. The Con Edison Energy Museum next door at No. 145 E 14th Street traces progress from Thomas Edison to solar power. There is a working model of Edison's 1882 generator, recreated factories and a cutaway view of underground New York.

Union Square ⑮

Map 9 A5. Ⓜ *14th St-Union Sq.* **Market** *Mon, Wed, Fri, Sat.*

Greenmarket day at Union Square

O PENED IN 1839, this park joined Bloomingdale Road (now Broadway) with the Bowery Road (Fourth Avenue or Park), and hence its name. Later, the centre of the square was lifted up for a subway to run beneath it. The park became popular with soapbox orators. During the Depression in 1930, more than 35,000 unemployed people rallied here, before marching on to City Hall to demand jobs. The square hosts a popular Greenmarket at which farmers from all over New York State sell their produce.

The Little Church Around the Corner ⑯

1 E 29th St. **Map** 8 F3.
🕻 684-6770. Ⓜ *28th St.* **Open** *9am–6pm daily.* 🕇 *11am Sun.*
🎦 🚻 📷 *Sun after 11am mass.* **Lectures, concerts, recitals.**

B UILT FROM 1849–56, the Episcopal Church of the Transfiguration is a tranquil retreat. It has been known by its nickname since 1870. When Joseph Jefferson tried to arrange the funeral of fellow actor George Holland, the pastor at a nearby church refused to bury a person of so lowly a profession. Instead, he suggested "the little church around the corner". The name stuck and the church has had special ties with the theatre ever since. Sarah Bernhardt attended services here.

The south transept window, by John La Farge, shows Edwin Booth playing Hamlet. Jefferson's cry of: "God bless the little church around the corner" is commemorated in a window in the south aisle:

CHELSEA AND
THE GARMENT DISTRICT

T HIS WAS OPEN farmland in 1750, by the 1830s it was a city suburb, and in the 1870s, with the coming of the elevated railroads *(see pp24–5)*, it became commercial. Music halls and theatres lined 23rd Street. Fashion Row grew in the shadow of the El, with department stores serving middle-class New York. But, as fashion moved uptown,

Statue of garment worker, at No. 555 7th Avenue

Chelsea drifted downhill. It became a warehouse district until the Els were removed and New Yorkers rediscovered the charm of the area's 19th-century town houses. While Chelsea's fortunes were waning, Herald Square to the north was looking up, as Macy's arrived and New York city's retailing and garment district quickly grew up around it.

Inside Chelsea's Empire Diner

SIGHTS AT A GLANCE

Historic Streets and Buildings
Empire State Building
pp134–5 ❷
General Post Office ❼
General Theological
Seminary ⓫

Chelsea Historic District ⓬
Hugh O'Neill Dry Goods
Store ⓮

Churches
Marble Collegiate Reformed
Church ❶
St John the Baptist Church ❺

Modern Architecture
Madison Square Garden ❻
Jacob K Javits Convention
Center ❽

Chelsea Piers Sports and
Entertainment Complex ❾

Monuments
Worth Monument ⓯

Parks and Squares
Herald Square ❸

**Landmark Hotels and
Restaurants**
Empire Diner ❿
Chelsea Hotel ⓭

Landmark Stores
Macy's ❹

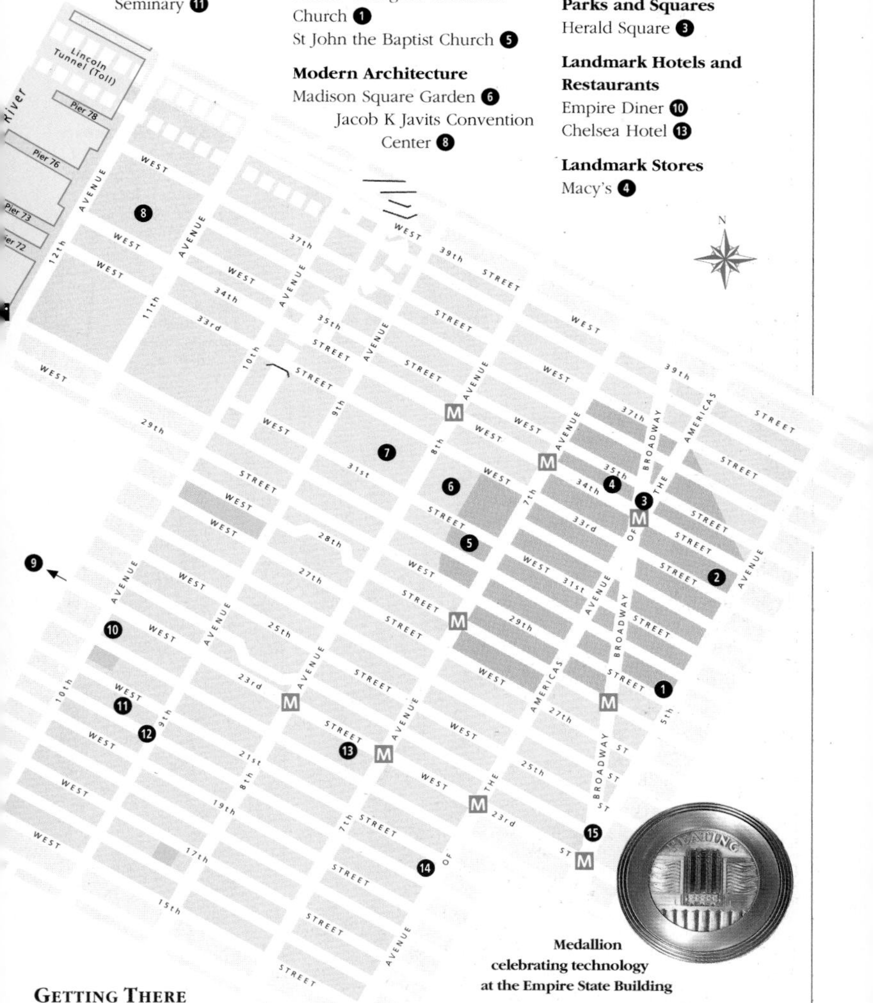

Medallion
celebrating technology
at the Empire State Building

GETTING THERE

To Chelsea take the 7th Ave/
Broadway 1 and 9 subway
trains to 18th or 23rd St. The
8th Ave A, C and E trains go to
23rd St. Buses include the M10
and M11, M14 or the M23
crosstown. To reach the area
around Macy's, take the 1 or 9
or the 2 and 3 express trains to
34th St/Penn Station. The 8th
Ave trains also stop at 34th St.

SEE ALSO

• *Street Finder*, maps 7 – 8

• *Where to Stay* pp274–5

• *Restaurants* pp290–92

KEY

▨	Street-by-Street map
Ⓜ	Subway station
⛴	Heliport

Street-by-Street: Herald Square

H ERALD SQUARE is named for the New York *Herald*, which had
its office there from 1894 to 1921. Today full of shoppers,
the area was once one of the raunchiest parts of New York.
During the 1880s and '90s, it was known as the Tenderloin
District and was filled with dance halls and bordellos. When
Macy's opened in 1901, the focus moved from flesh to fashion.
New York's Garment District now
fills the streets near Macy's
on and around Seventh
Avenue, also known as
"Fashion Avenue". To the
east on Fifth Avenue is
the Empire State Building,
with the city's best
eagle's eye views from
the observation deck.

Fashion Avenue is another name for the
stretch of Seventh Avenue around 34th
Street. This area is the heart of New York's
garment industry. The streets are full of
men pushing trolleys of clothes and furs.

**A&S Greeley Square
Plaza** is a branch of
Brooklyn's Abraham
& Straus. Once the
site of Macy's arch-
rival, Gimbel's, it
was remodelled
in 1988 for A&S.

**34th Steet-
Penn Station
subway (lines
1, 2, 3, 9)**

**The Ramada Hotel
Pennsylvania** was a
centre for the 1930s big
bands – Glenn Miller's
song *Pennsylvania 6-
5000* made its tele-
phone number
famous.

**St John
the Baptist Church**
*A beautiful set of carved
Stations of the Cross is
hung on the walls of the
white marble interior of
this church* ❺

The SJM Building is at 130 West
30th Street. Mesopotamian friezes run
around the outside of the building.

The Fur District is at the southern end
of the Garment District. Furriers ply their
trade between West 27th and 30th streets.

The Flower District,
around Sixth Avenue
and West 28th Street,
hums with activity in
the early part of the day
as florists pack their
vans with their highly
scented, brightly
coloured wares.

**28th Street
subway (lines N, R)**

★ **Macy's**
The biggest department store in the world has something for everyone ④

The Greenwich Savings Bank (now the CrossLand Savings Bank) is a Greek temple to banking with huge columns on three sides.

34th Street subway (lines B, D, F, N, Q, R)

Herald Square
The New York Herald Building's clock now occupies the place where Broadway meets Sixth Avenue ③

LOCATOR MAP
See Manhattan Map pp12–13

KEY

– – – Suggested route

| 0 metres | 100 |
| 0 yards | 100 |

★ **Empire State Building**
The observation deck of this quintessential skyscraper is a great place to see the city ②

Greeley Square is more of a traffic island than a square, but it does have a fine statue of Horace Greeley, founder of the New York Tribune.

Little Korea is where the city's Koreans do business. In addition to shops, there are restaurants nearby on West 31st and 32nd streets.

The Life Building at 19 West 31st Street housed *Life* magazine when it was a satirical weekly. Carrère and Hastings designed the building in 1894. It is now a hotel *(see p276)*.

Marble Collegiate Reformed Church
This 1854 church was built in the Gothic Revival style. It became famous when Norman Vincent Peale was pastor here ①

STAR SIGHTS

★ **Macy's**

★ **Empire State Building**

Marble Collegiate's Tiffany stained-glass windows

Marble Collegiate Reformed Church ❶

1 W 29th St. **Map** 8 F3. 686-2770. **M** 28th St. **Open** 9.30am–4pm Mon–Sat. ✝ Sep–Jun: 11.15am Sun; Jun–Sep: 10.30am Sun. 📷 during services. ♿

T HIS CHURCH is best known for its former pastor, Norman Vincent Peale, who wrote *The Power of Positive Thinking*. Another positive thinker, ex-president Richard M Nixon, attended services here when he was a lawyer in his pre-White House days.

The church was built in 1854 using the marble blocks that give it its name. At that time, Fifth Avenue was a dusty country road, and the cast-iron fence around the church kept livestock out.

The original white and gold interior walls were replaced with a stencilled gold *fleur-de-lis* design on a soft rust background. Two stained-glass Tiffany windows, depicting Old Testament scenes, were placed in the south wall in 1893.

Empire State Building ❷

See pp134–5.

Herald Square ❸

6th Ave. **Map** 8 E2. **M** 34th St-Penn Station. See **Shopping** p313.

N AMED AFTER the New York *Herald*, which occupied a fine Stanford White building here until 1921, the square was the hub of the rowdy Tenderloin district at the turn of the century. The ornamental clock is now all that is left of the Herald Building.

Herald Square is also the site of the now-defunct Gimbel Brothers Department Store, once arch rival to Macy's. (The rivalry was affectionately portrayed in the New York Christmas movie *A Miracle on 34th Street*.) In 1988 the store was converted into a vertical mall with a glittery neon front.

A&S Plaza on Herald Square

Macy's ❹

151 W 34th St. **Map** 8 E2. 695-4400 **M** 34th St-Penn Station. **Open** 10am–8.30pm Mon, Thu, Fri; 10am–7pm Tue, Wed, Sat; 11am–7pm Sun. See **Shopping** p311.

T HE "WORLD'S LARGEST STORE" covers a square block and the merchandise inside covers just about any item you could imagine in every price range.

Macy's was founded by a former whaler called Rowland Hussey Macy, who opened a small store at West 14th Street in 1857. The store's red star logo came from Macy's tattoo, a souvenir of his sailing days.

By the time Macy died in 1877, his little store had grown to a row of 11 buildings. It was to expand further under two brothers, Isidor and Nathan Straus, who had operated Macy's china and glassware department. By 1902 Macy's had outgrown its 14th Street premises and the firm acquired its present site. The eastern facade has a new

Macy's 34th Street facade

The nave of St John the Baptist Church

almost lost in the heart of the Fur District. The exterior has a single spire. Although the brownstone facade on 30th Street is dark with city soot, many treasures lie within this dull exterior. The entrance is through the modern Friary on 31st Street.

The sanctuary by Napoleon Le Brun is a marvel of Gothic arches in glowing white marble surmounted by gilded capitals. Painted reliefs of religious scenes line the walls; sunlight streams through the stained-glass windows. Also off the Friary is the Prayer Garden, a small, green and peaceful oasis with religious statuary, a fountain and stone benches.

New York Knickerbockers basketball and New York Rangers hockey teams. It is also the venue for a packed calendar of other events: rock concerts; championship tennis and boxing (plus outrageously staged wrestling); Ringling Bros and Barnum & Bailey Circus; an antiques show; a dog show; and more. There is also a 5,600-seat theatre.

In spite of some recent renovation work, Madison Square Garden lacks the panache of its earlier location, which combined a truly stunning Stanford White building with some extravagant entertainment *(see p124)*.

The massive interior of Madison Square Garden

Madison Square Garden ❻

4 Pennsylvania Plaza. **Map** 8 D2. 465-6741. M *34th St-Penn Station*. **Open** *Mon–Sun, times vary according to shows*. **Adm charge**. *See* **Entertainment** *p344*.

T HERE'S ONLY ONE good thing to be said for the razing of the extraordinarily lovely McKim, Mead & White Pennsylvania Station building in favour of this undistinguished 1968 complex: it so enraged city preservationists that they formed an alliance to ensure that such a thing would never be allowed to happen again.

Madison Square Garden itself, which sits atop underground Pennsylvania Station, is a cylinder of pre-cast concrete, functional enough as a 20,000-seat, centrally-located home for the famous

General Post Office ❼

421 8th Ave. **Map** 8 D2. 967-8585. M *34th St-Penn Station*. **Open** *24 hrs a day, every day, (incl public hols)*. *See* **Practical Information** *p361*.

D ESIGNED BY McKim, Mead & White in 1913, in a style to complement their 1910 Pennsylvania Station across the street, the Post Office is a perfect example of a public building of the Beaux Arts period. The imposing, two-block-long facade has a broad staircase leading to a facade adorned with 20 Corinthian columns and a pavilion at each end. The 280-ft (85-m) inscription across the full length is loosely based on a description by Herodotus of the Persian Empire's postal service: "Neither snow nor rain nor heat nor gloom of night stays these couriers from the swift completion of their appointed rounds."

entrance but still bears the bay windows and Corinthian pillars of the 1902 design. The 34th Street facade still has its original caryatids guarding the entrance, along with the clock, canopy and lettering.

The sea featured again in Macy's history in 1912 – a plaque by the main entrance commemorates the death of Isidor and his wife in the sinking of the *Titanic*.

Macy's sponsors New York's Thanksgiving Day parade and Fourth of July fireworks. The store's spring flower show draws thousands of visitors. But the recession has taken its toll even on this New York institution, and the 1990s have not been easy.

St John the Baptist Church ❺

210 W 31st St. **Map** 8 E3. 564-9070. M *34th St-Penn Station*. **Open** *6am–6pm daily*. *through-out the day*.

F OUNDED IN 1840 to serve a congregation of newly-arrived immigrants, today this small Roman Catholic church is

The Corinthian colonnade of the General Post Office

Empire State Building ②

Empire State Building

Aᴸᴛʜᴏᴜɢʜ ɪᴛ ʟᴏsᴛ its title as the world's tallest building to the World Trade Center in the 1970s, the Empire State is still New York's most famous skyscraper, a symbol of the city all over the world. Construction began only weeks before the Wall Street Crash of 1929 and, by the time it opened in 1931, space was so difficult to let that it was nicknamed "The Empty State Building". Only the immediate popularity of the observatories saved the building from bankruptcy – now over 85 million people have visited them.

102nd floor observatory

The Empire State was planned to be 86 storeys high, but then a 150-ft (46-m) mooring mast for zeppelins was added. Now the mast transmits TV and radio to the city and four states.

Symbols of the modern age are depicted in these bronze Art Deco medallions placed over the doorways.

CONSTRUCTION
The building was designed for ease and speed of construction. Everything possible was prefabricated and slotted into place at a rate of about four storeys per week.

Coloured floodlighting of the top 30 floors marks special and seasonal events.

High-speed lifts travel at up to 1,200 ft (366 m) per minute.

The framework is made from 60,000 tonnes of steel, and was built in 23 weeks.

Aluminium panels were used instead of stone around the 6,500 windows. The steel trim masks rough edges on the facing.

Ten million bricks were used to line the whole building.

Eleven minutes is all it takes fit runners to race up the 1,860 steps from the lobby to the 102nd floor, in the annual Empire State Run-Up.

Sandwich space between the floors houses the wiring, pipes and cables.

Over 200 steel and concrete piles support the 365,000-tonne building.

STAR FEATURES

★ **Fifth Avenue Entrance Lobby**

★ **Views from 86th and 102nd floor Observatories**

★ Views from the Observatories

The 86th floor has outdoor observation decks for bird's-eye views of Manhattan. From the 102nd floor, 1,250 ft (381 m) high, you can see more than 78 miles (125 km) on a clear day, but check the visibility rating in the lobby first.

Sky Boy

Photographer Lewis Hine vividly documented the hazards and bravery of 1930s construction. Here, a construction worker climbs up a cable. The wide Hudson River looks almost like a stream in the background.

Lightning Strikes

The Empire State is a natural lightning conductor and is struck up to 500 times a year. The outside deck is shut during storms, but it is safe to view from inside.

Empire State 1454 ft (443 m)

Eiffel Tower 1045 ft (319 m)

Great Pyramid 350 ft (107 m)

Big Ben 220 ft (67 m)

Pecking Order

New Yorkers are justly proud of their city's symbol, which towers above the icons of other cultures.

★ Fifth Avenue Entrance Lobby

A relief image of the skyscraper is superimposed on a map of New York State in the marble-lined lobby.

ENCOUNTERS IN THE SKY

The Empire State Building has been seen in many films. However, the finale from the 1933 classic *King Kong* is easily its most famous guest appearance, as the giant ape straddles the spire to do battle with army aircraft. In 1945 a real bomber flew too low over Manhattan in fog and struck the building just above the 78th floor. Luckiest escape was that of a young lift operator whose cabin plunged 79 floors to the basement. The emergency brakes saved her life.

THEATER DISTRICT

Lee Lawrie design in Rockefeller Center

It was the move of the Metropolitan Opera House to Broadway at 40th Street in 1883 that first drew lavish theatres and restaurants to this area. In the 1920s, movie palaces added the glamour of neon to Broadway, the signs getting bigger and brighter until the street became known as the "Great White Way".

After World War II, the pull of the movies waned and glitter was replaced by grime. Now a regeneration scheme has brought the public and the bright lights back. Pockets of calm also exist, away from the bustle. Explore the Public Library, or relax in Bryant Park. For the best of both worlds, though, visit Rockefeller Center.

Main Reading Room of the New York Public Library

Sights at a Glance

Historic Streets and Buildings
New York Yacht Club 5
American Standard Building 7
New York Public Library 8
Times Square 9
Group Health Insurance Building 11
Paramount Building 12
Shubert Alley 13
Alwyn Court Apartments 18

Museums
Intrepid Sea-Air-Space Museum 19

Modern Architecture
Rockefeller Center 1
MONY Tower 14

Parks and Squares
Bryant Park 6

Famous Theatres
Lyceum Theater 3
New Amsterdam Theater 10
City Center of Music and Drama 15
Carnegie Hall 16

Landmark Hotels and Restaurants
Algonquin Hotel 4
Russian Tea Room 17

Landmark Stores
Diamond Row 2

Getting There

Convenient subway routes are the 7th Ave/Broadway 1, 2, 3 and 9 trains to 50th or 42nd St, and N or R trains to 57th or 49th St. Other nearby lines include the 8th Ave A, C or E trains and 6th Ave D or F trains. Bus routes through the area are the M5, 6, 7, 10, the M34, M42, M50, M57 and the M58 Street crosstown.

See Also

- ***Street Finder***, maps 8, 11–12
- ***Where to Stay*** pp274–5
- ***Restaurants*** pp290–92

Key

- Street-by-Street map
- [M] Subway station
- ⛴ River boat boarding point

0 metres 500

0 yards 500

Mermaid and dolphin fountain in the Channel Gardens

Street-by-Street: Rockefeller Center

THE FIRST COMPLEX in the world to integrate offices with shops, entertainment, dining and gardens, Rockefeller Center is one of the most visited sights in New York. Night and day, throughout the year, the Center is alive with people. There are workers from some of the world's major companies, shoppers browsing in the stores and tourists admiring the wealth of American art and architecture. In winter skaters glide beneath the famous Christmas tree. You can rent skates and try it. The colourful flower displays change with the seasons.

The Winter Garden has housed hit revues and musicals since 1911.

Equitable Center has the Roy Lichtenstein *Mural with Blue Brushstroke (1984–5)* in its lobby.

Rockefeller Center expanded to the west in the 1960s with a series of four blocks providing a bland backdrop to the older buildings.

50th Street subway (lines 1, 9)

Cort Theater has a facade based on the Petit Trianon at Versailles, and a bust of Marie Antoinette overlooking the ticket lobby. Both *The Diary of Anne Frank* and *Sarafina!* were premiered here.

George M Cohan's statue, in front of the TKTS booth in Duffy Square, honours the man who wrote *Give my Regards to Broadway*.

GEORGE M COHAN

The Miller Building was "The Show Folks' Shoe Shop" before World War II. Four statues of American actresses by A Stirling Cooper are all that remain to show for its former role.

Lyceum Theater
This is the oldest New York theatre still in use, although it is "dark" more often than not these days. It was built in 1903 for producer Daniel Froman, who had an apartment in the building complete with a trap door looking down over the stage ❸

Detail from the facade of the Lyceum

Sun Triangle in the Lower Plaza mixes science and symbolism to show the relationship of the sun with the planets, using a reflecting pool and shining steel globes.

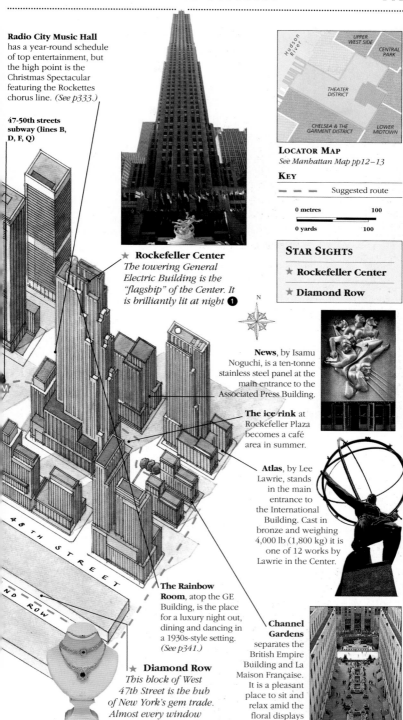

Radio City Music Hall has a year-round schedule of top entertainment, but the high point is the Christmas Spectacular featuring the Rockettes chorus line. *(See p333.)*

47-50th streets subway (lines B, D, F, Q)

LOCATOR MAP
See Manhattan Map pp12–13

KEY

– – –   Suggested route

0 metres   100

0 yards   100

STAR SIGHTS

★ **Rockefeller Center**

★ **Diamond Row**

★ **Rockefeller Center**
The towering General Electric Building is the "flagship" of the Center. It is brilliantly lit at night ❶

News, by Isamu Noguchi, is a ten-tonne stainless steel panel at the main entrance to the Associated Press Building.

The ice rink at Rockefeller Plaza becomes a café area in summer.

Atlas, by Lee Lawrie, stands in the main entrance to the International Building. Cast in bronze and weighing 4,000 lb (1,800 kg) it is one of 12 works by Lawrie in the Center.

The Rainbow Room, atop the GE Building, is the place for a luxury night out, dining and dancing in a 1930s-style setting. *(See p341.)*

★ **Diamond Row**
This block of West 47th Street is the hub of New York's gem trade. Almost every window gleams with jewels ❷

Channel Gardens separates the British Empire Building and La Maison Française. It is a pleasant place to sit and relax amid the floral displays and fountains.

The Rockefeller Center, looking towards the G E Building

Rockefeller Center ❶

Map 12 F5. **M** *47th-50th Sts.*
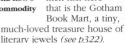

W HEN THE New York City Landmarks Preservation Commission unanimously voted to declare Rockefeller Center a landmark in 1985, they rightly called it "the heart of New York … a great unifying presence in the chaotic core of midtown Manhattan".

It is the largest privately-owned complex of its kind, and the inspiration for dozens of cities that try to emulate its almost perfect urban mix. The Art Deco design was by a team of top architects headed by Raymond Hood. Works by 30 artists can be found in foyers, on facades, and in the gardens.

The site, once a Botanic Garden owned by Columbia University, was leased in 1928 by John D Rockefeller, Jr as an ideal central home for a new opera house. When the 1929 Depression scuttled the plans,

Rockefeller, stuck with a long-term lease, decided to go ahead with his own development. The 14 buildings that were erected between 1931 and 1940 provided jobs for 225,000 people during the worst of the Depression. More development between 1957 and 1973 brought the Center to a total of 19 buildings in all.

In December 1932, Radio City Music Hall opened within the complex. Its dazzling shows have made it

Wisdom, **by Lee Lawrie, on the G E Building**

a New York institution, and the annual Christmas show featuring the Rockettes dance troupe is a perennial favourite.

Diamond Row ❷

47th St. **Map** 12 F5. **M** *47th-50th Sts. See* ***Shopping*** *p320.*

N EARLY EVERY SHOP window on 47th Street glitters with gold and diamonds. The buildings are filled with booths and workshops where jewellers vie for customers while, upstairs, millions of dollars change hands. The diamond district was born in the 1930s, when the Jewish diamond cutters of Antwerp and Amsterdam fled to America to escape Nazism. Hasidic Jews with black hats, beards and long sidelocks are still an integral part of the scene. Although mainly a wholesale district, individual customers are welcome. Bring cash, compare prices, haggle, and stay away if you know nothing about the value of diamonds. In the midst of all this, look for the sign saying "Wise men fish here" – that is the Gotham Book Mart, a tiny, much-loved treasure house of literary jewels *(see p322).*

Diamond Row's main commodity

Lyceum Theater ❸

149 W 45th St. **Map** 12 E5. **C** *Telecharge 239-6200.* **M** *42nd St-5th Ave. See* ***Entertainment*** *p330.*

T HE OLDEST New York theatre still going is a Baroque-style bandbox as frilly as a wedding cake. This 1903 triumph was the first theatre by Herts and Tallant, later renowned for their extravagant style. The Lyceum made history with a record run of 1,600 performances of the comedy *Born Yesterday.* It was the first theatre to be designated a Historic Landmark but, though it is safe from change, it is often dark, now that the Theater District has shifted westward.

The Rose Room in the Algonquin Hotel

Algonquin Hotel ❹

59 W 44th St. **Map** 12 F5. **C** 840-6800. **M** 42nd St-5th Ave. See **Where to Stay** p278.

THE EXTERIOR is a bit fussy – iron bay windows in vertical rows, red brick, too much detail – but it is the ambience, not the 1902 architecture, that makes the Algonquin special. In the 1920s, the Rose Room was home to America's best known luncheon club, the Round Table, with literary lights such as Alexander Woollcott, Franklin P Adams, Dorothy Parker, Robert Benchley and Harold Ross. All were associated with the *New Yorker* (Ross was the founding editor), whose 25 West 43rd Street headquarters had a back door opening into the hotel.

A recent renovation has preserved the old-fashioned, civilized feel of the Rose Room, as well as the cosy, panelled lobby where publishing types and theatre-goers still like to gather for drinks, settling into comfortable armchairs and ringing a small brass bell to summon the waiters.

New York Yacht Club ❺

37 W 44th St. **Map** 12 F5. **M** 42nd St-5th Ave. **Not open** to the public (access to members only).

A WHIMSICAL 1899 creation, this private club has the carved sterns of 18th-century sailing ships in the three bay windows. The prows of the ships are borne up by sculpted dolphins and waves, spilling over the windowsills and splashing down to the pavement.

This is the birthplace of the America's Cup yacht race, which was based in the US from 1857 to 1983. That was the year the much coveted prize was taken from the table where it had stood for more than a century, when the *Australia II* sailed to an historic victory.

The America's Cup, the coveted yachting prize

Bryant Park ❻

Map 8 F1. **M** 42nd St-5th Ave.

IN 1853, WITH the Public Library site still occupied by Croton Reservoir, Bryant Park (then Reservoir Park) housed a dazzling Crystal Palace, built for the World's Fair of that year (see p23).

In the 1960s the park was all but taken over by drug pushers and other undesirables. In 1989 the city closed and renovated it, reclaiming it for workers and visitors to relax in. Food is available at lunchtime and a Music & Dance Tickets Booth (see p329) offers half-price seats for same-day performances.

Storage stacks for over three million library books lie beneath the park.

Statue of poet William Cullen Bryant in Bryant Park

American Standard Building ❼

40 W 40th St. **Map** 8 F1. **M** 42nd St-Grand Central. **Not open** to the public.

THIS WAS the first major New York work by Raymond Hood, who went on to design the News Building (see p153) and Rockefeller Center. The structure, from 1924, is reminiscent of the Gothic building Hood was best known for at that time, Chicago's Tribune Tower. Here, the design is sleeker, giving the building the illusion of being taller than its actual 21 storeys. The black brick facade is set off by gold terracotta trim, evoking images of flaming coals: a comparison that would have suited its original owners well, since they made heating equipment. Stand across the street in Bryant Park to appreciate the striking golden tower top.

In 1989, the building was sold to a Japanese company. Their intention was to turn it into a hotel, but this did not happen and the building remains empty.

The American Standard Building seen from Bryant Park

New York Public Library **8**

5th Ave and 42nd St. **Map** 8 F1.
C 869-8089. **M** 42nd St-Grand
Central. **Open** Tue–Sat; hours vary.
Closed public hols.
Lectures, workshops, readings.

The doorway leading to the Main Reading Room

IN 1897 THE COVETED JOB of designing New York's main Public Library was awarded to architects Carrère & Hastings. Their plan was influenced by the library's first Director. He envisaged a light, quiet, airy place for study, where millions of books could be stored and yet be available to readers as promptly as possible. In the hands of Carrère & Hastings his vision came true in what is considered the epitome of New York's Beaux Arts period.

Built on the site of the former Croton Reservoir *(see p22)*, it opened in 1911 to immediate acclaim, despite having cost the city $9 million.

One of the Library's two stone lions, named Patience and Fortitude by Mayor LaGuardia

Barrel vaults of carved white marble over the stairs in the Astor Hall

The vast, panelled Main Reading Room stretches two full blocks and is suffused with daylight from the two interior courtyards. Below it are 88 miles (140 km) of shelves, holding over two million volumes. A staff of over 100 and a computerized dumb waiter can supply any book within 10 minutes.

The Periodicals Room holds 10,000 current periodicals, from 128 countries. On its walls are murals by Richard Haas, honouring New York's great publishing houses. The original library combined the collections of John Jacob Astor and James Lenox. Its collections today range from Thomas Jefferson's handwritten copy of the Declaration of Independence to T S Eliot's typescript of *The Waste Land*. More than 1,000 queries are

The Main Reading Room, with its original bronze reading lamps

answered daily, using the vast database of the CATNYP computer catalogue.

This library is the hub of a network of 82 branches, with nearly seven million users. Some branches are very well known, such as the New York Public Library for the Performing Arts at the Lincoln Center *(see p210)* and the Schomburg Center in Harlem *(see p227)*.

Times Square, ablaze with neon

Times Square ❾

Map 8 E1. Ⓜ *42nd St-Times Sq.*

KNOWN AS Longacre Square in the late 19th century, this was the home of horse traders, blacksmiths and stables, marking the edge of "Thieves' Lair", a haven for pickpockets. Oscar Hammerstein built the Victoria and Republic Theaters in 1899; and the Republic later became Minsky's, featuring the stylishly scandalous Gypsy Rose Lee. Broadway blossomed, and Times Square became the heart of the Theater District.

The Depression ruined many theatres, and Broadway's "guys and dolls" were replaced by much sleazier types. The 1980s saw a huge civic scheme to transform the square into a safe and vibrant place for theatregoers and tourists.

Times Square was named in 1904 after the 25-storey *New York Times* tower. The *Times* moved in on New Year's Eve with a fireworks display, and the celebration has continued every year, with a countdown to midnight, when a lighted ball is lowered to mark the new year. Thousands jam the square to watch and millions more follow the events on television across the country.

In 1928, the *Times* posted election returns on the world's first moving sign, a band of 14,800 lights running around the building. The newspaper has moved on, but the ever-busy newswire remains.

New Amsterdam Theater ❿

214 W 42nd St. **Map** 8 E1. Ⓜ *42nd St-Times Sq.* **Not open** to *the public.*

W C Fields (far left) and Eddie Cantor (holding top hat, right) in the 1918 *Ziegfeld Follies* at the New Amsterdam Theater

THIS WAS the most opulent theatre in the United States when it opened in 1903, and the first to have an Art Nouveau interior. It was owned for a time by Florenz Ziegfeld, who produced his famous *Follies* revue here between 1914 and 1918 – with Broadway's first $5 ticket price. He remodelled the roof garden into another theatre, the Aerial Gardens. This is one of a row of fine early theatres on 42nd Street that fell on hard times and became second-rate movie houses. It is now dark, and almost derelict.

The Art Deco top of the Paramount Building

Group Health Insurance Building ⓫

330 W 42nd St. **Map** 8 D1. Ⓜ *42nd St.* **Open** *office hours.*

THIS 1931 design by Raymond Hood was the only New York building selected for the influential International Style survey of 1932 *(see p41)*. Its unusual design gives it a stepped profile seen from east and west, but a slab effect viewed from north or south. The exterior's horizontal bands of blue-green terracotta have earned it the nickname "jolly green giant". Step inside to see the classic Art Deco lobby of opaque glass and stainless steel.

One block west is Theater Row, a pleasant group of Off-Broadway theatres and cafés.

Paramount Building ⓬

1501 Broadway. **Map** 8 E1. Ⓜ *34th St.*

THE FABULOUS ground floor movie theatre where bobby-soxers stood in line in the 1940s to hear Frank Sinatra perform is gone, but there's still a theatrical feel to the massive building designed by Rapp & Rapp in 1927. On each side are symmetrical setbacks, 14 in all, rising like building blocks to an Art Deco crown – a tower, clock and globe. In the heyday of the "great white way", the tower was lit, with an observation deck at the top.

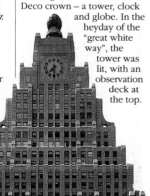

Shubert Alley ⑬

Between W 44th and W 45th St.
Map 12 E5. M *42nd St-Times Sq.*

THE PLAYHOUSES in the streets west of Broadway are rich in theatre lore – and in notable architecture. Two classic theatres built in 1913 are the Booth (No. 22 West 45th Street), named after actor Edwin Booth, and the Shubert (No. 221 West 44th), after theatre baron Sam S Shubert. They form the west wall of Shubert Alley, where aspiring actors lined up, hoping for a casting in a Shubert play.

A *Chorus Line* ran at the Shubert for a record 6,137 performances, until 1990; Katharine Hepburn starred earlier in *The Philadelphia Story*. Across from the 44th Street end of the Alley is the St James, where Rogers and Hammerstein made their debut with *Oklahoma* in 1941, followed by *The King and I*. Nearby is Sardi's, the restaurant where actors waited for opening night reviews. Irving Berlin staged *The Music Box Revue* opposite the other end of the Alley in 1921. His Music Box theatre has since housed many famous shows.

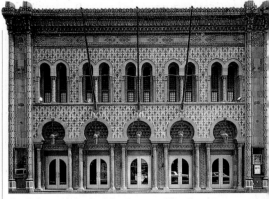

The tiled Moorish facade of the City Center of Music and Drama

MONY Tower ⑭

1740 Broadway. **Map** 12 E4.
M *57th St.* **Not open** to the public.

BUILT IN 1950, the head office of the Mutual of New York insurance company (now MONY Financial Services) has a weather vane which tells you everything except the wind direction. The mast turns green for fair, orange for cloudy, flashing orange for rain and white for snow. Lights moving up the mast mean warmer weather, lights going down mean get out your overcoat!

City Center of Music and Drama ⑮

131 W 55th St. **Map** 12 E3.
C 581-7907. M *57th St.* ☒ ♿
See **Entertainment** p334.

THIS HIGHLY ornate Moorish structure with its dome of Spanish tiles was designed in 1924 as a Masonic Shriners' Temple. It was saved from the developers by Mayor LaGuardia, to become a home for the New York City Opera and Ballet in 1943. When the troupes moved to Lincoln Center, City Center lived on as a major venue for dance. Recent renovation work has preserved the delightful excesses of the architecture.

Carnegie Hall ⑯

154 W 57th Street. **Map** 12 E3.
C 903-9600. M *57th St, 59th St.*
Museum open *11am–4.30pm Thu–Tue & during concerts.* ☒ ♿ ▣
▯ ▯ See **Entertainment** p338.

FINANCED BY millionaire philanthropist Andrew Carnegie, New York's first great concert hall opened in 1891 in what was then a suburb of the city. The terracotta and brick Italian Renaissance-style building is said to have among the best acoustics in the world. On opening night, when Tchaikovsky was a guest conductor, all of New York's finest families were in

Auditorium of the Shubert Theater, built by Henry Herts in 1913

attendance, though they sometimes had to queue for as long as an hour before they could alight from their horse-drawn carriages.

For many years Carnegie Hall was home to the New York Philharmonic, under conductors such as Arturo Toscanini, Leopold Stokowski, Bruno Walter and Leonard Bernstein. Carnegie Hall was never a venue for solely classical music. The only criterion is quality, and playing there quickly became an international symbol of success for both classical and popular musicians.

A campaign led by violinist Isaac Stern in the late 1950s saved the building from redevelopment as offices, and in 1964 the hall was made a national landmark. Interior renovation in 1986 brought the bronze balconies and the ornamental plaster back to their original splendour. The corridors are lined with memorabilia of artists who have performed here. In 1991, a museum opened adjacent to the first-tier level, telling the story of the illustrious first 100 years of "The House that Music Built".

Millionaire Andrew Carnegie

Today, top orchestras and performers from around the world still fill Carnegie Hall with their great music. A tour of the hall is also available.

Russian Tea Room ⑰

150 W 57th St. **Map** 12 E3.
Ⓒ 265-0947. Ⓜ *57th St.*
Closed for renovation until 1997.
See **Restaurants and Bars** *p303.*

T HIS IS A New York classic for Russian caviar, blinis and star-gazing at the many show-business luminaries who dine here, especially at lunch. The place is currently undergoing major renovation

Interior of the Russian Tea Room on West 57th Street

and will be closed until some time in 1997. When it reopens, a new celebrity chef, David Bouley, will be in residence.

Alwyn Court Apartments ⑱

180 W 58th St. **Map** 12 E3. Ⓜ *57th St.* **Not open** to the public.

Y OU CAN'T miss it – not with the fanciful crowns, dragons and other French Renaissance-style terracotta carvings covering the exterior of this 1909 Harde and Short apartment building. The ground floor has been altered and lost its cornice in the process, but the rest of the building is intact, an intricate stone tapestry, and one of a kind in the city.

The facade follows the style of François I, whose reign saw the building of some of the finest Loire châteaux, and whose symbol, a crowned salamander, can be seen above the entrance at 58th Street.

Residents and their guests are fortunate to be able to

Salamander on Alwyn Court

enjoy the interior courtyard, which features a dazzling display of the illusionistic skills of artist Richard Haas, in which plain walls are transformed into "carved" stonework.

Flight deck of the *Intrepid*

Intrepid Sea-Air-Space Museum ⑲

Pier 86, W 46th St. **Map** 11 A5.
Ⓒ 245-2533. Ⓕ 245-0072. Ⓜ *50th St.* **Open** *Jun–Aug: 10am–5pm daily; Sep–May: 10am–5pm Wed–Sun (last adm: 4pm).* **Adm charge**. ▯

O N THE *Intrepid*, a World War II US aircraft carrier, the control room and flight decks are open for exploration. Exhibits range from real fighter planes from the 1940s to space-age wonders like the A12, fastest spy plane in the world. The *Growler*, a guided-missile submarine, and the destroyer *Edson* are also here.

Pioneers Hall traces the development of flying and the workings of today's super-carriers; Technologies Hall looks at ocean exploration and the rockets of the future.

LOWER MIDTOWN

FROM BEAUX ARTS to Art Deco, this part of midtown boasts some fine architecture. Quiet, residential Murray Hill was named for a country estate that once occupied the site. By the turn of the century, it was home to many of New York's first families, including the financier J P Morgan whose library,

Brass door, Fred F French Building

now a museum, shows the grandeur of the age. The commercial pace quickens at 42nd Street, near Grand Central Terminal where tall office buildings line the streets. But few of the newer buildings have equalled the Beaux Arts Terminal itself or Art Deco beauties such as the Chrysler Building.

SIGHTS AT A GLANCE

Historic Streets and Buildings
Grand Central Terminal pp154–5 **2**
Home Savings of America **3**
Chanin Building **4**
Chrysler Building **5**
News Building **6**
Tudor City **7**
Helmsley Building **8**
Fred F French Building **12**
Sniffen Court **15**

Museums and Galleries
Pierpont Morgan Library pp162–3 **14**
Japan Society **11**

Modern Architecture
MetLife Building **1**
Nos. 1 and 2 United Nations Plaza **9**
United Nations pp158–61 **10**

Churches
Church of the Incarnation **13**

GETTING THERE
By subway, take the Lexington Ave 4, 5 or 6 trains to 42nd St-Grand Central. Buses M15, M101/102, M1, M2, M3 and M4 run along the area's avenues, while the M34 and M42 are the area's crosstown buses.

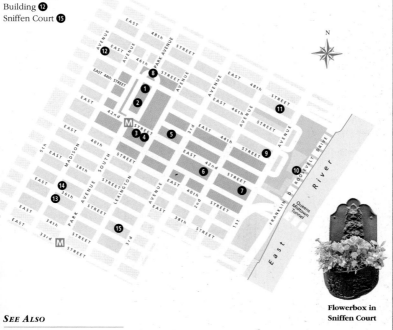

Flowerbox in Sniffen Court

KEY

| | Street-by-Street map |
| **M** | Subway station |

0 metres ——————— 500
0 yards ——————— 500

The stainless-steel-coated spire of the Chrysler Building

Street-by-Street: Lower Midtown

A WALK IN THE GRAND CENTRAL neighbourhood allows you to see an eclectic mix of New York architectural styles. Step back to appreciate the contours of the tallest skyscrapers, and step inside to experience the many fine interiors, from modern atriums such as the Philip Morris Building and Ford Foundation to the ornate details of the Home Savings Bank and the soaring spaces of Grand Central Terminal.

The Philip Morris Building is the headquarters of a tobacco company. It also houses a branch of the Whitney Museum which specializes in modern art.

MetLife Building
This skyscraper ruined the view along Park Avenue when it was built by Pan Am in 1963 ❶

★ Grand Central Terminal
The vast, vaulted interior is a splendid relic of the heyday of train travel ❷

Grand Central-42nd Street subway (lines S, 4, 5, 6, 7)

Chanin Building
Built for self-made real estate mogul Irwin Chanin in 1922, this building has a fine Art Deco lobby ❹

STAR SIGHTS

- ★ **Grand Central Terminal**
- ★ **Chrysler Building**
- ★ **Home Savings of America**
- ★ **News Building**

Brass door, Home Savings Bank

★ Home Savings of America
Formerly the headquarters of the Bowery Savings Bank, this is one of the finest bank buildings in New York. It was designed by the architects York & Sawyer to resemble a Romanesque palace ❸

The Mobil Building has a self-cleaning stainless steel facade which is embossed in geometric patterns to prevent it from warping. It was built in 1955.

Helmsley Building
The ornate entrance symbolizes the wealth of the New York Central Railroad, this building's first occupant 8

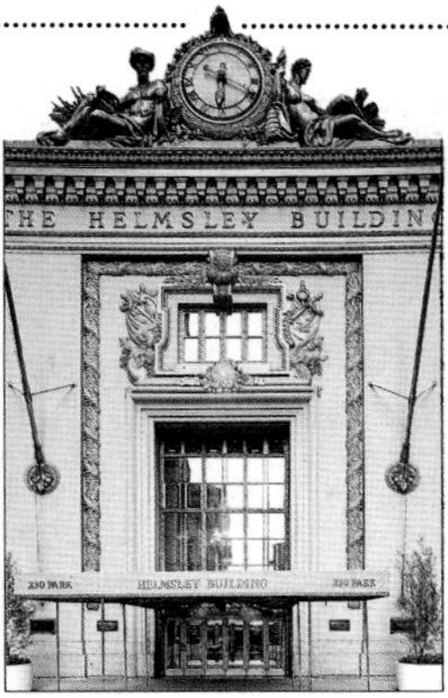
THE HELMSLEY BUILDING

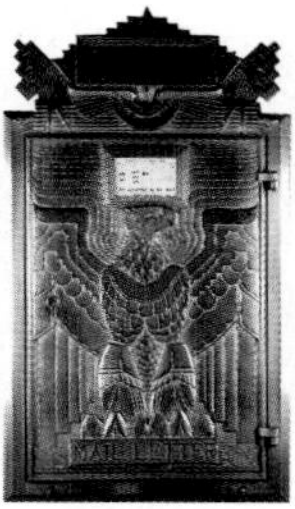

Mailbox in the Chrysler Building

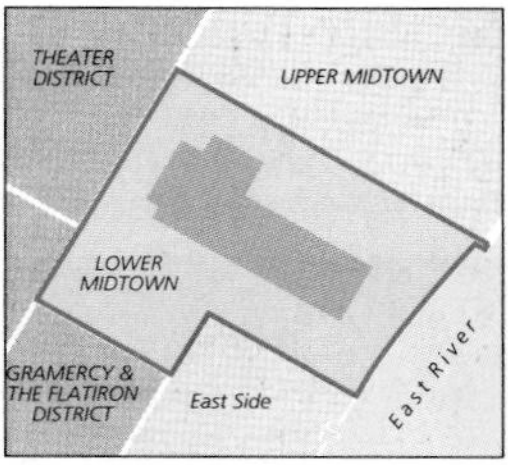
THEATER DISTRICT
UPPER MIDTOWN
LOWER MIDTOWN
GRAMERCY & THE FLATIRON DISTRICT
East Side
East River

LOCATOR MAP
See Manhattan Map pp12–13

KEY

Suggested route

0 metres 100

0 yards 100

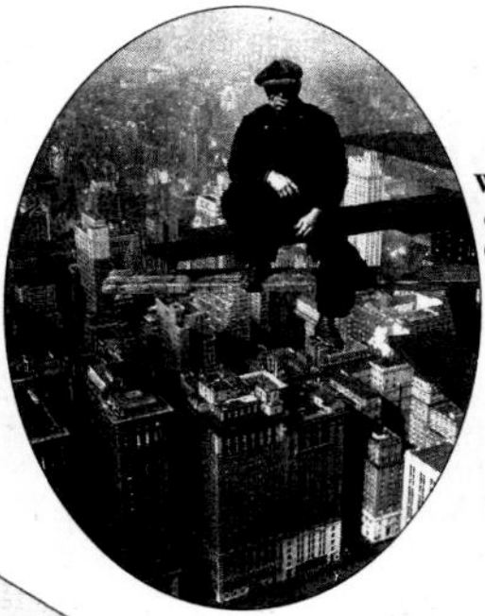

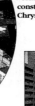

Worker resting during construction of the Chrysler Building

★ Chrysler Building
Ornamented with automotive motifs, this Art Deco delight was built in 1930 for the Chrysler car company 5

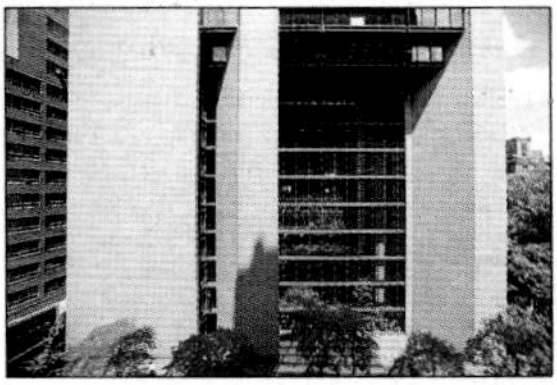

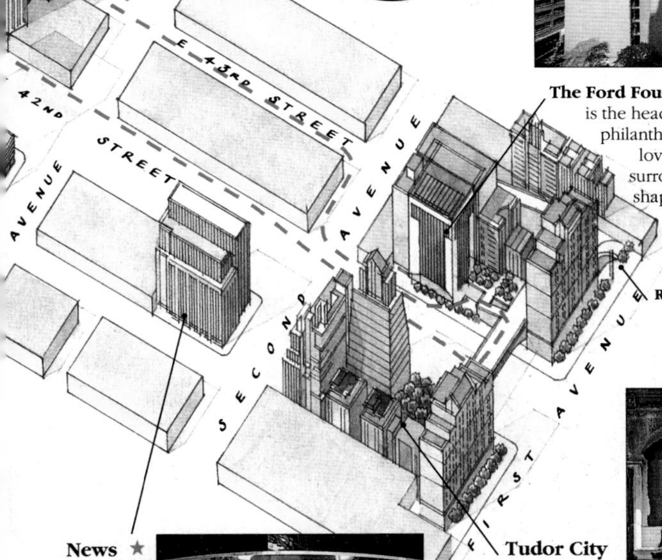
E 43RD STREET
42ND STREET
AVENUE
SECOND AVENUE
FIRST AVENUE

The Ford Foundation Building is the headquarters of Ford's philanthropic arm. It has a lovely interior garden surrounded by a cube-shaped building made of pinkish-grey granite, glass and steel.

Ralph J Bunche Park

News ★ Building
The Art Deco home of the Daily News *has a revolving globe in the lobby* 6

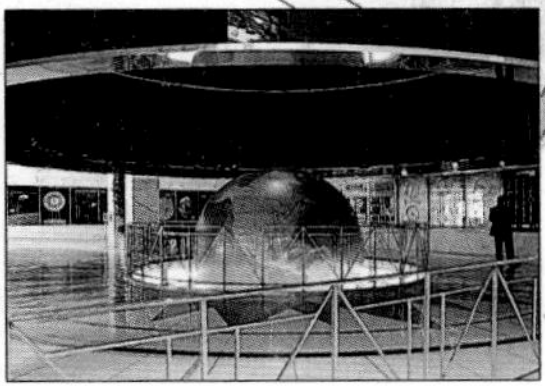

Tudor City
This 1928 complex has 3,000 apartments. It was built in the American Tudor style, and features fine stonework details 7

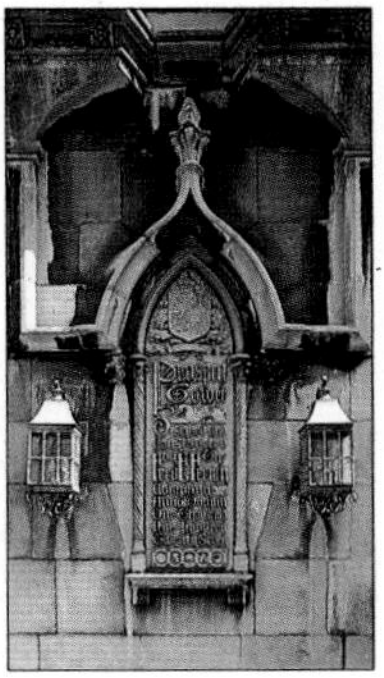

MetLife Building ❶

200 Park Ave. **Map** 13 A5.
M *42nd St-Grand Central.*
Open *office hours.* 🍴 🎫

Lobby of the MetLife Building

O NCE, THE SCULPTURES atop the Grand Central Terminal stood out against the sky. Then this colossus, formerly called the Pan Am Building and designed by Walter Gropius, Emery Roth and Sons and Pietro Belluschi, rose up in 1963 to block the Park Avenue view. It dwarfed the Terminal and aroused universal dislike. At the time it was the largest commercial building in the world, and the dismay over its scale helped thwart a later plan to build a tower over the Terminal itself.

It is ironic that the New York skies were blocked by Pan Am, a company that had opened up the skies as a means of travel for millions of people. When the company began in 1927, Charles Lindbergh, fresh from his solo trans-atlantic flight, was one of their pilots and an adviser on new routes. By 1936, Pan Am managed to introduce the first trans-Pacific passenger route, and in 1947 they introduced the first round-the-world route.

The building's famous roof-top heliport was abandoned in 1977 after a freak accident showered debris on to the

surrounding streets. Now Pan Am itself has gone, too, and in 1981 the entire building was sold to the Metropolitan Life organization.

Grand Central Terminal ❷

See pp154–5.

Home Savings of America ❸

110 E 42nd St. **Map** 9 A1.
M *42nd St-Grand Central.* **Open** *banking hours.*

M ANY CONSIDER this 1923 building the best work of the best bank architects of the 1920s. York & Sawyer chose the style of a Romanesque basilica for the uptown offices of the venerable Bowery Savings Bank (now Home Savings of America). An arched entry leads into the vast banking room, with a high beamed ceiling, marble mosaic floors and marble columns which support the stone arches that soar overhead.

Facade of Home Savings of America building

Between the columns are unpolished mosaic panels of marble from France and Italy. The rich detailing includes symbolic animal motifs such as a squirrel representing thrift and a lion for power.

Chanin Building ❹

122 E 42nd St. **Map** 9 A1.
M *42nd St-Grand Central.*
Open *office hours.*

Stonework detail of the Chanin Building

O NCE THE headquarters of one of New York's leading real estate developers, Irwin S Chanin, the 56-storey tower was the first skyscraper in the Grand Central area, a harbinger of things to come. It was designed by Sloan & Robertson in 1929, and is one of the best examples of the Art Deco period. A wide bronze band, patterned with birds and fish, runs the full length of the facade; the terracotta base is decorated with a luxuriant tangle of stylized leaves and flowers. Inside, Radio City's sculptor René Chambellan worked on the reliefs and the bronze grills, elevator doors, mailboxes, clocks and pattern of waves in the floor. The vestibule reliefs chart the career of Chanin, who was a self-made man.

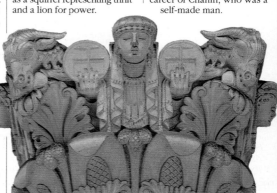

Carved detail in the banking hall of Home Savings of America

Chrysler Building [5]

405 Lexington Ave. **Map** 9 A1.
☎ *682-3070.* [M] *42nd St-Grand Central.* ***Open*** *office hours.*
🚫📷 ♿

Stainless steel gargoyle on the Chrysler Building

WALTER P CHRYSLER began his career in a Union Pacific Railroad machine shop, but his passion for the motor car helped him rise swiftly to the top of the new industry, to found, in 1925, the corporation bearing his name. His wish for a headquarters in New York that symbolized his company led to a building that will always be linked with the golden age of motoring. Following Chrysler's wishes, the stainless-steel Art Deco spire resembles a car radiator grill; the building's series of stepped setbacks are emblazoned with winged radiator caps, wheels and stylized automobiles; and there are gargoyles modelled on hood ornaments from the 1929 Chrysler Plymouth.

Though it lost the title of tallest building in the world to the Empire State Building only a few months after its completion in 1930, William Van Alen's 77-storey Chrysler Building and its shining crown are still among the city's best known and most loved landmarks.

The crowning spire was kept a secret until the last moment when, having been built in the fire shaft, it was raised into position through the roof, ensuring that the building would be higher than the Bank of Manhattan, then just completed downtown by Van Alen's great rival, H Craig Severance.

Van Alen was poorly rewarded for his labours. Chrysler accused him of accepting bribes from contractors and refused to pay him. Van Alen's career never recovered from the slur.

The stunning lobby, once used as a showroom for Chrysler cars, was perfectly restored in 1978. It is lavishly decorated with patterned marbles and granite from around the world and has chromed steel trims. A vast painted ceiling by Edward Trumball shows transport scenes of the late 1920s.

Elevator door at the Chrysler Building

Although the Chrysler Corporation never occupied the building as their headquarters, their name remains, as firm a fixture as the gargoyles.

Entrance to the News Building

News Building [6]

220 E 42nd St. **Map** 9 B1.
[M] *42nd St-Grand Central.*
Open *8am–6pm Mon–Fri.*

THE *DAILY NEWS* WAS founded in 1919, and by 1925 it was a million-seller. It was known, rather scathingly, as "the servant girl's bible", for its concentration on scandals, celebrities and murders, its readable style and its heavy use of illustration. Over the years it has stuck to what it does best, and for years the formula paid off handsomely. It revealed stories such as the romance of Edward VIII and Mrs Simpson, and has become renowned for its punchy headlines that sum up the mood of the moment. Though in recent years it has lost money, its circulation figures are still among the highest in the United States.

Its headquarters, designed by Raymond Hood in 1930, has rows of brown and black brick alternating with windows to create a vertical striped effect. Hood's lobby is familiar to many as that of the *Daily Planet* in the 1980s' *Superman* movies. It includes the world's largest interior globe, an illuminated, rotating geography lesson with details constantly updated. Bronze lines on the floor indicate the direction of world cities and the position of the planets. At night, the intricate Deco detail over the front entrance of the building is lit from within by neon.

Grand Central Terminal ②

IN 1871 CORNELIUS VANDERBILT opened a railway station on 42nd Street. Although often revamped, it was never large enough and was finally demolished. The present station opened in 1913. This Beaux Arts gem has been a gateway and a symbol of the city ever since. Its glory is the soaring main concourse and the way it separates auto, pedestrian and train traffic. The building has a steel frame covered with granites and marbles. Reed & Stem were in charge of the logistical planning; Warren & Wetmore the overall design. It is now being restored by the architects Beyer Blinder Belle.

42nd Street colonnaded facade

Statuary on the 42nd Street Facade
Jules-Alexis Coutan's sculptures of Mercury, Hercules and Minerva crown the main entrance.

Park Avenue ramp

Main concourse level

Subway

Cornelius Vanderbilt
The railway magnate was known as the "Commodore".

Commuters use the terminal. Half a million people pass through it each day. An escalator leads up into the MetLife Building and other nearby buildings can also be reached through tunnels.

Grand Central Oyster Bar
This popular venue, with its yellow Guastavino tiles, attracts over three million seafood lovers a year. But beware – the acoustics carry whispers from one vaulted corner to another (see p294).

STAR SIGHTS
★ **Grand Staircase**
★ **Main Concourse**
★ **Central Information**

VISITORS' CHECKLIST

E 42nd St at Park Ave.
Map 13 A5. 🎧 340-3000.
Ⓜ 4, 5, 6, 7 to Grand Central
Stn. 🚌 M104, M42. **Open**
5.30am–1.30am daily. 📷
♿ 🎧 Wed 12.30pm by
Municipal Arts Society (free).
🎧 935-3960. 🍴 ☐ ☐
Baggage check; lost & found.

★ **Main Concourse**
*This vast pedestrian area
with its high vaulted ceiling
is dominated by three great
arched windows, 75 ft
(23 m) high on
either side.*

Vaulted Ceiling
*A medieval manu-
script provided the
basis for French artist
Paul Helleu's zodiac
design containing
over 2,500 stars.
Lights pinpoint the
major constellations.*

The lower level is
linked to the other
levels by stairways
and by a clever
system of ramps.

Grand Staircase ★
*The double flight of
marble steps, styled
after the grand
staircase in the Paris
Opera House, is a
vivid reminder of the
glamorous days of
early rail travel.*

★ **Central Information**
*This four-faced clock tops the
travel information pagoda
on the main concourse.*

Tudor City ❼

E 42nd St. **Map** 9 B1.
Ⓜ *42nd St-Grand Central.*

THIS EARLY URBAN renewal
effort, developed between
1925 and 1928 by the Fred
F French Company, was
designed as a middle-class
city within the city. Rents
were modest, thanks to the
"large-scale production". There
are 12 buildings containing
3,000 apartments, a hotel,
shops, restaurants, a post office
and two small private parks, all
built in the Tudor Gothic style.
   Now a tranquil corner of
the modern city, in the mid-
19th century the area was the
haunt of criminals and was
known as Corcoran's Roost,
after Paddy Corcoran, the
leader of the notorious "Rag
Gang". The East River shore
was lined with glue factories,
slaughterhouses, breweries
and a gas works. Some were
still there when Tudor City
was planned, so its buildings
have few outward-facing
windows from which residents
might enjoy what is
now a great view
of the river.

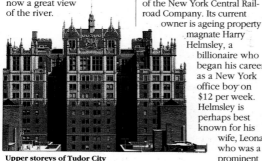
Upper storeys of Tudor City

Helmsley Building ❽

230 Park Ave. **Map** 13 A5.
Ⓜ *42nd St-Grand Central.* **Open**
office hours.

ONE OF THE GREAT New
York views looks south
down Park Avenue to the
Helmsley Building straddling
the busy traffic flow beneath.
There is just one flaw – the
monolithic MetLife Building
(which was built by Pan Am
as its corporate headquarters

Performance at the Japan Society

in 1963) that towers behind it,
replacing the building's
former backdrop, the sky.
   Built by Warren & Whetmore
in 1929, the Helmsley Building
was originally the headquarters
of the New York Central Railroad Company. Its current
owner is ageing property
magnate Harry
Helmsley, a
billionaire who
began his career
as a New York
office boy on
$12 per week.
Helmsley is
perhaps best
known for his
wife, Leona,
who was a
prominent
feature in all the advertisements for their hotel chain –
until her imprisonment in
1989 for tax evasion on a
grand scale. Many observers
believe that the extravagant
glitter of the building's
facelift is due to
Leona's over-
the-top taste
in decor.

Roman gods reclining against the Helmsley Building clock

Nos. 1 & 2 United Nations Plaza ❾

Map 13 B5. Ⓜ *42nd St-
Grand Central.*

THESE TWO
GREAT columns
of lovely blue-
green mirrored
glass are set at an
angle to one
another; the play of light and
reflections on their gleaming
sides and sloping setbacks
make them seem an ever-
changing, giant work of
modern art. The marble
and mirrored interiors are
also stunning. They
house streamlined,
modern offices and,
in No. 1, the
United Nations
Plaza Hotel
(*see p280*).
Here, the guest list frequently
includes many UN delegates
as well as a number of
visiting heads of state. Even
the stresses of international
diplomacy must ease when
you can float lazily in the
glassed-in swimming pool
enjoying the bird's-eye views
of the city and the United
Nations itself.

United Nations ❿

See pp158–61.

Japan Society ⓫

333 E 47th St. **Map** 13 B5.
Ⓒ *832-1155.* Ⓜ *42nd St-Grand
Central.* **Gallery open** *11am–5pm
Tue–Sun.* Ⓟ Ⓚ Ⓩ

THE HEADQUARTERS of the
Japan Society, which was
founded in 1907 to foster
understanding and cultural
exchange between Japan
and the United States,
was underwritten
by John D
Rockefeller
III at a cost

of some $4.3 million. The striking black building with its delicate sun grilles was designed by Tokyo architects Junzo Yoshimura and George Shimamoto in 1971. It includes an auditorium, a language centre, a research library, a museum gallery and serene, traditional Oriental gardens.

Changing exhibits open to the public include a variety of Japanese arts, from swords to kimonos to scrolls. The Society offers programmes of Japanese performing arts, lectures, language classes and many business workshops for American and Japanese executives and managers.

Fred F French Building ⑫

521 5th Ave. **Map** 12 F5.
Ⓜ *42nd St-Grand Central.* **Open** *office hours.*

Built in 1927 to house the best known real estate firm of the day, this is a fabulously opulent creation. It was designed by French's chief architect, H Douglas Ives, in collaboration with Sloan & Robertson, whose other work

Tiffany stained-glass window in the Church of the Incarnation

included the Chanin Building (see p152). They blended Near Eastern, ancient Egyptian and Greek styles with early Art Deco forms.

Multicoloured faïence ornaments decorate the upper facade, and the water tower is hidden in a false top level of the building. Its disguise is an elaborate one, with reliefs showing a rising sun flanked by griffins and bees and symbols of virtues such as integrity and industry. Winged Assyrian beasts ride on a bronze frieze over the entrances. These exotic themes continue into the vaulted lobby, with its elaborate polychrome ceiling decoration and 25 gilt-bronze doors.

This was the first building project to employ members of the Native Canadian Caughnawaga tribe as construction workers. They did not suffer from a fear of heights, and soon became highly sought-after scaffolders, helping to build many of the city's most famous skyscrapers.

Church of the Incarnation ⑬

205 Madison Ave. **Map** 9 A2.
📞 689-6350. Ⓜ *42nd St-Grand Central.* **Open** *11.30am–2.30pm Mon–Wed, Fri.* 🕐 *11am Sun.* 📷 ♿ *notify in advance.* ✉

This episcopal church and its parish house date from 1864, when Madison Avenue was home to the elite. Its patterned sandstone and brownstone exterior is representative of the period.

The interior includes an oak communion rail by Daniel Chester French, a chancel mural of the *Adoration of the Magi* by John La Farge, and stained-glass windows by La Farge, Louis Comfort Tiffany, William Morris and Edward Burne-Jones.

Pierpont Morgan Library ⑭

See pp162–3.

Sniffen Court ⑮

150–158 E 36th St. **Map** 9 A2.
Ⓜ *33rd St.*

Here is a delightful surprise: an intimate courtyard of ten brick Romanesque revival style carriage houses built by John Sniffen in the 1850s.

They are perfectly and improbably preserved off a busy block in modern New York. The house at the south end was used as a studio by the American sculptor Malvina Hoffman, whose plaques of Greek horsemen decorate the exterior wall.

Lobby of the Fred F French Building

Malvina Hoffman's studio

United Nations ❿

Founded in 1945 near the end of World War II with 51 members, the United Nations now numbers some 180 nations. Its aims are to preserve world peace, promote self-determination and to aid economic and social wellbeing around the globe. New York was chosen as the UN headquarters when John D Rockefeller, Jr donated $8.5 million for the purchase of the East River site. The chief architect was American Wallace Harrison, who worked with an international Board of Design Consultants. The 18 acre (7 ha) site is not on US territory. It is an international zone and has its own stamps and post office. Daily guided tours show visitors the various council chambers and General Assembly hall.

**Flag of the
United Nations**

**United Nations
Headquarters**

Secretariat
building

The Conference Building houses meeting rooms for the Security Council, the Trusteeship Council and the Economic and Social Council.

Trusteeship
Council

★ **Security Council**
Delegates and their assistants confer around the horseshoe-shaped table while verbatim reporters and other UN staff members sit at the long table in the centre.

Economic
and Social
Council

★ **Peace Bell**
Cast from the coins of 60 nations, this gift from Japan hangs on a cypress pagoda shaped like a Shinto shrine.

Rose Garden
Twenty-five varieties of rose adorn the manicured gardens on the East River.

STAR FEATURES

★ **General Assembly**

★ **Security Council**

★ **Peace Bell**

★ **Reclining Figure**

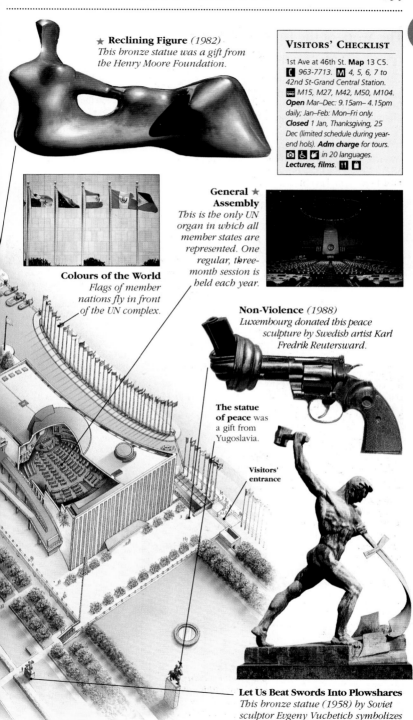

★ **Reclining Figure** (1982)
This bronze statue was a gift from the Henry Moore Foundation.

General ★ Assembly
This is the only UN organ in which all member states are represented. One regular, three-month session is held each year.

Colours of the World
Flags of member nations fly in front of the UN complex.

Non-Violence (1988)
Luxembourg donated this peace sculpture by Swedish artist Karl Fredrik Reutersward.

The statue of peace was a gift from Yugoslavia.

Visitors' entrance

Let Us Beat Swords Into Plowshares
This bronze statue (1958) by Soviet sculptor Evgeny Vuchetich symbolizes the main goal of the United Nations.

The Work of the United Nations

THE GOALS of the United Nations are pursued by three UN councils and a General Assembly comprising all member nations. The Secretariat carries out the administrative work of the organization. Guided tours allow visitors to see the Security Council Chamber and General Assembly Hall.

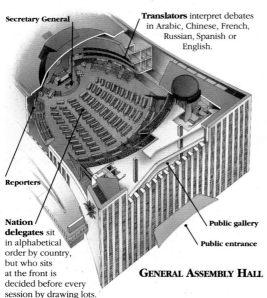

Secretary General

Translators interpret debates in Arabic, Chinese, French, Russian, Spanish or English.

Reporters

Nation delegates sit in alphabetical order by country, but who sits at the front is decided before every session by drawing lots.

Public gallery

Public entrance

GENERAL ASSEMBLY HALL

GENERAL ASSEMBLY

THE GENERAL ASSEMBLY is the governing body of the UN, and has regular sessions each year from mid-September to mid-December. Special sessions are also held when the Security Council or a majority of members request one. All member states are represented with an equal vote, regardless of size. The General Assembly may discuss any international problem raised by the members or by other UN bodies. While it cannot enact laws, recommendations strongly influence world opinion; these require a two-thirds majority vote.

Lots are drawn before each session to determine the seating in the chamber for the delegations. All 2,070 seats in the chamber are equipped with earphones which offer simultaneous translations in

several languages. The General Assembly also appoints the Secretary General (on the recommendation of the Security Council), approves the UN budgets and elects the non-permanent members of

Foucault's Pendulum **(Holland);**
its slowly rotating swing is proof
of the earth's rotation on its axis

the Councils. Together with the Security Council, it also appoints the judges of the International Court of Justice based in the Netherlands.

SECURITY COUNCIL

THE MOST POWERFUL part of the UN is the Security Council. It strives to achieve

Mural symbolizing peace and freedom by Per Krohg (Norway)

international peace and security, and intervenes in crises such as the fighting in Kuwait or the former Yugoslavia. It is the only body whose decisions member states are obliged to obey, and the only one in continuous session.

Five of its members – China, France, the Russian Federation, the United Kingdom and the United States – are permanent. The other nations are elected by the General Assembly to serve two-year terms.

When international conflicts arise, the Council's first tries to seek agreement by mediation. If fighting breaks out, it may issue cease-fire orders and impose military or economic sanctions. It could also decide to send UN peace-keeping missions into troubled areas to separate opposing factions until issues can be resolved through diplomatic channels.

Military intervention is the Council's last resort. UN forces may be deployed, and peace-keeping forces are resident in places such as Cyprus and the Middle East.

TRUSTEESHIP COUNCIL

THE SMALLEST OF the councils, this is the only UN body whose workload is decreasing. The council was established in 1945 with the goal of fostering peaceful independence for non-self-governing territories or colonies. Since then, more than 80 colonies have gained self-rule and the number of people living in dependent territories has been reduced from 750 million to about 3 million. The council currently consists of the five permanent members of the Security Council.

Zanetti mural (Dominican Republic) in the Conference Building depicting the struggle for peace

plays a key role as a spokes-person in the organization's peace-keeping efforts. The Secretary General is appointed by the General Assembly for a five-year term.

military support from members. As a result, it has had successes and failures in its efforts to keep the peace. In 1948, the UN declared South Korea the legitimate government of Korea and two years later, played a leading role in defending it against the invading armies of North Korea. In 1949, the UN helped negotiate a cease-fire between Indonesia and the Netherlands, and set up a conference which led to the Dutch granting independence to Indonesia. In 1974, the People's Republic of China, long refused membership in favour of Taiwan, gained UN membership, so restoring it to the international community.

The most persistent problems have been in the Middle East. When Israel was invaded by five Arab nations after it was declared a state in 1948, the UN negotiated a cease-fire; UN forces have been present in the area since 1974, but the status of the Palestinians is still unresolved.

The UN was instrumental in negotiating the independence of Cyprus from Britain in 1957, and in 1964 created a UN military force in Cyprus to keep peace between the Greeks and Turks.

Trusteeship Council Chambers

ECONOMIC AND SOCIAL COUNCIL

THE 54 MEMBERS OF this Council work to improve the standard of living and social welfare around the world, goals which consume 80% of the UN's resources. It makes recommendations to the General Assembly, to each member nation and to the UN's specialized agencies. The Council is assisted by com-missions dealing with regional economic problems, human rights abuses, population, narcotics and women's rights. It also works with the Inter-national Labour Organization, the World Health Organization, UNICEF, and other global welfare organizations.

SECRETARIAT

AN INTERNATIONAL STAFF of 16,000 works for the Secretariat to carry out the day-to-day work of the United Nations, providing services to all UN councils, commissions and agencies. The Secretariat is headed by the Secretary General, who

IMPORTANT EVENTS IN UN HISTORY

Soviet premier Krushchev speaking to the General Assembly in 1960

WITH NO PERMANENT police force to deal with disputes, the UN depends on voluntary compliance and

WORKS OF ART AT THE UN

The UN building has acquired many works of art and reproductions by major artists, many of them gifts from member nations. Most of them have either a peace or international friendship theme. The legend on Norman Rockwell's *The Golden Rule* reads "Do unto others as you would have them do unto you". Marc Chagall designed a large stained-glass window as a memorial to former Secretary General Dag Hammarskjöld, who was accidentally killed while on a peace mission in 1961. A Henry Moore sculpture graces the grounds. There are many other sculptures and paintings by the artists of many nations.

***The Golden Rule* (1985), a large mosaic by Norman Rockwell**

Pierpont Morgan Library ⑭

THE PIERPONT MORGAN LIBRARY came into being as the private collection of banker J Pierpont Morgan. In 1902, architects McKim, Mead & White designed a magnificent palazzo-style building to house it. Morgan's son, J Pierpont Morgan, Jr, established the library as a public institution in 1924. Today it has one of the world's finest collections of rare manuscripts, books and prints, displayed in a complex that includes the original library and J P Morgan, Jr's home.

Exterior of the original library building

★ **Garden Court**
This three-storey skylit garden area links the Library with the Morgan House.

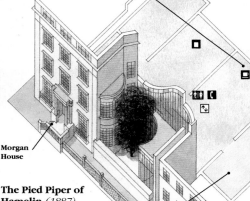

Morgan House

KEY TO FLOORPLAN

☐ Exhibition space
▨ Non-exhibition space

The Pied Piper of Hamelin (1887)
Kate Greenaway's vision of Robert Browning's poem is one of her finest works.

Forecourt Gallery

The Nursery Alice
Lewis Carroll's characters are immortalized in John Tenniel's classic illustrations (c. 1865).

Exhibition Room

STAR EXHIBITS

★ **Livre de la Chasse**

★ **Adam and Eve by Albrecht Dürer**

★ **Garden Court**

★ **Manuscript of Mozart's Horn Concerto in E-Flat Major**

Puss-in-Boots (1695)
This is an original page from the Tales of Mother Goose *by Charles Perrault.*

VISITORS' CHECKLIST

29 E 36th St. **Map** 9 A2.
685-0008. **M** 6 to 33rd St.
M1, M2, M3, M4. **Open**
10.30am–5pm Tue–Fri, 10.30am–
6pm Sat, noon–6pm Sun. **Closed**
1 Jan, 4 Jul, Thanksgiving, 25 Dec.
Adm charge. Concerts, lectures, film/video
presentations.

LIBRARY GUIDE

Mr Morgan's Study and the original library contain some of his favourite paintings, objets d'art and rare acquisitions. Medieval manuscripts and early books are in the Exhibition Room. The children's books are in the Forecourt Gallery.

West Room (Mr Morgan's Study)

★ Mozart's Horn Concerto in E-Flat Major
The six surviving leaves of this score are written in different coloured inks.

Rotunda

East Room
The walls are lined from floor to ceiling with triple tiers of bookcases. Murals show historical figures and their muses, and signs of the zodiac.

★ Adam and Eve (1504)
One of Albrecht Dürer's most celebrated works, this drawing reflects his quest for the perfect representation of the human figure.

Main entrance

★ Livre de la Chasse
This copy of Gaston Phébus's illustrated book on hunting was made in about 1410.

J PIERPONT MORGAN

J P Morgan (1837–1913) was not only a leading financier, but also one of the great collectors of his time. Rare books and original manuscripts were his passion, and inclusion in his collection was an honour. In 1909, when Morgan requested the donation of the manuscript of *Pudd'nhead Wilson*, Mark Twain responded: "One of my high ambitions is gratified".

UPPER MIDTOWN

1946 Cisitalia in the MoMA

UPMARKET NEW YORK in all its diversity is here, in this area of churches, synagogues, clubs, museums, luxury hotels, famous stores, trend-setting skyscrapers and pockets of luxury living. For almost 30 years from 1833, it was home to society names such as Astor and Vanderbilt. In the 1950s, architectural history was made when the Lever and Seagram buildings were erected. These first great modern towers marked midtown Park Avenue's change from a residential street to a prestigious office address.

SIGHTS AT A GLANCE

Historic Streets and Buildings
Villard Houses ❾
General Electric Building ⓫
Sutton Place and Beekman Place ⓱
Roosevelt Island ⓲
Fuller Building ⓴

Modern Architecture
Trump Tower ❷
IBM Building ❸
Lever House ⓭
Seagram Building ⓮
Citicorp Center ⓯

Museums and Galleries
Museum of Modern Art (MoMA) pp170–73 ❺
American Craft Museum ❻

Museum of Television and Radio ❼

Churches and Synagogues
St Thomas' Church ❹
St Patrick's Cathedral pp176–7 ❽
St Bartholomew's Church ❿
Central Synagogue ⓰

Landmark Hotels
Waldorf–Astoria ⓬
Plaza Hotel ㉑

Landmark Stores
Fifth Avenue ❶
Bloomingdale's ⓳

[Map of Upper Midtown showing Central Park, Grand Army Plaza, numbered sights, subway stations, East River, Roosevelt Island, Queensboro Bridge, Roosevelt Island Tram]

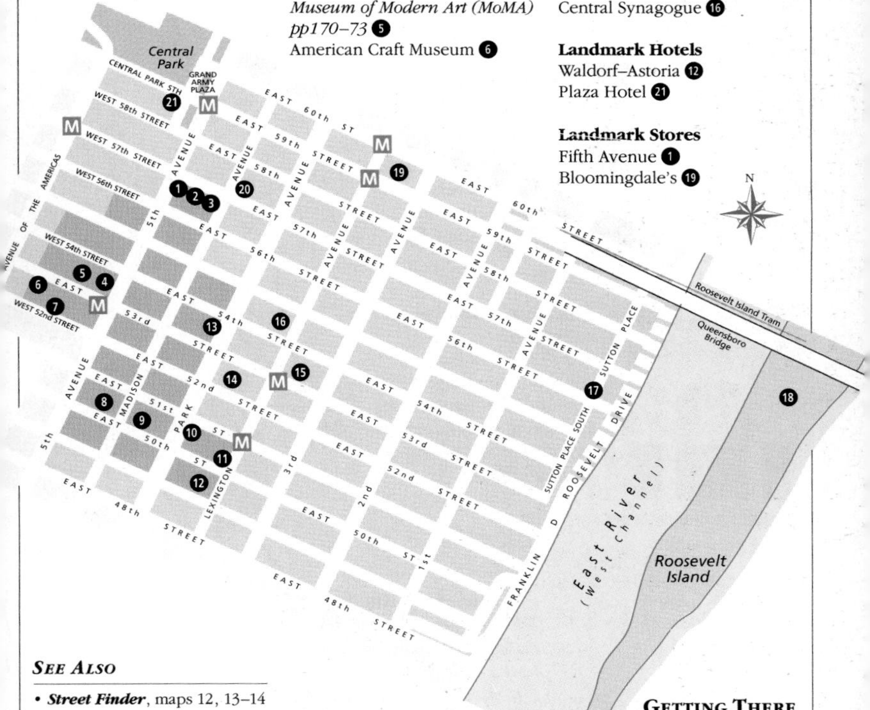

SEE ALSO

- *Street Finder*, maps 12, 13–14
- *Where to Stay* pp274–5
- *Restaurants* pp290–92

KEY

▨	Street-by-Street map
Ⓜ	Subway station

0 metres　500
0 yards　500

GETTING THERE
Take the Lexington Ave 4, 5 or 6 subways to 51st St, or the E or F to 5th Ave. Bus routes are the M15, M101/102 and M1, M2, M3 and M4. Crosstown buses are the M50, M57 and M58.

View down Fifth Avenue

Street-by-Street: Upper Midtown

T HE LUXURY STORES that are synonymous with Fifth Avenue first blossomed as society moved on uptown. In 1917, Cartier's acquired the mansion of banker Morton F Plant in exchange for a string of pearls, setting the style for other retailers to follow. But this stretch of Midtown is not simply for shoppers. There are three distinctive museums and an equally diverse assembly of architectural styles to enjoy, too.

Fifth Avenue
Today's carriage rides offer a taste of past elegance ❶

American Craft Museum
This is a showcase for crafts, from ceramics to furniture ❻

The University Club was built in 1899 as an elite club for gentlemen

St Thomas' Church
Much of the interior carving was designed by sculptor Lee Lawrie ❹

★Museum of Modern Art
This is one of the finest collections of modern art in the world ❺

Museum of Television and Radio
Exhibitions, seasons of special screenings, live events and a vast library of historic broadcasts are on offer at this media museum ❼

5th Avenue subway (lines E, F)

Saks Fifth Avenue has offered goods in impeccable taste to generations of New Yorkers. *(See p311.)*

★St Patrick's Cathedral
This, the largest Catholic cathedral in the United States, is a magnificent Gothic Revival building ❽

Olympic Tower
combines offices, apartments and a skylit atrium within its sleek walls.

Villard Houses
Five handsome brownstone houses now form part of the New York Palace hotel ❾

STAR SIGHTS

★ **Museum of Modern Art**

★ **St Patrick's Cathedral**

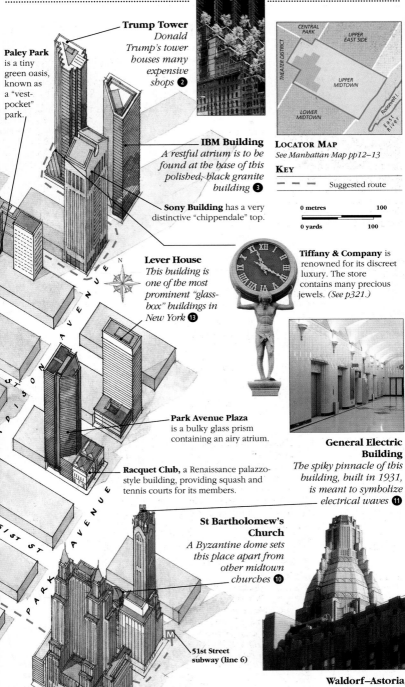

Trump Tower
Donald Trump's tower houses many expensive shops **2**

Paley Park is a tiny green oasis, known as a "vest-pocket" park.

IBM Building
A restful atrium is to be found at the base of this polished, black granite building **3**

Sony Building has a very distinctive "chippendale" top.

Lever House
This building is one of the most prominent "glass-box" buildings in New York **13**

Park Avenue Plaza is a bulky glass prism containing an airy atrium.

Racquet Club, a Renaissance palazzo-style building, providing squash and tennis courts for its members.

St Bartholomew's Church
A Byzantine dome sets this place apart from other midtown churches **10**

51st Street subway (line 6)

LOCATOR MAP
See Manhattan Map pp12–13

KEY

- - - - Suggested route

| 0 metres | 100 |
| 0 yards | 100 |

Tiffany & Company is renowned for its discreet luxury. The store contains many precious jewels. *(See p321.)*

General Electric Building
The spiky pinnacle of this building, built in 1931, is meant to symbolize electrical waves **11**

Waldorf–Astoria
Old-world elegance has attracted many famous guests to this hotel, including the Duke and Duchess of Windsor **12**

Window display at Bergdorf Goodman (see p311)

Fifth Avenue ❶

Map 4 F1–16 E1. **M** *5th Ave–53rd St.*

IN 1883, WHEN William Henry Vanderbilt built his mansion at Fifth Avenue and 51st Street, he started a trend that resulted in palatial residences stretching as far as Central Park, built for top families such as the Astors, Belmonts and Goulds. Only a few remain to attest to the grandeur of the era.

One such is the Cartier store at No. 651 Fifth Avenue, originally the home of Morton F Plant, millionaire and Commodore of the New York Yacht Club. As the retailers swept north up the avenue – a trend that began in 1906 – society gradually moved to better locations uptown. In 1917, Plant moved to a new mansion at 86th Street, and legend has it that he traded his old home to Pierre Cartier for a perfectly matched string of pearls.

Fifth Avenue has been synonymous with luxury goods ever since. From Cartier at 52nd Street to Tiffany and Berg-dorf Goodman at 57th, you will find a gamut of famous names symbolizing wealth and social standing today just as Vanderbilt and Astor did more than a century ago.

Trump Tower ❷

725 5th Ave. **Map** 12 F3. **C** *832-2000*. **M** *5th Ave–53rd St.* **Garden level, shops open** *10am–6pm Mon– Sat, noon–5pm Sun.* **Building open** *8am– 10pm daily.* **Adm free.** See **History** *p31.* 🅾 🅰 **Concerts.** 🍴 🖥 🚻

A GLITTERING, exorbitantly expensive apartment and office tower rises above a lavish six-storey atrium with layer upon layer of exclusive shops and cafés. Designed in 1983 by Der Scutt of Swanke, Hayden, Connell & Partners, the public space is lavished with pink marble, a waterfall, mirrors and glitz. It is the most opulent example of the new urban trend towards vertical shopping centres. The tower is a flamboyant monument to affluence by the developer Donald Trump, who himself became a symbol of the excesses of the 1980s.

Just next door, No. 727 is a complete contrast. This is Tiffany & Co, the prestigious jewellers founded in 1837. Famed for its exquisite window displays, its simple blue packaging is a status symbol in itself. It was immortalized in New York culture by Truman Capote's *Breakfast at Tiffany's*.

Entrance to Tiffany and Co, the exclusive jewellery emporium

IBM Building ❸

590 Madison Ave. **Map** 12 F3. **C** *745-5994.* **M** *5th Ave.* **Garden Plaza open** *7.30am–10pm daily.* 🚫 🅰 **Concerts.** 🖥 🚻

THIS 43-STOREY tower was designed by Edward Larrabee Barnes. Completed in 1983, it is a sleek, five sided prism of grey-green polished granite, with a cantilevered corner at 57th Street. The Garden Plaza, a light and spacious public atrium, offers rest and refreshment at café tables set out among the bamboo trees. It also houses a garden shop run by the New York Botanical Garden. Near the atrium is a work by American sculptor Michael Heizer, entitled *Levitated Mass.* Inside a low, stainless steel tank, a huge slab of granite seems to float on air while, beneath it, a sheet of water flows.

IBM's excellent Gallery of Science and Art is closed at present. Phone for current details.

Interior of the Trump Tower atrium

St Thomas' Church

St Thomas' Church ❹

1 W 53rd St. **Map** 12 F4.
【 757-7013. Ⓜ 5th Ave–53rd St.
Open 7am–6pm daily. ⊤ frequent.
∅ & 🔗

T HIS IS THE FOURTH home for this parish and the second on this site. Today's church was built between 1909 and 1914 to replace an earlier structure destroyed in a fire in 1905. The previous building had provided the setting for most of the large, glittering Fifth Avenue high society weddings of the late 19th century. The most lavish of these was the legendary ceremony of 1895 in which heiress Consuela Vanderbilt was married to the English Duke of Marlborough.

The limestone building, in French-Gothic style has a single asymmetrical tower and an off-centre nave, novel solutions to the architectural problems posed by the position, on a corner lot. The richly-carved, shimmering white screens behind the altar were designed by the architect Bertram Goodhue and the sculptor Lee Lawrie. Carvings in the choir stalls, dating from the 1920s, include modern inventions such as the telephone and radio, as well as Presidents Roosevelt and Wilson, and Lee Lawrie himself.

Museum of Modern Art ❺

See pp170–73.

American Craft Museum ❻

40 W 53rd St. **Map** 12 F4.
【 956-3535. Ⓜ 5th Ave–53rd St.
Open 10am–6pm Tue, Wed & Fri–Sun, 10am–8pm Thu. **Adm charge**. ∅ &
📽 Lectures, films.

T HERE IS NO BETTER place to experience the vitality of the contemporary American crafts movement than this, the showcase home of the American Crafts Council. On display are handmade quilts, ceramics, glass, textiles, wood, silver, furniture, paper and metalwork drawn from the museum's extensive collection of crafts, which date from 1900 to the present day. Founded in a brownstone on this site in 1956, the museum re-opened in 1987 in the three-storey atrium of an office tower. The reception desk is itself a work of art, designed and hand-carved in maple by James Schneider. The displays are not for sale.

Silver chalice by Ronald Hayes Pearson at the Craft Museum

Museum of Television and Radio ❼

25 W 52nd St. **Map** 12 F4.
【 621-6600. Ⓜ 5th Ave–53rd St. **Open** noon–6pm Tue–Sun (8pm Thu). Theatres and screening rooms close 9pm Fri. **Closed** public hols. **Adm charge**. ∅ & 📽 🔗 📷

I N THIS one-of-a-kind museum, visitors can watch and listen to a collection of news, entertainment, sports and documentary reports from radio and television's earliest days to the present. Pop fans can see the early Beatles, or a young Elvis Presley making his television debut. Sports enthusiasts can relive classic Olympic competitions. World War II footage might be chosen by students of history or by those who lived through the war. Six choices at any one

Beatles Paul, Ringo and John on the Ed Sullivan Show in 1964

time can be selected from a computer catalogue that covers a library of over 50,000 programmes. The selections are then played on small private consoles. There are larger screening areas and a theatre for 200, where retrospectives of artists, directors and topics are shown. Other areas include exhibits of photos, posters and memorabilia.

The museum was the brainchild of William S Paley, the late head of the CBS television network. It opened in 1975 as the Museum of Broadcasting on East 53rd Street. Its popularity soon led to the need for more space and in 1991 it moved into this hi-tech $50 million home in a building that, to many people, is reminiscent of an antique radio set.

1960s television star Lucille Ball

Museum of Modern Art ❺

Museum facade on West 53rd Street

THE MUSEUM of Modern Art contains one of the world's best and most comprehensive collections of modern art. It was founded in 1929 by wealthy patrons and has since set the standard for other museums of its kind, extending the boundaries of art to include many disciplines which are unrecognized by other galleries. The resulting mix is rich and stimulating, chronicling the development of modern art and the modern age.

Sculpture Garden
The Abby Aldrich Rockefeller Sculpture Garden is a beautiful and restful space.

Christina's World
(1948) Andrew Wyeth contrasts an overwhelming horizon with the minutely-studied surroundings of his handicapped neighbour.

STAR PAINTINGS

★ **The Starry Night by Vincent Van Gogh**

★ **Les Demoiselles d'Avignon by Pablo Picasso**

Bird in Space *(c. 1928)*
Constantin Brancusi's elegant bronze sculpture captures the sheer essence of flight.

GALLERY GUIDE
Changing exhibitions are displayed on the first floor. Painting and sculpture are exhibited on the second and third floors. Photography is on the second floor, prints are on the third floor. Architecture and design collections are on the fourth. Films are shown on the lower level.

Main entrance

Sculpture Garden

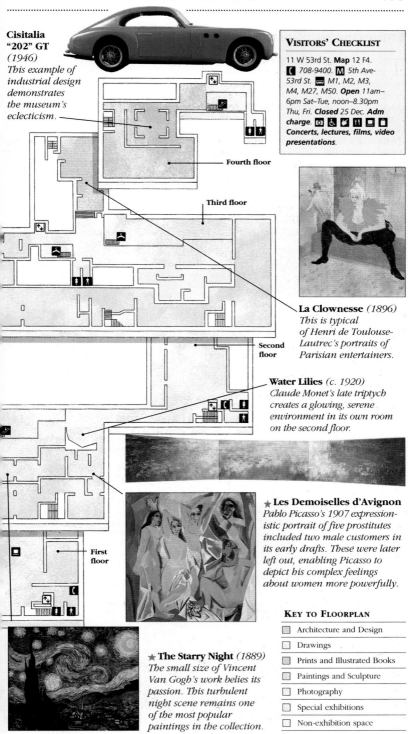

Cisitalia "202" GT *(1946)*
This example of industrial design demonstrates the museum's eclecticism.

VISITORS' CHECKLIST

11 W 53rd St. **Map** 12 F4.
708-9400. **M** 5th Ave-53rd St. **M1, M2, M3, M4, M27, M50. Open** 11am–6pm Sat–Tue, noon–8.30pm Thu, Fri. **Closed** 25 Dec. **Adm charge.** *Concerts, lectures, films, video presentations.*

Fourth floor

Third floor

La Clownesse *(1896)*
This is typical of Henri de Toulouse-Lautrec's portraits of Parisian entertainers.

Second floor

Water Lilies *(c. 1920)*
Claude Monet's late triptych creates a glowing, serene environment in its own room on the second floor.

★ **Les Demoiselles d'Avignon**
Pablo Picasso's 1907 expression-istic portrait of five prostitutes included two male customers in its early drafts. These were later left out, enabling Picasso to depict his complex feelings about women more powerfully.

First floor

★ **The Starry Night** *(1889)*
The small size of Vincent Van Gogh's work belies its passion. This turbulent night scene remains one of the most popular paintings in the collection.

KEY TO FLOORPLAN

- Architecture and Design
- Drawings
- Prints and Illustrated Books
- Paintings and Sculpture
- Photography
- Special exhibitions
- Non-exhibition space

Exploring the Collection

THE MUSEUM OF MODERN ART houses approximately 100,000 works of art, ranging from a collection of Post-Impressionist classics to an unrivalled collection of modern American art; and from fine examples of design to early masterpieces of photography and film.

1880s–1940s PAINTING AND SCULPTURE

The Persistence of Memory by the Surrealist Salvador Dali (1931)

The geometric, abstract art of the Constructivists is included in a strong display of works by Malevich, Lissitzky and Rodchenko: De Stijl's influence is seen in paintings by Piet Mondrian, including *Broadway Boogie Woogie*. An entire room is devoted to work by Matisse, such as *Dance I* and *The Red Studio*. Dali, Miró and Ernst feature among the collection of bizarre, strangely beautiful Surrealist works.

PAUL CEZANNE'S monumental *The Bather* and Vincent Van Gogh's passionate and transcendent *The Starry Night* are two of the seminal works in the museum's collection of late 19th-century painting. Both Fauvism and Expressionism are well represented with works by Matisse, Derain, Kirchner and others, while Pablo Picasso's *Les Demoiselles d'Avignon* marks a transition to a new style of painting.

The museum also has an unparalleled collection of Cubist paintings, providing an overview of a movement that radically challenged our perception of the world. Among the vast display are Picasso's *Girl with a Mandolin*, Georges Braque's *Man with a Guitar* and *Soda*, and *Guitar and Flowers* by Juan Gris. Works by the Futurists, who brought colour and movement to Cubism to depict the dynamic modern world, include Gino Severini's *Dynamic Hieroglyphic of the Bal Tabarin*, *Dynamism of a Soccer Player* by Umberto Boccioni, plus works by Balla, Carrà and Villon.

POSTWAR PAINTING AND SCULPTURE

AN EXTENSIVE display of postwar art begins on the third floor, with a series of works by Bacon, Dubuffet and others. The collection of Abstract Expressionist art includes Jackson Pollock's enigmatically stunning *One [Number 31, 1950]*, Willem de Kooning's *Woman, I*, Arshile Gorky's *Agony* and *Red, Brown, and Black* by

Dog (1952), an oil painting by British artist Francis Bacon

Mark Rothko. The following galleries exhibit works such as Jasper Johns' *Flag* and Robert Rauschenberg's *First Landing Jump*, composed from urban refuse, and *Bed*, composed of bed linen. The Pop Art on show includes Roy Lichtenstein's *Girl with Ball* and *Drowning Girl*, Andy Warhol's famous *Gold Marilyn Monroe* and Claes Oldenburg's *Giant Soft Fan*. Works after about 1965 are displayed on a rotating basis and can include works by Judd, Flavin, Serra and Beuys among many others.

DRAWINGS AND OTHER WORKS ON PAPER

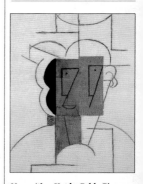

Man with a Hat by Pablo Picasso (1912), in collage and charcoal

THE MUSEUM of Modern Art has one of the most comprehensive collections of modern drawings anywhere in the world. This collection has a range of works in traditional mediums – pencil, ink and charcoal – and also in watercolour, gouache and collage. Some are early studies for famous paintings; Picasso's *Head of the Medical Student* is a study for *Les Demoiselles d'Avignon*. Special strengths are the works representing the School of Paris, Dada and Surrealism. The rotating exhibition on the department's second-floor galleries may include the works of Matisse, Ernst, Klee, Pollock, Dubuffet and Rauschenberg. At various times some of this collection is shown outside the drawings department to complement the museum's other exhibitions.

PRINTS AND ILLUSTRATED BOOKS

American Indian Theme II by Roy Lichtenstein (1980)

WIDE-RANGING examples of historical and contemporary printmaking include works in such traditional techniques as lithography, etching, screenprinting and woodcuts, as well as in more experimental techniques. There are fine examples of portraiture, notably a *Self-Portrait with Grimace* by Marc Chagall. The collection is strong in the works of Redon, Munch, Klee, Matisse, Picasso, Dubuffet, Villon and Johns. Prints by these and other artists are always on view in the constantly rotating exhibition in the department's second-floor galleries.

At the entrance to the Print galleries is a reading room containing catalogues and books about prints. The first gallery has a changing survey of printed art from the 1880s up to the 1950s. The next displays art from the 1960s onwards, introducing recent and contemporary work.

PHOTOGRAPHY

THE PHOTOGRAPHY collection begins with the invention of the medium around 1840. It includes pictures by fine artists, journalists, scientists and entrepreneurs, as well as amateur photographers. The first of the department's third-floor galleries is devoted to temporary exhibitions. The other galleries offer an ever-changing, chronological series of the collection's highlights. Included in these are photographs by Atget, Stieglitz, Lange, Arbus, Steichen,

FILM DEPARTMENT

With a collection of some 10,000 films and 4 million stills, the museum runs a wide range of programmes, including retrospectives of individual directors and actors, films in specific genres, and experimental work, as well as a broad range of other exhibitions. Film conservation is a key part of the department's work. Today's top directors are now donating copies of their films to help fund this expensive but vital work.

Film still of Charlie Chaplin and Jackie Coogan in *The Kid* (1921)

Cartier-Bresson and Kertesz, and a range of contemporary photographers, most notably Friedlander, Sherman and Nixon. There is an extensive variety of subject matter, covering delicate landscapes, scenes of urban desolation, abstract imagery and stylish portraiture, including some

Sunday on the Banks of the Marne, photographed by Henri Cartier-Bresson in 1939

beautiful gelatin-silver print nudes by the French Surrealist Man Ray. Together, they form a complete history of photographic art, and represent one of the finest collections in existence.

ARCHITECTURE AND DESIGN

THE MUSEUM of Modern Art was the first art museum to include utilitarian objects in its collection. These range from household appliances, stereo equipment, furniture, lighting, textiles and glassware to industrial ball bearings and silicon chips. Architecture is represented in the displays of scale models, drawings and photographs. Graphic design is shown in typography and posters. Architectural models and drawings are displayed in the first gallery, and selections from the design collection follow. Pinin Farina's Cisitalia car and the Bell helicopter are on permanent display in the fourth-floor galleries.

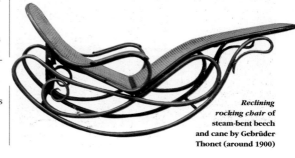

Reclining rocking chair of steam-bent beech and cane by Gebrüder Thonet (around 1900)

St Patrick's Cathedral **8**

See pp176–7.

Villard Houses **9**

457 Madison Ave (New York Palace Hotel). **Map** 13 A4. **C** 935-3960. **M** 51st St. **Urban Center open** 11am–5pm Mon–Wed, Fri, Sat.

HENRY VILLARD WAS a Bavarian immigrant who became publisher of the *New York Evening Post* and founder of the Northern Pacific Railroad. In 1881, he bought the land opposite St Patrick's Cathedral and hired McKim, Mead & White to design town houses, one for himself, the rest for sale. The inspired result has six four-storey houses built around a central court opening to the street and the church. The south wing was Villard's, but financial difficulties forced him to sell before it was finished.

Ownership passed to the Roman Catholic Archdiocese, but the houses were then threatened when the church outgrew its space in the 1970s. The problem was resolved when the Helmsley chain purchased air rights for the 51-storey Helmsley (now New York) Palace Hotel. The south wing became the formal entrance to the hotel and the grand public rooms of the Villard suite were incorporated as a tea room and lounge, restored to their former glory. The Urban Center occupies the entire north wing and it's large bookshop is the best place in New York to find architectural books on the city.

St Bartholomew's Church

St Bartholomew's Church **10**

109 E 50th St. **Map** 13 A4. **C** 751-1616. **M** 51st St. **Open** 8am–6pm daily. **Closed** public hols exc 25 Dec & Easter. **✝** 9am, 11am Sun. **Lectures, concerts**. on Sundays.

KNOWN FONDLY TO New Yorkers as "St Bart's", this Byzantine structure with its ornate detail, pinkish brick, open terrace and a poly-chromed gold dome brought colour and variety to Park Avenue in 1919.

Architect Bertram Goodhue incorporated into the design the Romanesque entrance portico done by Stanford White for the original 1903 St Bartholomew's on Madison Avenue, and marble columns from the earlier church were used in the chapel.

St Bartholomew's musical programmes are well known, their Jazz Nativity being a special favourite. They are now concentrating on classical, choral and organ music.

General Electric Building **11**

570 Lexington Ave. **Map** 13 A4. **M** Lexington Ave. **Not open** to the public.

IN 1931 ARCHITECTS Cross & Cross were commissioned to design a skyscraper that would be in keeping with its neighbour, St Bartholomew's Church. Not an easy task, but the result won unanimous acclaim. The colours were chosen to blend and contrast, and the design of the tower complemented the church's polychrome dome.

The General Electric Building on Lexington Avenue

View the pair from the corner of Park and 50th to see how well it works. However, the General Electric is no mere backdrop, but a work of art in its own right, and a favourite part of the city skyline. It is an Art Deco gem from its chrome and marble lobby to its spiky "radio waves" crown.

Walk one block north on Lexington Avenue to find a place much cherished by movie fans. It is right at this spot that Marilyn Monroe, in a billowing white frock, stood so memorably in the breeze from the Lexington Avenue Subway grating in the movie *The Seven-Year Itch*.

Villard Houses, now the entrance to the New York Palace Hotel

Waldorf–Astoria 12

301 Park Ave. **Map** 13 A5.
📞 *355-3000.* Ⓜ *Lexington Ave, 53rd St. See* **Where to Stay** *p281.*

THIS ART DECO classic, which covers an entire city block, was designed by Schultze & Weaver in 1931. The earlier Waldorf–Astoria Hotel at 34th Street was demolished to make way for the Empire State Building.

Winston Churchill and New York philanthropist Grover Whalen at the Waldorf–Astoria in 1946

Still deservedly one of New York's most prestigious hotels, the Waldorf–Astoria serves, too, as a reminder of a more glamorous era in the city's history. The 625-ft (190-m) twin towers, where the Duke and Duchess of Windsor lived, have hosted numerous celebrities, including every US President since 1931. The giant lobby clock, executed for the Chicago World's Fair of 1893, is from the original hotel, and the piano in the Peacock Alley cocktail lounge belonged to Cole Porter when he was a resident of the hotel's exclusive Towers.

Lever House 13

390 Park Ave. **Map** 13 A4.
📞 *888-1260.* Ⓜ *5th Ave-53rd St.* **Lobby open** *10am–5pm Mon–Sat.* **Closed** *public hols & Sun during summer.* 📷

IMAGINE A PARK AVENUE lined with sturdy, residential buildings – and then imagine the sensation when they were suddenly reflected here in the first of the city's glass-walled skyscrapers, one of the most influential buildings of the modern era. The design, by

The pool at the Four Seasons in the Seagram Building

Skidmore, Owings & Merrill, is simply two rectangular slabs of stainless steel and glass, one laid horizontally, the other stacked to stand tall above it, with light which pours in from every side. The crisp and bright design was always intended to symbolize many of the Lever Brothers' products – they make soaps and other washing products. Revolutionary though it was in 1952, Lever House is now dwarfed by the many imitators that have grown up around it, but its importance as an architectural pacesetter remains undiminished.

Lever House on Park Avenue

Seagram Building 14

375 Park Ave. **Map** 13 A4. 📞 *572-7000.* Ⓜ *5th Ave-53rd St.* 🎦 *3pm Tue.* 🍴

SAMUEL BRONFMAN, the late head of Seagram distillers, was prepared to put up an ordinary commercial building until his architect daughter, Phyllis Lambert, intervened and persuaded him to go to the best – Mies van der Rohe.

The result, which is widely considered the best of the many Modernist buildings of the 1950s, consists of two rectangles of bronze and glass which lets the light pour in.

Within is the exclusive Four Seasons Restaurant *(see p293)*, a landmark in its own right. Designer Philip Johnson has created two linked rooms of which the centrepiece of one is a pool, and the other a bar which is topped by a quivering Richard Lippold sculpture.

Office workers at lunch in the spacious Citicorp atrium

Citicorp Center 15

153 E 53rd St. **Map** 13 A4. Ⓜ *53rd St-Lexington Ave.* **Open** *7am–11pm daily.* 🍴 ⛪ **St Peter's Lutheran Church** 📞 *935-2200.* **Open** *9am–9pm daily* ✝ *8.45am, 11am Sun.* **Jazz vespers** *5pm Sun.* **Concerts** *daily except Mon.* **Theatre at St Peter's Church** 📞 *935-2200.*

AN ALUMINIUM-CLAD spire built on ten-storey stilts with a sliced-off roof, Citicorp Center is one of a kind and caused a sensation when it was completed in 1978. The unusual base design had to incorporate St Peter's Lutheran Church. The church is separate both in space and design, a granite sculpture below a corner of the tower. Step inside to see the handsome modern interior and the Erol Beker Chapel by sculptor Louise Nevelson. The church is well known for its organ concerts and jazz vespers, and has a small theatre. Citicorp's slanting top never functioned as a solar collector as intended, but it makes the building's outline an unmistakable landmark on the skyline.

Saint Patrick's Cathedral ❽

THE ROMAN CATHOLIC church originally intended this site for use as a cemetery, but in 1850 Archbishop John Hughes decided to build a cathedral instead. Many thought that it was foolish to build so far beyond the (then) city limits, but Hughes went ahead anyway. Architect James Renwick built New York's finest Gothic Revival building, and the largest Catholic cathedral in the United States. The

Fifth Avenue facade

cathedral, which seats 2,500 people, was completed in 1878, but the spires were added from 1885 to 1888.

Lady Chapel ★
This chapel honours the Blessed Virgin. The stained-glass windows portray the mysteries of the rosary.

Pieta
American sculptor William O Partridge created this statue of the Pieta in 1906; it stands at the side of the Lady Chapel.

★ **Baldachin**
The great baldachin rising over the high altar is made entirely of bronze. Statues of the saints and prophets adorn the four piers supporting the canopy.

STAR FEATURES

★ **Baldachin**

★ **Great Bronze Doors**

★ **Lady Chapel**

★ **Great Organ and Rose Window**

Cathedral Facade
The exterior wall is built of white marble. The spires rise 330 ft (101 m) above the pavement.

Stations of the Cross
Carved of Caen stone in Holland, these reliefs won first prize in the field of religious art at the Chicago World's Fair in 1893.

VISITORS' CHECKLIST

5th Ave and 50th St. **Map** 12 F4.
753-2261. 6 to 51st St;
E, F to 5th Ave. M1, M2,
M3, M4. **Open** 7.30am–8.30pm
daily. frequent Mon–Sat;
7am, 8am, 9am 10.15am, 12
noon, 1pm, 4pm, 5.30pm Sun.
**Concerts,
lectures.**

Shrine of St Elizabeth Ann Seton
The bronze statue and screen depict the life of the first native American to be canonized a saint, who founded the Sisters of Charity (see p76).

Great Organ ★ and Rose Window
Measuring 26 ft (8 m) in diameter, the rose window shines above the great organ, which has more than 7,000 pipes.

Main entrance

Great Bronze Doors ★
The massive doors weigh 20,000 lb (9,000 kg) and are adorned with statues which depict the saints of New York.

Central Synagogue 🖲

652 Lexington Ave. **Map** 13 A4.
⬛ 838–5122. **Ⓜ** 51st St, Lexington
Ave. **Open** noon–2pm Mon–Thu.
✡ 5.30pm Fri (but 8.15pm first Fri
each month),10.30am Sat. **🖉**

THIS IS NEW YORK'S oldest building in continuous use as a synagogue. It was designed in 1870 by Silesian-born Henry Fernbach, America's first prominent Jewish architect. He also designed some of SoHo's finest cast-iron buildings. The Central Synagogue is considered the city's best example of Moorish-Islamic Revival architecture. The congregation was originally founded in 1846 as Ahawath Chesed (Love of Mercy), by 18 newly-arrived immigrants, most of them from Bohemia, in much humbler surroundings on Ludlow Street on the Lower East Side.

The stencilled interior is a colourful mix of red, blue, ochre and gilt and was inspired by Victorian prints of a Moorish Palace in Spain called the Alhambra.

Banded "horseshoe" arches are an Hispano-Mooresque design.

The Ark holds the sacred scrolls of the Jewish Holy Book, The Torah.

The twin towers represent the two columns which stood outside Solomon's Temple. The domed minarets, which rise 122 ft (37 m) are onion-shaped and made of green copper.

The facade is an understated Moorish design in local brownstone.

Sutton Place and Beekman Place 🖲

Map 13 C3, 13 C5. **Ⓜ** 59th St.

SUTTON PLACE IS A posh and pleasant neighbourhood, delightfully devoid of busy traffic, made up of elegant low-rise apartment houses and town houses designed by noted architects. The arrival of New York society in the 1920s transformed an area that had once been the province of factories and tenements. No. 3 Sutton Square is the residence of the Secretary-General of the United Nations.

Look beyond Sutton Square and 59th Street for a glimpse of Riverview Terrace, a private street of five ivy-covered brownstones fronting on the river. The tiny parks at the end of 55th Street and jutting out at 57th Street offer views of the river and the Queensboro Bridge.

Smaller than Sutton Place, and even more tranquil, is Beekman Place, a virtually private two-block enclave of 1920s town houses and some small-scale apartments. Famous residents here have included Gloria Vanderbilt, Rex Harrison, Irving Berlin and members of the large Rockefeller family.

Between Beekman and Sutton Places is River House, a twin-towered apartment block built in 1931. Its squash and tennis courts, large private yacht moorings, pool and lavish ballroom gave it an immediate cachet which has stood the test of time, even

Park at Sutton Place, looking towards Queensboro Bridge and Roosevelt Island

though the moorings had to make way for FDR Drive.

At Turtle Bay Gardens, two rows of brownstone houses dating from the 1860s hide a charming, Italianate garden. Among the residents enticed by this privacy have been the film stars Tyrone Power and Katharine Hepburn, and modern composer Stephen Sondheim.

Roosevelt Island 🔞

Map 14 D2. **M** *59th St. Tram departs from 2nd Ave-60th St.*

SINCE 1976 a Swiss cable car has offered a quick ride across the East River to Roosevelt Island, with eagle's eye views of the city and the Queensboro Bridge.

Near the tram station are the remains of the Blackwell Farmhouse, which stood from 1796 to 1804 and gave the island its name until the 1920s. From the 1920s to the 1970s, when real estate developers set to work, it was Welfare Island, named for the hospitals, workhouse, almshouse and insane asylum that it once housed.

In 1927, Mae West was held in the penitentiary here for eight days after a "lewd performance". She requested, and got, her silk lingerie to wear under her prison uniform. The ruins of 19th-century hospitals still remain, as does an 1872 lighthouse built by an asylum inmate.

The island's new apartment buildings are not particularly noteworthy, but the trip is fun and the riverside promenade affords fine views of the city.

Bloomingdale's shop sign

Bloomingdale's 🔞

1000 3rd Ave. **Map** 13 A3.
C *355-5900.* **M** *59th St.*
Open *9.30am–9pm Mon–Fri, 9.30am–7pm Sat, 11am–7pm Sun.*
See **Shopping** *p311.*

FOR A WHILE in the booming 1980s, "Bloomies" was synonymous with the good life. Founded by Joseph and Lyman Bloomingdale in 1872, this famous department store had a bargain-basement image until the 3rd Avenue El was pulled down in the 1960s. Then came the store's transformation to the epitome of trendy, sophisticated shopping. But the late 1980s brought new ownership and eventual bankruptcy. While not as flashy as in the past, Bloomingdale's is operating normally and remains one of the city's best-stocked stores.

Fuller Building 🔞

41 E 57th St. **Map** 13 A3. **C** *André Emmerich Gallery 752-0124.* **Open** *10am–5.30pm Tue–Sat. Susan Sheehan Gallery 888-4220.* **Open** *10am–6pm Tue–Sat.* **M** *59th St.*

THIS SLIM-TOWERED black, grey and white 1929 beauty by Walker & Gillette is a prime example of geometric Art Deco design. The striking statues on either side of the clock above the entry are by Elie Nadelman. Step inside to see the intricate mosaic tile floors; one panel shows the Fuller Company's

former home in the Flatiron Building. The Fuller Building is a hive of exclusive art galleries, including the prestigious André Emmerich and Susan Sheehan galleries.

French Renaissance-style facade of the Plaza Hotel

Plaza Hotel 🔞

768 5th Ave. **Map** 12 F3.
C *759-3000.* **M** *59th St. See* **Where to Stay** *p281.*

THE CITY'S Grande Dame hotel was designed by Henry J Hardenbergh, known for the Dakota *(see p216)* and the original Waldorf-Astoria. Completed in 1907 at the exorbitant cost of $12.5 million, it was proclaimed "the best hotel in the world", with 800 rooms, 500 baths, a two-storey ballroom, five marble staircases, and 14- to 17-room apartments for families like the Vanderbilts and the Goulds *(see p49).*

The 18-storey cast-iron structure resembles a French Renaissance château on a larger scale. Much of the interior decoration came from Europe. The Palm Court still has mirrored walls and Italian carvings of the four seasons as supporting columns.

Former owner Donald Trump restored the hotel's original glitter (too much of it for some) with elaborate new Bavarian glass chandeliers, lush new carpet and miles of gold leaf. Venerable public areas have been refurbished without losing their original ambience and looks.

The clock statues above the Fuller Building entrance

UPPER EAST SIDE

AT THE TURN of the century, New York society moved to the Upper East Side – and stayed. Many of their Beaux Arts mansions are now museums and embassies, but the city's elite still occupy grand apartment buildings on Fifth and Park avenues. Chic shops and galleries line Madison. Further east, the area takes on an international tone with German Yorkville in the East 80s, Hungarian Yorkville to the south and little Bohemia, with its Czech population, below 78th Street. Many Germans, Czechs and Hungarians have moved away, but churches and some shops still remain.

African urn, Metropolitan Museum of Art

Looking down into the lobby of the Guggenheim Museum

Sights at a Glance

Historic Streets and Buildings
Seventh Regiment Armory 10
Henderson Place 14
Gracie Mansion 16

Museums and Galleries
International Center of Photography 1
Jewish Museum 2
Cooper-Hewitt Museum 3
National Academy of Design 4
Solomon R Guggenheim Museum pp186–7 5
Metropolitan Museum of Art pp188–95 6
Whitney Museum of American Art pp198–9 7
Frick Collection pp200–1 8
Asia Society 9
Society of Illustrators 12
Abigail Adams Smith Museum 13
Museum of the City of New York 19

Churches and Synagogues
Temple Emanu-El 11
Church of the Holy Trinity 17
St Nicholas Russian Orthodox Cathedral 18

Parks and Squares
Carl Schurz Park 15

Getting There

The Lexington Ave 4 and 5 express trains stop at 59th and 86th streets. The local (No. 6) also stops at 68th, 77th and 96th Streets. Buses include: M1, M2, M3 and M4 on Fifth/Madison Aves, M101/102 on Lexington/Third and M15 on First/Second. The crosstown buses are the M66, M72, M79, M86 and M96.

Key

- Street-by-Street map
- [M] Subway station
- Ferry terminal
- Heliport

0 metres 500

0 yards 500

Statue of Diana, National Academy of Design

See Also

- ***Street Finder***, maps 12–13, 16–17
- ***East Side Walk*** pp262–3
- ***Where to Stay*** pp274–5
- ***Restaurants*** pp290–92

Street-by-Street: Museum Mile

MANY OF NEW YORK'S museums are clustered in the Upper East Side, in homes ranging from the former Frick and Carnegie mansions to the modernistic Guggenheim by Frank Lloyd Wright. The displays are as varied as the architecture, running the gamut from old masters to photographs to decorative arts. Presiding over the scene is the vast Metropolitan Museum of Art, America's answer to the Louvre. Many of the museums stay open late on Tuesday evenings, and some offer free admission.

Jewish Museum
The most extensive collection of Judaica in the world is housed here. It includes coins, archaeological objects and ceremonial and religious artifacts ❷

Cooper-Hewitt Museum ★
The decorative arts, including ceramics, glass, furniture and textiles, are well represented here ❸

The Church of the Heavenly Rest was built in 1929 in the Gothic style. The madonna in the pulpit is by sculptor Malvina Hoffman.

National Academy of Design
The Academy, founded in 1825, moved here in 1940. Its fine collection includes paintings and sculptures by its members ❹

Graham House is an apartment building with a splendid Beaux Arts entrance. It was built in 1892.

★ **Solomon R Guggenheim Museum**
Floodlit at dusk, architect Frank Lloyd Wright's building looks purple. It is in the form of a spiral. Take the lift to the top and walk down through the collection to see some of the best modern art in the world ❺

STAR SIGHTS

★ Solomon R Guggenheim Museum

★ Cooper-Hewitt Museum

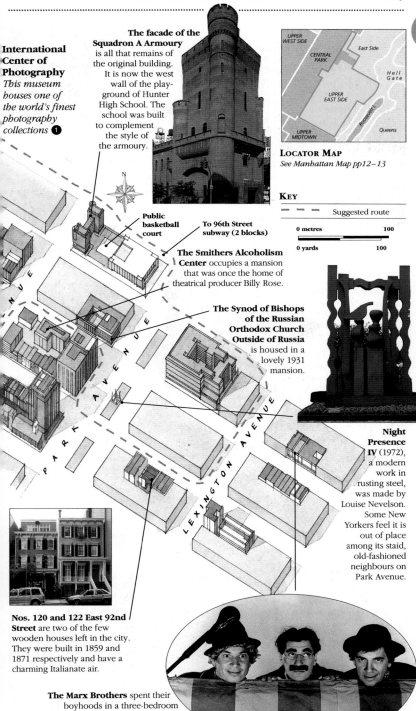

International Center of Photography
This museum houses one of the world's finest photography collections **①**

The facade of the Squadron A Armoury is all that remains of the original building. It is now the west wall of the playground of Hunter High School. The school was built to complement the style of the armoury.

LOCATOR MAP
See Manhattan Map pp12–13

KEY

– – –	Suggested route

| 0 metres | 100 |
| 0 yards | 100 |

Public basketball court

To 96th Street subway (2 blocks)

The Smithers Alcoholism Center occupies a mansion that was once the home of theatrical producer Billy Rose.

The Synod of Bishops of the Russian Orthodox Church Outside of Russia is housed in a lovely 1931 mansion.

Night Presence IV (1972), a modern work in rusting steel, was made by Louise Nevelson. Some New Yorkers feel it is out of place among its staid, old-fashioned neighbours on Park Avenue.

Nos. 120 and 122 East 92nd Street are two of the few wooden houses left in the city. They were built in 1859 and 1871 respectively and have a charming Italianate air.

The Marx Brothers spent their boyhoods in a three-bedroom apartment in a modest row house at No. 179 East 93rd Street.

International Center of Photography

International Center of Photography ❶

1130 5th Ave. **Map** 16 F2.
860-1777. Ⓜ *86th St, 96th St.*
Open *11am–8pm Tue, 11am–6pm
Wed–Sun.* **Closed** *public hols.* **Adm
charge**. 🚫 ✦ ▯

THIS MUSEUM, often referred to as the ICP, was founded by Cornell Capa in 1974 to conserve the work of such outstanding photojournalists as his brother Robert, who was killed on assignment in 1954. The ICP's collection of 12,500 original prints includes much work by some of the world's greatest photographers, such as Ansel Adams and Henri Cartier-Bresson. There are also excellent wide-ranging exhibitions, and a programme of films, lectures and classes.

One of upper Fifth Avenue's last grand residences, this brick six-storey Neo-Georgian house was built in 1915 for Willard Straight, a diplomat, financier and founder of the magazines *The New Republic* and *Asia*.

Jewish Museum ❷

1109 5th Ave. **Map** 16 F2.
423-3200. Ⓜ *86th St, 96th St.*
Open *11am–5.45pm Mon, Wed, Thu,
Sun, 11am–8pm Tue.* **Closed** *Fri, Sat,
major public & Jewish hols.* **Adm
charge**. 🚫 ♿ ✦ ▢ ▯

THE EXQUISITE château-like residence of Felix M Warburg, financier and leader of the Jewish community, was designed by C P H Gilbert in 1908. It now houses one of the world's largest collections of Jewish fine and ceremonial art, and historical Judaica. Renovation has almost doubled the display space. The stonework in the new extension is by the stonemasons of St John the Divine *(see pp224–5)*.

Objects have been brought here from all over the world, some at great risk of persecution to the donors. Covering 4,000 years, artefacts include Torah crowns, candelabras, kiddush cups, plates, scrolls and silver ceremonial objects.

There is a Torah ark from the Benguiat Collection, the exquisite faience entrance wall of a 16th-century Persian synagogue and the powerful *Holocaust* by sculptor George Segal. Changing exhibitions reflect Jewish life and experience around the world.

19th-century ewer and basin from Istanbul at the Jewish Museum

Cooper-Hewitt Museum ❸

2 E 91st St. **Map** 16 F2. *860-6868.*
Ⓜ *86th St.* **Open** *10am–9pm Tue,
10am–5pm Wed–Sat, noon–5pm Sun.*
Closed *public hols.* **Adm charge**. ♿
✦ ▯

ONE OF THE largest design collections in the world, this museum occupies the former home of industrialist Andrew Carnegie. It was amassed by the Hewitt sisters, Amy, Eleanor and Sarah. The museum opened in 1897 at Cooper Union *(see p118)*; the Smithsonian Institution acquired the collections in 1967, and the Carnegie Corporation offered the mansion.

Carnegie's house is an appropriate setting for the museum. He asked for "the most modest, plainest and most roomy house in New York", but the house set some new trends with its central

Cooper-Hewitt Museum entrance

heating, passenger lift and air conditioning. Visitors can still enjoy the fine wooden staircase, rich panelling and carving and sunny solarium.

National Academy of Design ❹

1083 5th Ave. **Map** 16 F3.
369-4880. Ⓜ *86th St.* **Open**
noon–5pm Wed–Sun, noon–8pm Fri.
Adm charge *except 5–8pm Fri.* 🚫

MORE THAN 6,000 paintings, drawings and sculptures, including works by Thomas Eakins, Winslow Homer, Raphael Soyer and Frank Lloyd Wright, comprise the collection of the National Academy of Design, founded in 1825 by a group of artists. The group's mission was (and is) to train artists and exhibit their work. In 1940, Archer Huntington, an art patron and philanthropist, donated his house, an attractive building with patterned marble floors and carved plaster ceilings. The grand entrance foyer has a statue of Diana by sculptor Anna Hyatt Huntington.

Statue of Diana in the National Academy of Design entrance foyer

Solomon R Guggenheim Museum ❺

See pp186–7.

Metropolitan Museum of Art ❻

See pp188–95.

Whitney Museum of American Art ❼

See pp198–9.

Frick Collection ❽

See pp200–1.

Asia Society ❾

725 Park Ave. **Map** 13 A1.
🄲 288-6400. Ⓜ 68th St.
Open 11am–6pm Tue–Sat (8pm Thu), noon–5pm Sun. **Closed** Mon, public hols. **Adm charge** exc 6–8pm Fri.
📷 🚫 🛗 ♿ 🛒 ♿

FOUNDED BY John D Rockefeller III in 1956 to increase American understanding of Asian culture, the Society is a forum for 30 countries from Japan to Iran, Central Asia to Australia.

Built in 1981, the eight-storey building is made of red granite. It was designed by Edward Larrabee Barnes. There are several galleries, one permanently devoted to Rockefeller's own collection of Asian sculptures, ceramics, bronzes and wood sculptures, amassed by him and his wife on frequent trips to the East.

Changing exhibits show a wide variety of Asian arts, and the Society has a full programme of films, dance, concerts and lectures. There is a well-stocked shop with books on Asia.

South Asian sculpture at the Asia Society

Entrance Hall of the Seventh Regiment Armory

Seventh Regiment Armory ❿

643 Park Ave. **Map** 13 A2.
🄲 439-0300. Ⓜ 68th St.
Open Mon–Fri by appt only.
Closed public hols. 📷 ♿ 🛒

FROM THE WAR of 1812 through two World Wars, the Seventh Regiment has played a vital role. They were an elite corps of "gentlemen soldiers" from prominent families, and their armoury is unlike any other in the US. Within the stern fortress-like exterior are extraordinary rooms filled with lavish furnishings of the Victorian era, objets d'art and regimental memorabilia.

The design by Charles W Clinton, a veteran of the regiment, had offices facing Park Avenue, with a vast drill hall stretching behind to Lexington Avenue. The reception rooms include the Veterans' Room and the Library by Louis Comfort Tiffany. The drill hall is now the venue for the Winter Antiques Show *(see p53)* and a favourite place to hold the city's many charity balls.

Temple Emanu-El ⓫

1 E 65th St. **Map** 12 F2.
🄲 744-1400. Ⓜ 68th St, 60th St.
Open 10am–4.45pm Sun–Fri, 10.45am–4.45pm Sat (last adm on Fri 3.30pm) **Closed** Jewish hols. ✡ 5.30pm Sun–Thu, 5.15pm Fri, 10.30am Sat. 📷 ♿ 🛒 ♿

THIS IMPRESSIVE limestone edifice of 1929 is one of the largest synagogues in the world, seating 2,500 in the main sanctuary alone. It is home to the oldest Reform congregation in New York. Among the many fine details are the bronze grille doors of the Ark, and stained glass showing the Shield of David and the Lion of Judah. The dominant feature of the Fifth Avenue exterior is the great recessed arch enclosing a magnificent wheel window. The Beth-El Chapel is a twin-domed structure with a Byzantine influence.

The synagogue stands on the site of the palatial home of the legendary society hostess, Mrs William Astor. She left her midtown mansion when her nephew, who was feuding with her, built the Waldorf Hotel next door. The formidable Mrs Astor moved to the Upper East Side, taking society with her, while her son built the Astoria Hotel on the site of her previous home.

The Ark at Temple Emanu-El

Solomon R Guggenheim Museum ❺

HOME TO ONE of the world's finest collections of modern and contemporary art, the Guggenheim building itself is perhaps the museum's greatest masterpiece. It was designed by architect Frank Lloyd Wright and has been likened to a giant white shell. As you walk along the spiral ramp that curves down and inwards from the dome, and visit the new Small Rotunda and Tower galleries, you will see special exhibitions featuring major works by many important 19th- and 20th-century artists. A new downtown site opened in 1992, the Guggenheim Museum SoHo *(see p105)*.

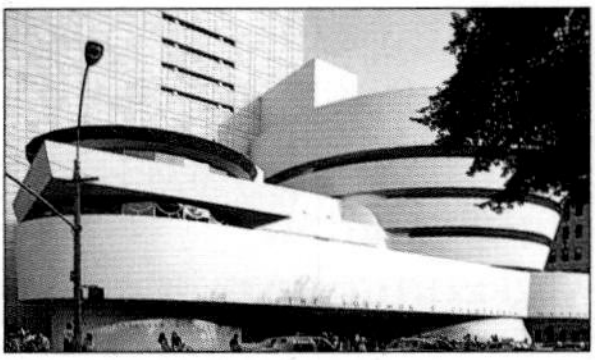

Fifth Avenue facade

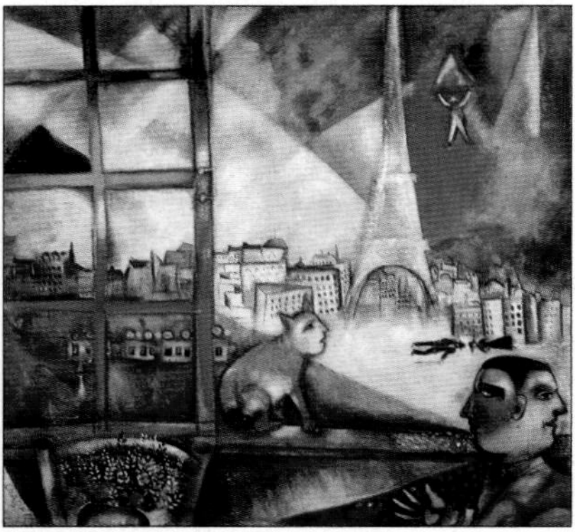

Paris Through the Window
The vibrant colours of Marc Chagall's 1913 masterpiece shine out from the canvas, conjuring up images of a magical and mysterious city where nothing is quite what it appears to be.

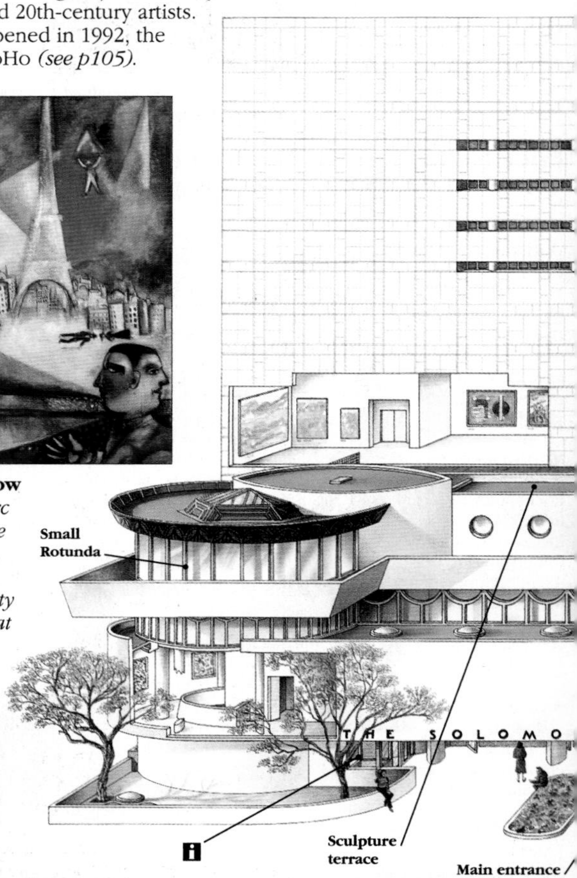
Small Rotunda
THE SOLOMO
[i]
Sculpture terrace
Main entrance

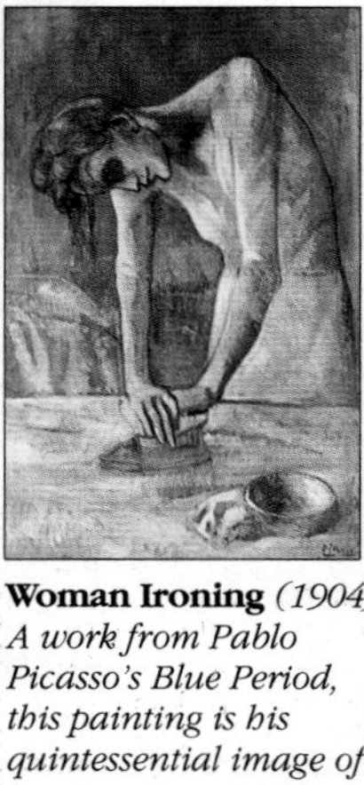

Woman Ironing *(1904)*
A work from Pablo Picasso's Blue Period, this painting is his quintessential image of hard work and fatigue.

Yellow Cow *(1911)*
Franz Marc's work was influenced by a German back-to-nature movement.

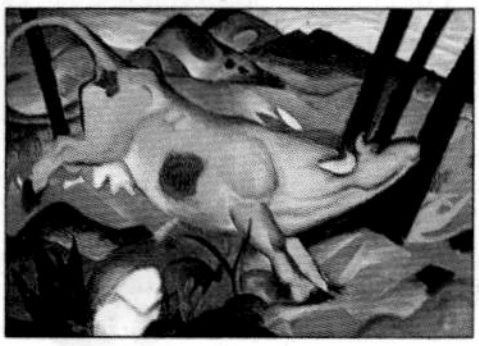

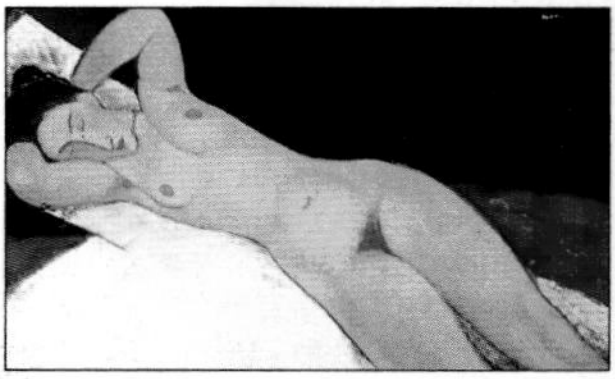

Nude *(1917)*
This sleeping figure is typical of Amedeo Modigliani's stylized work.

MUSEUM GUIDE

The Great Rotunda features special exhibitions. The Small Rotunda shows some of the museum's celebrated Impressionist and Post-Impressionist holdings. The new Tower galleries feature exhibitions of work from the permanent collection as well as contemporary pieces. A fifth-floor sculpture terrace overlooks Central Park. Not all of the collection is on show at any one time.

Tower

Great Rotunda

Before the Mirror *(1876)*
In trying to capture the flavour of 19th-century society, Edouard Manet often used the image of the courtesan.

VISITORS' CHECKLIST

1071 5th Ave at 89th St.
Map 16 F3. ☎ 423-3500.
Ⓜ 4, 5, 6 to 86th St. 🚌 M1, M2, M3, M4. **Open** 10am–6pm Sun–Wed, 10am–8pm Fri, Sat. **Closed** 25 Dec, 1 Jan. **Adm charge.** 📷 ♿ 🎭 **Concerts, lectures, performing art series.** 💻 📱

Woman Holding a Vase
Fernand Léger incorporated elements of Cubism into this work from 1927.

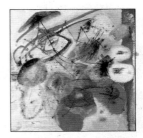

Black Lines *(1913) This is one of Vasily Kandinsky's earliest examples of his work in "non-objective" art.*

Woman with Yellow Hair
(1931) The gentle, voluptuous figure of Picasso's mistress often appears in his work.

FRANK LLOYD WRIGHT

During his lifetime, Wright was considered the great innovator of American architecture. Characteristic of his work are "prairie" style residences, and office buildings of concrete slabs, glass bricks and tubing. Wright received the Guggenheim commission in 1942, and was completed shortly after his death in 1959. It is his only New York building.

Interior of the Guggenheim's Great Rotunda

Metropolitan Museum of Art ❻

OUNDED IN 1870 by a group of artists and philanthropists who wanted an arts institution to rival those of Europe, this collection is thought to be the most comprehensive in the Western world. Works date from prehistoric times through to the present day. It moved to its current site in 1880 and houses collections from all continents, including ancient Egyptian art and American sculpture and decorative art since Colonial times.

The entrance of the Metropolitan Museum of Art

★ **Gertrude Stein** (1905–6)
This portrait of the American writer Gertrude Stein is by Pablo Picasso. The mask-like face shows his debt to African and Roman art.

Robert Lehman Collection

Pendant Mask
The kingdom of Benin (now part of Nigeria) was renowned for its art. This mask was made in the 16th century.

Seated Man with Harp
This statuette was made in the Cyclades c.3,000 BC.

Lower Floor

GALLERY GUIDE

Most of the collections are housed on the two main floors. Works from 19 curatorial areas are in the permanent galleries, with designated galleries for temporary exhibitions. Central on the first and second floors are European painting, sculpture and decorative art. Other collections can be found radiating out from the centre on both levels.

The Marriage Feast at Cana
This rare 16th-century panel painting by Juan de Flandes is part of the Linsky Collection

Bust of Diderot (1773)
Jean Antoine Houdon's bust was made for a Russian count.

★ **Portrait of the Princesse de Broglie**
This portrait, painted in 1853, was J A D Ingres' last.

First floor

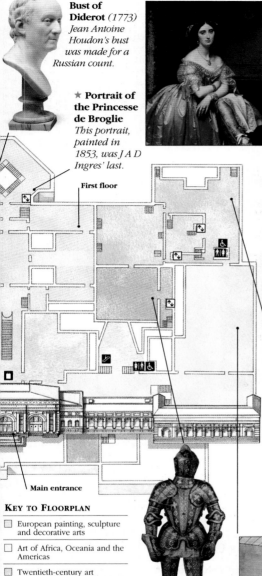

Main entrance

Tiffany Columns (c.1905)
The ornate columns are all that remain of Louis Comfort Tiffany's house in Oyster Bay.

STAR EXHIBITS

★ **Temple of Dendur**

★ **Portrait of the Princesse de Broglie by Ingres**

★ **Gertrude Stein by Pablo Picasso**

KEY TO FLOORPLAN

☐ European painting, sculpture and decorative arts
☐ Art of Africa, Oceania and the Americas
☐ Twentieth-century art
☐ American art
☐ Egyptian art
☐ Greek and Roman art
☐ Medieval art
☐ Arms and armour
☐ Costume Institute
☐ Special exhibitions
☐ Non-exhibition space

English Armour
This was made for George Clifford around 1580.

★ **Temple of Dendur** (15 BC)
The Roman emperor Augustus built this three-room temple. He is shown making offerings in its reliefs.

Metropolitan Museum of Art: Upper Levels

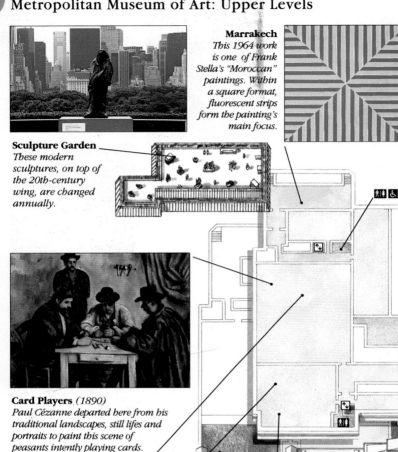

Marrakech
This 1964 work is one of Frank Stella's "Moroccan" paintings. Within a square format, fluorescent strips form the painting's main focus.

Sculpture Garden
These modern sculptures, on top of the 20th-century wing, are changed annually.

Card Players *(1890)*
Paul Cézanne departed here from his traditional landscapes, still lifes and portraits to paint this scene of peasants intently playing cards.

Islamic art

Second floor

First floor

★ **Cypresses** *(1889)*
Vincent Van Gogh painted this the year before he died. The heavy brushstrokes and the swirling style mark his late work.

STAR EXHIBITS

★ **Self-Portrait of 1660 by Rembrandt**

★ **George Washington Crossing the Delaware by Leutze**

★ **Cypresses by Vincent Van Gogh**

★ **Diptych by Jan van Eyck**

Eagle-Headed Winged Being Pollinating the Sacred Tree *(about 900 BC)*
This relief comes from an Assyrian palace.

★Diptych
(1425–30)
Flemish painter
Jan van Eyck was
one of the earliest
masters of oil
painting. These
scenes, of the
Crucifixion and
Last Judgment,
show him to be
a forerunner of
realism, too.

★ Washington Crossing the Delaware
In 1851 Emanuel Gottlieb Leutze painted
this romanticized – and inaccurate –
view of the famous crossing.

KEY TO FLOORPLAN

☐ European painting, sculpture and decorative arts

☐ Ancient Near Eastern and Islamic art

☐ Twentieth-century art

☐ American art

☐ Asian art

☐ Greek and Roman art

☐ Musical instruments

☐ Drawings, prints and photographs

☐ Special exhibitions

▨ Non-exhibition space

Astor Court

The Death of Socrates *(1787)*
Jacques Louis David shows
Socrates about to take poison,
rather than renounce his beliefs.

★ Self-Portrait *(1660)*
Rembrandt painted almost
100 self-portraits. This one
shows him at the age of 54.

THE ASTOR COURT

In 1979, 27 crafts-people from China, responsible for the care of Souzhou's historic gardens, came to New York to replicate a Ming-style scholar's garden in the Metropolitan Museum. They used centuries-old techniques and handmade tools that had been passed down for generations. It was the first cultural exchange between the United States and the People's Republic of China. The result is a quiet garden for meditation, a Western parallel to Souzhou's Garden of the Master of the Fishing Nets.

Exploring the Metropolitan

THE TREASURES OF "THE MET" include a vast collection of American art and more than 3,000 European paintings, including masterpieces by Rembrandt and Vermeer. There are also many Islamic exhibits, and the greatest collection of Egyptian art outside Cairo.

Mysterious in identity and origin, a rare 5,000-year-old copper head from the Near East

AFRICA, OCEANIA AND THE AMERICAS

A painted gold funerary mask (10th–14th century) from the necropolis of Batán Grande, Peru

NELSON ROCKEFELLER built the Michael C Rockefeller Wing in 1982 in memory of his son, who lost his life on an art-finding expedition in New Guinea. The wing showcases a superb collection of over 2,000 objects from Africa, the islands of the Pacific and the Americas.

Among the African works, the ivory and bronze sculptures from the royal kingdom of Benin (Nigeria) are outstanding as is the wooden sculpture by the Dogon, Bamana and Senufo peoples of Mali. From the Pacific come carvings by the Asmat people of New Guinea and decorations and masks from the Melanesian and Polynesian islands. From Mexico, Central and South America come pre-Columbian gold, ceramics and stonework. The wing also contains fine Native American artefacts by the Inuit and other groups.

AMERICAN ART

GILBERT STUART'S first portrait of George Washington, George Caleb Bingham's *Fur Traders Descending the Missouri*, John Singer Sargent's notorious portrait of *Madame X* and the monumental *George Washington Crossing the*

Delaware by Emanuel Leutze are among the icons of the American Wing. It holds one of the world's finest collections of American painting, including several works by Edward Hopper, and sculpture and decorative arts from colonial times to this century.

Period rooms, with original woodwork and furnishings, range from the saloon hall in which George Washington celebrated his last birthday, to the elegant prairie-style living room from the Little house in Minnesota, designed by Frank Lloyd Wright in 1912.

Engelhard Court is an indoor sculpture garden with large-scale architectural elements, including the lovely stained-glass and mosaic loggia from Louis Comfort Tiffany's Long Island estate and the facade of an 1824 United States Branch Bank that stood on Wall Street.

The Lighthouse at Two Lights (1929) by Edward Hopper

ANCIENT NEAR EASTERN AND ISLAMIC ART

MASSIVE STONE SCULPTURES of human-headed winged lions, once guardians of the 9th-century BC Assyrian

palace of Assurnasirpal II, sit at the entrance to the Ancient Near Eastern galleries. Inside is a collection spanning 7,000 years, rich in Iranian bronzes, Anatolian ivories, Sumerian sculptures, and Achaemenian and Sassanian works in silver and gold. An adjacent gallery area displays the diversity of Islamic art from the 7th to the 19th centuries: glass and metalwork from Egypt, Syria and Mesopotamia; royal miniatures from the courts of Persia and Mughal India; rugs of the 16th and 17th centuries; and an 18th-century room from Syria.

ARMS AND ARMOUR

MOUNTED KNIGHTS in full armour charge at each other across the equestrian court here. These galleries are a favourite with children and anyone moved by medieval romance or thrilled by power.

There are suits of armour, rapiers and sabres with hilts of precious stones and gold, firearms inlaid with ivory and mother-of-pearl, and colourful heraldic banners and shields.

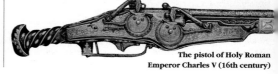

The pistol of Holy Roman Emperor Charles V (16th century)

Highlights include the armour of gentleman-pirate George Clifford, a favourite of Queen Elizabeth I. The rainbow-coloured armour of a 14th-century Japanese shogun and a collection of Wild West revolvers that once belonged to gun-maker Samuel Colt are also exhibited here.

ORIENTAL AND ASIAN ART

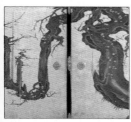

The Old Plum, a Japanese paper screen from the early Edo period (about 1650)

A SERIES of outstanding galleries contains master-pieces of Chinese, Japanese, Korean, Indian and Southeast Asian art, dating from the second millennium BC to the 20th century. A full-scale Ming-style Chinese scholar's garden was built by craftsmen from Souzhou as part of the first cultural exchange between the US and the People's Republic of China. The museum also has one of the finest collections of Sung and Yuan paintings in the world, Chinese Buddhist monumental sculptures, fine Chinese ceramics and jade and an important display of the arts of ancient China.

The full range of Japanese arts is represented in a breath-taking suite of ten galleries featuring chronological and thematic displays of Japanese lacquer, ceramics, painting, sculpture, textiles and screens. Indian, Southeast Asian and Korean galleries display superb sculptures and other arts from these regions.

COSTUME INSTITUTE

THERE IS ALWAYS a portion of the 45,000-piece collection of costumes, dating from the 17th century to the present, on display in new, state-of-the-art galleries. Here, the Institute maintains a definitive compendium of fashionable dress, from the elaborately embroidered dresses of the late 1600s to the shocking pink evening dresses of Elsa Schiaparelli, complete with hats, scarves, gloves, hand-bags and other accessories. There are also the designs of Worth, Quant and Balenciaga, as well as gowns from the Napoleonic and Victorian eras, the costumes of the Ballets Russes and even David Bowie's sequinned jockstrap.

The regional portion of the collection is rich with folk costumes from Europe, Asia, Africa and the Americas.

The Institute is so sophisticated in its understanding of conservation techniques that it has been called upon to advise NASA on the cleaning of astronauts' spacesuits.

A 17th-century European silk and satin doublet

DRAWINGS, PRINTS AND PHOTOGRAPHS

A NEW GALLERY puts on regular view selections from the museum's incredible holdings of drawings, prints, etchings and photographs.

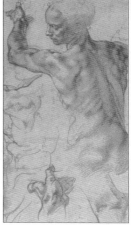

Michelangelo's studies of a Libyan Sibyl for the ceiling of the Sistine Chapel (1508)

The drawings collection is especially rich in Italian and French art from the 15th to 19th centuries. The works are exhibited on a rotating basis because of the light-sensitive nature of works on paper.

Highlights among the 4,000 drawings include works by Michelangelo, Leonardo da Vinci, Raphael, Ingres, Goya, Rubens, Rembrandt, Tiepolo and Seurat.

The encyclopedic print collection of 12,000 individual images (and almost the same number of illustrated books) includes major works by virtually every master printmaker, from an early German woodcut called *Virgin and Child* to some of Dürer's most accomplished works and Goya's *The Giant*. Influential gallery-owner Alfred Stieglitz's donation of his own extensive collection of photographs brought such gems as Edward Steichen's *The Flatiron* to the museum. It formed the core of a photography collection that is now also particularly strong in Modernist works dating from between the World Wars.

Ephemera such as posters and advertisements form another part of this collection.

EGYPTIAN ART

ONE OF THE MUSEUM'S finest
and best-loved areas is
the ancient Egyptian wing,
which displays every one of its
thousands of holdings, from
the prehistoric period to the
8th century AD. Objects range
from the fragmented jasper
lips of a 15th-century BC
queen to the massive Temple
of Dendur. Other amazing
archaeological finds, most of
them from museum-sponsored
expeditions undertaken early
in the 20th century, include
sculptures of the notorious
Queen Hatshepsut, who seized
the Theban throne in the 16th
century BC, 100 carved reliefs
of Amenhotpe IV's reign and
tomb figures like the blue
faïence hippo that has become
the museum's mascot.

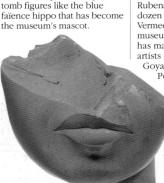

**Queen Tiye, wife of
Amenhotpe III (1417–1379 BC)**

EUROPEAN PAINTINGS, SCULPTURE AND DECORATIVE ARTS

THE HEART of the museum is
its awe-inspiring collection
of 3,000 European paintings.
The Italian works include

*Young Woman with a Water Jug
(1660) by Jan Vermeer*

Botticelli's *Last Communion
of Saint Jerome* and Bronzino's
Portrait of a Young Man. The
Dutch and Flemish canvases
are among the finest in the
world, with Brueghel's *The
Harvesters*, several works by
Rubens and Van Dyck, over a
dozen Rembrandts and more
Vermeers than any other
museum. The collection also
has masterpieces by Spanish
artists El Greco, Velázquez and
Goya, and by French artists
Poussin and Watteau.
Some of the finest
Impressionist and
Post-Impressionist
canvases reside
here: 30 Monets
including *Terrace at
Sainte-Adresse*, 17
Cézannes, and Van
Gogh's *Cypresses*.
In the Kravis wing
and adjacent galleries
are works from the
60,000-object collection of
European sculpture and
decorative arts, such as Tullio
Lombardo's marble statue of
Adam; a bronze statuette of a
rearing horse, after a model
by Leonardo; and dozens of
pieces by Degas and Rodin.
Period settings include the
patio from a 16th-century

Spanish castle and a series of
ornate 18th-century French
domestic interiors known as
the Wrightsman Rooms. The
Petrie European Sculpture
Court features French and
Italian sculpture in a beautiful
garden setting reminiscent of
Versailles in France.

GREEK AND ROMAN ART

A ROMAN SARCOPHAGUS from
Tarsus, donated in 1870,
was the very first work of art
in the Met's collections. It can
still be seen in the museum's
Greek and Roman galleries,
along with the breathtaking
wall panels from a villa that
was buried under the lava of
Vesuvius in AD 79, Etruscan
mirrors, Roman portrait busts,
exquisite objects in glass and
silver and hundreds of Greek
vases. A monumental 7th-
century-BC statue of a youth
shows the movement towards
naturalism in sculpture, and
the Hellenistic *Old Market
Woman* demonstrates how the
Greeks had mastered realism
by the 2nd century BC.

**An amphora by Exekias, showing
a wedding (6th century BC)**

LEHMAN COLLECTION

WHAT HAD BEEN one of the
the finest private art
collections in the world, that
of investment banker Robert
Lehman, came to the museum
in 1971. The Lehman Wing is
a dramatic glass pyramid
housing an extraordinarily
varied collection rich in Old
Masters and 19th-century
French paintings, drawings,

EGYPTIAN TOMB MODELS

In 1920, a Met researcher's torchbeam lit a room, hitherto
undiscovered for 2,000 years, in the tomb of the
nobleman Mekutra. Within were 23 tiny, perfect
replicas of his daily life, to
ensure his comfort in
the next world – his
house and garden,
fleet of ships and herd
of cattle. Mekutra himself is
there, too, on his boat, inhaling a
lotus bud and enjoying the music of his singer and harpist.

A panel from the stained-glass *Death of the Virgin* window, from the 12th-century cathedral of Saint-Pierre in Troyes, France

bronzes, Renaissance majolica, Venetian glass, furniture and enamels. Among the canvases are works by north European masters: Dutch and Spanish paintings, French masterworks, Post-Impressionists and Fauves.

MEDIEVAL ART

THE METROPOLITAN'S medieval collection includes works dating from the 4th to 16th centuries, roughly from the fall of Rome to the beginning of the Renaissance. It is split between the main museum and its uptown branch, the Cloisters *(see pp234–7)*. In the main building are a chalice once thought to be the Holy Grail, six silver Byzantine plates showing scenes from the life of David, a 1301 pulpit by Giovanni Pisano in the shape of an eagle, several monumental sculptures of the Virgin and Child, and a huge choir screen from Spain. Other exhibits include Migration jewellery, liturgical vessels, stained glass, enamels, ivories and 14th- and 15-century tapestries.

MUSICAL INSTRUMENTS

THE WORLD'S OLDEST piano, Andrés Segovia's guitars and a sitar shaped like a peacock are some of the features of a broad and sometimes quirky collection of musical instruments which spans six continents and dates from prehistory to the present. The instruments illustrate the history of music and performance, and most of them are conserved to remain in playable condition. Worth particular mention are instruments from the European courts of the Middle Ages and the Renaissance, rare violins, spinets and harpsichords, instruments inlaid with precious materials and a fully equipped traditional violin-maker's workshop, as well as African drums, Asian *pi-pas* or lutes and Native American pipes. Visitors can use audio equipment to hear many of the instruments playing the music of their day.

Stradivari violin from Cremona, Italy (1691)

TWENTIETH-CENTURY ART

SINCE ITS FOUNDATION in 1870, the museum has been acquiring contemporary art, but it was not until 1987 that a permanent home for 20th-century art was built – the Lila Acheson Wallace Wing. Other museums in New York have larger collections of modern art, but this display space is considered among the finest. European and American works from 1900 onwards are on view on three levels, starting with Europeans such as Picasso, Kandinsky and Bonnard. The collection's greatest strength lies in its collection of modern American art, with works by New York school "The Eight", including John Sloan, Modernists such as Charles Demuth and Georgia O'Keeffe, American Regionalist Grant Wood, Abstract Expressionist Willem de Kooning and Color Field painters such as Clyfford Still.

Grant Wood's view of *The Midnight Ride of Paul Revere* (1931)

Special areas house Art Nouveau and Art Deco furniture and metalwork, a large collection of works on paper by Paul Klee, and the Sculpture Gallery with its large-scale sculptures and canvases.

Gems of the collection include Picasso's portrait of Gertrude Stein, Matisse's *Nasturtiums and "Dance"*, Demuth's *I Saw the Figure 5 in Gold*, Jackson Pollock's *Autumn Rhythm*, and Andy Warhol's last self-portrait.

Each year the Cantor Roof Garden at the top of the wing features a new installation of contemporary sculpture that is all the more striking when viewed against the dramatic backdrop of the New York skyline and Central Park.

Book cover (1916) by illustrator N C Wyeth

Society of Illustrators **⑫**

128 E 63rd St. **Map** 13 A2. **☎** *838-2560.* **M** *Lexington Ave.* **Open** *10am–5pm Wed–Fri, 10am–8pm Tue, noon–4pm Sat.* 🖼 🚻 *restricted.* 🎬 🚻

ESTABLISHED IN 1901, this society was formed to promote the illustrator's art. Its notable roster included Charles Dana Gibson, N C Wyeth and Howard Pyle. It was at first concerned with education and public service, and held occasional exhibits. In 1981, the Museum of American Illustration opened in two galleries. Changing thematic exhibitions show the history of book and magazine illustration, with an annual exhibition of the year's finest American illustrations.

Abigail Adams Smith Museum **⑬**

421 E 61st St. **Map** 13 C3. **☎** *838-6878.* **M** *Lexington Ave, 59th St.* **Open** *11am–4pm Tue–Sun.* **Closed** *Aug, public hol.* **Adm charge.** 🚫 🎬 🚻

BUILT IN 1799, this federal-style stone stable once belonged to Abigail Adams Smith, President John Adams's daughter. The house burnt down in 1826; the stable

was renovated as an inn, then as a home and, later, as a shop selling colonial antiques.

It was acquired by the Colonial Dames of America in 1924 and turned into a charming re-creation of a Federal home. Costumed guides show visitors through the rooms, pointing out the treasures, including Chinese porcelain, Aubusson carpets, Sheraton chests and a Duncan Phyfe sofa. In one bedroom, a gown belonging to Abigail Adams Smith is stored in an antique wardrobe; the same room holds a baby's cradle and children's toys. An 18th-century-style garden has been planted around the house.

Henderson Place **⑭**

Map 18 D3. **M** *86th St.*

Queen Anne row houses at Henderson Place

NOW SURROUNDED by modern apartment blocks, this enclave of 24 red brick Queen Anne row houses was built in 1882. The row houses were commissioned by John C Henderson, a hat maker, as a self-contained community. The elegant Lamb & Rich design has grey slate roof gables, pediments, parapets, chimneys and dormer windows forming patterns, and a turret marks the corner of each block.

Carl Schurz Park promenade

Carl Schurz Park **⑮**

Map 18 D3. **M** *86th St.*

LAID OUT IN 1891, this park along the East River has a wide promenade over the East River Drive. It offers fine vistas of the river and the turbulent waters of Hell Gate, where the river meets Long Island Sound. It is named after Carl Schurz, a local who became Secretary of the Interior (1869–75). The first part of the promenade is the John Finlay Walk, named after an editor of the *New York Times* who was known for his hiking prowess. One of the city's most pleasant green escapes, the park's grassy areas are filled with basking New Yorkers on sunny days.

Gracie Mansion **⑯**

East End Ave at 88th St. **Map** 18 D3. **☎** *570-4751.* **M** *86th St.* **Open** *Mar–mid-Nov 10am–2pm Wed for pre-booked guided tours only.* **Adm charge.** 🚫 🚻 🚻

THIS GRACIOUS, balconied wooden 1799 country home is the official mayor's residence. Built by wealthy merchant Archibald Gracie, it is one of the best Federal houses left in New York.

The house was acquired by the city in 1887 and was the first home of the Museum of the City of New York. Mayor Fiorello LaGuardia moved in in 1942 after nine years in

Front view of Gracie Mansion

office, in preference to a 75-room palace on Riverside Drive – he said that even the more modest Gracie Mansion was much too fancy for him. LaGuardia, "The Little Flower" (from Fiorello), fought corruption in the city and reformed New York.

Church of the Holy Trinity ⑰

316 E 88th St. **Map** 17 B3.
📞 289-4100. Ⓜ 86th St. **Open** 9am–5pm Mon–Fri, 7.30am–2pm Sun. ✝ winter: 8.15am, 9.15am, 11am, 7pm Sun; summer: 8.15am, 10am.

Arched doorway of the Church of the Holy Trinity

D ELIGHTFULLY PLACED in a serene garden setting, this church was constructed in 1889 of glowing golden brick and terracotta in French Renaissance style. It boasts one of New York's best bell towers, which sports a handsome wrought-iron clock with brass hands. The arched doorway is richly decorated with carved images of the saints and prophets.

The complex was donated by Serena Rhinelander in memory of her father and grandfather. The land was part of the Rhinelander farm, which the family had owned for 100 years.

Further down the block at No. 350 is the Rhinelander Children's Center, also a gift, and the headquarters of the Children's Aid Society.

St Nicholas Russian Orthodox Cathedral ⑱

15 E 97th St. **Map** 16 F1.
📞 289-1915. Ⓜ 96 St. **Open** by appt. ✝ 6pm Sat, 10.00am Sun (Russian). 📷

T HIS REALLY IS "Moscow on the Hudson". Built in Muscovite Baroque style in 1902, it has five onion domes crowned with crosses, and blue and yellow tiles on a red brick and white stone facade. Among the early worshippers were White Russians who had fled the first uprisings at home, mostly intellectuals and aristocrats who soon became a part of New York society. Later, there were more waves of refugees, dissidents and defectors.

The cathedral now serves a scattered community, and the congregation is small. Mass is celebrated in Russian with great pomp and dignity.

The cathedral is filled with the scent of incense. The high central sanctuary has marble columns with blue and white trim above. Ornate wooden screens trimmed with gold enclose the altar. It is unique, an unexpected find on a side street in this staid part of Manhattan.

Facade and domes of St Nicholas Russian Cathedral

Facade of the Museum of the City of New York

Museum of the City of New York ⑲

5th Ave at 103rd St. **Map** 21 C5.
📞 534-1672. Ⓜ 103rd St. **Open** 10am–5pm Wed–Sat, 1pm–5pm Sun. **Closed** public hols. **Donations welcome.** 📷 ♿ 🖊 📱

F OUNDED IN 1923 and at first housed in Gracie Mansion, this museum is dedicated to New York's development from its earliest beginnings, shown in costumes, paintings, furnishings, toys and a range of fascinating memorabilia.

Housed in this handsome Georgian Colonial building since 1932, it is noted for the period rooms from actual homes, including John D Rockefeller's bedroom and dressing room, and for its wonderful collection of toys, dolls and doll's houses dating from 1769. Start with *The Big Apple* video, then visit the exhibition, "Broadway! 125 Years of Musical Theater". The second floor has a magnificent collection of silver objects dating from 1678 to 1984. The Alexander Hamilton Gallery contains furniture and paintings that once belonged to the first Secretary of the Treasury.

The impressive collection housed in the basement includes antique fire equipment, paintings, maps and prints all relating to city history.

Whitney Museum of American Art **❼**

T HE WHITNEY MUSEUM is the foremost
showcase for American art of this
century. It was founded in 1930 by sculptress Gertrude Vanderbilt Whitney after the
Metropolitan Museum of Art turned down
her collection of works by living artists
including George Bellows and Edward
Hopper. In 1966 the museum moved to
the present inverted pyramid designed
by Marcel Breuer. The Whitney Biennial
show of new work is the most significant
survey of new trends in American art.

The overhanging facade of the Whitney Museum

Green Coca-Cola Bottles
Andy Warhol's 1962 work reflects blandly upon mass-production, abundance and monopoly.

The White Calico Flower
Georgia O'Keeffe's enlarged flower paintings take on an abstract quality, as in this work from 1931.

Little Big Painting
The 1965 work by Roy Lichtenstein is a comic critique of Abstract Expressionist painting.

Early Sunday Morning *(1930)*
Edward Hopper's paintings often convey the emptiness of American city life.

MUSEUM GUIDE
There are no permanent displays here; the only item always on show is Alexander Calder's sculpture Circus, *situated on the first floor. Changing exhibitions occupy the second, third and fourth floors.*

Dempsey and Firpo
In 1924, George Bellows depicted one of the most famous prizefights of the century.

Three Flags (1958)
Jasper Johns's use of familiar objects in an abstract form was influential in the development of Pop Art.

Owh! In San Paõ (1951)
In this painting by Stuart Davis, abstract forms are combined with lettering to create a unique and distinctive American style.

Circus (1926–31)
Alexander Calder's fanciful creation is always on display.

Tango (1919)
This is considered Polish-born Elie Nadelman's greatest wood sculpture.

Hudson River Landscape (1951)
This steel sculpture is one of David Smith's most influential works.

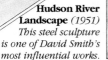

Frick Collection ⑧

THE PRICELESS ART collection of steel magnate Henry Clay Frick (1849–1919) is exhibited in a residential setting, amid the furnishings of his opulent mansion, providing a rare glimpse of how the extremely wealthy lived in New York's gilded age. Frick intended the collection to be a memorial to himself and bequeathed the entire house to the nation on his death. The collection includes old master paintings, French furniture, Limoges enamels and Oriental rugs.

Fifth Avenue facade of the Frick Collection

Colonnade Garden Court

The Harbour of Dieppe *(1826)*
J M W Turner was criticized by some sceptical contemporaries for depicting this northern European port suffused with light.

The White Horse *(1819)*
John Constable based this painting on a familiar scene from his Suffolk home.

Library

West Gallery

Limoges Enamel
The collection of enamels includes The Seven Sorrows of the Virgin *(1500–50).*

STAR PAINTINGS

★ **Sir Thomas More by Hans Holbein**

★ **Mall in St James's Park by Thomas Gainsborough**

★ **Officer and the Laughing Girl by Jan Vermeer**

★ **Lady Meux by James A M Whistler**

★ **Sir Thomas More** *(1527)*
Holbein's portrait of Henry VIII's Lord Chancellor was painted eight years before More's execution for treason.

Living Hall

GALLERY GUIDE
Of special interest are the skylit West Gallery, offering oils by Vermeer, Hals and Rembrandt; the East Gallery, featuring Whistler; the Library and Dining Room, devoted to English works; and the Living Hall with works by Titian, Bellini and Holbein.

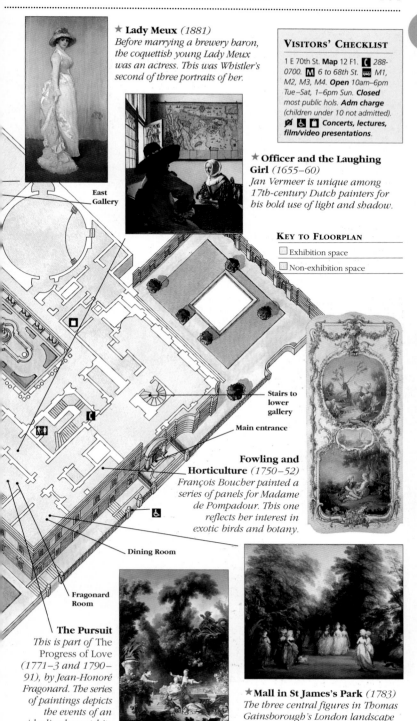

★ **Lady Meux** (1881)
Before marrying a brewery baron, the coquettish young Lady Meux was an actress. This was Whistler's second of three portraits of her.

East Gallery

★ **Officer and the Laughing Girl** (1655–60)
Jan Vermeer is unique among 17th-century Dutch painters for his bold use of light and shadow.

KEY TO FLOORPLAN

☐ Exhibition space
☐ Non-exhibition space

Stairs to lower gallery

Main entrance

Fowling and Horticulture (1750–52)
François Boucher painted a series of panels for Madame de Pompadour. This one reflects her interest in exotic birds and botany.

Dining Room

Fragonard Room

The Pursuit
This is part of The Progress of Love (1771–3 and 1790–91), by Jean-Honoré Fragonard. The series of paintings depicts the events of an idealized courtship.

★ **Mall in St James's Park** (1783)
The three central figures in Thomas Gainsborough's London landscape may be the daughters of George III.

CENTRAL PARK

THE CITY'S "BACK YARD" was created by Frederick Law Olmsted and Calvert Vaux in 1858 on an unpromising site – a mess of quarries, pig farms, swampland and squatters' shacks. Ten million cartloads of stone and earth turned this quagmire into a man-made 843-acre (340-ha) "natural" landscape. There are hills, lakes and meadows,

Statues, Delacorte Theater (see p206)

dotted with outcrops of Manhattan bedrock and planted with more than 500,000 trees and shrubs. Designed for scenic enjoyment, over the years the park has blossomed with playgrounds, skating rinks, tennis courts, ball fields and spaces for all kinds of games, from chess to croquet. Cars are banned at weekends, giving cyclists and joggers the right-of-way.

SIGHTS AT A GLANCE

Historic Buildings
The Dairy ❶
Belvedere Castle ❸

Monuments and Statues
Strawberry Fields ❷
Bethesda Fountain and Terrace ❺
Bow Bridge ❹

Lakes and Gardens
Conservatory Water ❻
Central Park Wildlife
Conservation Center ❼
Conservatory Garden ❽

SEE ALSO

• **Street Finder**, maps 12, 16

• **Restaurants** pp290–92

GETTING THERE

Subway lines B and C run the length of the park on the west side, with stops at 59th, 72nd, 81st, 86th, 96th and 103rd Sts. The 59th St/Columbus Circle stop is also served by the 1 and 9 Broadway/7th Ave lines, and the N and R Broadway local trains stop at 57th St and 5th Ave at the southern end of the park. Bus routes M1, M2, M3 and M4 run along the eastern edge of the park.

One of Central Park's mounted patrolmen

KEY

◻ Tour map

Ⓜ Subway station

0 metres   500
0 yards   500

Bird's-eye view of the park

A Tour of Central Park

O N A SHORT VISIT, a walking tour from 59th to 79th Streets takes in many of Central Park's loveliest features, from the dense, wooded Ramble to the open, formal spaces of Bethesda Terrace. Along the way, you will see man-made lakes and some of the 30 graceful bridges and arches, no two alike, that link some 58 miles (93 km) of footpaths, bridle paths and carriage drives in the park. A haven in summer, the park is several degrees cooler than the city streets around it.

★ **Strawberry Fields**
One of the park's most visited spots, this peaceful area was created in memory of John Lennon, who lived nearby ❷

★ **Bethesda Fountain and Terrace**
The richly-ornamented formal terrace overlooks the Lake and the wooded shores of the Ramble ❺

Wollman Rink was restored in the 1980s for future generations of skaters, by tycoon Donald Trump.

Central Park Wildlife Conservation Center
Three climate zones are home to over 100 species of animal ❼

The Pond

Plaza Hotel (see p179)

Frick Collection (see pp200–1)

Hans Christian Andersen's statue is a favourite Central Park landmark for children. It is situated on the west side of Conservatory Water, and is a venue for storytelling sessions in the summer.

★ **The Dairy**
This Victorian Gothic building houses the Visitor Center. Make it your first stop, to pick up a calendar of park events ❶

Bow Bridge
This cast-iron bridge links the Ramble with Cherry Hill via a graceful arch, 60 ft (18 m) above the Lake ❹

LOCATOR MAP
See Manhattan Map pp12–13

Alice in Wonderland is immortalized in bronze at the northern end of Conservatory Water with her friends, including the Cheshire Cat, the Mad Hatter and the Dormouse. Children love to climb up and slide down her toad-stool seat.

STAR SIGHTS

★ **The Dairy**

★ **Strawberry Fields**

★ **Belvedere Castle**

★ **Bethesda Fountain**

★ **Conservatory Water**

kota lding e p216)

San Remo Apartments
(see p212)

American Museum of Natural History
(see pp214–15)

E S T

Belvedere Castle

Metropolitan Museum *(see pp190–95)*

Obelisk

The Ramble is a wooded stretch of 37 acres (15 ha), criss-crossed by paths and streams. It is a paradise for birdwatchers – over 250 species have been spotted in the park, which is on the Atlantic migration flightpath.

Reservoir

Guggenheim Museum
(see pp186–7)

★ **Belvedere Castle**
From the terraces, visitors have unequalled views of the city and surrounding park. Within the stone walls is the Central Park Learning Center ❸

★ **Conservatory Water**
From March to November, this is the scene of model boat races each Saturday. Many of the tiny craft are stored in the boathouse that adjoins the lake ❻

The Carousel, part of the park's Children's Department

The Dairy ❶

Map 12 F2. 🕻 794-6564.
Ⓜ 5th Ave. **Open** Mar–Nov: 11am–5pm Tue–Sun (1pm–5pm Fri); Nov–Mar: 11am–4pm Tue–Sun (1pm–4pm Fri). **Slide show.** 🖬

NOW USED AS the park information centre, this charming building of natural stone was planned as part of the "Children's Department" of the park, which included a playground, the Carousel, a Children's Cottage and stable. In 1873, there were cows grazing on the meadows in front of the Dairy, a ewe and her lambs feeding nearby, and chickens, guinea fowl and peacocks roaming the lawn. City children could get fresh milk and other refreshments here. Over the years, the Dairy deteriorated, being

used as a shed until restoration in 1979, which followed original photographs and drawings. The Dairy is the best place to begin exploring the park, as maps and details of activities events can be obtained here. The less energetic can hire chess and checkers sets for use on the charming inlaid boards of the *kinderberg*, the pretty little "children's hill" nearby.

Strawberry Fields ❷

Map 12 E1. Ⓜ 72nd St.

THE RESTORATION of this teardrop-shaped section of the park was Yoko Ono's tribute in memory of her slain husband, John Lennon. They lived in the Dakota Building overlooking this spot *(see p216)*. Gifts for the garden came from all over the world. A mosaic set in the pathway, inscribed with the word *Imagine* (Lennon's most famous song), was a gift from the city of Naples in Italy.

This stretch of the park's landscape was designed by Vaux and Olmsted as a broad expanse. Now it is an international peace garden planted with 161 species of plant (one from every country of the world), with jetbread, witch hazel, roses, birches – and strawberries.

Belvedere Castle ❸

Map 16 E4. 🕻 772-0210.
Ⓜ 81st St. **Open** 11am–4pm Wed, Thu; 1–4pm Fri; 11am–5pm Sat, Sun. 🖬 ♿ to main floor only. 🖬

THIS STONE CASTLE atop Vista Rock, complete with tower and turrets, offers one of the best views of the park and the city from its rooftop lookout. Inside is the Central Park Learning Center, with a delightful Discovery Chamber telling young visitors about the surprising variety of park wildlife.

The view to the north from the castle allows you to look down in to

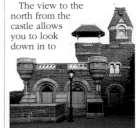

Belvedere Castle with its lookout over the park

the Delacorte Theater, home to the free productions of Shakespeare in the Park every summer, featuring bigname stars *(see p335)*. The theatre was the gift of George T Delacorte. Publisher and founder of Dell paperbacks, he was a philanthropist with a sense of fun, and it is to him that we owe many of the park's pleasures.

Bow Bridge ❹

Map 16 E5. Ⓜ 72nd St.

THIS IS ONE of the park's seven original cast-iron bridges, and is considered one of the finest. It was designed by Vaux as a bow tying together the two large sections of the lake. In the 19th century, when the Lake was used for ice skating, a red ball was hoisted from a bell tower on Vista Rock to signal that the ice was safe. The bridge gives expansive views of the park and the buildings bordering it on both the east and west sides.

A tranquil scene in Central Park, overlooked by exclusive apartments

An 1864 print of Bethesda Fountain and Terrace

Bethesda Fountain and Terrace ❺

Map 12 E1. **Ⓜ** *72nd St.*

Situated between the Lake and the Mall, this is the architectural heart of the park, a formal element in the naturalistic landscape. The fountain was dedicated in 1873. The statue, *Angel of the Waters*, marked the opening of the Croton Aqueduct system in 1842, bringing the city its first supply of pure water; its name refers to a Biblical account of a healing angel at the pool of Bethesda in Jerusalem. The Spanish-style detailing, such as the sculptured double staircase, tiles and friezes, was by Jacob Wrey Mould.

The terrace is one of the best spots to relax and take in some people-watching.

Conservatory Water ❻

Map 16 F5. **Ⓜ** *77th St.*

Better known as the Model Boat Pond, this stretch of water is home to model yacht races every weekend.

At the north end of the lake, a sculpture of Alice in Wonderland is a delight for children. It was commissioned by George T Delacorte in honour of his wife. He himself is immortalized in caricature as the Mad Hatter. On the west bank, free story readings are held at a statue of Hans Christian Andersen, portrayed reading from his own story *The Ugly Duckling* while its hero waddles at his feet. Like that of Alice, this statue is clambered on by small children, who like to snuggle in the author's lap.

Conservatory Water's literary links continue in to adolescence: it is here that J D Salinger's Holden Caulfield comes to tell the ducks his troubles in *The Catcher in the Rye*.

Central Park Wildlife Conservation Center ❼

Map 12 F2. **☎** *439-6500.* **Ⓜ** *5th Ave.* **Open** *Apr–Oct: 10.30am–5pm Mon–Fri, 10am–5.30pm Sat & Sun; Nov–Mar: 10am–4.30pm daily.* **Adm charge**. 📷 ♿ 🖺 🚻

Reopened in 1988 after four years of reconstruction, this imaginative zoo won plaudits for its creative and humane use of small space. More than 100 species of animals are represented in three climate zones, the Tropics, the Polar Circle and the California Coast. An equatorial rainforest is home to monkeys and free-flying birds, while penguins and polar bears populate an Arctic landscape that allows views both above and under water.

Near the entrance to the Children's Zoo next door is the much-loved Delacorte Clock, another example of the whimsical generosity of George T Delacorte. Every half-hour, bronze musical animals (such as a goat playing pan pipes) circle the clock playing nursery rhymes. Towards Willowdell Arch is another children's favourite – the memorial to Balto, lead dog of a team of huskies that made a heroic journey across Alaska to deliver serum for a diphtheria epidemic.

Statue of Balto, the heroic husky sled dog

Conservatory Garden ❽

Map 21 B5. **Ⓜ** *Central Pk N, 103rd St.* **☎** *860-1382.*

The Vanderbilt Gate on Fifth Avenue is the entry to three formal gardens filled with thousands of flowering trees and shrubs. The Central Garden has a large lawn with yew hedges, and ends in a semi-circle of hedges and shrubs crowned by a wisteria pergola. On either side are blooming Siberian crabapple trees. The South Garden spills over with perennials. The bronze statue in the reflecting pool is of Mary and Dickon, from Frances Hodgson Burnett's *The Secret Garden*. Beyond is a slope featuring thousands of native wildflowers, spreading into the park beyond. The North Garden, centred around the bronze *Fountain of the Three Dancing Maidens*, puts on a brief but brilliant display of annuals each summer.

Polar bear in the Wildlife Conservation Center

UPPER WEST SIDE

THIS AREA only became residential in the 1870s, when the Ninth Avenue El *(see pp24-5)* made commuting to midtown possible for the first time. When the Dakota, New York's first luxury apartment house, was built beween 1880 and 1884, the city finally began to grade and level

Indian mask, Museum of Natural History

the streets. Buildings soon sprang up along Broadway and Central Park West. The side streets, dating mainly from the 1890s, boast some fine brownstone row houses. Many cultural institutions can be found here, including Lincoln Center and the American Museum of Natural History.

SIGHTS AT A GLANCE

Historic Streets and Buildings
Twin Towers of Central Park West **1**
The Dakota **9**
Pomander Walk **13**
Riverside Drive and Park **14**
The Dorilton **17**

Museums and Galleries
Museum of American Folk Art **7**
New-York Historical Society **10**
American Museum of Natural History pp214–15 **11**
Hayden Planetarium **12**
Children's Museum of Manhattan **15**

Famous Theatres
Lincoln Center for the Performing Arts **2**
New York State Theater **3**
Metropolitan Opera House **4**
Lincoln Center Theater **5**
Avery Fisher Hall **6**

Landmark Hotels and Restaurants
Hotel des Artistes **8**
Ansonia Hotel **16**

GETTING THERE
By subway take the 7th Ave/Broadway 1, 2 and 3 trains or the 8th Ave A, C and E trains. Buses include the M10 (Central Park West), M7, M11, M104 and M5 or the M66, M72, M79, M86 and M96 crosstown buses.

SEE ALSO

• **Street Finder**, maps 11, 15

• **Where to Stay** pp274–5

• **Restaurants** pp290–92

Stone figure on the facade of the Hotel des Artistes

KEY

▨	Street-by-Street map
Ⓜ	Subway station

0 metres 500
0 yards 500

The facade of No. 14 Riverside Drive

Street-by-Street: Lincoln Center

LINCOLN CENTER was born when both the Metropolitan Opera House and the New York Philharmonic required homes and a large tract on Manhattan's west side was in dire need of revitalization. The notion of a single complex where different performing arts could exist side by side seems natural today, but in the 1950s, it was considered both daring and risky. Today Lincoln Center has proven itself by drawing audiences of five million each year. Proximity to its halls prompts both performers and arts lovers to live nearby.

★ **Lincoln Center for the Performing Arts**
Dance, music and theatre come together in this fine purpose-built complex. It is also a great place to sit around the reflecting fountain and people-watch **2**

Lincoln Center Theater
The Vivian Beaumont and the Mitzi E Newhouse theatres are both housed in this building **5**

Composer Leonard Bernstein's famous musical, *West Side Story*, which was based on the Romeo and Juliet theme, was set in the impoverished streets around what is now Lincoln Center. Bernstein was later instrumental in setting up the large music complex.

The Guggenheim Bandshell in Damrosch Park is the site of free concerts.

The New York State Theater
This is the home of the New York City Ballet, as well as an opera company. The theatre seats 2,737 people **3**

Metropolitan Opera House
Lincoln Center's focus is the Opera House. The café at the top of the lobby offers great views of the plaza **4**

The College Board Building is an Art Deco delight that now houses condominiums and the College Board (exams all American students must take to get into university).

Early American quilt

Museum of American Folk Art
Quilting and naive painting are some of the arts displayed here ❼

James Dean once lived in a one-room apartment on the top floor of No.19 West 68th Street.

LOCATOR MAP
see Manhattan Map pp12–13

KEY

− − − Suggested route

0 metres	100
0 yards	100

To 72nd Street subway (4 blocks)

★ **Hotel des Artistes**
Artists Isadora Duncan, Noel Coward and Norman Rockwell once lived here. It also houses a much praised restaurant (see p296) ❽

W 67TH STREET

65TH STREET

CENTRAL PARK WEST

The American Broadcasting Company is in a building that looks like a castle. It was once an armoury.

No. 55 Central Park West is the Art Deco apartment building that featured in the film *Ghostbusters*.

The Society for Ethical Culture was one of the city's first Art Nouveau buildings. It also houses a school.

To 59th Street subway (2 blocks)

Central Park West is home to many celebrities, who like the privacy of its exclusive apartments.

Century Apartments
The Century's twin towers are visible from the park, making it a New York landmark ❶

STAR SIGHTS

★ **Lincoln Center**

★ **Hotel des Artistes**

San Remo, a twin-towered apartment house designed by Emery Roth

Twin Towers of Central Park West ❶

Map 12 D1, 12 D2, 16 D3, 16 D5.
Ⓜ *59th St–Columbus Circle, 72nd St.*

AMONG THE MOST familiar landmarks on the New York skyline are the four twin-towered apartment houses on Central Park West. Built between 1929 and 1931, just before the Great Depression halted all luxury construction work, they are now among the most highly sought-after residences in New York.

Admired today for their grace and architectural detail, their design was in response to a city planning law allowing taller apartments if setbacks and towers were used.

Tenants of the San Remo (No. 145) have included Dustin Hoffman, Paul Simon and Diane Keaton. Madonna was turned down by the residents' committee and lives close by at No. 1 West 64th Street, next door to the New York Society for Ethical Culture. The towers on The Eldorado (No. 300), also designed by Emery Roth, are crowned by futuristic pinnacles that rise like a pair of twin rockets. The celebrity list here has included Groucho Marx, Marilyn Monroe and Richard Dreyfuss. The Majestic (No. 115) and the Century (No. 25) are both sleek classics by Art Deco designer Irwin S Chanin.

Lincoln Center for the Performing Arts ❷

Map 11 C2. 🎭 *875-5400.* Ⓜ *65th St.* ♿ 🎫 *875-5350.* 🍴 🅿 *See Entertainment pp338–9.*

IN MAY 1959, President Dwight D Eisenhower travelled to New York to turn a shovelful of earth, Leonard Bernstein lifted his baton, the New York Philharmonic and the Julliard Chorus broke into the *Hallelujah Chorus* – and New York's most important cultural centre was born.

It was soon to cover 15 acres (6 ha) on the site of the slums that had been the setting for Bernstein's classic musical *West Side Story*.

The plaza fountain is by Philip Johnson and the sculpture in the reflecting pool, *Reclining Figure*, is by Henry Moore.

Guided tours are the best way to see the complex.

New York State Theater ❸

Lincoln Center. **Map** 11 D2. 🎭 *870-5570.* Ⓜ *66th St.* ♿ 🎫 🍴 🅿 *See Entertainment pp334–5.*

THE HOME BASE for the highly acclaimed New York City Ballet and the New York City Opera, a troupe devoted to presenting opera at popular prices, is a Philip Johnson design. It was inaugurated in 1964.

Gargantuan white marble sculptures by Elie Nadelman dominate the vast four-storey foyer. The theatre seats 2,800 people. Because of its rhinestone lights and chandeliers both inside and out, some have described the theatre as "a little jewel box".

Metropolitan Opera House ❹

Lincoln Center. **Map** 11 D2. 🎭 *362-6000.* Ⓜ *66th St.* ♿ 🎫 🍴 🅿 *See Entertainment pp338–9.*

HOME TO THE Metropolitan Opera Company and the American Ballet Theater, "The Met" is certainly the most spectacular of Lincoln Center's buildings, and is the focal point of the plaza. Five great arched windows offer views of the opulent foyer and two radiant murals by Marc Chagall. (You won't see them in the mornings, as they are protected from the sun.)

Central Plaza at Lincoln Center

Inside there are curved white marble stairs, miles of plush red carpeting and exquisite starburst crystal chandeliers

Free open-air concerts are held at Guggenheim Bandshell

which are raised to the ceiling just before each performance. All the greats have sung here, including Maria Callas, Jessye Norman and Luciano Pavarotti. First nights are glittering, star-studded occasions.

The Guggenheim Bandshell, in Damrosch Park next to the Met, is a popular concert venue featuring music from opera to jazz. The high point of the season is the Lincoln Center Out-of-Doors Festival that takes place in August.

Lincoln Center Theater ❺

Lincoln Center. **Map** 11 C2.
📞 362-7600 (Beaumont and Newhouse), 870-1630 (Library).
Ⓜ 66th St. ♿ ✓ ⑪ ⬜ See *Entertainment* pp338–9.

Two theatres make up this innovative complex, presenting eclectic and often experimental drama.

The theatres are the 1000-seat Vivian Beaumont and the smaller, more intimate 280-seat Mitzi E Newhouse.

Some of New York's best modern playwrights have featured at the Beaumont. The theatre's inaugural per-formance in 1962 was Arthur Miller's *After the Fall*.

The size of the Newhouse suits workshop-style plays but it can still make the news with scoops such as Robin Williams and Steve Martin in a production of Samuel Beckett's *Waiting for Godot*.

Between the Metropolitan Opera and the Beaumont is the New York Public Library for the Performing Arts. Exhibits include historic cylinders of early Met perform-ances, some original scores, playbills and programmes.

Avery Fisher Hall ❻

Lincoln Center. **Map** 11 C2. 📞 875-5030. Ⓜ 66th St. ♿ ✓ ⑪ ⬜
See *Entertainment* p338–9.

Home to the New York Philharmonic, America's oldest orchestra, as well as Lincoln Center's own Great Performers, Mostly Mozart Festival and Jazz at Lincoln Center, Avery Fisher Hall opened in 1962 as Philharmonic Hall. While critics initially complained about the awful acoustics, several structural modifications, including one in 1992, have rendered the Hall an acoustic gem, comparing favourably with the great concert halls of the world.

For a small fee, the public can attend rehearsals on Thursday mornings.

Museum of American Folk Art ❼

Lincoln Sq. **Map** 12 D2.
📞 977-7170. Ⓜ 66th St.
Open 11.30am–7.30pm Tue–Sun.
Closed Mon. 🚫 ♿ ✓ ⬜

Concertgoers attending Lincoln Center events are among the many to discover and delight in this attractive small, modern gallery, which opened here in 1989 to show American folk art. The exhibits include quilts, carvings and paintings from the Museum's permanent collection as well as changing displays. There are also special

programmes for children and crafts demonstrations.

A huge weathervane, in the shape of an American Indian and named for the legendary chief Tammany, presides over the central atrium.

The museum plans a move to larger premises on West 53rd Street; but this venue will remain as a branch.

Copper weathervane from the Museum of American Folk Art

Hotel des Artistes ❽

1 W 67th St. **Map** 12 D2.
📞 362-6700. Ⓜ 72nd St. See *Restaurants* p296.

Built in 1918 by George Mort Pollard, these two-storey apartments were intended as working artists' studios but have attracted all manner of interesting tenants including Alexander Woollcott, Norman Rockwell, Isadora Duncan, Rudolph Valentino and Noël Coward. The Café des Artistes is well known for its misty, romantic Howard Chandler Christy murals and its fine cuisine.

Decorative figure on the Hotel des Artistes

The Dakota 9

1 W 72nd St. **Map** 12 D1. **M** *72nd St.* **Not open** *to the public.*

THE NAME AND STYLE reflect the fact that this apartment building was truly "way out West" when Henry J Hardenberg, the architect responsible for the Plaza Hotel, designed it in 1880–84. It was New York's first luxury apartment house and was originally surrounded by squatters' shacks and wandering farm animals. Commissioned by Edward S Clark, heir to the Singer Sewing Machine fortune, it is one of the city's most prestigious addresses.

The Dakota's 65 luxurious apartments have had many famous owners, including Judy Garland, Lauren Bacall, Leonard Bernstein and Boris Karloff, whose ghost is said to haunt the place. It was the setting for the film *Rosemary's Baby,* and the site of the tragic murder of former Beatle John Lennon. His widow, Yoko Ono, still lives here.

Carved Indian head over the entrance to the Dakota

New-York Historical Society 10

170 Central Park West. **Map** 16 D5. **C** 873-3400. **M** *81st St.* **Galleries open** *noon—5pm Wed–Sun.* **Library open** *noon–5pm Wed–Fri.* **Closed** *public hols.* **Adm charge** *for galleries.*

AUDUBON'S ORIGINAL *Birds of America* prints and over 150 Tiffany lamps are among

The Laserium at the Hayden Planetarium

the treasures of New York's oldest museum. Founded in 1804, the Society has a wide collection of paintings and decorative arts dating back to the 17th century. The portrait collection includes Gilbert Stuart's *George Washington.* There is fine furniture from the Federal period, plus an exceptional silver display.

The galleries reopened in 1995 after a two-year closure, despite a last-minute fire and continuing financial troubles.

American Museum of Natural History 11

See pp214–15.

Hayden Planetarium 12

Central Park West at 81st St. **Map** 16 D4. **C** 769-5920, 769-5100 *for times of shows.* **M** *81st St.* **Open** *10am–5.45pm Sun–Thu, 10am–8.45pm Fri, Sat.* **Closed** *Thanksgiving, 25 Dec.* **Adm charge.** 📷 ⓰ *limited.* 🔦

ADJOINING THE American Museum of Natural History is this planetarium, which was named after investment banker Charles Hayden who donated the original astronomical equipment. In the Sky Theater the Zeiss VI projector recreates the heavens on a vast dome. There are also 3-D laser light shows to rock music. Exhibits include a black light gallery with luminescent murals depicting a lunar landscape, a 14-tonne meteorite and, in the Guggenheim Space Theater, a scale model of the solar system, over 40 ft (12 m) in diameter. It shows the relative

size and speed of planets and satellites. Another exhibit focuses on the sun, explaining such things as why the sky is blue. Special children's shows are hosted by and feature the *Sesame Street* Muppets or *Star Wars* robots.

Pomander Walk 13

261–7 W 94th St. **Map** 15 C2. **M** *72nd St.*

LOOK THROUGH the gate for a delightful surprise – a double row of tiny town houses built in 1921 to look like the London mews setting of a popular play of the time.

Appropriately, it was much favoured as a home by movie actors, including Rosalind Russell, Humphrey Bogart and the Gish sisters.

Facade of Pomander Walk town house

Riverside Drive and Park 14

Map 15 B4. **M** *103rd St.*

RIVERSIDE DRIVE is one of the city's most attractive streets – broad, nicely shaded, and affording lovely views over the Hudson River. It is lined with the original opulent town houses as well as some newer apartment buildings. Look out for the houses designed at the end of the 19th century by local architect Clarence F True, at Nos. 40–46, 74–7, 81–9 and

105–7 Riverside Drive. Their curved gables, bays and arched windows seem to suit the curves of the road and the flow of the river.

The bizarrely named Cliff Dwellers' Apartments at No. 243 is a 1914 building with a frieze showing early Arizona cliff dwellers complete with masks, buffalo skulls, mountain lions and rattlesnakes.

Riverside Park was designed by Frederick Law Olmsted in 1880. He also laid out Central Park *(see pp202–5)*.

Soldiers' and Sailors' monument in Riverside Park

Children's Museum of Manhattan ❶❺

212 W 83rd St. **Map** 15 C4. **C** 721-1223. **M** 86th St. **Open** Sep–May: 1.30pm–5.30pm Mon, Wed, Thu; 10am–5pm Fri–Sun; Jun–Aug: 10am–5pm Wed–Mon. **Closed** 1 Jan, 25 Dec. **Adm charge**.

THIS PARTICULARLY imaginative participatory museum was founded in 1973 on the premise that children learn best through play. In the "Brainatarium" the magic of the human mind is revealed in a four-minute multi-media show projected on to the domed ceiling. Using hi-tech, hands-on equipment, children can explore the five senses – not just their own, but also those of birds, insects and animals.

Children's Museum entrance

The Time Warner Center for Media transforms children into budding camera operators, newscasters, animators and technicians in a state-of-the-art TV studio. At weekends and holiday times there are guest performers from puppeteers to storytellers in the 150-seat theatre. There is also a gallery for free play

Ansonia Hotel ❶❻

2109 Broadway. **Map** 11 C1. **M** 72nd St. **Lobby open** to the public.

THIS BEAUX ARTS gem was built in 1899 by William Earl Dodge Stokes, heir to the Phelps Dodge Company fortune, who brought architect Paul E M Duboy from France to execute a sumptuous apartment-hotel to rival the Dakota.

The most prominent features are the round corner tower and the two-storey mansard roof adorned with single and double dormers. Originally the building had a roof garden (complete with Dodge's menagerie: ducks,

Distinctive rounded turret of the Ansonia Hotel

chickens and a tame bear) and two swimming pools.

The hotel's thick, sound-muffling walls soon made it a favourite with the musical stars of yesteryear. Florenz Ziegfeld, Arturo Toscanini, Enrico Caruso, Leopold Stravinsky and Lily Pons were all once regular guests there.

The Dorilton ❶❼

171 W 71st St. **Map** 15 C5. **M** 72nd St. **Not open** to the public.

OPULENT DETAIL and an impressive high mansard roof adorn this apartment house. On the West 71st Street side of the building is a nine-storey-high gateway. To the modern eye, the Dorilton is gloriously over the top, but when it was first built in 1902 it provoked this reaction, reported by the *Architectural Record*: "The sight of it makes

Balcony on the Dorilton, supported by groaning figures

strong men swear and weak women shrink affrighted."

What would the critics have made of the Alexandria Condominium, at No. 135 West 70th Street, just a block away? Built in 1927 as the Pythian Temple, its current name stems from the lavish Egyptian-style motifs that adorned this former Masonic lodge. Many were stripped away when the building was converted to a condominium, but you can still see what the polychrome designs were like. There are lotus leaves, hieroglyphics, ornately carved columns, mythical beasts, and, in majestic splendour on the roof, two seated pharaohs.

MORNINGSIDE HEIGHTS AND HARLEM

MORNINGSIDE HEIGHTS, near the Hudson River, is home to Columbia University and two of the city's finest churches. Further to the east is Hamilton Heights, situated on the border of Harlem, America's most famous black community. Because Harlem is not New York's safest neighbourhood,

St Francis of Assissi, Museo del Barrio

perhaps the best way to see it is on a Sunday morning tour *(see p353)*. Many tours start in Hamilton Heights, move east to the St Nicholas Historic District, stop to enjoy the gospel choir at the Abyssinian Baptist Church, and then end with a southern-style brunch or lunch at Sylvia's, Harlem's best known restaurant.

Stained-glass window at the Cotton Club, showing Louis Armstrong

SIGHTS AT A GLANCE

Historic Streets and Buildings

Columbia University **1**
St Paul's Chapel **2**
Low Library **3**
Grant's Tomb **6**
City College of the City University of New York **7**
Hamilton Grange National Memorial **8**
Hamilton Heights Historic District **9**
St Nicholas Historic District **10**
Mount Morris Historical District **17**

Museums and Galleries

Schomburg Center for Research into Black Culture **12**
Studio Museum in Harlem **16**
Museo del Barrio **19**

Famous Theatres

Harlem YMCA **13**
Apollo Theater **15**

Churches

Cathedral of St John the Divine pp224–5 **4**
Riverside Church **5**
Abyssinian Baptist Church **11**

Parks and Squares

Marcus Garvey Park **18**

Landmark Restaurants

Sylvia's **14**

GETTING THERE

By subway, take the 7th Ave/Broadway local 1 and 9 trains to 116th St Columbia University. The M4, M5, M11 and M104 buses serve Columbia. For Harlem, take the A, B, C or D lines to 125th St, or the M1, M2, M7 or M101/102 buses.

SEE ALSO

Carved stone column, Cathedral of St John the Divine

KEY

Street-by-Street map

M Subway station

.0 metres   500

0 yards   500

Street-by-Street:
Columbia University

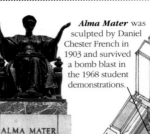

A GREAT UNIVERSITY is as much spirit as buildings. After admiring the architecture, linger a while on Columbia's central quadrangle in front of the Low Library, where you will see the jeans-clad future leaders of America meeting and mingling between classes. Across from the campus on both Broadway and Amsterdam Avenue are the coffee houses and cafés where students engage in lengthy philosophical arguments, debate the topics of the day or simply unwind.

Alma Mater was sculpted by Daniel Chester French in 1903 and survived a bomb blast in the 1968 student demonstrations.

**116th Street-
Columbia University
subway (lines 1, 9)**

The School of Journalism is one of Columbia's many McKim, Mead & White buildings. Founded in 1912 by publisher Joseph Pulitzer, it is the home of the Pulitzer Prize awarded for the best in literature and journalism.

Butler Library is Columbia's main library.

Low Library
With its imposing facade and high dome, the library dominates the main quadrangle. It was designed by McKim, Mead & White in 1895–7 ❸

★ **Central Quadrangle**
The earliest buildings were designed by McKim, Mead & White and built around a raised central quadrangle. This view looks across the quadrangle towards Butler Library ❶

St Paul's Chapel
*Designed by the architects Howells &
[Sto]kes in 1907, this church is known
for its fine woodwork and magnificent, vaulted interior. It is full of
light and has fine acoustics* **2**

**The Sherman
Fairchild
Center** was
built in 1977
to house the
university's
life sciences
departments.

LOCATOR MAP
See Manhattan Map pp12–13

KEY

‒ ‒ ‒ Suggested route

| 0 metres | 100 |
| 0 yards | 100 |

Student demonstrations put
Columbia University in the news in
1968. The demonstrations were
sparked by the university's plan to
build a gymnasium in nearby
Morningside Park. The protests forced
the university to build elsewhere.

116TH ST

MORNINGSIDE DRIVE

The Eglise de Notre Dame was built for
a French-speaking congregation. Behind
the altar is a replica of the grotto at
Lourdes, France, the gift of a woman
who believed her son was healed there.

★ **Cathedral of St
John the Divine**
*If this Neo-Gothic
cathedral is ever
finished, it will be
the largest in the
world. Although one third of the
structure has not yet been built, it
can hold 10,000 parishioners* **4**

STAR SIGHTS

★ **Columbia
University**

★ **Cathedral of St John
the Divine**

**Carved
stonework**
decorates the
facade of the
Cathedral.

Alma Mater statue at Low Library, Columbia University

Columbia University ➊

Main entrance at W 116th St.
Map 20 E3. **[** 854-1754.
M *116th St-Columbia Univ.* **[**

T HIS IS THE third location to
date of one of America's
oldest and finest universities.
Founded in 1754 as King's
College, its first site was close
to where the World Trade
Center now stands.

In 1814, when a move
uptown was proposed, the
university approached the
authorities for funding, but
was instead given a plot of
land valued at $75,000 on
which to build a new home. The
university never built on
the land itself, but leased it
out and spent the years from
1857 to 1897 in buildings
nearby. It finally sold the plot
in 1985 to the leaseholders,
Rockefeller Center Inc, for the
sum of $400 million.

The present campus was
begun in 1897 on the site of
the Bloomingdale Insane
Asylum. Architect Charles

McKim placed the university
on a terrace, serenely above
street level. Its spacious lawns
and plazas still create a sense
of contrast in the busy city.

At last count there were
over 19,000 students at this
campus, 10,400 men and
8,900 women. Columbia, an
Ivy League School, is noted
for its Law, Medicine and
Journalism Schools. Its highly
distinguished faculty and
alumni, past and present,
include 53 Nobel laureates.
Famous alumni include Isaac
Asimov, J D Salinger, James
Cagney and Joan Rivers.

St Paul's Chapel ➋

Columbia University. **Map** 20 E3.
[854-6625. **M** *116th St-Columbia
Univ.* **Open** *noon–4pm Mon–Fri (term
time), noon–2pm (breaks).* **Free organ
concerts** *noon Thu.* **[** *Sun.* **[** **[**

**Interior brick vaulting of
St Paul's Chapel dome**

C OLUMBIA'S MOST outstanding
building, built in 1904, is
a mix of Italian Renaissance,
Byzantine and Gothic. The
interior Guastavino vaulting is
of intricate patterns of aged
red brick; the whole chapel is
bathed in light from above.

The free organ concerts are
an exceptionally fine way to
appreciate the beauty and
acoustics of this church. The
Aeolian-Skinner pipe organ is
renowned for its fine tone.

Facade of St Paul's Chapel

Low Library ➌

Columbia University. **Map** 20 E3.
M *116th St-Columbia Univ.*

A CLASSICAL, columned
building atop three flights
of stone stairs, the library was
donated by Seth Low, a
former mayor and college
president. The statue in front
of it, *Alma Mater* by Daniel
Chester French, became
familiar as the backdrop to
the many 1968 anti-Vietnam
War student demonstrations.
The building is now used as
offices and its rotunda for a
variety of academic and
ceremonial purposes. The
books have now been moved
to Butler Library, across the
quadrangle. The university's
library collections total some
six million volumes.

Cathedral of St John the Divine ➍

See p224–5.

Riverside Church ➎

490 Riverside Dr at 122nd St.
Map 20 D2. **[** 870-6700. **M** *116th
St-Columbia Univ.* **Open** *9am–4pm
daily.* **[** *10.45am Sun.* **[** *with
prior permission.* **[** **[** *Carillon
bell concerts* *noon, 3pm Sun.*
Theatre **[** 864-2929.

A 21-STOREY STEEL frame with
a Gothic exterior, the
church design was inspired
by the cathedral at Chartres. It
was lavishly funded by John D
Rockefeller, Jr in 1930. The
Laura Spelman Rockefeller
Memorial Carillon (in honour
of Rockefeller's mother) is the
largest in the world, with 74

Columbia University's main courtyard and the Low Library

bells. The 20-tonne Bourdon or hour bell is the largest and heaviest tuned carillon bell ever cast. The organ, with its 22,000 pipes, is among the largest in the world.

At the rear of the second gallery is a figure by Jacob Epstein, *Christ in Majesty*, cast in plaster and covered in gold leaf. Another Epstein statue, *Madonna and Child*, stands in the court next to the cloister. The panels of the chancel screen honour eight men and women whose lives have exemplified the teachings of Christ. They range from Socrates to Michelangelo, and from Florence Nightingale to Booker T Washington.

For quiet reflection, enter the small, secluded Christ Chapel, patterned after an 11th-century Romanesque church in France. For views, take the elevator to the 20th floor and then walk the 140 steps to the top of the 392-ft (120-m) bell tower for a fine panorama of Upper Manhattan from the windy observation deck. (This is definitely not recommended when the bells are tolling.)

Mosaic mural in Grant's Tomb showing Grant (right) and Robert E Lee

Grant's Tomb ❻

W 122nd St and Riverside Dr.
Map 20 D2. 🔔 666-1640.
Ⓜ *116th St-Columbia Univ.* **Open**
9am–5pm daily. **Closed** *1 Jan, 4 Jul,
Thanksgiving, 25 Dec.* 📷 ✔ ♿

THIS GRANDIOSE monument honours America's 18th president, Ulysses S Grant, the commanding general of the Union forces in the Civil War.

The mausoleum contains the coffins of General Grant and his wife, in accordance with the president's last wish that they be buried together. After Grant's death in 1885, more than 90,000 Americans contributed $600,000 to build the sepulchre, which was inspired by Mausoleus's tomb at Halicarnassus, one of the seven Wonders of the Ancient World. The tomb was dedicated on Grant's

**General Grant on a
Civil War campaign**

75th birthday, 27 April 1897. The parade of 50,000 people, along with a flotilla of 10 American and five European warships, took more than seven hours to pass in review.

The interior was inspired by Napoleon's tomb at Les Invalides in Paris. Each sarcophagus weighs 8.5 tonnes. Two exhibit rooms feature displays on Grant's personal life and his presidential and military career. Surrounding the north and east sides of the building are 17 sinuously curved mosaic benches that seem totally out of keeping with the formal architecture of the tomb. They were designed in the early 1970s by the Chilean-born Brooklyn artist Pedro Silva and built by 1,200 local volunteers under his supervision. The colourful benches were inspired by the Spanish architect Antonio Gaudi's work in Barcelona. The mosaics depict a wide variety of subjects, ranging from the Inuits to New York taxis to Donald Duck.

A short walk north of Grant's Tomb is another, humbler, monument. An unadorned urn on a pedestal marks the resting place of a young child who fell from the riverbank and drowned in the 18th century. His grieving father placed a marker which reads simply "Erected to the memory of an amiable child, St Clair Pollock, died 15 July 1797 in his fifth year of his age".

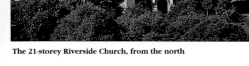

The 21-storey Riverside Church, from the north

Cathedral of St John the Divine 4

Cram's Gothic West Front

STARTED IN 1892 and still only two-thirds finished, this will be the largest cathedral in the world. The interior is over 600 ft (180 m) long and 146 ft (45 m) wide. Designed originally in Romanesque style by Heins and LaFarge, Ralph Adams Cram took over the project in 1911, devising a Gothic nave and west front. Medieval construction methods, such as the use of stone supporting buttresses, continue to be used to complete the cathedral, which is also a venue for theatre, music and avant-garde art.

Choir
Each of the choir's columns is 55 ft (17 m) tall and made of polished grey granite.

Nave
Rising to a height of over 100 ft (30 m), the piers of the nave are topped by graceful stone arches.

Rose Window ★
Completed in 1933, the stylized motif of the Great Rose is symbolic of the many facets of the Christian Church.

★ **West Front Entrance**
The portals of the cathedral's West Front are adorned with many fine stone carvings. Some are re-creations of medieval religious sculptures. Others, such as this apocalyptic vision of New York's skyline, by local stonemason Joe Kinkannon, highlight the cathedral's involvement in political and social issues of the day.

STAR FEATURES

★ **Rose Window**

★ **West Front Entrance**

★ **Bay Altars**

★ **Peace Fountain**

★ **Peace Fountain**
The sculpture is the creation of Greg Wyatt and represents nature in its many forms. It stands within a granite basin on the Great Lawn, south of the cathedral.

VISITORS' CHECKLIST

Amsterdam Ave at W 112th St.
Map 20 E4. 316-7540. **Box office** 662-2133. 1, 9 to Cathedral Pkwy (110th St).
M4, M5, M7, M11, M104.
Open 9am–5pm daily (8pm Sun).
Donation welcome.
Concerts, lectures, plays, art exhibitions.

Baptistry
The Gothic Baptistry has Italian, French and Spanish influences.

THE FINISHED DESIGN

Crossing tower

West towers

South transept

It will cost approximately $400 million to complete the cathedral. The south transept, crossing tower and west towers have yet to be finished. When the money is raised, the proposed design will take at least another 50 years to complete.

Pulpit

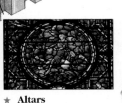

St Ambrose Chapel
Named after a 4th-century Italian bishop, the chapel is decorated with Renaissance-style iron work.

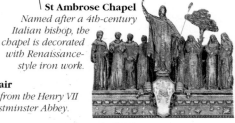

★ **Altars**
The bay altar windows are devoted to human endeavour. The sports window shows feats of skill and strength.

Bishop's Chair
This is a copy from the Henry VII chapel in Westminster Abbey.

TIMELINE

1800	1850	1900	1950

1823 Cathedral planned for Washington Square

1891 Site chosen and designated Cathedral Parkway

1909 Pulpit designed by Henry Vaughan

1911 Cram design replaces earlier ones

1967 Bronze lamps from former Penn Station installed on front steps

1873 Charter granted

1888 Competition to design cathedral won by Heins & LaFarge

1916 Ground broken for nave

1978 Third phase of building begins, and Stonemasons' Yard opened

1892 27 December (St. John's Day), cornerstone laid

1941 Work halted by World War II and does not resume until 1978

City College of the City University of New York ❼

Main entrance at W 138th St and Convent Ave. **Map** 19 A2. **☎** 650-7000. **Ⓜ** 137th St-City College.

SET HIGH on a hill adjoining Hamilton Heights, the original Gothic quadrangle of this college, built between 1903 and 1907, is extremely impressive. The material used for the buildings is Manhattan schist, a stone that had been excavated in building the IRT subway. Later, contemporary buildings were added to the school, which takes nearly 15,000 students.

Once free to all residents of New York, City College still offers an education at the city's lowest tuition rates. Three-quarters of the students are from minority groups and a large number of them are the first in their families to attend college.

Shepard Archway at City College of the City University of New York

Hamilton Grange National Memorial ❽

287 Convent Ave. **Map** 19 A1. **☎** 283-5154. **Ⓜ** 137th St-City College. **Not open** to the public.

BADLY SQUEEZED between a church and apartments is one of the city's most historic buildings, the 1802 columned wooden country home of Alexander Hamilton. He was one of the architects of the Federal government system, the first Secretary of the Treasury and founder of the National Bank. It is his face

Statue of Alexander Hamilton at Hamilton Grange

that appears on the $10 note. Hamilton lived here for the last two years of his life. He was killed in a duel with political rival, Aaron Burr, in 1804. Hamilton fired into the air.

The house was acquired by St Luke's Episcopal Church in 1889 and moved two blocks to this "temporary" site, where it is closed, pending further relocation and renovation.

Hamilton Heights Historic District ❾

W 141st–W 145th St. **Map** 19 A1. **Ⓜ** 137th St-City College.

ORIGINALLY THIS was a setting for the impressive country estates of the wealthy. Also known as Harlem Heights, it was developed during the 1880s following the extension of the El line (see p24) into the neighbourhood. The privacy of the enclave, on a high hill above Harlem, made it a very desirable location.

The section known as Sugar Hill was highly favoured by Harlem's elite – Chief Justice Thurgood Marshall, notable jazz musicians Count Basie, Duke Ellington and Cab Calloway, and boxer Sugar

Ray Robinson, five times world middleweight champion, have all lived there.

The handsome three- and four-storey stone row houses were built between 1886 and 1906 in a variety of styles mixing Flemish, Romanesque and Tudor influences. Still in fine condition, many are used as residences by the faculty of nearby City College.

Row houses in Hamilton Heights

St Nicholas Historic District ❿

202–250 W 138th & W 139th St. **Map** 19 B2. **Ⓜ** 135th St (B, C).

A STARTLING CONTRAST to the rundown surroundings, the two blocks here, known as the King Model Houses, were built in 1891 when Harlem was considered a neighbourhood for New York's gentry. They still comprise one of the city's most distinctive examples of row townhouses.

The developer, David King, chose three leading architects, who succeeded in blending their different styles to create a harmonious whole. The most famous of these was the firm of McKim, Mead & White,

Houses in St Nicholas district

Adam Clayton Powell, Jr (in dark suit) on a civil rights campaign

designers of the Pierpont Morgan Library *(see pp162-3)* and Villard Houses *(see p174)*, who were responsible for the northernmost row of solid brick Renaissance palaces. Their homes featured ground floor entrances rather than the typical New York brownstone stoops. Also, the elaborate parlour floors have ornate wrought-iron balconies below, as well as carved decorative medaillions above their windows.

The Georgian buildings designed by Price and Luce are built of buff brick with white stone trim. James Brown Lord's section of buildings, also Georgian in architectural style, feels much closer to Victorian, with outstanding red brick facades and bases constructed of brownstone.

Successful blacks were attracted here in the 1920s and 1930s, giving it the nickname Strivers' Row. Among them were celebrated musicians W C Handy and Eubie Blake.

Abyssinian Baptist Church ⓫

132 W 138th St. **Map** 19 C2.
📞 862-7474. **M** 135th St (2, 3).
✝ 11am Sun.

Nᴇᴡ ʏᴏʀᴋ's ᴏʟᴅᴇsᴛ black church, founded in 1808, became famous through its charismatic pastor, Adam Clayton Powell, Jr (1908–72), who became a congressman and civil rights leader. Under

his leadership it became the richest and most powerful black church in America. There is a room in the church which is entirely devoted to memorabilia from his life.

The church, which is housed in a fine 1923 Gothic building, welcomes visitors to its Sunday services which feature a superb gospel choir.

Schomburg Center for Research into Black Culture ⓬

515 Lenox Ave. **Map** 19 C2.
📞 491-2200. **M** 135th St (2, 3).
Open noon–8pm Mon–Wed, 10am–6pm Thu–Sat (exhibition hours vary). **Closed** public hols. 📷 with prior permission. ♿ 📹 📱

Hᴏᴜsᴇᴅ ɪɴ a sleek contemporary complex opened in 1991, this is the largest research centre of black and African culture in the United States. The immense collection was assembled by the late Arthur Schomburg, a black man of Puerto Rican descent, who was told by a teacher that there was no such thing as

Kurt Weill, Elmer Rice and Langston Hughes at the Schomburg Center

"black history". The Carnegie Corporation bought the collection in 1926 and generously gave it to the New York Public Library; Schomburg was made curator.

The library was the unofficial meeting place of the black literary renaissance of the 1920s, which included people like Langston Hughes, W E B Du Bois, Zora Neale Hurston and many other great writers of the day. It also hosted many literary gatherings and poetry readings.

The Schomburg Library has excellent facilities for conserving and making available the archive's many treasures, which include rare books, art and recordings. The library was planned and designed to double as a cultural centre and includes a theatre and two galleries which feature changing shows of art and photography.

Harlem YMCA ⓭

180 W 135th St. **Map** 19 C3.
📞 281-4100. **M** 135th St (2, 3).

Sociologist W E B Du Bois

Pᴀᴜʟ ʀᴏʙᴇsᴏɴ and many others made their first stage appearances here in the early 1920s. The Krigqa Players, organized by W E B Du Bois in the basement in 1928, was founded to counter the derogatory images of blacks often presented in Broadway reviews of the time. The "Y" also provided temporary lodgings for some notable new arrivals in Harlem, including writer Ralph Ellison.

Gospel singers performing at Sylvia's during Sunday brunch

Sylvia's ⑭

328 Lenox Ave. **Map** 21 B1.
☎ 996-0660. **Ⓜ** *125th St (2,3). See Restaurants p294.*

Harlem's best known soul food restaurant serves up southern-fried or smothered chicken, spicy ribs, black eyed peas, collard greens, candied yams, sweet potato pie and other southern delicacies

Sylvia's

(see p287). Sunday brunch is served to the accompaniment of gospel singers.

Take some time to explore the market at the corner of 125th Street and Lenox Avenue (opposite Sylvia's), extending for a block or more in either direction. This isn't a food market: it sells African clothing, jewellery and art of varying quality.

Apollo Theater ⑮

253 W 125th St. **Map** 21 A1.
☎ 749-5838. **Ⓜ** *125th St (A, B, C, D).* **Open** *at showtimes. See Entertainment p341.*

The Apollo opened in 1914 as a whites-only opera house. Its great fame came when Frank Schiffman, a white entrepreneur, took over in 1934. He then opened the theatre to all races and turned

it into Harlem's best known showcase, with legendary black artists such as Bessie Smith, Billie Holiday, Duke Ellington, and Dinah Washington performing.

Amateur nights on Wednesdays, with winners

Apollo Theater

determined by audience applause, were famous, and there was a long waiting list for performers. These amateur

nights launched the careers of Sarah Vaughan, Pearl Bailey, James Brown and Gladys Knight, among others, and they still attract hopefuls.

The Apollo was *the* place during the swing band era; following World War II, a new generation of musicians, such as Charlie "Bird" Parker, Dizzy Gillespie, Thelonius Monk and Aretha Franklin, continued the tradition.

Rescued from decline and refurbished in the 1980s, the Apollo still features top black entertainers performing the blues, jazz, gospel and dance.

Studio Museum in Harlem ⑯

144 W 125th St. **Map** 21 B2.
☎ 864-4500. **Ⓜ** *125th St (2, 3).* **Open** *10am–5pm Wed–Fri, 1pm–6pm Sat, Sun.* **Closed** *1 Jan, Thanksgiving, 25 Dec.* **Adm charge.**
Ⓥ ♿ 🎁 *Lectures, children's programmes, films.* 📷

The museum was founded in 1967 in a loft on upper Fifth Avenue with the mission of becoming the premier centre for the collection and exhibition of the art and artefacts of African-Americans.

The present premises, a five-storey building on Harlem's main commercial street, was donated to the museum by the New York Bank for Savings in 1979. The new museum opened in 1982. There are galleries on two levels for changing exhibitions featuring artists and cultural themes, and three galleries are devoted to the permanent collection of works by major black artists.

The photographic archives comprise one of the most

Exhibition space at the Studio Museum in Harlem

complete records in existence of Harlem in its heyday. A side door opens on to a small sculpture garden.

In addition to its excellent exhibitions, the Studio Museum also maintains a national artist-in-residence programme, and holds regular lectures, seminars, children's programmes and film festivals. An excellent small shop sells books and African crafts.

Mount Morris Historical District ⑰

W 119th–W 124th St **Map** 21 B2.
Ⓜ *125th St (2, 3).*

YOU CAN PLAINLY see that the late 19th-century Victorian-style town houses near Marcus Garvey Park were once grand. This was a favourite neighbourhood of German Jews moving up in the world from the Lower East Side. Time has not been kind, and this district shows how the area has deteriorated.

A few impressive churches, such as St Martin's Episcopal Church, remain. There are also some interesting juxtapositions of faiths to be seen: the columned Mount Olivet Baptist Church, at No. 201 Lenox Avenue, was once Temple Israel, one of the most imposing synagogues in

the city; and at the Ethiopian Hebrew Congregation, 1 West 123rd, housed in a former mansion, the gospel choir sings in Hebrew on Saturdays.

Marcus Garvey Park ⑱

120th–124th St. **Map** 21 B2.
Ⓜ *125th St (2,3).*

The flamboyant black nationalist leader Marcus Garvey

THIS HILLY, ROCKY two-block square of green is the site of New York's last fire watchtower, an open cast-iron structure built in 1856, with spiral stairs leading to the observation deck. The bell below the deck used to sound the alarm. Best to view it from a distance, however – this neighbourhood is not recommended for carefree wandering. Previously known as Mount Morris Park, it was renamed in 1973 in honour of Marcus Garvey. He came to Harlem from Jamaica in 1916 and founded the Universal Negro Improvement Agency, which promoted self-help, racial pride and a back-to-Africa movement.

Museo del Barrio ⑲

1230 5th Ave. **Map** 21 C5. Ⓒ *831-7272.* Ⓜ *103rd St (6).* **Open** *11am–5pm Wed–Sun.* **Donation expected.**
🚫 ♿ ▸

FOUNDED IN 1969, this is North America's only museum devoted to Latin American art, specializing in the culture of Puerto Rico. Exhibitions feature contemporary painting and sculpture, folk art and historical artefacts. The stars of the permanent collection are about 240 wooden Santos, carvings of the saints by folk artisans, and a reconstructed *bodega* or Latino corner grocery. Exhibits change often, but some of the Santos are always on display. The pre-Columbian collection contains rare artefacts from the Caribbean. Situated at the far end of Museum Mile, this unusual museum attempts to bridge the gap between the lofty Upper East Side and the cultural heritage of El Barrio (Spanish Harlem).

St Martin's Episcopal Church on Lenox Avenue

Folk art at the Museo del Barrio: one of the *Three Wise Men* (left) and the *Omnipotent Hand*

FURTHER AFIELD

THOUGH OFFICIALLY part of New York City, the boroughs outside Manhattan are quite different in feel and spirit. They are residential and don't have the skyscrapers that people associate with New York. The difference is evident even in the way residents describe a trip to Manhattan as "going into the city". Yet the outlying areas boast many attractions, including the city's biggest zoo, botanical gardens, museums, beaches and sports arenas. For a guided walk around Brooklyn see pages 264–5.

SIGHTS AT A GLANCE

Historic Streets and Buildings
Morris-Jumel Mansion **2**
George Washington Bridge **3**
Wave Hill **5**
Yankee Stadium **10**
Grand Army Plaza **17**
Park Slope Historic District **18**
Historic Richmond Town **23**
Alice Austen House **26**

Museums and Galleries
Audubon Terrace **1**
The Cloisters pp234–7 **4**
Van Cortlandt House Museum **6**

New York Hall of Science **13**
American Museum of the Moving Image and Kaufman Astoria Studio **14**
Brooklyn Children's Museum **15**
The Brooklyn Museum pp248–51 **20**
Jacques Marchais Center of Tibetan Art **24**
Snug Harbor Cultural Center **25**

Parks and Gardens
New York Botanical Garden pp240–41 **8**
International Wildlife Conservation Park pp242–3 **9**

Flushing Meadow-Corona Park **12**
Prospect Park **19**
Brooklyn Botanic Garden **21**

Famous Theatres
Brooklyn Academy of Music **16**

Cemeteries
Woodlawn Cemetery **7**

Beaches
City Island **11**
Coney Island **22**
Jamaica Bay Wildlife Refuge Center **27**
Jones Beach State Park **28**

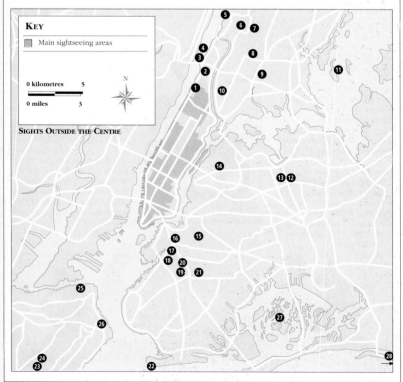

KEY

◻ Main sightseeing areas

0 kilometres   5
0 miles   3

N

SIGHTS OUTSIDE THE CENTRE

Jamaica Bay

Upper Manhattan

IT WAS IN UPPER Manhattan that the 18th-century Dutch settlers established their farms. Now a suburban area with little of the bustle of downtown Manhattan, it is a good place to escape the inner city for some relaxed museum and landmark sightseeing. The Cloisters *(see pp234–7)* displays a magnificent collection of medieval art, housed within original European buildings of the period. A piece of New York history is found at the Morris-Jumel Mansion in north Harlem. From his headquarters here, George Washington mounted the defence of Manhattan in 1776.

Audubon Terrace ❶

M *157th St.* **American Numismatic Society** *234-3130.* **Open** *9am–4.30pm Tue–Sat, 1–4pm Sun.*

American Academy of Arts and Letters *368-5900.* **Open** *during exhibitions.*

Hispanic Society of America *926-2234.* **Open** *10am–4.30pm Tue–Sat, 1–4pm Sun.* **Closed** *public hols.* **Donation expected.*

THIS 1908 complex of Classical Revival buildings by Charles Pratt Huntington is named after naturalist John James Audubon, whose estate once included this land. Audubon is buried in nearby Trinity Cemetery. His gravestone, a Celtic

Facade of the American Academy of Arts and Letters

cross, bears the symbolic images of this adventurous artist's career: the birds he painted, his palette and brushes, and his rifles.

The complex was funded by the architect's cousin, civic benefactor Archer Milton Huntington. His dream was that it should be a centre of culture and study. A central plaza contains statues by his wife, the sculptress Anna Hyatt Huntington.

Audubon Terrace contains several specialist museums that are worth seeking out. The American Numismatic Society is the leading American museum devoted to coinage and medals, and has one of the world's best

collections, with half a million photos and illustrations of coins. A permanent exhibition called "The World of Coins" traces the historical and political role of money, and the Society holds a vast library.

The American Academy of Arts and Letters was set up to honour American writers, artists, composers, and 75 honorary members from overseas. On the roll are writers John Steinbeck and Mark Twain, painters Andrew Wyeth and Edward Hopper, and the composer Aaron Copland. Exhibitions feature members' work. The library (for scholars, by appointment) holds old manuscripts and first editions.

Bronze door at the Academy

The Hispanic Society of America is a public museum and library based upon the personal collection of Archer M Huntington. The Spanish Renaissance-style main gallery holds works by Goya, El Greco and Velázquez. The National Museum of the American Indian, once here, has now reopened at the Custom House *(see p73).*

Statue of El Cid by Anna Hyatt Huntington at Audubon Terrace

Morris-Jumel Mansion ❷

Corner W 160th St and Edgecombe Ave. **C** *923-8008.* **M** *163rd St.* **Open** *10am–4pm Wed–Sun.* **Closed** *public hols.* **Adm charge.** ◻ ◻ *by appt.*

THIS IS ONE of New York's few pre-Revolutionary buildings. Now a museum, it was built in 1765 for Lt Col Roger Morris. His former military colleague George Washington used the house as temporary headquarters while defending Manhattan in 1776.

The house was bought and updated in 1810 by Stephen Jumel, a merchant of French-Caribbean descent, and his wife Eliza. The pair furnished the house with souvenirs of their many visits to France. Her boudoir contains her bed and "dolphin" chair, reputedly bought from Napoleon. Eliza's social climbing and love affairs scandalized New York society. It was rumoured that she let her husband bleed to death in 1832 so she could inherit his fortune. She later married Aaron Burr, aged 77, and divorced him three years later on the day he died.

The exterior of this wood-sided Georgian house with its classical portico and octagonal wing – the earliest in the colonies – has been restored. The museum exhibits include many original Jumel pieces.

The 3,500-ft (1,065-m) span of the George Washington Bridge

George Washington Bridge ❸

M *175th St.*

FRENCH ARCHITECT Le Corbusier called this "the only seat of grace in the disordered city". While not as famous a landmark as its Brooklyn equivalent, this bridge by engineer Othmar Ammann and his architect Cass Gilbert still has its character and history. Plans for a bridge linking Manhattan to New Jersey had been in the pipeline for

The lighthouse under Washington Bridge

more than 60 years before the Port of New York Authority raised the $59 million needed to fund the project. It was Ammann who suggested a road bridge rather than the more expensive rail link. Work began in 1927 and the bridge was finally opened in 1931. First across were two young roller skaters from the Bronx. Today the bridge is a vital link for commuter traffic and is in constant use.

Cass Gilbert had plans to clad the two towers with masonry but funds did not permit it, leaving an elegant skeletal structure 600 ft (183 m) in height and 3,500 ft (1,065 m) long.

Ammann had also allowed for a second deck in his original plan, and this lower deck was added in 1962, increasing the bridge's capacity enormously. Now the eastbound toll collection shows a traffic level of over 50 million cars per year.

Below the eastern tower is a lighthouse that was saved from possible demolition in 1951 by sheer force of public pressure. The reason for this unlikely protest has become part of the city's mythology. Many thousands of young New Yorkers and children all around the world have loved the bedtime story *The Little Red Lighthouse and the Great Gray Bridge*, and wrote letters to save the lighthouse. Author Hildegarde Hoyt Swift wove the tale around her two favourite New York landmarks.

The Cloisters ❹

See pp234–7.

Morris-Jumel Mansion, built in 1765, with its original colossal portico

The Cloisters ❹

The Cloisters seen from Fort Tryon Park

T HIS WORLD-FAMOUS museum of medieval art resides in a building constructed in 1934–8 from medieval cloisters, chapels and halls. Sculptor George Barnard founded the museum in 1914, having amassed architectural pieces and sculptures from many trips to medieval European sites. John D Rockefeller, Jr funded the Metropolitan Museum of Art's purchase of the collection in 1925 and later donated the present site at Fort Tryon Park.

Tomb Effigy of Jean d'Alluye
This tomb immortalizes the 13th-century Crusader.

Pontaut Chapter House

★ **Unicorn Tapestries**
The set of beautifully preserved tapestries, woven in Brussels around 1500, depicts the quest and capture of the mythical unicorn.

STAR EXHIBITS

★ **Unicorn Tapestries**

★ **Belles Heures de Jean, Duc de Berry**

★ **Annunciation Altarpiece by Robert Campin**

Boppard Stained-Glass Lancets (1440–47)
Below the lancet of Saint Catherine these angels display the arms of the coopers' guild, of which Catherine was patron.

Bonnefont Cloister

Trie Cloister

★ **Annunciation Altarpiece** (about 1425)
The Campin Room is the location of this small triptych by Robert Campin of Tournai, a magnificent example of early Flemish painting.

Saint-Guilhem Cloister
Intricate floral ornamentation can be found on the capitals of this cloister.

Romanesque Hall

Virgin and Child Frescoes
This 12th-century fresco is from the Catalonian church of San Juan de Tredós.

KEY TO FLOORPLAN

☐ Exhibition space

☐ Non-exhibition space

Upper floor

Lower floor

Cuxa Cloister
The reconstructed 12th-century cloister features Romanesque architectural detail and motifs.

Enthroned Virgin and Child
This elaborately-carved, ivory sculpture was made in England during the late 13th century.

Main entrance

GALLERY GUIDE
The museum is organized roughly in chronological order. It starts with the Romanesque period (1000 AD) and moves to the Gothic (1150 to 1520). Sculptures, stained glass, paintings and the gardens are on the lower floor. The Unicorn Tapestries are on the upper floor.

★ Belles Heures
This book of hours, a prayer book commissioned by Jean, Duc de Berry for his devotions, is illuminated by 94 miniatures in tempera and gold.

Exploring the Cloisters

KNOWN PARTICULARLY for its Romanesque and Gothic architectural sculpture, the Cloisters collection also includes illuminated manuscripts, stained glass, metalwork, enamels, ivories and paintings. Among its tapestries is the renowned *Unicorn* series. The Cloisters' splendid medieval complex is unrivalled in North America.

A 16th-century Flemish boxwood rosary bead from the Treasury

ROMANESQUE ART

A life-size 12th-century Spanish crucifix portraying Christ as the King of Heaven

FANCIFUL BEASTS and people, acanthus blossoms and scrollwork, top the columns around the Cloisters. Many are in the Romanesque style that flourished in the 11th and 12th centuries. The museum has numerous masterpieces of Romanesque art and architecture, showing the style's powerful, rounded arches and intricate details. Highly embellished capitals and warm, pink marble typify the 12th-century Cuxa Cloister from the Pyrenees in France. A griffin, a dragon, a centaur and a basilisk are among the creatures parading over the Narbonne Arch nearby. In the Romanesque Hall a golden-crowned Christ is depicted as triumphant over death.

In a more solemn style, the apse from the church of Saint-Martín in Fuentidueña, Spain, is a massive, rounded vault constructed from 3,000 blocks of limestone. It is decorated with a 12th-century fresco of the Virgin and Child.

More than 800 years ago, Benedictine and Cistercian monks sat on the cold stone benches in the Pontaut Chapter House. By the 19th century it had become so neglected that it was used as a stable. Its ribbed vaulting is a foretaste of the Gothic style to come.

GOTHIC ART

WHERE ROMANESQUE art was solid, the Gothic style that followed (from 1150 to around 1520) was open, with pointed arches, glowing stained-glass windows and three-dimensional sculpture. Gothic depictions of the Virgin and Child display exquisite craftsmanship.

The Gothic Chapel's brilliantly coloured windows show scenes and figures from Biblical stories. Life-size tomb sculptures include the effigy of the Crusader knight Jean d'Alluye. During the 1790s

Vaulted ceiling of the Pontaut Chapter House

the statue's original home, La Clarté-Dieu Abbey in France, was vandalised and the statue was used to bridge a stream.

In the Boppard Room, the lives of the saints are told in marvellous late-Gothic stained glass from Germany.

Robert Campin's Flemish masterwork, the *Annunciation* altarpiece, is the focus of the Campin Room. It is an intimate room with furnishings that might have belonged to a wealthy 15th-century family.

THE TAPESTRIES

THE CLOISTERS' tapestries are full of rich imagery and symbolism, and are among the museum's most highly prized treasures. The four *Nine Heroes Tapestries* bear the coat of arms of Jean, Duc de Berry, who was a brother of the King of France, and one of the greatest art patrons of the Middle Ages. These tapestries are one of only two sets that survived from the late 14th century; the other set belonged to Jean's brother, Louis, Duc d'Anjou.

Nine great heroes of the past – three pagan, three Hebrew, three Christian – are shown with members of the medieval court, from cardinals, knights and damsels to musicians.

In an adjacent room is the magnificent *Hunt of the Unicorn*, a series of seven tapestries woven in Brussels around 1500. It depicts the symbolic hunt, and capture by a maiden, of the mythical unicorn.

Although they were misused in the 19th century to protect fruit trees from frost damage,

MEDIEVAL GARDENS

More than 250 varieties of plant grown in the Middle Ages can be found in the Cloisters' gardens. The Bonnefont Cloister has herbal, medicinal and cooking plants. The Trie Cloister features plants shown in the *Unicorn Tapestries*, and reveals the use of flowers in medieval symbolism: roses (for the Virgin Mary), pansies (the Holy Trinity) and daisies (the eye of Christ).

Bonnefont Cloister

the tapestries are remarkably well preserved. They are also astonishing in detail, with

Julius Caesar, entertained by court musicians, in a *Nine Heroes* tapestry

literally hundreds of minutely observed plants and animals. Their story can be read as a tale of courtly love, but the series is also an allegory for the Crucifixion and the Resurrection of Christ.

THE TREASURY

IN MEDIEVAL TIMES, precious objects were stored in sanctuaries for safe keeping. At the Cloisters, they are to be found in the Treasury.

The collection includes several Gothic illuminated "books of hours". These were used for the private devotions of the nobility, such as the Limbourg brothers' *Belles Heures*, made for Jean, Duc de Berry, in 1410, and the tiny, palm-sized version by Gothic master Jean Pucelle for the Queen of France, around 1325.

Other religious artifacts range from a 13th-century English ivory Virgin to the 14th-century silver gilt and enamel reliquary shrine thought to have belonged to Queen Elizabeth of Hungary, along with censers, chalices, candlesticks and crucifixes.

Curiosities here include the "Monkey Cup", an enamelled beaker probably made for the 15th-century Burgundian court, showing mischievous monkeys robbing a sleeping peddler; an intricately carved rosary bead the size of a walnut; a 13th-century boat-shaped, jewelled saltcellar; and one of the oldest full sets of playing cards in existence.

Hunting images and symbols depicted in a 15th-century deck of playing cards

The west parlour of the Van Cortlandt House Museum

The Bronx

Once a prosperous suburb with a famous Grand Concourse lined with apartment buildings for the wealthy, the Bronx has now become an unfortunate symbol of urban decay. Still, diverse ethnic communities and charming areas, such as Riverdale at the northern end, remain. Two major attractions are the zoo and the New York Botanical Garden. New Yorkers still flock to the baseball park at Yankee Stadium, now more than 50 years old and maintaining loyalty to its old home in the Bronx.

Wave Hill 🟤

W 249th St and Independence Ave, Riverdale. **[** (718) 549-3200. **M** 231st St then bus Bx7, 10, 24. **Open** 9am–5.30pm Tue–Sun (9am–4.30pm mid Oct to mid May). **Adm charge** Sat, Sun; free Tue–Fri.

When city concrete begins to overwhelm, come to this 28-acre (11-ha) oasis of calm and beauty, with its fine views over to the New Jersey palisades across the Hudson River. The former estate of financier and conservationist George W Perkins, it has had a long series of distinguished tenants, including Theodore Roosevelt, Mark Twain and Arturo Toscanini. Perkins also

owned neighbouring estates, underneath which he built a subterranean recreation centre complete with bowling alley, and a tunnel leading into the main building.

The house and the grounds are open to the public. The house is frequently used for concerts. They often take place in the grand Armor Hall, designed in 1928 for Bashford Dean, who was then the curator of the collection of arms and armour at the Metropolitan Museum of Art.

The gardens were originally designed by Viennese landscape gardener, Albert Millard. There are also greenhouses, lawns, a herb garden and woodlands. Exhibitions range from sculpture to horticulture.

The adjoining Riverdale Park provides more attractive woodland, and pretty paths running alongside the river.

The interior of the grand Armor Hall at Wave Hill

Van Cortlandt House Museum 🟤

Van Cortlandt Park. **[** (718) 543-3344. **M** 242nd St, Van Cortlandt Park. **Open** 10am–4pm Tue–Fri, 11am–4pm Sat, Sun (last adm: 30 mins before closing). **Closed** most public hols. **Adm charge**. 🔲 🔲 🔲 See **The History of New York** pp18–19.

The facade of Van Cortlandt House

A restored 1748 Georgian-Colonial country manor built of rough stone, this was originally the family home of Frederick Van Cortlandt, a New Yorker who inherited great wealth and was related to many of the influential and rich families of his day.

The dining room was used as one of General George Washington's headquarters; the ground behind the house was once the scene of skirmishing during the Revolutionary War.

The interior has American period furnishings as well as a superb collection of delftware and a complete 17th-century Dutch bedroom.

On the exterior, look out for the carved faces in the keystones over the windows.

Woodlawn Cemetery 7

Jerome and Bainbridge Aves.
(718) 920-0500. M Woodlawn.
Open 9am–4.30pm daily. **Office closed** public hols.

Entrance to the Woolworth mausoleum

FOR A GLIMPSE into another kind of social history, visit Woodlawn Cemetery, the burial place of many a wealthy and distinguished New Yorker. Memorials and tombstones are set in beautiful grounds. F W Woolworth and many members of his family are interred in a mausoleum only a little less ornate than the building that carries the family name. The pink marble vault of meat magnate Herman Armour is oddly reminiscent of a ham.

Other New York notables buried here include Mayor Fiorello LaGuardia, Roland Macy, the founder of the great department store, the author Herman Melville and jazz supremo Duke Ellington.

New York Botanical Garden 8

See pp240–41.

International Wildlife Conservation Park 9

See pp242–3.

Yankee Stadium 10

E 161st St at River Ave, Highbridge.
(718) 293-6000. M 161st St.
See **Entertainment** pp344–5.

THIS IS THE HOME of the New York Yankees baseball team. Among Yankee heroes are two of the greatest players of all time: Babe Ruth and Joe DiMaggio (who was also famous for marrying, in 1954, the legendary actress, Marilyn Monroe).

The stadium was completed in 1923 by one Jacob Ruppert, the owner of the New York Yankees team. It became known as "the house that Ruth built" after the famous left-hander Babe Ruth. The Stadium had a face-lift in the mid-1970s, and now seats up to 54,000 people who come for sports, concerts and other events. If you go to a game, take the children along too.

Joe DiMaggio in action at Yankee Stadium in 1941

City Island 11

610 City Island Ave. M 6 to Pelham Parkway, then Bx29 to City Island.
North Wind Undersea Institute Museum (718) 885-0701.

SITUATED JUST off the northeast shore of the Bronx, City Island is a small nautical outpost with a very New England feel – it seems a world apart from New York City, and offers a total change of pace. Its scenic marinas are filled with sailing boats and its seafood restaurants would satisfy any sailor's appetite.

Diving helmet at the North Wind Undersea Institute Museum

Several America's Cup winners have been built in its boatyards.

The main entrance of the North Wind Undersea Institute Museum is constructed from the gaping 9-ft (2.75-m) jaw of a whale. It houses displays on the history of whaling and the only seals in the world that work for the police force. They are trained to retrieve sunken weapons and drugs and to undo the seat belts in submerged cars or planes and then to bring humans to the surface. The seals can sometimes be seen practising retrieving from the bottom of their tank.

City Island is now connected to the rest of the Bronx by bridge. Just to the north on the mainland is Orchard Beach, a very popular crescent of white sand edged with 1930s bathing huts. The best time to visit the beach is during the week, when it will be far less crowded.

An old tug boat at the North Wind Undersea Institute Museum

New York Botanical Garden ❽

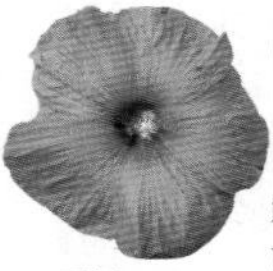

Hibiscus

ONE OF THE oldest and largest botanical gardens in America, founded in 1891, this pastoral oasis covers 250 acres (101 ha), including formal plantings and a large tract of unspoiled woodland along a winding river, one of the last remnants of New York's primeval forest. The showpiece is the Enid A Haupt Conservatory, which was added in 1902 and inspired by London's Crystal Palace and the Palm House at Kew Gardens. The garden is not simply a horticulturalist's paradise, however; it is also a centre for environmental and ecological research.

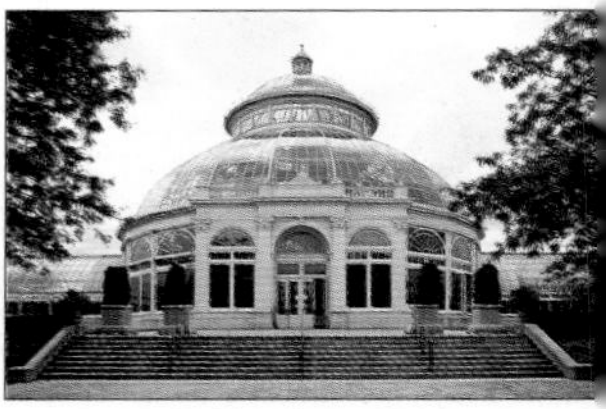

Entrance to Enid A Haupt Conservatory

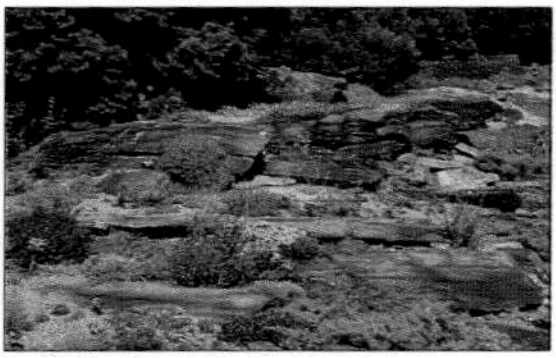

Rock Garden
Giant boulders, ledges, streams and a waterfall create an alpine habitat to display plants from the world's rocky and mountainous regions ④

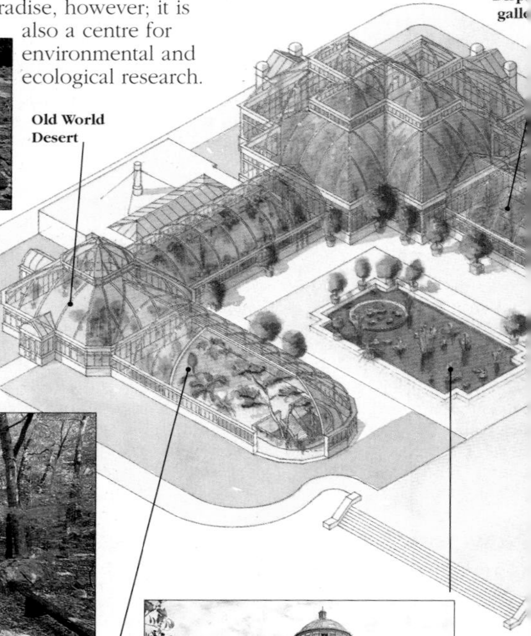

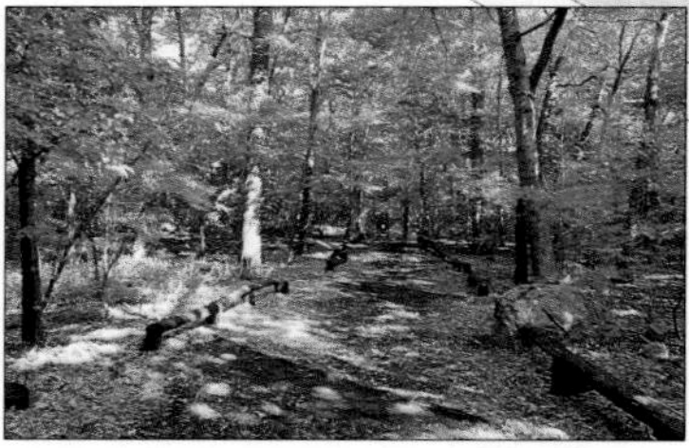

Botanical Garden Forest
One of New York City's last surviving natural forest areas includes red oak, white ash, tulip trees and hemlock ⑤

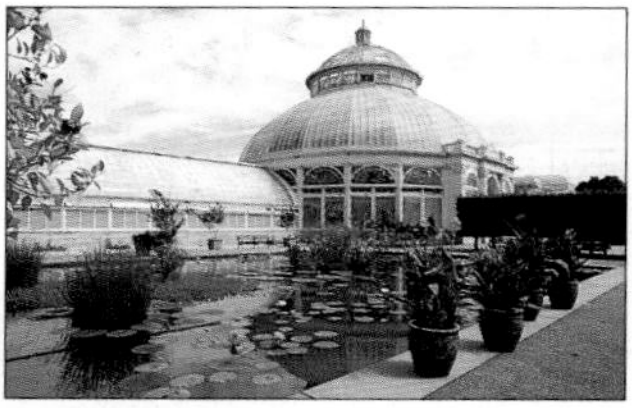

Hardy Pool
Exquisite aquatic plants from all over the world are displayed here.

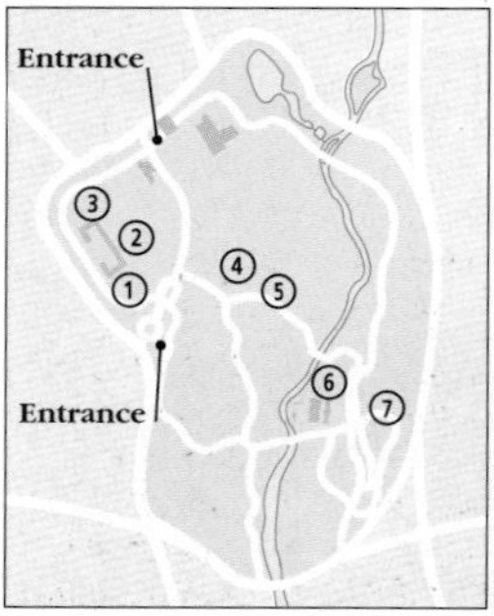

LOCATOR MAP

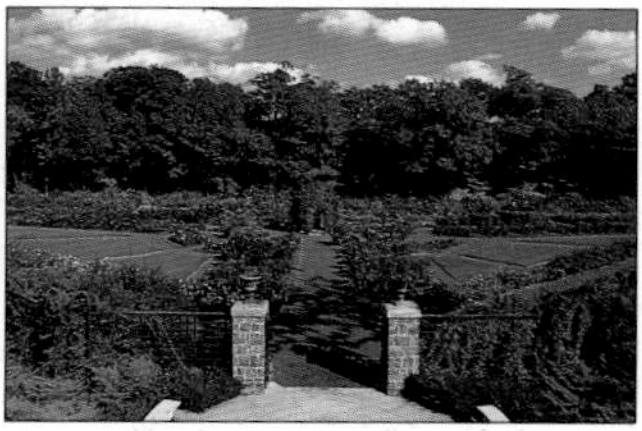

Rose Garden
Over 2,700 roses have been planted in the Peggy Rockefeller Rose Garden, laid out in 1988 according to the original 1915 design ⑦

Palm Court
Specimens of one quarter of the world's palm species are displayed here in a carefully controlled tropical environment.

VISITORS' CHECKLIST

Southern Blvd. **☎** *(718) 817-8700.* **Ⓜ** *4, D to Bedford Park Blvd.* **🚌** *Bx12, Bx19, Bx41.* **Open** *Nov–Mar: 10am–4pm Tue–Sun; Apr–Oct: 10am–6pm Tue–Sun (last adm to Conservatory: 1hr before closing).* **Note** *Newly restored Conservatory reopening in spring 1997.* **Adm charge.**
🎥 ♿ 🎫 🖥 🎦
Lectures.

The Enid A Haupt Conservatory consists of 11 areas, each with its own botanical or geographical theme. Temperature, light and humidity are all carefully controlled to simulate specific natural environments ①

Demonstration Gardens
Colourful displays are designed to inspire visitors with ideas for their own gardens ③

Jane Watson Irwin Perennial Garden
Flowering perennials are arranged in dramatic patterns according to height, shade and blooming time ②

Tropical pool

Tropical flora

Tropical New World Lowland Rainforest

Aquatic plants

Main entrance

Tropical New World Upland Rainforest

Snuff Mill Terrace Café
A new café near the Demonstration Gardens, with seating indoors and outdoors, is planned for spring 1997. In the meantime, light refreshments are served to Garden visitors on the terrace of the Lorillard Snuff Mill, by the Bronx River ⑥

International Wildlife Conservation Park ❾

FOUNDED IN 1899, the International Wildlife Conservation Park (formerly the Bronx Zoo) is the largest urban zoo in the USA, home to some 4,300 animals representing 764 species, living in realistic representations of their natural habitats. The Park is a leader in the perpetuation of endangered species, such as the hairy rhinoceros and the snow leopard. Its 265 acres (107 ha) of woods, streams and parklands include a children's zoo and a shuttle train that transports visitors around the sprawling park – visitors are also free to walk around. For the best overview of the different areas of the park take the Skyfari cable car.

Zoo Center entrance

Wildfowl Marsh

World of Darkness reverses the day/night cycle so visitors can see nocturnal animals like bats and bush-babies in action.

Mouse-House

Skyfari cable car

Carter Giraffe Building

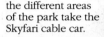

★ **African Plains**
Zebras, lions, cheetahs and gazelles roam the African Plains. Predators and prey are separated by a moat.

Africa
Oryxes find shelter under an African hut.

Asia entrance

Camel Rides
Children enjoy the zoo's experiences such as camel rides and other attractions.

Bengali Express monorail

★ **JungleWorld**
A glass-enclosed tropical rainforest harbours mammals, birds and reptiles from South Asia. The animals are kept apart from visitors by ravines, streams and cliffs.

Monkeys in JungleWorld

Baboon Reserve
Visitors wander along a dry riverbed to see wildlife in an Ethiopian mountain habitat.

Children's Zoo
Kids can crawl through a prairie dog tunnel, climb on a spider's web, try on a turtle shell, and pet and feed the animals.

The Zoo Center houses elephants, rhinos and tapirs.

Great Ape House

World of Reptiles

Southern Boulevard entrance

Aquatic Bird House

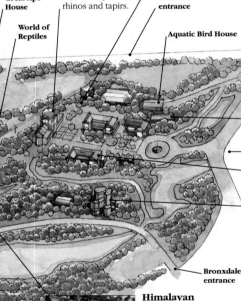

Dejur Aviary

Rainey Gate entrance

Monkey House

★ World of Birds
Exotic birds soar free in the natural surroundings of a rainforest. Simulated tropical thunderstorms occur each day at 2pm, and an artificial waterfall rushes down a 50-ft (15-m) fibreglass cliff.

Great hornbill

Bronxdale entrance

Himalayan Highlands
Endangered species, such as snow leopards and red pandas are kept here.

★ Wild Asia
The Bengali Express monorail journeys through forests and meadows of an Asian habitat, where elephants, rhinoceroses and Siberian tigers roam free.

Queens

A BIG, SPRAWLING borough, Queens has a wide variety of attractions and residential and commercial areas, including a business district known as Long Island City. Development of the borough accelerated after 1909, when the construction of Queensboro Bridge made commuting easier. The city's two main airports are located here and there are various ethnic enclaves, including the Greek neighbourhood of Astoria, and some Asian communities in Flushing, a district long popular with varied ethnic groups.

A 1900 Mutoscope at the Museum of the Moving Image

Flushing Meadow–Corona Park ⑫

Ⓜ *Willets Point-Shea Stadium. See **Entertainment** pp344–5.*

THE SITE of New York's two World's Fairs now offers expansive waterside picnic grounds and a multitude of attractions. These include the 50,000-seat Shea Stadium, the home of the New York Mets baseball team and a popular venue for rock concerts.

Flushing Meadow is also home to the US Tennis Center, where the prestigious United States Open is played. The courts are open for would-be Agassis, Grafs and Everts for the remainder of the year. In the 1920s this area was known as the Corona Dump, a nightmarish place of salt marshes and great piles of smouldering trash. In *The Great Gatsby*, author F Scott Fitzgerald dubbed it the "valley of ashes". It reeked of rotting garbage and glowed red at night. New York's Parks' Commissioner Robert Moses was the driving force behind its transformation. A whole mountain of rubbish was removed and the river was totally re-channelled. The marsh was drained and sewage works were built, helping to restore the abused area. This site was to serve as the venue for the 1939 World's Fair, at which a world on the brink of war saluted the elusive notion of world peace.

The Unisphere, symbol of the 1964 Fair, still dominates the remains of the fairground. This giant hollow ball of green steel, built by the US Steel Corporation, is 12 storeys high and weighs a massive 350 tonnes.

The 1964 World's Fair Unisphere at Flushing Meadow-Corona Park

New York Hall of Science ⑬

46th Ave and 111th St Flushing Meadows, Corona Park. Ⓒ *(718) 699-0005.* Ⓜ *111th St.* **Open** *10am–5pm Wed–Sun.* **Closed** *public hols.* **Adm charge.** ⓞ ⓑ ⓟ

THE SCIENCE PAVILION built for the 1964 World's Fair was designed with stained glass set in concrete panels. It is now a hands-on museum for science and technology, with exhibits on colour, light and physics. Children love to watch the giant video screens that can magnify the microbes in a drop of water, and the interactive video and laser optical exhibits.

The concrete curtain wall of the New York Hall of Science

American Museum of the Moving Image and Kaufman Astoria Studio ⑭

35th Ave at 36th St, Astoria. **Museum** Ⓒ *(718) 784-0077.* **Studio** Ⓒ *(718) 392-5600.* Ⓜ *36th St.* **Museum open** *noon–4pm Tue–Fri, noon–6pm Sat & Sun.* **Adm charge.** **Studio not open** *to public.* ⓞ ⓑ ⓟ

IN NEW YORK'S film-making heyday, Rudolph Valentino, W C Fields, the Marx Brothers and Gloria Swanson all made films here in the city's largest studio, opened by Paramount Pictures in 1920. When the movies went west, the Army took over, making training films here from 1941 to 1971.

The complex stood empty until the 1970s when Astoria Motion Picture and Television Foundation was founded to preserve it. *The Wiz*, Sidney Lumet's $24 million musical

Poster at the Museum of the Moving Image

starring Michael Jackson and Diana Ross, was made here, helping to pay for restoration. Today, the studios house the largest movie-making facilities

on the East Coast and are again in full use. *The Cotton Club* and Woody Allen's *Radio Days* were filmed here.

In 1981 one of the studio buildings was transformed into the American Museum of the Moving Image, with interactive displays on production and promotion and theatres for the screening of movies and television.

There is a lot of kitsch and memorabilia on display, from Annie Hall's outfits to the Star Trek costumes. The main gallery on the second floor draws from the permanent collection, containing over 60,000 movie artefacts. These include fun exhibits such as a mirror in which you can see your own head reflected above the

body of Sylvester Stallone as *Rocky*, Marilyn Monroe in *The Seven Year Itch* or Eddie Murphy in *Beverly Hills Cop*.

"Behind the Screen" looks at every aspect of film-making including editing, sound and costumes. Visitors can walk through the original set for Paul Newman's 1988 version of *The Glass Menagerie*. A cinema on the main floor has a full schedule of film and video programmes, ranging in variety from early silents to the most avant-garde.

Head for 31st Street for the heart of Astoria's big Greek enclave. Here and along Ditmars Boulevard and Broadway are legions of *zacharoplasteia* (pastry shops) and cafés, *tavernas* (restaurants) and *psistaria* (grills), nightclubs, 11 Greek Orthodox churches and a Greek cinema. Greek religious processions are very moving.

Brooklyn

The bandstand at Prospect Park *(see p246)*

I F BROOKLYN were a separate city, it would be the USA's fourth largest. It has a character all of its own. Many entertainment greats – Mel Brooks, Phil Silvers, Woody Allen and Neil Simon among them – celebrate their birthplace with great affection and humour. Brooklyn is the ultimate melting pot, with West Indians, Hasidic Jews, Russians, Italians and Arabs, to mention only a few groups, living side by side. Among the diverse neighbourhoods are the historic residential districts of Park Slope and Brooklyn Heights.

Brooklyn Children's Museum ⑮

145 Brooklyn Ave. 🅲 *(718) 735-4432.* Ⓜ *Kingston.* **Open** *2pm–5pm Wed–Fri, noon–5pm Sat, Sun. Jul, Aug; noon–5pm Mon, noon–5pm Wed–Sun.* **Closed** *1 Jan, Thanksgiving, 25 Dec.* **Donation expected.** 🅾 🅰

T HE BROOKLYN Children's Museum was the first to be designed especially for children and was founded in 1899. Since then, it has been a model, inspiration and consultant to the development of more than 250 museums for children across the country and all over the world. It is housed in a high-tech, specially designed underground building dating from 1976. It is one of the most imaginative and advanced children's museums anywhere.

The layout of the building is a maze of complex interconnected passageways running off

the main "people tube" – a huge drainage pipe that connects the four levels. This is not a passive place where children are meant to stand around and stare – the emphasis is on involvement and hands-on exhibits. Everywhere you look there are curiosities to be discovered, experienced, made or played with. There is even a walk-on piano like the one in the film *Big* – children of every age find it quite irresistible.

Special exhibitions and events are designed to help children learn about the planet, resolve their fears or problems, understand other cultures and to discover the past. The squeals of laughter and delight that are always heard are a sign of this well-designed and clever museum's success in teaching children and the young at heart.

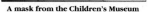

A mask from the Children's Museum

The facade of the Brooklyn Academy of Music

Brooklyn Academy of Music ⑯

30 Lafayette Ave. 📞 *(718) 636-4100.*
Ⓜ *Atlantic Ave.* **Adm charge.**
🚫 ♿ 🅿 *See* **Entertainment**
pp338–9.

H OME TO THE Brooklyn
Philharmonic, the
Academy (well known to all
as BAM) is Brooklyn's leading
cultural venue and the oldest,
founded in 1858. It offers
outstanding performances,
often tending towards the
innovative and avant-garde.

The classic 1908 building
was designed by Herts &
Tallant, and inaugurated with
a fine production of Gounod's
opera *Faust* featuring the
legendary Neapolitan tenor
Enrico Caruso. The list of the
greats who have performed
here is endless and includes
actress Sarah Bernhardt,
ballerina Anna Pavlova,
musicians Pablo Casals and
Sergei Rachmaninoff, poets
Edna St Vincent Millay and
Carl Sandburg, and statesman
Winston Churchill. Many
international touring groups
have made appearances here,
including Britain's Royal
Shakespeare Company.

The BAM Next Wave Festival
has presented a number of
well-known contemporary
artists, including
musicians Philip
Glass and David
Byrne, perform-
ance artist Laurie
Anderson, and
choreographers
Pina Bausch and
Mark Morris. The
Brooklyn Academy of Music
also runs the Majestic Theater
nearby, once a cinema and
now used for dance, drama
and music events.

Grand Army Plaza ⑰

Plaza St at Flatbush Ave.
📞 *(718) 965-8951.* Ⓜ *Grand Army
Plaza.* **Arch open** *for occasional
exhibitions.*

**The Soldiers' and Sailors' Arch at
Grand Army Plaza**

F REDERICK LAW OLMSTED and
Calvert Vaux laid out this
grand oval in 1870 as a gate-
way to Prospect Park. The
Soldiers' and Sailors' Arch and
its sculptures were added in
1892 as a tribute to the Union
Army. The bust of John F
Kennedy is the only official
New York monument to him.

In June, the plaza is the
centre of the Welcome Back
to Brooklyn Festival for the
famous – and not-so-famous
– people who were born in
the Brooklyn area.

Park Slope Historic District ⑱

Streets from Prospect Park W below
Flatbush Ave, to 8th/7th/5th avenues.
Ⓜ *Grand Army Plaza.*

Relief work on the Montauk Club

T HIS WONDERFUL enclave of
beautiful Victorian town
houses was developed on the
edge of Prospect Park in the
1880s. It served the upper-
middle-class professionals
who were able to commute
into Manhattan after the
Brooklyn Bridge was opened
in 1883. The shady streets
are lined with two- to five-
storey houses in every
architectural style popular in
the late 19th century, some
with the towers, turrets and
curlicues so representative of
the era. Particularly fine
examples are in Romanesque
Revival style, with rounded
entry arches.

The Montauk Club at 25
Eighth Avenue combines the
style of Venice's Ca' d'Oro
palazzo with the friezes and
gargoyles of the Montauk
Indians, after whom this
popular 19th-century
gathering place was named.

Prospect Park ⑲

📞 *(718) 965-8951.* 📠 *(718) 788-
8549.* Ⓜ *Grand Army Plaza.*
🎫 *(718) 287-3400.*

D ESIGNERS OLMSTED and Vaux
considered this park,
opened in 1867, better than
their earlier Central Park. The
Long Meadow, a sweep of
broad lawns and grand vistas,
is the longest unbroken swath
of green space in New York.

Olmsted's belief was that
"a feeling of relief is experienced by entering them [the
parks] on escaping from the
cramped, confining and
controlling circumstances of
the streets of the town". That

The facade of the Brooklyn Public Library on Grand Army Plaza

vision is still as true today as it was a century ago.

Among the many notable features are Stanford White's colonnaded Croquet Shelter, and the pools and weeping willows of the Vale of Cashmere. The Music Grove bandstand has major Japanese influences and hosts both jazz and classical music concerts throughout the summer.

A favourite feature of the park is the Camperdown Elm, an ancient and twisted tree planted in 1872. The Friends of Prospect Park raise money to keep it and all the park trees healthy. This old elm has inspired poems and paintings by many. Prospect Park has a wide variety of landscapes, from classical gardens dotted with statues to rocky glens with running brooks. A guided tour with a ranger is the best way to see the park.

Carousel horse in Prospect Park

The Brooklyn Museum ㉀

See pp248–51.

Brooklyn Botanic Garden ㉁

1000 Washington Ave. (718) 622-4433. Prospect Pk, Eastern Pkwy. **Grounds open** Apr–Sep: 8am–6pm Tue–Fri (10am Sat & Sun); Oct–Mar: 8am–4.30pm (10am Sat & Sun). **Closed** 1 Jan, Thanksgiving, 25 Dec. **Adm charge** for Japanese Garden, Sat & Sun.

THOUGH IT is not vast in size, you will find that this 50-acre (20-ha) garden holds many delights. The area was designed by the Olmsted Brothers in 1910, and features a traditional Elizabethan-style "knot" herb garden and one of North America's largest collections of roses.

The central showpiece is a Japanese hill-and-pond garden, complete with both a tea-house and Shinto shrines. In late April and early May the park promenade is aglow with delicate, Japanese cherry blossoms, which have prompted an annual festival featuring typical Japanese culture, food and music.

April is also the time for tourists to appreciate Magnolia Plaza, where some 80 trees display their beautiful, creamy blossoms against a backdrop of daffodils on Boulder Hill.

The Fragrance Garden is planted in raised beds, where the heavily scented, textured and flavoured plants are all labelled in Braille, giving blind visitors an opportunity to identify them as well.

The new conservatory now houses one of America's largest bonsai collections and some rare rainforest trees, which are providing scientists with medicinal extracts to produce life-saving drugs.

Brooklyn Botanic Garden lily pond

A beluga whale at the New York Aquarium

Coney Island ㉂

Boardwalk and W 8th St, Coney Island. Stillwell Ave, Coney Island. **New York Aquarium** (718) 265-3400.

IN THE MID-19TH century, the Brooklyn poet Walt Whitman composed many of his works on Coney Island, accompanied by the roar of the surf. At that time it was untamed Atlantic coastline, the tip of the nose on the great "whale" to which the poet compared Long Island.

By the 1920s, Coney Island was starting to bill itself as the "World's Largest Playground". It had grown from three huge fairgrounds built between 1887 and 1904 (Luna Park, Dreamland and Steeplechase Park), providing a popular combination of hair-raising rides and nearby beaches. The subway arrived in 1920, and the addition of the board-walk in 1921 ensured Coney Island's popularity throughout the Depression. Here was an escape from the city that cost little more than a few nickels.

A popular attraction is the New York Aquarium, which moved here from Battery Park in 1955, and is easily worth a day's visit. Today, Coney Island's boardwalk yields ocean views, the big wooden Cyclone roller coaster still rates screams and tourists will find Nathan's Famous still serves hot dogs that are, indeed, famous.

The Brooklyn Museum ⑱

WHEN IT OPENED in 1897, The Brooklyn Museum building, designed to be the largest cultural edifice in the world, was the greatest achievement of New York architects McKim, Mead & White. Though only one-fifth completed, the museum is today one of the most impressive cultural institutions in the United States, with a permanent encyclopedic collection of some 1.5 million objects which are housed in a grand structure of 450,000 sq ft (41,805 sq m).

North facade, designed by Stanford White

KEY TO FLOORPLAN

- ☐ African, Oceanic and New World art
- ☐ Asian art
- ☐ Prints, drawings and photographs
- ☐ Classical and Egyptian art
- ☐ Decorative arts
- ☐ Painting and sculpture
- ☐ Williamsburg murals
- ☐ Special exhibitions
- ☐ Non-exhibition space

Chinese Jar
Cobalt blue fishes and water plants adorn this 14th-century Yuan dynasty blue-and-white ceramic jar.

★ **Paracas Textile**
Over 2,000 years old, a woven mantle from Peru glows with colour and life.

Mother and Child
Figurines like this are carved by the Luluwa tribe of Zaire as amulets for pregnant or nursing women.

Third floor

Second floor

Sculpture Garden

First floor

West wing

Portico and main entrance

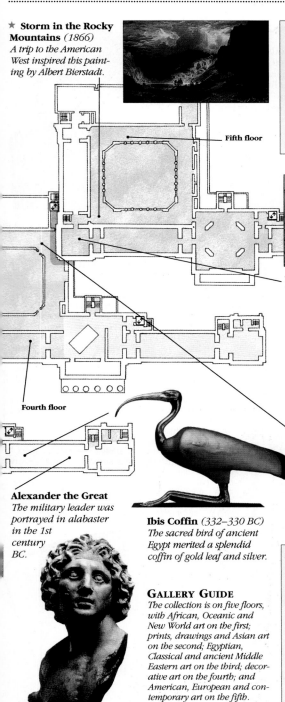

★ **Storm in the Rocky Mountains** (1866)
A trip to the American West inspired this painting by Albert Bierstadt.

Fifth floor

★ **The Ducal Palace at Venice** (1908)
The magical light of Venice was brilliantly captured by Impressionist Claude Monet.

★ **Parlour, Nicholas Schenk House**
This room re-creates middle-class life in 1820s Brooklyn.

Fourth floor

Alexander the Great
The military leader was portrayed in alabaster in the 1st century BC.

Ibis Coffin (332–330 BC)
The sacred bird of ancient Egypt merited a splendid coffin of gold leaf and silver.

GALLERY GUIDE
The collection is on five floors, with African, Oceanic and New World art on the first; prints, drawings and Asian art on the second; Egyptian, Classical and ancient Middle Eastern art on the third; decorative art on the fourth; and American, European and contemporary art on the fifth. There is special exhibition space on the first and fourth floors.

STAR EXHIBITS

★ **Paracas Textile**

★ **The Ducal Palace at Venice by Claude Monet**

★ **Storm in the Rocky Mountains – Mount Rosalie by Albert Bierstadt**

★ **Parlour, Nicholas Schenk House**

Exploring the Collection

T HE BROOKLYN MUSEUM houses one of the finest art
collections in the United States. Its strengths
include an outstanding collection of Native
American art from the Southwest; 28 American
period rooms; some exquisite examples of ancient
Egyptian and Islamic art; and many important
American and European paintings.

**Seated Buddha torso in limestone, from India
(late 3rd century AD)**

AFRICAN, OCEANIC AND NEW WORLD ART

T HE BROOKLYN Museum set
a precedent in the United
States in 1923 by exhibiting
African objects as works of art
rather than artefacts. Since
then, the African art collection
has grown steadily in both
importance and size.

Rare exhibits include an
intricately carved ivory gong
from the Benin kingdom of
16th-century Nigeria, one of
only five in existence.

The museum also houses a
very important collection of
Native American work, including totem poles, textiles and
pottery. A 19th-century deerskin shirt, once worn by a
chief of the Blackfoot tribe,
depicts his brave and daring
exploits in
battle.

Ancient American
artistic traditions
are represented by
Peruvian textiles,
Central American
gold and Mexican
sculpture. A
beautifully
preserved tunic
from Peru, dating
from AD 600, is so
tightly woven that its vibrant
symbolic designs appear to
have been painted onto the
cloth rather than woven in the
traditional manner.

The Oceanic collection
includes sculpture from the
Solomon Islands, Papua New
Guinea and New Zealand.

ASIAN ART

C HANGING EXHIBITIONS from
the museum's permanent
collection of Chinese,
Japanese, Korean,
Indian, Southeast
Asian and Islamic
art are always on
display. Japanese
and Chinese
paintings, Indian
miniatures and
Islamic
calligraphy
complement
the Asian
sculpture,
textiles and
ceramics.
The collec-
tions of
Japanese folk
art, Chinese cloisonné
(enamel work) and
Oriental carpets are of
particular note. Good
examples of Buddhist
art range from a variety
of Chinese, Indian
and Southeast Asian
Buddhas to a mandala-
patterned temple banner from
14th-century Tibet, painted in
rich, luminous watercolours.

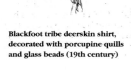

**Blackfoot tribe deerskin shirt,
decorated with porcupine quills
and glass beads (19th century)**

DECORATIVE ARTS

T HE FOCUS of the decorative
arts department is a very
stylish assembly of 28 superb
American period rooms.

The earliest is from a 17th-
century Brooklyn Dutch
house. It served as a parlour,
dining room and sleeping
area, with the enclosed "bed
boxes" built against the wall
opposite the fireplace. The
Moorish Smoking Room, from
John D Rockefeller's brownstone house, is an opulent
example of elegant New York
living during the 1880s. In
complete contrast, the most
recent room is a 1928–30 Art
Deco study from a Park
Avenue apartment, including
a secret walk-in bar hidden
behind panelling during the
Prohibition era *(see pp28-9).*

***Normandie* chrome pitcher, by
Peter Müller-Munk (1935)**

Also on exhibit is a wide selection from the museum's vast collection of furniture, ceramics, glass, pewter, silver and metalware, including a 1930s pitcher whose shape was inspired by the funnels of the ocean liner *Normandie*.

EGYPTIAN, CLASSICAL AND ANCIENT MIDDLE EASTERN ART

RECOGNIZED AS among the world's finest, the Egyptian collection holds many masterpieces. It begins with an early female figure dating from 3500 BC, and encompasses sculptures, statues, tomb paintings and reliefs as well as funerary paraphernalia. Of the latter, the most unusual is the coffin of an ibis, probably recovered from the vast animal cemetery of Tuna el-Gebel in Middle Egypt. The ibis was a sacred bird representing the god Thoth, and this coffin is made of solid silver and wood overlaid with gold leaf, with rock crystal for the bird's eyes. These galleries have been renovated into a state-of-the-art, hi-tech installation.

Among the artefacts from the Greek and Roman civilizations are statuary, pottery, bronzes, jewellery and mosaics.

Among the Ancient Near and Middle Eastern exhibits are an extensive collection of pottery and 12 alabaster reliefs from the Assyrian palace of King Ashur-nasir-pal II. These date from around 883-859 BC and depict the king fighting, overseeing his crops and purifying the "sacred tree", a major icon in Assyrian religion.

PAINTING AND SCULPTURE

THIS SECTION contains works from the 14th century to the present, including a well-known and outstanding 19th-century French art collection with works by Degas, Rodin, Monet, Cézanne, Matisse and Pissarro. It also boasts one of the largest holdings of Spanish

Pierre de Wiessant (about 1886) by Auguste Rodin, from his *Burghers of Calais* group

Colonial paintings and one of the best collections of North American paintings to be found in the United States.

The museum's 20th-century American collection includes, appropriately, *Brooklyn Bridge* by Georgia O'Keeffe.

The Sculpture Garden holds a collection of architectural ornamentation taken from demolished New York buildings, including statues that were rescued from the original Pennsylvania Station.

PRINTS, DRAWINGS AND PHOTOGRAPHS

THE PRINTS section displays examples by many masters, ranging from a rare woodcut print by Dürer entitled *The Great Triumphal Chariot* and works by Piranesi to an excellent Impressionist and Post-Impressionist collection. This includes works by Toulouse-Lautrec and Mary Cassatt, one of the few women and the only American associated with the Impressionist movement. There are lithographs by James McNeill Whistler, Winslow Homer engravings,

Rotherbide, an etching by James McNeill Whistler (1860)

and a superb selection of drawings by Fragonard, Paul Klee, Van Gogh, Picasso and Gorky, among others, many of them in black and white.

The photography collection consists mainly of 20th-century American photographs, including a 1924 portrait of Mary Pickford by Edward Steichen and shots by Margaret Bourke-White and Bernice Abbott. Contemporary examples include photographs by Robert Mapplethorpe.

Sandstone reliefs from Thebes in Egypt (around 760–656 BC), depicting the great god Amun-Re and his consort Mut

Staten Island

Apart from the famous ferry ride, Staten Island and its attractions are not well known to New Yorkers in general. Residents feel so ignored, they've talked about seceding from the city. Visitors who venture beyond the ferry terminal, however, will be pleasantly surprised to find hills, lakes and greenery with expanses of open space, amazing harbour views and well-preserved buildings dating from early New York. One of the biggest surprises here, is a cache of Tibetan art hidden away in a replica of a Buddhist temple.

Historic Richmond Town ㉓

441 Clarke Ave. **[** (718) 351-1611. **⁜** S74 from ferry. **Open** Jan–Mar: 1pm–5pm Wed–Fri; Apr–Jun & Sep–Dec: 1pm–5pm Wed–Sun; Jul–Aug: 10am–5pm Wed–Fri, 1pm–5pm Sat & Sun. **Adm charge.** **◙ ⑬ ✄ ▯**

Cologne at the General Store

There are now 29 buildings, 14 of which are open to the public, in New York's only restored village and outdoor museum. The village was first named Coccles-town, after the local shellfish, but was soon corrupted to "Cuckoldstown", much to the annoyance of the residents. By the end of the Revolutionary War the new name of Richmondtown had been adopted. It was the county seat until Staten Island was made part of the city in 1898, and has been preserved as an example of an early New York settlement.

The Voorlezer House, built in the Dutch era before 1696, is the oldest elementary school to be found in the country. The Stephens General Store, which opened in 1837, doubled as the local post office. It has been restored authentically right down to the contents on the shelves.

The well-renovated complex, set in 103 acres (42 ha), includes wagon sheds, a courthouse built in 1837, houses, several shops and a tavern. There are also seasonal workshops where traditional rural crafts are demonstrated to visitors.

St Andrew's Church (1708) and its old graveyard are just across the Mill Pond stream and the Historical Society Museum is in the County Clerk's and Surrogate's Office.

Jacques Marchais Center of Tibetan Art ㉔

338 Lighthouse Ave. **[** (718) 987-3500. **⁜** S74 from ferry. **Open** Apr–Nov: 1pm–5pm (last adm: 4.45pm) Wed–Sun; Dec–Mar: by appt. **Closed** public hols. **Adm charge.** **◙ ✄ ▯**

A hilltop provides a very tranquil setting for one of the largest collections of privately owned Tibetan art outside Tibet. The main building is a replica of a mountain temple with an authentic altar

The Voorlezer House at Richmond Town

in three tiers, crowded with gold, silver and bronze figures. Another building is used as a library. The garden has some stone sculptures, including life-size Buddhas. The museum was built in 1947 by Mrs Harry Klauber, a dealer in Asian art trading under the name of Jacques Marchais. The Dalai Lama paid his first visit here in 1991.

A gazebo at the Snug Harbor Cultural Center

Snug Harbor Cultural Center ㉕

1000 Richmond Terrace. **[** (718) 448-2500. **⁜** S40 from ferry to Snug Harbor Gate. **Grounds open** dawn–dusk daily. **Closed** 1 Jan, Thanksgiving, 25 Dec. **⑬** limited. **✄ ▯**

Founded in 1801 as a haven for aged sailors and now an arts centre, Snug Harbor is a complex of 28 historical buildings in various stages of restoration. The best are five stately Greek Revival gems, dating from 1831 to 1880. The oldest of these, the Main Hall, is now the Newhouse Center for Contemporary Art, but the ships at sea that decorate the stained-glass windows are a reminder of its origins.

Sacred sculpture at the Jacques Marchais Center of Tibetan Art

Other buildings house the award-winning Staten Island Children's Museum and the Veterans Memorial Hall, a restored chapel now used for indoor performances.

An annual sculpture festival and summer shows are held on the lawns. The grounds include the Staten Island Botanical Garden, with its noted orchid collection and a beautiful rose garden.

Snug Harbor is the legacy from a Scottish sailor, Robert Richard Randall, who became rich during the Revolutionary War, some say by piracy, and bequeathed his wealth to care for less fortunate seamen. His estate's trustees bought the property so that the sailors could enjoy its harbour views.

Clear Comfort, Alice Austen's lifetime residence

Alice Austen House 26

2 Hylan Blvd. (718) 816-4506.
S 51 from ferry to Hylan Blvd.
Open noon–5pm Thu–Sun. **Closed** public hols. **Donation expected.**
limited.

CLEAR COMFORT is a delightfully-named small cottage built around 1710, in a setting with splendid harbour views. This was the home of the photographer Alice Austen. Born in 1866, she lived in this house for most of her life. She documented life on the island, in Manhattan, and also on trips to other parts of the country and on her travels to Europe. She lost all her money in the stock market Crash of 1929 and her poverty forced her into a public poorhouse at the age of 84. One year later, her photographic talent was finally recognized by *Life* magazine, which published an article about her, earning her enough money to enter a nursing home. She left 3,500 negatives dating from 1880 to 1930. Today the Friends of Alice Austen House mounts exhibitions of her best work.

Even Further Afield

The village of Broad Channel at Jamaica Bay

Jamaica Bay Wildlife Refuge Center 27

Cross Bay Blvd at Broad Channel.
(718) 318-4340. Broad Channel. **Open** 8.30am–5pm daily.

THE MARSHES and uplands of the Refuge cover an area almost the size of Manhattan. Over 300 species of bird live here either seasonally or all year round. Situated on the main Atlantic migratory path, the Refuge is at its best in spring and autumn, when the skies are filled with skeins of geese and ducks. The park rangers conduct hikes and nature walks for weekend visitors – be sure to wear suitable shoes and clothes, and take along a zoom lens camera or binoculars to get the best from your visit. The only village at Jamaica Bay is named Broad Channel, a small collection of houses on pilings along the Cross Bay Boulevard. The Refuge and a 10-mile (16-km) stretch of beach and boardwalk at nearby Rockaway, are accessible by subway straight from the heart of Manhattan.

Jones Beach State Park 28

(516) 785-1600.
Long Island Railroad from Penn Station to Jones Beach. **Operates** 22 May–12 Sep. (718) 454-5477.
Jones Beach Theater
(516) 221-1000.
Beaches open 22 May–12 Sep.

JONES BEACH was the creation of New York's Parks' Commissioner Robert Moses *(see p244)*, who transformed this narrow spit of land into Long Island's most accessible and popular beach in 1929. There are sand dunes, surf on the Atlantic side and sheltered water in the bay. There is also pitch-and-putt golf, swimming pools, restaurants and the Jones Beach Theater, which hosts a variety of open-air concerts in the summer.

Robert Moses State Park is on the next island to the east, Fire Island, which is over 30 miles (48 km) long, yet less than 900 yds (800 m) across. Areas of the island are totally unspoiled and unpopulated, with long stretches of white sands, making it a great place for walking and cycling in peaceful surroundings.

Fire Island's communities are small and very varied – some are favoured by singles looking for the company of the opposite sex, others are sedate and family-orientated, others favourites with the big New York gay community.

Sunbathers basking at Jones Beach

FIVE GUIDED WALKS

WALKING IN NEW YORK is an excellent way to discover the human scale of the city. The following ten pages explore the unique character and charm of New York through five thematic walks. These range from an exploration of Greenwich Village and SoHo's literary and artistic connections *(see pp260–1)* to a trip across the Brooklyn Bridge for spectacular views and a glimpse of 19th-century New York *(see pp264–5).*

In addition, each of the 15 areas of Manhattan described in the *Area by Area* section of this book has a short walk on its *Street-by-Street* map, taking you past many of the interesting sights in that area. Various organizations and enthusiasts run walking tours of the city. These range from serious appraisals of architectural history to a guide to the ghosts of Broadway. Details of tour organizers are listed on page 353, or look at the listings in *New York* magazine. As in any major city, take extra care of your personal belongings while out walking *(see p356–7).* Plan your route ahead of time, walk during daylight hours and, if possible, go in a group.

Sculpture outside US Custom House, Lower Manhattan

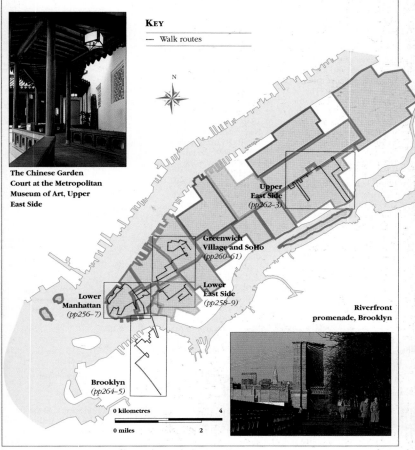

KEY

----- Walk routes

N

The Chinese Garden Court at the Metropolitan Museum of Art, Upper East Side

Upper East Side
(pp262–3)

Greenwich Village and SoHo
(pp260–61)

Lower East Side
(pp258–9)

Lower Manhattan
(pp256–7)

Riverfront promenade, Brooklyn

Brooklyn
(pp264–5)

0 kilometres   4

0 miles   2

Relaxing in Grove Street, Greenwich Village

A Two-Hour Walk in Lower Manhattan

This walk traces the tip of Manhattan from colonial capital to the World Financial Center, passing along the canyon-like streets of the financial district, with detours to the historic South Street Seaport as well as New York's newest neighbourhood, Battery Park City. For more details of sights in Lower Manhattan, see pages 64–79; for South Street Seaport, see pages 80–91.

Battery Park and Federal New York

Start at Battery Park ①, the tip of the island, named for the line of cannons that once protected the harbour. Visit Castle Clinton, an 1807 fort, to see dioramas of a changing New York. The shoreline is much further out than it used to be; much of the edge of Manhattan is built on landfill, including most of this park.

Walk a little further inland past the many statues and monuments and the handsome Beaux Arts US Custom House ②. The building is to become the new home of the Museum of the American Indian. Ironically, it was near to this spot, in 1626, that Peter Minuit acquired Manhattan Island from the local Indians, in exchange for $24 worth of beads and other trinkets.

Cross the street to Bowling Green, the city's first park, dating to 1633, and turn right on Whitehall, then left on to Pearl Street (which, as the old shoreline was once scattered with pearly shells). You'll soon come to the Fraunces Tavern ③, a restoration of the 1719 building where George Washington bade farewell to his troops after the War of American Independence. It is now a restaurant with a small museum upstairs. In this block are the last few small-scale Federal-style buildings found in the financial district.

Minuit memorial, Bowling Green

The Canyon of Wall Street

Walk up Broad Street, an avenue once split by a canal leading to the river. This was eventually filled in, resulting in one of the wider streets downtown. At Wall Street, look left between the high rises to Trinity Church, a square-towered structure built in 1846. Try to imagine a New York in which this 280 ft (85 m) steeple was (until 1860) the tallest point in New York. Among the many prominent early New Yorkers buried in the graveyard is Alexander Hamilton, whose ghost is said to haunt the nearby grave of Matthew Davis, Aaron Burr's second in the duel that took Hamilton's life.

At the junction of Broad and Wall Street stands the New York Stock Exchange ④. On weekdays, visitors can look down at the trading floor from a balcony. Nearby at No. 26 Wall Street is Federal Hall ⑤ where, in 1789, crowds of cheering New Yorkers saw George Washington take his oath of office as president.

The Immigrants' Memorial at Castle Clinton

From Nassau Street to City Hall

Turn uptown on to Nassau Street, a continuation of Broad Street, to see some of modern New York at Chase Plaza ⑥, the first open plaza in the financial district. At the north end of the plaza on Liberty Street is the massive, ornate Federal Reserve Bank ⑦, built in 1924 and famed for its five storeys of bullion vaults. At the far end of the block is the Legion Memorial Square which is now renamed Louise Nevelson

The tower of City Hall ⑨

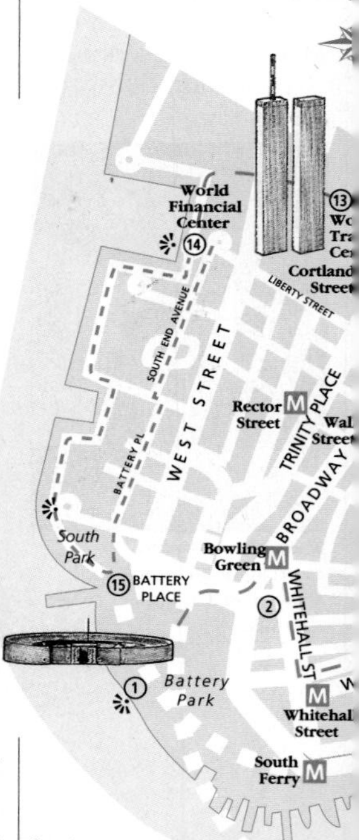
World Financial Center
14
13
Cortland Street
LIBERTY STREET
SOUTH END AVENUE
WEST STREET
Rector Street
TRINITY PLACE
BATTERY PL
BROADWAY
South Park
Bowling Green
15 BATTERY PLACE
2
WHITEHALL ST
Battery Park
1
Whitehall Street
South Ferry

0 metres 500

0 yards 500

Key

— Walk route

- Detour route

Good viewing point

[M] Subway station

Tips for Walkers

Starting point: *Battery Park.*
Length: *$2^1/_2$ miles (4 km).*
Getting there: *Take subway train 4 or 5 to Bowling Green; or the 1 or 9 to South Ferry. The Fifth Avenue bus M1 and Seventh Avenue-Broadway bus M6 are the closest bus routes.*
Stopping-off points: *Both the Seaport and the World Financial Center offer a good choice. At the Seaport, the best views are from Pier 17. At WFC, choose a café in the Winter Garden, a gourmet feast at the Hudson River Club or a "take-out" snack to munch along the promenade.*

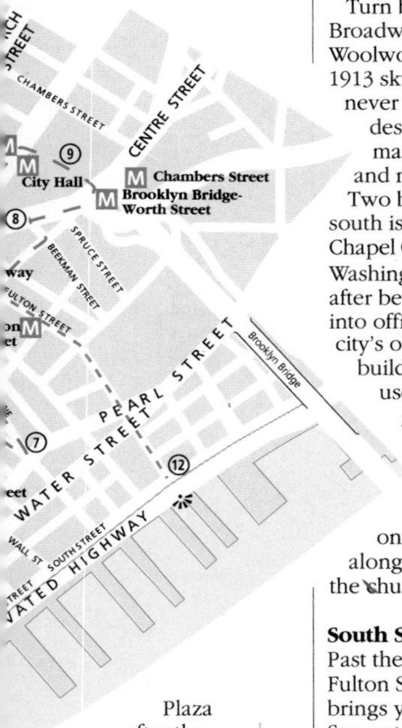

Plaza after the artist, who has seven sculptures on display here. Note the small 1815 building at No. 90 Maiden Lane opposite the south side of the plaza, a surprising survivor in the high-rise financial district. The fine cast-iron front was added in 1872. Continue north to Park Row ⑧ and the graceful

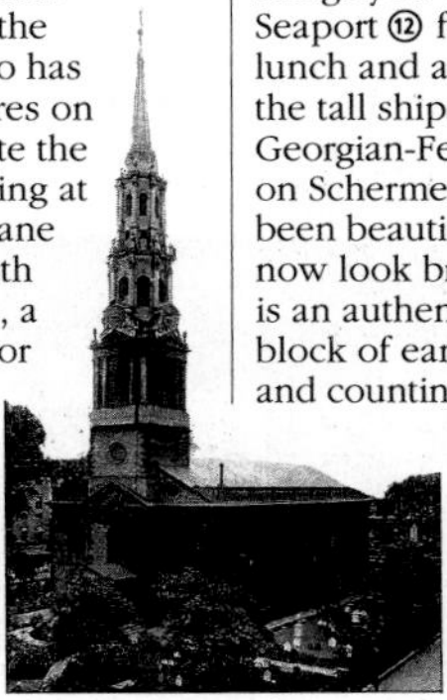
St. Paul's Chapel ⑪

The *Peking*, a four-masted barque, in South Street Seaport ⑫

Georgian City Hall ⑨, the seat of New York city government since 1812.

Turn back again on Broadway to No. 233, the Woolworth Building ⑩, a 1913 skyscraper that has never been surpassed in design. Inside is a marvellous interior and mosaic ceiling. Two blocks further south is St Paul's Chapel ⑪, where Washington prayed after being sworn into office. As the city's oldest public building in constant use, this Georgian gem was built in what was then a wheat field. The Hudson once flowed along the edge of the churchyard.

George Washington, Federal Hall ⑤

South Street Seaport

Past the church, a left turn on Fulton Street and a short walk brings you on to South Street Seaport ⑫ for a waterfront lunch and a tour of one of the tall ships. The red brick Georgian-Federal buildings on Schermerhorn Row have been beautifully restored and now look brand new, but this is an authentic New York block of early 1800s ware- and counting-houses. Sloppy Louie's, on South Street, is a good seafood restaurant. For a water view, stop off at the informal cafés on Pier 17.

From South Street to Battery Park City

Return along Fulton Street past Broadway and then cut through the sculpture-filled courtyard behind the twin towers of the World Trade Center ⑬, and detour for the views from the 107th floor observation deck. Across the street is the new World Financial Center ⑭, a vital part of the revival of lower New York. (Either use the over-pass from the north tower of the World Trade Center or cross over at Vesey Street.) The dazzling Winter Garden is a vast glass and steel atrium filled with tall palms, opening on to a landscaped promenade and a big marina on the Hudson River. The outdoor promenade continues along the river past the striking new Battery Park City ⑮.

Winter Garden at the World Financial Center ⑭

A 90-Minute Walk on the Lower East Side

THIS WALK PASSES through some of the old immigrant neighbourhoods that have given New York its unique texture, and gives you the chance to experience a taste of the character, cultures and cuisine of New York's most vibrant communities. Sunday is the best day for local colour. For more details of sights on the Lower East Side see pages 92–9.

The Lower East Side

Begin at the Lower East Side Tenement Museum ① at No. 97 Orchard Street between Delancey and Broome. This original tenement building is being restored to show how immigrants lived at the turn of the century. It features a gallery of exhibits on the immigrant experience, giving insights for the remainder of your walk.

Orchard Street itself ② was the centre of the Jewish Lower East Side. The pushcarts that once lined the block are gone, but the shops selling fashionable merchandise at discount prices still remain. The stores close on Saturday, the Jewish Sabbath, and so Sunday is the traditional shopping day.

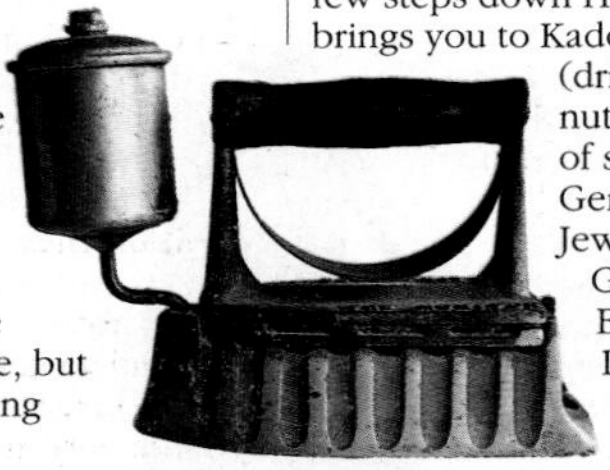

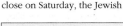

An 1885 iron from the Lower East Side Tenement Museum ①

Much of the Jewish heritage has gone, but there are some enticing reminders. Turn left on Grand Street and right on to Essex to the Essex Street Pickle Company ③ at No. 35, the shop in the film *Crossing Delancey*. Look for the barrels on the pavement and all the people lined up to buy. Just a few steps down Hester Street brings you to Kadouri Import (dried fruits, nuts and lots of spices) and Gertel's, an old Jewish bakery.

Go back up Essex, cross Delancey and at Rivington, turn right for tours and tastings at Schapiro's Winery ④ at No. 126. At No. 150 is Streit's Matzoh, the largest manufacturer of unleavened bread in New York.

A cultural mixture

Turn back on Rivington. Note the Spanish *bodegas* and the Chinese grocers serving the new restaurants in this once-Jewish area. This is a rather gritty street, but shows a true picture of new immigrant life. Across the street at the corner of Forsyth, a synagogue has been converted to a Spanish church ⑤. Detour right to No. 172 Forsyth ⑥. It looks like a junkyard until you see that the junk is in fact a series of strange sculptures by the Rivington School, an avant-garde art group. Back on Rivington, turn right on to Eldridge, a typical tenement street. The junction of Grand and Eldridge is the hub of the textile area, where the shops sell discount towels and linens. Beyond Canal Street is the Eldridge Street Synagogue ⑦, the first Eastern European synagogue in New York, now being carefully restored.

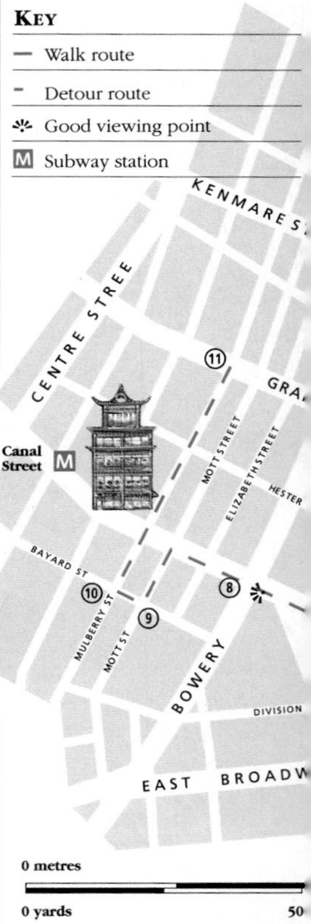
KEY
Walk route
Detour route
Good viewing point
[M] Subway station
KENMARE S
CENTRE STREET
GRA
MOTT STREET
ELIZABETH STREET
HESTER
Canal Street
BAYARD ST
MULBERRY ST
MOTT ST
BOWERY
DIVISION
EAST BROADW
0 metres
0 yards
50

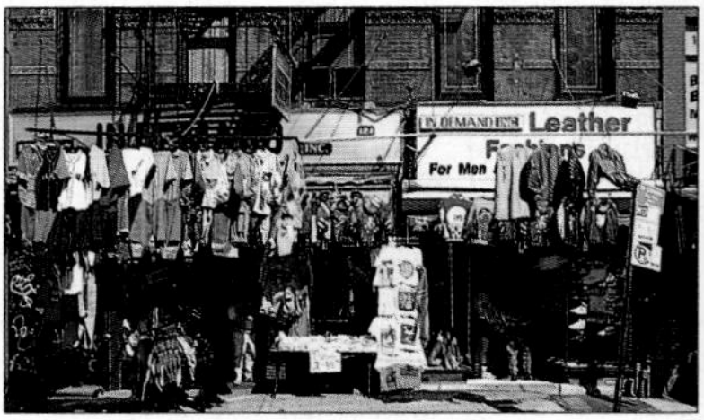
Leather
For Men

Clothes stalls in Orchard Street market ②

> **TIPS FOR WALKERS**
>
> ***Starting point:*** *Orchard Street.*
> ***Length:*** *2 miles (3.2 km).*
> ***Getting there:*** *Take the subway train F to Delancey; B, D or Q to Grand Street; J or M to Essex Street. The M15 bus stops at the corner of Delancey and Allen Streets. Returning from Chinatown-Little Italy, Canal Street station is served by the 4, 5, 6, N and R trains.*
> ***Stopping-off points:*** *Your walk will certainly whet your appetite, and you can break or end the tour with a pick of cuisine. Little Italy's cafés are perfect for coffee and luscious cakes. For more substantial fare, 20 Mott Street is recommended for Chinese food, or for Italian, Grotta Azzurra at 387 Broome Street. For a sampling of Jewish dairy delicacies such as blintzes, try Ratner's Dairy Restaurant at 138 Delancey Street.*

The Essex Street Pickle Company ③

Chinatown

Return to Canal Street and turn left. At the entry to the Manhattan Bridge, you'll see the World Trade Center towering in the distance, framed in stark contrast by the nearby tenements. Cross the Bowery; you'll see many jewellery shops, the remnants of the original Diamond District ⑧. As you continue, they give way to stalls selling an exotic array of vegetables, and butchers with rows of roast ducks in the windows. At No. 200 Canal Street is Kam Man Food Products, one of the largest Chinese markets found in the area.

Turn left from Canal to Mott Street and you'll know you are right in the heart of Chinatown by the ranks of Chinese neon signs. Even the banks and phone booths are shaped like pagodas. There are hundreds of restaurants here, from holes-in-the-wall to haute cuisine – giving a chance to taste the unusual produce. For spiritual sustenance visit the Eastern States Buddhist Temple ⑨.

At Bayard Street, step left to see all the Chinese political posters and messages on the Wall of Democracy, then turn back and to the right, to Mulberry Street. The curve next to Columbus Park was Mulberry Bend ⑩, once notorious for gang murders and mayhem.

An Italian deli in Little Italy ⑪

Little Italy

Turn and walk the other way on Mulberry Street and you are suddenly in Little Italy ⑪. Small in area though it is, and encroached on by Chinatown, this is still a wonderful neighbourhood full of old-world restaurants and stores selling home-made pasta, sausages, breads and pastries. The Italian population has dwindled over the years, as the younger generation has moved out. But a staunch community still remains, as does the area's Italian flavour.

The big event of the year is the Feast of San Gennaro, named for the patron saint of Naples. For eleven nights every September, Mulberry Street is jammed with thousands of locals and visitors enjoying the parades and the Italian food, with rows of stalls selling sizzling sausages.

Little Italy's foothold is Mott to Mulberry on Hester and then from Hester to Grand on Mulberry. If you turn right on to Grand Street you'll soon find yourself passing rows of Chinese grocers again.

Pretzel seller on Orchard Street ②

Kam Man Food Products at No. 200 Canal Street

A 90-Minute Walk in Greenwich Village and SoHo

A STROLL THROUGH the patchwork quilt of streets in Greenwich Village takes you to where New York's best-known writers and artists have lived, worked and played, and ends with a tour of SoHo's galleries and museums, where today's artists show their work. For more details on sights in Greenwich Village, see pages 106–13, and for SoHo, pages 100–5.

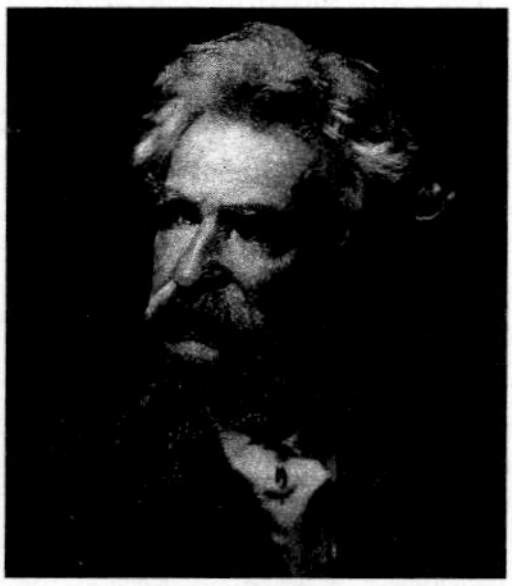

Author Mark Twain, who lived on 10th Street

West 10th Street

The junction of 8th Street and 6th Avenue ① has book, record and clothing shops nearby. Walk up Sixth to West Ninth Street for Jefferson Market Courthouse ② and Balducci's, a gourmet market.

Turn right along West 10th Street ③ to the Alexander Onassis Center for Hellenic Studies. A passageway at the front once led up to the Tile Club, a gathering place for the artists of the Tenth Street Studio, where Augustus Saint-Gaudens, John LaFarge and Winslow Homer lived and worked. Mark Twain lived at No. 24 10th Street, and Edward Albee at No. 50.

Across Sixth Avenue there is Milligan Place ④, a cluster of 19th-century houses, and Patchin Place ⑤, where the poets e e cummings and John Masefield both lived.

Further on is the Ninth Circle bar ⑥ which, when it first opened in 1898, was known as "Regnaneschi's". It was the subject of John Sloan's painting *Regnaneschi's Saturday Night.* Playwright Edward Albee first saw the question "Who's afraid of Virginia Woolf?" scrawled on a mirror here.

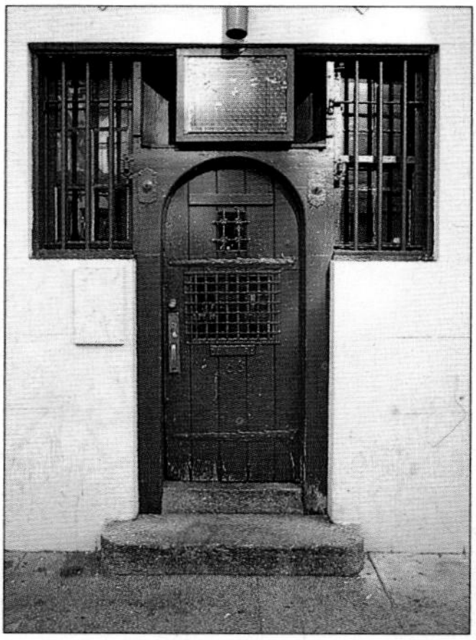

The doorway of Chumley's ⑩

Greenwich Village

Walk left on to Waverly Place past the Three Lives Bookshop, a typical Village literary gathering spot, to Christopher Street and to the triangular Northern Dispensary ⑦.

Follow Grove Street along Christopher Park to Sheridan Square, the busy hub of the Village. Left is the Circle Repertory Theater ⑧, which premieres the plays of Pulitzer Prizewinner Lanford Wilson.

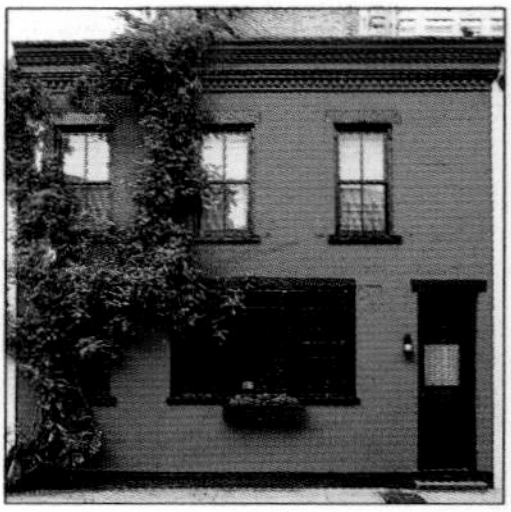

Facade in Washington Mews ⑬

Cross Seventh Avenue and bear left on to Grove Street. At the corner of Bedford Street, you can't miss "Twin Peaks" ⑨, a home for artists in the 1920s. Turn right on Bedford to the unmarked door at No. 86 of Chumley's ⑩, a saloon not much changed since 1928 when it was a speakeasy *(see p28).* Writers Dylan Thomas, Simone de Beauvoir, John Steinbeck, Ernest Hemingway, William Faulkner, J D Salinger, Jack Kerouac and many others all drank here. Covers of their books line the walls. At No. 75½ there is the narrowest house in the Village, which was once the home of feminist poet Edna St Vincent Millay.

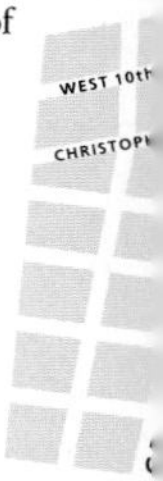

Walk up Carmine to Sixth Avenue and right at Waverly Place. At No. 116 ⑪, Anne Charlotte Lynch, an English teacher, held weekly gatherings in her town house for friends like Herman Melville and Edgar Allan Poe, who gave his first reading of *The Raven* here.

A detour left of half a block will bring you to MacDougal Alley ⑫, a lane of carriage houses in which Gertrude Vanderbilt Whitney had her studio. She opened the first Whitney Museum here in 1932, just behind the studio.

TIPS FOR WALKERS

Starting point: *8th St/6th Ave.*
Length: *2 miles (3.2 km).*
Getting there: *Take subway train A, B, C, D, E or F to West Fourth Street-Washington Square station (Eighth Street exit). Fifth Avenue buses M2 and M3 stop at Eighth Street. From here, walk one block west to Sixth. The M5 bus loops around Washington Square back to Sixth Avenue and Eighth Street.*
Stopping-off points: *The Pink Tea Cup, 42 Grove Street, is good for lunch. The SoHo Kitchen & Bar, 103 Greene Street, is a typical soaring SoHo space, also known for its superb selection of wines.*

Washington Square

Once back on to MacDougal, turn left to Washington Square North, to see the finest Greek Revival houses in the United States. Writer Henry James set his *Washington Square* in No. 18, his grandmother's home.

Then pause at Fifth Avenue to look back at Washington Square Park for a perfect view

Washington Square Park and Arch

of the twin towers of the World Trade Center framed by the Washington Square Arch.

Go across Fifth Avenue and opposite No. 2 is Washington Mews ⑬, an elegant carriage house complex. John Dos Passos, Edward Hopper, William Glackens and also Rockwell Kent were housed in the studio at No. 14a at various times.

Go back up Washington Square North, past some elegant houses, including that of writer Edith Wharton who lived at No. 7. Walk beneath the arch and across Washington Square Park. On the left as you leave the park, is the fine Judson Memorial Church and Tower ⑭ by Stanford White and the Loeb Student Center. The Center was once a boarding house, known as the "house of genius", and is where Theodore Dreiser wrote *An American Tragedy.*

SoHo

Walk south on Thompson, a typical Village street lined with clubs, cafés and shops. Turn left at Houston, SoHo's northern limit, and right on West Broadway, where the the city's galleries immediately begin to spring up, along with some very chic and arty boutiques.

Turn left at Spring Street for yet more tempting shops then right on to Greene Street ⑮, the heart of the Cast-Iron Historic District. Many of these fine buildings are now home to clusters of smart galleries. Upon turning left at the end of Greene Street to Canal Street, the end of SoHo, you will see just how quickly New York can change. This noisy street is full of hawkers and lots of cut-price electronics stores. Follow the action for a couple of blocks and then turn left up Broadway to the cutting edge of art, with the New Museum of Contemporary Art at No. 583 and also the Guggenheim Museum SoHo ⑯ found at No. 575 *(see p105).*

Cast-iron façade, Greene Street ⑮

KEY

— Walk route

🔆 Good viewing point

Ⓜ Subway station

```
0 metres        500
0 yards         500
```

A Two-Hour Walk on the Upper East Side

A PROMENADE ALONG upper Fifth Avenue and its environs will take you past the best remaining examples of New York's turn-of-the-century gilded age. A detour through the old German district of Yorkville leads to a riverside stroll to Gracie Mansion, the 1799 official residence of the city's mayor. For more details of sights on the Upper East Side, see pages 180–201.

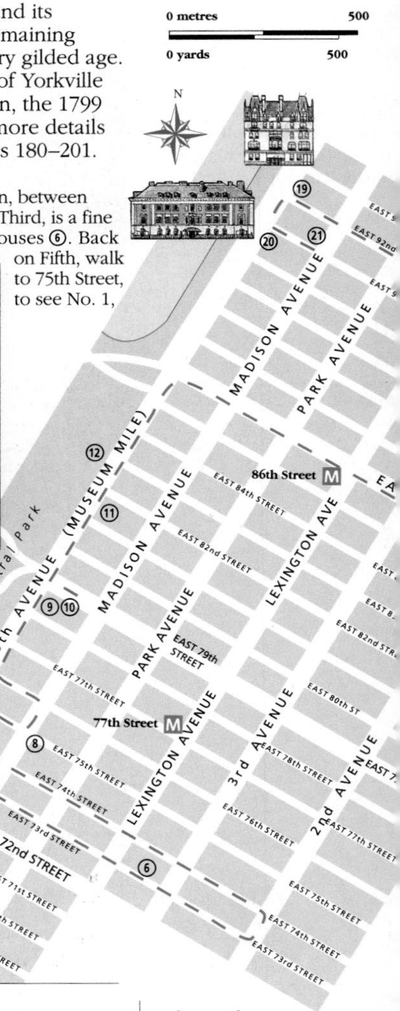
0 metres 500
0 yards 500
N
19
20
21
EAST 92nd
MADISON AVENUE
PARK AVENUE
5th AVENUE (MUSEUM MILE)
12
11
9 10
Central Park
86th Street M
EAST 84th STREET
EAST 82nd STREET
LEXINGTON AVE
EAST 82nd STR
EAST 79th STREET
EAST 80th ST
EAST 77th STREET
77th Street M
LEXINGTON AVENUE
3rd AVENUE
2nd AVENUE
EAST 78th STREET
EAST 77th STREET
7
8
EAST 75th STREET
5
EAST 74th STREET
4
EAST 73rd STREET
EAST 76th STREET
1
3
EAST 72nd STREET
2
6
EAST 71st STREET
EAST 70th STREET
EAST 69th STREET
EAST 75th STREET
EAST 74th STREET
EAST 73rd STREET

KEY

- Walk route
- Good viewing point
- [M] Subway station

From the Frick to the Met

Begin at the Frick mansion ①, built for coal magnate Henry Clay Frick in 1913–14. Allow some extra time to see Frick's art collection *(pp200–1)*. Many such mansions were built as New York's first families outdid each other with miniature Versailles, Loire-style châteaux and even Venetian palazzos. Most of the ones still standing have now become either institutions or else museums. The apartment building opposite is typical of those where today's affluent New Yorkers live.

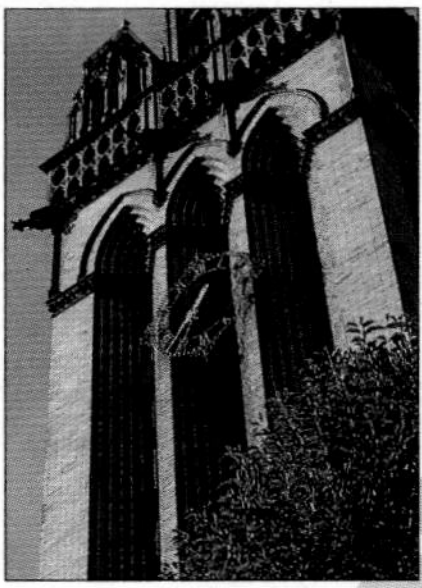

Church of the Holy Trinity ⑰

East on 70th are two of the city's top art galleries, the Knoedler Gallery and Hirsch & Adler ②. Walk up Madison to the corner of 72nd Street, to the big Polo-Ralph Lauren store ③, the 1898 French Renaissance home of Gertrude Rhinelander Waldo. Take a look inside to see the elegant restored interior.

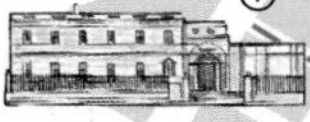

Walk back towards Fifth on the north side of 72nd, past two 1890s limestone beauties, now the Lycée Français de New York ④. Continue along Fifth Avenue to 73rd Street. Turn east to No. 11, Joseph Pulitzer's former home ⑤.

A few blocks on, between Lexington and Third, is a fine row of town houses ⑥. Back on Fifth, walk to 75th Street, to see No. 1, the former residence of Edward S Harkness, son of a founder of Standard Oil. It is now the Commonwealth Fund ⑦. At No. 1 East 78th, the tobacco millionaire James B Duke's 18th-century French-style château has now become the New York University Institute of Fine Arts ⑧. At 79th Street and Fifth, the former home of the financier Payne Whitney is now the French Embassy ⑨ and No. 2 East 79th is now the Ukrainian Institute of America ⑩. On the southeast corner of 82nd is Duke-Semans House ⑪, one of the few grand Fifth Avenue residences still in private hands. Save another day for The Metropolitan Museum of Art ⑫ at 82nd.

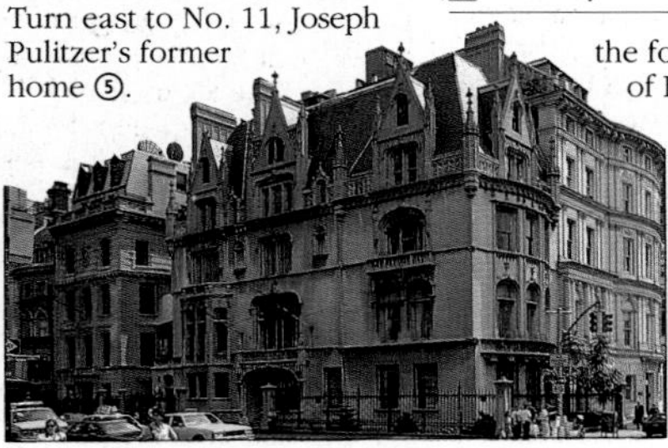

Ukrainian Institute of America ⑩

Carl Schurz Park Promenade

TIPS FOR WALKERS

Starting point: Frick Collection.
Length: 3 miles (4.8 km).
Getting there: Take subway train 6 to 68th Street and Lexington, then walk west three blocks to Fifth Avenue. Or take the M1, M2, M3 or M4 bus up Madison Avenue to 70th Street and walk one block west.
Stopping-off points: The cafés at the Whitney and Guggenheim museums are pleasant. Or sample the German fare at the Ideal luncheonette at No. 238 East 86th Street or the Heidelberg Café on Second Avenue off 86th Street. Madison Avenue between 92nd and 93rd has many places to eat, including Sarabeth's Kitchen, with its excellent weekend brunch.

Yorkville

Turn east on 86th Street for the vestiges of German Yorkville – Bremen House ⑬, Kleine Konditorei and Ideal, a luncheonette which serves large portions. Cross Second Avenue, then turn right to the Heidelberg Café and German deli, Schaller & Weber ⑭.

East River and Gracie Mansion

Henderson Place ⑮ at East End Avenue is a cluster of 24 red brick Queen Anne town houses. Carl Schurz Park opposite was named after the city's most prominent German immigrant, editor of *Harper's Weekly* and the *New York Post*. The park promenade atop the east River Drive leads to a view of Hell Gate, where the Harlem River, Long Island Sound and New York harbour meet. From the walkway you can see the back of Gracie Mansion ⑯, the mayor's official residence. The path west along the fence leads to a better view. Walk west on 88th Street past the Church of the Holy Trinity ⑰ and at Lexington Avenue go to 92nd Street and west past two of the few wooden houses left in Manhattan ⑱.

The Cooper-Hewitt Museum ⑳

Carnegie Hill

Back on Fifth Avenue, turn downtown past the Felix Warburg Mansion of 1908, now the Jewish Museum ⑲, and continue to 91st Street and the huge Andrew Carnegie home, now the Cooper-Hewitt Museum ⑳. Built in 1902 in the style of an English country manor, it gave the area the unofficial name of Carnegie Hill. The James Burden House ㉑ at No. 7, built for Vanderbilt heiress Adele Sloan in 1905, has a spiral staircase under a stained glass skylight that was known in society as "the stairway to heaven". At No. 9, the financier Otto Kahn's Italian Renaissance-style residence was a showplace with a drive-through porch and interior courtyard. It is now the Convent of the Sacred Heart School.

Wooden houses on 92nd Street ⑱

A Three-Hour Walk in Brooklyn

A TRIP ACROSS New York's most famous crossing leads to Brooklyn Heights, the city's first suburb. This neighbourhood has a 19th-century feel, mixed with a hint of Middle Eastern cultures. The riverfront promenade has unrivalled views of Manhattan. For more details of sights in Brooklyn, see pages 245–51.

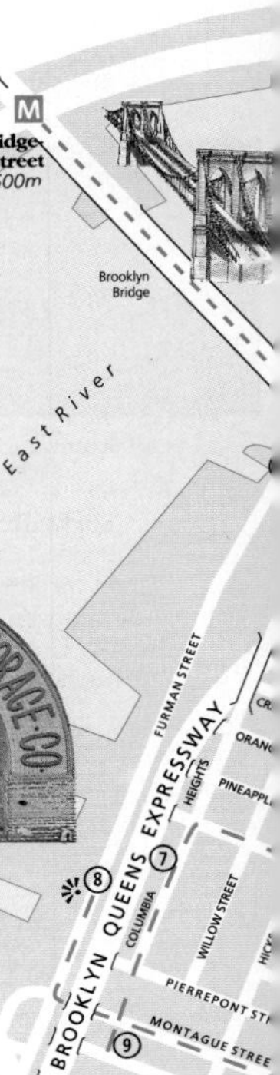

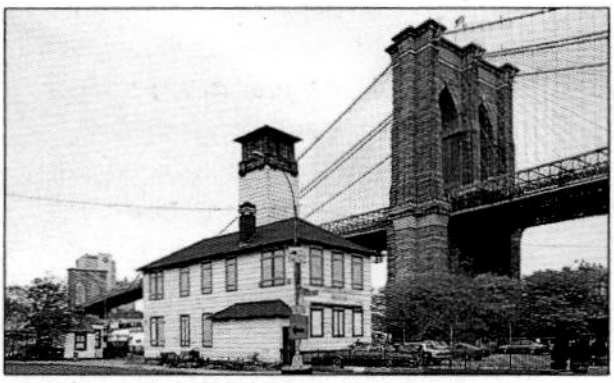

Fire Station on Old Fulton Street

Fulton Ferry Landing

About 3,580 ft (1 km) long, the Brooklyn Bridge span yields thrilling views of the lower New York skyline and prize photo opportunities. Take a taxi, or, if feeling energetic, walk across to Brooklyn.

On the far side, follow the Tillary Street sign to the right, turn right at the bottom of the stairs, then take the first path through the park and walk down Cadman Plaza West ① under the Brooklyn-Queens Expressway; here Cadman becomes Old Fulton Street. You can see the bridge on the right as you head to the river at Water Street and the Fulton Ferry landing ②. During the War of Independence, George Washington's troops fled to Manhattan from here. In 1814, this was the depot for the ferry connecting Brooklyn and Manhattan Island. This transformed Brooklyn Heights from a predominantly farming area to a residential district. The area is still a firm favourite with those working across the river. To the right are Bargemusic ③, a barge hosting chamber music concerts, and the River Café, its fine cuisine and views making it one of New York's most exceptional dining spots.

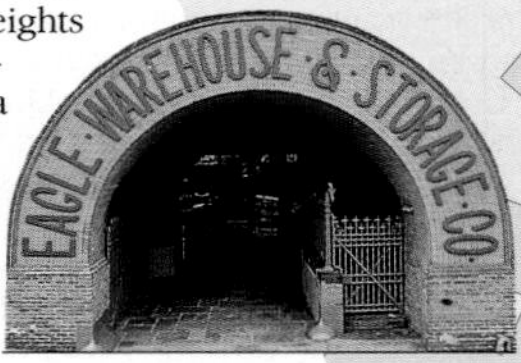

Eagle Warehouse ④

Brooklyn Heights

From the landing, turn right on to steep Everitt Street up Columbia Heights, past the former Eagle Warehouse ④ of 1893 to Middagh Street and along the streets of Brooklyn Heights. No. 24 ⑤ is one of the oldest houses, built in 1824.

Next turn right on Willow and left on Cranberry; here the town houses range from old, wooden clapboards to brick Federal-style to brownstones. Except for cars and a few modern buildings, you could be in the 19th century.

Many famous people live here. Truman Capote wrote *Breakfast at Tiffany's* and *In Cold Blood* in the basement of No. 70 Willow Street, and Arthur Miller once owned No. 155. Walt Whitman lived on Cranberry Street when he was editor of the *Brooklyn Eagle*. He set the type for his *Leaves of Grass* at a print shop near the corner of Cranberry and Fulton. The town houses now on the site are called Whitman Close.

Turn right along Hicks. The Hicks family, local farmers, inspired the name "hick" for a yokel. Turn left on Orange Street to the Plymouth Church ⑥, home of Henry Ward Beecher, an anti-slavery preacher. His sister, Harriet Beecher Stowe, wrote *Uncle Tom's Cabin*. At Clark Street, look left for

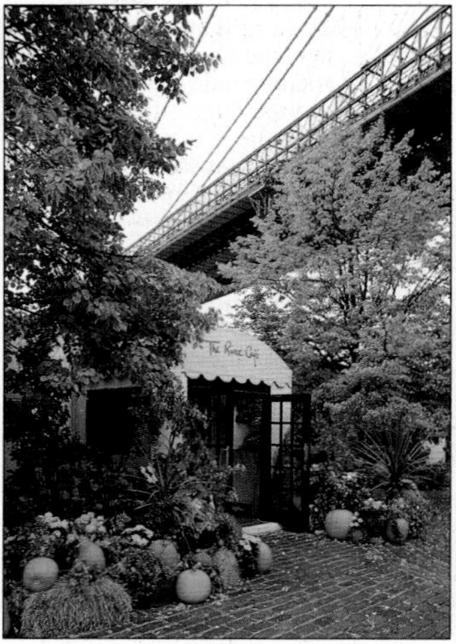

Entrance to the River Café

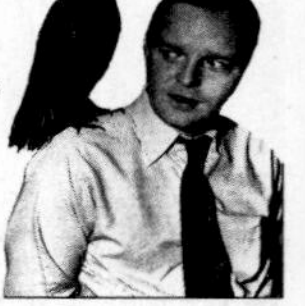

Truman Capote with feathered friend

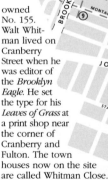

the marquees of Brooklyn's once-luxurious hotels such as the Towers. Follow Clark Street to Columbia Heights, where Norman Mailer lives at No. 142 ⑦. Other residents included invalid Washington Roebling, who, using a telescope, directed the construction of Brooklyn Bridge from his room at No. 110.

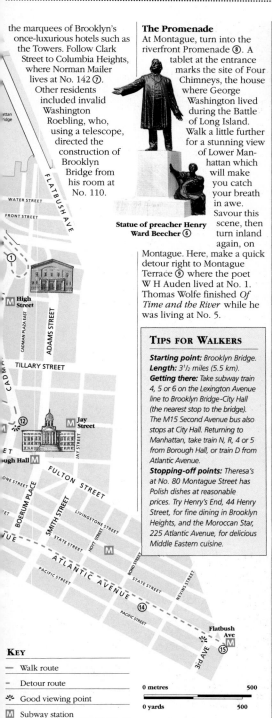

Statue of preacher Henry Ward Beecher ⑥

The Promenade

At Montague, turn into the riverfront Promenade ⑧. A tablet at the entrance marks the site of Four Chimneys, the house where George Washington lived during the Battle of Long Island. Walk a little further for a stunning view of Lower Manhattan which will make you catch your breath in awe. Savour this scene, then turn inland again, on Montague. Here, make a quick detour right to Montague Terrace ⑨ where the poet W H Auden lived at No. 1. Thomas Wolfe finished *Of Time and the River* while he was living at No. 5.

> **TIPS FOR WALKERS**
>
> *Starting point:* Brooklyn Bridge.
> *Length:* 3¹/₂ miles (5.5 km).
> *Getting there:* Take subway train 4, 5 or 6 on the Lexington Avenue line to Brooklyn Bridge-City Hall (the nearest stop to the bridge). The M15 Second Avenue bus also stops at City Hall. Returning to Manhattan, take train N, R, 4 or 5 from Borough Hall, or train D from Atlantic Avenue.
> *Stopping-off points:* Theresa's at No. 80 Montague Street has Polish dishes at reasonable prices. Try Henry's End, 44 Henry Street, for fine dining in Brooklyn Heights, and the Moroccan Star, 225 Atlantic Avenue, for delicious Middle Eastern cuisine.

The old Montague Street trolley, which led to the river and the ferry

Montague and Clinton Streets

Once back on Montague Street, walk to the heart of Brooklyn Heights with all its cafés and boutiques. The baseball team, the Brooklyn Dodgers, got their name from dodging trolley cars which once ran down the street. Walk to the intersection of Montague and Clinton to see the stained glass of the 1834 Church of St Ann and the Holy Trinity ⑩. Walk a block left on Clinton to Pierrepont Street for the Brooklyn Historical Society ⑪. A block further, at Court Street, is the 1849 Borough Hall ⑫, and the subway taking you back to Manhattan.

Brooklyn's Dodgers, who got their name from dodging trolley cars

Atlantic Avenue

Alternatively, stay on Clinton and walk five short blocks to Atlantic Avenue. A left turn here leads to a whole string of Middle Eastern emporia ⑬, such as Sahadi Imports at No. 187, with a huge selection of foods; Rashid at No. 191 sells Arabic publications and records; and the Damascus Bakery at No. 195 makes the most delicious filo pastries. A couple of blocks further on you will come to a host of antique shops ⑭. Arriving at Flatbush Avenue, look left to see the Brooklyn Academy of Music ⑮ and the grand front of Williamsburg Savings Bank. Look out for the signs to the subway back across the river.

KEY

— Walk route

- Detour route

❖ Good viewing point

Ⓜ Subway station

0 metres   500
0 yards   500

TRAVELLERS' NEEDS

WHERE TO STAY

Wıᴛʜ ᴏᴠᴇʀ 70,000 hotel rooms available, New York offers something for everyone. Top hotels are still not quite as expensive as those in Paris or London, but the best news for visitors is the increase in budget hotels. While many of these are basic rather than charming, they offer fair value. Other budget options are self-catering apartments and bed and breakfast in private

Cole Porter's piano, in the Waldorf–Astoria bar (see p281)

apartments, as well as youth hostels and YMCAs. From an inspection of over 200 hotels, we have selected 76 as the best of their kind. *Choosing a Hotel (pp274–5)* helps you make a choice based on your needs, but for more detailed descriptions, turn to the listings on pages 276–83. The map on page 272 highlights ten hotels, chosen as the best in their category.

Bathroom at the Paramount Hotel (see p277)

WHERE TO LOOK

Tʜᴇ ᴇᴀsᴛ sɪᴅᴇ, roughly between 59th and 77th Streets, is the traditional location for most luxury hotels, but the renovation of certain landmark midtown properties, such as the St Regis, and new hotels in famous chains from the Far East, such as the Peninsula Group, have spread the competition in the top ranges.

Business travellers tend to favour midtown, especially the moderately-priced hotels lining Lexington Avenue near Grand Central Terminal.

Those seeking relative quiet with access to midtown should look in the Murray Hill area, while theatre lovers should note the revival of the Times Square area. Hotels within walking distance of theatres offer an advantage, since all performances tend to end at the same time and cabs are hard to come by.

There are a number of good, inexpensive hotels around Herald Square, which is convenient for shopping.

The Upper West Side also specializes in less expensive hotels. This popular residential area is convenient for Lincoln Center and offers easy access to public transport.

The **New York Convention and Visitors Bureau** publishes a free, annually-updated leaflet called *The New York Hotel Guide*, listing current rates, toll-free numbers and fax numbers. Staff will offer advice about hotels, but do not make bookings.

HOTEL PRICES

Sᴏᴍᴇ ʜᴏᴛᴇʟs offer seasonal promotional rates and other off-peak reductions. For example, business travellers vacate hotels at the end of the working week, and you can

take advantage of bargain weekend deals, even in luxury hotels, as prices drop *(see Special Breaks p270)*. There is a growing number of all-suite hotels available in every price category. These offer extra space plus cooking facilities and a refrigerator. Most suites can accommodate up to four people, which makes them popular with families.

Café Botanica at the Essex House Hotel (see p278)

HIDDEN EXTRAS

Wʜᴇɴ ᴄᴀʟᴄᴜʟᴀᴛɪɴɢ the cost of hotels in New York, it is not enough simply to take into consideration the quoted room price. Hotel rooms have long been subject to extra taxes, but the former sliding scale, which favoured rates under $100, has now given way to a blanket, swingeing 16.25%, plus $2 per night occupancy tax.

Several hotels now include continental breakfast in the room price. This is a big

Lobby phones, to reach a guest staying in the hotel

Suite at the Millenium *(see p276)*

saving, since a standard hotel continental breakfast before tax costs about $5 per person in the cheaper hotels, soaring to over $15 in some of the really top hotels. To save money, head for the nearest deli or coffee shop and leave the hotel to business people having power breakfasts.

Hotel telephone charges are usually high; it may well be cheaper to use the pay phone in the lobby, particularly when calling overseas.

Tips are expected in the United States. Staff who take your luggage to the room are usually tipped a minimum of $1 per bag – more in a luxury hotel. The concierge need not be tipped for normal services such as arranging transport or making dinner reservations, but should be rewarded for exceptional services.

When you order anything from room service, check the menu to see whether a service charge will also be included in the bill; if not, a 15% tip will be in order.

Solo travellers will find that single room rates are usually at least 80% of the double rate and are sometimes the same as for two people.

FACILITIES

ALTHOUGH you'd expect hotel rooms in New York City to be noisy, most windows are double- or even triple-glazed to keep out the noise. Air-conditioning is almost a standard feature, so there is no need to open the windows in hot weather. Even so, some rooms are obviously quieter than others, if they are at the back of the hotel or overlooking a courtyard – check when booking.

Television, radio and at least one telephone are usually provided in every room, even in modest lodgings, and most hotel bedrooms have en-suite bathrooms. In budget and mid-priced hotels a shower, rather than a "tub" is the norm. Many mid-range hotels now offer fax points and machines in each room, a health club or exercise room and a full concierge service. Luxury facilities include mini-bars in the room, dual phones, private phone message systems and electronic check-out.

The hotels listed here are all within a few minutes' walk of a large number of shops and restaurants. Very few hotels have their own car park, but valets may park your car in areas reserved for guests' use in nearby public garages. A reduced (but still expensive) daily parking fee is normally payable. If there is no concierge at the hotel, front desk staff will be able to help with tourist information and to answer any queries.

The Art Deco lobby of the Edison Hotel *(see p277)*

HOW TO BOOK

IT IS ADVISABLE to make hotel reservations at least one month in advance. While it's unlikely that the hotel will be fully booked, you may well find that the best rooms and suites have been taken, especially if a major convention is taking place. The busiest periods are at Easter, the New York Marathon week in late October or early November, Thanksgiving in late November and Christmas.

Book directly with the hotel by telephone, letter or fax. Written confirmation of your telephone booking will be required, probably with a deposit as a guarantee of your arrival; any cancellation fees may be deducted from this. You can pay by credit card, international bank draft or money order, or dollar traveller's cheque. Advise the staff if you are going to arrive at the hotel after 6pm, or your room may be let again, unless you have prepaid with a credit card.

You can also book a hotel through your travel agent or air courier. Most hotels have a toll-free telephone number for use in the United States, but these numbers do not work from Europe and the UK. If the hotel is part of an international chain, an affiliated hotel in your country should be able to reserve a room for you.

SPECIAL BREAKS

HOTELS ARE BUSIEST during the week, when business travellers are in the city, so most of them offer cheap packages to encourage more weekend business. It's often possible to move from a standard to a luxury room for the weekend at the same rate.

A lower corporate rate is usually available to employees of large companies. But quite often, reservation clerks will grant you discounts on request without even asking for a company affiliation.

Some booking agencies offer discount rates. A good travel agent should be able to get the best current rates, but compare prices by contacting directly a discount reservation service such as Quikbook (see p269). They offer discounts between 20% and 50% on bookings, depending on the time of year. You book by credit card and receive a voucher to present to the hotel.

Package tours can also provide savings on the usual price. These rates may not oblige you to stay with a tour group, only to use their air and hotel arrangements. These packages may also include airport transfers, an additional saving. Airlines frequently have their own special deals, particularly during slow travel seasons. Again, a knowledgeable travel agent should be able to tell you the current best deals, but newspapers often advertise special, limited offers that can be booked directly. At off-peak times you may net even bigger savings than the package plans.

Lobby of the St Regis Hotel (see p282)

DIRECTORY

DISABLED TRAVELLERS

Mayor's Office for People with Disabilities
52 Chambers St, Room 206, NY, NY 10007.
☎ 788-2830.

BED AND BREAKFAST

Bed & Breakfast Bureau
306 8th Ave, Suite 111, NY, NY 10001. ☎ 645-4555.

Abode Bed and Breakfast Inc
PO Box 20022, NY, NY 10028. ☎ 472-2000.

At Home in New York
PO Box 407, NY, NY 10185.
☎ 956-3125.
FAX 247-3294.

Bed & Breakfast Network of New York
130 Barrow St, Suite 508, NY, NY 10014.
☎ 645-8134.

City Lights Bed & Breakfast Ltd
PO Box 20355, Cherokee Stn, NY, NY 10028.
☎ 737-7049.

New World Bed and Breakfast Ltd
150 5th Ave, Suite 711, NY, NY 10011.
☎ 675-5600.

Urban Ventures, Inc.
PO Box 426, Planetarium Station, NY, NY 10024.
☎ 594-5650.

YOUTH HOSTELS AND DORMITORIES

American Youth Hostel
891 Amsterdam Ave at W 103rd St, NY, NY 10025. **Map** 20 E5.
☎ 932-2300.

92nd St Y
1395 Lexington Ave, NY, NY 10128. **Map** 17 A2.
☎ 415-5650.

YMCA-Vanderbilt
224 E 47th St, NY, NY 10017. **Map** 13 A5.
☎ 756-9600.

YMCA-West Side
5 W 63rd St, NY, NY 10023. **Map** 12 D2.
☎ 787-4400.

CAMPING

Battle Row Campground
Claremont Rd, Old Bethpage, NY 11804.
☎ (516) 572-8690.

STUDENT LODGINGS

NYU Summer Housing
8 Washington Place, NY, NY 10003. ☎ 998-4621.

AIRPORT HOTELS

See p364.

DISABLED TRAVELLERS

By LAW, NEW hotels must provide facilities for disabled visitors, and many older buildings have been renovated to comply, too. Guide dogs are allowed in most hotels but it is advisable to check when booking.

This guide's disabled access information is based upon each hotel's own assessment of its suitability. Let the hotel know of any specific needs when booking. The **Mayor's Office for People With Disabilities** offers further information about hotels.

TRAVELLING WITH CHILDREN

American hotels generally have a very welcoming attitude towards children. Facilities like cots and lists of babysitters are normally widely available, and most hotel restaurants are happy to cater for young guests.

Travelling with children can be cheaper than anticipated. Many hotels do not charge for children if they stay in their parents' room, or make only a small charge for an extra bed. There is usually a limit of one or two children per room in these cases and most hotels stipulate that the children must be under a certain age, often 12. Parents of older children are expected to pay the full price, although the age limit is occasionally extended to 18. Ask about family deals when booking.

BED AND BREAKFAST

There is an increasing amount of bed-and-breakfast accommodation to be had in private apartments. This varies from a room in a flat with an owner-host in residence to an entire flat to yourself, with its own kitchen and bathroom, rented out while the owner is away.

Staying in a private apartment enables you to soak up the atmosphere of New York's neighbourhoods and to visit local restaurants, usually far more reasonably priced than those in midtown.

Entrance to the Peninsula Hotel *(see p281)*

Bed-and-breakfast lodgings can be found through many free booking services. Some booking agencies have a two-night minimum. Rates for unhosted apartments vary from about $70 to $200; and for a double room range from $60 to $90 a night, depending on whether you have a private bathroom. There is a wide range of apartments, from spacious and luxurious to cramped and dowdy. Your costs will rise if the address is remote, requiring frequent cabs. Ask about location and amenities when you book.

YOUTH AND BUDGET ACCOMMODATION

The city offers a youth hostel and many **YMCA** dormitories for those on a tight budget. For the longer-term visitor, the **92nd St Y**, a non-sectarian hostel and lively cultural centre, situated in the Upper East Side, has good-value rooms from about $30 to $50 a night.

There are no camp sites in Manhattan, and student accommodation is quite hard to come by unless you have an affiliation with one of New York's colleges.

Sky-high swimming pool at the UN Plaza Hotel *(see p280)*

USING THE LISTINGS
Hotel listings are on pages 276–83. Each hotel is listed according to the area and price category. The symbols after each hotel's address summarize the facilities it offers.

🛏 all rooms with bath and/or shower unless otherwise indicated
1️⃣ single-rate rooms available
🛏🛏 rooms for more than 2 people available, or an extra bed can be put in a double room
24 24-hour room service
📺 television in all rooms
🍸 minibar in all rooms
🚭 non-smoking rooms available
🏞 rooms with good view available
🔲 air conditioning in all rooms
🏋 gym/fitness facilities available in hotel
🏊 swimming pool in hotel
🛎 business facilities: message-taking service, fax machine for guests, desk and telephone in each room, and meeting room within hotel
🧒 children's facilities: cots, babysitting service
♿ wheelchair access
🛗 lift
🐾 pets allowed in bedrooms (always check when booking)
P valet parking available
🌳 garden/terrace open to guests
🍸 bar
🍴 restaurant
ℹ tourist information desk or personnel
💳 Credit cards accepted:
AE American Express
DC Diners Club
MC Mastercard/Access
V VISA
JCB Japanese Credit Bureau

Price categories for a double room with bath per night, including tax and service during high season:
$ under $150
$$ $150–$220
$$$ $220–$300
$$$$ $300–$400
$$$$$ over $400

New York's Best: Hotels

NEW YORK hotels range from the ultimate in luxury to surprisingly cheap and cheerful. All are within easy reach of shops, restaurants and transport. Some are of historical or literary interest, some are streamlined and hi-tech, others are old-fashioned and cosy. From this huge choice, certain hotels stand out, whether for character, comfort or good value. The hotels shown here have been selected from the listings on pages 276–83 as the best in their particular style or price range.

Plaza
This landmark hotel has been part of New York life for over 100 years. Refurbishment has restored its early glamour. (See p281.)

Wyndham
Book well in advance for a winning combination of homely charm and low prices. (See p280.)

Theater District

Paramount
Chic designer Philippe Starck set the style of this ultra-smart, yet sensibly-priced hotel. (See p278.)

Chelsea and the Garment District

Lower Midtown

Greenwich Village

Gramercy and the Flatiron District

SoHo and TriBeCa

Lower Manhattan

Seaport and the Civic Center

Lower East Side

Algonquin
Sip a cocktail in the spot where literary wit Dorothy Parker and her circle gathered in the 1920s. (See p278 and p143.)

Box Tree
Two brownstones have been converted into an intimate yet sumptuous inn, complete with superb restaurant. (See p281.)

Central Park

West e

Morningside Heights & Harlem

Upper East Side

Carlyle

Old-world elegance, stunning views of Central Park and the mellow jazz notes of Bobby Short in the Café Carlyle combine to make this luxury hotel superb. (See p282.)

Lowell

Luxurious suites offer all the comforts of a country house on the Upper East Side. There are also two restaurants on the premises. (See p282.)

Four Seasons

Modern fittings and hi-tech gadgetry combine with super-lative service at this IM Pei-designed hotel. (See p281.)

0 kilometres 2

0 miles 1

Pickwick Arms

Midtown's best bargain offers no-frills value for money in the heart of Manhattan. An unexpected bonus is the fine views of the encircling skyline from the simple, pleasant roof terrace. (See p280.)

UN Plaza

The soaring views from the bedrooms are outdone only by those from the glassed-in, 27th-floor pool. (See p280.)

Choosing a Hotel

THE 72 HOTELS listed in the following pages have all been individually inspected and assessed to help you make an informed decision. All the hotels are in Manhattan itself, within easy walking distance of museums, shops and restaurants. They are listed alphabetically in their price category.

		Number of Rooms	Large Rooms	Business Facilities	Children's Facilities	Recommended Restaurant	Concierge	Quiet Location	24-Hour Room Service
LOWER MANHATTAN (See p276)									
SoHo Grand Hotel	$$$	367		■					
Millenium Hilton	$$$$	561		■	●		●		●
NY Marriott Financial Center	$$$$	504		■	●		●		
GREENWICH VILLAGE (See p276)									
Washington Square Hotel	$	180					■	■	
GRAMERCY AND THE FLATIRON DISTRICT (See p276)									
Carlton	$	210		■	●			■	
Roger Williams	$	211	●					■	
The Inn at Irving Place	$$$	12	●					■	
CHELSEA AND THE GARMENT DISTRICT (See p276)									
Best Western Manhattan	$	147							
Herald Square Hotel	$	120							
Stanford	$	130			●				
Hotel Metro	$$$	157		■					
THEATER DISTRICT (See pp277–9)									
Edison	$	900						●	
Hampshire Hotel	$	50		■					
Iroquois	$	110		■					
Ramada Milford Plaza	$	1300							
Wellington	$	700		■					
Days Hotel Midtown	$$	366		■					
Hampshire Hotel and Suites	$$	200		■					
Howard Johnson Plaza	$$	300		■	●				
The Mansfield	$$	129					●		
Paramount	$$	610		■	●	■	●		●
Algonquin	$$$	165		■					
Crowne Plaza	$$$	770	●	■	●		●		●
Doubletree Guest Suites	$$$	460		■	●				
St Moritz	$$$	680							
Salisbury	$$$	320	●	■					
Essex House	$$$$	593		■	●	■	●		●
Michelangelo	$$$$	178	●	■	●		●		
Millennium Broadway	$$$$	629		■	●				
Le Parker Meridien	$$$$	691		■			●		●
Rihga Royal	$$$$	500	●	■	●		●		●
Royalton	$$$$	167		■	●	■	●		●
LOWER MIDTOWN (See pp279–80)									
Quality Hotel	$$	189		■					
Doral Court	$$$	199	●	■			■	●	■
Helmsley Middletowne	$$$	190							■

Price categories for a double room per night, including tax and service: $ under $150; $$ $150–$220; $$$ $220–$300; $$$$ $300–$400; $$$$$ over $400. CONCIERGE: Concierge available to advise, make reservations, etc.	BUSINESS FACILITIES: Message service; fax for guests; desk and telephone in each room; meeting room within the hotel. CHILDREN'S FACILITIES: Family rooms; cots; babysitting service; children's portions; high chairs in breakfast room restaurant. QUIET LOCATION: Quiet, residential neighbourhood or quiet street in a busy area.

	Price	NUMBER OF ROOMS	LARGE ROOMS	BUSINESS FACILITIES	CHILDREN'S FACILITIES	RECOMMENDED RESTAURANT	CONCIERGE	QUIET LOCATION	24-HOUR ROOM SERVICE
Jolly Madison Towers	$$$	246	●	●					
Morgans	$$$	113		●	●		●	●	●
Roger Smith	$$$	130	●	●	●				
Doral Park Avenue	$$$$	188		●		●	●	●	
Doral Tuscany	$$$$	121		●		●	●	●	
Sheraton Park Avenue	$$$$	150	●	●		●	●	●	●
United Nations Plaza	$$$$	428		●	●	●	●		●
UPPER MIDTOWN (See pp280–82)									
Pickwick Arms	$	400					●	●	
Hotel Beverly	$$	187	●	●	●		●		
Wyndham	$$	200	●					●	
Doral Inn	$$$	655		●			●		
Fitzpatrick Manhattan Hotel	$$$	92		●			●		
The Elysee	$$$	99		●	●				
New York Palace	$$$$	600	●	●	●	●	●		●
Plaza	$$$$	812	●	●	●	●	●		●
Waldorf–Astoria	$$$$	1410	●	●	●	●	●		●
Box Tree	$$$$$	13		●		●		●	●
Four Seasons	$$$$$	370	●	●		●	●		●
Peninsula	$$$$$	250	●	●	●	●	●		●
Pierre	$$$$$	206	●	●	●	●	●		●
Ritz-Carlton	$$$$$	428		●	●	●	●		●
St Regis	$$$$$	322	●	●	●	●	●		●
UPPER EAST SIDE (See pp282–3)									
Franklin	$$	53		●	●			●	●
Hotel Wales	$$	95		●			●	●	
Mark	$$$$	180	●	●	●	●	●	●	
Carlyle	$$$$$	175	●	●	●		●		●
Lowell	$$$$$	61	●		●	●	●	●	
Plaza Athénée	$$$$$	156	●	●	●	●	●		●
Regency	$$$$$	384		●	●	●	●		●
Stanhope	$$$$$	141	●	●	●	●	●		●
Westbury	$$$$$	231	●	●	●	●	●	●	●
UPPER WEST SIDE (See p283)									
Beacon	$	100					●	●	
Broadway American	$	200	●						
Excelsior	$	150	●					●	
Milburn	$	90	●	●	●		●	●	●
Radisson Empire	$$	375		●	●	●	●		●
Mayflower	$$$	377	●	●				●	

LOWER MANHATTAN

SoHo Grand Hotel

27 Grand Street, NY, NY 10012. **Map** 4
D4. **(** 965-3000. **FAX** 965-3113.
Rooms: 367. 🛏 1 TV 🍸 🛁 ☷
☰ 🛗 📶 🕭 ⊗ 📞 ¶¶ 🍴 🍸
AE, DC, MC, V, JCB. $$$

The first hotel in arty SoHo
opened in 1996, a stylish, well-
located haven in an area ideal for
browsing. The two-level lobby,
designed to evoke the architec-
tural spirit of the neighbourhood,
boasts massive brick and cast stone
columns, exposed steel ceiling
beams and a staircase of translu-
cent glass and iron suspended by
cables. Compact contemporary
guest rooms in neutral tones offer
king-size beds, and two-line
phones with voice mail. Vintage
photographs of New York adorn
the walls. The hotel includes a
fitness room and a bistro which
serves American fare.

Millenium Hilton

55 Church St, NY, NY 10007.
Map 1 B2. **(** 693-2001
FAX 571-2317. *Rooms*: 561. 🛏
1 ☷ 24 TV 🍸 🛁 ☷ ☰
☰ 🛗 📶 🕭 ⊗ 📞 ¶¶ 🍴
AE, DC, MC, V. $$$

At 58 storeys high, the sleek
Millenium is designed to appeal to
the well-heeled who have business near Wall Street. Rooms are
not particularly large, but make
excellent use of space with furnishings that give the illusion of
being built-in. Bathrooms are in
dramatic black marble, lighting
fixtures are the very latest design,
and there are conveniences such
as two-line telephones with
speaker and conference capabilities, voice mail and a video
system that can be used to order
room service or settle the bill.
Most rooms face the World Trade
Center; lower floors overlook the
courtyard while higher locations
offer sight of the river. Some of
the most pleasant views are from
the side, where the fitness centre
and large pool face the leafy
churchyard of St Paul's Chapel.

New York Marriott
Financial Center

85 West St, NY, NY 10006. **Map** 1 B3.
(385-4900. **FAX** 227-8136. *Rooms*:
504. 🛏 1 TV 🍸 🛁 ☷ ☰
☰ 🛗 📶 🕭 ⊗ 📞 ¶¶ 🍴 🍸
AE, DC, MC, V, JCB. $$$$

The standard rooms and amenities
of this hotel are redeemed by some
welcome features, such as an
indoor pool and health club and

the outstanding views of the
Hudson River from higher floors.
Rates drop substantially at weekends, making this a good base for
exploring Lower Manhattan.

GREENWICH VILLAGE

Washington Square
Hotel

103 Waverly Pl, NY, NY 10011.
Map 4 E2. **(** 777-9515.
FAX 979-8373. *Rooms*: 180. 🛏 170.
1 TV 🛁 ☷ 🛗 📶 🕭 ¶¶
🍸 AE, MC, V, JCB. $

This small hotel, just off the square
in the heart of Greenwich Village,
has tiny rooms but much to recommend it nevertheless. Marble,
lattice-work and plants give an
old-world look to the lobby, while
the narrow hallways are accented
with Mexican tiles. The rooms are
decorated with cheerful fabrics,
bathrooms are new and there is a
restaurant and a small fitness
centre. Above all, it is the only
hotel at the centre of the Village.

GRAMERCY AND THE
FLATIRON DISTRICT

Carlton

22 E 29th St, NY, NY 10016. **Map** 8 F3.
(532-4100. **FAX** 889-8683.
Rooms: 210. 🛏 1 ☷ TV 🛁
☰ 🛗 📶 🕭 🍸 ¶¶ 🍴 🍸 AE,
DC, MC, V. $

Renovation of this Beaux Arts building has provided a budget option
with a cheerful lobby, decent
rooms and modern bathroom
fixtures, though the hallways still
need sprucing up. There's a convenient little café off the lobby.

Roger Williams

28 E 31st St, NY, NY 10016.
Map 8 F3. **(** 684-7500. **FAX** 576-
4343. *Rooms*: 211. 🛏 1 ☷ TV
🛁 ☰ 🕭 🍸 AE, DC, MC, V. $

Complete renovation by the
Gotham Hospitality Group is
turning the Roger Williams into a
spiffy, moderately priced hotel that
fits the Gotham model. Until the
changes are complete late in 1997,
the older rooms are a bargain that
includes continental breakfast.

The Inn at Irving Place

54 Irving Place, NY, NY 10003. **Map** 9
A5. **(** 533-4600. **FAX** 533 4611.
Rooms: 12. 🛏 ☷ TV ☰ ⊗ 🍸
🍸 AE, MC, V, JCB. $$$

This discreet 19th-century town
house is straight out of a Jane
Austen novel. The sitting room
with high ceilings and ornate
plasterwork and the 12 guest
rooms are filled with antiques
denoting understated elegance.
Bedrooms have brass, iron or
carved headboards, Victorian
armoires, wooden-armed settees,
chaise longues and period lamps,
and each has a fireplace (non-
working). The 20th-century
intrudes only with additions such
as dual line telephones, cable
television and videos. Guests can
enjoy breakfast in a charming
dining room/bar, where an elegant
five-course tea is also served in
the afternoon. The neighbourhood,
near Gramercy Park, is another
evocation of Old New York.

CHELSEA AND THE
GARMENT DISTRICT

Best Western
Manhattan

17 W 32nd St, NY, NY 10001.
Map 8 E3. **(** 736-1600. **FAX** 563-
4007. *Rooms*: 147. 🛏 1 ☷ TV
🛁 ☷ ⊗ 📞 ¶¶ 🍸 AE, MC, V,
JCB. $

This new budget entry on the "Little
Korea" block is a winner, recently
renovated with fresh black-and-
white décor, smart contemporary
furnishings and new bathroom
fixtures. The theme is New York,
with attractive Manhattan photos
in the halls and fun touches like
a Statue of Liberty lamp in each
room. Comfortable suites accom-
modate four and are an excellent
choice for families.

Herald Square Hotel

19 W 31st St, NY, NY 10001.
Map 8 F3. **(** 279-4017. **FAX** 643-
9208. *Rooms*: 120. 🛏 108. 1 ☷
TV ☰ 🕭 🍸 AE, MC, V, JCB. $
See p131.

This tiny budget hideaway has
been renovated with taste. The
gilded cherub over the front door
remains from the time when the
Beaux Arts building, designed by
Carrere and Hastings, was the first
home of *Life Magazine*, a satirical
magazine in its earliest incarnation.
Vintage *Life* covers now adorn the
hallways. The rooms are quite
small, but pleasantly decorated
and bathrooms are modern. The
location near Macy's is very conve-
nient for Herald Square shopping
and the Javits Convention Center.
The neighbourhood, unfortu-
nately, lacks a wide range of
restaurants but "Little Korea"
is only a block away, with a
variety of inexpensive eateries.

Stanford

43 W 32nd St, NY, NY 10001.
Map 8 F3. ☎ 563-1480. **FAX** 629-0043. **Rooms:** 130. ▮▮ ① ▦ TV
▮ ▮ ▮ ▮ ▮ ▮ ▮ ▮ ☒ AE, DC, MC, V. $

Particularly popular with Asian visitors, this clean, modern hotel on the "Little Korea" block is very good value for money. In addition to the standard hotel facilities of a telephone, TV and radio, the comfortable rooms also come with a fridge. The Stanford offers an American coffee shop as well as the Gam Mee Ok restaurant which features good Korean cuisine. The location is convenient for Herald Square as well as Madison Square Garden and the Javits Convention Center (see p136).

Hotel Metro

45 W 35th St, NY, NY 10001.
Map 7 C2. ☎ 947-2500. **FAX** 279-1310. **Rooms:** 157. ▮▮ ▮ ▦ TV
▮ ▮ ▮ ▮ ▮ ☒ AE, DC, MC, V. $$$

A bright, recent arrival, the Metro sets a breezy, sophisticated tone with a spacious contemporary Deco-Revival lobby, and walls adorned with oversized Greta Garbo and Marlene Dietrich photos, old movie posters and vintage New York scenes. Rooms are a good size with a tailored black-and-tan colour scheme, striped wallpapers and amenities such as fridges and hair dryers. There is a small exercise room on the top floor, and the roof terrace, with its smashing views of the Empire State Building, becomes an outdoor bar during the summer months. Guests can also enjoy a spacious double sitting room off the lobby where a complimentary breakfast is served and coffee is available throughout the day. Understandably popular with younger visitors in the fashion industry, the Hotel Metro is a well-priced choice for all.

THEATER DISTRICT

Edison

228 W 47th St, NY, NY 10036.
Map 12 E5. ☎ 840-5000.
FAX 719-9541. **Rooms:** 900. ▮▮ ①
▦ TV ▮ ▮ ▮ ▮ ☒ AE, DC, MC, V, JCB. $

After its recent restoration, this vintage building has become one of the best value hotels to be found in the Theater District. The Art Deco lobby, brass doorways and period light fixtures of the original 1931 hotel have all been beautifully restored. Rooms have also been refurbished, and now

boast updated bathrooms and some new soft furnishings. The hotel has a café, restaurant and bar.

Hampshire Hotel

132 W 45th St, NY, NY 10036.
Map 12 E5. ☎ 921-7600.
FAX 719-0171. **Rooms:** 50. ▮▮ ①
▦ TV ▮ ▮ ▮ ▮ ▮ ☒ AE, DC, MC, V, JCB. $

A modest, reasonably priced choice in a very convenient location for theatre-goers, the Hampshire Hotel has recently been remodelled with very attractive new furnishings and bathrooms. A free continental breakfast is served in a pleasant room off the lobby.

Iroquois

49 W 44th St, NY, NY 10036.
Map 12 F5. ☎ 840-3080.
FAX 398-1754. **Rooms:** 110. ▮▮ ①
▦ TV ▮ ▮ ▮ ▮ ▮ ▮ ▮ ▮ ☒ AE, DC, MC, V, JCB. $

A budget choice on the same block as the Algonquin and Royalton, the Iroquois is unpretentious and comfortable. It has a friendly, multilingual staff to take care of the many foreign visitors who keep it booked. Several suites also have kitchenettes. The location is handy for shopping and theatres.

Ramada Milford Plaza

270 W 45th St, NY, NY 10036.
Map 11 C5. ☎ 944-8357.
FAX 869-3600. **Rooms:** 1300.
▮▮ ① ▦ TV ▮ ▮ ▮ ▮ P ▮
▮ ▮ ☒ AE, DC, MC, V. $

Big and bustling, this 28-storey, 1300-roomed hotel is a favourite with tour groups who appreciate its location in the heart of the Theater District. Don't expect frills, but there are conveniences such as exercise equipment and a restaurant and bar on site, as well as videos available on request.

Wellington

7th Ave at 55th St, NY, NY 10019.
Map 12 E4. ☎ 247-3900.
FAX 581-1719. **Rooms:** 700. ▮▮ ①
▦ TV ▮ ▮ ▮ ▮ P ▮ ▮ ▮
☒ AE, DC, MC, V. $

A favourite with tour groups, this big budget hotel offers a convenient midtown location and amenities that include a coffee shop, lounge and restaurant on the premises. Smallish rooms offer updated baths, suites and a number of rooms also provide kitchenettes. Family rooms with two bathrooms are also available.

Days Hotel Midtown

790 8th Ave, NY, NY 10019. **Map** 12 D5. ☎ (1800) 572-6232. **FAX** 974-0291. **Rooms:** 366. ▮▮ ① ▦ TV
▮ ▮ ▮ T ▮ P ▮ ▮ ▮
☒ AE, DC, MC, V. $$

An outdoor rooftop swimming pool (open May–mid Sep) is the main attraction at this otherwise predictable Loews chain hotel in the Theater District. The entire hotel was recently renovated, including the lobby, which has some sleek banquettes and an attractive Art Deco chandelier. The rates are moderate, especially for families, as children under 18 can stay in their parents' room free. Definitely worth consideration.

Hampshire Hotel and Suites

157 W 47th St, NY, NY 10036.
Map 12 D5. ☎ 768-3700.
FAX 768-3403. **Rooms:** 200. ▮▮ ①
▦ TV ▮ ▮ ▮ ▮ ▮ ▮ ▮ ▮ ▮
☒ AE, DC, MC, V, JCB. $$

A multi-lingual staff welcomes guests from all parts of the world at this modest hotel. It is convenient for theatre-goers, has small, recently renovated bedrooms with new bathroom fixtures, and offers complimentary continental breakfasts. No frills, but decent value.

Howard Johnson Plaza

851 8th Ave, NY, NY 10019.
Map 12 D4. ☎ 581-4100.
FAX 974-7502. **Rooms:** 300. ▮▮ ①
▦ TV ▮ ▮ ▮ ▮ ▮ P ▮ ▮ ☒
AE, DC, MC, V, JCB. $$

Though it bears the name of a chain of motels, this lodging is also under upmarket Loews management and it may exceed your expectations. Comfortable, decent-sized rooms have recently been refurbished. Many rooms have spacious areas for seating and lots of work space, and there is an on-site restaurant. A garage is available for parking. Children under 18 can stay free with their parents. For the price, it's a reasonable choice.

The Mansfield

12 W 44th St, NY, NY 10036. **Map** 11 B5. ☎ 944-6050. **FAX** 764-4477.
Rooms: 129. ▮▮ ① ▦ TV ▮ ▮
▮ ▮ ▮ ☒ AE, MC, V, JCB. $$

Adding to the hotel riches on this block is this treasure built in 1904 as a lodging for well-heeled bachelors. It has recently been restored by the Gotham Hospitality Group, whose architecturally interesting and moderately priced hotels are an increasing and welcome presence in the city. The original cast iron detailing and stonework, coffered ceilings, graceful mahogany and steel staircases have been restored. Rooms are chic modern, with sleigh beds made of iron and wire mesh, and sleek stainless steel washbasins in the bathroom. On the main floor are a sitting room with a period skylight and a lovely book-lined library where a harpist plays and concerts are held. Rates include parking, breakfast, complimentary cappuccino all day and an after-theatre dessert buffet, as well as a library of tapes, CDs and videos for the TV, video and CD player in every room.

Paramount

235 W 46th St, NY, NY 10036. **Map** 12 E5. ☎ *764-5500.* [FAX] *575-4892.* ***Rooms**: 610.* 🛁 [1] 👪 [24] [TV] 🚭 ▤ 🏋 💼 👶 ⇅ 🍸 🍴 [i] 💳 *AE, DC, MC, V, JCB.* $$

Philippe Starck's spectacular floating stairway and lighting, inspired by the art of Joan Miró, are the first things you see in the Paramount Hotel. Ian Schrager designed it for the young and hip, and to prove that inexpensive hotels need not be boring. Playful design, such as prints of Vermeer's *Lacemaker* as headboards, manage to distract from the tiny rooms. Amenities include a children's play room and a branch of Dean & DeLuca *(see p326)*, with takeaway food. There's a business centre, and a video library to supply the video recorders in every room. The bar, known as Whiskey, is one of the hottest spots in town.

Algonquin

59 W 44th St, NY, NY 10036. **Map** 12 F5. ☎ *840-6800.* [FAX] *944-1419.* ***Rooms**: 165.* 🛁 [1] 👪 [TV] 🚭 ▤ 💼 ♿ ⇅ 🍸 🍴 [i] 💳 *AE, DC, MC, V, JCB.* $$$ *See p143.*

The Round Table of the 1920s may have gone, but the Algonquin still maintains its famous literary tradition. It is a favourite haunt of publishers, writers and theatrical types – even the friendly bartender is rumoured to have written a couple of novels. Renovation has considerably freshened the décor and modernized most bathroom fixtures, but the old-fashioned feel of the rooms, which make up in cosiness what they lack in size, has been very carefully preserved.

Crowne Plaza

1605 Broadway, NY, NY 10019. **Map** 12 E4. ☎ *977-4000.* [FAX] *333-7393.* ***Rooms**: 770.* 🛁 [1] 👪 [24] [TV] 🥃 🚭 ☀ ▤ 🏋 🏊 💼 👶 ♿ ⇅ 🐕 [P] 🍸 🍴 [i] 💳 *AE, DC, MC, V, JCB.* $$$

For those who want a really big hotel right on Broadway, there is much to recommend the Crowne Plaza, aptly described by one reviewer as "brassy and classy". Public spaces are flashy and fun and, while their furnishings are predictable, the rooms are large and higher floors have some really great views of New York or the Hudson River. Guests can choose from three restaurants and have the use of a well-equipped business centre, a health club and the added luxury of New York's largest indoor hotel swimming pool.

Doubletree Guest Suites

1568 Broadway, NY, NY 10036. **Map** 12 E5. ☎ *719-1600.* [FAX] *921-5212.* ***Rooms**: 460.* 🛁 [1] 👪 [TV] 🚭 ▤ 🏋 💼 👶 ♿ ⇅ [P] 🍴 [i] 💳 *AE, DC, MC, V.* $$$

Broadway buffs, business travellers and families will find spacious quarters here and a quiet haven from the busy scene outside. Part of a 43-storey office building atop the Palace Theater, the setting is suitably dramatic for the Theater District, with a sky-lit third-floor lobby, klieg lighting and sleek playful Deco décor. The well-equipped two-room suites offer three phone lines with call waiting and voice mail, two remote-control TV sets, a bar, fridge, microwave, coffee maker and ironing board. Guests also have free use of a fitness centre and children's playroom, access to a café, and room service from 6am–4am. Everyone gets the Doubletree trademark chocolate chip cookies at night.

St Moritz

50 Central Park S, NY, NY 10019. **Map** 12 E3. ☎ *755-5800.* [FAX] *319-9658.* ***Rooms**: 680.* 🛁 [1] 👪 [TV] 🚭 ☀ ▤ ⇅ [P] 🍸 🍴 [i] 💳 *AE, DC, MC, V, JCB.* $$$

Standing in a superb location opposite Central Park, and with one of the best pavement cafés in the city, the refurbished St Moritz is a solid choice in the moderate-price category – especially for rooms facing the park. While not posh, the décor is comfortable and most bathrooms have been updated. Rumplemayer's, the famous ice-cream parlour, is just off the lobby. Don't count the calories, just enjoy the experience.

Salisbury

123 W 57th St, NY, NY 10019. **Map** 12 E3. ☎ *246-1300.* [FAX] *977-7752.* ***Rooms**: 320.* 🛁 [1] 👪 [TV] 🚭 ▤ 💼 ⇅ [i] 💳 *AE, DC, MC, V, JCB.* $$$

Comfortably old-fashioned, the Salisbury is a really good deal in a wonderful location. It is right across from Carnegie Hall and an easy walk to the best Fifth Avenue shops. Rooms are fairly undistinguished, but a decent size, and many of them have well-equipped kitchenettes, a bonus for families. The ambience is friendly and warm and the neighbourhood is convenient and safe.

Essex House

160 Central Park S, NY, NY 10019. **Map** 12 E3. ☎ *247-0300.* [FAX] *315-1839.* ***Rooms**: 593.* 🛁 👪 [24] [TV] 🥃 🚭 ☀ ▤ 🏋 💼 👶 ♿ ⇅ 🐕 [P] 🍸 🍴 [i] 💳 *AE.* $$$$

A multi-million dollar renovation by the Nikko hotel chain of Japan has transformed the Essex House into dramatic Art Deco. There are stunning black marble columns standing tall in the lobby, coffered ceilings, etched brass lift doors and newly enlarged windows, through which views of Central Park can be enjoyed. Rooms are not overly large, but guests who have views of the park may never actually notice. All of the rooms are decorated in tasteful, traditional English-style décor, and guests are treated to bathrobes, shoe shines, turn-down service and 24-hour room service. The hotel also offers a health spa and a business centre.

Michelangelo

152 W 51st St, NY, NY 10019. **Map** 12 E4. ☎ *765-1900.* [FAX] *541-6604.* ***Rooms**: 178.* 🛁 👪 [24] [TV] 🚭 ▤ 🏋 💼 👶 ♿ ⇅ [P] 🍸 🍴 [i] 💳 *AE, DC, MC, V, JCB.* $$$$

A classy hotel situated just off Broadway, this New York outpost of Italy's Starhotels has spacious rooms averaging 475 sq ft (46 sq m) and an unusual choice of room furnishings: Empire, Country French or Art Deco. Marble bathrooms come with oversize tubs and TVs. Guests enjoy a complimentary continental breakfast, videos and a video library, and a 24-hour fitness facility. Business travellers can choose SmartDesk rooms, conveniently equipped with computers, printer/fax/copiers, and fax modems.

Millennium Broadway

145 W 44th St, NY, NY 10036. **Map** 12 E5. ☎ *768-4400.* [FAX] *768-0847.* ***Rooms**: 629.* 🛁 [1] 👪 [TV] 🥃 🚭 ☀ ▤ 🏋 💼 👶 ♿ ⇅ [P] 🍸 🍴 [i] 💳 *AE, DC, MC, V, JCB.* $$$$

Sleek and streamlined, this high-tech mecca boasts a striking modernistic lobby and staff dressed all in robot-like grey. Rooms are fairly small for the price, but are compensated for by a large cache of gadgetry, which includes voice mail in four languages and an in-room system that allows guests to access airline schedules and restaurant menus, order tickets and make theatre reservations, review accounts and then check out of the hotel electronically. Hotel amenities include a fitness centre and a business centre. The Millennium Broadway is especially recommended for business travellers, who can make use of the extensive meeting room and conference facilities.

Le Parker Meridien

118 W 57th St, NY, NY 10019.
Map 12 E3. **C** 245-5000.
FAX 708-7477. **Rooms:** 691. 🛏 1
🈹 24 📺 🍸 🏊 🎿 🎾 🍴 🔔 🚹 ⬆
🚭 📺 🅿 🕗 🍴 ℹ 🗂 *AE,*
DC, MC, V. $$$$$

The two main attractions at Le Parker Meridien are the soaring public spaces and the exceptionally good fitness facilities. There is a rooftop pool, jogging track, squash courts and racquet-ball court, plus a well-equipped health club. The entrance, a two-storey, block-long arcade, is very impressive, and the colourful Montparnasse bar is a great place for a relaxing drink. Recently refurbished rooms are in a smart Neo-Classical motif and come with fax, hairdryer and CD player.

Rihga Royal

151 W 54th St, NY, NY 10019.
Map 12 E4. **C** 307-5000.
FAX 765-6530. **Rooms:** 500. 🛏 24
📺 🍸 🏊 🎿 🍴 🚹 🔔 ⬆
🅿 🍴 ℹ 🗂 *AE, DC, MC, V,*
JCB. $$$$$

In the line-up of the many luxury hotels near Broadway, the all-suite Rihga Royal really does stand out: at 54 storeys high, it is one of New York's tallest hotels. Rooms on the upper floors offer spectacular panoramic views. Each elegant suite has a living room with bay windows and one or two bedrooms, separated with mirrored French doors. Décor is classic and comfortable, and amenities in the rooms include dressing areas, minibars with icemakers, three telephones, two TVs, including cable TV and movie channels, a video and an electronic room safe. Guests can also make the most of a business and fitness centre, free newspapers, shoe shines and the added convenience of transport laid on from the hotel to Wall Street.

Royalton

44 W 44th St, NY, NY 10036.
Map 12 F5. **C** 869-4400.
FAX 869-8965. **Rooms:** 167. 🛏 1
🈹 24 📺 🍸 🏊 🎿 🍴 🍴 🚹 ⬆
🚭 🅿 🍴 ℹ 🗂 *AE, DC, MC,*
V. $$$$$

Ian Schrager, who began revolutionizing New York hotels with Morgans on Madison Avenue, really pulled out all the stops with the amazing Royalton. Philippe Starck's design includes a space-age lobby, curving hallways and rooms rigged out like first-class cabins in a sleek ocean liner, with big beds built in like bunks. Who likes this sort of thing? Well, the celebrity guest list includes directors David Lynch and Oliver Stone, actors Dudley Moore, Sean Penn and John Malkovich, the Manhattan Transfer singing group and other musical stars including Hammer and heavy-metal band Guns 'n' Roses. The 44 restaurant attracts trendy editorial types for lunch, and the small round bar, aptly called 44 Round, is equally popular.

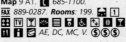

LOWER MIDTOWN

Quality Hotel

3 E 40th St, NY, NY 10016. **Map** 8 F1.
C 447-1500. **FAX** 213-0972.
Rooms: 189. 🛏 1 🈹 📺 🏊
🍴 🔔 ⬆ 🍸 ℹ 🗂 *AE, DC,*
MC, V. $$

A Canadian company which is best known for its motels has provided this clean, contemporary, no-frills midtown hotel with very reasonable rates. The décor is, unsurprisingly, motel-like, but the rooms are fitted out with functional work tables and comfortable sitting areas, remote-control TV and clock-radios, and guests receive complimentary morning newspapers and coffee. Many rooms have sofa-beds for children, who can stay free in their parents' room. The location is within easy walking distance of theatres and good shopping.

Doral Court

130 E 39th St, NY, NY 10016.
Map 9 A1. **C** 685-1100.
FAX 889-0287. **Rooms:** 199. 🛏 1
🈹 📺 🍸 🏊 🍴 🔔 ⬆ 🍸
🍴 ℹ 🗂 *AE, DC, MC, V.* $$$

This is the least assuming of three popular Doral properties in the civilized Murray Hill area, and the Doral Court is an appealing hotel. Among its many features are a small, warm, wood-panelled lobby and cheerful, light and airy rooms with entry foyers, walk-in closets,

dressing areas and fluffy bathrobes. Other niceties include large TVs, videos, and guest privileges at the nearby Doral Fitness Center. Ask for one of the four rooms on the 15th floor for terraces with skyline views.

Helmsley Middletowne

148 E 48th St, NY, NY 10017.
Map 13 A5. **C** 755-3000.
FAX 832-0261. **Rooms:** 190. 🛏 1
🈹 📺 🏊 🍴 🔔 ⬆ 🅿 🗂 *AE,*
DC, MC, V, JCB. $$$

Of the city's several Helmsley hotels, the Middletowne Hotel is the least glitzy. It is a good bet for those who like the ambience of a smaller hotel but who also want a safe, convenient East Side location. The lobby is tiny and the rooms are small, but the bedrooms have a pleasant atmosphere, as they have been redecorated in bright colours and fresh fabrics. All rooms have fridges, and many come with well-fitted kitchenettes.

Jolly Madison Towers

22 E 38th St, NY, NY 10016.
Map 9 A1. **C** 802-0600.
FAX 447-0747. **Rooms:** 246. 🛏 1
🈹 📺 🍴 🍴 🔔 ⬆ 🍸 ℹ
🗂 *AE, DC, MC, V.* $$$

A comfortable mid-range hotel, the Madison Towers is nothing fancy – but then neither are the rates. The rooms are reasonably large, and are being redecorated by the Jolly chain from Italy. The hotel offers a good health spa equipped with whirlpool and sauna. The pleasant Whaler Bar has a fireplace and murals with a nautical theme.

Morgans

237 Madison Ave, NY, NY 10016.
Map 9 A3. **C** 686-0300. **FAX** 779-8352. **Rooms:** 113. 🛏 1 🈹 📺
🍸 🏊 🍴 🍴 🔔 ⬆ 🅿 🚭
🕗 ℹ 🗂 *AE, DC, MC, V.*
$$$

There are no hotel clichés at this first hot property of Ian Schrager, not even a sign out front. French designer Andrée Putman's black-and-white minimalist world is clean and uncluttered, from the optical-illusion cube carpeting in the lobby to the bold tiles and stainless steel washbasins in the bathroom. Furniture in the smallish rooms is functional – built-in sofas, window seats that lift to accommodate suitcases and clutter. All rooms come with a CD player and private phone line; fax and computers are available on request. There is complimentary continental breakfast, afternoon tea service and dining at the Asia de Cuba restaurant.

For key to symbols *see p271*

Roger Smith

501 Lexington Ave, NY, NY 10017.
Map 13 A1. **C** 755-1400.
FAX 319-9130. **Rooms**: 130. 🛏 1
🔲 📺 🔛 🍴 ⛑ 🗼 🏋 🅿
🍷 🍽 🛗 *AE, DC, MC, V.*
💲💲💲

This used to be just yet another commonplace commercial hotel, but some artistic new owners have done wonders. The lobby has been transformed with paintings and sculpture and all the rooms have been refurbished; no two are alike and some have four-poster beds. Continental breakfast is offered on the balcony level, and Lily's Restaurant serves good continental food.

Doral Park Avenue

70 Park Ave, NY, NY 10016. **Map** 9 A1.
C 687-7050. **FAX** 949-5924.
Rooms: 188. 🛏 1 🔛 📺 🍷 ▤
🔛 🖥 ⛑ 🏋 🍷 🍽 🛗 *AE, DC, MC, V.* 💲💲💲💲

A Murray Hill oasis attracting sophisticated travellers who prefer smaller hotels, the Doral Park Avenue has distinctive Neo-Classical décor. Tranquil bedrooms in muted colours have such luxurious amenities as marble bathrooms, well-stocked minibars and TV movies. Guests also have use of the Doral Fitness Center. In warm weather, the Odyssey Lounge moves outside with a pleasant pavement café.

Doral Tuscany

120 E 39th St, NY, NY 10016.
Map 9 A1. **C** 686-1600. **FAX** 779-7822. **Rooms**: 121. 🛏 1 🔛 📺
🍷 ▤ 🔛 🖥 ⛑ 🍷 🍽 🛗 🗄 *AE, DC, MC, V.* 💲💲💲💲

The most expensive of the Murray Hill Doral trio, the Tuscany attracts a loyal clientele who appreciate such details as fresh flowers, walk-in closets, TV and telephone in the bathroom, and fridges stocked with free soft drinks. Guests can use the Doral Fitness Center across the street, or request exercise bicycles in their own rooms. The aptly named Time and Again restaurant has a good reputation.

Sheraton Park Avenue

45 Park Ave, NY, NY 10016.
Map 9 A2. **C** 685-7676.
FAX 889-3193. **Rooms**: 150. 🛏 1
🔛 24 📺 🔛 🖥 ▤ 🔛 🖥
🔛 🅿 🍷 🍽 🛗 🗄 *AE, DC, MC, JCB.* 💲💲💲💲

The Sheraton Park Avenue is decorated in English style, with wood-panelled walls, Chippendale furnishings and an entire library of leather-bound books. Bedrooms are comfortable, with long floral curtains, mantelpieces and prints of old New York on the walls. There's a fine restaurant and a bar, and a concierge is always on duty. Understated, in a quiet location, it feels almost like a country inn.

United Nations Plaza

1 United Nations Plaza, NY, NY 10017.
Map 13 C5. **C** 758-1234. **FAX** 702-5051. **Rooms**: 428. 🛏 1 24 📺
🗼 🚰 🔛 🖥 🔛 🖥 🔛 🗄 🔛
🅿 🍷 🍽 🛗 🗄 *AE, DC, MC, V, JCB.*
💲💲💲💲 *See p156.*

There is no more dramatic setting in New York than Kevin Roche's soaring skyscraper towering above the city, which is usually filled with an international clientele from the nearby United Nations. The sleek, marble lobby has chrome accents and massive floral bouquets are displayed here. Pastel-hued and very comfortable modern bedrooms begin on the 28th floor, and provide truly spectacular views. The 27th floor has a fitness centre and a glass-enclosed swimming pool, and on the 38th floor is the only indoor hotel tennis court in Manhattan. The artwork throughout the hotel is unique, taken from the hotel's collection of antique tapestries and textiles gathered from every UN nation. The hotel also offers butler service, and provides complimentary transport to Wall Street and other business locations and to the Theater District.

UPPER MIDTOWN

Pickwick Arms

230 E 51st St, NY, NY 10022.
Map 13 B4. **C** 355-0300.
FAX 755-5029. **Rooms**: 400. 🛏 235.
1 📺 🔛 🚰 🔛 🍷 🍽 🛗 🗄
🗄 *AE, DC, MC, V.* 💲

With a good and safe Eastside address, this is the best Midtown choice in the budget range. The comfortable lobby is adorned with columns, sofas and a sparkling chandelier. Plain but pleasant bedrooms offer TV, a small safe and room service. The single rooms with a shared bathroom are very cheap. The studios offer extra space and a sofa-bed for additional family members. On the premises are a decent coffee shop and a Spanish restaurant. It's a good hotel to relax in and enjoy the city views from the attractive rooftop garden.

Hotel Beverly

125 E 50th St, NY, NY 10022. **Map** 13
A4. **C** 753-2700. **FAX** 759-7300.
Rooms: 187. 🛏 1 🔛 📺 🚰 🔛
🔛 🖥 🅿 🍷 🍽 🛗 🗄 *AE, DC, MC, V, JCB.* 💲💲

The Beverly is an unpretentious, friendly, family-owned hotel. It provides spacious suites, some old-fashioned, comfortable furnishings, and caring service at rates well below those of many of its neighbours. It is a good choice for business travellers on a budget as well as for families with children. The hotel also has a reasonable restaurant and a coffee shop.

Wyndham

42 W 58th St, NY, NY 10019.
Map 12 F3. **C** 753-3500. **FAX** 754-5638. **Rooms**: 200. 🛏 1 📺 ▤ 🖥
🔛 🍷 🍽 🗄 *AE, DC, MC, V.* 💲💲

It is important to book well in advance to get a room in the hotel that many consider to be New York's best buy. The very homely warm atmosphere is enhanced by the fact the owners themselves reside here. Exceptionally large rooms are individually furnished and decorated and, although a little threadbare in places, they all have a personal charm and warmth. This is a favourite place for actors, especially those seeking long-term lodgings during a Broadway run. The low prices mean that there is no room service, but there is a decent restaurant in the hotel.

Doral Inn

541 Lexington Ave, NY, NY 10022.
Map 13 A5. **C** 755-1200.
FAX 319-8344. **Rooms**: 655.
🛏 1 📺 🚰 🔛 🖥 🔛 🖥
🍽 🛗 🗄 *AE, DC, MC, V, JCB.*
💲💲💲

One of several decent commercial hotels near Grand Central, the Doral Inn provides good value for money. It has well-decorated, moderately-priced lodgings and offers extras such as a complimentary health club with a sauna and squash courts, a 24-hour café and a convenient and money-saving laundry room. The hotel is also popular with tour groups, which accounts for the occasional queues at the check-in counter.

Fitzpatrick Manhattan Hotel

687 Lexington Ave, NY, NY 10022.
Map 13 A3. **C** 355-0100.
FAX 355-1371. **Rooms**: 92. 🛏 1
📺 ▤ 🔛 🖥 🅿 🍷 🍽 🛗 🗄
🗄 *AE, DC, MC, V, JCB.* 💲💲💲

Emerald-green carpet, Waterford chandeliers and lots of Irish prints are unmistakable clues that this is a new American outpost for a Dublin-based hotelier. Further hints include a portrait of the Irish president and suites named after past presidents of the Irish

Republic. This is a renovation of a former apartment hotel with just 92 rooms, more than half of them suites, which are much better value than the rather small single rooms. Amenities offered to the guests include cable TV, voice mail, computer and fax outlets. Guests also get membership privileges at the Excelsior Club, an excellent nearby fitness centre. Fitzers, the in-house restaurant and bar, features delicious Dublin Bay prawns and oak-smoked salmon.

The Elysee

60 E 54th St, NY, NY 10022.
☎ *753-1066.* [FAX] *980-9278.*
***Rooms**: 99.* 🛎 [1] 👪 [TV] 🚭 ≡ 🏋 🔒 👶 ♿ ⇅ [P] 🍷 🍴 ℹ
💳 *AE, DC, MC, V, JCB.* [$][$][$][$]

In a world of look-alike hotels, the 99-room Elysee stands out. Named rather than numbered rooms have a home-like quality, each individually furnished with comfortable reading areas and antique pieces such as fruitwood commodes or carved desks that look as though they might have been in the family for years. Some rooms have kitchenettes and terraces, and all have sleek, marble baths. Rates include continental breakfast as well as afternoon tea served in a pretty second-floor sitting room, where the menu changes to complimentary wine and cheese after 5pm. The murals in the Monkey Bar are famous, including Hirschfeld caricatures of Tallulah Bankhead, Joe DiMaggio, the Gish Sisters, Tennessee Williams and other former residents of the hotel. The Piano Suite boasts a Steinway that once belonged to Vladimir Horowitz.

New York Palace

455 Madison Ave, NY, NY 10022.
☎ *888-7000.* [FAX] *303 6000.* ***Rooms**: 600.* 🛎 [1] 👪 [24] [TV] 🚭 ☀ ≡ 🔒 👶 ♿ ⇅ 🐕 [P] 🍷 🍴 ℹ
💳 *AE, DC, MC, V, JCB.* [$][$][$][$]

The New York Palace incorporates an unusual blend of the opulent 1882 landmark Villard Houses with a contemporary 55-storey tower. Oversize guest rooms have been handsomely refurbished in traditional European style, with a safe, mini-bar and fax machine installed in every room. Rooms on the upper floors have dazzling views. Other amenities include a spa and fitness centre and a well-equipped business centre. The Stanford White-designed interiors of the Villard Houses, inspired by the Palazzo della Cancelleria in Rome, will be occupied in early 1997 by Le Cirque *(see p296)*, one of Manhattan's finest and most celebrated French restaurants.

Plaza

5th Ave at 59th St, NY, NY 10019.
Map 12 F3. ☎ *759-3000.*
[FAX] *759-3167.* ***Rooms**: 812.*
🛎 👪 [24] [TV] 🍸 🚭 ☀ ≡ 🏋 🔒 👶 ♿ ⇅ 🐕 [P] 🍷 🍴 ℹ
💳 *AE, DC, MC, V, JCB.* [$][$][$][$]
See p179.

There are smarter hotels and more elaborate rooms in New York, but for location, lobby and history, nothing compares with the Plaza. It is a National Landmark, a local fixture and has been a favourite for almost 100 years. The Plaza presides over Grand Army Plaza at the entrance to Central Park, and rooms facing the park have really fabulous green vistas. Among the Plaza's many amenities are a business centre, theatre ticket desk, meeting and banqueting rooms, several shops and restaurants, a barber and hair salon.

Waldorf–Astoria

301 Park Ave, NY, NY 10022.
Map 13 A5. ☎ *355-3000.*
[FAX] *759-9209.* ***Rooms**: 1410.*
🛎 [1] 👪 [24] [TV] 🍸 🚭 ≡ 🏋 🔒 👶 ♿ ⇅ [P] 🍷 🍴 ℹ
💳 *AE, DC, MC, V, JCB.* [$][$][$][$]
See p175.

There are really two Waldorfs: the big business-orientated hotel and the ultra-exclusive Towers, with its own private entrance and smart concierge and without doubt some of the most elaborate and beautifully furnished quarters in the city. The Towers is the frequent choice of presidents and visiting top dignitaries. The main lobby is quite magnificent. It has been restored to its 1931 Art Deco glory, with bas-relief friezes and grill-work setting off the beautifully painted murals, deep mahogany panelling and elegant marble columns. The marvellous giant clock, dating from 1893, once stood in the legendary original hotel on 34th Street. Famous Peacock Alley is still a very popular place to go for drinks.

Box Tree

250 E 49th St, NY, NY 10017.
Map 13 B5. ☎ *758-8320.*
[FAX] *308-3899.* ***Rooms**: 13.* 🛎 [1]
👪 [24] [TV] ≡ 🔒 🐕 🍷 🍴 ℹ
💳 *AE.* [$][$][$][$][$]

Only the red carpet on the front steps gives a clue that these two town houses in a row of look-alike brownstones are actually New York's most unusual lodging. The Box Tree is an opulent 13-room inn with its own restaurant. It reflects the extravagant tastes of Bulgarian-born owner, Augustin Paege, who, having bought the brownstone next door, hopes to increase the number of rooms available. The rooms are small but sumptuous, with formal curtains, chandeliers, fur throws and working marble fireplaces. Each room has an individual theme, with décor ranging from Chinese to English Gothic or 1930s Paris. Rates are high, but they do include a substantial restaurant credit per night. Children under the age of five are not welcome in the hotel.

Four Seasons

57 E 57th St, NY, NY 10022.
☎ *758-5700.* [FAX] *758-5711.*
***Rooms**: 370.* 🛎 [1] 👪 [24] [TV] 🍸 🚭 ☀ ≡ 🏋 🔒 ♿ ⇅ 🐕 [P] 🌿 🍷 🍴 ℹ 💳 *AE, DC, MC, V, JCB.*
[$][$][$][$][$]

IM Pei's 52-storey triumph is an updated, slim, soaring limestone evocation of New York's Art Deco prime. Breaking the predictable mould of traditional Old World décor found in the city's luxury hotels, the soaring pillared 33 ft high (10 m) grand foyer is as austere and awesome as a monument. Rooms are the city's largest with exquisite custom-made modernistic furnishings and bedside buttons for everything – to open the curtains, pull down the blinds, turn off the lights. Many have foyers and dressing rooms and all have enormous marble bathrooms with giant tubs and separate glass stall showers. Lacking no amenity and with peerless service, the Four Seasons was accorded five-star status just after it opened in 1993. For those who wish for luxury in an urbane modern mode and can afford the lofty tab, this is New York's prime lodging.

Peninsula

700 5th Ave, NY, NY 10019.
Map 12 F4. ☎ *247-2200.*
[FAX] *903-3949.* ***Rooms**: 250.*
🛎 👪 [24] [TV] 🍸 🚭 ☀ ≡ 🏋 🏊 🔒 👶 ⇅ [P] 🌿 🍷 🍴 ℹ 💳 *AE, DC, MC ,V, JCB.*
[$][$][$][$][$]

Since the noted Peninsula group from Hong Kong took over at the hotel, things have been looking up at the 1905 Beaux Arts landmark, the former Gotham Hotel. Guests go up a sweeping double stairway to the elegant lobby, resplendent with antiques and massive floral arrangements. The Art Nouveau bedrooms are gracious and some of the baths come with 6 ft (2 m) whirlpool tubs. A highlight of the hotel is the rooftop-level fitness centre, health spa and pool. The Pen-Top bar opens on to a terrace in summer and is always a pleasant place to go for a drink because of the grand city views.

Pierre

2 E 61st St, NY, NY 10021.
Map 12 F3. ☎ *838-8000.*
[FAX] *940-8109.* ***Rooms**: 206.*
🛁 [1] ⊞ [24] [TV] 🍾 🚭 ❄ 💼 👶 🧍 ♿ ⇅ 🐕 [P] 🍸 🍴 [i] 💳 *AE, DC, MC, V, JCB.*
$$$$$

Limousines stand outside the door, awaiting the presidents who are among the clientele of this luxurious and cosseting hotel. The Pierre is a member of Canada's highly esteemed Four Seasons group. Half the rooms are leased on a permanent basis. Both lobby and bedrooms are full of antiques and old-world elegance, and are lovelier than ever after recent refurbishing. Amenities and service are top of the line, and the Café Pierre is one of New York's top places for business breakfasts.

Ritz–Carlton

112 Central Park South, NY, NY 10019. **Map** 12 E3. ☎ *757-1900.*
[FAX] *757-9620.* ***Rooms**: 228.* 🛁 [1] ⊞ [24] [TV] ❄ 💼 👶 🧍 ♿ ⇅ [P] 🍸 🍴 [i] 💳 *AE, DC, MC, V, JCB.* $$$$$

Lavish renovation has completely changed the décor and made this one of New York's most elegant boutique hotels. The look is luxe old world European, with crystal chandeliers, Oriental rugs and many gilt-trimmed French furnishings. Guest rooms have been enlarged and a fitness centre added. The splendid Central Park views needed no improvement. The Fantino restaurant is winning praise for its northern Italian menu, and the bar remains a favourite gathering place. Guests enjoy a full breakfast buffet.

St Regis

2 E 55th St, NY, NY 10022.
Map 12 F4. ☎ *753-4500.*
[FAX] *787-3447.* ***Rooms**: 322.* 🛁 ⊞ [24] [TV] 🍾 🚭 💼 🏋 👶 🧍 ♿ ⇅ [P] 🍸 🍴 [i] 💳 *AE, DC, MC, V, JCB.* $$$$$

John Jacob Astor's Beaux Arts beauty, the toast of New York society back in 1904, has emerged from a $100 million, three-year restoration looking almost as good as new. Decorated in muted blues and greens, the high-ceilinged rooms contain silk wall coverings and Louis XV reproduction furniture. The St Regis Roof is the scene of glittering social events, and Maxfield Parrish's mural of King Cole once more reigns behind the King Cole Bar. The price for all this luxury is one of the highest room rates in the whole of New York.

Upper East Side

Franklin

164 E 87th St, NY, NY 10028.
☎ *369-1000.* [FAX] *369-8000.*
***Rooms**: 53.* 🛁 [1] ⊞ [TV] 🚭 ❄ 💼 🏋 🏊 👶 🧍 ⇅ [P] [i] 💳 *AE, MC ,V.* $$

The Gotham hoteliers have transformed the 53-room Franklin Hotel into a reasonably priced entry compensating for small space with high style. Tall bouquets and an original Picasso print greet guests in the tiny lobby. Sandblasted steel, polished black granite, rich cherrywood and soft black leather are used throughout. Custom furnishings and built-ins are designed to fool the eye. Each room comes with a video and TV, and a library offers free videos of classic films. Rates include complimentary continental breakfast as well as on-site parking. The neighbourhood is rich in museums, shops and restaurants.

Hotel Wales

1295 Madison Ave, NY, NY 10128.
Map 17 A3. ☎ *876-6000.*
[FAX] *860-7000.* ***Rooms**: 95.* 🛁 [TV] ❄ 💼 🏋 [P] 🍸 🍴 [i] 💳 *AE, MC, V.* $$

A small turn-of-the-century, almost European hotel, this Gotham Hospitality Group property is one of a kind in New York. While far from luxurious, it has genteel charm, thanks to caring renovation that has restored the fireplaces, marble stairs and oak wood panelling of the original 1901 hotel. The marble sinks and brass fixtures in the bathrooms are also originals. Complimentary breakfast and tea are served in a Victorian parlour on the second floor, decorated with charming antique illustrations from children's books. The room also hosts musical recitals and Sunday chamber music concerts. The location is perfect for museum-hopping, and the neighbourhood has a wide choice of restaurants.

Mark

25 E 77th St, NY, NY 10021.
Map 16 F5. ☎ *744-4300.*
[FAX] *744-2749.* ***Rooms**: 180.* 🛁 [24] [TV] 🍾 💼 👶 🧍 ♿ ⇅ 🍸 🍴 [i] 💳 *AE, DC, MC, V, JCB.* $$$$

Discreet, contemporary elegance is the hallmark of this Upper East Side sanctuary, with Biedermeier furniture, marble floors and 18th-century Piranesi prints on the walls. There is a 24-hour concierge service. The bedrooms have formal curtains matching the bedspreads, fresh plants, antique prints and bathrooms in marble or black-and-white Italian ceramic tile. Fine linen and down pillows are used in all rooms and most have pantries with minibars. The Edwardian, wood-panelled Mark's Restaurant gets high marks from reviewers, and its drawing room ambience makes it a favourite spot for afternoon tea.

Carlyle

35 E 76th St, NY, NY 10021.
Map 16 F5. ☎ *744-1600.*
[FAX] *717-4682.* ***Rooms**: 175.* 🛁 [1] ⊞ [24] [TV] 🍾 ❄ 💼 🏋 👶 🧍 ⇅ 🐕 [P] 🍸 🍴 [i] 💳 *AE, DC, MC, V.* $$$$$

A hushed lobby, filled with antiques and tapestries, welcomes guests to what many consider to be New York's best hotel. An Upper East Side luxury outpost, the Carlyle has a reputation for exceptional personal service. The rooms are large and in understated good taste, decorated in traditional style and floral prints. Each has a kitchenette as well as a video, stereo, CD player, dedicated fax line and a multiple-line hands-free phone. Several of the rooms have private terraces and dining rooms. A fitness centre and sauna are available to all guests. Despite its subdued luxury, the Carlyle is lively by night, a popular spot for drinks amid the amusing murals in Bemelmans' Bar, and songs by cabaret star Bobby Short in the Café Carlyle.

Lowell

28 E 63rd St, NY, NY 10021. **Map** 13 A2. ☎ *838-1400.* [FAX] *838-9194.*
***Rooms**: 61.* 🛁 [1] [TV] 🍾 💼 🧍 ♿ ⇅ 🐕 [P] 🍸 🍴 [i] 💳 *AE, DC, MC, V, JCB.* $$$$$

This intimate, luxurious all-suite hotel was built in 1926 and retains its old-world charm. Service is excellent, and the 61 suites offer such persuasive niceties as wood-burning fireplaces, libraries, real plants, fresh flowers, marble baths and full kitchens. Eclectic decor mixes French, Art Deco and Oriental pieces, always in the best of taste. The Pembroke Room on the second floor seats just 35 people and is a delightful place for tea or weekend brunch in a serene setting of lace curtains and discreet European character. The Post House restaurant is also highly regarded.

Plaza Athénée

37 E 64th St, NY, NY 10021.
Map 12 F2. ☎ *734-9100.*
[FAX] *772 0958.* ***Rooms**: 156.* 🛁 [1] ⊞ [24] [TV] 🚭 💼 👶 ♿ ⇅ 🐕 [P] 🍸 🍴 [i] 💳 *AE, DC, MC, V, JCB.* $$$$$

The New York version of the Paris hotel is an elite enclave. It is very exclusive, with opulently appointed, albeit small, rooms and a host of amenities, including fresh flowers, shoe trees, safes, kitchenettes, bathrobes and room humidifiers. Décor is Louis XVI and every room has a replica of the gilt clock found in the famous Paris hotel. The hotel's restaurant, Le Régence, receives good reviews for its food, served beneath a cloud-painted ceiling (see p297). The reader survey in *Institutional Investor Magazine* has often named the hotel number one in Manhattan.

Regency

540 Park Ave, NY, NY 10021.
Map 13 A2. 759-4100.
FAX 826-5674. **Rooms**: 384.
AE, DC, MC, V, JCB.

Hollywood moguls are likely to be among those alighting from the limousines in front of the Regency, many of them bound for magnificent suites. The name reflects the Regency décor that the rooms share, and the lobby is filled with mirrors and gilt. The Regency's 540 Restaurant is where New York's "power breakfast" was born; you can see the bigwigs almost every morning, wheeling and dealing over muffins and croissants. The hotel gives first-class service to all guests and has every amenity, including 24-hour room service, a fitness centre and business centre.

Stanhope

995 5th Ave, NY, NY 10028. **Map** 17 A4. 288-5800. FAX 517-0088.
Rooms: 141.
AE, DC, MC, V.

Small and opulent, the Stanhope stands in a superb spot right across the street from the Metropolitan Museum of Art. It has a Parisian-style terrace café which is one of the city's most popular. The public rooms are heavily adorned with French antiques. Each of the bedrooms is furnished with Louis XVI reproduction furniture and, besides the usual conveniences, comes equipped with CD and cassette players. Even if you can't afford to stay here, it is worth coming for tea in Le Salon, a room with the feel of an indoor garden.

Westbury

15 E 69th St, NY, NY 10021. **Map** 12 F1. 535-2000. FAX 535-5058.
Rooms: 231. AE, DC, MC, V, JCB.

Set amid the exclusive boutiques and galleries of Madison Avenue, the quiet Westbury exudes English charm. The rooms are pretty, and the lobby is a wonderful oasis of calm with its tapestries and huge bouquets of flowers. Indeed, the entire hotel seems wonderfully civilized. A health club has been added and the gracious Polo restaurant is a long-time favourite in the neighbourhood.

UPPER WEST SIDE

Beacon

2130 Broadway, NY, NY 10023.
Map 15 C5. 787-1100.
FAX 724-0839. **Rooms**: 100. AE, DC, MC, V, JCB.

The smartest of the budget hotels sprouting on the Upper West Side, the Beacon is named after the famous theatre next door. The recently refurbished lobby is stylish, with a floor of black and white tiles and an Oriental-style rug. Bedroom furnishings are unimaginative but adequately comfortable, and rooms are equipped with full kitchenettes.

Broadway American

2178 Broadway, NY, NY 10024.
Map 15 C5. 362-1100.
FAX 787-9521. **Rooms**: 430. 40.
AE, DC, MC, V.

The Broadway American is a good find for budget-watchers. This recently renovated Upper West Side lodging is decorated in sparse Art Deco style, with bright, abstract modern art downstairs and some whimsical touches in the rooms. Room amenities include cable TV and fridges, and guests have use of kitchen facilities, a laundry, and vending machines on each floor. There is also a 24-hour café on the premises. Rooms with shared bathrooms are excellent value.

Excelsior

45 W 81st St, NY, NY 10024. **Map** 15 D4. 362-9200. FAX 721-2994.
Rooms: 150. AE, MC, V.

An understated, reliable option on the Upper West Side, the Excelsior has a gracious, welcoming lobby and large, comfortable, old-fashioned rooms that lack fancy furnishings. Most of the accommodation is in suite form, but even individual rooms come equipped with money-saving kitchens. For the best views, ask for a room right at the front, overlooking the Museum of Natural History.

Milburn

242 W 76th St, NY, NY 10023.
Map 16 D5. 362-1006.
FAX 721-5476. **Rooms**: 90.
AE, DC, MC, V.

Newly refurbished and pleasantly decorated with art posters, this modest West Side hotel offers some reasonably sized studios (the best buys) and a few two-room suites, all with fully equipped kitchens, including a microwave and a fridge. Bathrooms are new, and there is an in-house laundry for guests' use. The location is convenient for the Lincoln Center, and for the many interesting shops and restaurants to be found on increasingly trendy Broadway and the rest of the Upper West Side.

Radisson Empire

44 W 63rd St, NY, NY 10023.
Map 12 D2. 265-7400
FAX 765-4913. **Rooms**: 375.
AE, DC, MC, V.

The old Empire has a totally new lease of life, thanks to fairly recent stylish renovations. The high-ceilinged lobby now has the look of a Tudor castle, with some unusual wrought-iron candelabra and a beautiful carved mantelpiece. Rooms are pleasantly decorated with floral patterns. The hotel is almost close enough to Lincoln Center to hear the arias. Music lovers will be pleased to note that each room comes equipped not only with TV and video but with a stereo, tape deck and CD player. The Empire Café is convenient for pre-concert dining.

Mayflower

15 Central Park West, NY, NY 10023.
Map 12 D2. 265-0060.
FAX 265-2026. **Rooms**: 377.
AE, DC, MC, V, JCB.

Situated opposite Central Park and an easy walk from Lincoln Center, the Mayflower has a genteel air – perhaps shabbily genteel is a better description, as the rooms are well overdue for renovation. It remains pleasantly comfortable and unpretentious though, and bedrooms have the added convenience of small kitchenettes and fridges. The hotel is very popular with those who appreciate the location and the frequent opportunities to rub elbows with Lincoln Center performers at the Conservatory Café. Park views from rooms at the front on the higher floors are glorious, and are well worth the extra expense.

RESTAURANTS AND BARS

N EW YORKERS love to eat well, and there are over 25,000 restaurants in the five boroughs catering for them. They avidly read the restaurant reviews in magazines, such as *New York* and *Where*, to ensure they are seen in the latest fashionable eaterie. It's all taken very seriously – one bad review can close down a restaurant. The restaurants in

The classic Manhattan cocktail

our listings have been selected as the best that New York can offer. *Choosing a Restaurant* on pages 290–92 will help narrow down your choice, and the map on page 288 shows the highlights of the list. For lighter refreshment, *Light Meals and Snacks* on pages 304–6 picks some of the best places to go for a quick snack.

RESTAURANT MENUS

M EALS IN MOST restaurants consist of three courses: the appetizer (or starter), an entrée (the main course) and dessert. Virtually all New York restaurants, except fast food places, serve you rolls and butter just after you're seated, at no extra charge – it's all part of the expected service.

You may also be offered a *lagniappe* – or appetizer, such as a small dollop of mousse or a tiny triangle of quiche – before you order.

A typical New York deli *(see p304)*

PRICES

Y OU WILL ALWAYS find a restaurant in New York to suit your budget. At inexpensive luncheonettes, diners and fast food chains, $5 will buy you a filling meal. There are also hundreds of acceptable, even first-rate, restaurants where you can eat well at a moderate cost – around $20 per person for a filling and decent meal, not including drinks – in attractive surroundings. For dinner at a "hot ticket" New American venue with a star chef, the bill could be upwards of $40 to $60 per person, excluding drinks. Many top restaurants do, however, offer fixed-price (or, as they are known in New York, prix fixe) meals. These are normally much cheaper than the à la carte menu. Lunch is also less expensive than dinner in such places, and in many, because of the profusion of expense account diners, lunch is also the busiest period of the day.

US. The most commonly accepted credit cards are VISA, Mastercard and American Express. Dollar traveller's cheques are also welcome in many restaurants. Luncheonettes and coffee shops accept cash only. In fast food chains, you order at the counter and then pay cash in advance.

DINING ON A BUDGET

D ESPITE THE TALES of $200 expense account lunches, there are ways to stretch a meal budget in New York.

Order fewer courses than you would normally. American portions are huge, and an appetizer is often big enough for a light main course. You could share one with your companion, or choose two appetizers and no entrée.

Be wary of ordering special "dishes of the day". They are often more expensive than items on the printed menu.

Ask your waiter if there is a prix fixe menu. Many of the expensive restaurants offer

Interior of Zen Palate *(see p300)*

these at lunch and dinner – in the early evening it may often be called the pre-theater menu. Or try a prix fixe lunch buffet, these are popular in

Street-corner hot dog stand

Appetizers at the upmarket restaurants are often the chef's most creative dishes – many diners request two appetizers and no entrée. Italian menus offer a pasta dish as a second course before the main course, but most non-Italian-Americans order it as their main course. Coffee is served at the end of the meal in all restaurants above the diner or coffee-shop level. Your coffee cup may be refilled until you refuse any more.

The cheeseboard is a rarity in New York restaurants. A few top French restaurants offer one, but it is not an American custom, especially in these cholesterol-conscious days.

TAXES AND TIPPING

N EW YORK CITY sales tax of 8.25% will be added to your bill. Service is not usually included. Tipping can run from 10% at a coffee shop to 25% at the fanciest places. Many New Yorkers just double the sales tax for a tip, and then adjust it as the service dictates.

The bill is known as the "check" in the

the Indian restaurants found around Manhattan and offer excellent value for money.

Go to bars featuring happy hours. They often offer a variety of hors d'oeuvres, like Spanish *tapas*, which can make a meal in themselves. If you really want to try an upmarket restaurant, go for lunch. It is often a lot cheaper than dinner. If you want to see inside the restaurants every visitor has heard about, just go to have a drink. The atmosphere is more important than the food anyway.

Avoid breakfast in your hotel. Even its coffee shop will be much more expensive than a diner or luncheonette.

Hours

Breakfast hours are usually from 7am to 10.30 or 11am. Sunday brunch is a popular meal, served at most upmarket restaurants between about 11am and 3pm. Lunch runs from 11.30am or noon to 2.30pm at most places, but the busiest time of the day is 1pm. Dinner is usually served from 5.30 to 6pm onwards. The most popular time is around 7.30 to 8pm.

Some restaurants stop serving at 10pm during the week, or 11pm on Friday and Saturday. Certain informal restaurants, especially Chinese, are open all day, from 11.30 am to 10pm. Diners are also open long hours, from 7am to midnight in some cases.

Poolside at the Four Seasons ***(see p293)***

Dress Codes

Few restaurants demand that male diners dress formally, though a jacket is required at classy restaurants, and jacket and tie at the very best. At most places, for both men and women, "casual but smart" suffices. Women tend to dress up when dining at the expensive restaurants. If unsure, check the dress code when making a reservation.

Waiting in style at the Café at Grand Central Terminal ***(see p309)***

Reservations

It is prudent to make reservations at any restaurant above the luncheonette/fast food level, especially at weekends. A few of the trendiest restaurants won't even accept reservations except for groups of six or more. It is essential to make reservations for lunch at a midtown restaurant. But you may still be seated at the bar, even if you have booked a table.

Smoking

Smoking is now illegal in restaurants with 35 or more seats. Many places provide separate rooms for smokers, but do phone ahead for details.

Children

When eating out with children, ask if there's a child's menu with half-portions. The prices are reduced, sometimes by half. Well-behaved children are accepted in most New York restaurants, but if yours are unpredictable stick to Chinatown Chinese or family-run Italian restaurants, burger bars, delis, cafés, fast food chains and luncheonettes. A few of the more upmarket restaurants have facilities for babies or toddlers; others may not be so well equipped. Dining out in the more formal New York restaurants is certainly not a family affair.

Wheelchair Access

While many restaurants may be able to accommodate a wheelchair, it is always best to mention your requirements when making your reservation. Many diners and luncheonettes cannot cater for disabled customers because of lack of space.

Using the Listings

Key to symbols in the listings on pp293–303.

☎ telephone number
🍴 fixed-price menu available
[V] vegetarian or vegetarian specialities
🚸 high chairs and/or children's portions
☂ outdoor eating
♿ wheelchair access to all or part of restaurant
👔 jacket and tie required
♫ live music
🍷 excellent wine list
★ highly recommended
💳 credit cards accepted
AE American Express
DC Diners Club
MC Mastercard/Access
V VISA
JCB Japanese Credit Bureau

Price categories for a three-course meal for one, including a half-bottle of house wine and all unavoidable extra charges (sales tax and service):

$ Under \$25
$$ \$25–\$35
$$$ \$35–\$50
$$$$ \$50–\$70
$$$$$ Over \$70

What to Eat in New York

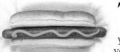

Hot dog

THE VARIETY OF FOOD found in New York is as varied as its cultural and ethnic makeup and you can find virtually any food you want. If you fancy a hearty simple meal, such as marinated vegetables, pasta or salami, visit one of the many Italian restaurants found in every neighbourhood. For a more sophisticated meal try a Japanese restaurant for sushi and sashimi – considered as good as anywhere in Japan. Or you could try some traditional Jewish foods, like pastrami, blintzes and bagels, found in most delis and luncheonettes. Spicy curries can be found in the many Indian restaurants around Manhattan. If you are really hungry, visit a steakhouse for juicy steaks, fresh seafood and some especially wicked desserts.

Bagel
This chewy, Jewish bread roll is most popularly served with lox (smoked salmon) and cream cheese.

Pancakes
Thick, sweet pancakes are usually served with maple syrup as part of a full breakfast. Fresh or dried fruit may be mixed into the batter before cooking.

Bacon is often sweet-cured streaky, fried very crisp.

"Home fries" are chunky sautéed potatoes.

Whole-meal toast

Eggs "over easy" are lightly fried on both sides.

Breakfast or Brunch
Breakfast (or brunch if eaten midmorning) can consist of anything from home fries, eggs, bacon and toast to sweet pancakes all in huge portions, often with unlimited coffee.

French Toast
A breakfast dish of sliced bread dipped in egg then fried and often served with syrup.

Egg Cream
This classic deli drink is made with iced milk, chocolate syrup and soda water.

Corned Beef on Rye
Cured beef is served on rye bread with mild mustard and a dill pickled gherkin.

Burger and Fries "To Go"
A takeaway beefburger and chips often comes with salad and onion rings too.

Giant Pretzel
This savoury bread twist is sold on every street corner.

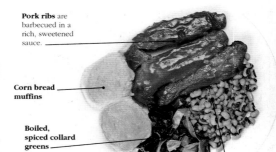

Pork ribs are barbecued in a rich, sweetened sauce.

Corn bread muffins

Boiled, spiced collard greens

Black-eyed peas

Clam Chowder
The Manhattan version of this shellfish soup is made with tomatoes and garnished with dry biscuits.

Soul Food
The cuisine of Harlem stems from America's Deep South. Simple foods are cooked with spices for a unique flavour.

Pizza
The street food of Little Italy is available all over the city – this uptown version is topped with artichoke hearts.

Sushi
Japanese cuisine, like this ultra-fresh raw fish and rice, is a New York favourite.

Dim Sum
Tiny steamed dumplings, stuffed with fish, meat or vegetables, are a speciality of Chinatown.

Waldorf Salad
Created in the 1930s at the Waldorf Hotel, it's made out of apples, nuts and leaves.

Cappuccino and Cookies
Frothy coffee is sprinkled with chocolate and served with tiny biscuits in the cafés around New York.

Apple Pie à la Mode
This traditional American dessert is only "à la mode" when served with ice cream.

New York Cheesecake
This thick, baked Jewish dessert may be served plain or glazed with fruit.

Banana Split
Some New York ice cream concoctions will feed a family. No one will mind if you order extra spoons and share.

New York's Best: Restaurants, Cafés and Bars

Restaurants can be found all over New York, catering to all tastes and pockets, and open at all times of the day or night. In the past, New York's eating habits reflected the city's ethnic heritage, and to some extent they still do – witness the huge rise in the number of Italian, Chinese and Japanese restaurants, and the enduring popularity of the traditional Jewish deli. However, with 37 pages of restaurant listings in the New York telephone directory, you can find virtually any cuisine you crave, from Californian, New American, Cajun and southern barbecue to Thai, Vietnamese, Indian, Afghan, Burmese and Philippine. The restaurants here are just a few New York favourites, selected from the listings on pages 293–303 as the best in their particular field.

Carnegie Delicatessen
Try the giant "pastrami on ry at this typical deli. (See p306.

Zen Palate
The excellent vegetarian cuisine offered here is a clever blend of Oriental styles. (See p300.)

Union Square Café
This is the place to sample New American cuisine at its best. Seafood and desserts are both excellent. (See p295.)

Florent
This bistro is open round the clock for authentic food and atmosphere. (See p306.)

Caffè Vivaldi
Of many charming coffee houses in New York, this is a favourite for its delicious, sticky pastries. (See p306.)

Golden Unicorn
Chinatown's best Chinese food is served here. Their range of dim sum is not to be missed. (See p300.)

Greenwich Village

Gram
the
Di

SoHo and
TriBeCa

Lower
Manhattan

Seaport
and the
Civic
Center

McSorley's Old Ale House
For atmosphere alone, this is Neu York's best bar. Sample the poten house beer with care. (See p309.)

Café des Artistes
This New York classic is famed for both its saucy 1930s murals and its unmissable chocolate dessert platter. (See p296.)

Mezzaluna
It's just a short walk from Museum Mile to some of the best pizzas in town. (See p306.)

Serendipity 3
Eccentric Victoriana amuses the adults, but kids vote this café a hit for its ice-cream sundaes. (See p306.)

The Four Seasons
Outstanding European and American food is served in two stunning rooms, one panelled in rosewood, the other centred around a pool. (See p293.)

Oyster Bar, Grand Central Terminal
The best seafood restaurant in Manhattan is this golden, vaulted room in the main railway station. The all-American wine list is excellent, too. (See p294.)

Hatsuhana
The freshest and most varied sushi available makes this Japanese restaurant stand out from the rest. Take a seat at the sushi bar itself to watch the skilled chefs at work. (See p301.)

Upper West Side

Central Park

Upper East Side

Upper Midtown

lower Midtown

EAST RIVER

kilometres   2

miles   1

Choosing a Restaurant

THE RESTAURANTS in this section have been selected for their good value or exceptional food. The chart highlights some factors which may influence your choice. For details see pages 293–303. Details of *Light Meals and Snacks* are on pages 304–6 and for some of New York's best *Bars* see pages 307–9.

	Page Number	Fixed-Price Menu	Late Opening	Children's Facilities	Tables Outside	Quiet Restaurant	Vegetarian Dishes	Seafood Specialities
LOWER MANHATTAN								
Hudson River Club *(American)* $$$$	294	●		●				
Layla *(Middle Eastern)* $$$$	302	●	■	●	■		■	
Windows on the World *(American)* ★ $$$$$	295	●				●		
SEAPORT AND THE CIVIC CENTER								
Bo Ky *(Chinese)* $	299	●		●				
LOWER EAST SIDE								
Canton *(Chinese)* $$	299							
Oriental Garden *(Chinese)* $$	300		■	●				●
Golden Unicorn *(Chinese)* $$$	299	●	■	●				
Sammy's Famous Roumanian *(Jewish/Romanian)* $$$$	303							
SOHO AND TRIBECA								
Penang Malaysian Cuisine *(Malaysian)* $	301		■				■	
Mekong *(Vietnamese)* $$	301	●			■		■	
Saalam Bombay *(Indian)* $$	302	●			■		■	
Savoy *(Mediterranean)* $$	294			●		●	■	●
Honmura An *(Japanese)* $$$	300	●				●	■	●
Provence *(French)* $$$	297		■	●	■			
Alison on Dominick Street *(French)* $$$$	295	●				●		●
Chanterelle *(French)* $$$$	296	●				●		
Montrachet *(French)* ★ $$$$	297	●		●				
TriBeCa Grill *(American)* $$$$	295	●			■		■	
Zoë *(American)* $$$$	295			●			■	●
GREENWICH VILLAGE								
Moustache *(Middle Eastern)* $	302	●	■				■	
Riodizio *(Brazilian)* $	303		■				■	
Cendrillon *(Malaysian/Philipino)* $$	301	●						
Cent' Anni *(Italian)* $$$$	298						■	
Il Mulino *(Italian)* $$$$	298		■	●			■	
La Métairie *(French)* $$$$	296		■					
Nobu *(Japanese)* ★ $$$$	300	●		●		●	■	●
Gotham Bar & Grill *(American)* $$$$$	293	●		●			■	
EAST VILLAGE								
Iso *(Japanese)* $$$	300	●	■					●
GRAMERCY AND THE FLATIRON DISTRICT								
An American Place *(American)* $$$	293			●			■	
Mesa Grill *(American)* $$$	294					●		●
Verbena *(American)* $$$	295			●	■	●	■	●
C.T/Claude Troisgros *(French)* $$$$	296	●	■	●	■		■	●
Gramercy Tavern *(American)* ★ $$$$	294	●						
Lola *(Caribbean)* $$$	303		■	●				
Periyali *(Greek)* $$$$	303				■			
Union Square Cafe *(American)* ★ $$$$	295			●			■	
The Water Club *(American)* $$$$	295	●	■		■			●

Price categories include a three-course meal for one, half a bottle of house wine, and all unavoidable extra charges such as sales tax and service.
ⓢ under $25
ⓢⓢ $25–$35
ⓢⓢⓢ $35–$50
ⓢⓢⓢⓢ $50–$70
ⓢⓢⓢⓢⓢ over $70.

★ Means highly recommended.

FIXED-PRICE MENU
A fixed price for a set meal which is a lot cheaper than normal menu prices.
LATE OPENING
Last orders at or after 11.30pm excluding Sunday.
CHILDREN'S FACILITIES
High chairs and/or child portions.
QUIET RESTAURANT
No piped music; peaceful atmosphere.
VEGETARIAN DISHES
Vegetarian restaurant, or restaurant with good vegetarian selection.

	Price	Page Number	Fixed-Price Menu	Late Opening	Children's Facilities	Tables Outside	Quiet Restaurant	Vegetarian Dishes	Seafood Specialities
CHELSEA AND THE GARMENT DISTRICT									
Da Umberto (*Italian*)	ⓢⓢⓢⓢ	298							●
Le Madri (*Italian*) ★	ⓢⓢⓢⓢ	298			■		■	■	
THEATER DISTRICT									
Afghan Kebab House (*Afghan*)	ⓢ	302	●						
Siam Inn (*Thai*)	ⓢ	301	●		●			■	
Jewel of India (*Indian*)	ⓢⓢ	302	●					■	
Tang Pavilion (*Chinese*)	ⓢⓢ	300	●					■	
Zen Palate (*Southeast Asian*)	ⓢⓢ	301	●	●				■	
B Smith's (*American*)	ⓢⓢⓢ	293							
Cabana Carioca (*Brazilian*)	ⓢⓢⓢ	303			●				
Orso (*Italian*)	ⓢⓢⓢ	298		■				■	
Tapika (*American*)	ⓢⓢⓢ	294	●						
Barbetta (*Italian*)	ⓢⓢⓢⓢ	297	●	■			●		
Osteria del Circo (*Italian*) ★	ⓢⓢⓢⓢ	298	●		●			■	
Remi (*Italian*)	ⓢⓢⓢⓢ	299		■		■			
Trattoria Dell'Arte (*Italian*)	ⓢⓢⓢⓢ	299		■		■			●
Le Bernardin (*French*)	ⓢⓢⓢⓢⓢ	295	●						●
Les Célébrités (*French*) ★	ⓢⓢⓢⓢⓢ	296	●		●		●		
Palio (*Italian*)	ⓢⓢⓢⓢⓢ	298						■	
The Rainbow Room (*American*) ★	ⓢⓢⓢⓢⓢ	294	●	■	●				
Russian Tea Room (*Russian*)	ⓢⓢⓢⓢⓢ	303	●	■				■	
San Domenico (*Italian*) ★	ⓢⓢⓢⓢⓢ	299		■			●	■	
LOWER MIDTOWN									
Ambassador Grill (*American*)	ⓢⓢⓢ	293	●		●		●	■	
Grand Central Oyster Bar (*American*) ★	ⓢⓢⓢ	294	●		●				●
Tropica (*Caribbean*)	ⓢⓢⓢⓢ	303	●		●			■	●
Sparks Steakhouse (*American*)	ⓢⓢⓢⓢⓢ	294							●
UPPER MIDTOWN									
Zarela (*Mexican*)	ⓢⓢ	303							
Arizona 206 (*American*)	ⓢⓢⓢ	293		■	●			■	●
Chin Chin (*Chinese*)	ⓢⓢⓢ	299	●	■	●	■		■	●
Le Colonial (*Vietnamese*)	ⓢⓢⓢ	301	●					■	
Dawat (*Indian*)	ⓢⓢⓢ	302	●					■	
Hatsuhana (*Japanese*)	ⓢⓢⓢ	300	●						●
Il Nido (*Italian*)	ⓢⓢⓢ	298			●				
Sushisay (*Japanese*)	ⓢⓢⓢ	300							●
Vong (*Thai*) ★	ⓢⓢⓢ	301	●			■	●	■	
Bice (*Italian*)	ⓢⓢⓢⓢ	297				■			
La Caravelle (*French*)	ⓢⓢⓢⓢ	296	●				●		
Darbar (*Indian*)	ⓢⓢⓢⓢ	302			●		●	■	
Felidia (*Italian*)	ⓢⓢⓢⓢ	298						■	
La Grenouille (*French*)	ⓢⓢⓢⓢ	296	●		●			■	
Inagiku (*Japanese*)	ⓢⓢⓢⓢ	300							●
Lutèce (*French*)	ⓢⓢⓢⓢ	297	●						
Shun Lee Palace (*Chinese*)	ⓢⓢⓢⓢ	300							●
Lespinasse (*French*) ★	ⓢⓢⓢⓢ	297					●	■	
Aquavit (*Scandinavian*)	ⓢⓢⓢⓢⓢ	302	●						●

Price categories include a three-course meal for one, half a bottle of house wine, and all unavoidable extra charges such as sales tax and service.
$ under $25
$$ $25–$35
$$$ $35–$50
$$$$ $50–$70
$$$$$ over $70.

★ Means highly recommended.

FIXED-PRICE MENU
A fixed price for a set meal which is a lot cheaper than normal menu prices.
LATE OPENING
Last orders at or after 11.30pm excluding Sunday.
CHILDREN'S FACILITIES
High chairs and/or child portions.
QUIET RESTAURANT
No piped music; peaceful atmosphere.
VEGETARIAN DISHES
Vegetarian restaurant, or restaurant with good vegetarian selection.

Restaurant	Page Number	Fixed-Price Menu	Late Opening	Children's Facilities	Tables Outside	Quiet Restaurant	Vegetarian Dishes	Seafood Specialties
La Côte Basque (French) $$$$$	296	●				●		
The Four Seasons (American) ★ $$$$$	293	●				●		●
Le Périgord (French) $$$$$	297	●				●		●
The '21' Club (American) $$$$$	295	●				●	■	
UPPER EAST SIDE								
Bangkok House (Thai) $$	301							●
Pamir (Afghan) $$	302						■	
Arcadia (American) ★ $$$$	293	●		●	■			
Coco Pazzo (Italian) $$$$	298						■	
Daniel (French) ★ $$$$	296	●		●	■		■	
Jo Jo (French) $$$$	296		■			●		
Aureole (American) ★ $$$$$	293	●			■	●	■	
Le Cirque (French) $$$$$	296	●						●
Le Régence (French) $$$$$	297	●						●
Parioli Romanissimo (Italian) $$$$$	298						■	
Sign of the Dove (American) $$$$$	294	●			■	●		
UPPER WEST SIDE								
Lemongrass Grill (Thai) $	301	●	■				■	
Monsoon (Thai/Vietnamese) $	301	●	■				■	
Barney Greengrass (Jewish) $$	302	●	■	●				
Ollie's Noodle Shop & Grill (Chinese) $$	299		■	●				●
Rain (Southeast Asian) $$	301			●			■	
Santa Fe (American) $$	294		■				■	
Carmine's (Italian) $$$	297			●				
Shun Lee West (Chinese) $$$	300		■				■	
Picholine (French/Mediterranean) $$$	303	●	■	●				
Café des Artistes (French) ★ $$$	296	●	■					●
MORNINGSIDE HEIGHTS AND HARLEM								
Sylvia's (American) $	294			●				
The Terrace (French) $$$$	297	●				■		●
BROOKLYN								
Moroccan Star (Moroccan) $	302	●		●				
Gage & Tollner (American) $$$	293	●		●				●
Peter Luger (American) $$$$	294	●		●				
The River Café (American) ★ $$$$$	294	●				■		
QUEENS								
The Water's Edge (American) $$$$$	295			●	■			●

AMERICAN

Three types of American cuisine are likely to be found in New York restaurants: Standard American, New American and Regional American.

Standard American cuisine generally consists of grilled meats, deep-fried seafood, chips and fresh tossed salads. Served in huge portions at reasonable prices this food will be found in restaurants in almost every neighbourhood.

New American cuisine is a spin-off from French nouvelle cuisine. Portions are generally small – and foods are chosen for interesting textures and colour combinations. Adapting the old, regional recipes and using fresh local ingredients with the infusion of Oriental items – such as ginger, soy, garlic, curry and fresh coriander – has become a touchstone of this cooking style. New American restaurants are easily among the very best and most expensive in New York.

Also to be found in the city is Regional American food. Cuisines in this category range from New England's seafood to southern barbecued ribs and soul food, which is traditionally eaten by African-Americans. Cajun cuisine may include blackened fish, crayfish or gumbo (soup, stew with poultry, rice, seafood, tomatoes and sausage). Californian cuisine uses mainly natural, fresh ingredients, often combining Asian food with nouvelle techniques. Restaurants serving regional food tend be in the middle of the price range, though southern soul food is cheaper.

Ambassador Grill

United Nations Plaza Hotel, 1 United Nations Plaza. **Map** 13 C5. 702-5014. **Open** 7–10.30am, noon–2pm, 6–10.30pm daily. 🍴🍷🛗🎵🅿️ 🈂️ AE, DC, MC, V. $$$

American cuisine, with a French flourish, is served to a mixed clientele of UN business people and mature East Siders in this comfortable mirrored setting. Prices are reasonable, considering the quality of the food and the locality. By far the best buy is the all-you-can-eat Sunday lobster-and-champagne brunch buffet.

An American Place

2 Park Ave. **Map** 9 A2. 684-2122. **Open** 11.45am–3pm Mon–Fri, 5.30–10pm Mon–Sat. 🆚🍴🛗🅿️ 🈂️ AE, DC, MC, V. $$$

Chef-proprietor Larry Forgione has made a name for himself and his New American cooking style in this restaurant reminiscent of a 1930s hotel dining room. His inventive menu frequently changes and might include grilled boneless quail with cornbread stuffing, or crisp free-range duck with a minted wildflower honey glaze.

Arcadia

21 E 62nd St. **Map** 12 F2. 223-2900. **Open** noon–2.30pm Mon–Sat, 6–10.30pm Mon–Sat. **Closed** some hols. 🍴🏃🛗🍷🎵🅿️ ★ 🈂️ AE, DC, MC, V. $$$$

For the practising gourmet, a visit to this posh, well-decorated uptown brownstone is essential. The chef/co-owner Anne Rosenzweig is one of the top young New American chefs. Virtually everything on the menu is appealing and dining here can be a memorable experience. Unfortunately, its popularity means it gets a bit crowded and the noise levels can then become intrusive.

Arizona 206

206 E 60th St. **Map** 13 B3. 838-0440. **Open** noon–3pm Mon–Sat, 5.30–11.30pm Fri, Sat, 5.30–10.30pm Sun. 🆚 🈂️ AE, DC, MC, V. $$$

For a different experience, step into this adobe-like interior, with its whitewashed-walls, cosy wood fires, wood tables and knotty pine floors. An imaginative blend of the southwest with New American flair produces dishes such as barbecued *foie gras* and roasted quail with polenta. Dinner is the best time to eat here, though it's noisy and crowded. The attached Arizona 206 Café is cheaper, with a different menu, but also wonderful food.

Aureole

34 E 61st St. **Map** 12 F3. 319-1660. **Open** noon–3pm Mon–Fri, 5.30–11pm Mon–Sat. 🍴🛗🍽️🆚🅿️🍷★ 🈂️ AE, DC, MC, V. $$$$

In an old, well-restored brownstone, long, narrow rooms are brightened by floral arrangements and bas relief decorations. The garden is the place to be in warm weather. The American-cum-French menu changes often and offers a rare dining experience. Recent gems include oak-smoked salmon with vegetable citrus salad, and aubergine-crusted Maine cod with bay prawns. A prix fixe menu offers excellent value for rarefied food.

B Smith's

771 8th Ave. **Map** 12 D5. 247-2222. **Open** noon–11pm Mon–Thu, noon–12.30pm Fri, Sat, noon–10.30pm Sun. 🛗🎵🈂️ AE, DC, V, MC. $$$

Run by Barbara Smith, a former model, this high-ceilinged restaurant is a magnet for New York's showbiz types and after-theatre crowd. Surprisingly, the stylish Southern and Mediterranean food is both good and reasonably priced. Upstairs, in a vast glass-enclosed space, is B Smith's Rooftop Café, where there is live music every night of the week.

The Four Seasons

99 E 52nd St. **Map** 1 3A. 754-9494. **Open** noon–2pm Mon–Fri, 5–11.15pm Mon–Sat. **Closed** some hols. 🍴🛗🍷🎵 occasionally. 🍷★ 🈂️ AE, DC, MC, V, JCB. $$$$

This restaurant, established in 1961, continues to attract power-lunch regulars to its magnificent, high-ceilinged Grill Room. More romantic, and a good place for a pre-theatre prix fixe dinner, is the spacious Pool Room, with its marble pool. Wherever you sit, you'll enjoy a consistently delicious meal of New American and continental dishes. The game dishes, including fillet of buffalo, baby lamb and all meat dishes are superb, and don't miss the dessert cart. This will be an expensive treat that will not disappoint.

Gage & Tollner

372 Fulton St, Brooklyn. (718) 875-5181. **Open** 11.30am–10pm Mon–Fri, 3.30–10pm Sat. 🍴🏃🛗🈂️ AE, DC, MC, V. $$$

It's worth the subway ride to Gage and Tollner for some of the area's best seafood, served in a restaurant that could pass as a set for the film *Gaslight*. Oysters and broiled clam-bellies are here, as are South Carolina specialities like Charleston she-crab soup (crab meat and crab eggs mixed with cream, onion and sherry). At lunch the clientele is mostly local politicos; at night it's more eclectic and interesting, but take a taxi.

Gotham Bar & Grill

12 E 12th St. **Map** 4 E1. 620-4020. **Open** noon–2.30pm Mon–Fri, 5.30–10pm Mon–Thu, 5.30–11pm Fri, Sat, 5.30– 9.30pm Sun. 🍴🆚🍷🅿️ 🈂️ AE, DC, MC, V. $$$$

Housed in a former warehouse, amid a Neo-Classical setting of columns, high ceilings and a pink marble bar, you will find what is probably the best food in this part of town. Alfred Portale is a young and gifted French-trained chef whose seafood dishes are wonderful, but who also has a flair with game such as grilled saddle of rabbit. It is pricey, but makes for a great New American food experience.

For key to symbols *see p285*

Gramercy Tavern

42 E 20th St. **Map** 8 F5.
[477-0777. **Open** noon–11pm
Mon–Thu, noon–11.30pm Fri, Sat,
5–11pm Sun. 🍴⑨ ♿ 🚻 V T 💳
★ 🎴 AE, DC, MC, V. $$$$

This newcomer, the creation of
Danny Meyer of the Union Square
Café, has inventive New American
fare in a setting that could pass for
a French country inn. You might
try such dishes as roasted scallops
with truffle *coulis* or marinated
salmon with minted *couscous* and
crème fraîche. Desserts are uni-
formly wonderful. Food in the
Tavern Room is also good and
much less expensive.

Grand Central Oyster Bar

Grand Central Station, Lower Level.
Map 9 A1. [490-6650. **Open**
11.30am to last sitting at 9.30pm
Mon–Fri. **Closed** some hols. 🚻 ♿
🍽 ★ 🎴 AE, DC, MC, V, JCB.
$$$

Some of the best seafood in New
York is served in this cavernous,
simple space below the city's main
railway station. At lunch you can't
hear yourself think, let alone talk,
as sound bounces off the vaulted
tile arches and ceilings. But the
fish and shellfish are always fresh
and simply prepared – and
surprisingly well-priced. There's
also a lengthy Californian wine list.

Hudson River Club

250 Vesey St. **Map** 1 A2. [786-
1500. **Open** 11.30am–3pm Mon–Fri,
5–10pm Mon–Sat, 11.30am–3.30pm
Sun. **Closed** some hols. 🍴⑨ 🚻 ♿
T 🎴 AE, DC, MC, V. $$$$

Situated on the second floor in
one of the World Financial Center
towers, this elegant club-like
restaurant offers views of the
harbour and the Statue of Liberty.
The original menu highlights the
foods and wines of the Hudson
River Valley for a stylish clientele.

Mesa Grill

102 5th Ave. **Map** 8 F5. [807-
7400. **Open** noon–2.15pm Mon–Fri,
11.30am–3pm Sat, Sun, 5.30–10pm
Mon–Thu, 5.30–10.30pm Fri, Sat. ♿
🎴 AE, DC, MC, V. $$$

Spicy, inventive renderings of
southwestern US dishes, mainly
from Arizona and New Mexico,
are served in a former clothing
showroom, now turned into a
spacious and colourful evocation
of the west. It attracts the trend-
setting crowd with its unusual
combinations of grilled foods
at very reasonable prices.

Peter Luger Steakhouse

178 Broadway, Brooklyn. [(718)
387-7400. **Open** 11.45am–10pm
Mon–Thu, 11.45am–11pm Fri, Sat,
1–10pm Sun. 🍴⑨ 🚻 ♿ 🎴 $$$$

Carnivores call this the best steakhouse in all five boroughs and
worth the taxi ride to indulge in
an enormous well-charred porter-
house steak or double lamb chops.
The main dining room resembles a
German beer-hall, with oak wain-
scoting and exposed wood beams,
and the same kind of intimacy. The
waiters deal with their customers
with a brusque good humour –
rare for New York steakhouses.

The Rainbow Room

65th floor, GE Building, 30 Rockefeller
Plaza. **Map** 12 F5. [632-5000.
Open 5.30pm–1am Tue–Sat, 6–9pm
Sun. 🍴⑨ ♿ V 🚻 T 🎵 ★
🎴 AE, MC. $$$$

This is definitely a place for
special occasions, with splendid
American, French and continental
food, dancing to a live band and
a celestial view of New York. The
luxurious Art Deco setting
anticipates a comparable bill.

The River Café

1 Water St, Brooklyn. **Map** 12 F5.
[(718) 522-5200. **Open** noon–
11pm daily. 🍴⑨ ♿ T 🚻 🎵
★ 🎴 AE, DC, MC, V. $$$$

This delightful site on the East
River has spectacular skyline views
of Manhattan, and also features
creative New American cooking
with excellent seafood, as well as
prix fixe and six-course tasting
menus. Night time is the lovers'
favourite here, but views are great
at lunch and brunch and it's easier
to reserve a window table then.

Santa Fe

72 W 69th St. **Map** 11 C1.
[724-0822. **Open** 11am–midnight
Mon–Fri, 10am–midnight Sat, Sun.
♿ ✈ V 🎴 AE, DC, MC, V. $$

A good bet for Lincoln Center-
goers, this decorative south-
western restaurant with its own
fireplace has been dishing up good,
spicy New Mexican fare for years.

Savoy

70 Prince St. **Map** 4 D3. [219-
8570. **Open** noon–3pm daily,
6–10.30pm Mon–Thu, 6–11pm
Fri, Sat, 6–10pm Sun. ✈ V 🚻
🎴 AE, DC, MC, V. $$$

With its welcoming fireplace,
Savoy is a hit with SoHo's success-

ful artistic types who can afford
the prices. The menu sometimes
tends to be too creative, pairing
too many competing flavours. But
it is always intriguing, emphasiz-
ing fresh locally grown ingredients,
such as *penne* with rabbit,
chanterelles, corn and walnuts.

Sign of the Dove

1110 3rd Ave. **Map** 13 B2. [861-
8080. **Open** noon–2.30pm Tue–Fri,
11.30am–2.30pm Sat & Sun,
6–11pm Mon–Fri, 5.30–11.30pm
Sat, 6–10pm Sun. 🍴⑨ 🎵 🏧
🎴 AE, DC, MC, V. $$$$$

Couples gravitate to this romantic
hideaway of small rooms with well-
spaced tables, brick archways and
mirrors. On starlit summer nights,
dine in the conservatory with its
sliding roof. It is one of the city's
prime restaurants for its elegant
New American/French food, such
as fillet steak with *foie gras*.

Sparks Steakhouse

210 E 46th St. **Map** 13 B5.
[687-4855. **Open** noon–3pm
Mon–Fri, 5–11pm Mon–Thu,
5–11.30pm Fri, Sat. 🚻 T 🎴 AE,
DC, MC, V. $$$$

This machismo place, which may
remind you of *The Godfather*, is a
business lunch favourite. As such,
the decibel level rises quickly.
Steaks are the main menu item,
though there are good lobsters too.
The wine list is exceptional.
Service is typically brusque.

Sylvia's

328 Lenox Ave. **Map** 21 B1.
[996-0660. **Open** 7.30am–
10.30pm Mon–Sat, 1–7pm Sun.
Closed Christmas. 🚻 ♿ 🎵
🎴 AE. $ See p228.

For a unique American cuisine
experience, head for this soul food
heaven in Harlem (going by taxi is
recommended), Barbecue ribs,
fried chicken, black-eyed peas,
collard greens and ham are a
few things to try in this homey
outpost of South Carolina home
cooking, where the waiters may
call you "dear". The Sunday
gospel brunch is also terrific.

Tapika

950 8th Ave. **Map** 13 D5.
[397-3737. **Open** noon–2pm
daily, 5.30–11pm Mon–Fri, 5–
11.30pm Sat, Sun. 🍴⑨ ♿ ✈ V
🎴 AE, DC, MC, V. $$$

Tapika has more going for it than
just its Carenegie Hall location.
The colourful décor was designed
by David Rockwell (who also did
Nobu) and the southwestern

cuisine is brightly innovative. You might try coriander-crusted tuna or tequila-cured salmon, two of many delicious dishes. Brunch is great too.

TriBeCa Grill

375 Greenwich St. **Map** 4 D5.
(941-3900. **Open** 11.30am–3pm Mon–Fri, 5.30–10.45pm Sun– Thu, 5.30–11.15pm Fri, Sat, 11.30am– 3pm Sun. 🍴 🔽 ♿ 🎵 ⛳
🍽 AE, DC, MC, V. $$$$

You may see co-owner Robert De Niro here, as well as many other stars, especially at the large round bar that is the centrepiece of this brick-walled bistro. The inventive American food is surprisingly good, despite the frenetic nature of the place. Save room for one of the many delicious desserts.

The '21' Club

21 W 52nd St. **Map** 12 F4. **(** 582-7200. **Open** noon–2.30pm, 5.30–10.30pm Mon–Fri; 5.30–11.15pm Sat. **Closed** Sat in May–Aug. 🍴 🔽
⛳ 🍽 🍽 AE, DC, MC, V.
$$$$

Although 21's heyday is long past, this former speak-easy, in three attached brownstones with a black iron fence and jokey statues outside, has developed a younger showbiz-and-political clientele for the overpriced Amercan food and somewhat formal town house ambience. New owners, the Orient-Express Hotels, Inc., suggest more changes in the near future.

Union Square Café

21 E 16th. **Map** 8 F5. **(** 243-4020.
Open noon–2.30pm Mon–Sat, 6–10.30pm Mon–Thu, 6–11.30pm Fri, Sat, 5.30–10pm Sun. 🔽 🚻 ⛳ ★
🍽 AE, DC, MC, V. $$$$

This is one of New York's premier restaurants, famous for its imaginative American/Italian/French dishes. Attractive but not ostentatious, the café is moderately priced, despite all the hype, and the staff are unusually friendly. Almost everything on the seasonal menu is delicious, from a starter of rosemary gnocchi with gorgonzola, walnuts, pancetta and leeks to a main course of cornmeal-and-sage-fried rabbit with creamy polenta. Needless to say, desserts are also consistently superb.

Verbena

54 Irving Place. **Map** 9 A5.
(260-5454. **Open** noon–2.30pm, 5–10.30pm daily. ⛳ 🔽 🔽 🚻
🍽 AE, DC, MC, V. $$

This new restaurant with a charming herb garden at the back has a youthful chef-owner, Diane Forley,

who uses the best natural ingredients in a creative (sometimes overly-so) New American menu. Memorable moments include butternut squash ravioli, oxtail terrine, and seared tuna with minted cucumber. Brunch is especially nice in the garden.

The Water Club

500 E 30th St. **Map** 9 C3.
(683-3333. **Open** noon–11.30pm daily. 🍴 ⛳ 🎵 🍽 AE, DC, MC, V. $$$$

Located in a glass-enclosed, skylit pier which connects two large barges, the Water Club offers sweeping East River views and some intriguing seafood dishes, such as spiced seared yellowfin tuna and sautéed red snapper with lobster dumplings.

The Water's Edge

44th Drive & East River, Long Island City. **(** (718) 482-0033. **Open** noon–3pm Mon–Fri, 6–11pm Mon–Sat. 🚻 ⛳ 🎵 🍽 ⛳ 🍽
🍽 AE, DC, JCB, MC V. $$$$

From this large dining room's windows, you'll have a wide-angle view of the Chrysler Building and other Manhattan landmarks across the river. New American food prepared with a certain amount of flair and live music add to the often magical experience here. There's a free ferry service from 34th Street to the restaurant dock.

Windows on the World

1 World Trade Center, 107th Fl, West St. **Map** 1 B2. **(** 938-1111. **Open** 5–10.30pm Mon–Thu, 5–11.30pm Fri, Sat, noon–2pm, 11am–3pm, 5–10pm Sun. 🍴 🚻 ⛳ 🍽 🍽
★ 🍽 AE, DC, MC, V. $$$$

Located 107 storeys above the harbour in the World Trade Center, with stunning views, this is an ideal place for seeing events in the harbour, such as the Fourth of July celebrations. Recent elaborate renovations have made the place even more attractive. The food is expensive, but a prix fixe menu helps considerably. It is a membership club at breakfast and lunch, with an extra charge for non-members.

Zoë

90 Prince St. **Map** 4 E3. **(** 966-6722.
Open noon–3pm, 6–10.30pm daily.
🔽 🚻 ⛳ 🍽 🍽 AE, DC, MC, V.
$$$$

Inside a 19th-century landmark building, Zoë has loft-like high

ceilings, high columns and an open kitchen. The SoHo artists and young professional clientele appreciate its New American cuisine, extensive microbrewery beer and American wine lists. Grilled meats and fish are specialities, such as grilled loin of lamb with potato-horseradish gratin and herb-roasted salmon. Brunch is a great time to eat here.

FRENCH

Fine dining in New York usually means French. The fashionable, long-established French restaurants tend to be expensive, serving haute cuisine in a setting profuse with fresh floral arrangements. Most are located on the Upper East Side. In many of them the chef-proprietor is French with long restaurant experience. Some places in the Theater District are less fancily decorated and less pricey, though still traditional in menu. Many newer places feature nouvelle cuisine and can also be very costly. Prix fixe lunch, dinner and pre-theatre menus lower the prices.

Bistros have become newly popular, as a means of serving simple French fare at lower prices in informal settings with less fussiness. All three types, haute, nouvelle and bistro, are at their very best in New York.

Alison on Dominick Street

38 Dominick St. **Map** 4 D4. **(** 727-1188. **Open** 5.30–10.30pm Mon–Thu, 5.30–11pm Fri, Sat, 5.30–9.30pm Sun. 🍽 AE, DC, MC, V. $$$$

You'll find a creative rendering of French/Mediterranean/New American cuisines in this rather off-the-track, romantic place. The setting is sleek and stylish. The bar at the front is a scene in itself, and the dining room is dark, cosy and conducive to intimate dining.

Le Bernardin

155 W 51st St. **Map** 10 E4.
(489-1515. **Open** noon–2.30pm Mon–Fri, 6–10.30pm Mon–Thu, 5.30–11pm Fri, Sat. **Closed** some hols. 🍴 ⛳ 🍽 🍽 AE, DC, MC, V, JCB. $$$$

To New York food-lovers, seafood and Le Bernardin are synonymous. This is a large and beautiful, if somewhat austere, room with teak ceiling, pale blue walls and tapestry-covered chairs. The fish is served undercooked to let the freshness speak for itself, and is minimally sauced. While very expensive, for a seafood fancier it is worth every penny. You might consider the prix fixe lunch.

Café des Artistes

1 W 67th St. **Map** 12 D2. **[** 877-3500. **Open** noon–3pm, 5.30pm–midnight Mon–Sat, 10am–3pm, 5–11pm Sun. **Closed** Christmas Day. **[†][T]** after 5pm. ★ **[** AE, DC, MC, V, JCB. **$$$$**

This boisterous, jolly café is on everyone's list of favourites. The 1934 murals of frolicking nymphs, by Howard Chandler Christy, set the light-hearted tone, and the excellent French food extends it. Desserts are a speciality here, especially the Hungarian *tortes* (small cakes), and lavish chocolate creations that only the very strong-willed can resist. The theatre and media personalities who drop by add to the *joie de vivre*.

La Caravelle

33 W 55th St. **Map** 12 F4. **[** 586-4252. **Open** 12.30–2.30pm Mon–Fri, 5.30–10.30pm Mon–Sat. **[†][T][** AE, DC, JCB, MC, V. **$$$$**

For over 30 years this bastion of haute cuisine has been serving classic French food in a comfortable, softly-lit room to an upmarket, regular clientele. With a new chef, there have been some new flourishes in the kitchen, but the fresh *foie gras*, Dover sole and other seafood dishes are old favourites that are consistently good. Lunch, dinner, and pre-theatre prix fixe menus are also available.

Les Célébrités

Essex House Hotel, 160 Central Park South. **Map** 12 E3. **[** 484-5113. **Open** 6–10pm Tue–Sat. **[†][][** **[T]** ★ **[** AE, DC, MC, V. **$$$$$**

Within a short space of time, this luxurious dining room, off the lobby of the Essex House Hotel, has become one of New York's top French restaurants. The setting is sumptuous in a theatrical way, with huge gilded columns, thick carpeting, paintings by showbiz people – and a mere 14 tables. The food is remarkably good with many elegant touches, such as veal tenderloin filled with *foie gras*, truffles and wild mushrooms, or rabbit loin and leg stuffed with aubergine caviar and black olives.

Chanterelle

2 Harrison St. **Map** 4 D5. **[** 966-6960. **Open** noon–2.30pm, 6–10.30pm Tue–Sat. **Closed** some hols. **[†][][T][** AE, DC, MC, V. **$$$$**

This TriBeCa establishment seats 60 people in a handsome setting,

with high ceilings, wood walls, columns, and stunning flower arrangements. The creative French menu changes daily, but you might encounter such dishes as striped bass with sage and red butter or salmon sauté with fresh rhubarb. Desserts are wonderful, and there is a cheese tray, a rarity in New York. At lunch there is an à la carte and prix fixe menu; at dinner only prix fixe and tasting menus.

Le Cirque

455 Madison Ave. **Map** 13 A2. **[** 794-9292. **Open** noon–2.30pm, 5.45–10.15pm Mon–Sat. **[†][][T][** AE, DC, MC, V. **$$$$$**

Long considered one of New York's finest restaurants, Le Cirque should blossom even more when it re-opens in new, spacious quarters at the New York Palace Hotel early in 1997. To be expected are Le Cirque's usual floral extravaganzas, Limoges china, exquisitely prepared French food and a prix fixe lunch menu offering good value. Past performance augurs well for the move of this illustrious restaurant, as ownership and management are expected to remain intact.

La Côte Basque

5 E 55th St. **Map** 12 F4. **[** 688-6525. **Open** noon–2pm Mon–Sat, 6–10.30pm Mon–Fri, 5.30–11pm Sat. **Closed** some hols. **[†][][T][** AE, DC, JCB, MC, V. **$$$$$**

In a new location just a block from the old, this outpost of traditional French cuisine continues to serve its classic *cassoulets*, with more modern dishes such as roast duckling in a honey/Grand Marnier/black cherry sauce. The setting is as comfortable as ever. Even the mural of the Basque Coast and the old wooden beams have been transported to the new site. The upmarket, knowledgeable clientele appreciate one of the city's most extensive wine lists.

C.T./Claude Troisgros

111 E 22nd St. **Map** 9 A4. **[** 995-8500. **Open** noon–2.30pm, 5.30–11.30pm daily. **[†][][** **[V][** **[** AE, DC, MC, V. **$$$$**

If you are the offspring of the famous French cooking family, it's no surprise that you know something about food. Here in a Gramercy Park locale, Claude Troisgros' lively restaurant offers a stimulating menu of French dishes, some with a Caribbean twist, such as tuna *carpaccio* with fresh heart of palm and roasted duck breast with a passion fruit

purée. Prix fixe lunch and pre-theatre menus help to ease the severe economic pain.

Daniel

Surrey Suite Hotel, 20 E 76th St. **Map** 16 F5. **[** 288-0033. **Open** noon–2pm, 5.45–11pm Mon–Sat. **[†][** **[][V][][T]** ★ **[** AE, DC, MC, V. **$$$$$**

Chef-owner Daniel Boulud, formerly of Le Cirque, has created a floral bower with fabulous displays of seasonal flowers as a backdrop for some of the very best modern French cooking in town. It would be hard to surpass the honey and cumin-glazed leg of venison with *foie gras* or a seasonal dish like shad roe sautéed with sun-dried tomatoes, toasted almonds and black olives. The entire menu, at lunch or dinner, is a catalogue of unusual and inspiring creations, beautifully executed. The lunch and dinner prix fixe menus, while not cheap, offer excellent value in this otherwise ultra-expensive restaurant. The wine list, as you would expect, is exemplary.

La Grenouille

3 E 52nd St. **Map** 12 F4. **[** 752-1495. **Open** noon–3pm, 5.45–11pm Tue–Sat, noon–2pm, 5.45–10pm Sun. **[†][][V][][T][** AE, DC, MC, V. **$$$$$**

La Grenouille has everything one expects of a superior French restaurant: dazzling floral displays, unobtrusive service, expertly prepared food, and an extensive wine list. Lunch is the time to be here, both for the well-priced prix fixe menu and to people-watch the fashion industry clientele.

Jo Jo

160 E 64th St. **Map** 13 A2. **[** 223-5656. **Open** noon–2.30pm, 6–11.30pm Mon–Fri, 6–11.30pm Sat. **[][** AE, MC, V. **$$$$**

Jo Jo is the creation of chef Jean-Georges Vongerichten, who also owns Vong. The setting is a Paris-style town house. The quieter upstairs is best for a tête-à-tête meal, but the downstairs dining room with mirrored walls is more glamorous and livelier. The prices aren't too hefty for some very good, inventive bistro food. There's also a prix fixe lunch menu.

Lespinasse

St Regis Hotel, 2 E 55th St.. **Map** 12 F4. **[** 339-6719. **Open** 7–10.30am Mon–Fri, 7–11.30am Sat & Sun, noon–2pm, 6–10pm daily. **[][** **[V][][** ★ **[** AE, DC, MC, V. **$$$$$**

One of New York's most expensive restaurants, Lespinasse is also one of the very best. The dining room is sedate to the point of dullness, relieved by a few dignified floral displays. But it's the food here that matters, elegant French with an Asian accent. Words can't convey the finesse of dishes such as quail salad with endive in an almond-honey vinaigrette, herbed risotto with mushroom *fricasée*, and seared loin and *confit* of rabbit in rosemary-mustard sauce. Desserts are also spectacular. There is an interesting, if pricey, four-course vegetarian tasting menu.

Lutèce

249 E 50th St. **Map** 13 B4.
(752-2225. **Open** noon–2pm Tue–Fri, 6–10pm Mon–Sat. **Closed** Aug, some hols. **⊙** **&** **□** **▤** AE, DC, JCB, MC. **$$$$$**

For decades, this was New York's authoritative French restaurant. But with new ownership and chef and the advent of many other excellent restaurants, Lutèce has lost some of its lustre. Its country look, however, is still appealing and it remains an attractive place to dine – try the grilled squab with asparagus and morels or guinea hen baked in cabbage leaves. There's a prix fixe menu that makes an occasional splurge more possible.

La Métairie

189 W 10th St. **Map** 3 C2.
(989-0343. **Open** noon–midnight daily. **&** **▼** **▤** AE, DC, MC, V. **$$$$**

This tiny, crowded bistro, with room for a mere 20 customers, not only has plenty of charm, but good robust, country French food, and a setting which is marvellous for a romantic dinner for two.

Montrachet

239 W Broadway. **Map** 4 E5. **(** 219-2777. **Open** noon–2pm Fri, 6–10pm Mon–Thu, 6–11pm Fri, Sat. **⊙** **▥** **&** **□** **★** **▤** AE. **$$$$**

In this popular TriBeCa restaurant, the three large, high-ceilinged loftlike dining rooms are spacious but unpretentious. The menu offers a panoply of inventive contemporary French dishes – and desserts must be sampled. The extensive wine list is well-priced as is the food, especially the lunch specials.

Le Périgord

405 E 52nd St. **Map** 13 C4.
(755-6244. **Open** noon–3pm Mon–Sat, 5.30–11.30pm daily. **Closed** some hols. **⊙** **□** **▥** **▤** AE, DC, MC, V. **$$$$$**

This established restaurant is a favourite of UN people who appreciate impeccably prepared dishes, with service to match, in a setting of quiet elegance. Fresh flowers, soft lighting and a low noise level all add up to a superlative dining experience.

Provence

38 MacDougal St. **Map** 4 D3.
(475-7500. **Open** noon–3pm, 6–11.30pm daily. **Closed** some hols. **⚘** **⏧** **&** **▤** AE, MC, V. **$$$**

This is a well-priced Greenwich Village bistro, whose country French décor, dried flowers and garden for warm-weather dining, all suggest Provence. A menu of café fare includes braised monkfish, Provençal fish soup and pan-roasted lamb with ratatouille and other southern French favourites.

Le Régence

Hotel Plaza Athénée, 37 E 64th St. **Map** 13 A2. **(** 606-4647. **Open** 7–10am, noon–2.30pm, 6–9.30pm daily. **⊙** **&** **□** **▤** AE, DC, MC, V. **$$$$$**

Crystal chandeliers and a cloud-painted ceiling add to the classical splendour of this dining experience. Dishes are prepared with great inventiveness, making this a most memorable French restaurant. It is expensive, but there's a prix fixe dinner menu.

The Terrace

400 W 119th St. **Map** 20 F3.
(666-9490. **Open** noon–2.30pm Mon–Fri, 6–10pm Tue–Sat. **⊙** **♫** **⏧** **□** **▤** AE, DC, MC, V. **$$$$$**

Although somewhat overpriced, everything is redeemed by the breathtaking view of the city. Service can be erratic, but the setting invites lovers with its candlelit tables and compelling French menu. Take a taxi there and back, as the neighbourhood is dubious.

ITALIAN

Italian restaurants vie with Chinese for being the most popular with New Yorkers and the most prolific. Little Italy and Greenwich Village have long been strongholds of southern Italian cooking, but northern Italian cuisine has become increasingly popular in the 1990s, and restaurants featuring it have blossomed all over the city. The southern cuisine consists of hearty, more peasant-style food, while northern cuisine is more sophisticated. Another difference is price: southern Italian restaurants range from cheap to moderate;

northern ones are more expensive. In southern Italian restaurants you may find formica-topped tables and a cheerful, noisy, informal atmosphere. The food usually features soups, many prawn and veal *entrées*, vegetable dishes such as *aubergine parmigiana* (aubergine, cheese and tomato sauce), plenty of rich tomato-based sauces and deep-fried mozzarella.

Northern Italian restaurants have a tendency to be more formal, elegant and pricey. They feature a variety of pastas in rich cream and cheese sauces, polenta, gnocchi, risotto, game birds, venison, truffles, many kinds of wild mushrooms, diverse herbs and breads such as *foccacia* and *bruschetta*.

Barbetta

321 W 46th St. **Map** 12 D5. **(** 246-9171. **Open** noon–2pm, 5pm–midnight Mon–Sat. **⊙** **&** **□** **▥** **▤** AE, DC, MC, V. **$$$$**

In warm weather, the beautiful garden of this 19th-century town house is so tranquil it's hard to believe that Broadway is just a stone's throw away (literally). The excellent Piedmontese Italian food served in this elegant restaurant is pricey, but a prix fixe pre-theatre menu offers good value. There is an extensive wine list.

Bice

7 E 54th St. **Map** 12 F4. **(** 688-1999. **Open** noon–11pm, daily. **⏧** **&** **▤** AE, DC, MC, V. **$$$$**

A magnet for the rich, famous and expense account types, this Art Deco offspring of Milan's Bice is packed steadily. It is no wonder: the northern Italian food is light with freshly made pastas, such as lobster ravioli or pasta with quail and *arugula* (rocket). The bill is as heady as the ambience and the staff's snobbish attitudes.

Carmine's

2450 Broadway. **Map** 15 C2.
(362-2200. **Open** 5–11pm Mon–Thu, 5pm–midnight Fri & Sat, 2–10pm Sun. **Closed** Thanksgiving, 25 Dec. **⚘** **&** **▤** AE. **$$$**

Carmine's is the sort of southern Italian restaurant you would expect to find in Little Italy, but with Upper West Side casualness. This rollicking, cavernous Sicilian restaurant is best enjoyed in a group; single portions could feed armies. It is popular with families who like plates piled high with food for relatively little money – and those who don't mind an uneven culinary performance and the possibility of waiting in long queues. Another branch is located at 200 W 44th St (221-3800).

For key to symbols see p285

Cent' Anni

50 Carmine St. **Map** 4 D3. █ 989-9494. **Open** noon–2.30pm, 5.30–11pm Mon–Thu, noon–2.30pm, 5.30–11.30pm Fri, 5.30–11.30pm Sat, 5–10.30pm Sun. **Closed** 25 Dec, 1 Jan, 10 days in July. ▼ ⬥ ▣
⬥ AE. $$$$$$

This West Village favourite earns good reviews for its robust, Florentine-style food and unusual Tuscan wines at pretty reasonable prices. Service can be erratic and crowds ensure high noise levels. For a classic Village experience, however, it's fine. You might try the *grigliata mista* (mixed grill plate of rabbit, lamb, sausage and quail).

Coco Pazzo

23 E 74th St. **Map** 16 F5. █ 794-0205. **Open** noon–3pm, 6–11.30pm daily. **Closed** one wk Aug. ▼ ⬥ ▣
⬥ AE, MC, V. $$$$$$

This trendy, softly-lit, contemporary-looking trattori is a favourite with beautiful people, and is part of the Le Madri stable of stylish, upmarket Italian restaurants. The tables are close together, the noise level can be distracting and the service can be slow, but these points should not deter the dedicated food-lover from the remarkable risotto with seafood, and the assortment of delicious, mostly northern specialities.

Da Umberto

107 W 17th St. **Map** 8 E5. █ 989-0303. **Open** noon–3pm Mon–Fri, 5.30–11pm Mon–Sat. **Closed** 25 Dec, 1 Jan. ▣ AE.
$$$$

In a tawny, softly-lit front dining room and an airier skylit one in the back, which is probably the brighter lunch choice, hearty Tuscan fare, strong on game and roasts, is served. You can watch through glass windows as large portions of baked pheasant with herbs, veal chops with cognac and pork studded with garlic are dished up in the kitchen. It's pretty good value for money.

Felidia

243 E 58th St. **Map** 13 B3. █ 758-1479. **Open** noon–2.30pm, 5–11pm Mon–Fri, 5pm–midnight Sat. ▼ ▣ ▣ ▣ AE, DC, MC, V.
$$$$

Dinner in this much-acclaimed restaurant in an East Side brownstone is comfortably rustic, with rows of brightly polished copper pots, partial brick walls and open wine racks. The Italian regional food derives mostly from

Trieste, with dishes such as *gnocchi al ragu d'agrello* (potato dumplings with lamb ragu and artichokes) and *krafi all' Istriana* (fresh pasta "pillows" stuffed with three cheeses, raisins, rum and citrus rind).

Le Madri

168 W 18th St. **Map** 8 E5. █ 727-8022. **Open** noon–3pm daily, 6pm–12.30pm Mon–Sat, 5–10.30pm Sun. **Closed** one wk Sep. ▼ ▣ ▣
★ ▣ AE, MC, V. $$$$$$

Named after the female cooks, "the mothers", who turn out some of the most exquisite northern Italian food in the city, Le Madri continues to shine as one of New York's most fashionable restaurants. The dining room is low-key, but enlivened by lavish floral arrangements and food displays. Risotto, *osso buco* (veal shank stew), gourmet pizzas and various pastas are among the specialities. There are good vegetarian dishes as well.

Il Mulino

86 W 3rd St. **Map** 4 D3. █ 673-3783. **Open** noon–2.30pm Mon–Fri, 5–11.30pm Mon–Sat. **Closed** July, some hols. ▼ ▣ ▣ ▣ AE. $$$$$$

Almost too dark at dinner, Il Mulino's exposed brick walls, bent-wood chairs and cramped quarters seem more agreeable at lunch when there are fewer customers. Aficionados love the *lagniappe* (small appetizer) of delicious fried courgettes, served the minute you sit down. Less agreeable is the long wait at the bar before you are seated, even with a reservation. Though expensive, this is the best Italian in Greenwich Village.

Il Nido

251 E 53rd St. **Map** 13 B4. █ 753-8450. **Open** noon–3pm, 5.30–11pm Mon–Sat. **Closed** 4 Jul, Thanksgiving, Christmas. ▼ ▣ ▣
▣ AE, DC, MC, V. $$$

One of the earliest northern Italian restaurants to open in New York, Il Nido has been overshadowed recently by newer stars. But its charming Tuscan farmhouse interior prepares you for many delicious dishes, like the risotto Nido and grilled *scampi* with anchovy caper sauce. A place for upmarket and business clientele, dining here is a fairly dressy affair.

Orso

322 W 46th St. **Map** 12 D5. █ 489-7212. **Open** noon–midnight Sun–Tue, Thu, Fri, 11.30am–midnight Wed, Sat. **Closed** 25 Dec. ▼
▣ MC, V. $$$

There are many Theater District Italian restaurants, but only one Orso, a favourite of journalists, theatre people and their agents. Its Broadway convenience, cheerful décor, with open kitchen and bright skylight, large pizzas and other Italian standbys contribute to its bustling popularity. There is a respectable Italian wine list. The limited menu has enough choices at medium prices, especially pastas, to keep you satisfied.

Osteria del Circo

120 W 55th St. **Map** 11 B4. █ 265-3636. **Open** 11.30am–2.45pm Mon–Sat, 5.30–11pm daily. ⬥ ▣
▼ ▣ ★ ▣ AE, MC, V. $$$$$$

It is no wonder that Circo is so dazzling. It has the imprimatur of Sirio Maccioni, owner of the fabulous Le Cirque, whose sons run this newcomer with similar panache. The circus motif with bright banners overhead can be seen throughout the stylish restaurant; even the tables are set as though inside a big, open circus tent. One can watch the chefs at work in the open kitchen. The food is refined northern Italian. Flash-seared beef carpaccio in an aromatic herb crust, gnocchi with prawns and black truffle ragu, and *calamaretti ripieni* (squid filled with prawns and vegetables) are among many notable dishes. This is not a place to worry about the price; just sit back, enjoy the high-powered celebrity scene, and savour the wonderful food.

Palio

151 W 51st St. **Map** 12 E4. █ 245-4850. **Open** noon–2.30pm Mon–Fri, 5.30–11pm Mon–Sat. **Closed** some hols. ▼ ⬥ ▣ ▣ ▣ AE, DC, MC, V. $$$$$$

Palio is a favourite of upmarket Broadwayites and office workers in the Equitable Assurance Tower, in which the restaurant is located. The restaurant has a popular street-level bar with a vivid, 124-ft (38-m) long, wrap-around mural of Siena's famous Palio (horse race festival) by Sandro Chia. Upstairs, the dining room is pretty, though northern Italian food can be uneven – superb one evening, routine the next. Dishes to savour include fillet steak in a hazelnut crust, loin of venison in a juniper berry sauce and the risottos. A pleasant quick lunch at the bar and a pre-theatre menu are also available.

Parioli Romanissimo

24 E 81st St. **Map** 16 F4. █ 288-2391. **Open** 6–11pm Mon–Sat. ⬥ ▣ ▣ ▣ AE, DC, MC, V. $$$$$$$

This handsome, low key restaurant housed in an Upper East Side town house has the aura of a private club, complete with fireplace. In this setting the classic Italian cuisine and service are virtually flawless, as indeed they should be at the rarefied prices charged. This is possibly the priciest Italian restaurant in town.

Remi

145 W 53rd St. **Map** 12 E4. ☎ *581-4242.* ***Open*** *11.45am–2.30pm Mon–Fri, 5.30–11.30pm Mon–Sat, 5.30–10pm Sun.* ***Closed*** *Thanksgiving, 25 Dec.* ♿ 🪑 🍸 💳 *AE, DC, MC, V.* $$$$

For deal-makers at lunch and the pre- and post-theatre crowd at dinner, this lively, noisy restaurant is the place to be seen. Adam Tihany designed the spectacular décor (he also did the new Osteria del Circo). There is a mural of Venice, reddish Brazilian maple floors with stripes of birch, comfortable chairs and banquettes, and a glass wall facing a flower-bedecked atrium, where diners may eat in mild weather. The service is very attentive and the fine Venetian food is prepared with brio. The pasta dishes, such as the homemade ravioli Marco Polo, filled with fresh tuna and ginger in a light tomato sauce, are especially creative. Desserts are stunning, as is the lengthy Italian wine list, which includes more than four dozen types of grappa.

San Domenico

240 Central Park South. **Map** 12 E3. ☎ *265-5959.* ***Open*** *11.30am–2.30pm Mon–Fri, 5.30–11.30pm daily.* [V] ♿ [T] 🍸 ★ 💳 *AE, DC, MC, V.* $$$$$

Soft lighting, Florentine terracotta floors, well-spaced tables, supple leather chairs and impeccable service make this a luxurious and romantic setting for some of the best and most imaginative northern Italian food in town. Risotto with white truffles, snails in brown sauce and grilled eel in vine leaves with balsamic vinegar are a few of the many superlative dishes on the menu. A well-priced pre-theatre menu is available early evening.

Trattoria dell'Arte

900 7th Ave. **Map** 12 E3. ☎ *245-9800.* ***Open*** *noon–2.30pm daily, 5–11.30pm Mon–Sat, 5–10.30pm Sun.* ***Closed*** *Christmas Day.* [V] 🪑 💳 *AE, MC, V.* $$$$

The two main advantages here, according to the Carnegie Hall-going clientele, are the bright, clever Milton Glazer interior designs and what is possibly the biggest antipasto bar in the city. Share an amazingly well-priced platter of delicious antipasto items, enjoy the exuberant décor of "body parts" sculpture, people-watch the celebrities who gather here, and then head across the street for the music. The rest of the menu, even the pizza, is somewhat uninspired.

CHINESE

Chinese restaurants are as numerous as Italian ones in New York. They range from takeaway outlets and cheap eateries – found in almost every neighbourhood and extensively throughout Chinatown – to more formal, expensive restaurants, located mostly in Midtown or on the Upper East Side. For those visitors dining on a tight budget, a Chinese meal is probably the cheapest option.

Many Chinese restaurants in New York are of the chop-suey-chow-mein variety, Americanized for decades. The better Chinese restaurants are as good as any to be found outside Hong Kong and Taiwan. A large local Chinese population has created a much more demanding clientele. On the whole, by far the most authentic places are to be found in Chinatown while the uptown restaurants tend to be more chic, serving, in some instances, Westernized nouvelle Chinese fare.

Szechuan and Hunan cooking swept New York in the 1980s, creating a demand for the hot, sour and peppery cuisines of those regions of China. Of late, New Yorkers have become more interested in the delicate subtlety of Cantonese cooking. Most Chinese restaurants have large menus, enabling you to sample both spicy and mild dishes. Desserts at a Chinese restaurant tend to be limited, usually to ice-cream, tinned lychees or pineapple.

Dim sum, which are small steamed or fried dumplings and other nibbles, are mainly served in Chinatown on weekend mornings and early afternoons, and are treated as a Chinese brunch. Diners choose their dishes from trolleys wheeled from table to table, generally drinking hot tea as an accompaniment.

Bo Ky

80 Bayard St. **Map** 4 F5. ☎ *406-2292.* ***Open*** *8am–9.30pm daily.* ***Closed*** *two days Chinese New Year.* 🍴 🚸 ♿ $

This noisy and bustling, no-frills Chinatown restaurant has shared tables and waiters who speak limited English. But the many seafood noodle dishes and soups are filling, delicious and good value. The Vietnamese items on the menu are often the best.

Canton

45 Division St. **Map** 5 A5. ☎ *226-4441.* ***Open*** *noon–10pm Wed–Thu, noon–11pm Fri, Sat, noon–9.30pm Sun.* ***Closed*** *4 weeks mid-July–mid-August.* $$

The Canton offers better standards than those usually found in Chinatown restaurants, in décor, service and food. Prices are also higher, but its ardent fans think it's worth it, especially for the Cantonese seafood dishes. No credit cards are accepted, nor is there a licence for alcohol, but you may bring your own wine or beer.

Chin Chin

216 E 49th St. **Map** 13 B5. ☎ *888-4555.* ***Open*** *11.30am–midnight daily.* 🍴 [V] 🚸 🪑 🍸 💳 *AE, DC, MC, V.* $$$

An upmarket Chinese restaurant with western décor, Chin Chin has a wide and interesting range of dishes from all over China (many prepared with a Western accent). Try some of the offbeat items, such as vegetable duck pie with crepes or Chinese ratatouille casserole. As Chinese restaurants go, this is on the pricey side.

Golden Unicorn

18 E Broadway. **Map** 5 A5. ☎ *941-0911.* ***Open*** *8am–midnight daily.* 🍴 🚸 💳 *AE, MC, V.* $$$

This huge, attractive, mirrored, two-storey Hong Kong-style palace has some of the most delicious *dim sum* in town, as well as savoury Cantonese dishes. Noise, crowds and staff outfitted with walkie-talkies may be off-putting, but the large numbers of Chinese families attest to the restaurant's authenticity. A special winner on the menu is the shark-fin dumpling in fragrant broth.

Ollie's Noodle Shop & Grille

2315 Broadway. **Map** 15 C4. ☎ *362-3111.* ***Open*** *11.30am–midnight Sun–Thu, 11.30am–1am Fri, Sat.* ***Closed*** *Thanksgiving.* 🚸 💳 *AE, MC, V.* $$

In this plain luncheonette-type noodle restaurant the many different soups available, with wontons, vegetables, meats and/or seafood, are hearty, satisfying and particularly budget-friendly.

For key to symbols *see p285*

Oriental Garden

14 Elizabeth St. **Map** 4 F5.
(619-0085. **Open** 8.30am–2am
daily. **♿ 🈂 ☆** AE, MC, V. **$$**

Expect to share formica-topped
tables with strangers in this jam-
packed, noisy restaurant. Don't let
the dreary décor or occasional
surly waiter put you off, for the
seafood is among Chinatown's
best. *Dim sum* and other
Cantonese dishes are also good.

Shun Lee Palace

155 E 55th St. **Map** 13 A4.
(371-8844. **Open** noon–11pm
daily. **Closed** Thanksgiving. **♿ 🈂**
☆ AE, DC, MC, V. **$$$$$**

In the forefront of East Side
Chinese chic for more than 20
years, this popular place has a
devoted clientele for its spacious
elegance and slightly upmarket
Cantonese and Szechuan menu
(there's even a spa cuisine menu
for the diet-conscious). The wine
list is long for a Chinese restaurant
and prices are very fair for the
neighbourhood. The casserole
dishes are house specialities.

Shun Lee West

43 W 65th St. **Map** 11 D2.
(595-8895. **Open** noon–midnight
daily. **Closed** Thanksgiving. **🈂 ♿**
☆ AE, DC, MC, V. **$$$**

Handy for the Lincoln Center, this
West Side cousin of Shun Lee
Palace has just as devoted a
coterie, though both food and
service can be slightly erratic,
especially at peak times. When
"on", its Szechuan dishes have
real sizzle and snap. Regional
winners include softshell crab in
black bean sauce and dry,
shredded Szechuan beef.

Tang Pavilion

65 W 55th St. **Map** 11 B4.
(956-6888. **Open** 11.45am–
10.30pm daily. **🈂 ☆ 🈂**
☆ AE, DC, MC, V. **$$**

Finding such a low-key and
pleasantly upmarket Chinese
restaurant near Carnegie Hall is
good news. That the food is so
tasty and prices so fair makes the
Tang Pavilion even more of an
asset. You might try the Shanghai
specialities, a rarity in New York.

JAPANESE

After Chinese, Japanese restau-
rants are the most common Asian
restaurants in New York and serve
perhaps the best Japanese food
this side of Tokyo. Most are
located in the Midtown area and

serve traditional dishes, such as
sukiyaki (vegetables and meat
simmered in broth), *tempura* (vege-
tables or seafood deep-fried in
gossamer-light batter) and *teriyaki*
(meat or chicken marinaded seve-
ral times in soya sauce, sweet rice
wine and sugar, dried, then grilled).
  Many Japanese restaurants have
sushi bars in the front or back,
where you can sit and eat, choos-
ing from a tempting array of fresh,
uncooked seafood in a display
case in front of you. Sushi (cooked,
vinegared rice wrapped around
raw fish or barely-cooked prawns)
and sashimi (raw fish accom-
panied by a dip of soya, ginger
and *wasabi*, Japanese horseradish)
are extremely popular and are
always eaten with chopsticks.

Hatsuhana

17 E 48th St. **Map** 12 F5.
(355-3345. **Open** 11.45am–
2.45pm, 5.30–10pm Mon–Fri,
5–10pm Sat. **🈂 ☆** AE, DC,
MC, V. **$$$**.

Just why this Japanese sushi and
sashimi restaurant is so revered
and constantly so crowded may
not seem apparent at first glance.
But connoisseurs have long since
considered it to have the very
best, freshest and most varied
sushi in town. The best seats in
the house are at the sushi bar,
where you can watch the skilled
chefs carry out their work.

Honmura An

170 Mercer St. **Map** 4 E3.
(334-5253. **Open** noon–2.30pm
Wed–Sat, 6–10pm Tue–Thu, 6–
10.30pm Fri, Sat, 6–9.30pm Sun.
Closed 1st week Jan, 4th July
weekend, Labor Day weekend.
🈂 🈂 ☆ AE, DC, MC, V. **$$$**

The elegant and stylish Honmura
An raises noodle-making to an art
form and its SoHo setting adds to
its artistic appeal. The homemade
udon and soba noodle dishes are
particularly delicious.

Inagiku

Waldorf–Astoria Hotel, 301 Park Ave.
Map 13 A5. **(** 355-0440. **Open**
noon–2.30pm Mon–Fri, 5.30–
10pm daily. **Closed** some hols.
♿ ☆ AE, DC, JCB, MC, V.
$$$$

With its tasteful, formal Japanese
décor, kimono-clad waitresses,
and tatami-mat dining rooms,
Inagiku is a unique dining expe-
rience. Specialities are *tempura*,
teriyaki and the traditional *Kaiseki*,
a full course dinner comprising a
dozen or so dishes served in a
designated order. The large selec-
tion of ingredients is seasonal.

Iso

175 2nd Ave. **Map** 4 F1.
(777-0361. **Open** 5.30pm–
midnight Mon–Sat. **Closed** some
hols, one week summer. **🈂 ☆**
☆ AE, DC, MC, V. **$$$**

Iso combines walls hung with
modern art, the freshest sushi
imaginable and a casual East
Village ambience. Add moderate
prices and it's no wonder this has
become a neighbourhood favourite.

Nobu

105 Hudson St. **Map** 3 B1. **(** 219-
0500. **Open** noon–2.30pm, 5.30–
11pm Mon–Fri, 5.30pm–midnight
Sat, 5.30–11pm Sun. **🈂 ☆ 🈂 🈂**
★ ☆ AE, DC, MC, V. **$$$$**

Nobu has become a "hot ticket"
for its superb sushi and sashimi
and the iconoclastic whimsy of
its chef's creations (in which non-
Japanese ingredients are added to
classic dishes). A clever décor fits
the arty TriBeCa locale perfectly.
Prices are rather high, but offbeat
delights such as rock prawns
tempura with spicy red pepper
oil and Kumamoto oysters with
Maui onion salsa give a new
fillip to the Japanese menu.

Sushisay

38 E 51st St. **Map** 13 A4. **(** 755-
1780. **Open** noon–2.15pm,
5.30–10.15pm Mon–Fri, 5pm–9pm
Sat. **☆** AE, DC, MC, V. **$$$**

This understated and tranquil
Japanese dining room is just
below street level. Sushi and
sashimi are the best choices here,
especially at the always-crowded
sushi bar, where you can select
favourites from the display. Service
is cheerful and quick at the sushi
bar, but can be slow elsewhere.
Go for the sushi; dishes on the
regular menu are more humdrum.

SOUTHEAST ASIAN

The Thai mania that swept the US
a few years ago never took too
strong a hold in New York. Many
of the hole-in-the-wall Thai res-
taurants known for spicy food and
modest prices have given way to
more sophisticated restaurants that
combine Thai and European
cuisines, using Thai ingredients,
such as lemongrass, *galanga*
(similar to ginger root), kaffir lime
leaves, garlic, tamarind, fresh
coriander and hot chilli oil, and
western cooking techniques.
  There has been a recent upsurge
in New York of other Southeast
Asian restaurants, especially
Vietnamese, which often have
an overlay of the French in

presentation and décor. The "Euro-peanizing" of these cuisines has led to a toning down of the spiciness, though there is still enough sizzle for most Caucasian palates.

Bangkok House

1485 1st Ave. **Map** 17 C5. 249-5700. **Open** noon–3pm Mon–Fri, 5–11pm Mon–Thu & Sun, 5–11.30pm Fri, Sat. AE, MC, V.

You will find reasonably authentic, well-spiced Thai food in Bangkok House's romantic setting of spacious tables and comfortable chairs, enhanced by helpful staff. Prices range from inexpensive to high, depending on what you order.

Cendrillon

45 Mercer St. **Map** 4 E2. 343-9012. **Open** 11am–4pm, 6–11pm Tue–Sun. AE, DC, MC, V.

The setting is a spacious, restful one in bustling SoHo, the food is Malaysian and Filipino, artistically presented, and the prices are modest. Sweet potato noodle with spicy grilled squid is one of many pleasing dishes.

Le Colonial

149 E 57th St. **Map** 13 B3. 752-0808. **Open** noon–3pm, 5.30–10.30pm Mon–Fri, 5.30–midnight Sat, 5.30–10.30pm Sun. AE, DC, MC, V.

A celebrity favourite, Le Colonial uses pre-war Vietnam as a theme, but its Vietnamese food and well-dressed clientele are strictly 1990s. The food can be very spicy, but its always fresh, low in calories and quite delicious. Try the tasty crisp-seared whole red snapper or the Vietnamese ravioli and prawns in coconut curry sauce.

Lemongrass Grill

2534 Broadway. **Map** 15 C4. 666-0888. **Open** noon–11.30pm Sun–Thu, 11.30am–midnight Fri, Sat. MC, V.

Countering other restaurants' moves upmarket, this inexpensive Thai restaurant offers fiery delights that include delicious soups and noodle dishes, served in a tropical setting. There are other branches in Greenwich Village and Brooklyn.

Mekong

44 Prince St. **Map** 4 D3. 343-8169. **Open** 11am–11pm daily. AE, MC, V.

Softly lit but not fancy, this cheerful little Vietnamese restaurant does a good job of serving authentic dishes at reasonable prices for its SoHo location.

Monsoon

435 Amsterdam Ave. **Map** 15 C4. 580-8686. **Open** 11.30am–11.30pm daily. AE, MC, V.

With a successful blend of Thai and Vietnamese dishes, Monsoon is popular for its surprisingly low prices and satisfying amalgam of both cuisines.

Penang Malaysian Cuisine

109 Spring St. **Map** 3 C4. 274-8883. **Open** 11.30am–midnight Mon–Sat, 7–11pm Sun. AE, MC, V.

This has become a popular SoHo hangout for its unusual, slightly exotic Malaysian food and vibrant tropical setting. The pompano fish in black bean sauce is one of many delicious dishes to choose from. There is a slightly cheaper branch in Queens (321-2078).

Rain

100 W 82nd St. **Map** 15 B4. 501-0776. **Open** noon–3pm Mon–Fri, noon–4pm Sat & Sun, 6–11pm Mon–Thu, 6pm–midnight Fri, 5pm–midnight Sat. AE, MC, V.

Trendy, noisy and crowded, this new restaurant brings touches of Thailand, Vietnam and Malaysia to its menu. A haunt of celebrities, the restaurant boasts good food, such as crispy whole fish, and a huge beer list. Service can be a little slow at times.

Siam Inn

916 8th Ave. **Map** 12 D5. 489-5237. **Open** 11.45am–3pm, 5.30–10pm Mon–Fri, 5–10pm Sat, Sun. AE, DC, MC, V.

Décor is just a notch above the diner level in this tiny, crowded restaurant, but the authentic food compensates, and the price is right – low. Hot, fresh, spicy Thai dishes are served in generous portions by friendly staff. *Plalad prig* (deep-fried seabass in a chilli-garlic sauce) is one of many very good dishes. The prix fixe dinner is a good option and excellent value for money. There is another branch nearby called Siam Inn Too at 854 8th Avenue (757-4006).

Vong

200 E 54th St. **Map** 13 A4. 486-9592. **Open** noon–2.15pm daily, 6–10.45pm Mon–Fri, 6–11.15pm Sat, 6–9.45pm Sun. ★ AE, DC, MC, V.

Probably the hippest of the French-accented Thai restaurants, the copper-toned Vong looks as beautiful as its elegantly presented food tastes. Memorable dishes include sweetbreads roasted on a liquorice satay and sautéed *fois gras* with ginger and mango. Desserts are as mouth-watering as the rest of the menu. Prices are moderate for the quality of the food.

Zen Palate

663 9th Ave. **Map** 12 D3. 582-1669. **Open** 11.30am–2.30pm Mon–Fri, 5.30–11.30pm daily. AE, DC, MC, V.

Zen Palate is a stylish vegetarian restaurant located in the Theater District. Many original dishes with a Thai, Chinese and Japanese flair are served with considerable panache. There is another branch located at 34 E Union Square (614-9291). A takeaway service is available at both branches.

INDIAN AND AFGHAN

Indian restaurants in New York have only recently become more adventurous, but they still have a way to go to match the standard of Indian restaurants in London, for example. Even so, they offer some of the best dining values in the city, with many featuring a lunchtime buffet that is a real bargain. Some of the cheapest Indian restaurants can be found on E 6th Street between 1st and 2nd Avenue. Most Indian menus feature curries and other lamb, chicken, prawn and vegetable dishes. Due to New York's scarcity of pure vegetarian restaurants, Indian ones make a fine substitute. Some restaurants have tandoori ovens and specialize in chicken dishes and breads baked in the oven's dry heat. While most Indian restaurants have alcohol licences, the best drink with Indian food is beer. For non-drinkers, a yoghurt-based drink called lassi is a refreshing substitute, while mango lassi makes a sweet alternative to traditional Indian desserts, which are often too sweet for most western palates.

There are just a few Afghan restaurants in New York also reasonably priced and informal. Afghan food is similar to Indian, with some interesting variations, though less spicy and diverse.

Light Meals and Snacks

YOU CAN GET A SNACK almost anywhere and anytime in Manhattan. New Yorkers seem to eat endlessly – on street corners, in bars, luncheonettes, delis, before and after work and long into the night. Casual eating in New York might include soft pretzels or char-roasted chestnuts from a corner stand; a huge sandwich from a deli; a Greek *gyro* sandwich (roasted lamb in pitta bread) from street vendors; a pre-theatre snack at a café or coffee bar; or a post-party binge at an all-night diner or bistro. While street fare is generally cheap, the quality and culinary skills vary greatly.

DELIS

DELICATESSENS are a New York institution, a great source for a hefty lunchtime sandwich. Try the wonderful corned beef and pastrami sandwiches at the famous **Carnegie Delicatessen**, considered by many to be New York's best deli.

Some delis, such as **Katz's Deli**, cater for those who enjoy traditional kosher food. Most deli business is, however, takeaway and as such delis are bustling places serving huge sandwiches at relatively cheap prices. Counter staff are typically surly and impatient and rudeness has almost become a trademark of the **Stage Deli**, which is now more of a tourist stop than the showbiz favourite it used to be.

For New York ethnic Jewish flavour, try the **Second Avenue Delicatessen**, well-known for its home-made soups, pickles, corned beef sandwiches, chopped liver and other kosher goodies. **Zabar's** is a takeaway heaven for yuppies who put up with the crowds for superb smoked fish, pickles and salads.

Aficionados say the best pastrami sandwiches and other favourites are to be found at the **Pastrami King** in Queens.

CAFÉS, BISTROS AND BRASSERIES

CAFÉS, BISTROS and the larger brasseries have become "in" places in New York in recent years. In general, they serve lunch and dinner, but they also serve light snacks. The new **Café Centro**, above Grand Central Station, is particularly busy and noisy during lunchtime, and is a favourite with business types. The Provence/Mediterranean fare includes fish soups and some succulent desserts. **The Brasserie**, a longtime landmark, has reliable French food and is open 24 hours a day. A real sleeper in the Carnegie Hall area is **Table d'Hôte**. Small and romantic, it serves good French/American fare with an inventive flair. Downtown, **Odeon** is a TriBeCa favourite for its brasserie menu and late hours. **Raoul's** in SoHo is a French bistro with a relaxed ambience that keeps artists and other habitués coming back for reliable, informal food. **Elephant and Castle**, a minimally decorated café, is a Greenwich Village standby for soup-salad-omelette lunches and other light snacks. Its real forte is breakfast and brunch, served in ample portions at modest prices. The bar scene is lively too. Tiny **Chez Jacqueline** is also a favoured Village spot. Its French bistro fare and proximity to several off-Broadway theatres make it popular with the young, hip and international crowd for a moderately priced dinner or late supper.

In the Theater District, try the Cuban **Victor's Café 52**. Large, lively and Latin, it is known for authentic Cuban food served in giant portions at medium prices. **Chez Josephine** is an exuberant bistro-cabaret with live jazz piano playing. The scene is the main attraction here, although the French food is excellent.

La Boite en Bois, small but delightfully French, serves delicious French bistro food and is conveniently close to the Lincoln Center. In the same vicinity is **Vince and Eddie's**, a tiny gem known for reliable, often superb American food.

Sarabeth's, on Upper West Side, defies categorizing, but might best be dubbed a café. The best time to visit is for breakfast or weekend brunch, when families wolf down wonderful waffles, French toast, pancakes and omelettes. There are two other branches.

The Gramercy area's **Les Halles** is about as all-out French bistro as New York gets. At its late-night peak, the decibel level is high, but regulars think the *frites* and beef dishes are worth the noise and crowds. It's open all night.

PIZZERIAS

PIZZA IS AVAILABLE all over New York, from street stalls and fast-food places which sell it by the slice for a few dollars, to a traditional Neapolitan pizzeria.

Some pizzerias offer something more. **Arturo's Pizzeria** uses a coal-oven for crisp, thin-crusted bases with the added inducement of live jazz. **Mezzogiorno** has a Tuscan menu and wonderful pizzas with unusual toppings. The crowded **Mezzaluna** also specializes in brick-oven, thin crusted pizza, as does the popular **John's Pizzeria**, whose many fans (including Woody Allen) consider it to be Manhattan's best.

Brooklyn boasts two top pizzerias, **Patsy's Pizza** and Coney Island's **Totonno Pizzeria**, both well worth the trip for real pizza aficionados.

Generally, pizza parlours are good places to go for a cheap, simple meal, especially with children. Most pizza places won't take reservations, so the popular ones may have long queues at mealtimes.

HAMBURGER BARS

YOUR NOSE may lead you to some of the cheaper burger and hot dog bars on the street. However, there are many places in New York where you can buy a better quality burger, even though prices for a top grade all-beef burger can go up to $10.

Hamburger Harry's offers reasonably priced, large, juicy and mesquite-grilled burgers, with a choice of over a dozen toppings and a huge fresh salad. There are cheap burgers at **Papaya King**, but their speciality is all-beef hotdogs and fresh papaya juice.

Bright and basic, the five outlets of **Jackson Hole** offer fat, juicy, meaty burgers in 28 varieties popular with kids. Adults might prefer less glare and smarter décor, but they will like the low prices. It's also a good place to try the quintessential New York drink, the egg cream (*see p286*).

Beer Bar is a new gathering place where professional types like to hang out. Besides an unusual beer menu, the burgers are delicious.

New York's best burgers may well be found at the **Corner Bistro** in Greenwich Village. Not only are the burgers tasty and reasonably priced, but the beer selection is good too and the 4am closing makes this a great late night stop.

DINERS AND LUNCHEONETTES

Diners and luncheonettes, also called sandwich or coffee shops, can be found all over town. Food is usually indifferent but served in huge, cheap platefuls. Despite the name luncheonette, such places are usually open from breakfast until late evening, and you can call in at almost any hour for coffee and something basic and filling to eat.

A recent trend with diners has seen 1990s replicas of the old 1930s cheap-eats places. One such retro-diner is the chic Empire Diner (*see p136*). The **Broadway Diner** in Midtown is a faithful re-creation of a 1940s diner. It offers a good American breakfast, including thick-cut chips and home-made corned beef hash with poached eggs.

Jerry's attracts a SoHo art and celebrity crowd who love the inventive sandwiches,

salads, desserts and huge breakfasts. Also attracting a hip art crowd is **Florent**, a West Village diner with reliable French food served round-the-clock. The **Kiev** is very plain, but famous for its Jewish-Eastern European specialities, like borscht. **The Coffee Shop** in Union Square serves Brazilian-American fare and is open all night.

On the Upper East Side, Eli Zabar's **E.A.T.** sells top quality, but pricey Jewish favourites – like mushroom barley soup and *challah* bread, as well as some sinful desserts.

Devotees swear by **Viand**, a spic-and-span East Side luncheonette, with cheap, ample American breakfasts, good burgers, egg creams and the best turkey sandwiches in town. **Veselka** is not the usual New York sandwich shop – what makes it special is the Polish/Ukrainian food, all at rock-bottom prices.

TEAROOMS

About the only place you can be absolutely sure of getting a cup of real, brewed tea is at a formal, prix fixe afternoon tea in a lounge at one of New York's pricier hotels, from 3pm to 5pm.

Afternoon tea in the **Plaza Hotel**'s Palm Court has cream cakes and hot buttered scones galore. For an extra smart tea, on Chippendale furniture, visit the **Carlyle** hotel. The **Hotel Pierre** offers one of the better buys in hotel prix fixe teas. Tea at the **Waldorf–Astoria** comes with Devonshire cream, while the elegant tea at the **Stanhope** hotel is abundant enough to carry you through to a late dinner.

A proper afternoon tea (with 25 teas to choose from) can also be found at the **T Salon**, in the lower level of the Guggenheim Museum's SoHo branch. Uptown, **L'Après-Midi à Bendel's** features a full-fledged afternoon tea. Teatime, Japanese style, can be enjoyed at the **Tea Box** in the Takashimaya department store. A cheaper tea is served at **Book-Friends Café**, tucked behind a display in this Chelsea bookshop.

COFFEE AND CAKES

You can get a decent cup of coffee for as little as 75 cents with endless free refills, at most diners, luncheonettes and coffee shops. There is a new trend for coffee bars which serve a variety of gourmet and speciality coffees, such as cappuccino, expresso and café latte. Some ice cream parlours and patisseries also serve good coffee, along with decadently luscious pastries.

Some of the most charming coffee houses are in Little Italy, such as **Caffè Biondo**, which serves cappuccino and sinful sweets and **Caffè Vivaldi** with relatively cheap coffees, teas and desserts, served on marble tables. **Caffè Ferrara**, going strong since 1892, has moderately-priced Italian pastries, good coffee and outdoor seating. **Caffè Dante** is a favourite with students who like to sit outside in warm weather.

The European-style outdoor **Fledermaus Café**, in South Street Seaport, serves fine coffee and is a good place to watch the passing scene.

Like an old time Viennese café, **Kaffeehaus**, in Chelsea, offers a selection of excellent Viennese pastries and coffees *mit schlag* (with whipped cream) in a cosy turn-of-the-century setting. The modern Austrian dishes make this a worthwhile dinner stop as well. At **Caffè Bianco**, uptown, desserts are fabulous, the coffee is good, and prices are low. The much pricier **Les Délices Guy Pascal** has delicious French pastries. **Sant' Ambroeus** is a luxurious outpost of the Milanese *pasticceria,* with decadent desserts and an expresso bar. **Rumpelmayer's** is New York's quintessential old-fashioned ice cream parlour and is the best place to have an egg cream (*see p286*) or an ice cream fantasia. A close runner-up is **Serendipity 3**, famous for its Victoriana, elaborate ice cream creations, coffee and mid-afternoon snacks. **Barnes & Noble Café** is a happy refuge for coffee and a pastry while browsing at one of New York's largest bookstores.

DIRECTORY

LOWER EAST SIDE

Caffè Biondo
141 Mulberry St.
Map 4 F5.

Caffè Ferrara
195 Grand St.
Map 4 F4.

Fledermaus Café
1 Seaport Place.
Map 2 E2.

Katz's Deli
205 E Houston St.
Map 5 A3.

SOHO AND TRIBECA

Jerry's
101 Prince St.
Map 4 D3.

Mezzogiorno
195 Spring St.
Map 4 D4.

Odeon
145 W Broadway.
Map 1 B1.

Raoul's
180 Prince St.
Map 4 D3.

T Salon
Guggenhein SoHo,
142 Mercer St.
Map 4 E2.

GREENWICH VILLAGE

Arturo's Pizzeria
106 W Houston St.
Map 4 E3.

Caffè Dante
79 MacDougal St.
Map 4 D3.

Caffè Vivaldi
32 Jones St. **Map** 3 C2.

Chez Jacqueline
73 MacDougal St.
Map 4 D2.

Corner Bistro
331 W 4th St.
Map 3 C1.

Elephant and Castle
68 Greenwich Ave.
Map 3 C1.

Florent
69 Gansevoort St
Map 3 B1.

EAST VILLAGE

Kiev
117 2nd Ave.
Map 4 2F.

Second Avenue Delicatessan
156 2nd Ave.
Map 4 F1.

Veselka
144 2nd Ave.
Map 4 F1.

GRAMERCY AND THE FLATIRON

Book-Friends Café
16 W 18th St.
Map 8 F5.

The Coffee Shop
29 Union Sq.
Map 9 A5.

Les Halles
411 Park Ave.
Map 9 A3.

CHELSEA AND THE GARMENT DISTRICT

Kaffeehaus
131 8th Ave.
Map 8 D2.

THEATER DISTRICT

Broadway Diner
1726 Broadway.
Map 12 E4.

Carnegie Delicatessen
854 7th Ave.
Map 12 E4.

Chez Josephine
414 W 42nd St.
Map 7 B1.

Hamburger Harry's
145 W 45th St.
Map 12 E4.

Rumpelmayer's
St Moritz Hotel,
50 Central Park S.
Map 12 F3.

Stage Deli
834 7th Ave.
Map 12 E4.

Victor's Café 52
236 W 52nd St.
Map 11 B4.

EAST SIDE MIDTOWN

Beer Bar
MetLife Building,
200 Park Ave. **Map** 9 A2.

Café Centro
MetLife Building,
200 Park Ave. **Map** 9 A2.

UPPER MIDTOWN

Barnes & Noble Café
Citicorp Building,
160 E. 54th St. **Map** 13 A4.

The Brasserie
100 E 53rd St. **Map** 13 A4.

Plaza Hotel
Palm Court, 768 5th Ave.
Map 12 F3.

The Tea Box
Takashimaya, 693 5th Ave.
Map 12 F2.

Waldorf–Astoria
301 Park Ave.
Map 13 A5.

UPPER EAST SIDE

Caffè Bianco
1486 2nd Ave.
Map 17 B5.

Carlyle
35 E 76th St.
Map 17 A5.

Les Délices Guy Pascal
1231 Madison Ave.
Map 17 A3.

E.A.T.
1064 Madison Ave.
Map 17 A4.

Hotel Pierre
2 E 61st St.
Map 12 F3.

Jackson Hole
232 E 64th St.
Map 13 B2.

John's Pizzeria
408 E 64th St.
Map 13 C2.

Mezzaluna
1295 3rd Ave.
Map 17 B5.

Papaya King
983 3rd Ave.
Map 13 B3.

Sant' Ambroeus
1000 Madison Ave.
Map 17 A5.

Serendipity 3
225 E 60th St.
Map 13 B5.

Stanhope
995 5th Ave.
Map 17 A4.

Table d'Hôte
44 E 92nd St.
Map 16 F2.

Viand
673 Madison Ave.
Map 13 A2.

UPPER WEST SIDE

L'Après-Midi à Bendel's
Bendel's, 712 5th Ave.
Map 12 F3.

La Boite en Bois
75 W 68th St.
Map 11 C1.

Sarabeth's
423 Amsterdam Ave.
Map 15 C4.

Vince and Eddie's
70 W 68th St.
Map 11 C1.

Zabar's
2245 Broadway.
Map 15 C2.

BROOKLYN

Patsy's Pizza
19 Old Fulton St.
Map 2 F2.

Totonno Pizzeria
1524 Neptune Ave.
Map 7 C5.

QUEENS

Pastrami King
124 Queens Blvd,
Kew Gardens.

New York Bars

NEW YORK BARS play a huge role in the life and culture of the city. Many New Yorkers spend the evening in a succession of bars, because each usually offers something more than just alcohol. There may be additional inducements, such as excellent food, live music, dancing or a particularly large selection of beers. Brew pubs, which serve meals and brew beer on the premises, are a recent phenomemon. Bars suiting every taste and budget are to be found all over the city.

RULES AND CONVENTIONS

BARS GENERALLY stay open from around 11am to midnight. Some stay open to 2 or 4am, when they must close by law. Many bars have what used to be called a "happy hour" (a term now slightly discredited because of a campaign against alcohol). Call it by any name, but between 5pm and 7pm, many bars offer twofers (two drinks for the price of one) and a variety of free snacks.

The legal minimum drinking age is 21; if the bartender suspects you are younger, you'll be "carded", or asked to show some identification to prove your age. Children are not usually taken into bars.

It is common to "run a tab" and pay your bill just before you leave. Tipping the bartender is expected – 10% of the bill or about 50 cents for a single drink. Shots are not pre-measured, so if you want a bigger drink, it can help to "belly up" to the bar and tip the bartender accordingly for his or her generosity. If you sit at a table, you'll be served there and be charged more.

A round of drinks can be expensive. A good way to save money is by buying a quart (95 cl) or a half gallon (190 cl) pitcher of beer.

Avoid the "free drinks for ladies" bars, which are often just pick-up joints. Some of New York's pubs did not admit women until forced by law to do so, a few years ago. Even today, many women feel uncomfortable drinking alone in certain places. Safer bets for single women are hotel bars or singles bars, although it may still be difficult to avoid harassment.

WHAT TO DRINK

YOU CAN GET almost any alcoholic drink you fancy in New York bars; the most popular drink is ice-cold beer. Mainstream bars serve standard beers from big producers like Budweiser, Coors and Miller, and high-profile imports such as Bass ale, Becks and Heineken, and even draft Guinness. Some bars, especially the old pubs and certain chic new bars, have a much wider variety of beers, imported and small domestics. These include locally made products by Neptune, New York's only microbrewery, and the popular Brooklyn Lager. There is a vogue now, especially among the young, for microbrewery products. A microbrewery is a small producer of flavourful beers often based on traditional European (German/Belgian/English) styles.

Other popular drinks include cocktails; rum and coke; dry martinis; Scotch or bourbon, either "straight up" (without ice), or on the rocks (with ice); vodka-and-tonic and gin-and-tonic. Wine, especially white wine, is also widely available at bars, though the "wine bar" concept has never really caught on in New York.

FOOD

MOST BARS SERVE some sort of food throughout the day. It is usually convenience food like burgers, chips, salads, sandwiches and small snacks like delicious spicy chicken wings. Happy hour is an excellent time to fill up on free snacks and hot starters in the smarter New York bars. Most bar kitchens stop serving food just before midnight.

FASHIONABLE BARS

YOU'LL probably have to queue to watch the bored and beautiful at the **Bowery Bar**, one of the hippest (and most overrated) bars on the current scene. The bar's pretentiousness belies its humble beginnings as a gas station.

Much more fun is the funky late night scene at **Bar Six**, a West Village hangout for the cool and quirky, with microbrewery beers and food that has a Moroccan accent. Also downtown is **SoHo Kitchen and Bar**, a handsome loft-like space with tiered dining areas, a long brick bar, good pizzas, a lengthy wine lists with some 400 wines and a good range of beers. The **Odeon** is another good place to catch the lively SoHo–TriBeCa scene.

On the Upper East Side, the bar at **Mortimer's** is a place to observe what passes these days for high society without paying exorbitant prices for the restaurant's ordinary food.

There is a new vogue for cigar bars that encourage smokers. **The Cigar Room at Trumpets** has a 36 premium cigar menu and a large single malt Scotch list. Its attached *intime* dining room is also cigar-friendly. At **Bar and Books** you can inhale, sip and nibble snacks before a fireplace in a club-like library setting, with live jazz on weekends. In the same venue is the Beekman Bar and Book.

BARS WITH VIEWS

FINANCIAL TYPES gravitate towards the **Edward Moran Bar and Grill** in the World Financial Center for a beer and the views from the terrace of the harbour and Statue of Liberty. **City Lights** also offers a view of the statue, as well as 130 varieties of Scotch and some 75 gins. In warm weather **BP Café**, a friendly outdoor café, is the latest Midtown scene. The **Tavern on the Green** has magical views of Central Park. Inside, the glitz of mirrored walls and chandeliers may overwhelm you, but the garden is a pure delight.

HISTORIC AND LITERARY BARS

IF YOU SAMPLE only one New York bar, it should probably be **McSorley's Old Alehouse**, an old Irish saloon, often dubbed "McSurly's" because of the staff. It's been on the same site since 1854, making it one of New York's oldest bars. It offers a good choice of beers and a tasty ploughman's lunch.

The Ear Inn dates from 1812 when the first tavern opened on this SoHo site. Now the haunt of poets and writers, its cramped, dark interior and long wooden bar ooze authenticity.

Greenwich Village has some of the city's oldest bars, such as **Chumley's**, which retains its character as a Prohibition era speakeasy. It's particularly snug in winter, when an open fire burns in the hearth.

Dylan Thomas's old favourite, the **White Horse Tavern**, is an unpretentious 1880s landmark still going strong and crowded with literary and collegiate types. There's an outside café used in warm weather.

Peculier Pub is a beer-lover's paradise, with over 360 varieties of beer from all over the world. You must, however, be willing to tolerate the sometimes snappish and uninformed staff.

A good, though rather touristy, place for a drink in the financial district is the atmospheric **Fraunces Tavern**, first built in 1719 *(see p76)*. Another oldie, dating to 1864, is **Pete's Tavern**, a prime hangout in the Gramercy Park area that is busy until 2am. It is known for its Victoriana, its house brew called Pete's Ale, and the many beers on tap. In the same area, the **Old Town Bar** has been a typically Irish pub since 1892 and is now favoured largely by advertising types.

No longer the celebrity scene it once was, **Sardi's** is still a hangout for *New York Times* reporters and is worth a stop to inspect the "who's who" celebrity caricatures lining the walls and for the generous drinks served in the second floor bar.

After work, crowds head to **P. J. Clarke's**, a long time favourite New York saloon dating back to the 1890s, with Irish bartenders and an incredibly bustling *après*-office scene. **Elaine's**, also on the East Side, remains a haunt of New York and visiting literary types. Sit close to Elaine's table where the meeting-and-greeting action takes place. The food is nothing much.

Near Carnegie Hall is the unobtrusive **P. J. Carney's** which has been a watering hole for musicians and artists since 1927. It serves Irish ales and a good shepherds pie.

YOUNG HANGOUTS

BREW PUBS, where the house beer is brewed on the premises, are currently the rage with the 20s-to-30s crowd, as are bars with sizeable beer lists that feature a variety of microbrewery and imported beers. One of the first and still going strong is **Zip City Brewing Company**. You can watch the brewing process at the gleaming copper kettles in the centre of the room, while drinking the fresh suds. In the same neighbourhood is the **Heartland Brewery**, the busiest, and, some think, best of the new brewpubs, with five beers, including the India Pale Ale which is outstanding, and many seasonals, such as cranberry and pumpkin ales.

The **Westside Brewing Company** uptown is a favourite youth and neighbourhood hangout, popular for its house ales and fruit beers. Also popular is the **Yorkville Brewery & Tavern**, which has a sports bar feel in what used to be a German neighbourhood. The beer list is extensive and there is typical pub fare served at the bar.

Brews in the Garment District has a huge beer list, good grub and an upstairs club with live music, making it a pub-crawlers favourite.

For homesick Brits, the **Manchester** is a name to reckon with. In a cosy publike setting, you'll find Watneys or Newcastle Brown Ale on tap, just two of 18 draft beers and 40 bottled ones which are not widely available in New York.

In the East Village is bustling **d.b.a.**. Depending on whom you ask, the initials might stand for "don't bother to ask" or "draft beer available". There are 14 draft beers on tap, along with scores of microbrews and 50 single malt whiskeys to choose from.

A popular beer stop uptown for the college-age crowd is the loud and noisy **Brother Jimmy's BBQ**, where you can snack on old-fashioned southern barbeque ribs.

In South Street Seaport, the **North Star Pub** is housed in a building dating back to 1821. It has much to recommend it for those in search of a good selection of English and Irish beers on tap and some 70 single malt whiskies.

Park Slope Brewery Company, in two Brooklyn locations, is another brewpub favoured by the young for its 12 homebrews and seasonal beers, as well as its decent pub grub and lively ambience.

SINGLES BARS

THE CHANCE TO MEET new people is offered in singles bars, which are still extremely popular. These are located all over the city, with a large concentration in midtown on the East Side. Prices in such places can be inflated, with beer costing $3 and up.

The Art Deco styled **Beer Bar**, with its interesting beer list and beer-tasting menus, is currently new and "with it". There is a frenetic singles scene at **Live Bait**, which is good for model-gazing and for its passable southern food.

GAY AND LESBIAN BARS

GAY BARS CAN be be found in Greenwich Village, with many also in SoHo, the East Village, Chelsea and Murray Hill. Lesbian bars are mostly in Greenwich Village and the East Village. For current listings, check the *Native* newspaper and the *Village Voice* or ring the Gay and Lesbian Switchboard *(see p343)*.

HOTEL BARS

CENTRALLY LOCATED in mid town, the Algonquin Hotel *(see p143)* was a famous literary haunt in the 1920s and early 1930s. Its Lobby

ar and Blue Bar are both
ood places for a quiet pre-
inner or pre-theatre drink.
  The round bar in the hand-
ome lobby lounge of the
endy **Royalton Hotel** is a
erfect spot for a drink while
watching the theatrical crowds
rifting in and out. This is a
avourite meeting place for
onde-Nast staffers. Also in the
heater District, the **Whiskey
ar** in the Paramount Hotel
as floor-to-ceiling windows
nd is usually frequented by
ashion and theatre types.

In Lower Midtown is the **Sun
Garden**, a glassed-in tiered
space, particularly pleasant
on bright afternoons when the
sun streams through the glass.
  The **Bull and Bear** in the
Waldorf–Astoria, dating back
to the Prohibition era, exudes
comfort and a sense of history.
There are many exotic drinks
and Bull and Bear ale on tap.
  Uptown, the **Oak Room**
at the Plaza Hotel is a posh
place to impress people,
drink and converse in earnest
tones – but at a high price.

The **King Cole Room** at the
St Regis Hotel is named after
the mural behind the bar, by
Maxfield Parrish, which adds
colour to a stylish room.
  For nostalgic British visitors
and anglophile New Yorkers,
Journeys in the Essex House
Hotel has an English club
ambience, with hunting prints
and mahogany panelling.
  It's good value at the
Warwick Bar in the Warwick
Hotel, especially during
happy hour, when free,
delicious snacks are served.

DIRECTORY

LOWER MANHATTAN

Bowery Bar
40 E 4th St. **Map** 4 F2.

City Lights
1 World Trade Center,
107th fl, West St.
Map 1 B2.

**Edward Moran
Bar and Grill**
World Financial Center.
250 Vesey St. **Map** 1 B2.

Fraunces Tavern
54 Pearl St. **Map** 1 C4.

North Star Pub
93 South St, South St
Seaport. **Map** 2 D3.

SoHo AND TRiBeCa

The Ear Inn
326 Spring St. **Map** 3 C4.

Odeon
145 W Broadway.
Map 4 E4.

**SoHo Kitchen
and Bar**
103 Greene St. **Map** 4 E3.

GREENWICH VILLAGE

Bar Six
502 6th Ave. **Map** 4 D1.

Chumley's
86 Bedford St.
Map 3 C2.

Peculier Pub
145 Bleecker St.
Map 4 D3.

**White Horse
Tavern**
567 Hudson St.
Map 3 C1.

EAST VILLAGE

d.b.a.
41 1st Ave. **Map** 5 A1.

**McSorley's Old
Alehouse**
15 E 7th St. **Map** 4 F2.

GRAMERCY

**Heartland
Brewery**
35 Union Square W.
Map 9 A5.

Live Bait
14 E 23rd St. **Map** 8 F4.

Old Town Bar
45 E 18th St. **Map** 8 F5.

Pete's Tavern
129 E 18th St. **Map** 9 A5.

CHELSEA AND THE GARMENT DISTRICT

Brews
156 E 34th St. **Map** 9 A2.

**ZIP City Brewing
Company**
3 W 18th St. **Map** 8 F5.

THEATER DISTRICT

P. J. Carney's
906 7th Ave. **Map** 12 E3.

Royalton Hotel
44 W 44th St. Fifth Ave.
Map 12 F5

Sardi's
234 W 44th St.
Map 12 F5.

Warwick Bar
Warwick Hotel, 65 W
54th St. **Map** 12 F4.

Whiskey Bar
Paramount Hotel, 235 W
46th St. **Map** 12 E5.

LOWER MIDTOWN

Beer Bar
Metlife Bldg, 200 Park
Ave. **Map** 9 A2.

BP Café
Bryant Park, 25 W 40th St.
Map 7 B1.

**The Cigar Room at
Trumpets**
Grand Hyatt Hotel,
Grand Central Station,
E 42nd St.
Map 13 A5.

Sun Garden
Grand Hyatt Hotel, Grand
Central, 42nd St.
Map 9 A1.

UPPER MIDTOWN

Bar and Books
889 1st Ave. **Map** 13 C2.

Bull and Bear
Ground fl, Waldorf–Astoria
Hotel, Lexington Ave at E
49th St. **Map** 13 A5.

King Cole Room
St Regis Hotel,
2 E 55th St. **Map** 12 F5.

Manchester
920 2nd Ave. **Map** 13 B5.

Oak Room
Plaza Hotel, 768 5th Ave.
Map 12 F3.

P. J. Clarke's
915 3rd Ave.
Map 13 B4.

UPPER EAST SIDE

**Brother Jimmy's
BBQ**
1461 1st Ave.
Map 17 C3.

Elaine's
1703 2nd Ave.
Map 17 B4.

Mortimer's
1057 Lexington Ave.
Map 17 A5.

**Yorkville Brewery
and Tavern**
1359 1st Ave.
Map 13 C5.

UPPER WEST SIDE

Journeys
Essex House Hotel,
160 Central Park S.
Map 12 E3.

**Tavern on the
Green**
Central Park, W 67th St.
Map 12 D2.

**Westside Brewing
Company**
340 Amsterdam Ave.
Map 15 C2.

BROOKLYN

**Park Slope
Brewing Company**
356 6th Ave.
Map 4 D1.
One of several branches.

SHOPPING

ANY VISITOR to New York will inevitably include shopping in their plan of action. The city is the consumer capital of the world: a shopper's paradise which is a constant source of entertainment, with dazzling window displays and a staggering display of goods. Everything is available here, from high fashion to some rare

Tiffany's clock

children's books, state-of-the-art electronics and a mouthwatering array of exotic food. If you must have a personal hovercraft, read-in-the-dark spectacle attachments, a designer bed for your pet gerbil or a Wurlitzer jukebox, this is the city of your dreams. Whether you have $50,000 or $5, New York is the place to spend it.

BEST BUYS

NEW YORK is a bargain-hunter's dream, with huge reductions on anything from household goods to designer clothes. Some of the best shops are on Orchard Street and Grand Street on the Lower East Side, where shops sell designer goods at

The 1920s-style Henri Bendel store *(see p311)*

20–50% below the retail price. You can find just about every item of clothing imaginable here, in addition to tableware, shoes, home furnishings and electronics. Shops in this area are closed on Saturday – the Jewish Sabbath – but are usually open all day Sunday.

Another great area for fashion bargain-hunters is the trendy Garment District, roughly between Sixth and Eighth avenues from 30th to 40th Street. The hub of it – Seventh Avenue – was renamed as Fashion Avenue in the early 1970s. Here, many different designers and manufacturers have showrooms, some of which are open to the public. They also have sales of many of their samples, announced on notices posted around the

area. Often the best time to go and visit these stores is just before one of the major gift-giving holidays.

SALES

ONE WORD you are likely to see all over the city, no matter what time of year you visit, is "Sale". So before you pay full price for anything, check the sale goods first. The best sales are during New York's sale seasons, which run from mid-June until the end of July and from 26 December until February. For information, look out for notices in the local papers. A word of warning: along midtown Fifth Avenue there are signs announcing "Lost Our Lease" sales. But many of the shops have had these signs up for years and are best avoided.

HOW TO PAY

MOST SHOPS accept major credit cards, although there will often be a minimum purchase price. If you want to use your traveller's cheques, identification is needed. Personal cheques drawn in another currency will be refused. Some stores only take cash, especially during sales.

The Bulgari entrance at Hotel Pierre *(see p282)*

OPENING HOURS

MOST SHOPS in New York are normally open from 10am to 6pm, Monday to Saturday. Many department stores, though, are open all day Sunday and until 9pm at least two nights a week. The best time to avoid crowds is weekday mornings. The most crowded times are lunch hours (noon to 2.30pm), Saturday mornings, sales and holidays.

TAXES

THE NEW YORK city sales tax, 8.25%, is added to the price when you pay. But you may still be asked to pay duty on goods at customs if you exceed the allowance. However, if the goods are sent direct, you won't have to pay sales tax.

Cut-price designer dress at a New York sale

SHOPPING TOURS

I F YOU CAN'T face the thought of braving the shops by yourself, why not go on one of the many shopping tours available in New York? Apart from visiting the main department stores, options include a visit to private designer showrooms, auction houses and fashion shows. Some operators will customize tours to suit your requirements.

Convention Tours Unlimited
📞 545-1160.

Guide Service of New York
📞 408-3332.

Doorway to Design
📞 221-1111.

The Intrepid New Yorker
📞 534-5071.

A magnificent shop display offering household goods

experience of a lifetime.

Barney's New York is a favourite among the young professional New Yorkers. It specializes in excellent, but expensive, designer clothes. A branch for men is located in the glittering World Financial Center.

Bergdorf Goodman is luxurious, very elegant and understated. It carries top-quality contemporary fashions at high prices, specializing in European designers. The men's store is right across the street.

Almost every visitor to New York includes **Bloomingdale's** *(see p179)* on their sightseeing list. "Bloomies" is the Hollywood film star of the department stores, with many eyecatching displays and seductive goods. Its ambience is of a luxurious Middle Eastern bazaar, filled with wealthy, immaculately dressed New Yorkers seeking out the newest, trendiest fashions. Bloomingdale's also

Window displays at Bloomingdale's *(see p179)*

DEPARTMENT STORES

M OST OF New York's large department stores are in midtown Manhattan. Be sure to allow plenty of time to explore the ones you are interested in, as all these stores tend to be enormous, with an amazing range of goods. If at all possible, avoid going at weekends and around holiday perids – the crowds can be overwhelming. Prices are often high, but you can get bargains during the sales.

Stores such as Saks Fifth Avenue, Bloomingdale's and Macy's provide a diverse and extraordinary range of shopping services, including doing the shopping for you. But then you would miss out on what may be the shopping

has a high reputation for household goods and gourmet food – it has a shop devoted entirely to caviar. Extensive shopping services and amenities include a noted restaurant, Le Train Bleu *(see p306)*, and a theatre ticket discount agency.

Everything found in **Henri Bendel's**, from the Art Deco jewels to beautiful hand-made shoes, is displayed as though each is a priceless work of art. The store, which is laid out in a series of 1920s-style boutiques, is exclusive and sophisticated, and has a good selection of creative and innovative women's fashions.

Lord & Taylor is renowned for its classic and much more conservative fashions for men and women. The store places an emphasis on US designers.

You need a strong pair of legs, comfy shoes and lots of spare time to wander around.

Macy's, the self-proclaimed largest store in the world *(see p132–3)*, manages to sprawl over an entire city block. It has ten floors, and sells everything imaginable from tiny tin openers to massive TVs.

Saks Fifth Avenue is synonymous with style and elegance. It has long been considered one of the city's top-quality department stores, with service to match. It sells stunning designer clothes for men, women and children.

ADDRESSES

Barney's New York
660 Madison Ave. **Map** 13 A3.
📞 826-8900.
Upper Level, 2 World Financial Center.
Map 1 A2.
📞 945-1600.

Bergdorf Goodman
754 5th Ave. **Map** 12 F3.
📞 753-7300.

Bloomingdale's
1000 3rd Ave. **Map** 13 B3.
📞 355-5900.

Henri Bendel
712 5th Ave. **Map** 12 F4.
📞 247-1100.

Lord & Taylor
424 5th Ave. **Map** 8 F1.
📞 391-3344.

Macy's
151 W 34th St. **Map** 8 E2.
📞 695-4400.

Saks Fifth Avenue
611 5th Ave. **Map** 12 F4.
📞 753-4000.

New York's Best: Shopping

Designer shoes from Madison Avenue

I N A CITY where you can literally shop 24 hours a day the best plan is to shop the way New Yorkers do, by neighbourhood – each has its own character and specialities. Here are highlights of the best shopping districts – where they are and what you will find there – compiled from the detailed listings on pages 314–27. If time is tight, you could simply head for one of the huge department stores *(see p311)* or, if window shopping is your preference, stroll along Fifth Avenue, home to Manhattan's most glittering stores *(see opposite)*.

Greenwich and East Villages

Explore around Eighth Street and St Mark's Place for shoes and avant-garde fashions, books, ethnic goods and flea markets. Move to lower Broadway for antiques (often "retro" 20th century). (See pp108–9 and pp116–17.)

SoHo

The area bordered by Sixth Avenue, Lafayette, Houston and Canal streets is bustling with contemporary art galleries, antiques, crafts, exclusive or unusual gifts and fashions. Weekend brunchtime gallery-hopping is very popular. (See pp102–3.)

Lower East Side

Sunday is the day when New Yorkers and visitors flock to Canal, Delancey, Orchard and Essex streets for great bargains in fashions, shoes, jewellery, electronics and household goods. (See pp94–5.)

South Street Seaport

This is a browser's paradise of crafts, gifts, toys, souvenirs, books both antiquarian and new, and antiques with a strong seafaring connection. (See pp82–3.)

Columbus and Amsterdam Avenues

These are New York hot spots for exclusive but trendy designer-wear, quirky antiques, esoterica and upmarket gift shops. (See pp210–11.)

Madison and Lexington Avenues

Shoppers come here for classics in art and antiques, designer clothes and shoes. The museum shops are also nearby. (See pp182–83.)

East 57th and 59th Streets

Exclusive antiques and high fashion are found on 57th Street – and be sure not to miss Bloomingdale's. (See p179.)

| 0 kilometres | 2 |
| 0 miles | 1 |

FIFTH AVENUE

Trump Tower Shopping Mall

Harry Winston

Saks Fifth Avenue

Tiffany's

Cartier

Herald Square and the Garment District

Here, you'll find Macy's, a store that occupies an entire block. The surrounding area (especially Seventh Avenue) is the fashion wholesale centre with big discounts during the sales – but many stores only accept cash. (See pp130–31.)

From Saks to Tiffany's

Top retailers have their flag-ship store on world-famous Fifth Avenue.

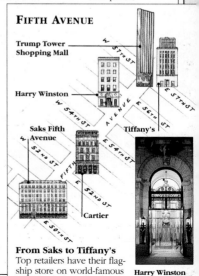

Harry Winston *(see p320)*

New York Originals

NEW YORK IS A CITY where just about every kind of shop, no matter how esoteric, will always attract customers. Dozens of tiny shops, scattered around the city, specialize in myriad products ranging from butterflies and bones to traditional Tibetan treasures and Shamrock sprigs from Ireland. Coming across these in some tucked-away corner is what makes shopping in New York such an entertaining experience.

SPECIALIST SHOPS

FOR BEAUTIFUL BRASS, onyx and pewter chess sets, and the opportunity to play a decent game, make a move to the **Chess Shop**. **Big City Kites and Darts** has kites in all different kinds of weird and wonderful shapes, from fiery dragons to cuddly teddy bears, plus enough accessories to satisfy even the most dedicated kite flyer. For those with a bit more energy, **Blades** sells and hires out skates and skateboards for the brave, plus all the safety equipment to go with them.

If you're on the lookout for different or unusual buttons a visit to **Tender Buttons** is a must. Whether you want your buttons made from enamel, wood or Navajo silver – or perhaps made into cuff links or earrings – you'll find what you want among the millions they have in stock.

Leo Kaplan Ltd is the place to go if you collect paperweights and **Rita Ford's Music Boxes**, a 19th-century style of shop, stocks a tuneful and extensive range of music boxes. For unusual phones the **Phone Booth** stocks every possible design including juicy puckered lips, Snoopy dogs and hamburgers.

The **New York Firefighter's Friend** sells an intriguing range of items related purely to firefighting, including mini toy fire engines, firemen's jackets, badges, scaled-down uniforms for children, stuffed toy dalmatians (these are their mascots) and lots of different T-shirts including a popular one with NYFD (New York Fire Department) on one side and "Keep back 200 feet" on the other – children love it.

For the true romantic who wants to impress, everything sold by **Only Hearts** is heart-shaped, including pillows, soap and jewellery. The **Magickal Childe** is an occult emporium full of potions, tarot cards and fragrant incense (note: there's no phone here and hours are erratic). Step straight into the space age at **Star Magic**, to buy celestial maps, holograms, prisms and scientific toys.

Cologne made specially for George Washington and the official soap of the White House during the Eisenhower era are just some of the many fascinating items for sale at **Caswell-Massey Ltd**, the oldest pharmacy in the city.

Guitar gurus will want to visit **Rudy's**, Manny's or Sam Ash's guitar shop. Not only is there a chance you'll bump into Eric Clapton or Lou Reed – both have their guitars made in this area – but you'll find the widest and best choice of instruments in the city.

Bibliophiles will find a range of gifts in both the **New York Public Library Shop** (see p144) (they sell bookends of the lions guarding the main entrance) and the **Pierpont Morgan Library shop** (see pp162–3), including bookmarks and writing paper.

University logos and college colours dominate the many knick-knacks and accessories at **The Yale Club** gift shop and **The Princeton Club**.

The Shop at One East (Temple Emanu-El) sells all manner of Judaica and other miscellaneous household gifts for the Jewish home. **Hebrew Religious Articles** carries one of the largest selections of Jewish religious items in the city.

The Cathedral Shop at the Cathedral of St John the Divine is a crafts fair where you can buy jewellery and religious items made locally.

MEMORABILIA

AT LINCOLN CENTER, the **Metropolitan Opera Shop** has records, libretti, tiny binoculars and many other opera-related gifts and cards. The **Performing Arts Shop** downstairs is a real treasure-trove of theatre, opera, ballet and music memorabilia. For ballet fans, everything from Nureyev T-shirts to dance records can be found at the **Ballet Shop**. For thousands of rare and old film stills and posters visit **Jerry Ohlinger's Movie Material Store**.

If you're looking for an old Wurlitzer jukebox or a Coke machine, go to **Back Pages Antiques**. The **Carnegie Hall Shop** carries musically-themed cards, T-shirts, games, posters, tote bags and much more. For something truly original and very American, be sure to visit **Lost City Arts** and **Urban Archaeology** in SoHo. Between these two shops, you'll unearth all sorts of relics from America's past, from Barbie Doll lunch boxes to fittings from the traditional ice cream parlours and old-fashioned barbershops.

TOYS, GAMES AND GADGETS

FOR CHILDREN'S GIFTS, don't miss the legendary **FAO Schwarz**. This is a massive store crammed from floor to ceiling with luxury toy cars, enormous stuffed animals and every kind of electronic toy imaginable. There are always horrendously large crowds at Christmas, when you might have to queue to get in. The **Children's General Store** is one of the city's newest – and cleverest – children's toy stores. **The Enchanted Forest** (see p102) is indeed a magical experience for children. Its handmade toys are artfully displayed among the trees of the enchanted forest, which was devised and built by a theatrical set designer.

Penny Whistle Toys sells a huge selection of quality toys, games and all kinds of different dolls.

For games that will appeal to children and adults, the **Game Show** has puzzles and games galore, from real classics like Monopoly to the latest yuppie favourite. **Red Caboose** is for fans of model railways. **Toys 'R' Us** doesn't have Schwarz's style but has over a million toys at reasonable prices.

If you're looking for a self-stirring saucepan or a pair of electric socks, then go to **Hammacher Schlemmer**. There are hi-tech gadgets galore, some more fascinating than practical, but this was the first shop to sell the steam iron and pop-up toaster.

MUSEUM SHOPS

SOME OF NEW YORK'S best souvenirs can be found in the city's many museum shops. In addition to the usual range of books, posters and cards, there are reproductions of the exhibits on show, including jewellery and sculpture. The **American Craft Museum** (see p169) has a really excellent selection of local American crafts in addition to original works for sale. As well as realistic model dinosaurs, rubber animals, minerals and rocks, the

American Museum of Natural History (see pp214–15) has a variety of recycled products and earth-awareness gifts, which include posters, bags and T-shirts with environmental messages, and a large selection of native American handicrafts. There is also a junior shop with items like shell sets, magnets and toys.

The **Asia Society Bookstore and Gift Shop** (see p185) has a striking selection of Oriental prints, posters, art books, toys and jewellery, all designed to spread a greater knowledge of Asia among Americans. Items related to interior design are on offer at the **Cooper-Hewitt** (see p184). One of New York's largest collections of Jewish ceremonial objects, including menorahs and Kiddish cups, books and jewellery is found in the small shop at the **Jewish Museum** (see p184).

For reproduction prints of famous paintings, a visit to the **Metropolitan Museum of Art** (see pp188–95) gift shop is a must. There is also an enormous book department. The traditional **Museum of American Folk Art** (see p213) prides itself on its

American country crafts, including wooden toys, quilts and weathervanes, which are mostly original. Works by crafts people who currently have pieces on display in the museum are also sold.

The **Museum of the City of New York** (see p197), specializes in pictures of old New York. The **Museum of Modern Art/MOMA Design Store** (see pp170–73) has a highly-praised selection of innovative home furnishings, toys and home kitchenware, inspired by international designers such as Frank Lloyd Wright and Le Corbusier.

For a selection of nautical items, including charts, maps, model ships and scrimshaw, go to the **South Street Seaport Museum Shops** (see pp82–5). The **Whitney Museum's Store Next Door** (see pp198–9) only stocks American-made items, including jewellery, wooden toys and also goods which complement the current exhibitions. The **Hayden Planetarium** (see p216) has an interesting gift shop for budding astronomers, with books on all aspects of astronomy plus star-finders and charts, cards and prints.

THE BEST OF THE IMPORTS

NEW YORK is a massive melting pot of different nationalities, cultures and ethnic groups. Most have made their mark on New York's diverse culture in one way or another and each are represented by shops that sell food or goods that are particular to that group.

Some of the most interesting and unusual shops include **Alaska on Madison**, which has a huge collection of Eskimo art, and the exquisite **Chinese Porcelain Company** which has a mass of Chinese decorative arts and furniture. **Back From Guatemala** has jewellery and decorative arts from Central and South America, and **Himalayan Crafts and**

Tours stocks everything from paintings to Tibetan rugs. A truly amazing collection of emerald-green goods can be found in **Shamrock Imports**, which also sells hand-knitted Irish sweaters.

Things Japanese has beautifully-made crafts and unusual books. **Surma** is a Ukrainian general store which sells hand painted eggs and linens. **Common Ground** has native American baskets, weavings and jewellery, and **Tibet West** has textiles and silver bracelets.

ADDRESSES

Alaska on Madison
937 Madison Ave.
Map 17 A1.
(879-1782.

Back From Guatemala
306 E 6th St. **Map** 5 A2.
(260-7010.

Chinese Porcelain Company
475 Park Ave. **Map** 13 A3.
(838-7744.

Common Ground
19 Greenwich Ave. **Map** 1 B1.
(989-4178.

Himalayan Crafts and Tours
2007 Broadway. **Map** 11 C1.
(787-8500.

Shamrock Imports
Manhattan Mall, 901 6th Ave.
Map 8 E1.
(564-7474.

Surma
11 E 7th St. **Map** 4 F2.
(477-0729.

Things Japanese
127 E 60th St.
Map 13 A3.
(371-4661.

Tibet West
19 Christopher St. **Map** 3 C2.
(255-3416.

DIRECTORY

SPECIALIST SHOPS

Big City Kites and Darts
1201 Lexington Ave.
Map 17 A4.
472-2623.

Blades
120 W 72nd St.
Map 11 C1.
787-3911.
One of several branches.

Caswell-Massey Ltd
518 Lexington Ave.
Map 13 A5.
755-2254.

The Cathedral Shop
Cathedral of St John the
Divine, 1047 Amsterdam
Ave. **Map** 20 E4.
222-7200.

Hebrew Religious Articles
45 Essex St. **Map** 5 B4.
674-1770.

Leo Kaplan Ltd
967 Madison Ave.
Map 17 A5.
249-6766.

Magickal Childe
35 W 19th St.
Map 8 F5.

New York Firefighter's Friend
263 Lafayette St.
Map 4 F3.
226-3142.

New York Public Library Shop
5th Ave at 42nd St.
Map 8 F1.
930-0678.

Only Hearts
386 Columbus Ave.
Map 15 D5.
724-5608.

Phone Booth
12 E 53rd St.
Map 12 F4.
564-0900.

Pierpont Morgan Library Shop
Madison Ave at 36th St.
Map 9 A2.
685-0610.

The Princeton Club
15 W 43rd St. **Map** 8 F1.
596-1200.

Rita Ford's Music Boxes
19 E 65th St.**Map** 12 F2.
535-6717.

Rudy's
169 W 48th St.
Map 12 E5.
391-1699.

The Shop at One East
Temple Emanu-El,
1 E 65th St. **Map** 12 F2.
744-1400.

Star Magic
745 Broadway. **Map** 4 E2.
228-7770.

Tender Buttons
143 E 62nd St.
Map 13 A2.
758-7004.

The Chess Shop
230 Thompson St.
Map 4 D3.
475-9580.

The Yale Club
50 Vanderbilt Ave.
Map 13 A5.
661-2070.

MEMORABILIA

Back Pages Antiques
125 Greene St.
Map 4 E4.
460-5998.

Ballet Company
1887 Broadway.
Map 12 D2.
246-6893.

The Carnegie Hall Shop
881 7th Avenue.
Map 12 E3.
903-9610.

Jerry Ohlinger's Movie Material Store
242 W 14th St.
Map 3 C1.
989-0869.

Lost City Arts
275 Lafayette St.
Map 4 F3.
941-8025.

Metropolitan Opera Shop
Metropolitan Opera
House, Lincoln Center,
136 W 65th St.
Map 11 C2.
580-4090.

Performing Arts Shop
Metropolitan Opera
House, Lincoln Center,
136 W 65th St.
Map 11 C2.
580-4356.

Urban Archaeology
285 Lafayette St.
Map 4 F3.
431-6969.

TOYS, GAMES AND GADGETS

The Children's General Store
2473 Broadway.
Map 15 C4.
580-2723.

The Enchanted Forest
85 Mercer St.
Map 4 E4.
925-6677.

FAO Schwarz
767 5th Ave.
Map 12 F3.
644-9400.

Game Show
474 6th Ave.
Map 12 E5.
633-6328.

Hammacher Schlemmer
147 E 57th St.
Map 13 A3.
421-9000.

Penny Whistle Toys
448 Columbus Ave.
Map 16 D4.
873-9090.
One of several branches.

Red Caboose
23 W 45th St.
Map 12 F5.
575-0155.

Toys 'R' Us
Herald Center,
1293 Broadway.
Map 8 E2.
594-8697.

MUSEUM SHOPS

American Craft Museum
40 W 53rd St. **Map** 12 F4.
956-6047.

American Museum of Natural History
W 79th St at Central Park
West. **Map** 16 D5.
769-5100.

Asia Society Bookstore and Gift Shop
725 Park Ave. **Map** 13 A1.
288-6400.

Cooper-Hewitt
2 E 91st St. **Map** 16 F2.
860-6878.

Hayden Planetarium
Central Park West at
W 81st St. **Map** 16 D4.
769-5900.

Jewish Museum
1109 5th Ave. **Map** 16 F2.
423-3200.

Metropolitan Museum of Art
5th Ave at 82nd St.
Map 16 F4.
535-7710.

Museum of American Folk Art
2 Lincoln Sq. **Map** 12D2.
496-2966.

Museum of the City of New York
5th Ave at 103rd St.
Map 21 C5.
534-1672.

Museum of Modern Art/MOMA Design Store
44 W 53rd St.
Map 12 F4.
767-1050.

South St Seaport Museum Shops
207 Front St.
Map 2 D2.
748-8600.

The Whitney Museum's Store Next Door
943 Madison Ave.
Map 13 A1.
606-0200.

Fashion

WHETHER YOU'RE LOOKING for an old pair of bargain basement 501s or the kind of ballgown Ivana Trump would wear, you're sure to find it in New York. The city is the fashion focus of America and an important centre of clothing manufacture and design. New York's mass of clothing shops, like its restaurants, reflects the different styles and cultures found in the many districts throughout the city. To save time it's probably best to visit one area at a time. Alternatively visit one of the department stores for an excellent selection of fashion for all.

AMERICAN DESIGNERS

MANY AMERICAN designers sell their creations in boutiques within the large department stores, or have exclusive shops of their own. One of the most famous is Geoffrey Beene, known for sophisticated looks that are casual and comfortable.

Bill Blass is the king of American fashion He uses many different colours, wild patterns, innovative shapes and a lot of wit, all of which have proved very popular. Liz Claiborne's designs are always elegantly simple, casual and reasonably priced. You'll find everything you could possibly need from tennis whites to smart office clothes for women.

The late Perry Ellis's style lives on with clothes designed by Marc Jacobs, known especially for his sportswear. James Galanos is an exclusive designer for the rich and famous, making one-off *couture* clothes at way-off prices. At the opposite extreme, perhaps, is Betsey Johnson who is very popular with wafer-thin extroverts who love to go to wild parties and wear figure-hugging fashions.

In recent years, Donna Karan is a name that appears everywhere. Her simple, smart and great-looking designs work for everything from exercise clothes to black tie wear. Calvin Klein now has his name on place settings and sunglasses in addition to underwear, jeans and a whole range of clothes. He is renowned for comfortable, sensous and well-fitting – plus very hip – looks. Ralph Lauren is well-known for his aristocratic and expensive clothes, a "look" favoured by the exclusive and posh Ivy League, horsey set. Joan Vass specializes in moderately-priced but exciting, colourful and innovative knitwear.

CUT-PRICE DESIGNER CLOTHES

IF YOU'RE on the lookout for cut-price designer clothes, **Designer Resale**, **Encore** and **Michael's** sell a huge range. Oscar de la Renta, Ungaro and Armani are just some of the top designers the shops have on offer. These shops only sell perfect and near-perfect clothing, much of which has never been worn before.

MEN'S CLOTHES

IN THE CENTRE of midtown, you'll find two of the city's most highly-regarded mens-wear stores – **Brooks Brothers** and **Paul Stuart**. Brooks Brothers is something of a New York institution, famous for its traditional, conservative clothing such as smart button-down shirts and Chinos. There is also an ultra-conservative woman's line. Paul Stuart prides itself on its very British look and offers a stylish array of superbly-tailored fashions.

Go to the top-quality department store **Bergdorf Goodman Men** to find beautifully-made Turnbull & Asser shirts and marvellous suits by Gianfranco Ferré or Hugo Boss.

Barney's New York has one of the most comprehensive men's departments in America, with a huge range of clothes and accessories. A smaller Barney's, at the World Financial Center, specializes in a selection of smarter business clothes and suits for city slickers. The **Polo/Ralph Lauren** department store is packed from floor to ceiling with the so-called King of American Sportswear's simple and timeless fashions and his many stylish accessories.

Matsuda sells very expensive, avant-garde Japanese chic for men and women. **Bijan Designer for Men** is so exclusive that customers have to book an appointment before they can even see any clothes.

The Custom Shop Shirt-makers specializes in custom-made suits and shirts in beautiful materials. Go to **Burberry Limited** if you're looking for that classic British trenchcoat.

J Press sells classic and conservative clothes. Uptown designer menswear boutiques include the renowned **Beau Brummel** with a selection of very stylish European clothes and for superb designer bargains, go and visit **Moe Ginsburg** for one of New York's largest selections of men's Italian clothing. Many menswear shops also have women's departments.

CHILDREN'S CLOTHES

IN ADDITION to an excellent range of children's shops within the large department stores, there are several shops around the city that sell children's clothing exclusively. Take a look at **Bonpoint** for French-style charm.

Gapkids and BabyGap shops, often in the **Gap** shops, are well known for comfortable, long-lasting cotton overalls, sweatpants, denim jackets, sweatshirts and leggings. The wonderfully-named **Peanut Butter & Jane** sells trendy but particularly comfortable togs. **Space Kiddets** has everything from bibs and booties to cowboy and cowgirl clothes.

WOMEN'S CLOTHES

WOMEN'S FASHION is more status-orientated than trend-setting, with a heavy emphasis on designer chic. Most of New York's really fashionable shops are found in the midtown area around Madison and Fifth avenues. These include some of the major department stores (see p311), which stock a range of American designers, including Donna Karan, Ralph Lauren and Bill Blass.

Top international names such as **Chanel**, **Fendi**, and **Valentino** also have shops here, as does one of the outstanding American designers, **Geoffrey Beene**. There is also a handful of popular ready-to-wear stores, including **Ann Taylor**, much favoured by young, busy professionals looking for stylish, comfortable clothing.

Right at the heart of this area stands the pink-marbled Trump Tower, which houses a selection of exclusive shops.

Madison Avenue is packed with smart-set designers, who have everything you could ever need, including **Givenchy** who sells show-stopping gowns at phenom-enal prices, Valentino who has classic Italian clothes and **Emanuel Ungaro** who is relatively unintimidating and has something to suit most tastes and physiques from beautifully tailored jackets to matronly full-figured and boldly patterned print dresses. **Missoni** is famous for richly textured sweaters in sumptuous wools and colourful patterns. **Yves St Laurent Rive Gauche** has evening gowns, one-of-a-kind jackets, extravagant blouses and beautifully-cut trouser suits.

Sophisticated Italian looks are also presented by Italian style kings **Giorgio Armani** and **Gianni Versace**. **Romeo Gigli's** Milanese clothing is so exclusive that his shop has no name on the door. **Gucci**, one of the oldest Italian shops in America, is only for the wealthy and status-conscious.

The Upper West Side has many shops competing for attention with eye-catching fashions including **Betsey Johnson's** shop, with her whimsical and relatively cheap designs. **Charivari** now has a very successful chain of stores which specialize in ultra-hip casual fashions. **French Connection** is known for its affordable separates, both casual and for the office. **Variazioni** has become *the* place to get a little black dress.

The villages – the East Village in particular – are the best places to go for second-hand clothing and 1950s rock 'n' roll gear. Go to the villages to hang out, and to sample the ever-changing scene of interesting shops run by new and young designers and art school graduates.

Cheap Jack's carries a huge selection of second-hand Levi's as well as hundreds of denim and leather jackets. **Dorothy's Closet** has classic dresses from the 1920s to the 1960s. **Big Drop** has a great selection of perfectly-fitting little black dresses. **Screaming Mimi's** is where you could unearth that pair of velvet bell-bottoms or go-go boots you've always dreamed of having. A more mainstream shop is **The Gap**, a chain store selling lots of moderately-priced, casual and comfortable clothes for men, women and children.

Recently SoHo has come to rival Madison Avenue for designer boutiques specializing in expensive but interesting clothes – the fashions here are far more avant-garde. You'll find **Yohji Yamamoto**, among other esoteric stores. **Comme des Garçons** sells minimalist Japanese chic.

More accessible is one of SoHo's most famous stores, the **Canal Jean Co**, which has all the latest SoHo looks at affordable prices. **What Comes Around Goes Around** is the place to go for vintage jeans. Take a look around **Wearable Energy** for wall-to-wall spandex.

SIZE CHART
For Australian sizes follow the British and American conversions.

Children's clothing

American	2-3	4-5	6-6x	7-8	10	12	14	16 (size)
British	2-3	4-5	6-7	8-9	10-11	12	14	14+ (years)
Continental	2-3	4-5	6-7	8-9	10-11	12	14	14+ (years)

Children's shoes

American	7½	8½	9½	10½	11½	12½	13½	1½	2½
British	7	8	9	10	11	12	13	1	2
Continental	24	25½	27	28	29	30	32	33	34

Women's dresses, coats and skirts

American	4	6	8	10	12	14	16	18
British	6	8	10	12	14	16	18	20
Continental	38	40	42	44	46	48	50	52

Women's blouses and sweaters

American	6	8	10	12	14	16	18
British	30	32	34	36	38	40	42
Continental	40	42	44	46	48	50	52

Women's shoes

American	5	6	7	8	9	10	11
British	3	4	5	6	7	8	9
Continental	36	37	38	39	40	41	44

Men's suits

American	34	36	38	40	42	44	46	48
British	34	36	38	40	42	44	46	48
Continental	44	46	48	50	52	54	56	58

Men's shirts

American	14	15	15½	16	16½	17	17½	18
British	14	15	15½	16	16½	17	17½	18
Continental	36	38	39	41	42 . 43	44	45

Men's shoes

American	7	7½	8	8½	9½	10½	11	11½
British	6	7	7½	8	9	10	11	12
Continental	39	40	41	42	43	44	45	46

DIRECTORY

Cut-Price Designer Clothes

Designer Resale
324 E 81st St.
Map 17 B4.
(734-3639.

Encore
1132 Madison Ave.
Map 17 A4.
(879-2850.

Michael's
1041 Madison Ave.
Map 17 A5.
(737-7273.

Men's Clothes

Barney's New York
669 Madison Ave.
Map 13 A3. (593-7800.
One of several branches.

Beau Brummel
421 Broadway.
Map 4 E2.
(219-2666.
One of several branches.

Bergdorf Goodman Men
754 5th Ave. **Map** 12 F3.
(753-7300.

Bijan Designer for Men
699 5th Ave. **Map** 12 F4.
(758-7500.

Brooks Brothers
346 Madison Ave.
Map 9 A1. (682-8800.

Burberry Limited
9 E 57th St. **Map** 12 F3.
(371-5010.

The Custom Shop Shirtmakers
618 5th Ave. **Map** 12 F4.
(245-2499.
One of several branches.

J Press
7 E 44th St. **Map** 12 F5.
(687-7642.

Matsuda
156 5th Ave. **Map** 8 F4.
(645-5151.

Moe Ginsburg
162 5th Ave. **Map** 8 F4.
(242-3482.

Paul Stuart
Madison Ave at 45th St.
Map 13 A5.
(682-0320.

Polo/Ralph Lauren
Madison Ave at 72nd St.
Map 13 A1. (606-2100.

Children's Clothes

Bonpoint
1269 Madison Ave.
Map 17 A3.
(722-7720.

Gapkids
657 3rd Ave.
Map 9 B1.
(697-9007.
One of several branches.

Peanut Butter & Jane
617 Hudson St.
Map 3 B1.
(620-7952.

Space Kiddets
46 E 21st St. **Map** 8 F4.
(420-9878.

Women's Clothes

Ann Taylor
645 Madison Ave.
Map 13 A3.
(832-2010.
One of several branches.

Betsey Johnson
248 Columbus Ave.
Map 16 D4.
(362-3364.
One of several branches.

Big Drop
174 Spring St.
Map 3 C4.
(966-4299.

Canal Jean Co
504 Broadway.
Map 4 E4.
(226-0737.

Chanel
5 E 57th St.
Map 12 F3.
(355-5050.

Charivari 57
18 W 57th St.
Map 12 F3.
(333-4040.

Charivari Madison
1001 Madison Ave.
Map 17 A5.
(650-0078.

Charivari 72
58 W 72nd St.
Map 12 F3.
(787-7272.

Cheap Jack's
841 Broadway.
Map 4 E1.
(777-9564.

Comme des Garçons
116 Wooster Street.
Map 4 E3.
(219-0660.

Dorothy's Closet
335 Bleecker St.
Map 3 C2.
(206-6414.

Emanuel Ungaro
792 Madison Ave.
Map 13 A2.
(249-4090.

Fendi
720 5th Ave.
Map 12 F3.
(767-0100.

French Connection
304 Columbus Ave.
Map 12 D1.
(496-1470.
One of several branches.

The Gap
354 6th Ave.
Map 8 E1.
(777-2420.
One of several branches.

Geoffrey Beene
783 5th Ave.
Map 12 F3.
(935-0470.

Gianni Versace
816 Madison Ave.
Map 13 A2.
(744-5572.

Giorgio Armani
815 Madison Ave.
Map 13 A2.
(988-9191.

Givenchy
954 Madison Ave.
Map 13 A1.
(772-1040.

Gucci
685 5th Ave.
Map 12 F4.
(826-2600.

Missoni
836 Madison Ave.
Map 13 A1.
(517-9339.

Romeo Gigli
21 E 69th St.
Map 10 F1.
(744-9121.

Screaming Mimi's
22 E 4th St.
Map 4 E2.
(677-6464.

Valentino
825 Madison Ave.
Map 13 A2.
(772-6969.

Variazioni
309 Columbus Ave.
Map 16 D2.
(874-7474.

Wearable Energy
73 W Houston St.
Map 4 D3.
(475-0026.

What Comes Around Goes Around
351 Broadway.
Map 4 E2.
(343-9303.

Yohji Yamamoto
103 Grand St.
Map 4 E4.
(966-9066.

Yves St Laurent Rive Gauche
855 Madison Ave.
Map 13 A1.
(472-5299.

Accessories

IN ADDITION TO the following shops, all of the major Manhattan department stores have extensive accessory departments stocking a range of hats, gloves, bags, jewellery, watches, scarves, shoes and umbrellas.

JEWELLERY

MIDTOWN FIFTH AVENUE is where to find the most dazzling jewellers. By day, windows glisten with gems from around the world; by night they are empty – the jewels safely locked away. The most sensational shops are all within a couple of blocks of one another and include the museum-like **Harry Winston**, which showcases its coveted jewels from around the world. **Buccellati** is well-respected for its innovative Italian creations and excellent workmanship. **Bulgari** has an impressive collection that ranges in price from a mere couple of hundred to over a million dollars.

Housed in a Renaissance palazzo, **Cartier** is a jewel in itself, and sells its beautiful baubles at unthinkable prices. **Tiffany & Co** has ten floors of glittering crystal, diamonds and other jewels just waiting to be packed up for you and taken away in the store's signature sky-blue boxes.

Diamond Row, a one-block area on 47th Street (between Fifth and Sixth avenues), is lined with shops displaying hundreds of thousands of dollars worth of diamonds, gold, pearls and other exotic jewels from around the world. Try not to miss the **Jewelry Exchange**, a complex where 60 different craftsmen sell their wares direct to the public. Boisterous bargaining is very much alive here, so be prepared to play the game.

HATS

THE CITY'S OLDEST hat shop is **Worth & Worth**, which has the largest collection of hats in the city. You can get everything you could possibly want here from original Australian bush hats to silk toppers and romantic, magical frothy concoctions. Try **Lola**

Millinery for some unique, whimsical hats. **Suzanne Millinery** is the hat-maker to the stars, very popular with celebrities such as Whoopi Goldberg and Ivana Trump. **Don Marshall Millinery** has been worn everywhere by the rich and famous since 1946.

UMBRELLAS

THE MINUTE IT STARTS to rain in New York, hundreds of street vendors selling umbrellas seem to sprout like mushrooms. Their umbrellas, at just a few dollars, are without doubt the cheapest in the city, but are unlikely to last much longer than the duration of the downpour. For good-quality umbrellas, you'll find a fine selection of Briggs of London at **Worth & Worth**. There is a wide range of styles at **Uncle Sam** from small Mickey Mouse styles that start at about $10 to enormous tent-like umbrellas, and both trendy patterns and more traditional tartans and stripes at **Barney's New York**. World-famous **Gucci** have umbrellas to match their ties. There are expensive and telescopic ones found at **Hanae Mori**, and doorman-sized ones in solid black or the university's traditional colours of black and orange at **The Princeton Club**. **The Yale Club** has blue ones which are emblazoned with a white "Y".

HANDBAGS AND BRIEFCASES

TWICE A YEAR, during the January and August sales, a serpentine queue of buyers wraps around the corner of 48th Street and Madison Avenue waiting to get into **Crouch & Fitzgerald**. An old New York institution, it sells handbags, briefcases and luggage. All the well-known brands are sold here, including Judith Leiber, Ghurka, Cooney

& Bourke and Louis Vuitton, as well as the firm's own line. Elsewhere in the city there are several exclusive shops such as **Bottega Veneta** and **Prada**, where handbags are displayed like precious works of art, with prices to match. Younger and trendier places include **Furla**, well-respected for its Italian designs, and the stylish **Il Bisonte**. Current must-have designer Rafé Totengco's soft suede pastel pouches are found at **TG-170** and **Big Drop**. **The Coach Store** is known for its simple, classic American handbags made of thick, strong leather.

For cut-price designer handbags go to the legendary **Fine & Klein** and for bargain briefcases galore, from slim envelopes to thick lawyer's bags, a visit to the **Altman Luggage Company** is a must.

SHOES AND BOOTS

MANHATTAN SHOE stores are well-renowned for their extensive selections of shoes and boots – you'd be very unlucky not to find what you want at a price you can afford.

Most of the large department stores in New York also have shoe departments where you can find designer-label shoes in addition to their own brands. **Bloomingdale's** (see p179) has a huge and efficient women's footwear department and **Brooks Brothers** has one of the best selections of traditional men's shoes in the city, with service to match.

For both men's and women's shoes, the most exclusive shops are around the midtown area. **Susan Bennis/Warren Edwards** has fabulous shoes made from exotic and often unusual materials. **Ferragamo** sells classic styles crafted in Florence. Go to **Botticelli** for whimsical shoe fashions. For stylish shoes at decent prices, head for **Sigerson Morrison** in Little Italy.

For cowboy boots, head for **Billy Martin's**. There's an enormous selection of handmade boots from basic, no-frills "ropers" that real American cowboys wear to crocodile leather boots that sell for thousands of dollars. Billy Martin's also stocks all sorts of western garb, so you can walk out looking like Clint Eastwood. For beautiful custom-made boots, try **Buffalo Chips Bootery**.

For the latest and best in children's shoes, **East Side Kids** prides itself on keeping up with the latest, trendiest

fashions for kids. **Little Eric** has unusual, eye-catching footwear and **Shoofly** has imported shoes in all styles. **Harry's** carries a wonderful selection of sensible shoes.

For discounted shoes, the greatest concentration of shops are around West 34th Street and West 8th Street, between Fifth and Sixth avenues, and Orchard Street.

LINGERIE

EXPENSIVE and exquisite items of hand-made silk lingerie can be found at **Montenapoleone**.

More affordable is **Victoria's Secret**, which offers two floors of beautifully-made underclothes in satin, silk and most everything else.

Books and Music

As the publishing capital of America, it's not surprising that New York has the country's best selection of bookshops. These range from huge general interest stores to hundreds of esoteric bookshops specializing in everything from sci-fi to suspense, new and old.

Music lovers will also find sounds for all tastes at reasonable prices, plus thousands of rare recordings.

GENERAL INTEREST BOOKSHOPS

Top of most New Yorkers' list of bookshops – for best prices as well as selection of titles – is **Barnes & Noble** on Fifth Avenue, reputedly the world's largest bookstore and packed high with over three million books on every imaginable subject. The sales annex across the street has thousands of amazing bargains.

Several blocks away is the main branch of New York's famous **Strand Book Store**. "The Strand", as those in the know refer to it, has an astonishing two million copies of second-hand books at some of the best prices in town. Upstairs there is a rare book room for first editions. **Doubleday Book Shop** is very good for new titles, best-sellers and travel books. **B Dalton's** flagship store on Fifth Avenue is stacked with the latest bestsellers, and **Coliseum Books** has a vast selection of paperbacks.

In midtown, **Rizzoli** has an enormous selection of photography, foreign language, music and art books as well as many children's books and videos. **Gotham Book Mart**, a New York institution, is a tiny shop where you can find hundreds of out-of-print books and limited editions.

Shakespeare & Co offers a sensational selection of titles and is open late every night.

SPECIALIST BOOKSHOPS

For the best selection of art books in the city, visit **Hacker Art Books**. **Urban Center Books** has titles on urban planning and conservation issues.

Books and Co is a magnet for literati, with an emphasis on poetry, art and philosophy.

The city's largest selection of out-of-print books, especially for art and literature, can be found at **Academy Book Store**. Rare, out-of-print and old books about New York are the *raison d'être* of **New York Bound Bookshop**. The **Biography Bookshop** is the only midtown store specializing in diaries, letters, biographies and autobiographies. Theatre buffs will find everything they need at the **Applause Theater & Cinema Books**.

For hundreds of titles on science, business, technology and computers visit **McGraw-Hill Bookstore**.

Books on murder, mystery and suspense are the preserve of two shops: **Murder Inc** and **Mysterious Bookshop**. **Forbidden Planet** is the place to go for old and brand-new science fiction books and comics. The **Village Comics** has thousands of old and new comics.

Bank Street Book Store has one of the best selections of current children's books. **Books of Wonder** has rare children's books.

The **Travelers' Bookstore** is run by three extremely knowledgeable bibliophiles who not only know every book they sell (both fiction and non-fiction), but every corner of the globe too, it seems. **The Complete Traveler** stocks a wide selection of travel books and guides for your journey, on everywhere from Alabama to Zimbabwe, as does the **The Civilized Traveler**. The latter also carries travel accessories from portable high-tech gadgets to an array of leather bags. There are also travel videos for rent, an ongoing schedule of lectures and seminars on worldwide travel issues by some well-known travellers, and special interest trip services.

For an excellent range of maps visit the large **Rand McNally Map & Travel Store** and the **Hagstrom Map & Travel Store**. Cookery books are on the menu at **Kitchen Arts & Letters**, with lots of hard-to-find out-of-print and original books.

Radicals should head for **Revolution Books** or **St Mark's Bookshop**. The **Oscar Wilde Memorial Bookshop** has a wide selection of gay and lesbian texts.

RECORDS, TAPES AND COMPACT DISCS

The best Manhattan record shop is **Tower Records**, which is stocked with almost everything from bebop to rap. This is closely followed by **HMV** and **Virgin**. **J&R Music World** is a complete home entertainment department store. **Record Explosion** carriers a huge selection of CDs at very low prices.

Those looking for deleted records should make their way to **Gryphon Records**, a treasure-trove for collectors. The **Academy Book Store** has an excellent choice of classical, jazz and opera recordings. **Footlight Records** is for lovers of Broadway musicals and film soundtracks and **House of Oldies** has a massive stock of deleted and rare records to suit all tastes.

Bleecker Bob's Golden Oldies record shop has everything from imports, rock and punk to rare jazz. Try **Midnight Records** for imports, re-issues, American garage rock and psychedelia.

SHEET MUSIC

Just behind Carnegie Hall is one of the best shops for classical sheet music – **Joseph Patelson Music House Ltd**. The **Frank Music Company** has a huge collection of classical music scores. **Charles Colin Publications** specializes in jazz. For chart music and pop tunes try **Colony Record and Music Center** in the Brill Building.

DIRECTORY

GENERAL INTEREST BOOKSHOPS

B Dalton
666 5th Ave.
Map 12 F4.
(247-1740.

Barnes & Noble
105 5th Ave. **Map** 8 F5.
(807-0099.
One of several branches.

Coliseum Books
1771 Broadway.
Map 12 D3.
(757-8381.

Doubleday Book Shop
724 5th Ave. **Map** 12 F3.
(397-0550.
One of several branches.

Gotham Book Mart
41 W 47th St. **Map** 12 F5.
(719-4448.

Rizzoli
31 W 57th St. **Map** 12 F3.
(759-2424.
One of several branches.

Shakespeare & Co
2259 Broadway.
Map 15 C4.
(580-7800.

Strand Book Store
828 Broadway.
Map 4 E1.
(473-1452.

SPECIALIST BOOKSHOPS

Academy Book Store
10 W 18th St.
Map 8 F5.
(242-4848.

Applause Theater & Cinema Books
211 W 71st St.
Map 11 C1.
(496-7511.

Bank Street Book Store
610 W 112th St.
Map 21 A4.
(678-1654.

Biography Bookshop
400 Bleecker St.
Map 3 C2.
(807-8655.

Books and Co
939 Madison Ave.
Map 17 A5.
(737-1450.

Books of Wonder
132 7th Ave.
Map 8 E5.
(989-3270.

The Civilized Traveler
2003 Broadway.
Map 11 C1.
(875-0306.

The Complete Traveler
199 Madison Ave.
Map 9 A2. (685-9007

Forbidden Planet
840 Broadway.
Map 4 E1. (473-1576.

Hacker Art Books
45 W 57th St. **Map** 12 F3.
(688-7600.

Hagstrom Map & Travel Store
57 W 43rd St. **Map** 8 F1.
(398-1222.

Kitchen Arts & Letters
1435 Lexington Ave.
Map 17 A2.
(876-5550.

McGraw-Hill Bookstore
1220 6th Ave. **Map** 12 E4.
(512-4100.

Murder Inc
2486 Broadway.
Map 15 C2.
(362-8905.

Mysterious Bookshop
129 W 56th St. **Map** 12 E3.
(765-0900.

New York Bound Bookshop
50 Rockefeller Plaza.
Map 12 F5.
(245-8503.

Oscar Wilde Memorial Bookshop
15 Christopher St.
Map 3 C2.
(255-8097.

Rand McNally Map & Travel Store
150 E 52nd St.
Map 13 A4.
(758-7488.

Revolution Books
9 W 19th St.
Map 7 C5.
(691-3345.

St Mark's Bookshop
31 3rd Ave.
Map 5 A2.
(260-7853.

Travelers' Bookstore
Time Warner Building,
22 W 52nd St.
Map 12 F4.
(664-0995.

Urban Center Books
457 Madison Ave.
Map 13 A4.
(935-3592.

Village Comics
163 Bleecker St.
Map 4 D3.
(777-2770.

RECORDS, TAPES, COMPACT DISCS

Academy Book Store
See Specialist Bookshops.

Bleecker Bob's Golden Oldies
118 W 3rd St.
Map 4 D2.
(475-9677.

Footlight Records
113 E 12th St.
Map 4 F1.
(533-1572.

Gryphon Records
251 W 72nd St.
Map 11 D1.
(874-1588.

HMV
2081 Broadway.
Map 15 C5.
(721-5900.
One of several branches.

House of Oldies
35 Carmine St.
Map 4 D3.
(243-0500.

J&R Music World
15, 23, 27 & 33 Park Row.
Map 1 C2.
(732-8600.

Midnight Records
263 W 23rd St.
Map 8 D4.
(675-2768.

Record Explosion
384 5th Ave.
Map 8 F3.
(736-5624.
One of several branches.

Tower Records
692 Broadway.
Map 4 E2.
(505-1500.
One of several branches.

Virgin Megastore
45th & Broadway.
Map 12 E5.
(921-1020.

SHEET MUSIC

Charles Colin Publications
315 W 53rd St.
Map 12 D4.
(581-1480.

Colony Record and Music Center
1619 Broadway.
Map 12 E4.
(265-2050.

Frank Music Company
250 W 54th St.
Map 12 D4.
(582-1999.

Joseph Patelson Music House Ltd
160 W 56th St.
Map 12 E4.
(757-5587.

Art and Antiques

ANY ART-LOVING VISITOR to New York could easily spend their whole time gallery-hopping around the several hundred galleries found throughout New York. Antique lovers could happily hunt out bargains at the many flea markets, or browse through European and American fine antiques at one of the more exclusive antique centres. Lovers of Americana will also find a wealth of such pieces for sale. To find out what's on offer during your stay, pick up a copy of *Art Now Gallery Guide,* a free monthly listing available at most galleries and bookstores, or check the local papers.

ART GALLERIES

ONE OF THE BIGGEST names in SoHo is **Leo Castelli**, a fanatical supporter of Pop Art during the early 1960s and now spotlighting new artists. **Mary Boone Gallery** has established Neo-Expressionist artists such as Julian Schnabel. The **Pace Gallery** exhibits current stars, especially well-known painter-photographers, and the trendy gallery **Jay Gorney Modern Art** deals in contemporary art and sculpture. The **John Weber Gallery** features new talent but is famous for its many Minimalists and Conceptualists. **Metro Pictures** is a treasure-trove of experimental pieces.

Among the exclusive 57th Street galleries is the venerable **Sidney Janis Gallery**, which displays 20th-century masters. **Holly Solomon Gallery** has European and American cont-emporary painting, drawing and sculpture, while **Marian Goodman Gallery** show-cases European avant-garde.

Along the Upper East Side is **Knoedler & Company**, which exhibits contemporary paintings by modern masters. **Gagosian Gallery** has great works by Lichtenstein and Johns, and the **Hirschl & Adler Galleries** feature a good selection of European and American fine art.

AMERICAN FOLK ART

IF YOU'RE in the market for American folk art, go to **Susan Parrish Antiques** and **Kelter-Malcé** for a selection of hooked rugs, American furniture and other Americana. Similar goods are at **Brian Windsor**. **American Hurrah**

Antiques has a good selection of quilts, native American art and paintings. **Laura Fisher** at the Manhattan Art & Antiques Center *(see below)* sells everything from decoys to hooked rugs.

ANTIQUE CENTRES AND SECOND-HAND ANTIQUES

IN ADDITION TO hundreds of small shops selling every-thing from tiger teeth to multi-million-dollar paintings, Manhattan is home to **The Manhattan Art & Antiques Center** which has dozens of dealers under one roof. **Irving Barber Shop Antiques** is filled with fabulous second-hand finds at astoundingly good prices.

AMERICAN FURNITURE

FOR FURNITURE from the 17th-, 18th- and 19th-centuries, try **Bernard & S Dean Levy**, **Eagles Antiques**, **Leigh Keno American Furniture** or the highly-regarded **Israel Sack**. **Judith James Milne** sells early American country furniture and a splendid collection of quilts. Go to **Thomas K Woodard American Antiques & Quilts** for a truly wonderful selection of Shaker pieces.

Collectors of Art Deco or Art Nouveau furniture should pay a visit to **Alan Moss**, which is full of furniture and decorative items. **Macklowe Gallery & Modernism** has a massive collection of fine Art Nouveau furniture. **Minna Rosenblatt** and **Lillian Nassau** have Tiffany lamps and many Art Nouveau and Art Deco pieces. There is a handful of retro shops, though numbers are

growing all the time, including **Depression Modern** and **Mood Indigo,** for treasures from the 1930s and 1940s.

INTERNATIONAL ANTIQUES

IF YOU'RE LOOKING for English antiques, try **Florian Papp** and **Kentshire Galleries**. For European pieces, visit **Betty Jane Bart Antiques**, **Kurt Gluckselig Antiques**, **The Little Antique Shop**, **Linda Horn Antiques**, **La Belle Epoque** and **Pierre Deux**. Oriental dealers include **Doris Leslie Blau**, **E & J Frankel** and **Flying Cranes Antiques**.

FLEA MARKETS

NEW YORK does not have a Portobello Road or a Marché aux Puces. However, it does have a number of year-round weekend markets. The best time to go is at the crack of dawn. Most flea markets don't officially open until 9 or 10am, but the haggling starts as early as 6am. If you arrive early you may be lucky enough to unearth some valuable piece of Americana like a Barbie lunch box or a Soupy Sales record.

Visit the **Annex Antiques Fair and Flea Market** for everything from second-hand clothing to antique furniture. The weekend **Canal Street Flea Market** has bric-a-brac; the **Columbus Avenue Flea Market** has new and second-hand clothing and furniture. For information on all street fairs and flea markets check Friday's *New York Times*.

AUCTION HOUSES

MANHATTAN'S TWO most celebrated auction houses are **Christie's** and **Sotheby's**, selling collectibles ranging from coins, jewels and vintage wines to fine and decorative arts. Items for sale are usually previewed several days before the auctions. For information on previews and auctions, check the Friday and Sunday editions of the *New York Times*.

DIRECTORY

ART GALLERIES

Gagosian Gallery
980 Madison Ave.
Map 17 A5.
📞 744-2313.

Hirschl & Adler Galleries
21 E 70th St. **Map** 12 F1.
📞 535-8810.
One of several branches.

Holly Solomon Gallery
172 Mercer St. **Map** 4 E3.
📞 941-5777.

Jay Gorney Modern Art
100 Greene St. **Map** 4 E4.
📞 966-4480.

John Weber Gallery
142 Greene St. **Map** 4 E4.
📞 966-6115.

Knoedler & Company
19 E 70th St. **Map** 13 A1.
📞 794-0550.

Leo Castelli
420 W Broadway.
Map 4 E4.
📞 431-5160.

Marian Goodman Gallery
24 W 57th St. **Map** 12 F3.
📞 977-7160.

Mary Boone Gallery
417 W Broadway.
Map 4 E4.
📞 752-2929.

Metro Pictures
150 Greene St. **Map** 4 E4.
📞 925-8335.

Pace Gallery
32 E 57th St. **Map** 12 F3.
📞 421-3292.

Sidney Janis Gallery
110 W 57th St. **Map** 12 E3.
📞 586-0110.

AMERICAN FOLK ART

American Hurrah Antiques
766 Madison Ave.
Map 13 A2.
📞 535-1930.

Brian Windsor
272 Lafayette St.
Map 4 F4.
📞 274-0411.

Kelter-Malcé
74 Jane St.
Map 3 C1.
📞 675-7380.

Laura Fisher
Manhattan Art & Antiques
Center, 1050 2nd Ave.
Map 13 B4.
📞 838-2596.

Susan Parrish Antiques
390 Bleecker St.
Map 3 C2.
📞 645-5020.

ANTIQUE CENTRES AND SECOND-HAND ANTIQUES

Irving Barber Shop Antiques
210 E 21st St.
Map 9 A4.
no phone.

The Manhattan Arts & Antiques Center
1050 2nd Ave.
Map 13 A3.
📞 355-4400.

AMERICAN FURNITURE

Alan Moss
436 Lafayette St.
Map 4 F2.
📞 473-1310.

Bernard & S Dean Levy
24 E 84th St.
Map 16 F4.
📞 628-7088.

Depression Modern
150 Sullivan St.
Map 4 D3.
📞 982-5699.

Eagles Antiques
1097 Madison Ave.
Map 17 A5.
📞 772-3266.

Israel Sack
730 5th Ave.
Map 12 F3.
📞 399-6562.

Judith James Milne
506 E 74th St.
Map 17 C5.
📞 472-0107.

Leigh Keno American Furniture
19 E 74th St. **Map** 16 F5.
📞 734-2381.

Lillian Nassau
220 E 57th St. **Map** 13 B3.
📞 759-6062.

Macklowe Gallery & Modernism
667 Madison Ave.
Map 13 A3.
📞 644-6400.

Minna Rosenblatt
844 Madison Ave.
Map 13 A1.
📞 288-0257.

Mood Indigo
181 Prince St.
Map 4 E3.
📞 254-1176.

Thomas K Woodard American Antiques & Quilts
506 E 74th St.
Map 17 A5.
📞 988-2906.

INTERNATIONAL ANTIQUES

La Belle Epoque
280 Columbus Ave.
Map 12 D1.
📞 362-1770.

Betty Jane Bart Antiques
1225 Madison Ave.
Map 17 A3.
📞 410-2702.

Doris Leslie Blau
724 5th Ave.
Map 12 F3.
📞 586-5511.
By appointment only.

E & J Frankel
1040 Madison Ave.
Map 17 A5.
📞 879-5733.

Florian Papp
962 Madison Ave.
Map 17 A5.
📞 288-6770.

Flying Cranes Antiques
1050 2nd Ave.
Map 13 B4.
📞 223-4600.

Kentshire Galleries
37 E 12th St. **Map** 4 E1.
📞 673-6644.

Kurt Gluckselig Antiques
1050 2nd Ave.
Map 13 B4.
📞 758-1805.

Linda Horn Antiques
1015 Madison Ave.
Map 17 A5.
📞 772-1122.

The Little Antique Shop
44 E 11th St.
Map 4 E1.
📞 673-5173.

Pierre Deux
367 Bleecker St.
Map 3 C2.
📞 243-7740.
One of several branches.

FLEA MARKETS

Annex Antiques Fair and Flea Market
24th to 27th Sts at 6th Ave.
Map 8 E4.
📞 243-5343.
Open Sat and Sun.

Canal Street Flea Market
335 Canal St.
Map 4 E5.
Open every weekend Mar–Dec.

Columbus Avenue Flea Market
Columbus Ave, between
76th and 77th St.
Map 16 D5.
📞 721-0900.
Open Sun.

AUCTION HOUSES

Christie's
502 Park Ave.
Map 13 A3.
📞 546-1000.

Sotheby's
1334 York Ave.
Map 13 C1.
📞 606-7000.

Food and Household Goods

Nᴇᴡ ʏᴏʀᴋ's sᴛʀɪᴋɪɴɢ cultural and ethnic diversity is celebrated in its food – the city's food shops provide a truly international feast. There is also a dazzling array of household goods, electronics and photographic equipment available almost everywhere you turn.

GOURMET GROCERIES

Sᴄᴀᴛᴛᴇʀᴇᴅ ᴀʀᴏᴜɴᴅ town are a handful of famous food emporia which are tourist attractions in themselves. When shopping for gourmet food remember to visit the department stores, which often rival the specialist food stores.

Balducci's in Greenwich Village is a real Italian delight, with its own brands of cold meats, pastas, salami and fish. Food has been elevated into an art form at **Dean & Deluca**, a chic delicatessen – don't miss the huge range of take-away food. **Russ & Daughters** is one of the first gourmet shops, known as an "appetizing" store, full of food to help remind immigrants of home, and famous for cream cheese, chocolates and bagels. **Zabar's** is arguably the finest food store in the world with huge crowds jostling for the excellent smoked salmon, bagels, caviar and cheese.

William Poll has a good selection of picnic hampers as well as a great variety of prepared dishes. For pâté de foie gras, Scottish smoked salmon, caviar and hand-made chocolates go to **Caviarteria**.

SPECIALIST FOOD AND WINE SHOPS

Fᴀʙᴜʟᴏᴜs ʙʀᴇᴀᴅ and cake shops abound but one of the best is **Poseidon Greek Bakery**, renowned for its filo pastry. **H & H Bagels** bakes 60,000 of the best bagels in Manhattan every day. **Vesuvio** has Italian bread and some unusual pepper biscuits. Try **Fung Wong** for delicious Chinese pastries or purchase a traditional Sicilian loaf from **A Zito & Son's Bakery**.

Cheese lovers should visit **Ben's Cheese Shop**, with its varieties of farmer's cheese. Great confectionery shops include **Li-Lac** for hand-made chocolates and **Mondel Chocolates** for chocolate animals. **Economy Candy** has a huge selection of dried fruit but for a real treat go to **Teuscher** who stock fresh champagne truffles flown in direct from Switzerland.

Myers of Keswick imports English food. For something more exotic, **Kam Man Food Products** is an original oriental grocery. The **Italian Food Center** has great olive oils, dried pastas and sausages. Go to **Jefferson Market** for meat and fish, and **Citarella's** for its amazing display of seafood. **Angelica's Herbs and Spices** has around 2,000 varieties of herbs and spices.

For fine burgundies **Acker, Merrall & Condit** has an enviable reputation. Go to **Garnet Liquors** for upmarket wines and champagnes at bargain prices. **SoHo Wines and Spirits** has an extensive selection of single-malt Scotch whisky. **Sherry-Lehmann** is New York's top wine merchant.

As well as a good selection of wine shops New York also has a number of coffee shops. Among the best are **Oren's**, **The Sensuous Bean**, **M Rohrs** and **Porto Rico Importing Company**. All have a great selection to tempt the coffee connoisseur.

For fruit and vegetables at reasonable prices visit a farmers' market, but be sure to get there early. Among the most popular are **City Hall**, **Upper West Side**, **St Mark's in-the-Bowery**, and **Union Square**. For information on the city's markets phone: 788-7900.

HOUSEHOLD GOODS

Mᴏsᴛ ᴏꜰ ᴛʜᴇ department stores sell a wide range of household goods. For a specialist shop, try **Broadway Panhandler**, a cook's heaven with outstanding baking and pastry-making equipment.

Bridge Kitchenware is a household name among most restaurateurs. **Williams-Sonoma** has many cooking utensils and cookbooks. **Zabar's** has an excellent selection of cooking utensils.

Baccarat, **Daum**, **Lalique** and **Villeroy & Boch** are where you'll find the finest crystal, china and silverware. Other upmarket shops include **Orrefors Crystal**, **Kosta Boda** and **Tiffany & Co**. Go to **Avventura** for crystal and china and, for the best of inexpensive, utilitarian American china, visit **Fishs Eddy**. Also visit **Ceramica** for lovely hand-made Italian pottery, and **La Terrine** and **Steuben Glass** for exquisite hand-painted ceramics.

Cheap linens can be found in most department stores. But for silk sheets and luxurious linens visit **Porthault** and **Pratesi**. **ABC Carpet & Home** has an enviable reputation for home furnishings as does **Ad Hoc Softwares** for its bed linens and bathroom accessories. For the lowest prices, shop-hop on Grand Street on the Lower East Side.

ELECTRONICS AND PHOTOGRAPHIC EQUIPMENT

Pᴇʀʜᴀᴘs ᴛʜᴇ ᴍᴏsᴛ competitive retailers in New York are the ones that sell electronics. Whatever you're buying, it pays to shop around. For the best buys of the week, check Tuesday's *New York Times*. If you're buying electrical goods to take back to Europe, make sure they are compatible with the voltages and formats (many electrical goods in the US are made to different standards).

47th Street Photo sells equipment from cameras to fax machines. Another popular shop for electrical equipment is **Uncle Steve's**. **J&R Music World** sells very competitively-priced equipment. **Nobody Beats the Wiz** is a large electronics chain that prides itself on never knowingly being undersold. For a wide variety of computers, videos and cameras try **Willoughby's**.

DIRECTORY

GOURMET GROCERIES

Balducci's
424 Ave of the Americas.
Map 4 D1.
673-2600.

Caviarteria
29 E 60th St. **Map** 12 F3.
759-7410.

Dean & DeLuca
560 Broadway. **Map** 4 E3.
431-1691.

Russ & Daughters
179 E Houston St.
Map 5 A3.
475-4880.

William Poll
1051 Lexington Ave.
Map 17 A5.
288-0501.

Zabar's
2245 Broadway.
Map 15 C4.
787-2000.

SPECIALIST FOOD AND WINE SHOPS

A Zito & Son's Bakery
259 Bleecker St. **Map** 3 C2.
929-6139.

Acker, Merrall & Condit
160 W 72nd St.
Map 11 C1.
787-1700.

Angelica's Herbs and Spices
147 1st Ave.
Map 5 A1.
677-1549.

Ben's Cheese Shop
181 E Houston St.
Map 5 A3.
254-8290.

Citarella's
2135 Broadway.
Map 15 C5.
874-0383.

City Hall Green Market
Centre St and Chambers St.
Map 1 C1.

Economy Candy
108 Rivington St.
Map 5 A3.
254-1531.

Fung Wong
30 Mott St. **Map** 4 F3.
267-4037.

Garnet Liquors
929 Lexington Ave.
Map 13 A1.
772-3211.

H & H Bagels
2239 Broadway.
Map 15 C4. 595-8000.

Italian Food Center
186 Grand St. **Map** 15 C4.
925-2954.

Jefferson Market
450 Ave of the Americas.
Map 12 E5. 533-3377.

Kam Man Food Products
200 Canal St. **Map** 4 F5.
571-0330.

Li-Lac
120 Christopher St.
Map 3 C2. 242-7374.

M Rohrs
1692 2nd Ave. **Map** 17 C3.
427-8319.

Mondel Chocolates
2913 Broadway.
Map 20 E3. 864-2111.

Myers of Keswick
634 Hudson St.
Map 3 C2.
691-4194.

Oren's
1144 Lexington Ave.
Map 17 A4.
472-6830.

Porto Rico Importing Company
201 Bleeker St. **Map** 3 C2.
477-5421.

Poseidon Greek Bakery
629 9th Ave. **Map** 12 D5.
757-6173.

St Mark's in-the-Bowery Greenmarket
E 10th St at 2nd Ave.
Map 4 F1.

The Sensuous Bean
66 W 70th St. **Map** 12 D1.
724-7725.

Sherry-Lehmann
679 Madison Ave.
Map 13 A3.
838-7500.

SoHo Wines and Spirits
461 W Broadway.
Map 4 E4.
777-4332.

Teuscher
25 E 61st St. **Map** 12 F3.
751-8482.

Union Square Greenmarket
E 17th St and Broadway.
Map 8 F5.

Upper West Side Greenmarket
Columbus Ave at 77th St.
Map 16 D5.

Vesuvio
160 Prince St. **Map** 4 E3.
925-8248.

HOUSEHOLD GOODS

ABC Carpet & Home
888 Broadway.
Map 8 F5.
473-3000.

Ad Hoc Softwares
410 W Broadway.
Map 4 E3.
925-2652.

Avventura
463 Amsterdam Ave.
Map 15 C4.
769-2510.

Baccarat
625 Madison Ave.
Map 13 A3.
826-4100.

Bridge Kitchenware
214 E 52nd St.
Map 13 B4.
688-4220.

Broadway Panhandler
520 Broadway.
Map 4 E4.
966-3434.

Ceramica
59 Thompson St.
Map 4 D4.
941-1307.

Daum
694 Madison Ave.
Map 13 A3.
355-2060.

Fishs Eddy
2176 Broadway.
Map 15 C5.
873-8819.

Kosta Boda
58 E 57th St.
Map 12 F3.
753-3442.

Lalique
680 Madison Ave.
Map 13 A3.
355-6550.

Orrefors Crystal
58 E 57th St. **Map** 13 A3.
753-3442.

Porthault
18 E 69th St. **Map** 12 F1.
688-1660.

Pratesi
829 Madison Ave.
Map 13 A2.
288-2315.

Steuben Glass
715 5th Ave. **Map** 12 F3.
752-1441.

La Terrine
1024 Lexington Ave.
Map 13 A1.
988-3366.

Tiffany & Co
See p321.

Villeroy & Boch
974 Madison Ave.
Map 17 A5.
535-2500.

Williams-Sonoma
20 E 60th St. **Map** 12 F3.
980-5155.
One of several branches.

Zabar's
See Gourmet Groceries.

ELECTRONICS AND PHOTOGRAPHIC EQUIPMENT

47th St Photo
67 W 47th St. **Map** 13 A5.
921-1287.
One of several branches.

J&R Music World
See p322.

Nobody Beats the Wiz
212 E 57th St. **Map** 13 A3.
754-1600.
One of several branches.

Uncle Steve's
343 Canal St. **Map** 4 E5.
226-4010.
One of several branches.

Willoughby's
110 W 32nd St. **Map** 8 E3.
564-1600.

ENTERTAINMENT IN NEW YORK

NEW YORK IS a non-stop entertainment extravaganza, every day, all year round. Whatever your taste, you can be sure the city will satisfy it on both a grand and an intimate scale. The challenge is to take advantage of as many of the entertainments as possible. If it's theatre, you can enjoy a mainstream success on Broadway, or take a chance on an experimental production performed

Performance by the New York City Ballet

in a loft. If it's music, there's the magnificence of opera at the Met, or a jazz group blowing in a club in the Village. You can catch a spectacle of avant-garde dance in a café, or try your own avant-garde dancing in one of the city's warehouse-sized clubs. Cinemas abound. But perhaps best of all is just wandering the streets and watching the vast show that is New York.

PRACTICAL INFORMATION

FIND OUT what's on in the arts and leisure listings of the *New York Times* and the *Village Voice* newspapers, and *New York* and *The New Yorker* magazines. These

TKTS discount ticket booth

briefly describe the entertainment on offer and tell you which credit cards are accepted. At your hotel ask for *Where*, a free weekly magazine containing maps and information on the many different attractions.

Hotel staff may be able to answer some of your queries, and should also carry a wide selection of brochures and leaflets. They may also be willing to book tickets. Some hotel TVs have a New York visitor information channel.

The efficient **New York Convention and Visitors Bureau** *(see p352)* is the city's official tourism data distribution point for literature, TV shows and schedules of events. They also have free and cut-price tickets such as "twofers" – which used to mean two for the price of one, but now just refers to a hefty discount.

NYC On Stage is a telephone hotline for theatre, dance and music, **Broadway Line** gives brief descriptions of current shows, schedules and the different prices, while **Moviephone** gives recorded information on all the films.

BOOKING TICKETS

POPULAR SHOWS may well be booked for weeks ahead so reserve your seats well in advance. Theatre box offices are open daily, except on Sundays, from 10am until one hour after the performance begins. Call in person, or telephone the box office or a ticket agency and order your seats by credit card. The biggest agencies are **Hit-Tix**, **Telecharge**, **Ticketmaster** and **Ticket Central**. A small handling fee of a few dollars will always be charged.

An independent ticket agent may also be able to find seats – good ones include **Prestige Entertainment** and **Union Tickets**; others are listed in the New York Yellow Pages. Fees will vary according to demand and availability of tickets.

New York magazine has a free phone hotline with information on ticket availability. This is open from 10.30am to 4.40pm Monday to Friday.

CUT-PRICE TICKETS

DISCOUNTS on tickets for plays and musicals are sold on the day of performance by non-profit **TKTS** booths. Discounts range from 25 to 50% but the price will include a small handling fee and must be paid for in cash or by traveller's cheque.

There is a TKTS booth on Broadway, where matinée tickets are sold from 10am to 2pm every Wednesday and Saturday; evening tickets from 3pm to 8pm and Sunday tickets from noon until 7pm. The booth at the 2 World Trade Center mezzanine sells tickets from 11am to 5.30pm Monday to Friday and 11am to 3.30pm on Saturday. Saturday matinée tickets can be bought here on Fridays.

On the third floor of Bloomingdale's *(see p179)*, a **Ticketmaster** outlet sells a few day-of-performance tickets at discounts of 10 to 75% (with a small charge) in normal shopping hours.

Bobby Short singing at the Café Carlyle *(p343)*

The Booth Theater on Broadway *(see p333)*

Ticketmaster now also sells tickets via its own website. If you have access to the internet, you can find them at www.ticketmaster.com. The **Hit Show Club** sells vouchers which can be exchanged at theatre box offices for discounted tickets.

Some shows offer standing-room tickets on the day at a bargain price. It's often the only way to catch a sold-out show at short notice.

TOUTS AND "SCALPERS"

IF YOU DECIDE to buy from a "scalper" (a ticket tout), be warned that the wrong day, wrong price, counterfeit tickets and outrageous prices are among the risks you face.

FREE TICKETS

FREE TICKETS to TV shows, concerts and special events are offered at the **New York Convention and Visitors Bureau** which is open from 9am to 6pm Monday to Friday and 10am to 6pm at weekends. Look in the "Cheap Thrills" listings in the *Village Voice* for events such as poetry readings, recitals and experimental films. During the popular New York Shakespeare Festival, free tickets are given out on a first-come, first-served basis, and are restricted to one ticket per person. The queue forms from noon on the day of the performance at the **Delacorte**

Theater, in Central Park. Veteran playgoers have even learnt to take along a picnic, rugs and cushions.

Free tickets for TV video-taping sessions are available by writing to the networks or from their on-street agents at **Rockefeller Center.**

Royale Theater at night *(see p333)*

HANDICAPPED ACCESS

BROADWAY THEATRES reserve a few spaces and cut-price tickets for wheelchair-bound people and attendants. Call **Ticketmaster** or **Telecharge** for information on shows and also to book tickets. For Off-Broadway theatres, call their box offices. Some theatres offer useful equipment for the hearing-impaired. **Tap** can arrange sign language for Broadway theatres, and **Hands On** for Off-Broadway.

USEFUL ADDRESSES

Broadway Line
[563-2929.

Delacorte Theater
Entrance via 81st St
at Central Park W.
Map 16 E4.
[861-7277.

Hands On
[672-4898 (Voice/TDD).

Hit Show Club
8th floor, 630 5th Ave.
Map 12 D5.
[581-4211.

Hit-Tix
[239-6200.

Moviephone
(see p337)
[777-FILM.

New York Convention and Visitors Bureau
2 Columbus Circle.
Map 12 D3.
[397-8222.

Prestige Entertainment
[697-7788.

Network Tickets
ABC.
67th St and Columbus Ave.
[456-3537.
CBS.
524 W 57th St.
[975-2476
NBC.
30 Rockefeller Plaza.
[664-3055.

NYC On Stage
1501 Broadway.
Map 12 D2
[768-1818.

Tap
[221-1103 (Voice),
719-4537 (TDD).

Telecharge
[239-6200.

Ticket Central
[279-4200.

Ticketmaster
[307-7171.
Bloomingdale's Department Store.
Lexington Ave at 59th St.
Map 13 A3.
[705-2122.

TKTS
Broadway at W 47th St.
Map 12 E5.

2 World Trade Center.
Map 1 B2.

New York's Best: Entertainment

Greenwich Village jazz club

NEW YORK is one of the great entertainment capitals of the world. Top names in every branch of the arts are drawn here to perform, and often to live and work. Sporting action is also guaranteed and as for nightlife, New York lives up to its reputation as "the city that doesn't sleep". From the huge choice on offer, there are some venues and events which stand out as classics of their kind; this selection has been chosen from the listings on pages 332–47 as among those not to be missed. Even if you experience only one of them you will have been part of something as essentially New York as the Empire State Building.

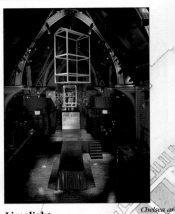

Limelight
Nightclubs come and go, but this converted church has become a firm favourite with New York's night owls.
(See p342.)

Chelsea and Garment

Madison Square Garden
Top sporting action is found at "the Garden", including home games for basketball team the New York Knicks and ice hockey's Rangers, and the Golden Gloves boxing tournament. (See p344.)

Greenwich Village

SoHo and TriBeCa

Seaport and the Civic Center

Lower Manhattan

Lower East Side

HUDSON RIVER

Film Forum
At New York's most stylish arts cinema you can see the latest foreign and American independent releases or catch up with a movie classic in a wide range of retrospectives.
(See p336.)

Village Vanguard
The jazz clubs of Greenwich Village have played host to all the great names in jazz. Fans can catch the stars of today and tomorrow at the world-famous Village Vanguard and the Blue Note. (See p340.)

Philharmonic Rehearsals
The Thursday morning rehearsals at Avery Fisher Hall are often open to the public at a fraction of the normal ticket price. (See p338.)

Metropolitan Opera House
Book well ahead and prepare to pay high prices to see the giants of the opera world. (See p338.)

Shakespeare in Central Park
If you are a summer visitor, set aside a day to get one of the rare free tickets for the Delacorte Theater's open-air Shakespeare featuring top Hollywood and Broadway names. (See p332.)

The Nutcracker
The Christmas event for children of every age is performed each year at Lincoln Center by the New York City Ballet. (See p334.)

0 kilometres | 2
0 miles | 1

The Fantasticks
The tiny Sullivan Street Playhouse has been home to America's longest running play since May 1960. New Yorkers who saw it when they were young are now taking their own children to the show. (See p332.)

Carnegie Hall
Conveniently situated in the Theater District, Carnegie Hall is famous the world over as a showcase for the best in the musical arts. A backstage tour gives a fascinating insight into "the house that music built". (See p338.)

Theatre and Dance

NEW YORK IS FAMOUS for its extravagant musicals and its ferocious critics. It is one of the world's greatest theatre and dance centres, featuring every kind of production imaginable. Whether your preference is for the glitz and glamour of a Broadway blockbuster or something truly experimental, you'll find it here.

BROADWAY

BROADWAY HAS long been synonymous with New York's Theater District, but the majority of Broadway theatres are actually scattered between 41st and 53rd streets, and from Sixth to Ninth avenues, with a few around the much improved Times Square. Most were built between 1910 and 1930 during the heyday of vaudeville and the likes of the famous Ziegfeld Follies. The **Lyceum** (see p142) is the oldest theatre still in operation (1903) and the **Majestic** is the newest (1986). Broadway theatres experienced a slump during the 1980s but are now enjoying a revival by a combination of cost-cutting, using big names to draw in the crowds and urban renewal of the Broadway district.

This is where you will find the "power productions" – the big, highly-publicized dramas, musicals and revivals starring many Hollywood luminaries in (it is hoped) sure-fire money spinners. Recent hits include well-known international imports *Dancing at Lughnasa,* and *Les Misérables,* New York originals such as *Falsettos* and *Jelly's Last Jam* and great revivals like *Guys and Dolls –* Damon Runyon's nostalgic snapshot of the Broadway district and its denizens.

OFF-BROADWAY AND OFF-OFF-BROADWAY

THERE ARE about 20 Off-Broadway stages and 300 Off-Off-Broadway stages whose works will sometimes transfer to Broadway. Off-Broadway theatres have from 100 to 499 seats and Off-Off-Broadway showplaces have fewer than 100. Both range from the well-appointed to the improvised, sited in lofts, churches and even garages.

Off-Broadway became very popular during the 1950s as a reaction to the commercialism of Broadway. It was also an ideal place for more cautious producers to try out works considered too avant-garde or unsuitable for Broadway at much lower operating costs. During the last two decades Off-Off-Broadway theatres have become the venue for the more experimental pieces as these same producers have moved even further afield.

Off-Broadway theatres are found all over Manhattan from Greenwich Village's the **Sullivan Street Playhouse** (where the longest-running show in New York, *The Fantasticks*, plays) to Central Park's open-air **Delacorte Theater**. Some are even in the traditional Broadway district. Further afield can be found the **Brooklyn Academy of Music (BAM)** (see p246), the **Manhattan Theater Club** and the **92nd Street Y**. In these venues you will always find lively, unusual and experimental showcases for new talent and lots of uninhibited productions.

The Off-Broadway theatres mounted the first productions in New York of the works of playwrights like Sean O'Casey, Tennessee Williams, Eugene O'Neill, Samuel Beckett, Jean Genet, Eugene Ionesco and David Mamet. They host new and very often irreverent treatments of the classics and every imaginable theatrical presentation is floated.

Sometimes a more intimate, smaller Off-Broadway stage suits a production much better than a larger more established theatre would, as proved by long-running successes such as the *The Fantasticks* and the *Three-penny Opera*. Of course, there are flops occasionally – but that's show business.

PERFORMANCE THEATRE

THIS EXTREMELY avant-garde art form can be found in several Off- and Off-Off-Broadway locations. Accurate descriptions and categorizations are almost impossible but expect the bizarre and outlandish. The most likely venues to find this are **La MaMa**, **PS 122**, **CBGB's 313 Gallery**, **92nd Street Y**, **Symphony Space** and the Joseph Papp **Public Theater** (see p118). The latter is perhaps the most influential theatre in New York. It was founded in the 1950s by the late director Joseph Papp, who introduced neighbourhood tours to bring theatre to people who had never seen it before.

The Public Theater created hits like *Hair* and *A Chorus Line* but it is most famous for its many free summer performances of Shakespeare at the Delacorte Theater, Central Park (see p206). It usually has several productions running, and at 6pm on the day of performance, "Quiktix" cut-price tickets (limited to two per person) are sold in the Public Theater lobby.

THEATRE SCHOOLS

NEW YORK is the best place in the country to see actors learning their trade. Foremost among the acting schools is **The Actors' Studio**. The late Lee Strasberg, the advocate of method acting – in which the actor aims for complete identification with the character being played – was its guru. His students have included Dustin Hoffman, Al Pacino and Marilyn Monroe. Its "in progress" productions feature current trainees and are usually open to the public. Sandy Meisner trained many actors, including Lee Remick, at the **Neighborhood Playhouse School of the Theater**. Its plays are also open to the public. The **New Dramatists** began in 1949 to help develop new playwrights, helping the careers of the likes of William Inge. Play readings are open to the public and free.

Broadway Theatres

1 **Ambassador**
215 W 49th St.
☎ *239-6200.*

2 **Barrymore**
243 W 47th St.
☎ *239-6200.*

3 **Belasco**
111 W 44th St.
☎ *239-6200.*

4 **Booth**
222 W 45th St.
☎ *239-6200.*

5 **Broadhurst**
235 W 44th St.
☎ *239-6200.*

6 **Broadway**
1681 Broadway.
☎ *239-6200.*

7 **Brooks Atkinson**
256 W 47th St.
☎ *307-4100.*

8 **Circle in the Square – Uptown**
1633 Broadway.
☎ *239-6200.*

9 **Cort**
138 W 48th St.
☎ *239-6200.*

10 **Eugene O'Neill**
230 W 49th St.
☎ *239-6200.*

11 **Gershwin**
222 W 51st St.
☎ *307-4100.*

12 **John Golden**
252 W 45th St.
☎ *239-6200.*

13 **Helen Hayes**
240 W 44th St.
☎ *307-4100.*

14 **Imperial**
249 W 45th St.
☎ *239-6200.*

15 **Longacre**
220 W 48th St.
☎ *239-6200.*

16 **Lunt–Fontanne**
205 W 46th St.
☎ *307-4100.*

17 **Lyceum**
149 W 45th St.
☎ *239-6200.*

18 **Majestic**
245 W 44th St.
☎ *239-6200.*

19 **Marquis**
1535 Broadway.
☎ *307-4100.*

20 **Martin Beck**
302 W 45th St.
☎ *239-6200.*

21 **Minskoff**
Broadway at 45th St.
☎ *307-4100.*

22 **Music Box**
239 W 45th St.
☎ *239-6200.*

23 **Nederlander**
208 W 41st St.
☎ *307-4100.*

24 **Neil Simon**
250 W 52nd St.
☎ *307-4100.*

25 **Palace**
1564 Broadway.
☎ *307-4100.*

26 **Plymouth**
236 W 45th St.
☎ *239-6200.*

27 **Richard Rodgers**
226 W 46th St.
☎ *307-4100.*

28 **Roundabout**
1530 Broadway.
☎ *869-8400.*

29 **Royale**
242 W 45th St.
☎ *239-6200.*

30 **St James**
246 W 44th St.
☎ *239-6200.*

31 **Shubert**
225 W 44th St.
☎ *239-6200.*

32 **Virginia**
245 W 52nd St.
☎ *239-6200.*

33 **Walter Kerr**
219 W 48th St.
☎ *239-6200.*

34 **Winter Garden**
1634 Broadway.
☎ *239-6200.*

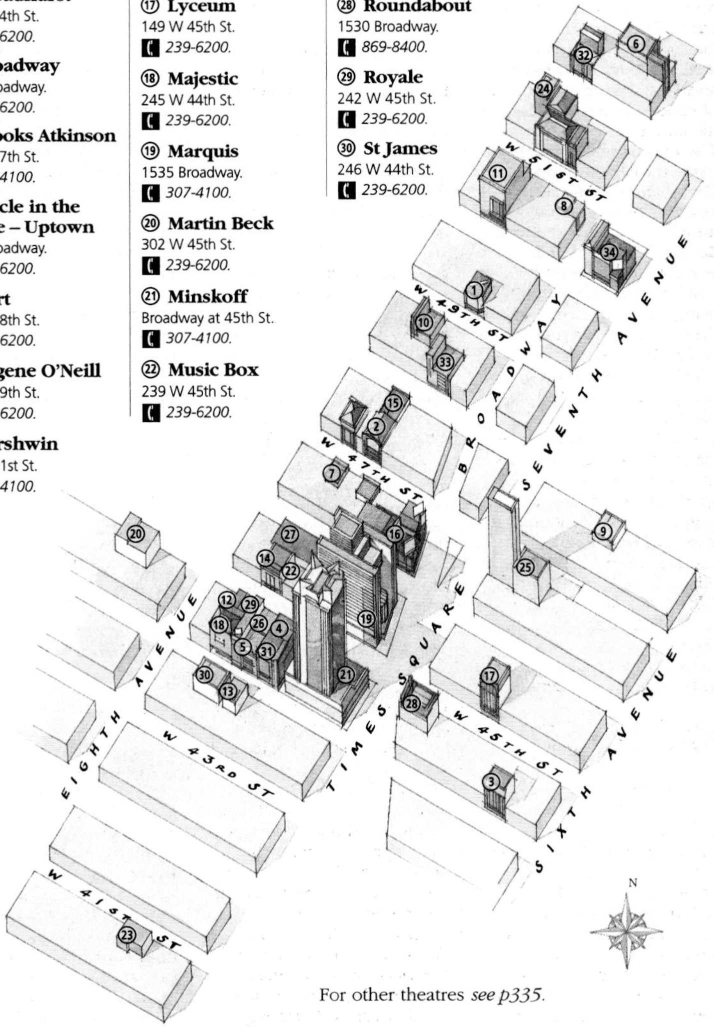

For other theatres *see p335.*

BALLET

AT THE HEART of the dance world is Lincoln Center *(see p212)*, where the New York City Ballet performs pieces in the **New York State Theater**. This company was created by the legendary and brilliant choreographer George Balanchine *(see p46)* and is probably still the best in the world. The current director, Peter Martins, was one of Balanchine's best dancers and continues the strict policy of ensemble dancing rather than "star turns". The season runs from November to February and late April to early June. The ballet school at the **Juilliard Dance Theater** also presents a spring workshop every year and this is a good chance to see budding stars.

The American Ballet Theatre appears at the **Metropolitan Opera House**, which also hosts many visiting foreign companies such as the Kirov, Bolshoi and Royal Ballets. Its repertoire includes 19th-century classics such as *Swan Lake* and works by modern choreographers like Twyla Tharp and Paul Taylor.

CONTEMPORARY DANCE

NEW YORK is the centre of many of the most important movements in modern dance. The **Dance Theater of Harlem** is world famous for its modern, traditional and ethnic productions. Other havens of experimental dance include the **92nd Street Y** and the **Merce Cunningham Studio** in Greenwich Village. The unusual **Dance Theater Workshop** has a packed programme as well as an art gallery. **The Kitchen**, **La MaMa**, **Symphony Space** and **PS 122** are all multi-media venues with the latest in contemporary dance, performance art and avant-garde music. Choreographer Mark Morris's company performs at the **Manhattan Center**. **City Center** *(see p146)* is a favourite venue for dance fans, and used to house the New York City Ballet and the American Ballet Theatre well before Lincoln Center was

built. As well as featuring the Joffrey Ballet, City Center has been the venue for performances by all the great contemporary artists, including Alvin Ailey's blend of modern, jazz and blues and the companies of modern dance masters Merce Cunningham and Paul Taylor. Try to avoid the mezzanine as the view is restricted.

The city's single most active venue for dance is probably the **Joyce Theater** where well-established companies such as the Feld Ballet, along with bold newcomers and visiting troupes, perform.

Each spring the Festival of Black Dance at the **Brooklyn Academy of Music (BAM)** *(see p246)* features everything from ethnic dance to hip-hop. During autumn the "Next Wave" festival of music and dance is held, which celebrates international and American avant-garde dance and music. During winter the American Ballet Festival is held here.

During June, **New York University** *(see p113)* holds a Summer Residency Festival with lecture-demonstrations, rehearsals and performances, and **Dancing in the Streets** organizes summertime dance performances all over the city.

Throughout the month of August, **Lincoln Center Out of Doors** has a programme of free dance events on the plaza with ethnic and experimental groups such as the American Tap Dance Orchestra.

The **World Financial Center** *(see p69)* has a free series at the Winter Garden with dance companies such as the National Dance Institute.

At different times of the year, **Radio City Music Hall** holds several accomplished and spectacular shows, with different companies from all over the world. At Christmas and Easter, it features the Rockettes dance troupe.

Choreographers and dance companies frequently present works-in-progress and recitals to the public. Among the most interesting venue for these is the **Alvin Ailey's Repertory Ensemble**. The **Hunter College Dance Company** performs new works by its student choreographers and

the **Isadora Duncan International Center for Dance** recreates her original dances. For contemporary choreographers the best place to go is **Juilliard Dance Theater**.

PRICES

THEATRE is extremely expensive to produce and ticket prices tend to reflect this. Even Off- and Off-Off-Broadway tickets are not cheap anymore. At one time, all tickets to previews of new plays sold at a much reduced price, but not so today: you can expect to pay exactly the same as post-opening tickets. Preview tickets are a lot easier to get hold of, though, and it's fun to see a show before the reviews are in and to make up your own mind.

For Broadway theatre you can expect to pay $15–50; for musicals, up to $65; Off-Broadway, $15–40. For dance, $7–30 is the usual range, with up to $60 for the American Ballet Theatre. The **Music and Dance Booth** *(see p329)* in Bryant Park sells half-price day-of-performance tickets and it is worth queuing.

TIMES OF PERFORMANCE

THE GENERAL RULES for theatre hours are: closed on Mondays (except for most musicals) with matinees on Wednesdays, Saturdays and sometimes Sundays. These usually begin at 2pm and evening performances at 8pm. Be sure to check the correct dates and times of the performance beforehand.

BACKSTAGE TOURS AND LECTURES

FOR THOSE INTERESTED in the mechanics of the theatre and anecdotes on the stars, **Backstage on Broadway** conducts some fascinating backstage tours. The **92nd Street Y** organizes talks giving an insider's view of the theatre, with famous directors, actors and choreographers taking part. Writers are often invited along to read or discuss their current works. **Radio City Music Hall** also hold tours.

DIRECTORY

OFF-BROADWAY

92nd Street Y
Lexington Ave.
Map 17 A2.
(415-5420.

Actors' Playhouse
100 7th Ave S.
Map 3 C1.
(463-0060.

American Place
111 W 46th St.
Map 12 E5.
(840-3074.

Brooklyn Academy of Music
30 Lafayette Ave.
((718) 636-4100.

CBGB's 313 Gallery
313 Bowery. **Map** 4 F2.
(677-0455.

Circle in the Square – Downtown
159 Bleecker St.
Map 4 D3.
(254-6330.

Circle Repertory
99 7th Ave. **Map** 3 C2.
(486-0177.

Delacorte Theater
Central Park. (81st St.)
Map 16 E4.
(861-7277.

John Houseman
450 W 42nd St.
Map 7 C1.
(967-9077.

Lambs Theater
130 W 44th St.
Map 12 E5.
(997-1780.

Manhattan Theater Club
City Center, 131 W 55th St.
Map 12 E4.
(645-5848.

Provincetown Playhouse
133 MacDougal St.
Map 4 D2.
(777-2571.

Public Theater
425 Lafayette St.
Map 4 F2.
(539-8500.

Sullivan Street Playhouse
181 Sullivan St.
Map 4 D3.
(674-3838.

Symphony Space
2537 Broadway.
Map 15 C2.
(864-5400.

Vivian Beaumont
Lincoln Center.
Map 11 C2.
(362-7600.

OFF-OFF-BROADWAY

The Kitchen
512 W 19th St. **Map** 7 C5.
(255-5793.

Living Theater
(865-3957.
Touring group. Ring for info.

Mabou Mines
(254-1109.
Touring group. Ring for info.

Performing Garage
33 Wooster St.
Map 4 E4.
(966-3651.

Theater at St Peter's Church
Citicorp Center, 619 Lexington Ave.
Map 13 A4.
(935-2200.

PERFORMANCE THEATRE

92nd Street Y
See Off-Broadway.

CBGB's 313 Gallery
See Off-Broadway.

La MaMa
74a E 4th St.
Map 4 F2.
(475-7710.

PS 122
150 1st Ave. **Map** 5 A1.
(477-5288.

Public Theater
See Off-Broadway.

Symphony Space
See Off-Broadway.

THEATRE SCHOOLS

The Actors' Studio
432 W 44th St.
Map 11 C5.
(757-0870.

Neighborhood Playhouse School of the Theater
340 E 54th St.
Map 13 B4.
(688-3770.

New Dramatists
424 W 44th. **Map** 11 C5.
(757-6960.

DANCE

92nd Street Y
See Off-Broadway.

Alvin Ailey American Dance Center
211 W 61st St. **Map** 11 3C.
(767-0940.

Brooklyn Academy of Music
See Off-Broadway.

City Center
131 W 55th St.
Map 12 E4.
(581-7907.

Dance Theater of Harlem
466 W 152nd St.
(690-2800.

Dance Theater Workshop
219 W 19th St. **Map** 8 E5.
(924-0077.

Dancing in the Streets
131 Varick St. **Map** 4 D4.
(989-6830.

Hunter College Dance Company
695 Park Ave.
Map 13 A1.
(772-5011.

Isadora Duncan International Center for Dance
91 Claremont Ave.
Map 20 D2.
(662-4591.

Joyce Theater
175 8th Ave at 19th St.
Map 8 D5.
(242-0800.

Juilliard Dance Theater
60 Lincoln Center Plaza, W 65th St.
Map 11 C2.
(769-7406.

The Kitchen
See Off-Off Broadway.

La MaMa
See Performance Theatre.

Lincoln Center Out of Doors
Lincoln Center, Broadway at 64th St. **Map** 11 C2.
(362-6000.

Manhattan Center
311 W 34th St.
Map 8 D2.
(307-4100.

Merce Cunningham Studio
55 Bethune St.
Map 3 B2.
(691-9751.

Metropolitan Opera House
Lincoln Center, Broadway at 65th St.
Map 11 C2.
(362-6000.

Music and Dance Booth
See page 329.

New York State Theater
Lincoln Center, Broadway at 65th St. **Map** 11 C2.
(870-5570.

New York University
Tisch Hall, 111 2nd Ave.
Map 4 F1.
(998-1984.

PS 122
See Performance Theatre.

Radio City Music Hall
50th St Ave of the Americas. **Map** 12 F4.
(247-4777.

Symphony Space
See Off-Broadway.

World Financial Center
West St between Vesey and Liberty St. **Map** 1 B2.
(945-0505.

BACKSTAGE TOURS

92nd Street Y
See Off-Broadway.

Backstage on Broadway
(575-8065.

Radio City Music Hall
(632-4041.

Cinema

NEW YORK is a film buff's paradise. Apart from new US releases, which show months in advance of London, many classic and foreign films are screened here.

The city has always been the testing ground for new developments in films and it continues to be a hotbed of new and innovative talent. Many of the cinema's most famous directors like Spike Lee, Martin Scorsese and Woody Allen were born and bred in New York and the city's influence can be seen in many of their films. They, and others, can often be seen filming on the streets of the city – many of New York's landmarks have become famous after appearing in films.

Most of the TV networks based in New York offer free tickets to the taping of their TV shows. Watching the taping of a show, such as *The David Letterman Show* or *Donahue,* is popular with New Yorkers and visitors alike.

FIRST-RUN CINEMAS

NEW YORK REVIEWS and box office returns are so vital to a film's success that most major American films have their premieres in Manhattan's top cinemas. First-run films are shown mainly at the City Cinema chains, Loews, Guild and Cineplex Odeon, which are scattered widely around the city. Some cinemas have recorded information giving the names and duration of the different films then showing, starting times and ticket prices.

Programmes start at noon and are repeated every two to three hours until midnight. You should expect to queue for most evening and weekend performances of the more popular films. Advance booking using a credit card is possible at some cinemas for an additional charge of about $1 per ticket. Matinées (usually before 4pm) are easier to get into. Senior citizens pay a reduced price for tickets: the required age may be over 60, 62 or 65 depending on the policy of the cinema.

NEW YORK FILM FESTIVAL

A HIGH POINT of the year for American film buffs is the New York Film Festival, now in its third decade. Organized by the **Film Society of Lincoln Center**, the festival starts in late September and continues for two weeks at the many Lincoln Center cinemas. Outstanding new films from the US and abroad are entered in a competition which has no prizes except for the huge prestige of winning an award. The successful films go on to have a limited release in New York's many art houses.

FOREIGN FILMS AND ART HOUSES

FOR THE LATEST foreign and independent films, go to the **Angelika Film Center**, which has six screens and an up-market coffee bar. Other good venues are the plush **Carnegie Hall Cinema** and the stylish **Film Forum** and **Lincoln Plaza Cinema**. The Plaza has many foreign and art films, as does the **68th St Playhouse**. For Asian, Indian and Chinese films, you should visit the **Asia Society**. The

FILM CERTIFICATES

Films in the US are graded as follows:
G General audiences, all ages admitted.
PG Parental guidance suggested. Some material unsuitable for children.
PG-13 Parents strongly cautioned. Some material inappropriate for children under age 13.
R Restricted. Children under 17 need to be accompanied by a parent or adult guardian.
NC-17 No children under 17 admitted.

ON LOCATION

Many New York locations have played starring roles in films. Here are a few:

The Brill Building (1141 Broadway) was Burt Lancaster's penthouse in *Sweet Smell of Success.*
The Brooklyn Bridge was a great backdrop in Spike Lee's *Mo' Better Blues.*
Brooklyn Heights and the **Metropolitan Opera** appeared in *Moonstruck.*
Central Park has shown up in countless films, including *Love Story* and *Marathon Man.*
No. 55 Central Park West will be remembered as Sigourney Weaver's home in *Ghostbusters.*
Chinatown played a major role in *Year of the Dragon.*
The Dakota was where Mia Farrow lived in the classic, *Rosemary's Baby.*
The Empire State Building is still standing after *King Kong*'s last heroic battle.
Grand Central Station is famous for Robert Walker's meeting with Judy Garland in *Under the Clock* and the magical ballroom sequence in *The Fisher King.*
Harlem's tenements were the seedy settings for the jazz musicians and dancers in *The Cotton Club.*
Katz's Deli is the backdrop in the memorable café scene between Billy Crystal and Meg Ryan in *When Harry Met Sally...*
Little Italy appeared in *The Godfather I* and *II.*
Madison Square Garden was the setting for the dramatic climax of *The Manchurian Candidate.*
The Russian Tea Room is where Dustin Hoffman had lunch with his stunned agent in *Tootsie.*
Tiffany & Co was Audrey Hepburn's favourite shop in *Breakfast at Tiffany's.*
The United Nations Building featured in the thriller *North by Northwest.*
Washington Square Park was where Robert Redford and Jane Fonda walked *Barefoot in the Park.*

French Institute screens many French films with English subtitles and plays host to the Asian American International Film Festival. The **Cinema 3** located in the Plaza Hotel shows new films in elegant surroundings. **Cinema Village** runs special film events such as the Festival of Animation.

The **Walter Reade Theater** houses the Film Society of the Lincoln Center, offering retrospectives of international cinema as well as celebrations of contemporary works, such as the popular annual Spanish Cinema Now festival.

CLASSIC FILMS AND MUSEUMS

RETROSPECTIVES OF films by particular directors or featuring specific actors are shown at the **Film Society of Lincoln Center**, the **Public Theater** and the **Whitney Museum of American Art** *(see pp198–9)*. The extensive **Museum of Modern Art** *(see pp170–3)* is one of the best places to see a wide range of classic and silent movies. The museum also screens films on art and culture.

The **American Museum of the Moving Image** *(see p244)* screens old films and also has many exhibits of memorabilia from the film industry. The **Museum of Television & Radio** *(see p169)* has regular screenings of classic films; you can also see or hear specific television or radio programmes. Students interested in classic, new and experimental cinema will appreciate the really huge wealth of material at the **Anthology Film Archives.**

"Naturemax", which is at the **American Museum of Natural History**, shows environmental films using the most up-to-date technology – like IMAX, 70 mm film which has incredible clarity of image – projected on to huge screens.

On Saturday mornings, take your young film-goers to the **Film Society of Lincoln Center** where special children's shows are held.

TELEVISION SHOWS

A NUMBER of TV programmes originate in New York. By writing ahead several months in advance, you may be able to see one or more of them as they are being taped for broadcast. These include the highly popular Phil Donahue and David Letterman shows. To request free tickets for programmes made by **ABC,** **CBS** and **NBC**, write to each company individually. Another good source of free tickets is the New York Convention and Visitors Bureau *(see p352)*. On weekday mornings on 5th Ave around **Rockefeller Plaza**, free tickets for a number of TV programmes are sometimes distributed by the programme's production staff. There's absolutely no way that you can plan for this. It's simply a matter of good luck and being in the right place at the right time.

For those who want to get a glimpse of what goes on behind the scenes of TV, NBC organizes studio tours, usually from 9am to 4pm Monday to Saturday.

CHOOSING WHAT TO SEE

IF YOU FEEL bewildered by the huge range of films on offer in New York, have a look at the detailed listings found in the art sections of *New York* magazine, the *New York Times*, the *Village Voice* and *The New Yorker*. "Moviephone", a free telephone service, gives recorded information on details of all the latest films. For the first run of a film, you can expect to pay around $7.50.

FILM VENUES

68th St Playhouse
3rd Ave.
Map 13 B1.
C 734-0302.

ABC
See p329.

American Museum of the Moving Image
35th Ave and 36th St
Astoria, Queens.
C (718) 784-0077.

American Museum of Natural History
Central Park W at 79th St.
Map 16 D5.
C 769-5650.

Angelika Film Center
18 W Houston St.
Map 4 E3.
C 995-2000.

Anthology Film Archives
32 2nd Ave at 2nd St.
Map 5 C2.
C 505-5181.

Asia Society
725 Park Ave. **Map** 13 A1.
C 517-2742.

Carnegie Hall Cinema
7th Ave at 56th St.
Map 12 E3.
C 265-2520.

CBS
See p329.

Cinema 3
2 W 59th St.
Map 12 F3.
C 752-5959.

Cinema Village
22 E 12th St.
Map 4 F1.
C 924-3363.

Film Forum
209 W Houston St.
Map 3 C3.
C 727-8110.

French Institute
55 E 59th St.
Map 12 F3.
C 355-6160.

Moviephone
C 777-FILM.

Museum of Modern Art
11 W 53rd St.
Map 12 F4.
C 708-9480.

Museum of Television & Radio
25 W 52nd St.
Map 12 F4.
C 621-6600.

NBC
See p329.

New York Film Festival
C 875-5600.

Public Theater
425 Lafayette St.
Map 4 F4.
C 539-8500.

Rockefeller Plaza
47th–50th St, 5th Ave.
Map 12 F5.

Walter Reade Theater/Film Society of the Lincoln Center
70 Lincoln Center Plaza.
Map 12 D2.
C 875-5600.

Whitney Museum of American Art
945 Madison Ave.
Map 13 A1.
C 570-3600.

Classical and Contemporary Music

NEW YORKERS HAVE A voracious appetite for music. Live concerts by the world's most celebrated musical performers may be enjoyed at famous halls throughout the year, and younger, newer artists and exotic imports find welcoming audiences.

PRACTICALITIES

FIND OUT WHAT's on in New York by checking out the listings in the *New York Times* and the *Village Voice* newspapers, and in *New York Time Out* and *The New Yorker* magazines.

CLASSICAL MUSIC

THE ORCHESTRA in residence at **Avery Fisher Hall** in Lincoln Center *(see p213)* is the New York Philharmonic. It is also the annual venue for the popular "Mostly Mozart" series and Young People's Concerts. The **Alice Tully Hall**, in Lincoln Center, is an acoustic gem and home to the Chamber Music Society.

One of the world's premier concert halls is the revamped **Carnegie Hall** *(see p146)*. Upstairs in the Weill Recital Hall there are quality performances for reasonable prices.

The **Brooklyn Academy of Music (BAM)** *(see p246)* is the home of the Brooklyn Philharmonic, which has recently gone into partnership with the Metropolitan Opera to produce lesser-known works.

The **Merkin Concert Hall** is host to some top chamber ensembles and soloists. For really excellent acoustics, go to the **Town Hall**. The **92nd Street Y** Kaufmann Concert Hall also offers a lively menu of music and dance. Popular museum venues include the **Museum of Modern Art's** sculpture garden for chamber and contemporary music, the

Frick Collection and the **Symphony Space**, both of which offer a varied programme ranging from gospel to Gershwin, classical to ethnic. The beautiful Grace Rainey Rogers Auditorium in the **Metropolitan Museum of Art** is for chamber music and soloists, while **Bargemusic**, in Brooklyn, presents chamber music and soloists against the stunning backdrop of Manhattan's famous skyline.

The **Juilliard School of Music** and the **Mannes College of Music** are both considered excellent. Their students and faculties give lots of free recitals, and there are shows by many leading orchestras, chamber music groups and opera companies. The **Manhattan School of Music** offers an excellent program of over 400 events per year, from classical to jazz.

At 9.45am on the Thursdays of the New York Philharmonic concerts, the evening show is rehearsed at **Avery Fisher Hall** in Lincoln Center. Audiences are often admitted to listen, and rehearsal tickets are available at low prices. Phone beforehand to check.

OPERA

DOMINATING the city's operatic scene is **Lincoln Center** *(see p212)*, home to the New York City Opera, and the **Metropolitan Opera House**, which has its own operatic company. The Met is the jewel in the crown, offering top international performers, but it is often criticized for being unadventurous. More accessible and dynamic is the New York City Opera. Its performances range from *Madame Butterfly* to *South Pacific*, with subtitles above the stage to help the audience understand the plot.

Lower-priced, quality performances are staged by the

up-and-coming singers at the **Village Light Opera Group**, the **Amato Opera Theater**, the **American Chamber Opera Co**, and the students at the **Juilliard Opera Center** in Lincoln Center.

CONTEMPORARY MUSIC

NEW YORK is one of the most important places in the world for contemporary music. Exotic, ethnic and experimental music is played in many first-rate venues. The **Brooklyn Academy of Music (BAM)** is the standard-bearer of the avant-garde. Each autumn the Academy holds a festival of music and dance called "Next Wave" which has helped launch the careers of many musicians, including Philip Glass.

An annual festival of serious modern music called "Bang on a Can" is performed at the **Ethical Culture Society Hall** and features composers like Pierre Boulez and John Cage. Experimentalists, such as Davie Weinstein with his "audio-visual acid test" music – a mix of CD players, amplified instruments, keyboards and sound effects – perform at the **Dance Theater Workshop**.

Other venues include the **Asia Society** *(see p185)*, with its jewel of a theatre for many visiting Asian performers, and **St Peter's Church**.

BACKSTAGE TOURS

BEHIND-THE-SCENES tours are offered by **Lincoln Center** and **Carnegie Hall**, which also holds a "Tour and Tea" package in the Russian Tea Room *(see p147)*.

RELIGIOUS MUSIC

FEW EXPERIENCES are more moving than an Easter concert in the vast **Cathedral of St John the Divine** *(see pp224–5)*. Seasonal music is also offered at many of the city's museums, and in almost every other available space, from Grand Central Station's main concourse *(see pp154–5)* to bank and hotel lobbies.

CLASSICAL RADIO
New York has four good FM radio stations that broadcast classical (and a selection of other) music: WQXR at 96.3, WKCR at 89.9, WNYC at 93.9 and WNCN at 104.3.

For jazz vespers in a stunning modern building, visit **St Peter's Church** (see p175). Most of these concerts are free for everyone, but you are encouraged to contribute.

AL FRESCO

FREE OUTDOOR concerts during the summer are to be found in **Bryant Park**, **Washington Square** and **Lincoln Center's Damrosch Park**. The annual concerts on Central Park's Great Lawn and in Brooklyn's Prospect Park are performed by the New York Philharmonic and the Metropolitan Opera. In good weather keep a look out for all the strolling musicians who perform at South Street Seaport, right on the steps of the **Metropolitan Museum of Art** (see pp188–95) and also around Washington Square.

MUSIC FOR FREE

THROUGHOUT the year free musical performances are given at the **Citicorp Atrium** (see p175), the fascinating **IBM Garden Plaza** (see p168), **The Cloisters** (see pp234–7) and the **Whitney Museum's** Philip Morris Building (see p150). Sunday afternoon recitals are held at **The Dairy** in Central Park (see p206). You will also find music in the Winter Garden and Plaza of the **World Financial Center** (see p69) and **Federal Hall** (see p68). At **Lincoln Center** be sure not to miss the free performances held in the **Juilliard School of Music** and the **Library Museum of the Performing Arts**.

Other very popular venues include the **Mark Goodson Theater** (for chamber music) and the **Theodore Roosevelt Birthplace** (see p125).

Free concerts and talks in churches include **St Paul's Chapel** and the **Trinity Church** (see p68).

MUSIC VENUES

92nd Street Y
1395 Lexington Ave.
Map 17 A2.
996-1100.

Amato Opera Theater
319 Bowery at 2nd St.
Map 4 F2.
228-8200.

American Chamber Opera Co
6 E 87th St. **Map** 16 F3.
781-0857.

Asia Society
70th St at Park Ave.
Map 13 A1.
517-2742.

Backstage Tours
903-9790.

Bargemusic
Fulton Ferry Landing,
Brooklyn. **Map** 2 F2.
(718) 624-4061.

Brooklyn Academy of Music
30 Lafayette Ave, Brooklyn.
(718) 636-4100.

Bryant Park
Map 8 F1.
983-4143.

Carnegie Hall
881 7th Ave. **Map** 12 E3.
247-7800.

Cathedral of St John the Divine
Amsterdam Ave and
112th St.
Map 20 E4.
316-7400.

Citicorp Atrium
Lexington Ave at 53rd St.
Map 13 A4.
559-9095.

The Cloisters
Fort Tryon Park.
923-3700.

The Dairy
Central Park. **Map** 12 F2.
794-6564.

Dance Theater Workshop
See Dance p335.

Ethical Culture Society Hall
2 W 64th St. **Map** 12 D2.
874-5210.

Federal Hall
Broad St at Wall St.
Map 1 C3.
866-2086.

Frick Collection
1 E 70th St. **Map** 12 F1.
288-0700.

IBM Garden Plaza
590 Madison Ave.
Map 13 A3.
745-3500.

Lincoln Center
155 W 65th St.
Map 11 C2.
875-5400.

Alice Tully Hall
875-5050.

Avery Fisher Hall
875-5030.

Damrosch Park
875-5400.

Juilliard Opera Center
769-7406.

Juilliard School of Music
799-5000.

Library Museum of the Performing Arts
870-1630.

Metropolitan Opera House
362-6000.

Manhattan School of Music
120 Claremont Ave.
Map 20 E2.
749-2802.

Mannes College of Music
150 W 85th St.
Map 15 D3.
580-0210.

Mark Goodson Theater
2 Columbus Circle.
Map 12 D3.
841-4100.

Merkin Concert Hall
129 W 67th St. **Map** 11 D2.
362-8719.

Metropolitan Museum of Art
5th Ave at 82nd St.
Map 16 F4.
570-3949.

Museum of Modern Art
Sculpture garden
11 W 53rd St. **Map** 12 F4.
708-9480.

NYC On Stage
1501 Broadway.
Map 12 D2.
768-1818.

St Paul's Chapel
Broadway at Fulton St.
Map 1 C2.
602-0747.

St Peter's Church
54th St at Lexington Ave.
Map 13 A4.
935-2200.

Symphony Space
2537 Broadway.
Map 15 C2.
864-5400.

Theodore Roosevelt Birthplace
28 E 20th St.
Map 8 F5.
260-1616.

Town Hall
123 W 44th St.
Map 12 E5.
840-2824.

Trinity Church
Broadway at Wall St.
Map 1 C3.
602-0800.

Village Light Opera Group
227 W 27th St. **Map** 8 E3.
279-4200.

Washington Square
Map 4 D2.

Whitney Museum
(Philip Morris Building)
Park Ave at 42nd St.
Map 9 A1.
878-2550.

World Financial Center
West St at Vesey St.
Map 1 A2.
945-0505.

Rock, Jazz and World Music

THERE'S EVERY IMAGINABLE form of music in New York, from stadium rock to the sounds of the 1960s, Dixieland jazz or country blues, soul and world music and street musicians. The city's music scene changes at a dizzying pace, with many new arrivals (and departures) almost daily, so there's no way to predict what you may find when you arrive. Musical standards also vary.

PRICES AND PLACES

AT CLUBS EXPECT a cover charge and possibly a one- or two-drink minimum (at $5 or more) requirement. The prices for concerts range from $8 to $40 for the major venues, with about $12 to $15 the norm. Many of the smaller concert venues are arranged for seating in certain areas and dancing in others – often with different prices for each.

The top international bands are usually to be found in the huge arenas at **Shea Stadium** in Flushing Meadows or at **Meadowlands** and **Madison Square Garden** *(see p133)*. Here the likes of Elton John, Bruce Springsteen and David Bowie perform. Tickets for these events sell out very fast, so buy as many as you need as soon as you hear of a concert, unless you don't mind paying a lot for them through an agent or ticket tout. During the summer, big outdoor concerts are held at Jones Beach *(see p253)* and **Central Park SummerStage**.

Medium-sized venues for mainstream bands include the Art Deco palace of **Radio City Music Hall** and the **Beacon Theater**, by far the most popular live music venue in the Upper West Side area.

Many leading rock venues are basically bars with music. They will often book different bands every night, so check the listings in the *New York Times*, *Village Voice*, *New York* magazine or phone the venue to find out what's happening and at what time during that particular week.

ROCK MUSIC

ROCK COMES IN many forms: gothic, industrial, techno, psychedelic, post-punk funk, indie and alternative music are among the latest crazes. If you prefer to see more of a band than a giant video screen, the following venues have a much more intimate, friendly atmosphere and culturally significant **CBGB**, New York's sleazy, dungeon-like cradle of new wave, launched bands such as The New York Dolls, Talking Heads and Blondie in the 1970s and is still a showcase for new indie bands.

The **Knitting Factory** has live jazz and new music. The **Limelight** is a good bet for the latest sounds and the newest groups. **The Mercury Lounge** is another of the most happening music spots, featuring hot new bands being groomed for MTV. **Tramps** is in a loft where relatively unknown rock groups play, as do the occasional famous country and blues musicians. Mega-star Bruce Springsteen played his first recorded concert in the 1970s at the **Bottom Line**, and it still remains a record industry showcase for new and up-and-coming bands.

Bands appearing at the **Academy** range from indie stalwarts such as Ride and the Soupdragons to Ice-T's controversial Body Count. Located in the old meat-packing district, **The Cooler** is a hip new home for ravers. Alternative rock, avant-garde jazz and innovative DJs make this a great place to dance. The subterranean space is huge and wild.

The **Palladium** is a vast, old theatre which has been really spectacularly revamped for dancing and rock concerts. **Roulette** continues New York's tradition of pioneering innovative music and has avant-garde sounds which are performed by appropriately named groups such as Woof, Quack and Miaow.

JAZZ

THE ORIGINAL Cotton Club and Connie's Inn which were once crucibles of jazz are long gone, as are the former speakeasies of West 52nd Street. But some living legends still play, while others carry on the old traditions of Duke Ellington, Count Basie and other big bands.

In Greenwich Village jazz temples from the 1930s survive today and continue to foster great music. Foremost among them is the **Village Vanguard**, where some of the most highly revered jazz memories linger and newer ones are being fashioned by groups such as the McCoy Tyner and Branford Marsalis trios. **Blue Note** hosts big bands at high prices but has an excellent atmosphere.

The **Knitting Factory** and the **Bottom Line** tend to feature much more contemporary and avant-garde jazz, while **Zinno** offers an appealing blend of northern Italian food and guest appearances by some top-flight musicians.

The **Birdland** features ex-Mingus alumni and musicians such as Bud Shank. Expect the great sounds of Dixieland jazz or small unknown groups in **Cajun**, a friendly, New Orleans-style restaurant.

Michael's Pub features jazz-pop singers and revues. Its really big draw is the New Orleans Funeral and Ragtime Orchestra, a Dixieland septet of uneven capabilities, which has been led by clarinettist-cum-film-maker Woody Allen on most Monday nights for the last 23 years.

One of the hottest tickets in town is the Sunday jazz brunch at **Sweet Basil**, which often features the trumpeter Doc Cheatham and his band. A sophisticated newcomer, club and restaurant **Iridium** features progressive jazz. **Time Café** presents the Mingus Big Band workshop every Wednesday. If you are ever in New York in June, don't miss the annual **JVC Jazz Festival**, where famous jazz icons such as Oscar Peterson, Nina Simone and BB King are still actively making music at various venues all around Manhattan. For any information phone beforehand.

The end of July sees the annual Classical Jazz Series at Lincoln Center's **Alice Tully Hall**. The music ranges from Duke Ellington's New York sounds, under the direction of Wynton Marsalis, to Johnny Dodds' traditional New Orleans-style jazz.

FOLK AND COUNTRY MUSIC

FOLK, ROCK MUSIC and R&B (rhythm and blues) can be found at the famed but much faded **Bitter End**, which once showcased James Taylor and

Joni Mitchell, but currently specializes in new talent as does **Kenny's Castaways**, a bar for local hopefuls.

For state-of-the-art folk music with an Irish flavour, try **Sin-e**. You might catch Sinead O'Connor giving an unadvertised performance. Also good for folk, check out the **Sidewalk Café**.

BLUES, SOUL AND WORLD MUSIC

FOR BLUES, soul and world music, options include the **Apollo Theater** in Harlem (see p228). For nearly 60 years the near legendary Wednesday Amateur Nights have "discovered" stars such as James Brown and Dionne Warwick. **China Club** is a

soul music venue which also stages rock groups and hosts impromptu jamming by visiting rock stars. There is also dancing. This is currently one of the hottest places in town to be seen.

The **Cotton Club** is not the original venue, but it does offer top blues, jazz and a real Sunday gospel brunch on Harlem's main street. **Manny's Car Wash** runs the gamut of blues, rock and soul with appearances by the likes of Bo Diddley Jr, Tino Gonzales and a free Sunday "Blues Jam". Don't miss "Mambo Mondays" with Nestor Torres at **SOB's** (Sounds of Brazil), a world music venue specializing in the many Afro-Latin rhythms. Finally, there's **Wetlands**, a classic soul music venue.

DIRECTORY

MUSIC VENUES

Beacon Theater
2124 Broadway.
Map 15 C5.
496-7070.

Central Park SummerStage
Rumsey Playfield.
Map 12 F1.
360-2777.

Madison Square Garden
7th Ave 33rd St.
Map 8 E2.
465-MSG1.

Meadowlands
50 Route 120
East Rutherford, N J.
(201) 935-3900.

Radio City Music Hall
See Dance p335.

Shea Stadium
126th St at Roosevelt Ave.
Flushing, Queens.
(718) 507-8499.

ROCK MUSIC

Academy
234 W 43rd St. **Map** 8 E1.
249-8870.

Bottom Line
15 W 4th St. **Map** 4 D2.
228-6300.

CBGB
315 Bowery. **Map** 4 F2.
982-4052.

Cooler
416 W 14th St. **Map** 3 B1.
229-0785.

Knitting Factory
47 E Houston St. **Map** 4 F3.
219-3055.

Limelight
47 W 20th St. **Map** 8 F4.
473-7171.

Mercury Lounge
217 E Houston St.
Map 5 A3. 260-4700.

Palladium
126 E 14th St. **Map** 4 F1.
473-7171.

Roulette
228 W Broadway. **Map** 4 E5.
219-8242.

Tramps
45 W 21st St. **Map** 8 F4.
727-7788.

JAZZ

Alice Tully Hall
See Classical Music p339.

Birdland
2745 Broadway. **Map** 22 E5.
581-3080.

Blue Note
131 W 3rd St. **Map** 4 D2.
475-8592.

Bottom Line
See Rock Music.

Cajun
129 8th Ave. **Map** 8 D5.
691-6174.

Iridium
44 W63rd St. **Map** 12 D2.
582 2121.

JVC Jazz Festival
501-1390.

Knitting Factory
See Rock Music.

Michael's Pub
211 E 55th St. **Map** 13 B4.
758-2272.

Sweet Basil
88 7th Ave S. **Map** 8 E5.
242-1785.

Time Café
380 Lafayette St. **Map** 4 F2.
533-7000.

Village Vanguard
178 7th Ave South.
Map 3 C1.
255-4037.

Zinno
126 W 13th St.
Map 3 C1.
924-5182.

FOLK AND COUNTRY

Bitter End
147 Bleecker St.
Map 4 E3.
673-7030.

Kenny's Castaways
157 Bleecker St. **Map** 4 E3.
473-9870.

Sidewalk Café
94 Ave A.
Map 5 B2.
473-7373.

Sin-e
122 St Mark's Pl.
Map 5 A2.
982-0370.

BLUES, SOUL AND WORLD MUSIC

Apollo Theatre
253 W 125 St.
Map 19 A1.
749-5838.

China Club
2130 Broadway.
Map 15 C5.
877-1166.

Cotton Club
666 W 125th St.
Map 22 F2.
663-7980.

Manny's Car Wash
1558 3rd Ave.
Map 17 B3.
369-2583.

SOB's
204 Varick St.
Map 4 D3.
243-4940.

Wetlands
161 Hudson St.
Map 4 D5.
966-4225.

Clubs, Dance Halls and Piano Bars

NEW YORK'S NIGHTLIFE and club scene is legendary. Whatever your preference – be it for a noisy disco, stand-up comedy or the soothing melodies of a Harry Connick, Jr soundalike in a piano bar – you'll be really spoilt for choice. There was a rash of big discos in the 1980s, but relatively few of these have survived the recent trend towards the comfort and style of "supper clubs".

PRACTICALITIES

THE BEST and hippest time for clubbing is during the week – it's also a lot cheaper. Take a fair amount of money and some ID to prove you're old enough to drink (which is over 21) but beware, all the drinks are very expensive.

The trendiest clubs roll on until 4am or later. Fashions and club nights change all the time, so go to Tower Records on Broadway for all the latest leaflets, check club details in the listings magazines (see p328) and read the Village Voice. The most interesting places nowadays are often popularized by word of mouth. Your best bet is to go somewhere like the **Limelight** and hope someone will tell you where to go on to – often invitations to other clubs are given out there as well.

DANCING

NEW YORKERS thrive on music and dancing. The dance floors available all around the city range from the handkerchief-sized **Hors d'Oeuvrerie** – for jazz, dancing, a 107th-floor view, and hors d'oeuvres – to a few huge basketball-court-sized places, such as the **Roseland**. This has ballroom dancing every Thursday and Sunday and is New York's classic Broadway ballroom, revealing a tantalizing glimpse of older Broadway culture. It also has a decent, mega-size, 700-seater restaurant-cum-bar.

For mainstream, danceable music, the **Rainbow Room** is reliable. For rock and roll, there's the fun **China Club**, and if you want something really different, try **Barbetta**, where Boris and Yvgeny play a combination of gypsy music and Viennese waltzes. The **Copacabana**, which when it originally opened starred the likes of Dean Martin and Frank Sinatra, is now a disco alternating with live bands. It also stages wild parties on the last Thursday of every month with go-go boys, drag queens and disco divas, so prepare either to be outrageous, or to be outraged.

The **Limelight**, which started as an enormous 1980s disco, has been transformed into a mixed venue which has ground-floor dancing as well as spectator seats up in the balconies. It always advertises upcoming features. To book tickets ahead telephone Ticketmaster (see p329).

Some of the most popular clubs for disco dancing, which also feature the latest music groups, are Ritz, the Academy, Marquee, CBGB, Tramps, Manny's Carwash and the Knitting Factory (see p340). Few of these have strict membership policies. Be sure to get there early and be prepared to queue for entry.

NIGHTCLUBS

NIGHTCLUBS are the places to see a show. New York shows are less flashy than in the 1940s and 1950s, but still have a variety of acts. Expect to pay a cover charge; many of the clubs also require that you have at least two drinks.

The Ballroom is a simple, breezy room which adjoins a Spanish restaurant and often has vocalists singing hits from Broadway musicals. **Maxim's** usually has one room open that features revues, and another with singers. For some spectacular views, an elegant room, revues and singers, go to the **Rainbow & Stars**. **Swing Street Café** is a theatre supper club. The smart **Supper Club** surrounds you with gold lamé draperies and features big band music downstairs. Cabaret singers perform upstairs in their intimate Blue Room. **Tatou** is very expensive to eat in, and acts range from jazz to disco. Central Park's venerable indoors/outdoors **Tavern on the Green** now offers jazz in its Chestnut Room.

GAY AND LESBIAN VENUES

THE PAST TWO decades have seen the arrival of clubs and restaurants specifically geared to gay and lesbian clientele. Although the entertainment is varied, transvestite revues predominate. Though all the clubs are open to heterosexuals and often to the opposite sex too, some can make "interlopers" feel extremely uncomfortable. The current popular gay cabarets include **Duplex**, which has a mix of stand-up comics and comedy sketches. The very fashionable nightclubs and bars for men include the trendy, uptown **Town House**, a piano bar with restaurant, and **Julius**, known as Greenwich Village's top neighbourhood bar. **Don't Tell Mama** is a long-established gay bar, with musical revues and spoofs.

Henrietta Hudson and **Crazy Nanny's** cater solely for women, as does **Grolier**. **Marie's Crisis** piano bar is a mixed venue and **Splash** is open daily with a happy hour between 5pm and 9pm.

The Village Voice has good listings of what's happening in the gay communities, and the Gay Yellow Pages covers the gay scene. If you need more information phone the **Gay and Lesbian Switchboard**.

COMEDY SHOWCASES

MANY OF New York's best current comedy clubs or showcases have evolved from earlier "improvisational" comedy. Leading the pack are the **Boston Comedy Club**, **Improvisation** and

Caroline's. Also good for a visit are the **Comic Strip**, **Stand-Up New York**, **Rebar**, **55 Grove St**, **Dangerfield's**, and **Comedy Cellar**. Each club presents a nightly batch of comics.

PIANO BARS AND HOTEL "ROOMS"

CABARETS HAVE become a New York institution. Such cosy, just-for-listening places are often called "rooms" and are located in hotels. Most operate from Tuesday to Saturday (usually with a cover charge or drink minimum) and most take credit cards.

The **Algonquin's** Oak Room has had song stylists such as Michael Feinstein. For a classic piano lounge with a panoramic Manhattan view visit the **Beekman Tower**. The "long-distance hummer" award goes to the suave and sophisticated Bobby Short, who has played his piano for over a quarter of a century at the atmospheric Café Carlyle in the **Carlyle Hotel**. Located in the same hotel is the

Bemelman's Bar, which is decorated with whimsical murals and attracts a crowd who enjoy the urbaneness of first-class crooners.

Hear tinkling keys and fine songs in the lounge of the **Drake Swissôtel**. Performers such as Barbara Cook play the **Hilton Hotel's** Club 53 and Café Pierre's singer-pianist Kathleen Landis holds court at the **Pierre Hotel**. Piano music is heard at the Ambassador Lounge in the **UN Plaza Park Hyatt Hotel**.

DIRECTORY

DANCING

Barbetta
321 W 46th St.
Map 12 D5.
📞 246-9171.

China Club
See p341.

Copacabana
617 W 57th St.
Map 11 B3.
📞 582-2672.

Hors d'Oeuvrerie
1 World Trade Center.
Map 1 B2.
📞 938-1111.

Knitting Factory
See p341.

Limelight
See p341.

Rainbow Room
30 Rockefeller Plaza.
Map 12 F4.
📞 632-5100.

Roseland
239 W 52nd St.
Map 12 E4.
📞 247-0200.

NIGHTCLUBS

The Ballroom
253 W 28th St.
Map 8 E3.
📞 244-3005.

Maxim's
680 Madison Ave.
Map 13 A3.
📞 751-5111.

Rainbow & Stars
30 Rockefeller Plaza.
Map 12 F4.
📞 632-5000.

Supper Club
240 W 47th St.
Map 12 D5.
📞 921-1940.

Swing Street Café
253 E 52nd St.
Map 13 B4.
📞 754-4862.

Tatou
151 E 50th St. **Map** 13 A4.
📞 753-1144.

Tavern on the Green
Central Park west side at 67th St.
Map 12 D2.
📞 873-3200.

GAY AND LESBIAN VENUES

Crazy Nanny's
21 7th Ave South.
Map 3 C1.
📞 366-6312.

Don't Tell Mama
343 W 46th St.
Map 12 D5.
📞 757-0788.

Duplex
61 Christopher St.
Map 3 C2.
📞 255-5438.

Gay and Lesbian Switchboard
📞 777-1800.

Henrietta Hudson
438 Hudson St.
Map 3 C3.
📞 243-9079.

Julius
159 W 10th St.
Map 4 D1.
📞 929-9672.

Marie's Crisis Café
59 Grove St.
Map 3 C2.
📞 243-9323.

Town House
236 E 58th St.
Map 13 B4.
📞 754-4649.

COMEDY SHOWCASES

55 Grove St
Map 3 C2.
📞 366-5438.

Boston Comedy Club
82 W 3rd St. **Map** 4 D2.
📞 477-1000.

Caroline's
1626 Broadway.
Map 12 E5.
📞 757-4100.

Comedy Cellar
117 MacDougal St.
Map 4 D2.
📞 254-3480.

Comic Strip
1568 2nd Ave.
Map 17 B4.
📞 861-9386.

Dangerfield's
1118 1st Ave.
Map 13 C3.
📞 593-1650.

Improvisation
433 W 34th St.
Map 7 C2.
📞 279-3446.

Rebar
127 W 16th St. **Map** 8 E5.
📞 627-1680.

Stand-Up New York
236 W 78th St.
Map 15 C5.
📞 595-0850.

PIANO BARS AND HOTEL "ROOMS"

Algonquin Hotel
Oak Room, 59 W 44th St.
Map 12 F5.
📞 840-6800.

Beekman Tower
3 Mitchell Pl.
Map 13 C5.
📞 355-7300.

Carlyle Hotel
35 E 76th St.
Map 17 A5.
📞 744-1600.

Drake Swissôtel
440 Park Ave.
Map 13 A3.
📞 421-0900.

Hilton Hotel
Club 53, 53 Ave of the Americas. **Map** 12 E4.
📞 586-7000.

Pierre Hotel
Café Pierre, 2 E 61st St.
Map 12 F3.
📞 940-8185.

UN Plaza Park Hyatt Hotel
1 UN Plaza at 44th St.
Map 13 C5.
📞 758-1234.

Sport and Fitness

NEW YORKERS ARE SPORT-MAD, and there are activities to suit every taste. If you're a doer not a viewer, you can choose from health clubs and horseback riding to pumping iron and swimming, playing tennis or jogging. Spectator sport is provided by two professional baseball teams, two hockey teams, a basketball team and two football teams, while for tennis fans there are the US Open and Virginia Slims tournaments.

PRACTICALITIES

THE EASIEST WAY to get hold of your tickets is through Ticketron or Ticketmaster (see p329). For the big games, you may need a ticket agent.

AMERICAN FOOTBALL

THE CITY'S two professional American football teams are the New York Giants and the New York Jets. They both play home games across the river at **Giants Stadium** in New Jersey. Tickets for the Giants are almost impossible to obtain, but they may be available for the Jets.

BASEBALL

TO CAPTURE the essence of this American institution, first-time spectators should go to **Yankee Stadium**, home of the New York Yankees. **Shea Stadium**, the Mets' base, is also convenient. The season runs from April to September.

BASKETBALL

THE NEW YORK KNICKS play their home games from October to April at **Madison Square Garden**; you may also catch the ever-popular Harlem Globetrotters there.

BICYCLING

THE BEST PLACE to cycle is in Central Park during the weekend, when it is closed to cars. Bikes may be hired from **AAA Bicycle Rentals**.

BOXING

PROFESSIONAL boxing matches are more often seen on Paramount's wide TV screen than in the flesh at **Madison Square Garden**.

FITNESS CENTRES, GYMS AND HEALTH CLUBS

FACILITIES INCLUDING jogging tracks, Nautilus and swimming pools are now found in hotels such as the UN Plaza or Peninsula (see pp280–81). Many of the commercial gyms and health clubs are only open to those with an annual membership, but it is possible to use the facilities at a **YMCA** if you are a member, or buy a day pass.

GOLF

PRACTISE YOUR swing at the **Randalls Island Golf Center** or play mini-golf at the **Wollman Memorial Rink**. The city owns several courses in the boroughs, such as **Pelham Bay Park** in the Bronx and **Silver Lake** on Staten Island. For information, call 360-8204; or to make a reservation, phone 225-GOLF.

HORSE-RIDING AND RACING

THE ONLY riding stable in Manhattan is **Claremont Riding Academy**. You can ride in its indoor arena, or go hacking in Central Park.

Harness racing, in which horses pull small buggies, takes place all year round at **Yonkers Raceway**. Flat racing is held daily, except Tuesday, from October to May at the **Aqueduct Race Track**, and from May to October at the **Belmont Park Race Track**.

ICE HOCKEY

THE ICE FLIES, as do the players' fists, when the New York Rangers meet their competition at **Madison Square Garden**. The season runs from October to April.

ICE SKATING

THE OUTDOOR Rockefeller **Plaza Rink** is glamorous. **Lasker Skating (City) Rink** is an outdoor pool in summer. The **Wollman Memorial Rink** has ice skating in winter, roller skating and mini-golf in summer. Indoor sites include **Rivergate Ice Rink** and the **Ice Studio**.

INDOOR SPORTS AND RACQUET GAMES

A LARGE SPORTS complex called **Hackers, Hitters & Hoops** has batting cages, mini-golf, ping-pong, racquet-ball (similar to squash) and other activities. There's also the **Printing House Fitness & Racquet Center**.

JOGGING

SOME PARKS are safe for joggers, others are not, so be guided by your concierge. None is safe after dark, at dusk or before dawn. The most popular route is around the reservoir in Central Park. The **International Running Center** has weekly running clinics and races.

MARATHON

TO BE ONE of the 25,000 who enter the New York marathon, you have to sign up six months in advance. The race is held on the first Sunday in November. Phone 860-4455 for information.

SPORTS BARS

TOP BARS include **The Sporting Club**, which has a huge electronic scoreboard with right-up-to-the-second information, and nine life-size TV screens. At **Mickey Mantle's** you can watch the fixtures on ten elephantine video screens.

SWIMMING

MANY MANHATTAN hotels have pools with free access during your stay. If yours does not, look for the public pools listed in the Yellow Pages "Government Offices" section. There are also various outdoor pools.

Try the spectacular Jones Beach State Park *(see p253)* along Long Island's shoreline.

TENNIS

THE TOP TENNIS tournament in New York is the US Open, played each August at the **National Tennis Center**. Also good is the women's Virginia Slims Championships in November at **Madison Square Garden** *(see p133)*.

If you want to play tennis rather than watch it, look in the telephone directory under

"Tennis Courts: Public and Private". For private courts, you can expect to pay up to about $50 an hour. For public courts, you will need a $50 permit, available from the **NY City Parks & Recreation Department**. You will also need an identity card before you are allowed on to play. Courts must be reserved at least a week in advance. **Crosstown Tennis** and the **Manhattan Plaza Tennis Center** are two possibilities.

TRACK AND FIELD

THE MILLROSE GAMES are normally held in the beginning of February and the

Amateur Athletic Union (AAU) championships, where most of the top athletes usually appear, in late February at **Madison Square Garden**.

OTHER ACTIVITIES

IN CENTRAL PARK, options include hiring rowing boats from **Loeb Boathouse** or playing chess – pick up the pieces from The Dairy *(see p206)*. Bowling is available at the **Leisure Time Recreation Center**. Pool is catered for in bars and pool halls such as the **Julian Billiard Academy** and **Chelsea Billiards**. Further afield are fishing trips from **Sheepshead Bay**.

SPORTS ADDRESSES

AAA Bicycle Rentals
The Boathouse, Central Park. **Map** 16 F5.
(775-1800.

Aqueduct Race Track
Ozone Park, Queens.
((718) 641-4700.

Belmont Park Race Track
Hempstead Turnpike, Long Island.
((718) 641-4700.

Chelsea Billiards
54 W 21st St. **Map** 8 E4.
(989-0096.

Claremont Riding Academy
175 W 89th St.
Map 15 C3.
(724-5100.

Crosstown Tennis
14 W 31st St.
Map 8 F3.
(947-5780.

Giants Stadium
Meadowlands
East Rutherford, N J.
((201) 935-8222. *New York Giants.*
((201) 935-8500. *New York Jets.*

Hackers, Hitters & Hoops
123 W 18th St. **Map** 8 E5.
(929-7482.

Ice Studio
1034 Lexington Ave.
Map 17 A5.
(535-0304.

International Running Center
9 E 89th St. **Map** 17 A3.
(860-4455.

Julian Billiard Academy
138 E 14th St.
Map 4 F1.
(598-9884.

Lasker Skating (City) Rink
110th St at Lenox Ave.
Map 21 B4.
(996-1184.

Leisure Time Recreation Center
625 8th Ave. **Map** 8 D1.
(268-6909.

Loeb Boathouse
Central Park. **Map** 16 F5.
(517-4723.

Madison Square Garden
7th Ave at 33rd St.
Map 8 E2.
(465-MSG1.

Manhattan Plaza Tennis Center
450 W 43rdSt.
Map 7 C1.
(594-0554.

Mickey Mantle's
42 Central Park South.
Map 12 E3.
(688-7777.

National Tennis Center
Flushing Meadows Park, Queens.
((718) 760-6200.

NY City Parks & Recreation Department
Arsenal Building
64th St and 5th Ave.
Map 12 F2.
(408-0100.

Pelham Bay Park
Bronx.
((718) 885-1258

Plaza Tennis
Rockefeller Center.
1 Rockefeller Plaza, 5th Ave.
Map 12 F5.
(332-7654.

Printing House Fitness & Racquet Center
422 Hudson St.
Map 3 C3.
(243-3777.

Randalls Island Golf Center
Randalls Island.
Map 22 F2.
(427-5689.

Rivergate Ice Rink
401 E 34th St.
Map 9 C2.
(689-0035.

Shea Stadium
126th St at Roosevelt Ave, Flushing, Queens.
((718) 507-TIXX or (718) 507-8499.

Sheepshead Bay
(For information on fishing trips call Mike's Tackle & Bait Shop.)
((718) 646-9261.

Silver Lake
915 Victory Blvd
Staten Island.
((718) 447-5686 or (718) 225-4653.

The Sporting Club
99 Hudson St.
Map 4 D5.
(219-0900.

Wollman Memorial Rink
Central Park. 5th Ave at 59th St. **Map** 12 F2.
(396-1010.

Yankee Stadium
River Ave at 161st St
The Bronx.
((718) 293-6000.

YMCA 47th St
224 E 47th St.
Map 13 B5.
(756-9600

YMCA 92nd St
1395 Lexington Ave.
Map 17 A2.
(427-6000.

YMCA West Side
5 W 63rd St.
Map 12 D2.
(787-4400.

Yonkers Raceway
Yonkers
Westchester County.
((914) 968-4200.

Late-Night New York

N EW YORK IS INDEED a city that never sleeps. If you wake up in the middle of the night – with a craving for fresh bread, a need to be entertained or an urge to watch the sun rise over the Manhattan skyline – there are plenty of options to choose from.

BARS AND CLUBS

T HE BEST and friendliest bars are often the Irish ones. Singalongs happen at **Katie O'Toole's** on Thursdays, and daily (except Mondays) at **Tommy Makem's**. Have a late-night dry martini at the **Temple Bar**. The best piano bars are in the hotels: try the Café Carlyle in the **Carlyle Hotel** or the Oak Room in the **Algonquin Hotel**.

For hot American jazz until 4am, go to **Sweet Basil** or the **Blue Note**. Traditional jazz and swing entertain the diners and dancers at the **Rainbow Room** and the **Red Blazer Too**. **Cornelia Street Café** is a snug and lively nook for prose, poetry and theatre readings. Poetry, theatre and Latin music are on offer at the **Nuyorican Poets Café**.

MIDNIGHT MOVIES

S PECIAL MIDNIGHT showings and a youthful crowd can be found at Eighth Street Playhouse. Late shows are also screened at the Angelika Film Center and the Film Forum. *(See pp336–7.)*

SHOPS

O N FIFTH AVENUE, the huge Doubleday Book Shop is open to 10pm; the St Mark's Bookshop and Shakespeare & Company Booksellers are also open late. The Upper West Side HMV is open til midnight, East Side HMV until 10pm. Both Tower Records shut at midnight, as does Gryphon Records. Bleecker Bob's Golden Oldies Record Shop stays open until 3am on weekends *(see Shopping pp322–3)*. Late-night video stores include the huge **Palmer Video Store** and **Mrs Hudson's Video Store**, both on Hudson.

Among the many Village clothing stores that stay open late on weekends are the **Antique Boutique** (open until midnight) and **Trash and Vaudeville** (open till 8pm on Fridays and Saturdays). For aspirin, toothpaste and those other essentials, **Kaufman Pharmacy** is open 24 hours a day, **Plaza Pharmacy** until 11pm every night.

TAKEAWAY FOOD AND GROCERIES

A FEW TAKEAWAY food stores are open 24 hours a day, including the **Delmonico Gourmet Food Market** and the **West Side Supermarket**. Many Korean greengrocers also stay open all night. The **Food Emporium** is a supermarket chain open until midnight (around the clock at the York Avenue branch). On Saturdays, **Zabar's** stays open until midnight. Liquor stores are usually open until 10pm and many deliver your order to your apartment.

For the best in bagels, go to **H & H Bagels East**, **Bagels On The Square** and **Jumbo Bagels and Bialys**. There are many pizzerias and Chinese restaurants which stay open late, and most deliver. Many ice cream parlours shut late.

DINING

C LUBBERS AND trendies often frequent **La Jumelle**, **Florent** and **Les Halles** for a variety of good French dishes. Twentysomethings will seek out the **Coffee Shop** for late-night beer and Brazilian food. You'll find delicious and legendary sandwiches at the **Carnegie Deli**. **Caffè Reggio** in Greenwich Village has been a favourite for late-night coffee, tea and cakes since 1927. It is now possible to find good food in certain supper clubs. **Le Bar Bat** is popular for its bat cave décor and the Vietnamese cuisine.

Tatou's offers some real old-fashioned Creole food with jazz in the background, and at the 1930s **Rainbow Room**, the continental dishes add to the magic of this special place.

SPORT

T HERE IS round-the-clock play at **Chelsea Billiards** or until 5am at the **Billiard Club** at weekends. Have late-night beers and burgers with the New York University crowd at **Bowlmore Lanes** bowling alley.

SERVICES

I N LONG ISLAND CITY, **Midnight Express Cleaners** picks up garments until midnight and has them ready the next day. It also delivers until midnight. **Tudor City Flowers** will take your order for flowers 24 hours a day. On Thursdays hairdresser **George Michael of Madison Avenue/Madora Inc** is open until 10pm and will also make house calls.

TOURS AND VIEWS

O NE OF NEW YORK'S most enjoyable walks is along the Hudson River at the World Financial Center's **Battery Park City**, open (and safe) at all hours. Piers 16 and 17 at South Street Seaport attract strollers and revellers all night long and the **Harbour Lights** restaurant on Pier 17 is open until 4am for a middle of the night pick-me-up. Or check out lighting-up time by taking a **Circle Line** two-hour tour of the night-time harbour.

Try the Riverview Terrace at Sutton Place: the benches offer a peaceful and quiet place to watch the sun rise over the East River, Roosevelt Island and Queens. Two of the most sensational views with the Manhattan backdrop are (looking west) from the **River Café** and (looking east) from **Arthur's Landing** restaurant.

Take a trip on the **Staten Island Ferry** *(see p76)* to see the Statue of Liberty and the Manhattan skyline in the dawn light, or a take a taxi across

Brooklyn Bridge (see pp86–9) to watch the sun rise over New York harbour. Go to the **Beekman Tower Hotel's** Top of the Tower for some panoramas of the city's East Side up to 1am. Perhaps the ultimate view is from the **Empire State Building**: its Observation Deck (see pp134–5) stays open until midnight. Have breakfast 107 floors up, at the World Trade Center's **Windows on the World** restaurant, overlooking the city, river and harbour.

Château Stables offer rides in horse-drawn carriages and **Island Helicopter** run spectacular flights over the glittering city at night. If you want to experience some-thing a little bit different, try one of **Marvelous Manhattan Tours'** escorted evening bar-hopping walks, or see the night lights with **Happy Apple Tours**. And if you still can't sleep, visit the bustling **Fulton Fish Market** at 6am – tours are offered by the South Street Seaport Museum (see p84), from April through to November.

DIRECTORY

BARS AND CLUBS

Algonquin Hotel
See Piano Bars p343.

Blue Note
See Jazz p341.

Carlyle Hotel
See Piano Bars p343.

Cornelia Street Café
29 Cornelia St. **Map** 4 D2.
(989-9318.

Katie O'Toole's
134 Reade St. **Map** 1 B1.
(226-8928.

Nuyorican Poets Café
236 E 3rd St. **Map** 5 A2.
(505-8183.

Rainbow Room
See Dancing p343.

Red Blazer Too
349 W 46th St.
Map 12 D5.
(262-3112.

Sweet Basil
See Jazz p341.

Temple Bar
332 Lafayette St.
Map 4 F4.
(925-4242.

Tommy Makem's
130 E 57th St. **Map** 12 E3.
(759-9040.

SHOPS

Antique Boutique
712–714 Broadway.
Map 4 E2.
(460-8830.

Kaufman Pharmacy
See Survival Guide p357.

Mrs Hudson's Video Library
573 Hudson St.
Map 3 C2.
(989-1050.

Palmer Video Store
470 Hudson St. **Map** 3 C3.
(463-9377.

Plaza Pharmacy
251 E 86th St. **Map** 17 B3.
(427-6940.

Trash and Vaudeville
4 St. Mark's Pl. **Map** 5 A2.
(982-3590.

TAKEAWAY FOOD AND GROCERIES

Bagels On The Square
7 Carmine St. **Map** 4 D3.
(691-3041.

Delmonico Gourmet Food Market
55 E 59th St. **Map** 12 F3.
(751-5559.

Food Emporium
1498 York Ave.
Map 17 C4.
(879-9555.

H & H Bagels East
1550 2nd Ave. **Map** 17 B4.
(734-7441.

Jumbo Bagels and Bialys
1070 2nd Ave. **Map** 13 B3.
(355-6185.

West Side Supermarket
2171 Broadway. **Map** 15 C5.
(595-2536.

Zabar's
2245 Broadway. **Map** 15 3C.
(787-2000.

DINING

Caffè Reggio
119 MacDougal St.
Map 4 D2.
(475-9557.

Carnegie Deli
Restaurants and Bars p306.

Coffee Shop
Restaurants and Bars p306.

Florent
Restaurants and Bars p306.

La Jumelle
55 Grand St. **Map** 4 E4.
(941-9651.

Le Bar Bat
311 West 57th St.
Map 12 D3.
(307-7228.

Les Halles
Restaurants and Bars p306.

Rainbow Room
Restaurants and Bars p297.

Tatou
151 East 50th St.
Map 13 A4.
(753-1144.

SPORT

Billiard Club
220 W 19th St.
Map 8 E5.
(206-POOL.

Bowlmore Lanes
110 University Pl.
Map 4 E1.
(255-8188.

Chelsea Billiards
See Sport p345.

SERVICES

George Michael of MadisonAvenue/ Madora Inc
420 Madison Ave.
Map 13 A5.
(752-1177.

Midnight Express Cleaners
25–15 41 Ave,
Long Island City.
(921-0111.

Tudor City Flowers
5 Tudor City Place.
Map 9 B1.
(986-1490.

TOURS AND VIEWS

Arthur's Landing
Port Imperial Marina,
Pershing Circle,
Weehawken, NJ.
((201) 867-0777.

Battery Park City
West St. **Map** 1 A3.

Beekman Tower Hotel
1st Ave 49th St.
Map 13 C5.
(355-7300.

Château Stables
608 W 48th St.
Map 15 B3.
(246-0520.

Circle Line
W 42nd St. **Map** 15 B3
(563-3200 .

Marvelous Manhattan Tours
((800) 926-8795.

Empire State Building
See pp134–5.

Fulton Fish Market Tours
(748-8590.

Happy Apple Tours
((800) 421-4518.

Harbour Lights
89 Fulton St.
Map 2 D2.
(227-2800.

Island Helicopter
(683-4575.

River Café
See Restaurants and Bars p294.

Staten Island Ferry
See Getting Around New York p76.

Windows on the World
See Restaurants and Bars p295.

CHILDREN'S NEW YORK

YOUNG VISITORS soon catch the contagious excitement in the air in New York. Attractions for all ages abound, and plenty are designed especially for children. More than a dozen theatre companies, two zoos and three imaginative museums are just for the young, backed up with special events at many museums and parks. The chance to visit a TV studio is a treat, and New York's own Big Apple Circus is a perennial delight. With more to do than can ever be squeezed into a single visit, you'll never hear the cry "I'm bored!" and, best of all, there's no need to spend a fortune to have fun.

A young visitor making New York his very own playground

PRACTICAL ADVICE

NEW YORK is family-friendly. Many of its hotels allow children in parent's rooms free, and will supply cribs if needed. Most museums charge half price or less for children, while others are free. Children under 44 in (112 cm) also ride free on subways and buses when accompanied by an adult. Travel between 9am and 4pm to avoid rush hours.

Supplies such as nappies and medicines are readily available, and the Kaufman Pharmacy *(see p357)* is open 24 hours a day. Finding changing tables in public toilets is less easy, but no-one objects if a counter is used. Best bets are the facilities in libraries, hotels and department stores. Most hotels will arrange babysitters; another reliable source is the **Baby Sitters' Guild**.

To find out more about the range of current activities for children, get a copy of the free quarterly calendar of events, available from the New York Convention and Visitors Bureau *(see p352)*. Weekly listings can be found in *New York* magazine.

NEW YORK ADVENTURES

THE CITY can seem like a giant amusement park for youngsters. Elevators whisk you sky-high for bird's-eye views from atop the world's highest buildings. Or you can set sail on the classic **Circle Line** tour around Manhattan; the sailboat ***Petrel*** ; a choice of tall ship or paddlewheeler from South Street Seaport *(see p84)*; or the bargain round-trip on the Staten Island Ferry *(see p76)*. The Roosevelt Island Tram *(see p179)* is a Swiss cable car offering an airborne ride over the East River. Central Park *(see pp202–7)* is a source of rides of every kind, from the old-fashioned charm of the carousel to real horse-back and pony-and-trap rides. Children who prefer a faster pace can join the rollerblade skaters who cruise around the park, away from the traffic, every weekend.

Cooling off in a fountain in Central Park

MUSEUMS

WHILE MANY of New York's museums appeal to all ages, some are designed just for the young. High on the list is the imaginative Children's Museum of Manhattan *(see p217)*, a multi-media world in which children can produce their own videos and newscasts. Further afield are the **Staten Island Children's Museum**, where a huge climb-through ant hill is one of the favourite items, and the Brooklyn Children's Museum *(see p245)*. The *Intrepid* Sea-Air-Space Museum *(see p147)* is a real aircraft carrier, with exhibits including the fastest spy plane in the world. Finally, be sure to see the dinosaur displays at the American Museum of Natural History *(see pp214–15)*.

OUTDOOR FUN

IN SUMMER, all of New York comes out to play. Central Park is a child's wonderland, from skating rinks to

Skating with Santa at Rockefeller Center

boating lakes, cycle paths to crazy golf. The park has free entertainment galore, such as guided walks by park rangers on Saturdays, miniature sailboat races and summer storytelling. The zoo is relatively small in scale, which makes it just right for children.

Young children will be fascinated by the International Wildlife Conservation Park *(see pp242–3)*, where there are plenty of friendly animals to be petted.

Orchard and **Rockaway** beaches and Coney Island *(see p247)*, are just a subway ride away. Winter brings the chance to skate at Rockefeller Center *(see p142)*, or in Central Park on a rink fringed with views of skyscrapers.

INDOOR FUN

NEW YORK children's theatre is of a quality and variety to match that for adults. Some favourite companies include the **PaperBag Players** and **Theatreworks, USA**, whose productions sell out fast; schedules and book early.

The New York City Ballet's annual Christmas season of *The Nutcracker* at Lincoln Center *(see p212)* opens at about the same time that the **Big Apple Circus** sets up its tent nearby. Ringling Brothers and Barnum & Bailey Circus is in action at Madison Square Garden *(see p133)* for several weeks each spring.

Opportunities for youngsters to work off energy in winter are many, from indoor skating rinks to bowling alleys.

SHOPPING FOR TOYS

THERE WILL be no complaints about shopping trips if they include **F A O Schwarz**,

Centrepiece clock at toy shop F A O Schwarz

one of the world's biggest and best toy shops. Another children's favourite is **Enchanted Forest** and youngsters are welcomed for educational and entertaining storytelling sessions at children's bookshops such as **Books of Wonder**.

EATING OUT

HAMBURGERS-and-pasta chain **Ottomanelli's Cafés** is very popular with children; and even adults find it hard to finish their huge burgers, but of course it's fun trying. The lively **Hard Rock Café** is another hit, and most children enjoy the foods on offer around Chinatown and Little Italy. For a quick, hot snack, the pizza-by-the-slice emporiums are worth a try, or stave off any hunger pangs with pretzels and hot dogs from street vendors. Sure to sweeten young dispositions are the legendary ice-cream parlours at Rumplemayer's *(see p305)* and **Peppermint Park**. If all else fails, McDonalds has more than 40 branches dotted throughout Manhattan.

Storytelling session at South Street Seaport

SURVIVAL
GUIDE

PRACTICAL INFORMATION

VISITORS TO New York are treated very much the same as anyone else. While you may not be given special treatment, as long as you follow a few guidelines on personal security (see pp356–7) you'll be able to explore the city as freely as any native New Yorker. Buses and subway trains (pp372–5)

Visitors resting on the steps of the Metropolitan Museum of Art

are reliable and cheap; there are lots of cashpoint machines (pp358–9), and money can be easily exchanged at banks, hotels and bureaux de change. The wide range of prices offered by all the hotels (pp274–5), restaurants (pp290–92) and various entertainments (pp328–347) means your New York trip needn't drive you to destitution.

SIGHTSEEING TIPS

NEW YORK'S rush hours extend from 8 to 10am, 11.30am to 1.30pm and 4.30 to 6.30pm, Monday to Friday. During these times, every form of public transport will be crowded, and the streets will be much harder to navigate on foot. Plan your day accordingly.

It's worth trying to visit a cluster of sights in the same area – see the *Street-by-Street* plans of each area – instead of exhausting yourself rushing from one distant attraction to another. Buses are a comfortable and reliable way to get around, and you'll see the city as you travel.

It's best to avoid passing through certain areas of the city, especially at particular times (pp356–7). Public toilets in train stations, bus stations and subways should always be avoided. They attract many drug users and the homeless, even when there's an attendant.

If you need help with street directions or, for whatever reason, feel a need to get off the street, try and find a hotel doorman. There is one on duty at the entrance to most hotels 24 hours a day.

Hotel doorman

OPENING HOURS

BUSINESS HOURS are generally from 9am to 5pm with no lunchtime closing. Only banks close earlier, at 3pm, although some do have longer hours

(8am–6pm) and are open on Saturday mornings. Many museums close on Mondays and major holidays. Some open on Tuesday or Thursday evenings during certain seasons (phone for details).

MUSEUMS

IN NEW YORK, "museums" is used as a blanket term to include institutions that might in Europe be called "galleries". The city's museums are described on pages 34 to 37. Museums in the city either charge admission, starting at around $2, or require a "donation". There are usually discounts for senior citizens, students and children. The leading museums schedule free guided tours and lectures. Museum Mile (see pp182–3), on or near Fifth Avenue, groups a number of major museums close together. Of these, the Frick Collection and the Cooper-Hewitt design museum are small enough to see in only a couple of hours, but the larger Guggenheim and Whitney museums may take far longer.

ETIQUETTE

IT IS NOW ILLEGAL to smoke in *any* public space or building in New York. Some restaurants provide separate rooms for smokers, but it is best to check by phone in advance for details.

Business travellers need not bring a gift for their American hosts. Such tokens are not

expected and they may even be considered improper. If you do bring something, it should be cheap and representative of where you live.

Tipping is an integral part of New York life: for taxi drivers leave 10 to 15%; waiters 15 to 20%, cocktail waiters 15%, hotel room service 10% (when not added to the bill); coat check $1; hotel maids $1 or $2 per day after the first day; hotel bellhops about $1 per bag; hair stylists 15 to 20% and barbers 10 to 20%.

TOURIST INFORMATION

ADVICE ON ANY aspect of life in New York is available from the **New York Convention and Visitors Bureau**. Attendants will answer any questions you may have. The bureau's literature racks and information desk are loaded with information. The 24-hour touch-tone phone line offers help outside office hours.

Useful information New York Convention and Visitors Bureau, 2 Columbus Circle. **Map** 12 D3.
[(800) 692-8474. **Open** 9am–6pm Mon–Fri, 10am–6pm Sat, Sun.

Information racks at the New York Convention and Visitors Bureau

ENTERTAINMENT LISTINGS

A NUMBER of cheaply priced or even free publications listing current exhibitions and leisure activities are available at newsstands, hotels or galleries throughout New York.

Among the more popular ones are *New York* magazine and *The New Yorker's*, "Goings On About Town" roster. Both magazines list offerings at the city's many museums, clubs, theatres, galleries, restaurants, cinemas, colleges and libraries, and impending auctions.

The *Village Voice* focuses on events in SoHo, TriBeCa and Greenwich Village, plus other major exhibitions in the city. The *New York Times*

Friday and Sunday editions list current exhibitions and shows in their respective "Weekend" and "Arts and Leisure" sections. *Art News* is a monthly magazine that lists major events in the art world as well as having reviews of the latest exhibitions and impending auctions.

There are also various free magazines. The weekly *Where* is distributed through hotel concierges and lists major museums, their opening hours, locations and any exhibitions they have on. *Art Now/New York Gallery Guide* is released in art galleries each month. It lists current exhibitions and has maps showing where they are located.

New York **magazine which has comprehensive entertainment listings for all of New York**

GUIDED TOURS

However you want to see New York – with the help of a pre-recorded walk or by an exciting trip in a helicopter, boat or horse-drawn carriage – organized sight-seeing trips, planned by someone else, can save a lot of time, effort and often money.

Boat Tours

Circle Line
Sightseeing Yachts
Pier 83, W 42nd St.
Map 7 A1.
☎ 563-3200.
A three-hour trip circumnavigating Manhattan.

Circle Line Statue of Liberty Ferry
South Ferry,
Battery Park.
Map 1 C4.
☎ 269-5755.

Spirit of New York
99 Wall St.
Map 2 D3.
☎ 741-4266. *Cruises include lunch or dinner.*

Staten Island Ferry
South Ferry.
Map 2 D4.
☎ 806-6940.
Manhattan–Staten Island.

World Yacht, Inc
Pier 81 W 41st St.
Map 2 D5.
☎ 630-8100.
Cruises include lunch, dinner and entertainment.

Helicopter tour

Carriage Tours

59th St at Fifth Ave and along Central Park S.
*Horse-drawn carriages gather outside the Plaza Hotel (**Map** 12 F3), days and evenings. The usual itinerary takes in Central Park.*

Coach Tours

Allied Tours
165 W 46th St.
Map 12 E5.
☎ 869-5100.

Gray Line of New York
254 W 54th St.
Map 12 E4.
☎ 397-2600.

Short Line Tours/American Sightseeing NY
166 W 46th St.
Map 12 F5.
☎ 800-631-8405.

Helicopter Tours

Island Helicopter
Sightseeing
E 34th St and East River.
Map 9 C2. ☎ 683-4575.

Liberty Helicopter Tours
Heliport at W 30th St and Twelfth Ave. **Map** 7 B3.
☎ 967-6464.

Walking Tours

Backstage on Broadway
228 W 47th St.
Map 12 E5.
☎ 575-8065.
Behind-the-scenes tours of Broadway shows.

Big Onion Walking Tours
PO Box 250201,
Columbia University.
Map 20 E3.
☎ 439-1090.
Historical and ethnic.

CityWalks
410 W 20th St. **Map** 7 C5.
☎ 989-2456.
Historic neighbourhoods.

Harlem Spirituals, Inc.
1697 Broadway.
Map 12 E4.
☎ 757-0425.
Harlem's history and culture.

Museum of the City of New York
103rd St and Fifth Ave.
Map 21 C5.
☎ 534-1672.
Architecture and history.

NBC Studio Tour
30 Rockefeller Plaza.
Map 12 F5.
☎ 664-3055.

92nd Street YMCA
1395 Lexington Ave.
Map 17 B5.
☎ 427-6000.
Culture and history.

Talk-a-Walk
30 Waterside Plaza.
Map 9 C4.
☎ 686-0356.
Recorded itineraries.

Carriage ride in Central Park

DISABLED TRAVELLERS

DISABLED PEOPLE will find New York more accessible than most cities. Many of the city's buses have ramps which can be placed to help people in wheelchairs board. The buses also "kneel" to help those with restricted mobility.

Hotels, large stores and office buildings are also often well-equipped for wheelchair access and some museums offer tours for deaf, blind and disabled people. Several city theatres have systems to aid hearing-impaired patrons as do a growing number of telephones. *Access Guide to New York City*, free from the **Junior League of the City of New York**, lists buildings that are accessible to the disabled.

Useful information Junior League of the City of New York, 130 E 80th St. **Map** 17 A4. **C** *288-6220*. The Mayor's Office for People with Disabilities. **C** *788-2830*.

A New York city bus "kneeling" to help the elderly board

CUSTOMS AND IMMIGRATION

AT PRESENT ALL British an Canadian passport holders, whether they are holiday-maker, business traveller or student, do not need visas if staying in the US for 90 days or less. Australians and New Zealanders require passports, visas and onward passage tickets. Some nationals also require proof they have $500 or more. Check with a travel agent if in any doubt.

Customs allowances per person when you enter the US are 200 cigarettes, 50 cigars,

2 kilograms (4.4 pounds) of tobacco; no more than 1 litre (1.8 pints) of alcohol; gifts which are worth no more than $100; no meat or meat products (even in tins), seeds, growing plants, or fresh fruit.

Upon arrival at one of New York's airports, you should follow signs stating "other than American passports" to immigration counters where your passport will then be inspected and stamped. Once you have reclaimed your baggage from the appropriate area (again, follow the signs) you will be approached by a customs officer. He or she will examine the customs declaration you should have received and filled in on your flight, and direct you either towards the exit or to a customs inspector who will then search your luggage.

According to American customs officials, only 5% of all travellers will have to have their luggage searched. There are no red or green customs channels – you're cleared and free to go once the customs officer has seen your fully completed declaration.

STUDENT TRAVELLERS

MANY MUSEUMS and theatres allow students a discount on admission. To receive this, however, you will need to carry some proof of your student status at all times.

An International Student ID Card can be purchased quite cheaply, provided you have the right credentials, from the **New York Student Center** or the **Council on International Educational Exchange**. At the same time, make sure you ask for a copy of the *ISIC Student Handbook*. This invaluable booklet identifies places and services throughout the US that offer a range of discounts to card holders. Included are accommodation, various museums, theatres, tours and attractions, night clubs, restaurants and even Carey transportation (buses from Manhattan to New York's airports, *see p363*).

Normally, it is extremely difficult to obtain permission to work in the USA, but

students are an exception. Any branch of the Student Travel Association in the UK, Australia or New Zealand will be able to help you with details of working holidays in New York. In London, contact the **University of London Union** for advice.

STUDENT INFORMATION

International Educational Exchange
205 E 42nd St. **Map** 9 B1.
C *661-1414*.

New York Student Center
895 Amsterdam Ave.
Map 20 E5.
C *666-3619*.

University of London Union
Malet St, London WC1E 78Y.
C *0171-580 9551*.

CONVERSION CHART

Bear in mind that 1 US pint (0.5 litre) is a smaller measure than 1 UK pint (0.6 litre).

Imperial system:
1 inch = 2.5 centimetres
1 foot = 30 centimetres
1 mile = 1.6 kilometres
1 ounce = 28 grams
1 pound = 454 grams
1 US pint = 0.5 litre
1 US gallon = 3.8 litres

Metric system:
1 millimetre = 0.04 inch
1 centimetre = 0.4 inch
1 metre = 3 feet 3 inches
1 kilometre = 0.6 mile
1 gram = 0.04 ounce

International Student ID Card

New York daily newspapers

A newspaper-dispensing machine

NEWSPAPERS, TELEVISION AND RADIO

YOU CAN BUY foreign newspapers, usually the previous day's issue, at **Hotalings**. Stockists also include airports, hotels and newsstands near international business areas like the World Trade Center and Wall Street.

Comprehensive schedules of TV programmes can be found in the weekly *TV Guide* magazine and the television section of Sunday's *New York Times*.

The choice of TV stations available in New York is vast. CBS operates on channel 2, NBC on channel 4 and ABC on channel 7. PBS offers cultural and educational fare, including some vintage BBC programmes, on channel 13. Cable TV offer anything from The Arts and Entertainment network to the Disney Channel to public access.

AM radio stations include WCBS News (880Hz) and WFAN Sports (660Hz). Among the many FM stations are WNEW rock (102.7M), WBGO jazz (88.3M) and WNCN classical (104.3M).
Useful information Hotalings,142 W 42nd St. **Map** 8 E1. 840-1868.

ELECTRICAL APPLIANCES

ALL AMERICAN electric current flows at a standardized 115–120 volts AC (alternating current). You will need to bring an adapter plug and a voltage convertor that fits standard US electrical outlets. US plugs have two flat prongs.

Most modern New York hotels provide wall-mounted electric hair dryers. In addition, some hotels have wall plugs capable of powering both 110 and 220 volt electric shavers, but little else – not even radios. It can, in fact, be very dangerous to connect anything more powerful. If you bring along sophisticated electrical appliances with you, be certain to take a battery pack as well. Remember that you will also need an adapter to recharge your spare batteries.

Few New York hotels have electric clothes presses in rooms and very few offer the added luxury of coffee or tea makers. However, if you do want to press or iron your clothes, room service should be able to provide you with an iron.

Standard plug

EMBASSIES AND CONSULATES

Australian Consulate General
636 Fifth Ave. **Map** 12 F5.
408-8400.

British Consulate General
845 Third Ave. **Map** 13 B4.
745-0202.

Canadian Consulate General
1251 Sixth Ave and 50th St.
Map 12 E4. 596-1601.

Consulate-General of Ireland
345 Park Ave. **Map** 13 A4.
319-2555.

New Zealand Embassy
37 Observatory Circle, NW, Washington, DC 20008.
(202) 328-4880.

RELIGIOUS SERVICES

THERE ARE SOME 4,000 places of worship in New York, catering for almost any faith. Most hotels have lists of local organizations and service times. Among the leading churches and temples are:

Catholic
St Patrick's Cathedral
Fifth Ave at 50th St.
Map 12 F4.
753-2261.

Episcopalian
St Bartholomew's
109 E 50th St. **Map** 13 A4.
751-1616.

Jewish
Reform
Temple Emanu-El
Fifth Ave at 65th St.
Map 12 F2.
744-1400.

Orthodox
Fifth Avenue Synagogue
5 E 62nd St. **Map** 12 F2.
838-2122.

Lutheran
St Peter's
619 Lexington Ave. **Map** 17 A4.
935-2200.

Methodist
Christ Church United Methodist
520 Park Ave. **Map** 13 A3.
838-3036.

Nondenominational
Riverside Church
122nd St at Riverside Dr.
Map 20 D2.
870-6700.

Riverside Church

Personal Security and Health

Police badge

IN 1990, NEW YORK was a distant 30th on the Federal Bureau of Investigation's total crime index of American cities. This ranks it below towns like Boston and Columbus, Ohio, neither of which has New York's international reputation for violent crime. The city's police force concentrates on foot patrols in tourist areas, and security is being beefed up in midtown, in the transit system and at airports. While there are places where any traveller would be foolish to tread after dark – and sometimes in daylight – if you keep your wits about you and stick to the following guidelines, you should enjoy a trouble-free visit.

Curtis Sliwa, founder of the Guardian Angels

LAW ENFORCEMENT

THE NEW YORK police department has round-the-clock foot, horse and motor patrols. These are concentrated in specific areas at critical times; for instance, the theatre district during show times. There are also platoons of parking violations officers and a small army of transit police who patrol the subway stations and trains.

You will probably also see youths wearing red berets. As their T-shirts proclaim, they are Guardian Angels. Always unarmed, these safety patrols "police" the subways and midtown streets. Although tolerated by the police and often a welcome sight, they have no official powers.

GUIDELINES ON SAFETY

BE ALERT and walk as if you know where you're going. Avoid making eye contact and confrontations with down-and-outs.

If someone asks you for money, be careful; do not be drawn into conversation.

Never use deserted streets. At night, if you can't afford a taxi, try to travel with a group and avoid such areas as the Lower East Side, Chinatown, midtown west of Broadway (except the Lincoln Center plaza) and uptown, generally north of 82nd Street. Even the side streets around Times Square and the Broadway theatres can be unsafe. The Financial District (except for the World Financial Center) is deserted after business hours, and some TriBeCa and SoHo streets can be risky after dark if you are alone.

Parks are often used for drug-dealing. They are safest when there is a crowd for a rally, concert or other event. If you want to go for a jog, ask your hotel concierge for a map of safe routes and follow his or her advice. Keep your wallet in an inconspicuous place and have enough change handy for phone calls and bus fares. It's best not to have to dig into your purse or wallet while standing in a queue. Never stop to count your money on the street. Defeat purse-snatchers by carrying your bag with the clasp facing towards you and the shoulder strap across your body.

Leave valuable jewellery at home or stored at your hotel. If you wear it casually, it will only mark you out as a target for robbery or worse.

Do not allow anyone except hotel and airport personnel to carry your luggage or parcels.

Stow your valuables and camera in a locked suitcase or dresser or closet safe when you do leave your hotel room.

Mounted police officers

LOST AND FOUND

THE CHANCES of recovering anything you lose in New York are poor. There is no city-wide lost and found

Two armed New York City police officers

Cap and badge worn by city police

office. If you do happen to misplace something, ask your hotel concierge where you should start looking for it.

USEFUL INFORMATION

Lost and Found Offices
Bus and subway services
(718) 625-6200.

Taxis
222-8294.

Missing Credit Cards
American Express
(800) 528-4800 (freephone).

Diners Club
(800) 234-6377 (freephone).

JCB
(800) 366-4522 (freephone).

MasterCard
(800) 627-8372 (freephone).

VISA
(800) 336-8472 (freephone).

TRAVEL INSURANCE

TRAVEL INSURANCE is highly recommended, mainly because of the high cost of medical care. There are many types of coverage, with prices dependent on the length of your trip and the number of people covered on the policy.

Among the most important features are: accidental death, dismemberment, emergency medical and dental care, trip cancellation, and baggage and travel document loss. There are many policies that include all these items. Your travel agent or insurance company should recommend a suitable policy.

MEDICAL TREATMENT

BE PREPARED to undergo an expensive experience: some of the city's practitioners and facilities are among the

best around, and medical fees in the US are unregulated. Be sure to protect yourself well with insurance. A few physicians and dentists may accept credit cards but they are much more likely to want payment in cash or traveller's cheques. Hospitals accept most credit cards *(see p358).*

Kaufman's Pharmacy, open throughout the night

EMERGENCIES

IN THE UNLIKELY event of you being involved in a medical emergency, proceed at once to a **Hospital Emergency Room**. Should you need an ambulance, telephone 911 and one will be sent. If you have all your medical insurance properly arranged, you won't have to worry about costs.

Unless you are particularly impoverished, it is better to avoid the overworked and regularly overcrowded city-owned hospitals listed in the telephone book blue pages. Instead, you can opt for one of the many private hospitals listed in the yellow pages in the telephone directory. Or dial 411 and ask the operator to give you the number of the nearest public or private hospital to you. Other options include asking your hotel to call a doctor or dentist to visit you in your room, or find one yourself by telephoning the **Doctors Emergency Service** or **Dental Emergency Service**. For more general advice and information ring **Travelers' Aid**, a national organization geared to helping travellers.

CRISIS INFORMATION

All Emergencies
911 (or 0). This alerts police, fire and medical services.

Animal Attack
566-2068 for medical help in case of dog bites, etc.

Crime Victims Hot Line
577-7777.

Dental Emergency Service (24-hour)
679-3966 (9am–8pm); 679-4172 (8pm–9am).

Doctors on Call
(718) 238-2100.

Hospital Emergency Rooms
St Vincent's.
11th St and Seventh Ave.
Map 3 C1.
604-7998.

St Luke's Roosevelt.
58th St and Ninth Ave.
Map 12 D3.
523-6800.

National Organization of Women (NOW)
260-4422.

Pharmacy (24-hour)
Kaufman's
557 Lexington Ave at 50th St.
Map 13 A4.
755-2266.

Poison Control Center
764-7667.

Robberies, Muggings or Assaults
911 for instant police help.

Sex Crimes Report Line
267-7273.

Travelers' Aid
944-0013.

New York ambulance

Banking and Currency

N EW YORK IS THE NATION'S banking centre. It has a
wealth of local, regional and major national banks,
plus some retail branches of the leading foreign banks.
NatWest and Barclays are well-represented in New
York; the banks of Australia, Canada, Ireland, Montreal,
Nova Scotia and Scotland all have offices or branches.

BANKING

N EW YORK banks are gen-
erally open weekdays
from 9am to 3pm. There are,
however, a number of banks
that open earlier or close
late evening to suit commuters'
needs. Tellers are behind a
counter. At most banks, all the
tellers will cash traveller's
cheques and exchange your
foreign currency.

Automated teller machine (ATM)

AUTOMATED TELLER MACHINES

A CONVENIENT development in
banking has been the
introduction of the automated
teller machine (ATM). These
are found in nearly all bank
lobbies and enable you to
obtain American currency 24
hours a day by electronically
tapping into your own bank
account. ATMs usually issue
American banknotes in $20
denominations.

Before you leave for the US,
check with your own bank
which New York City banks
and ATM systems will accept
your bank card, and the fees
and commissions charged on
each transaction. Most ATM
machines are in either the
Cirrus or Plus networks. They

accept various US bank cards,
MasterCard and VISA cards
and certain others. Among
the many advantages of ATMs
is the swift, secure exchange
of your money at the wholesale rate used between the
banks when they make their
million-dollar deals.

On a more cautionary note,
robberies of customers using
ATMs have recently increased
in New York. It is therefore
prudent to use them only in
daylight hours or when the
streets are crowded.

CREDIT CARDS

M ASTERCARD, American
Express, VISA, JCB
and Diners Card are widely
accepted throughout the
United States, regardless of
which company or bank
issues them. These cards
can also be used to obtain
cash advances from various
ATM machines. They may
also be upgraded to confer
higher spending limits. In
the US you can use a credit
card to pay for nearly
everything imaginable, from
groceries to restaurant and
hotel bills, and telephone
orders for cinema and theatre
tickets. Major expenses such
as tours, travel packages and
expensive rentals are all best
paid for by credit card. Try to
avoid carrying huge sums of
money around with you.

CASHING CHEQUES

D OLLAR TRAVELLER'S cheques
issued by American
Express and Thomas Cook
are widely accepted without
commission by most of New
York's department stores,
shops, hotels and restaurants.
Traveller's cheques in other
currencies, including sterling,
are unlikely to be so well
received. They can usually be
exchanged by your hotel

**Foreign currency exchange
counter at Chequepoint USA**

cashier, but may require a
visit to a bank. Exchange
rates are printed daily in the
New York Times and *Wall
Street Journal*, and may be
posted in the windows of
banks that invite currency-
exchange business. American
Express cheques are always
exchanged without discount
or fee when presented at
American Express offices.
Major hotels have cashiers
equipped to exchange your
traveller's cheques.

Foreign exchange brokers
are few. Among the most
solidly established are
**Thomas Cook Currency
Services** and **MTB Banking
Corporation**. The ones listed
on the opposite page have late
opening hours. Others are
listed in the city's telephone
yellow pages under *Foreign
Exchange Brokers*. Expect to
pay a fee, which will vary
widely from one place to the
next, plus a commission.

There are scores of hole-in-
the-wall cheque-cashing shops
in Manhattan. They are listed
in the yellow pages classified
section. They may not be
willing to cash your traveller's
cheques though, and they are
very unlikely to accept or
cash foreign cheques.

EXCHANGE ADDRESSES

**Thomas Cook Currency
Services**
Rockefeller Center, 630 Fifth Ave.
Map 12 F5. 757-6915.
One of several other branches.

MTB Banking Corporation
90 Broad St.
Map 1 C3. 858-3300.

Coins

American coins (actual size shown) come in 25, 10, 5 and 1 cent pieces. 50 cent and $1 coins are also minted but are rarely used. Each value of coin has a more popular name: 25 cent pieces are called quarters, 10 cent pieces are called dimes, 5 cent pieces are called nickels and 1 cent pieces are known as pennies.

25 cent coin (a quarter)

10 cent coin (a dime)

5 cent coin (a nickel)

1 cent coin (a penny)

Bank Notes

Units of currency in the United States are dollars and cents. There are 100 cents to a dollar. Notes, which are known as bills, come in $1, $5, $10, $20, $50 and $100 denominations; $2 bills are printed but very rarely circulated. A "buck" is the popular slang for a dollar.

Emblem on US currency

1 dollar bill ($1)

5 dollar bill ($5)

20 dollar bill ($20)

50 dollar bill ($50)

100 dollar bill ($100)

AFTER-HOURS FOREIGN CURRENCY EXCHANGE

American Express
Bloomingdale's, 59th St and Lexington Ave. **Map** 13 A3. 705-3171. **Open** 10am–6pm Mon–Sat. One of several branches.

Chequepoint USA
551 Madison Ave and 55th St. **Map** 13 A4. 837-7881. **Open** 8am–8pm Mon–Fri, 10am–8pm Sat, 10am–6pm Sun.

Harold Reuter & Co
Grand Central Station. **Map** 13 A5. No telephone. **Open** 7am–7pm Mon–Fri, 8am–3pm Sat & Sun.

Kara International
1225 Broadway, Suite 813. **Map** 12 E4. 725-5270. **Open** 9am–6pm Mon–Fri, 9am–3.30pm Sat.

Thomas Cook
1590 Broadway. **Map** 12 E5. 265-6049. **Open** 9am–7pm Mon–Sat. Also at 41 E 42nd St. 883-0400. **Open** 9am–5pm Mon–Sat.

Using New York's Phones

Sign for public payphones

PUBLIC PAYPHONES can be found at many street corners, in hotel and office building lobbies, restaurants, bars, theatres and department stores. Very few use credit cards and none use prepaid phone cards. Most are coin operated and take 5, 10 and 25 cent coins. Hotels are free to set their own rates and so calls made from your room can often be a lot more expensive than public payphones. Avoid this by making calls from a public phone in the lobby.

NEW YORK TIME

New York is on Eastern Standard Time. When making international calls, first calculate the time of day in the country you are calling. For the UK, add 5 hours; for Australia, add 15 hours and for New Zealand, add 17 hours.

PUBLIC TELEPHONES

THE STANDARD payphone has a hand receiver, 12-button key pad, and is pillar or wall-mounted. In some locations the payphone may belong to an independent operating company. This can be confusing since the payphones often look similar and are sometimes found in phone banks. The independents, though, can often prove slightly more expensive.

Independently operated payphone

Regulations require each public payphone to post information about charges, toll-free numbers and how to make calls using other carriers. Look for the New York Telephone Company name or logo on the box to be sure the phone will reach all numbers at the standard rates. To complain about the service, call the **Public Service Commission**.

Useful information Public Service Commission ((800) 342-3355 (freephone).

PAYPHONE CHARGES

WITHIN the New York boroughs, the standard charge, around 25 cents, buys five minutes' talking time. If your call lasts more than five minutes, the operator will request additional payment.

Domestic long-distance rates for direct-dial calls decrease by 35% from day rates after 5pm and 60% after 11pm on weekdays. At weekends the 60% discount also applies, except for Sundays from 5 to 11pm when the 35% rate resumes. These discounts also apply to calls to Canada, but they take effect an hour later.

USING A COIN-OPERATED PHONE

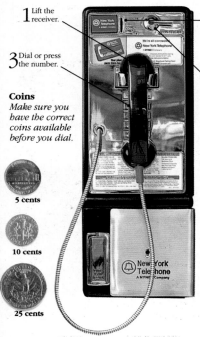

1 Lift the receiver.

3 Dial or press the number.

Coins
Make sure you have the correct coins available before you dial.

5 cents

10 cents

25 cents

2 Insert the necessary coin or coins. The coin drops as soon as you insert it.

4 If you do not want to make a connection or the call does not get through, retrieve the coin by pressing the coin return.

5 If the call is answered and you talk longer than the allotted five minutes, the operator will interrupt and ask you to deposit some more coins into the phone. Payphones do not give change.

A New York Telephone Company phone stand

International long-distance rates for calls dialled directly vary from country to country. For calls to the UK the discount rate starts at 1pm, then drops to an economy rate from 6pm until 7am the next day.

USEFUL NUMBERS

Local Directory Inquiries
411.

Main Post Office
967-8585.

Operator Assistance
0.

Speaking Clock
976-1616.

International Directory Inquiries
00.

REACHING THE RIGHT NUMBER

• Two prefixes (area codes) are used in New York: 212 for Manhattan and 718 for Brooklyn, the Bronx, Queens and Richmond (Staten Island). An 800 prefix means the call will be free.
• To ring a number outside your own area, first dial 1. For example, to dial Queens from Manhattan dial 1 (718) (number).
• To call long distance from a payphone: dial 0 followed by the area code and then the number. The operator will answer and tell you how much money you need to deposit.
• To make an international direct call: dial 011 followed by the country code (New Zealand: 64, Australia: 61; UK: 44), then the city or area code (minus the first 0) and the local number.
• To make an international call via the operator: dial 01 followed by the country code, the city code (minus the first 0) and then the local number.
• International Directory Inquiries are on 00. If you have problems, call international operator assistance on 01.
• **In an emergency, dial 911.**

Sending A Letter

US state mail logo

APART FROM post offices, letters can be posted at your hotel concierge desk (which usually also sells stamps); in letter slots in office building lobbies; in air, rail and bus terminals; and in the occasional street postbox. These are always painted blue, or red, white and blue. Mail in most postboxes is not picked up at weekends. Post offices are shown on the *Street Finder* maps *(see pp378–9)*.

POSTAL SERVICES

THE CITY'S main **General Post Office** is open 24 hours a day. Stamps can be bought here or from coin-operated machines in pharmacies, department stores and bus and rail locations. There is a 25% charge on the stamps bought anywhere other than a post office. All letters go first class.

The federal post office has two special delivery services available at extra cost. The **Express Mail** service is for next-day delivery and the **Priority Mail** service is for two-day delivery. Priority Mail will also pick up letters on weekdays for an extra charge. These services are very easy to use – just ask at any post office.

Colourful US stamps

Private express mail can be arranged through hotel concierges or with one of the delivery services listed in the telephone book. Two international companies are **DHL** and **Federal Express**.

Useful information General Post Office, 421 Eighth Ave. **Map** 8 D2. 967-8585. Priority Mail and Express Mail (800) 222-1811. Federal Express (800) 238-5355. DHL (800) 225-5345.

POSTE RESTANTE

LETTERS AND parcels are kept for 30 days at the General Post Office's General Delivery window. Mail can be sent to other post offices by giving the postal code or name. Address mail with: Name, Post Restante, c/o General Delivery, New York, NY 10001.

Express Mail

Priority Mail

Postboxes
Postboxes can be few and far between on New York streets, and it may be easier to find a post office (see Street Finder pp378–9). Instructions on how to use each postbox are written on the box. If you use Express or Priority services, weigh your letters at a post office to work out which stamps are needed.

Standard postbox

GETTING TO NEW YORK

MANY INTERNATIONAL airlines have direct flights to New York. It is also very well served by charter and domestic services. Price wars between airlines have reduced fares, and domestic flights now prove a viable alternative to bus and train tickets; group tour package prices are often

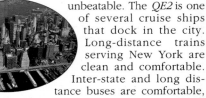

Aerial view of Manhattan

unbeatable. The *QE2* is one of several cruise ships that dock in the city. Long-distance trains serving New York are clean and comfortable. Inter-state and long distance buses are comfortable, air-conditioned with on-board toilets. For information on arriving in New York see the map on pages 366–7.

AIR TRAVEL

NEW YORK CAN be reached by air direct from most major cities. The flight from London takes about eight hours. However, there are no direct flights from Australia or New Zealand. Instead, the airlines fly to the west coast, which takes around 14 hours, land, refuel and then continue on to New York.

Among the main carriers to New York are **Continental**, **British Airways**, **American Airlines**, **Virgin Atlantic** and **United Airlines**. All international flights arrive at Newark or JFK airports *(see pp364–5)*.

APEX (Advance Purchase Excursion) tickets for the scheduled airlines are usually the cheapest return fares apart from package tours. But they must be bought in advance and are valid for a stay of 7 to 30 days. Some airlines offer cheaper fares if you limit your stay to specified periods. Senior citizens may also receive discounts. You can reserve a flight by phone using your credit card.

AIRLINE NUMBERS

Major Carriers

American Airlines
📞 *(800) 433 7300 (freephone).*

British Airways
📞 *(800) 247-9297 (freephone).*

Continental
📞 *(800) 231-0856 (freephone).*

United Airlines
📞 *(800) 241-6522 (freephone).*

Virgin Atlantic
📞 *(800) 862-8621 (freephone).*

Discount ticket agents

ATAB (Air Travel Advisory Bureau). A British organization that will recommend a discount agency.
📞 *(0171) 636-5000.*

SEA TRAVEL

NEW YORK IS a regular port of call for the *QE2* which docks there, via Southampton, some 25 times a year. It also makes annual voyages that extend to Australia and New Zealand. Sea travel offers an expensive and lengthy, but

Long-distance Greyhound coach

relaxing, way of travelling to New York. Ships dock at the Hudson River piers in midtown Manhattan, a short taxi or bus ride from most hotels.

COACH TRAVEL

ALL LONG-DISTANCE buses such as **Greyhound Coaches**, arrive in the city at the **Port Authority Bus Terminal**. Buses from here also connect with the three airports. With over 6,000 coaches arriving and leaving daily and carrying some 172,000 passengers, the atmosphere can seem chaotic. Many midtown hotels are also accessible by bus directly from the terminal.
Useful information Greyhound Coaches 📞 *(800) 231-2222 (24 hrs).* Port Authority Bus Terminal. W 40th St and Eighth Ave. **Map** 8 D1. 📞 *564-8484 (24 hrs).*

TRAIN TRAVEL

AMTRAK TRAINS from Canada, upstate, southern, northeastern and western states all stop at Penn Station *(see p376).* Metro North lines from upstate and Connecticut arrive at Grand Central Terminal.

Ocean liner approaching Manhattan

New York Airports

Transatlantic jet

THE THREE MAIN airports (Newark, JFK and LaGuardia) are all well connected to central Manhattan. Look for uniformed "skycaps" – scarlet-capped porters wearing distinctive badges who will help you with your luggage. Never trust anyone else to help carry your bags – you will be unlikely to see them ever again. Taxi dispatchers will help you into a licensed taxi at the taxi area.

GETTING INTO MANHATTAN

THE GROUND Transportation centre at each airport will give you information on the ways you can continue your trip. The most useful services, operating from LaGuardia and JFK, are the **Carey Airport Express** and **Gray Line Air Shuttle**. The former stops at Grand Central; the latter will drop you anywhere in Manhattan between 23rd and 63rd streets. The shuttle is more expensive than buses, but the door-to-door service saves a taxi fare. New Jersey Transit buses and **Olympia Airport Express** also go to Manhattan.

Shared vehicle rides are offered at JFK and LaGuardia by **Classic Airport Share Ride** and **Westchester Express**. You can share taxi fare and tolls with up to three other people. Many car rental

Ground Transportation

Signposting for connections to Manhattan at LaGuardia

firms have courtesy telephones at the baggage-reclaim areas. Telephone numbers for your advance reservations are listed on page 370.

COACH COMPANIES

Carey Airport Express
(718) 632-0500/0509.

Classic Airport Share Ride *(516) 567-5100.*

Gray Line Air Shuttle
315-3006.

Olympia Airport Express
964-6233.

Westchester Express
(914) 592-9200.

Taxi dispatcher

LAGUARDIA (LGA)

PRINCIPALLY SERVING business travellers, LaGuardia lies 8 miles (13 km) east of Manhattan on the north side of Long Island in Queens.

Upon arrival, you can hire luggage trolleys cheaply from the baggage-reclaim area next to the luggage carousels. Skycaps are on hand to assist you. Baggage can also be left in the Tele-Trip business centre on the departure level. Bureaux de change are located around the Central Terminal.

Uniformed taxi dispatchers at the airport are on duty at peak hours; or ask one of the Port Authority Police for help. Only use yellow taxis licensed by the city. The cost of tolls, plus a small surcharge after 8pm and all day Sunday, will be added to the fare shown on the meter (about $25–30 to central Manhattan). **Useful information** Airport Information Service *(718) 533 3400.*

Check-in desk at LaGuardia

PLAN OF LAGUARDIA AIRPORT

A frequent free bus service runs between each of the terminals and car parks. Buses and taxis into the city and its suburbs depart from the first floor of the Central Terminal building.

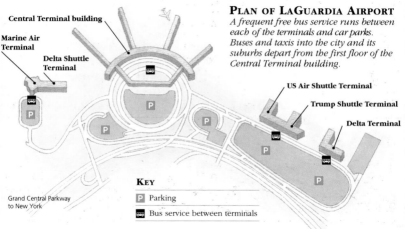

Central Terminal building

Marine Air Terminal

Delta Shuttle Terminal

US Air Shuttle Terminal

Trump Shuttle Terminal

Delta Terminal

Grand Central Parkway to New York

KEY

P Parking

🚌 Bus service between terminals

JFK Airport

New York's main inter-national airport, JFK, lies 15 miles (24 km) southeast of Manhattan, in the borough of Queens. American Airlines, British Airways, Delta, TWA, and United have their own arrivals buildings, complete with customs and immigration facilities. Other airlines use the International Arrivals Building.

Luggage trolleys can be hired from the baggage-re-claim area. Your bags can also be left at the check-in

Main Hall at the International Arrivals Building, JFK

Airport information signs at JFK

counter of the International Arrivals Building. Bureaux de change are in all terminals.

The Ground Transportation services desk is on the ground level near the baggage-reclaim area. Transport into Manhattan can be arranged and booked from here 24 hours a day.

The quickest way to reach Manhattan is by helicopter. But the price for a 15-minute flight is double or more the cost of a taxi fare. Courtesy phones are provided by the car-hire companies. Most have a shuttle

service to their rental offices. Taxis queue at stands outside the terminals. A trip to the city centre normally takes about an hour and costs around $30.

Buses can take up to an hour and a half to the city centre, but the Carey Airport Express bus service is very reliable, relatively cheap and safe, and operates 24 hours a day.

For early morning flights there are hotels very near the airport. City centre hotels can be booked from the Meegan Services reservation desk.

Useful Addresses

Airport Information Service
🅖 *(718) 244-4444.*

Hilton JFK Airport
138–10 135th Ave, Queens.
🅒 *(718) 322-8700.*

Holiday Inn JFK
144–02 135th Ave, Queens.
🅒 *(718) 659-0200.*

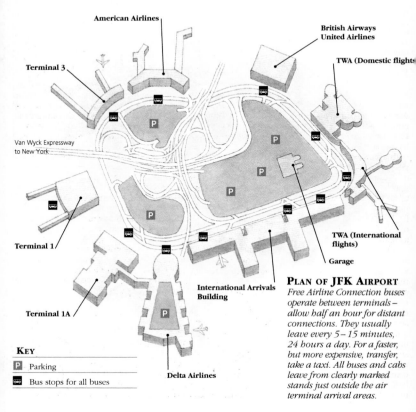

American Airlines

British Airways
United Airlines

TWA (Domestic flights)

Terminal 3

Van Wyck Expressway
to New York

Terminal 1

TWA (International flights)

Garage

Terminal 1A

International Arrivals Building

Delta Airlines

Plan of JFK Airport

Free Airline Connection buses operate between terminals – allow half an hour for distant connections. They usually leave every 5 – 15 minutes, 24 hours a day. For a faster, but more expensive, transfer, take a taxi. All buses and cabs leave from clearly marked stands just outside the air terminal arrival areas.

Key

🅿 Parking

🚌 Bus stops for all buses

NEWARK AIRPORT

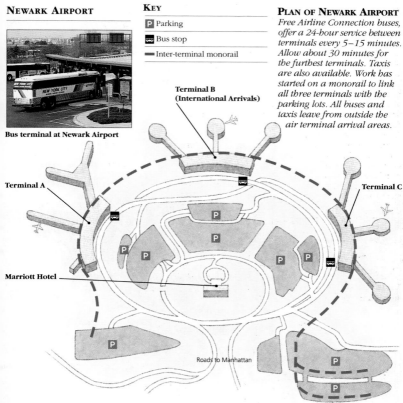

Bus terminal at Newark Airport

KEY

🅿 Parking

🚌 Bus stop

━ Inter-terminal monorail

**Terminal B
(International Arrivals)**

Terminal A

Terminal C

Marriott Hotel

Roads to Manhattan

PLAN OF NEWARK AIRPORT

*Free Airline Connection buses,
offer a 24-hour service between
terminals every 5–15 minutes.
Allow about 30 minutes for
the furthest terminals. Taxis
are also available. Work has
started on a monorail to link
all three terminals with the
parking lots. All buses and
taxis leave from outside the
air terminal arrival areas.*

N EWARK, NEW YORK'S second largest international airport, is located about 16 miles (26 km) southwest of Manhattan, in New Jersey.

All international flights arrive at Terminal "B". Baggage trolleys are available for hire near the luggage carousels in the baggage-reclaim area on the ground level. There is, however, no left luggage office. Bureaux de change are available in each terminal.

The Ground Transportation services desk, open 24 hours a day, is next to the baggage-reclaim area. Courtesy phones are provided by limousine and car hire companies. Many of these have a free shuttle service to their rental offices.

If you want a taxi, queue up at one of the many taxi stands located outside most arrival areas. Uniformed taxi dispatchers will also help you hail a cab. Never accept a ride into town from anyone

who approaches you in the terminal: they will probably have no insurance and could charge an outrageous fare. The journey into Manhattan will take about 40 minutes and will cost you up to $30.

Buses and coaches can take anything from 40 minutes to an hour to arrive in Manhattan, but cost no more than $10. Electronic boards around the terminal list departure times of all these services.

For early morning flights, there are hotels located in and around the airport grounds. City hotels can be booked on arrival through the courtesy

phones which are linked directly to various Manhattan hotels. At Newark, these are located in all three terminals.

USEFUL ADDRESSES

**Airport Information
Service**
📞 *(201) 961-2000.*

**Holiday Inn
International**
1000 Spring St, Elizabeth, N J.
📞 *(800) 465-4329.*

Marriott Hotel
Newark Airport grounds.
📞 *(800) 228-9290.*

Monitors showing ground transport information, Newark Airport

Arriving in New York

THIS MAP SHOWS the links between New York's three airports and the centre of Manhattan. It also illustrates rail connections linking New York to the rest of the United States and Canada. Travel information, including journey times for subway, bus, coach and helicopter services, is listed in each information box. The passenger ship terminal, once New York's key point of arrival for the flood of post-war immigrants, is located a short distance from the centre of Manhattan. The Port Authority Bus Terminal, nearby, provides services across the city.

Ships at the passenger terminal

🛳 PASSENGER SHIP TERMINAL

Piers 88–92 for QE2 and other cruise ship arrivals and departures.

Passenger Ship Terminal

Port Author[ity] Bus Termin[al]

🚌 PORT AUTHORITY BUS TERMINAL

All long-distance buses arrive and depart here; links to all city airports.

🚆 PENN STATION

*Long-distance trains from **Canada** and other US states arrive and depart here; daily commuter train services to **Long Island** and **New Jersey**.*
🚆 *Amtrak, Long Island Rail Road and New Jersey Transit services.*
Ⓜ *A, C, E, 1, 2, 3, 9.*

Penn Station

Chelsea and the Garment District

KEY

🛫	Airport *see pp363–5*
🛳	Seaport *see p362*
🚆	Rail link *see p362*
🚌	Bus station/link *see p362*
Ⓜ	Subway link *see pp374–5*
🚤	Water shuttle
🚁	Helicopter link *see p364*

— Carey Airport Express and Gray Line Air Shuttle *see p363*

— Water shuttle

— Helicopter *see p364*

— Long Island Rail Road *see pp376–7*

— New Jersey Transit buses *see p363*

— Olympia Airport Express *see p363*

— Shuttle bus *see p364*

— Subway line A *see p374*

Greenwich Village

Gray Line A[ir] Shuttle buse[s] take passen[gers] to any poin[t] between 23rd and 63rd str[eets]

SoHo and TriBeCa

East Village

Seaport and the Civic Center

Lower East Side

World Trade Center
Ⓜ Metro North.
A, C, E, 2, 3.

Lower Manhattan

Pier 11

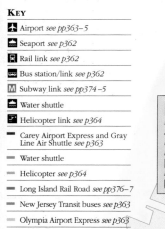

✈ NEWARK

Bus service to central Manhattan every 20–30 mins.
🚌 ***Olympia Airport Express** every 20–30 mins to the **World Trade Center**, **Penn Station** and **Grand Central Terminal**.*
🚌 ***New Jersey Transit** buses every 15–20 mins to the **Port Authority Bus Terminal**.*

Delta Water Shuttle from LaGuardia

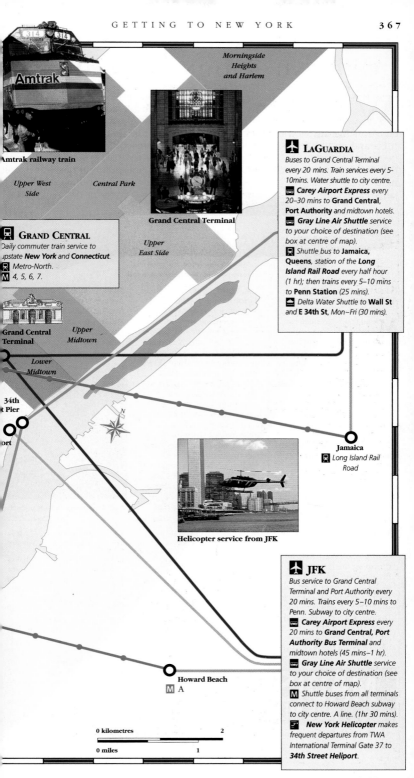

Amtrak railway train

Morningside Heights and Harlem

Upper West Side

Central Park

Grand Central Terminal

🚆 GRAND CENTRAL
Daily commuter train service to upstate **New York** and **Connecticut**.
🚆 Metro-North.
Ⓜ 4, 5, 6, 7.

Grand Central Terminal

Upper East Side

Upper Midtown

Lower Midtown

34th St Pier

✈ LAGUARDIA
Buses to Grand Central Terminal every 20 mins. Train services every 5–10mins. Water shuttle to city centre.
🚌 *Carey Airport Express* every 20–30 mins to **Grand Central, Port Authority** and midtown hotels.
🚌 *Gray Line Air Shuttle* service to your choice of destination (see box at centre of map).
Ⓡ Shuttle bus to **Jamaica, Queens,** station of the **Long Island Rail Road** every half hour (1 hr); then trains every 5–10 mins to **Penn Station** (25 mins).
🚢 *Delta Water Shuttle* to **Wall St** and **E 34th St**, Mon–Fri (30 mins).

Jamaica
🚆 Long Island Rail Road

Helicopter service from JFK

✈ JFK
Bus service to Grand Central Terminal and Port Authority every 20 mins. Trains every 5–10 mins to Penn. Subway to city centre.
🚌 *Carey Airport Express* every 20 mins to **Grand Central, Port Authority Bus Terminal** and midtown hotels (45 mins–1 hr).
🚌 *Gray Line Air Shuttle* service to your choice of destination (see box at centre of map).
Ⓜ Shuttle buses from all terminals connect to Howard Beach subway to city centre. A line. (1hr 30 mins).
🚁 *New York Helicopter* makes frequent departures from TWA International Terminal Gate 37 to **34th Street Heliport**.

Howard Beach
Ⓜ A

| 0 kilometres | 2 |
| 0 miles | 1 |

GETTING AROUND NEW YORK

WITH OVER SIX thousand miles of streets, walking around New York could prove difficult. But the city is a network of districts and many of the major sites can be visited area by area. Taxis are best for door-to-door transit but can be held-up in traffic jams, especially during rush hours. The city's bus service is reliable and cheap, but is often slow. The subway is quick, cheap and reliable, but first-time users can find the system confusing. There are no weekly or day passes valid for all forms of public transport, but buses and train systems have their own forms of travel passes.

Stretch limousine, the preferred transport for New York's glitterati

NEGOTIATING THE AVENUES AND STREETS

MANHATTAN'S avenues run approximately north to south; its streets (except in the older areas) run east to west. Fifth Avenue is used as an arbitrary centre line for the measurement of East and West addresses; No. 5 West 40th Street is, for example, a few doors west of Fifth Avenue on 40th Street, and No. 5 East 40th is a few doors to the east.

Most streets in midtown are one-way. In general, traffic is eastbound on even-numbered streets and westbound on odd-numbered streets. Avenues also tend to be one-way, alternating northbound or southbound.

First, Third, above 23rd Street, Madison, Eighth, Avenue of the Americas (6th Ave), and Tenth avenues, are all northbound, while Second, Lexington, Fifth, Seventh, Ninth and Broadway below 59th Street are southbound. There is two-way traffic on York, Park, Eleventh, Twelfth and Broadway above 60th Street.

Although most city blocks north of Houston Street are rectangular, they are not very uniform: east–west blocks are three or even four times longer than north–south blocks.

When asking directions from a New Yorker, you may get confused over certain streets. For instance, Avenue of the Americas, is still known as Sixth Avenue, and Seventh Avenue is often called Fashion Avenue. Many intersections and tiny plazas have also been given titles commemorating famous people or local events.

Rush-hour gridlock in Manhattan

FINDING AN ADDRESS

A useful formula has been devised to help pinpoint any **Avenue Address**. By dropping the last digit of the address, dividing the remainder by 2, then adding or subtracting the **Key Number** given here, you will discover the nearest cross street. For example: to find No. 826 Lexington Avenue first you have to drop the 6, divide 82 by 2, which is 41, then add **22** (the key number). Therefore, the nearest cross street is 63rd Street.

Avenue Address	Key Number	Avenue Address	Key Number
1st Ave	+3	9th Ave	+13
2nd Ave	+3	10th Ave	+14
3rd Ave	+10	Amsterdam Ave	+60
4th Ave	+8	Audubon Ave	+165
5th Ave, up to 200	+13	Broadway above	
5th Ave, up to 400	+16	23rd St	-30
5th Ave, up to 600	+18	Central Park W, divide	
5th Ave, up to 775	+20	full number by 10	+60
5th Ave 775–1286,		Columbus Ave	+60
do not divide by 2	-18	Convent Ave	+127
5th Ave, up to 1500	+45	Lenox Ave	+110
5th Ave, up to 2000	+24	Lexington Ave	+22
(6th) Ave of the		Madison Ave	+26
Americas	-12	Park Ave	+35
7th Ave below		Park Ave South	+08
110th St	+12	Riverside Drive, divide	
7th Ave above		full number by 10	+72
110th St	+20	St Nicholas Ave	+110
8th Ave	+10	West End Ave	+60

MADISON AVENUE

A road sign for Madison Avenue positioned at an intersection with a street

However, the maps in this guide use the place names that most New Yorkers know and regularly use.

PLANNING YOUR JOURNEY

THE STREETS and sidewalks are busiest during the rush hours – 8 to 10am, 11.30am to 1.30pm and 4.30 to 6.30pm, Monday to Friday. Throughout these periods it is better to face the crowds on foot than attempt any journey by bus, taxi or subway. At other times of day and during certain holiday periods *(see p53)*, the traffic is often much lighter and you should reach your destination quickly.

There are, of course, a few exceptions. Fifth Avenue should always be avoided on parade days (St Patrick's Day and Thanksgiving Day are the worst). Celebrity visits or one of the regular demonstrations at City Hall *(see p90)* can cause major disruption to the traffic. The area around Seventh Avenue, south of 42nd Street, is likely to be busy during the day with the truck and handcart traffic of New York's garment industry.

WALKING

MOST INTERSECTIONS between avenues and streets have lampposts with name-markers and electric traffic signals. The traffic lights show red (stop) and green (go) for vehicles and "Walk–Don't Walk" for pedestrians. You

Pedestrian crossing

Do not cross the road

You may cross the road

will quickly come to realize, however, that most New York pedestrians rely on their eyes and judgment rather than on the numerous "Walk" signs.

Remember that vehicles keep to the right. There are no cautionary "Look Left" signs to alert you to the direction of oncoming traffic. There are, however, numerous one-way streets, so it's best to look both ways before you cross Beware, too, of cars, trucks and taxis turning the corner behind you as you start to cross the road.

There are pedestrian crossings at some intersections. These are officially designated pedestrian crossing points, although they are more often than not ignored by both pedestrians and motorists alike. Do not rely on them. The city has few underground subways for pedestrians.

Circle Line tour boat

Staten Island Ferry leaving Battery Park

FERRIES

There are two ferries of interest to visitors *(see also p353)*: the Circle Line runs a ferry to the Statue of Liberty and Ellis Island several times each day from Battery Park at the southern tip of Manhattan. The 24-hour Staten Island ferry service from Battery Park travels the channel, offering splendid sea views of Manhattan, the Statue of Liberty, the bridges and Governors Island for only 50 cents. You can also stay on board and return to Manhattan without having to pay any extra charge.

CYCLING

FOR VISITORS who want to cycle around New York it is probably safer to stick to park pathways (in Central Park and along the East and Hudson rivers) and to use them only during daylight hours. You can rent bikes at AAA Bicycle Rentals in Central Park.
Useful information AAA Bicycle Rentals. 861-4137.

Cyclist in Central Park

Driving in New York

HEAVY TRAFFIC AND EXPENSIVE rental cars make driving in New York a frustrating experience. You must wear a seat belt. The speed limit is 35 mph (56 km/h) – which is difficult to exceed because of Manhattan's potholes and traffic. Most streets are one-way and there are traffic lights at every corner. Driving is on the right.

Traffic queuing on Sixth Avenue

HIRING A CAR

TO HIRE A CAR you must be able to prove you are at least 25 years old. You will need a valid driver's licence (an International Driver's Licence is useful but not essential) and a recognized credit card otherwise you will have to pay a large deposit.

Unless you are adequately covered by your own insurance policy, you should also take out damage and liability protection, as vandalism and theft are common. Refill with petrol before you return the car or you'll pay double the street price for fuel. It is cheaper to hire a car in the city than at the airports.

TRAFFIC SIGNS

Black and white pedestrian striped markings on many street crossings mean that pedestrians have right of way. At intersections, they indicate that traffic should keep out when the traffic light is red. Unlike the rest of New York State, you can never turn right on a red light.

Traffic flows in a single direction

PARKING

PARKING IN Manhattan is difficult and costly. Car parks (parking garages) always post their rates at the entrance. Some hotels include parking charges in their room rates.

In some areas there are meters at the kerb for short term (20–60 minutes) parking. Don't be tempted to park at out-of-order meters – you may receive a parking ticket. Yellow street and kerb markings mean no parking.

"Alternate side" parking applies on most of the city's side streets. Cars may usually be left all day and night but must be moved to the other side of the street before 8am the next day. For specific information call the **Transportation Department.**

PENALTIES

IF YOU RECEIVE a parking ticket, you have seven days to pay the required fine or to appeal against it. If you have any queries about your ticket call the **Parking Violations Bureau** between 8.30am and 7pm on any weekday.

New York's tow-away brigades are extremely active, and one-third of cars towed suffer damage. If you cannot find your car at its parking place, first of all call the traffic department's tow-away office. The pound is open 24 hours a day, Monday to Saturday. You can redeem your car for a hefty fine of $150, plus $5 per day storage fee. Traveller's cheques, certified cheques, money orders and cash are all accepted. There is an ATM machine *(see p358)* on the premises. If you have rented the car, the rental contract must be produced and only the authorized driver (you'll need your licence) may collect the car. If your car is not there, report its loss to the police.

Useful information Police █ *911;* Parking Violations Bureau █ *477-4430;* Traffic Dept, Tow Pound, Pier 76, West 38th St and Twelfth Ave. **Map** 7 1B. █ *788-7800;* Transportation Dept █ *442-7070.*

Police Department traffic officer

CAR HIRE AGENCIES

IF YOU WISH TO rent a car while in New York, agencies are listed in the telephone directory under *Automobile Renting.* The major rental companies include:

Avis
█ *(800) 331-1212.*

Budget
█ *(800) 527-0700.*

Dollar
█ *(800) 800-4000.*

Hertz
█ *(800) 654-3131.*

National
█ *(800) 227-7368.*

Entry prohibited

50mph (80km/h) speed limit

Give way to all vehicles

Stop at intersection

New York's Taxis

New York taxi cab

Aʟʟ ʟɪᴄᴇɴsᴇᴅ ᴛᴀxɪ cabs are yellow. If their roof numbers are lit up, they are available for hire and can be flagged down. Occupied cabs have their top lights switched off. Taxis that are not on duty have their "Off-Duty" sign lit. Only licensed cabs are authorized to pick up people who hail them from the street; accepting a ride from anyone else can be dangerous and expensive.

Tᴀᴋɪɴɢ ᴀ Cᴀʙ

Eᴠᴇʀʏ ʏᴇʟʟᴏᴡ ᴄᴀʙ has a meter and many can issue printed receipts. A taxi can carry up to four passengers with a single fare covering everyone on board.

Taxi stands are scarce; hotels, Penn Station and Grand Central Terminal are by far the best places to seek cabs.

Licensed taxis undergo periodic inspections and are insured against accidents and losses. Non-licensed or "gypsy" cabs are unlikely to have these safeguards.

As soon as the cab driver accepts your custom the meter starts ticking at around $1.50. The fare increases by about 25 cents after each additional 292 yards (320 metres). Surcharges will then be added for waiting time and journeys between 8pm and 6am. A few drivers now accept credit cards but most will want to be payed in cash. Tip the driver no more than 15%.

Cab driving is a traditional occupation of newly arrived immigrants and, as such, communication can be a problem. Although owners of licensed cabs must pass exams in English comprehension and the layout of the city they will not necessarily understand either. Make sure your driver understands exactly

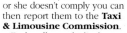

A printed receipt available from most taxi cabs

where you want to go before you start your journey.

By law, a driver must take you anywhere in the city unless the off-duty sign is lit and the roof light is off. The driver should not ask you your destination until after you've sat down, and must follow your requests not to smoke, to open or close a window, and to pick up or drop off passengers as you direct. If he or she doesn't comply you can then report them to the **Taxi & Limousine Commission**.

Each yellow cab displays the driver's photograph and registered number next to the meter. Drivers can be sullen, or try to overcharge or not cooperate with some of your requests. Make a note of the driver's number or the licence or receipt number (if you have requested one) and report it to a policeman.

Heavy one-way traffic on one of the city's avenues

Tᴀxɪ Nᴜᴍʙᴇʀs

Taxi & Limousine Commission
📞 302-8294.

Yellow Cab Information
📞 840-4572.

Lost Property
📞 302-8294.

If you would prefer to use a radio-dispatched taxi, call:

Bell Radio Taxi
📞 691-9191
or (800) 344-3974 (freephone).

Big Apple Car
📞 517-7010
or (800) 251-5001 (freephone).

Chris Limousines
📞 (718) 356-3232.

A meter will display your fare as it mounts up. Additional costs are then shown separately.

The roof-light illuminates the cab's number as well as the driver's "Off-Duty" sign.

Charge rates are listed clearly on the outside of the front passenger door.

Travelling by Bus

THE CITY'S 3,700 BLUE AND WHITE buses cover more than 200 routes in the five boroughs. Many run 24 hours a day, every day. The buses are modern, clean and air-conditioned. Travelling by bus is a good way to take in many of New York's sights. Buses are also considered very safe and tend not to get too crowded. Smoking is forbidden on all public buses and animals (except guide dogs) are not allowed.

TICKETS

FARES MUST BE PAID using a subway token, bought from a station or an "out-of-system" site like McDonald's, a MetroCard *(see p374)*, or with the correct change (only 5, 10 and 25 cent coins are accepted – no notes). The fare is a flat one, so you won't get any change.

Subway or bus token

If you need to change buses to reach your destination, you can request a free paper transfer when you pay your fare. This is valid for an hour and allows you to travel on any connecting bus.

There are discount fares for senior citizens and the disabled. Most buses can "kneel" which helps elderly people board *(see p354)*.

Be sure to have the correct fare ready before you board, so you don't attract attention by opening your wallet.

Bus transfer

RECOGNIZING YOUR BUS

Each bus stop serves more than one route, so look for the route number posted on the lighted strip above the wind-screen at the front of the bus. Ask the driver if he or she will be calling at your stop.

Exit the bus through the double doors towards the rear.

RIDING THE BUS

BUSES WILL ONLY stop at the designated bus stops. They follow north–south routes on the major avenues, stopping every two or three blocks. Crosstown buses, running east–west, stop at every block *(see p368)*. Many routes run a daily, 24-hour service, which becomes a lot less frequent during the evening and at night; other bus services only operate during the peak hours of 7am to 10pm.

Bus stops are marked by red, white and blue signs and yellow paint along the kerb. Most also have bus shelters. A route map and schedule is posted at each stop. When you have identified your bus, enter at the front door and deposit your coins or a subway token in the fare box. Ask the driver if the bus goes near your destination and request the stop at the nearest

The fare box is just inside the entrance doors, next to the driver.

Bus stops often have three-sided, glass-walled shelters.

This bus map shows the route and main stopping-off points for route M15.

point. The majority of New York's bus drivers are very friendly and will call out loud when they approach the stop you wanted.

To request a stop when travelling on the bus, press the vertical call strip between the windows. A "Stop Requested" sign, near the driver's head, will light up.

Leave through the double door located towards the rear of the bus. The driver will activate the door release as soon as the bus has stopped, but you then have to push the door to open it. If you do not keep a firm grip on the door handle, it is liable to swing back and hit you.

Route numbers appear on the front and side of the bus.

Enter the bus through the doors at the front.

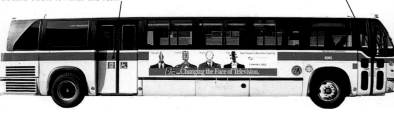

LONG-DISTANCE COACHES

COACHES TO THE rest of the USA and Canada leave from the **Port Authority Bus Terminal**. The terminal at the Manhattan end of the George Washington Bridge is for local coaches to northern New Jersey and New York's Rockland County.

Tickets for coaches leaving from the main terminal are sold at its Ticket Plaza main concourse. The long-distance bus company, Greyhound Coaches, and the commuter line, Short Line coaches, each has its own ticket counter. There are no reservations on Greyhound coaches, but Short Line do take bookings.

There are hygienic toilets with attendants on duty which are open from 6am to 10pm.

A long-haul Greyhound coach arriving in New York

BUS AND COACH INFORMATION

Route Maps
Available from MTA, 370 Jay St, Brooklyn, NY 11201.

Travel Information
(*(718) 330-1234 (24 hrs).*

Port Authority Bus Terminal
West 40th St and Eighth Ave.
Map 8 D1.
(*564-8484.*

George Washington Bridge Terminal
178th St and Broadway.
(*564-1114.*

Lost Property
(*(718) 625-6200.*

SIGHTSEEING BY BUS

For a pleasant and cheap alternative to a tour bus, hop on a city bus and see New York with the New Yorkers. Bus route M1 goes from 59th Street, along Fifth Avenue and onward to the Battery, returning north via the Wall Street area and Madison Avenue. Route M5 gives fine views of the Hudson River as buses travel north on Riverside Drive to the George Washington Bridge at 178th Street. Route M104 travels from the United Nations at First Avenue across 42nd Street, through Times Square, then follows Broadway north by Lincoln Center to Columbia University at 125th Street.

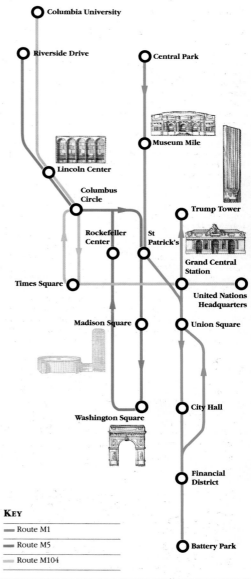

Columbia University
Riverside Drive
Central Park
Museum Mile
Lincoln Center
Columbus Circle
Trump Tower
Rockefeller Center
St Patrick's
Grand Central Station
Times Square
United Nations Headquarters
Madison Square
Union Square
Washington Square
City Hall
Financial District
Battery Park

KEY

Route M1
Route M5
Route M104

Using the Subway

New York subway logo

THE SUBWAY is the quickest and most reliable way to travel in the city. The vast system extends over 714 miles (1142 kilometres) and has 469 stations. Most routes operate 24 hours a day, throughout the year. Night services are less frequent, and fewer trains run at weekends. In the last few years the subway system has been completely upgraded and the trains are now air-conditioned, well lit and modern.

NEW YORK SUBWAY

MANY SUBWAY entrances are marked by illuminated spheres: green where the token booth is manned around the clock, red where there is restricted entry. Others are marked by a sign bearing the name of the station and the numbers or letters of the routes passing through it.

The subway system runs 24 hours a day, but some routes do have restricted operating times. The basic service is between 6am and midnight.

Always bear in mind that there are two types of train. Local trains call at all stations and express trains are faster and call at fewer stops. Both types of stop are distinguished on every subway map.

Safety on the subway has improved tremendously. If you travel between the rush hours of 8am to 6pm anywhere south of Central Park you should be safe. However, women should not travel alone after the evening rush hour

and no-one should travel to the outer boroughs, like the Bronx and Harlem, unless with a large group of people. Stand in well-lit spots, use the central carriages and avoid eye contact with unsavoury characters. In an emergency, contact the guard on the station.
Subway information New York City Transit Authority [(718) 330-1234; Metrocard Customer Service [(212) 638-7622

SUBWAY TOKENS

THE FARE is the same no matter how far you travel on the subway. There are no discount passes. Purchase a token from an attendant in a booth, from a token machine or from over 100 McDonalds. By 1997, the MetroCard, which is used in place of the token, will be available from all subway stations. The price of the MetroCard ranges from $5 to $80 depending on the number of journeys you plan to take.

Subway token and MetroCard

READING THE SUBWAY MAP

Each route is identified on the subway map *(see inside back cover)* by colour, by the names of the stations at each end of the line, and by a letter or number. For instance, the green (6) route links Woodlawn and Utica avenues, and is served by the No. 4 trains. Local and express stops and interchange points are identified. The letters and numbers

below the station names indicate which routes serve that particular station. A letter or number in heavy type indicates that trains on that route stop there between 6am and midnight; letters in lighter type mean that the route is served by a part-time service only; a boxed letter or number shows the last stop on the line. The maps posted in all the subway stations have a comprehensive guide which explains the trains and timetable of each route.

Ⓐ——— Line letter

———— Local stop

●——— Express stop

○——— Express and local stop

Free local transfers

Free express transfers

42 Street–Times Square

N·R Ⓢ

1·2·3 ⑦ 9

Express and local stops

Light type Part-time service

Boxed type Last stop on this line (full or part-time)

Free transfers from line to line

Bold type Full-time service

This station's green sphere shows that it is staffed continuously

MAKING A JOURNEY BY SUBWAY

1 There is a map of the subway system on the back inside cover of this book. Large-scale maps are also positioned in prominent areas in every station, usually very near the token booth.

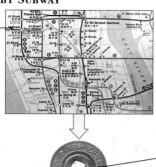

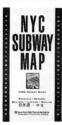

Subway map

Booth with agent

2 Buy a token from an agent in a booth or from a token machine.

Token machine

3 Deposit the token in the turnstile to pass through to the platform.

Token deposit slot

4 Follow the directions for the train you want. For safety, stay in sight of the token booth as you wait for your train; at night, stay in one of the yellow off-hours waiting areas.

→ Uptown Local ① ⑨

Off-hours waiting area

5 Each train displays its route number or letter in the appropriate colour, and the names of the terminal stations.

242 St–Van Cortlandt Park Bronx
South Ferry Manhattan

Route indicator

6 Once aboard, you will find a system map next to the door on each side of the carriage. Use it to follow your progress. Stops are announced on the public address system, and you will also see the station names at each platform. The doors are operated by the driver. For safety, be sure to enter a well-populated carriage.

① ⑨ Broadway Skip-Stop Express

7 After leaving the train, look for signs giving directions to the exit. If you need to change trains then follow the signs to the connecting platforms.

→ Exit **33 St** Penn Station
7 Av Madison Square Garden
Amtrack LIRR NJ Transit

Travelling by Train

NEW YORK HAS TWO main train stations. Grand Central Terminal is served by commuter trains from New York's suburbs and Connecticut, while Pennsylvania (Penn) Station is the terminal for long-haul services from the rest of the US and also Canada. Most commuter trains have no buffet cars on board, so it's best to buy any food and drink you want before boarding the train. Seat reservations are only available on the long-haul intercity services.

An Amtrak train

GRAND CENTRAL TERMINAL

GRAND CENTRAL Terminal *(see pp154–5)* on Park Avenue between 41st and 42nd streets is the main terminal for **Metro-North** Railroad trains (Hudson, New Haven and Harlem lines) which run to the north and east of New York, and serve southwest Connecticut, Westchester, Dutchess and Putnam counties. From Grand Central you might travel by train to destinations such as the International Wildlife

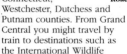

Conservation Park *(see pp242–3)* and President Franklin Roosevelt's large Hyde Park estate.

Train numbers 4, 5 and 6 on the green line and number 7 on the purple line serve Grand Central subway station. There is a shuttle service which links Grand Central to Times Square. Many bus lines stop at Grand Central.

PENN STATION

PENN STATION, between Seventh and Eighth avenues and from 31st to 33rd streets, is a modern terminal which was rebuilt in 1963 underneath the Madison Square Garden complex *(see p133)*. Commuter trains, New Jersey Transit trains and **Amtrak** trains from Canada and other parts of America terminate at this station. There are no luggage trolleys, but redcap porters are on hand to help.

You will find taxis at street level. Buses run downtown on Seventh Avenue and uptown on Eighth Avenue. The blue A, C, and E subway lines run on the Eighth Avenue side of the station; the red 1, 2, 3 and 4 lines run on the Seventh Avenue side. The ticket counters and waiting rooms are at street level while the trains actually leave from the level below.

From Penn Station, you could head for New Jersey and Long Island or further afield on Amtrak trains to such destinations as Canada, Philadelphia or Washington.

Long Island Rail Road logo

Adjoining Penn Station are the many ticket offices and departure points of the **Long Island Rail Road (LIRR)**. This is primarily a commuter railroad, but it also has trains running to the resorts of Long Island, such as the Hamptons and Montauk Point.

PATH TRAINS

PATH TRAINS operate round the clock between New Jersey stations (Harrison, Hoboken, Jersey City and Newark) and Penn Station in Manhattan. They also stop at Christopher Street, the World Trade Center, Ninth, 14th, 23rd and 33rd streets and Avenue of the Americas.

LIRR train at Penn Station

AMTRAK

AMTRAK IS THE US national railroad passenger service linking New York with other American cities and Canada. Some Amtrak trains have carriages with reclining seats; others have dining facilities and lounge cars. Sleeper carriages are available on all long-haul routes. Some fast trains operate on certain Amtrak routes, such as the **Metroliner** between Boston and Washington via New York.

Tickets can be bought at Penn Station, as well as from Amtrak Travel Centers. Buy your ticket before getting on the train as there is a penalty for buying tickets on board. Senior citizens receive a 15% discount; the conductor will ask for proof of age. There are no student discounts. Seat reservations organized over the phone with a credit card need to be made at least 10 days in advance of travel, as the tickets are posted to you.

Amtrak also offers a Great American Vacations package and various promotional fares during the year. Ask for information when you book.

Grand Central Terminal

Information board at Penn Station

TICKETS AND TRAVEL

TICKETING AREAS at all train stations are well lit and generally crowded at all times of the day. Ticket offices will accept most credit cards, as well as cash. There are a variety of ticket types, most of which are based on a one-way fare; a return fare is simply twice the single fare. If you are planning a number of trips, Metro-North and LIRR offer weekly passes which are excellent value for money.

Train times, destination and gate numbers are continually updated on numerous large information boards. Look out for signs indicating the major interim stops and transfer points, listed next to the gate for departing trains.

Wait for the opening of the gate posted for your train. The carriages are all one class, and have no reserved seating. The conductor will ask to see your ticket only after the train has left the station.

Both Penn Station and Grand Central Terminal have minimal facilities for travellers waiting for their trains, but both have toilet facilities.

TRAIN INFORMATION

Amtrak Travel Centers
12 West 51st St. **Map** *12 F4.*
1 East 59th St. **Map** *12 F3.*
1 World Trade Center. **Map** *1 B2.*
☏ *(800) USA-RAIL or*
(800) 872-7245.

Long Island Rail Road (LIRR)
☏ *(718) 217-LIRR (Information).*
☏ *(212) 643-5228 (Lost property).*

Metroliner
☏ *(800) 523-8720.*

Metro-North
☏ *532-4900 (Information).*
☏ *340-2555 (Lost property).*

PATH Trains
☏ *(800) 234-7284.*

DAY TRIPS BY TRAIN

There are some beautiful places outside New York city, which, if your time allows, are well worth a visit. Below is a list of some recommended sights within 125 miles (200 km) of New York city centre. For futher details ring the New York Convention and Visitors Bureau *(see p352).*

A scenic view of Tarrytown

Stony Brook
Peaceful north shore village. Entrance to the Three Villages historic district.
🚊 *58 miles (93 km) east. Long Island Rail Road from Penn Station. 2 hrs.*

The Hamptons
Chic bars and boutiques in a weathered, historic setting. The Beverly Hills of Long Island.
🚊 *100 miles (161 km) east. Long Island Rail Road from Penn Station. 2 hrs, 50 min.*

Montauk Point
State park on the eastern-most tip of Long Island; windswept ocean views.
🚊 *120 miles (193 km). LIRR from Penn Station. 3 hrs.*

Westbury House, Old Westbury
John Phipps's 1906 recreation of a Charles II mansion with exquisite English formal gardens.
🚊 *24 miles (39 km) east. Long Island Rail Road from Penn Station. 40 min.*

Tarrytown
Washington Irving's home "Sunnyside" and Jay Gould's mansion.
🚊 *25 miles (40 km) north. Metro-North from Grand Central, then taxi. 40–50 min.*

Hyde Park
Springwood estate of Franklin D Roosevelt and the Vanderbilt mansion.
🚊 *74 miles (119 km) north. Metro-North from Grand Central to Poughkeepsie, then bus. 2 hrs.*

New Haven, Connecticut
Home of Yale University.
🚊 *74 miles (119 km). Metro-North from Grand Central Terminal. 1 hr, 46 min.*

Hartford, Connecticut
Mark Twain's riverboat-style house, Atheneum Museum and Old State House.
🚊 *112 miles (180 km) north. Amtrak from Penn Station. 2 hrs, 45 min.*

Winterthur, Delaware
Henry du Pont's collection of Early American art, museum and gardens.
🚊 *116 miles (187 km) south. Amtrak from Penn Station to Wilmington, then bus to Winterthur. 2 hrs.*

Yale University in New Haven, Connecticut

STREET FINDER

THE MAP REFERENCES given with all sights, hotels, restaurants, bars, shops and entertainment venues described in this book refer to the maps in this section (*see* How Map References Work *opposite*). These maps cover the whole of Manhattan. A complete index of street names and all the places of interest marked on the maps can be found on the following pages.

The key map *(below)* shows the areas covered by the *Street Finder*, within the various districts. The maps include all of Manhattan's sight-seeing areas (which are colour-coded), with all the districts important for hotels, restaurants, bars, shops and entertainment venues.

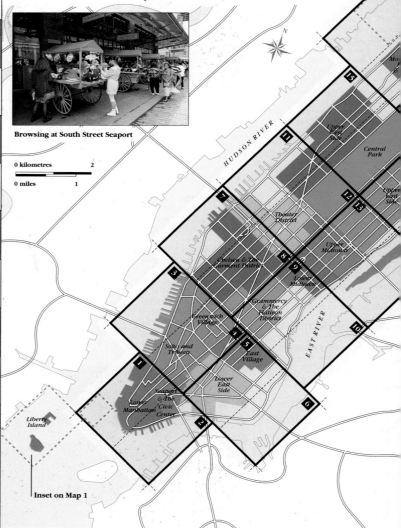

Browsing at South Street Seaport

| 0 kilometres | 2 |
| 0 miles | 1 |

Inset on Map 1

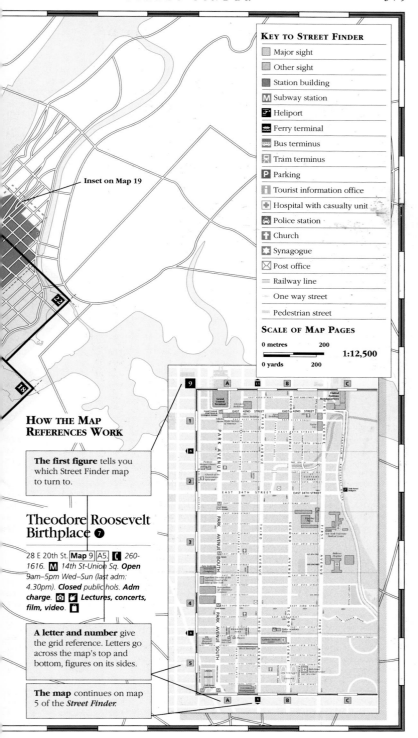

Inset on Map 19

KEY TO STREET FINDER

	Major sight
	Other sight
	Station building
M	Subway station
	Heliport
	Ferry terminal
	Bus terminus
	Tram terminus
P	Parking
i	Tourist information office
+	Hospital with casualty unit
	Police station
	Church
	Synagogue
⊠	Post office
=	Railway line
—	One way street
	Pedestrian street

SCALE OF MAP PAGES

0 metres	200	
		1:12,500
0 yards	200	

HOW THE MAP REFERENCES WORK

The first figure tells you which Street Finder map to turn to.

Theodore Roosevelt Birthplace ➐

28 E 20th St. **Map 9** **A5.** **C** 260-1616. **M** 14th St-Union Sq. **Open** 9am–5pm Wed–Sun (last adm: 4.30pm). **Closed** public hols. **Adm charge.** 📷 🎬 **Lectures, concerts, film, video.** 🚻

A letter and number give the grid reference. Letters go across the map's top and bottom, figures on its sides.

The map continues on map 5 of the *Street Finder.*

Street Finder Index

Each place name is followed by its borough (unless in Manhattan) and then by its Street Finder reference

Each place name is followed by its borough (unless in Manhattan) and then by its Street Finder reference

Each place name is followed by its borough (unless in Manhattan) and then by its Street Finder reference

Each place name is followed by its borough (unless in Manhattan) and then by its Street Finder reference

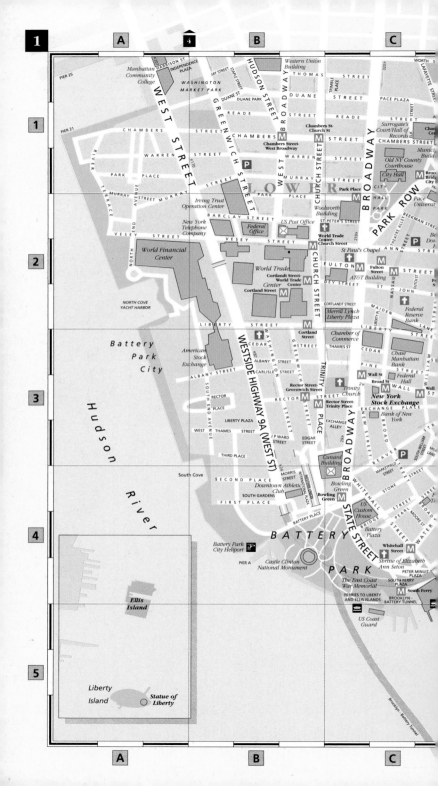

NORTH 9TH STREET

NORTH 8TH STREET

NORTH 7TH STREET

NORTHE 6TH STREET

NORTH 5TH STREET

NORTH 4TH STREET

NORTH 3RD STREET

METROPOLITAN AVENUE

NORTH 1ST STREET

GRAND STREET

SOUTH 1ST STREET

SOUTH 2ND STREET

SOUTH 3RD STREET

SOUTH 4TH STREET

SOUTH 5TH STREET

SOUTH 6TH STREET

SOUTH 8TH STREET

SOUTH 9TH ST

SOUTH 11TH ST

BERRY STREET

WYTHE AVENUE

KENT AVENUE

BEDFORD AVENUE

#215

DUNHAM PLACE

BROADWAY

375TH

BERRY STREET

WYTHE STREET

AVENUE

DIVISION AVENUE

RIVER

Williamsburg Bridge

Fireboat Station

EAST

AST

chletic Field

RIVER

PARK

FRANKLIN D ROOSEVELT DRIVE

MANGIN STREET

Y PLACE

STREET

SOUTH

STREET

SAMUEL A L SQUARE

CHERRY STREET

CHERRY STREET

PARK

CORLEARS HOOK PARK

VIADUCT

Corlears Hook

PIER 44

Wallabout Channel

US Naval Reserve Center

Wallabout Bay

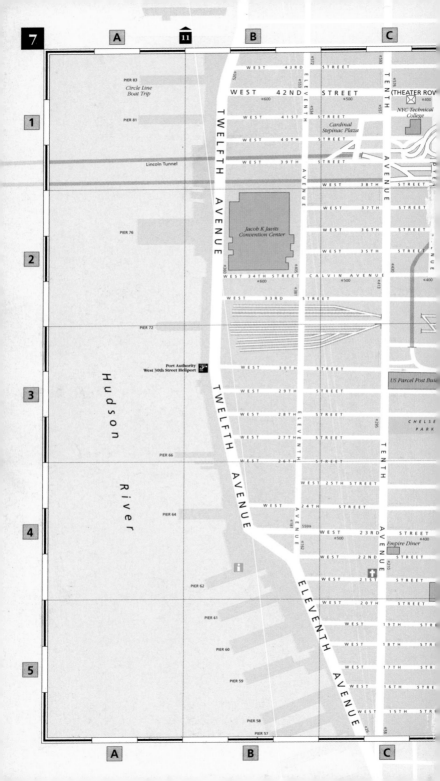

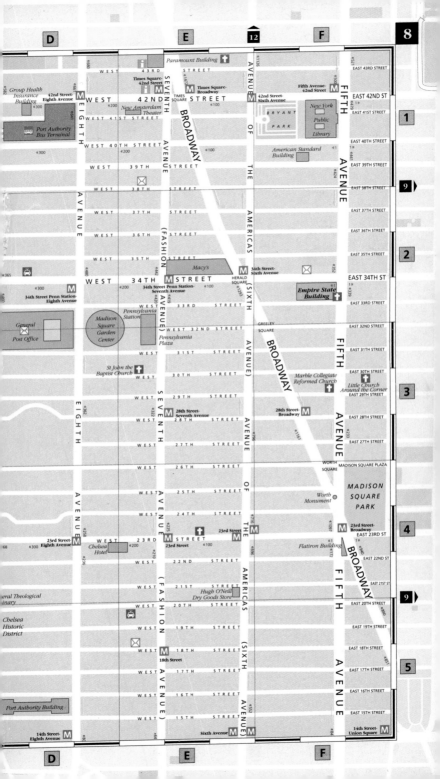

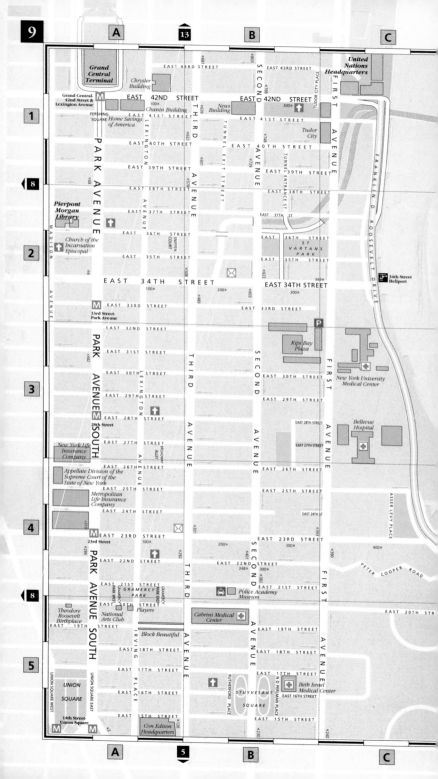

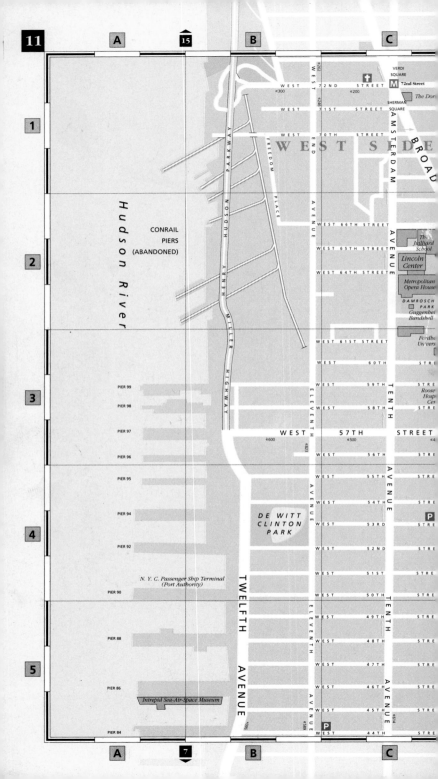

A B C

15

1

2

3

4

5

7

WEST 72ND STREET
«300 «240 «200

VERDI SQUARE
72nd Street M
SHERMAN SQUARE
The Dor

WEST 71ST STREET

WEST 70TH STREET

W E S T   S I D E

BROAD
AMSTERDAM

WEST 66TH STREET

AVENUE

AVENUE

The
Juilliard
School

Lincoln
Center

WEST 65TH STREET

WEST 64TH STREET

Metropolitan
Opera House

DAMROSCH PARK

Guggenhei
Bandshell

Fordha
Univers

WEST 61ST STREET

WEST 60TH STREET

WEST 59TH STREET

TENTH

Roose
Hosp
Cen

WEST 58TH STREET

ELEVENTH

WEST 57TH STREET
«600 «823 «500 «4

WEST 56TH STREET

WEST 55TH STREET

AVENUE

AVENUE

WEST 54TH STREET

AVENUE

P

WEST 53RD STREET

DE WITT
CLINTON
PARK

WEST 52ND STREET

WEST 51ST STREET

WEST 50TH STREET

TENTH

N. Y. C. Passenger Ship Terminal
(Port Authority)

PIER 90

TWELFTH

ELEVENTH

WEST 49TH STREET

WEST 48TH STREET

PIER 88

AVENUE

WEST 47TH STREET

WEST 46TH STREET

PIER 86

AVENUE

TENTH

Intrepid Sea-Air-Space Museum

WEST 45TH STREET

PIER 84

AVENUE

P

WEST 44TH STREET

Hudson River

CONRAIL
PIERS
(ABANDONED)

HENRY HUDSON PARKWAY

FREEDOM PLACE

MILLER HIGHWAY

PIER 99

PIER 98

PIER 97

PIER 96

PIER 95

PIER 94

PIER 92

A B C

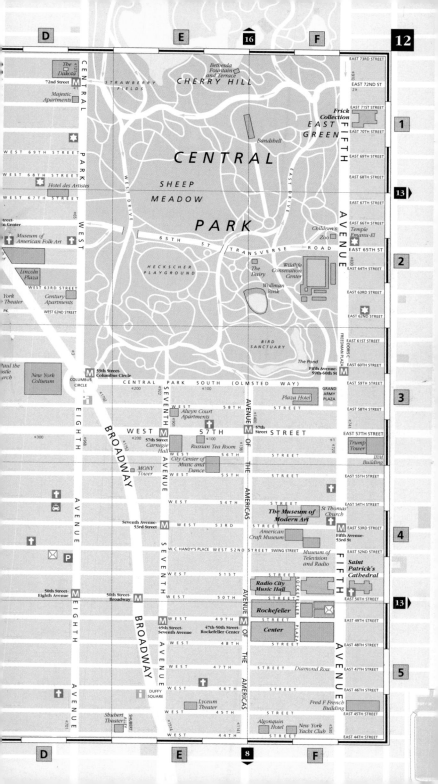

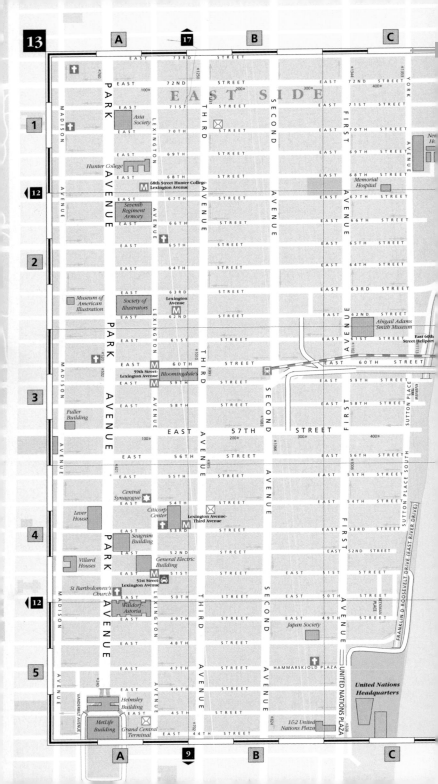

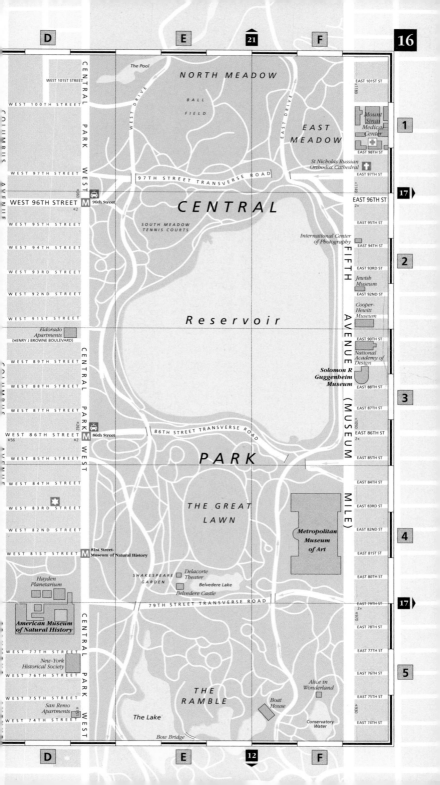

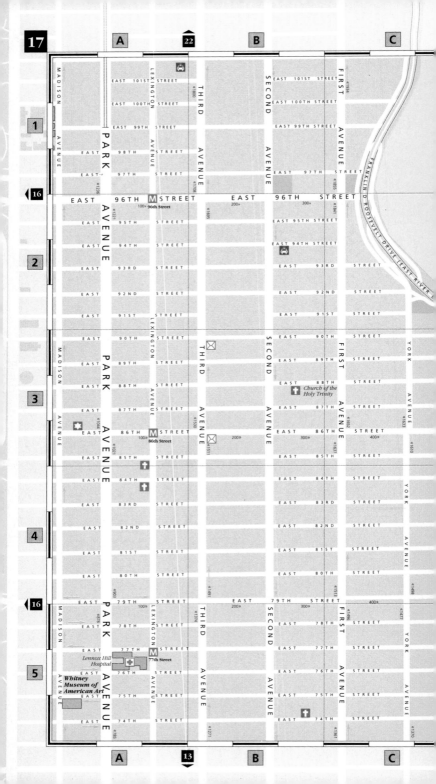

East River

Triborough Bridge

Hell Gate

SHORE BOULEVARD

ASTORIA PK SOUTH

1

Pot Cove

MILL ROCK PARK

12TH STREET

14TH STREET

26TH AVENUE

4TH STREET

9TH STREET

2ND STREET

3RD STREET

1ST STREET

8TH STREET

27TH STREET

AVENUE

2

28TH AVENUE

ASTORIA BOULEVARD

MAIN AVENUE

WELLING STREET

30TH AVENUE

VERNON BOULEVARD

30TH STREET

30TH ROAD

Gracie Mansion

CARL

SCHURZ

PARK

LIGHTHOUSE PARK

Hallets Cove

30TH DRIVE

12TH STREET

31ST AVENUE

3

GRACIE SQ

GRACIE TERRACE

FDR DRIVE (EAST RIVER DRIVE)

FRANKLIN D ROOSEVELT DRIVE (EAST RIVER DRIVE)

ROOSEVELT ISLAND

West Channel

East Channel

MAIN STREET

31ST DRIVE

BROADWAY

33RD AVENUE

33RD ROAD

13TH STREET

4

RAINEY PARK

VERNON BOULEVARD

34TH AVENUE

9TH STREET

10TH STREET

11TH STREET

12TH STREET

STREET

5

BLACKWELL PARK

35TH AVENUE

19

A   B   C

145th Street Ⓜ

JACKIE ROBINSON PARK

145th Street Ⓜ

1

WEST 145TH STREET

WEST 144TH STREET

WEST 143RD STREET

HAMILTON PLACE

WEST 142ND STREET

Aunt Len's Doll and Toy Museum

Hamilton Grange National Monument

WEST 141ST STREET

AMSTERDAM AVENUE

CONVENT AVENUE

HAMILTON TERRACE

EDGECOMBE AVENUE

BRADHURST AVENUE

ST NICHOLAS AVENUE

FREDERICK DOUGLAS BOULEVARD (EIGHT AVENUE)

ADAM CLAYTON POWELL JR BOULEVARD (SEVENTH AVENUE)

LENOX AVENUE

WEST 145TH STREET

WEST 144TH STREET

WEST 143RD STREET

WEST 142ND STREET

WEST 141ST STREET

2

Hamilton Heights

WEST 140TH STREET

WEST 139TH ST

WEST 138TH STREET

WEST 136TH ST

City College of the University of NY

St Nicholas Historic District

Abyssinian Baptist Church ✝

Schomburg Center for Research in Black Culture

WEST 140TH STREET

WEST 139TH STREET

WEST 138TH STREET

WEST 137TH STREET

WEST 136TH STREET

ST NICHOLAS PARK

3

WEST 135TH STREET

135th Street Ⓜ

WEST 135TH STREET

135th Street Ⓜ

Harlem YMCA

WEST 134TH STREET

WEST 133RD STREET

WEST 132ND STREET

WEST 131ST STREET

21 ▼

4

Hudson

5

River

A   B   C

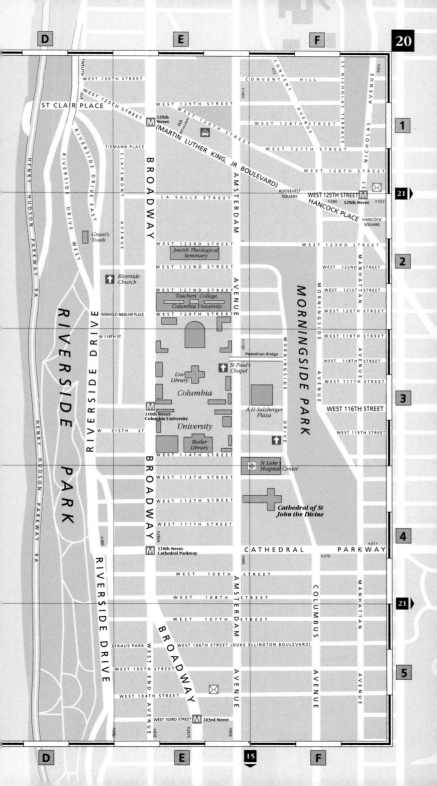

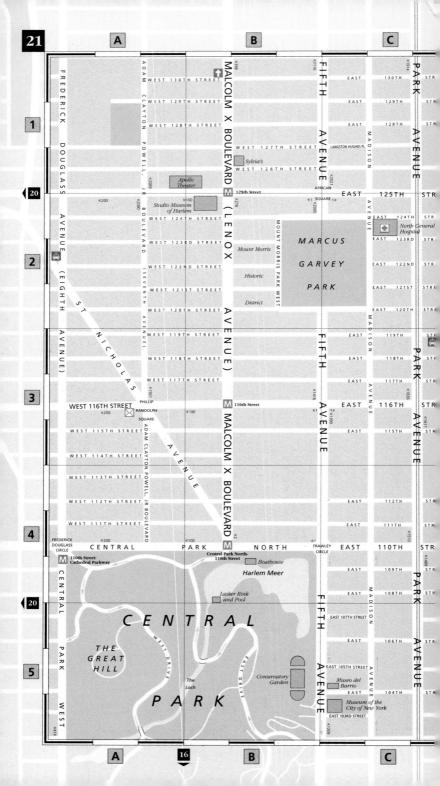

1

2

3

4

5

Harlem River

Willis Avenue Bridge

EAST 127TH STREET

EAST 126TH STREET

(TIN LUTHER KING, JR BOULEVARD)   200»

#2238

#2281

THIRD   AVENUE

SECOND   AVENUE

RONALD E McNAIR PLACE

SYLVAN PL

LOUIS GUVILLIER PARK

FRANKLIN D ROOSEVELT DRIVE

PALADINO   AVENUE

Triborough   Bridge

RANDALL'S

ISLAND

PARK

FIRST   AVENUE

EAST 120TH STREET

PLEASANT   AVENUE

EAST 119TH STREET

EAST 118TH STREET

EAST 117TH STREET

#2254

IS   MUÑOZ   MARIN   BOULEVARD)

#103   200»   300»   #238   400»

EAST 115TH STREET

EAST 114TH STREET

JEFFERSON

PARK

FRANKLIN D ROOSEVELT DRIVE (EAST RIVER DRIVE)

EAST 113TH STREET

EAST 112TH STREET

EAST 111TH STREET

#2135

EAST 110TH STREET

#2002

EAST 109TH STREET

#1981

EAST 108TH STREET

THIRD   AVENUE

SECOND   AVENUE

FIRST   AVENUE

Benjamin

Franklin

Plaza

97TH STREET

EAST 106TH STREET

RECREATION   PIER

Harlem

River

EAST 105TH STREET

EAST 104TH STREET

#2001

EAST 103RD STREET

Foot Bridge

General Index

Guys and Dolls (Runyon) 332
Gyms, Fitness Centres and Health
 Clubs 344, 345

H

H & H Bagels 326, 327
H & H Bagels East 346, 347
Haas, Richard 48, 59
 Alwyn Court Apartments 147
 Brooklyn Bridge mural 83
 Greene St murals 104
 New York Public Library murals
  144
 SoHo mural 103
Hacker Art Books 322, 323
Hackers, Hitters & Hoops 344, 345
Hagstrom Map & Travel Store
 322, 323
Hair 30
Hairdressers 352
Hale, Nathan 20, 90
Hall of Records 85
Hallowe'en Parade 52
Hamburger Harry's 305, 306
Hamilton, Alexander 21
 Bank of New York 57
 burial place 68, 256
 Hamilton Grange National
  Memorial 226
 New York Post 21
 statue 226
Hamilton (Alexander) Gallery 197
Hamilton Grange National
 Memorial 226
Hamilton Heights Historic District
 226
Hammacher Schlemmer 315, 316
Hammarskjöld, Dag
 Chagall's memorial 161
Hammerstein I, Oscar 145
Hammerstein II, Oscar 49, 146
Hammett, Dashiell 48
Hampshire Hotel and Suites 247, 277
Hamptons, The 377
Hands On 328, 329
Handy, W C 227
Hanover Square 56
Hanukkah Menorah 53
Harbour Lights 346, 347
Harbour of Dieppe (Turner) 200
Hard Rock Café 305, 306, 349
Harde and Short 147
Hardenbergh, Henry J
 The Dakota 41, 216
 Plaza Hotel 179
Haring, Keith 48
Harkness, Edward S 262
Harlem, Morningside Heights 16,
 43, 218–29
 The Cotton Club (film) 336
Harlem Heights 226
Harlem Spirituals, Inc 353
Harlem Week 51
Harlem YMCA 227
 area map 219
Harper, James 126
Harper's Weekly 263
Harrison, Rex 178
Harrison, Wallace 158
Harrison Street 105
Harry's New York Bar 309
Hartford, Connecticut 377
Hastings, Thomas
 Eternal Light Flagpole 124
 Forbes Building and Galleries 112
 New York Public Library 144

Hatsuhana 301
 New York's Best: Restaurants,
  Cafés and Bars 289
 restaurant choosing guide 291
Haughwout Building 104
 Street-by-Street map 103
Haupt (Enid A) Conservatory
 240–41
Hawley, Irad 112
Hayden, Charles 216
Hayden Planetarium 37, **216**
 area map 209
 Planetarium shop 315, 316
Hayes (Helen) 333
Hebrew Religious Articles 314, 316
Heidelberg Café 263
Heins and LaFarge 224–5
 Cathedral of St John the Divine
  224–5
Heisman Trophy 55
Helicopter Tours 353
Hell Gate 196
Helleu, Paul 155
Hell's Kitchen 42
 Irish community 44
Helmsley, Harry 49, **156**
Helmsley, Leona 49, 156
Helmsley Building 41, 156
 Street-by-Street map 151
Helmsley Middletowne 274, 280
Helmsley Palace Hotel (now New
 York Palace) 174, 305, 306
Hemingway, Ernest 260
Henderson, John C 196
Henderson Place 196
Hendrick, Chief of the Iroquois
 18
Hendricks, Harmon 110
Henrietta Hudson 342, 343
Henry, O
 Gift of the Magi, The 123
 Last Leaf, The 110
Hepburn, Audrey 110
Hepburn, Katharine
 Shubert Alley 146
 Turtle Bay Gardens 179
Hepworth, Barbara 60
Herald Square 132
 area map 129
 New York's Best: Shopping
  312–13
 Street-by-Street map 130–31
Herald Square Hotel 274, 276
Herter Brothers 124
Herts, Henry 146
Herts & Tallant 142, 246
Hertz 370
Hewitt sisters 184
Heye (George Gustav) Center 73
Hicks family 264
Hill, Joe 45
Hilton Hotel 343
Hilton JFK Airport 364
Himalayan Crafts and Tours 315
Hine, Lewis 135
Hip Sing 96
Hirschl & Adler Galleries 324, 325
 Street-by-Street map 102
 walking tour 262
Hispanic community 43, 44
 Puerto Rican Day Parade 51
 walking tour 258
Hispanic Society of America 232
Historic Richmond Town 19, 252
 museums beyond Manhattan 37
 Richmond County Fair 52

Historical Society Museum 252
Hit Show Club 329
Hit-Tix 328, 329
HMV 322, 323, 346
Hoffman, Dustin 108
 Actors' Studio 332
 San Remo 212
Hoffman, Malvina
 Church of the Heavenly Rest 182
 Sniffen Court 157
Hofmann, Hans 48
Holbein, Hans 200
Holiday, Billie 228
Holiday Inn Crowne Plaza 274, 278
Holiday Inn Downtown 274, 276
Holiday Inn International 365
Holiday Inn JFK 364
Holland, George 127
Holland Tunnel 28
Holy Trinity, Church of the 197
Home Savings of America **96**, **152**
 Street-by-Street 95, 150
Homer, Winslow 260
 National Academy of Design 184
Honmura An 290, 301
Hood, Raymond
 American Standard Building 143
 Group Health Insurance Building
  41, 145
 News Building 153
 Rockefeller Center 142
Hope, Bob 45
Hopper, Edward 261
 American Academy and Institute
  of Arts and Letters 232
 Early Sunday Morning 198
 Forbes Building and Galleries
  112
 The Lighthouse at Two Lights 192
 Washington Square 113
Horn (Linda) Antiques 324, 325
Hors d'Oeuvrerie 309, 342, 343
Horse-Riding and Racing 344, 345
Hospital Emergency Rooms 357
Hotalings 355
Hotel des Artistes 213
 area map 209
 Street-by-Street map 211
Hotel Pierre 310
Hotel Reservations A Meegan
 Services 269
Hotels 268–83
 airports 363–5
 bars 308–9
 bed and breakfast 270, 271
 booking 270
 booking agencies 269
 breakfast 269
 children 271
 disabled travellers 271
 hotel choosing guide 274–5
 facilities 269
 hidden extras 268
 listings symbols 271
 New York's Best: Hotels 272–3
 payment 270
 prices 268
 room service 269
 special breaks 270
 student lodgings 270
 tipping 269
 where to look 268
 youth hostels and dormitories
  270
Houdini, Harry 47, 124
Houdon, Jean Antoine 189

P

Pace Gallery 324, 325
  Fuller Building 179
  Street-by-Street map 103
Pace University 59
Pacino, Al 332
Palace 333
Paley, William S 169
Paley Park 166–7
Palio 291, 299
Palladium 340, 341
Palm Court 241
Palmer Video Store 346, 347
Pamir 292, 302
Pan Am Building see MetLife Building
Panache 318, 319
Papaya King 305, 306
PaperBag Players 349
Papp, Joseph
  Public Theater 116, 332, 335
  Shakespeare Festival 118
Papp (Florian) 324, 325
Paracas Textile 248
Paramount 277
  hotel choosing guide 274
  New York's Best: Hotels 272
Paramount Building 145
Paramount Pictures 244–5
Paris Through the Window
  (Chagall) 186
Park Avenue Plaza 167
Park Slope Historic District 246
Park Theater 91
Parker, Charlie "Bird" 49
  Apollo Theater 228
Parker, Dorothy 143
Parking and Garages
  hotels 269
  Parking Violations Bureau 370
Parrish, Maxfield 309
  St Regis 282
Parrish (Susan) Antiques 324, 325
Passports and Visas 354
Patchin Place 111
  Street-by-Street map 109
  walking tour 260
Patelson (Joseph) Music House Ltd 322, 323
PATH Trains 376, 377
Paul, Les 340
Pavarotti, Luciano 213
Pavlova, Anna 246
Peace Bell, United Nations 158
Peacock Alley 175, 281
Peale, Norman Vincent 131, 132
Peanut Butter & Jane 318, 319
Peculier Pub 308, 309
Pei, I M 136
Peking 84
Pelham Bay Park 344, 345
Pelli, Cesar 69
Pendant Mask 188
Peninsula 275, 281
  gym facilities 344
Pennsylvania Station 27, 30, 133, 362, 376
  arrival map 366
Penny Whistle Toys 314, 316
Peppermint Park 349
Performing Arts Shop 314, 316
Performing Garage 102
Periyali 290, 303
Perkins, George W 238
Perrault, Charles 162
Persistence of Memory, The (Dali) 172
Personal security and health 356–7

Peterson, Oscar 341
Pete's Tavern 308, 309
  Street-by-Street map 123
Petit, Philippe 72
Petrel 348, 349
Petrie European Sculpture Court 194
Phébus, Gaston 163
Philharmonic Rehearsals 331
Philip Morris Building 150
Phipps, John 377
Phone Booth 314, 316
Picasso, Pablo
  Brooklyn Museum 251
  Metropolitan Museum of Art 195
  Museum of Modern Art 173
  Bust of Sylvette 113
  Girl with a Mandolin 172
  Head of the Medical Student 172
  Les Demoiselles d'Avignon 171, 172
  Man with a Hat 172
  Picasso's portrait of Gertrude
  Stein 188, 195
  Woman Ironing 186
  Woman with Yellow Hair 187
Pickford, Mary 251
Pickwick Arms 275, 280
  New York's Best: Hotels 273
Pied Piper of Hamelin (Browning) 162
Pier 17 58, 257
  Street-by-Street map 83
Pierpont Morgan Library 162–3
  area map 149
  New York's Best: Museums 34
  New York's Libraries 37
  prints and photography 36
Pierpont Morgan Library Shop 314, 316
Pierre 41, 275, 282, 305, 306
Pierre de Wissant (Rodin) 251
Pig Heaven 292, 300
Pilothouse, The 82
Pioneer 83, 84
Piranesi, Giambattista 251
Pisano, Giovanni 195
Pissarro, Camille 251
Pizzeria Uno 304, 306
P.J. Carney's 308, 309
P.J Clarke's 307, 309
Place des Antiquaires 324, 325
Planet Hollywood 305, 306
Plant, Morton F 166, 168
Players, The 126
  Street-by-Street map 122–3
Plaza Athénée 275, 283
Plaza Fifty 269
Plaza Hotel **179**, 281, 305, 306
  area map 165
  hotel choosing guide 275
  New York's Best: Hotels 272
Plaza Pharmacy 346, 347
Plaza Rink 344, 345
Plymouth 333
Plymouth Church 264
Poe, Edgar Allan 48, 109, 124, 260
Poison Control Center 357
Police 356
Police Academy Museum 37, **127**
  area map 121
Police Headquarters Building 96
  Street-by-Street map 94–95
Police Plaza 59
Polish community 45
  Pulaski (Casimir) Day Parade 52
Pollard, George Mort 213

Pollock, Jackson 48
  Museum of Modern Art 172
  Autumn Rhythm 195
Pollock, St Clair 223
Polo/Ralph Lauren 317, 319
  walking tour 262
Pomander Walk 216
Pomodoro, Arnoldo 61
Pons, Lily 217
Port Authority Bus Terminal 366, 373
Porter, Cole 175
Porthault (D) & Co 326, 327
Portrait of the Princesse de Broglie
  (Ingres) 189
Poseidon Greek Bakery 326, 327
Postal Services 361
Postwar New York 30–1
Poussin, Nicolas 194
Powell, Jr, Adam Clayton 227
Power, Tyrone 179
Practical Information
  banking and currency 358–9
  credit cards 358
  customs and immigration 354
  disabled travellers 354
  electrical appliances 355
  Embassies and Consulates 355
  entertainment listings 353
  etiquette 352
  guided tours 353
  measurement conversion 354
  museums 352
  New York time 360
  newspapers, TV and radio 355
  opening hours 352
  personal security and health 356–7
  religious services 355
  sending a letter 361
  sightseeing tips 352
  student travellers 354
  telephones 360–61
  toilets 352
  tourist information 352
  travel insurance 357
Prada 320, 321
Pratesi 326, 327
President's Day 53
Press (J) men's clothes 317, 319
Prestige Entertainment 328, 329
Princeton Club, The 314, 316
  club's shop 320, 321
Printing House Fitness & Raquet Center 344, 345
Printing House Square 90–91
Prohibition 28–9
Prospect Park 24, **246–7**
  area map 231
  outdoor concert venue 339
Provence 290, 297
PS 122 332, 335
Public Service Commission 360–61
Public Theater (Papp, Joseph) **118**, 332, 335, 337
  area map 115
  Street-by-Street map 116
Pucelle, Jean 237
Puck Building 99
Pudd'nhead Wilson (Twain) 163
Puerto Rican Day Parade 51
Puerto Rico 229
Pulaski (Casimir) Day Parade 52
Pulitzer, Joseph 262
  School of Journalism, Columbia University 220
Pusterla, Attilio 85
Pyle, Howard 196

Acknowledgments

DORLING KINDERSLEY would like to thank the many people whose help and assistance contributed to the preparation of this book.

MAIN CONTRIBUTOR
Eleanor Berman has lived in New York for almost 40 years. Her travel articles are widely published and she is the author of *Away for the Weekend: New York,* a favourite since 1982. Her other books include *Away for the Weekend* guides for the Mid-Atlantic, New England and Northern California, *Travelling on Your Own,* and *Reflections of Washington, DC.*

MUSEUM CONTRIBUTORS
Michelle Menendez, Lucy O'Brien, Heidi Rosenau, Elyse Topalian, Sally Williams.

DORLING KINDERSLEY wishes to thank the following editors and researchers at Websters International Publishers: Sandy Carr, Matthew Barrell, Sara Harper, Miriam Lloyd, Ava-Lee Tanner, Celia Woolfrey.

ADDITIONAL PHOTOGRAPHY
Edward Hueber, Eliot Kaufman, Karen Kent, Norman McGrath, Howard Millard, Paul Solomon, Chuck Spang, Chris Stevens.

ADDITIONAL ILLUSTRATIONS
Steve Gyapay, Kevin Jones, Dinwiddie MacLaren, Janos Marffy, Chris D Orr, Nick Shewring, John Woodcock.

CARTOGRAPHY
Advanced Illustration (Cheshire), Contour Publishing (Derby), Europmap Ltd (Berkshire). Street Finder maps: ERA-Maptec Ltd (Dublin) adapted with permission from original survey and mapping by Shobunsha (Japan).

CARTOGRAPHIC RESEARCH
Roger Bullen, Tony Chambers, Ruth Duxbury, Ailsa Heritage, Jayne Parsons, Laura Porter, Donna Rispoli, Joan Russell, Jill Tinsley, Andrew Thompson.

DESIGN AND EDITORIAL ASSISTANCE
Keith Addison, Ron Boudreau, Linda Cabasin, Michelle Clark, Carey Combe, Diana Craig, Maggie Crowley, Guy Dimond, Tom Fraser, Alex Gray, Marcus Hardy, Sasha Heseltine, Pippa Hurst, Kim Inglis, Jane Middleton, Helen Partington, Leigh Priest, Nicki Rawson, Marisa Renzullo, Ellen Root, Liz Rowe, Anaïs Scott, Anna Streiffert, Clare Sullivan, Andrew Szudek.

SPECIAL ASSISTANCE
Beyer Blinder Belle, John Beatty at the Cotton Club, Peter Casey at the New York Public Library, Nicky Clifford, Linda Corcoran at the International Wildlife Conservation Park, Susan Ely at the Morgan Library, Jane Fischer, Deborah Gaines at the New York Convention and Visitors Bureau, Dawn Geigerich at the Queens Museum of Art, Peggy Harrington at St John the Divine, Pamela Herrick at the Van Cortlandt House, Marguerite Lavin at the Museum of the City of New York, Robert Makla at the Friends of Central Park, Gary Miller at the New York Stock Exchange, Laura Mogil at the American Museum of Natural History, Fred Olsson at the Shubert Organization, Dominique Palermo at the Police Academy Museum, Royal Canadian Pancake House, Lydia Ruth and Laura I Fries at the Empire State Building, David Schwartz at the American Museum of the Moving Image, Joy Sienkiewicz at the South Street Seaport Museum, Pam Snook at the New York City Transit Authority, staff at the Lower East Side Tenement Museum, Msgr Anthony Dalla Valla at St Patrick's Cathedral.

RESEARCH ASSISTANCE
Christa Griffin, Steve McClure, Sabra Moore, Jeff Mulligan, Marc Svensson, Vicky Weiner, Steven Weinstein.

PHOTOGRAPHIC REFERENCE
Duncan Petersen Publishers Ltd.

PHOTOGRAPHY PERMISSIONS
DORLING KINDERSLEY would like to thank the following for their kind permission to photograph at their establishments: American Craft Museum, American Museum of Natural History, Aunt Len's Doll and Toy Museum, Balducci's, Home Savings of America, Brooklyn Children's Museum, The Cloisters, Columbia University, Eldridge Street Project, Federal Hall, Rockefeller Group, Trump Tower.

PICTURE CREDITS
t = top; tc = top centre; tr = top right; cla = centre left above; ca = centre above; cra = centre right above; cl = centre left; c = centre; cr = centre right; clb = centre left below; cb = centre below; crb = centre right below; bl = bottom left; bc = bottom centre; br = bottom right.

Every effort has been made to trace the copyright holders and we apologize in advance for any unintentional omissions. We would be pleased to insert the appropriate acknowledgments in any subsequent edition of this publication.

Works of art have been reproduced with the permission of the following copyright holders: © ADAGP, Paris and DACS, London 1993: 67cl (*Four Trees,* April 1971–July 1972, by Jean Dubuffet), 105cl, 170bl, 186tl, 187crb, 199crb; *Alice In Wonderland,* 1959 © Jose de Creeft/DACS, London/VAGA, New York 1993: 53cl, 205cl; © DACS 1993: 34tr, 113tc, 160tr (donated by the Norwegian Government, 1952), 171cb, 172cr, 186bl, 187cra, 187bl, 188cla; © Estate of STUART DAVIS/DACS, London/VAGA, New York 1993:

199cr; © DEMART PRO ARTE BV/DACS 1993: 172cl; *The American Merchant Mariners Memorial*, 1991, © MARISOL ESCOBAR/DACS, London/VAGA, New York 1993: 55bc; © JASPER JOHNS/DACS, London/VAGA, New York 1993: 199ca; © ROY LICHTENSTEIN/DACS 1993: 140tr (commissioned by The Equitable Life Assurance Society of the United States), 173tl, 198clb; © Estate of DAVID SMITH/DACS, London/VAGA, New York 1993: 199bl.

© 1993 THE GEORGIA O'KEEFFE FOUNDATION/ARS, New York: 198c; © 1993 FRANK STELLA/ARS, New York: 190tr.

By permission of ELLSWORTH KELLY: 35cr.

By permission of E JAN NADELMAN: 199br.

.Printed by permission of the NORMAN ROCKWELL FAMILY TRUST © 1961 the Norman Rockwell Family Trust: 161br.

© 1993 THE ANDY WARHOL FOUNDATION FOR THE VISUAL ARTS, INC: 198cla.

© THE WHITNEY MUSEUM OF AMERICAN ART, NY: 35br (*The Brooklyn Bridge: Variation On An Old Theme*, 1939, by Joseph Stella), 198bl.

The Publishers are grateful to the following museums, companies and picture libraries for permission to reproduce their photographs:

ALGONQUIN HOTEL, N.Y: 272bl; AQUARIUS, UK: 169c; AMERICAN MUSEUM-HAYDEN PLANETARIUM, NY: 216tl; AMERICAN MUSEUM OF THE MOVING IMAGE: Carson Collection © Bruce Polin 245t; AMERICAN MUSEUM OF NATURAL HISTORY, NY: 37bl, 214ca; ASHMOLEAN MUSEUM, Oxford: 15tc; THE ASIA SOCIETY, NY: 185cl; AVERY ARCHITECTURAL AND FINE ART LIBRARY, Columbia University in the City of New York: 135cl; AVERY FISHER HALL: © N McGrath 1976 331tr.

© THE GEORGE BALANCHINE TRUST: *Apollo*, choreography by George Balanchine, photo by P Kolnik 5tc; *Stravinsky Violin Concerto*, choreography by George Balanchine, photo by P Kolnik 328tc; George Balanchine's *The Nutcracker*, SM, photo by P Kolnik 331cb; THE BETTMANN ARCHIVE, NY: 16bcl, 17cra, 17cr, 17bl, 18cl, 20cbr, 20bl, 20–21, 23br, 25cra, 26cla, 26cra, 26crb, 30cla, 31tl, 41tl, 43cbl, 47cr, 47bc, 49c, 54-55b, 71tl, 74cla, 79crb, 79br, 109bl, 175cla, 183br, 207t, 210cl, 223cr, 229t, 239tr, 265tr; BETTMANN NEWSPHOTOS/REUTERS: 31tr; BETTMANN/UPI: 27cra, 27bc, 28bcr, 29br, 30cra, 30bl, 30br, 31br, 44cl, 47cra, 48cl, 49bl, 72c, 72ca, 78cl, 151c, 161c, 264br, 265cr; BLOOMINGDALE'S: 27cbr; BFI: courtesy of Paramount Pictures 46b; © Roy Export Company Establishment 173tr; THE BRITISH LIBRARY, London: 14;

BROOKLYN HISTORICAL SOCIETY: (detail) 89tl; THE BROOKLYN MUSEUM: 34clb (*Climbing Into The Promised Land*, 1908, photo by Lewis Wick Hine), 36bl, 37c, 248cra, 248bl, 249t, 249cra, 249c, 249bl, 250t, 250br, 251cr, 251bl; The Cantor Collection 251cl; photo by J Kerr 248c, 250bl; photo by P Warchol: 249cr; BROWN BROTHERS: 67br, 71bl, 82cra, 90t, 104br.

CAMERA PRESS: 28cbr, 28bl, 31cb, 125cr; R Open 48tr; T Spencer 30cb; THE CARLYLE HOTEL, NY: 273tr, 328bc; CARNEGIE HALL: © H. Grossman 331br; J ALLAN CASH: 31bl, 362cr; CBS ENTERTAINMENT/DESILU TOO: "Vacation from Marriage" 169br; COLORIFIC!: A Clifton 373cl; Colorific/ Black Star: 79cra; T Cowell 221cr; R Fraser 74t; H Matsumoto 368cr, 371tr; D Moore 29bl; T Spiegel 13cr, 348tr; CULVER PICTURES, INC: (inset) 9 , 17crb, 18cbl, 19bl, 21tl, 21br, 24tl, 24cl, 27cb, 27bl, 46tr, 47cb, 48br, 49tr, 74bl, 75cra, 75cb, 76tl, 78crb, 83c, 83crb, 119bl, 122tc, 125bl, 135cr, 145c, 147cl, 227t, 227bc, 227cr, 257bl, 259crb.

DAILY EAGLE: (detail) 89cl; DAILY NEWS: 354tl, 354tr.

ESSEX HOUSE, NY: 268cr; COLLECTION THE EQUITABLE LIFE ASSURANCE SOCIETY: Photo by G Gorgoni 140tr; ESTO: P Aaron 330bl; MARY EVANS PICTURE LIBRARY: 22br, 46clb, 47br, 87br, 104bl.

CHRIS FAIRCLOUGH COLOUR LIBRARY: 369bcl; THE FORBES MAGAZINE COLLECTION, NY: 112tl; FRAUNCES TAVERN MUSEUM, NY: From the exhibit "Come All You Gallant Heroes" The World of the Revolutionary Soldier December 4, 1991 to August 14, 1992: 20cla; Copyright THE FRICK COLLECTION, NY: 35bl (*St Francis In The Desert* by Giovanni Bellini), 200ca, 200cl, 200clb, 200b, 201tl, 201ca, 201cr, 201bc, 201br.

GARRARD THE CROWN JEWELLERS: 143c; THE SOLOMON R GUGGENHEIM MUSEUM, NY: *Blue, Green, Yellow, Orange, Red*, 1966, by Ellsworth Kelly, photo by D Aronowitz 35cr; photo by D Heald 186tl, 186bl, 186bc, 186br, 187t, 187cra, 187crb, 187bl.

ROBERT HARDING PICTURE LIBRARY: 362tc, 362bl; HARPERS NEW MONTHLY MAGAZINE: 87tl; HARPERS WEEKLY: 351c; MILTON HEBALD: *Prospero and Miranda* 203t, *Romeo and Juliet* 331cr; THE HOTEL MILLENIUM, NY: 269tl.

THE IMAGE BANK: front endpaper bl, 89br; M Hilaire 75t; P McConville 377c; M Melford 10t, 377br; P Miller 367tr; A Satterwhite 75br.

THE JEWISH MUSEUM, NY: 182tr, 184c.

Copyright © 1993 K-III MAGAZINE CORPORATION: . All rights reserved. Reprinted with the permission of *New York* Magazine 352tr; THE KOBAL COLLECTION: 211tc.

FRANK LESLIE'S ILLUSTRATED NEWSPAPER: 86br, 87tr, 267c; LIBRARY OF CONGRESS: 18bc, 21cla, 25bl, 25br; LIFE MAGAZINE © Time Warner Inc/Katz/A Feininger: 8–9; GEORG JOHN LOBER: *Hans Christian Anderson*, 1956, 204br; THE LOWELL HOTEL, NY: 273cl; MARY ANN LYNCH: 310bc, 356cl.

MADISON SQUARE GARDEN: 132r, 330cr; MAGNUM PHOTOS: © H Cartier-Bresson 173c; Erwitt 33cr; G Peres 12br, 92; JACQUES MARCHAIS CENTER OF TIBETAN ART: 252bc; THE MAYFAIR HOTEL, NY: 273cr; METRO-NORTH COMMUTER RAILROAD: F English 154tr, 154cla; THE METRO-POLITAN MUSEUM OF ART, NY: 33bl (*Young Woman With A Waterjug* by Johannes Vermeer), 35crb (*Figure of a Hippopotamus*, faience, Egypt, 12th Dynasty), 180tc, 188cla, 188clb, 188bc, 188br, 189tl, 189tr, 189cr, 189bl, (photo Al Mozell) 189br, 190tr, 190c, 190bl, 190br, 191tl, 191tr, 191c, 191bl, 192tl, 192tr, 192c, 192b, (detail) 193tl, 193tr, 193b, 194t, 194cl, 194cr, 194b, 195tl, 195cr, 195bl, 234tr, 234cl, 234cr, 234b, 235ca, 235cr, 235bl, 235br, 236tl, 236tr, 237tr, 237c, 237b; MORRIS-JUMEL MANSION, INC NY: 17tl; A Rosario 21crb; THE MUSEUM OF THE CITY OF NEW YORK: 15b, 16cra, 16–17, 17tr, 18ca, 19crb (photo J Parnell), 20tl, 20cbl, 22tl (attributed to Samuel Lovett Waldo), 22cla, 22clb, 23cr, 23crb, 23bc, 24cb, 25tl, 25crb, 25cb, 26bl, 27tr, 28tl, 28cr, 29tc, 29c, 30tr, 35tr (silver porringer), 87cr (Talfour); THE MUSEUM OF MODERN ART, NY: 33ca (*The Starry Night* by Vincent Van Gogh, 1889), 34t (*The Goat* by Pablo Picasso, 1950), 6bl (Cisitalia "202" GT car), 165tc, 170c, 170bl, 171tc, 171cra, 171crb, 171cb, 171bl, 172cl, 172cr, 172bc, 173tl, 173b.

NATIONAL BASEBALL LIBRARY, Cooperstown, NY: 4tr, 23bl, 28cl; NATIONAL MUSEUM OF THE AMERICAN INDIAN/SMITHSONIAN INSTITUTION: 16c; NATIONAL PARK SERVICE: Ellis Island Immigration Museum 78ca, 78br; Statue of Liberty National Monument 75bl; THE NEW MUSEUM OF CONTEMPORARY ART, NY: 105cl; NEW YORK CITY TRANSIT AUTHORITY: 374bc; Collection of THE NEW YORK HISTORICAL SOCIETY: 47tr; THE NEW YORKER MAGAZINE INC: Cover drawing by Rea Irvin, © 1925, 1953, All rights reserved, 28bcl; THE NEW YORK PALACE, NY: 25tr; NEW YORK POST: 354tl; NEW YORK PUBLIC LIBRARY: Special Collection Office, Schomburg Center for Research in Black Culture 28ca, 29cla; Stokes Collection 21tr; NEW YORK STATE DEPARTMENT OF MOTOR VEHICLES: 370b; THE NEW YORK TIMES: 354tl; NPA: © CNES 1993 10b; THE PENINSULA, NY: 271bc; PERFORMING ARTS LIBRARY: Clive Barda: 210bl; Collection of THE PIERPONT MORGAN LIBRARY, NY: 34cr (*Blanche of Castille and King Louis IX of France, author dictating to a scribe*, moralized Bible, c1230), 162bc, 162clb, 162br, 163tl, 163c, 163bl, 163br; POPPERFOTO: 29cra, 29cr, 71crb, 260cla; PLAZA HOTEL, NY: 272tr.
COLLECTION OF THE QUEENS MUSEUM OF ART: purchased with funds from the George and

Mollie Wolfe World's Fair Fund 29cbr; Official souvenir, purchase 30cbr.

RENSSELAER POLYTECHNIC INSTITUTE: 86–87, 87bl; REX FEATURES LTD: 376tl; Sipa-Press 52tr, 52br; Courtesy of the ROCKEFELLER CENTER © The Rockefeller Group, Inc: 29cbl.

LUIS SANGUINO: *The Immigrants*, 1973, 256b; THE ST. REGIS, NY: 270c; SCIENTIFIC AMERICAN: 18 May 1878 edition 86tr; 9 November 1878 edition 88bl; THE SOCIETY OF ILLUSTRATORS: 196tl; SPECTRUM COLOUR LIBRARY: 376bl; FRANK SPOONER PICTURES: Gamma 158cl; Gamma/B Gysenbergh 367tl; Liaison/Gamma/Anderson front endpaper clb, 158tl, 159cla; Liaison/Levy/Halebian: 42tr, 45c; Sygma/ A Tannenbaum 47ca.

TURNER ENTERTAINMENT COMPANY: 135br, 183br.

UNITED AIRLINES: Goldstag 363tl; UNITED NATIONS, NY: 159cra, 160tr, 160bc, 161tc, 161cla, 161br; © US POSTAL SERVICE: 361t, © THE US POSTAL SERVICE 1981: 361ca, © US POSTAL SERVICE 1991: 361c. Used with permission; UN PLAZA HYATT HOTEL, NY: 273bl.

© JACK VARTOOGIAN, NY: 61bc, 156t.

JUDITH WELLER: *The Garment Worker* 128t; LUCIA WILSON CONSULTANCY: Ivar Mjell 2–3, 13br, 164; Collection of THE WHITNEY MUSEUM OF AMERICAN ART, NY: 198cla, 198c, 198clb, 199t, 199ca, 199cr, 199crb (purchase with funds from a public fundraising campaign in May 1982. One half of the funds were contributed by the Robert Wood Johnson Jr. Charitable Trust. Additional major donations were given by The Lauder Foundation; the Robert Lehman Foundation, Inc.; the Howard and Jean Lipman Foundation, Inc; an anonymous donor; The TM Evans Foundation, Inc.; MacAndrews & Forbes Group Incorporated; the DeWitt Wallace Fund, Inc; Martin & Agnes Gruss; Anne Phillips; Mr and Mrs Laurance S. Rockefeller; the Simon Foundation, Inc.; Marylou Whitney; Bankers Trust Company; Mr and Mrs Kenneth N Dayton; Joel and Anne Ehrenkranz; Irvin and Kenneth Feld; Flora Whitney Miller. More than 500 individuals from 26 states and abroad also contributed to the campaign), 199bl, 199br (purchased with funds from the Mr and Mrs Arthur G Altschul Purchase Fund, the Joan and Lester Avnet Purchase Fund, the Edgar William and Bernice Chrysler Garbisch Purchase Fund, the Mrs Robert C Graham Purchase Fund in honour of John I H Baur, the Mrs Percy Uris Purchase Fund and the Henry Schnakenberg Purchase Fund in honour of Juliana Force); WHEELER PICTURES: 78t.

YU YU YANG: *Untitled*, 1973, 57br.

The Manhattan Subway

How to Use this Map

Transit Authority service operates 24 hours a day, but not all routes operate at all times. Train identification letters or numbers below station names on this map show the basic, seven-day-a-week service from 6am to midnight. A **bold** letter or number at a station indicates that trains always operate and always stop at the station between 6am and midnight. A light letter or number indicates that the train either does not operate at all times or sometimes skips the station.

This map gives details of Manhattan subway services only. A free copy of the full NYC Subway Map is available from all subway stations. A large-scale map is also displayed at each station. For specific enquiries, call the NYCTA Travel Information Center on (718) 330-1234 from 6am–9pm daily.

The nearest subway station is listed for every sight in this book. For more details on travelling on the New York subway, see pages 374–5.

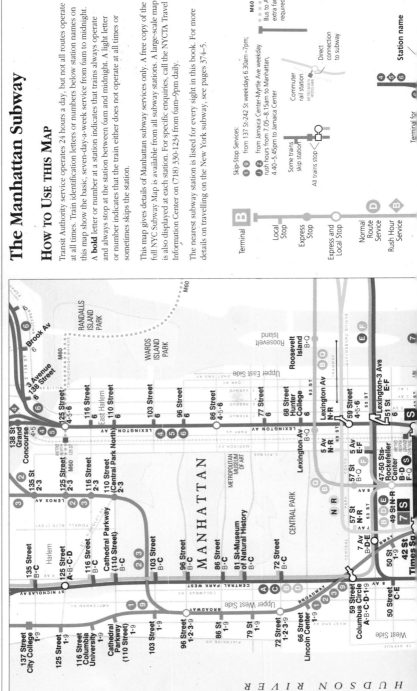

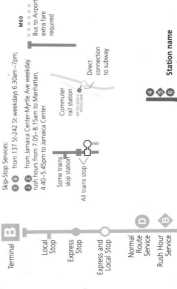

Skip-Stop Services:

❶❾ from 137 St–242 St weekdays 6.30am–7pm;

❷❾ from Jamaica Center–Myrtle Ave weekday rush hours from 7.05–8.15am to Manhattan, 4.40–5.45pm to Jamaica Center

Some trains skip station

All trains stop

Ⓑ Terminal

Local Stop

Express Stop

Express and Local Stop

Ⓓ Normal Route Service

Ⓑ Rush Hour Service

M60 Bus to Airport extra fare required

Direct connection to subway

Commuter rail station

METRO-NORTH WOODLAWN

④ ⑤ ⑥ **Station name**

Terminal for